WOMEN'S STUDIES
ENCYCLOPEDIA

WOMEN'S STUDIES ENCYCLOPEDIA

Revised and Expanded Edition

A–F

Edited by

Helen Tierney

Greenwood Press
Westport, Connecticut

Library of Congress Cataloging-in-Publication Data

Women's studies encyclopedia / edited by Helen Tierney.—Rev. and
    expanded ed.
        p.   cm.
    Includes bibliographical references and index.
    ISBN 0–313–29620–0 (alk. paper)
        1. Women—United States—Encyclopedias.   2. Women—Encyclopedias.
    3. Feminism—Encyclopedias.   I. Tierney, Helen.
    HQ1115.W645   1999
    305.4'03—dc21   98–14236

British Library Cataloguing in Publication Data is available.

A CD-ROM version of *Women's Studies Encyclopedia:
Revised and Expanded Edition* is available from Greenwood
Press, an imprint of Greenwood Publishing Group, Inc.
(ISBN 0-313-31074-2).

Library of Congress Catalog Card Number: 98–14236
ISBN: 0–313–29620–0 (set)
ISBN: 0–313–31071–8 (A–F)
ISBN: 0–313–31072–6 (G–P)
ISBN: 0–313–31073–4 (Q–Z)

First published in 1999

Greenwood Press, 88 Post Road West, Westport, CT 06881
An imprint of Greenwood Publishing Group, Inc.
www.greenwood.com

Printed in the United States of America

The paper used in this book complies with the
Permanent Paper Standard issued by the National
Information Standards Organization (Z39.48–1984).

10 9 8 7 6 5 4 3 2 1

Every reasonable effort has been made to trace the owners of copyright materials in this
book, but in some instances this has proven impossible. The editor and publisher will be
glad to receive information leading to more complete acknowledgments in subsequent print-
ings of the book and in the meantime extend their apologies for any omissions.

Contents

Acknowledgments

Our sister, Helen Tierney, the editor of this *Women's Studies Encyclopedia*, died on October 31, 1997, when the encyclopedia was almost complete, but before she had acknowledged the myriad of individuals who made this book possible. Helen worked on this edition, almost to the exclusion of everything else, for the better part of two and a half years because she considered the availability of information about women of the utmost importance—their contributions to literature, art, science, learning, philosophy, religion, and their place in history. Her family has taken the few remaining steps necessary to see this project to completion.

The encyclopedia is a collaborative effort of many women and men who have given generously of their time, experience, and expertise. Acknowledgment and special thanks are due to all those who contributed articles and to the consultants whose advice and counsel were essential in choosing topics, in recommending the professionals who wrote the articles, and in reviewing articles. Acknowledgment and thanks are due to Helen's colleagues in the Women's Studies Program and the History Department of the University of Wisconsin for their assistance and support, particularly Gloria Stephenson for her help with articles Helen was working on at the time of her death. We do not know all the names of the many individuals who provided their generous assistance along the way, but we would like to express our deepest appreciation to them on Helen's behalf.

The Family of Helen Tierney

Introduction

The *Women's Studies Encyclopedia* contains information about women from all fields and disciplines of study, written in nonspecialist language and in a style accessible to all readers. The idea for the encyclopedia grew out of the discovery, when I first began to organize a course in women's history, that to teach about women, information from beyond the confines of my own area of expertise was essential. Conversations with colleagues interested in offering introductory women's courses or courses in their own disciplines showed that we all shared the same problem: a need for knowledge outside our own fields of interest but with neither the time nor the training to find and understand the results of current research in disciplines other than our own.

Students discovering the then brand-new world of women's studies, male colleagues interested either in broadening their own courses to include something about the other half of humanity or at least in finding out "what the fuss was all about," and women in the "real world" of business and homemaking also evinced interest in a reference that would offer basic information with the latest research and reflection about women from a feminist perspective. The encyclopedia tries to meet these needs.

Since the publication of the first edition of the *Women's Studies Encyclopedia*, research on women has proceeded rapidly; feminist thought has grown and branched out; conditions for women have changed markedly in some areas of life, for good and for ill, and little in others; material conditions in various areas of the world have offered new opportunities or set back advances. Less than ten years after its publication, many articles in the *Encyclopedia* had become out-of-date. In fact, the rapid changes taking place in Eastern Europe a decade ago were making some articles obsolete even before the third volume was published.

Since the early 1980s there has been an increase in women's studies and feminist reference materials, but the need for a multidisciplinary reference tool that touches on all facets and aspects of the female condition is still needed. To better meet that need, the new edition of the *Encyclopedia* has been somewhat enlarged, but, of course, three volumes cannot do more than scratch the surface. There are new articles; some articles have been completely rewritten; many others have been revised or updated. Some omissions have been corrected, and the number of articles in some areas has increased. There is more complete coverage of violence against women, as well as additional materials on women in public life. There are also more articles on contemporary conditions for women in specific countries or regions, but it was impossible to cover every country and every region of the world.

The entries in the *Encyclopedia* are meant to convey information to an educated audience without expertise in the subject under discussion. The bibliographic apparatus is, therefore, limited. The references included at the end of many of the articles are meant primarily to direct readers to works from which they may obtain a fuller explanation, more detailed information, or different perspectives on a subject.

The focus, as in the first edition, is on the American experience. Although a wide array of articles deal with women in other areas of the world and other cultures or on women in general, unless otherwise specified articles deal with women in the United States.

The articles are not written from a single feminist perspective. One aim in inviting contributions was to incorporate as wide a variety of feminist approaches as possible, so that all shades of opinion, from those so conservative that some will deny they are feminist, to the most radical, are represented. They do not, therefore, necessarily represent or agree with my own perspective.

As in the first edition, uniformity of organization and structure for articles of such widely varying subjects was not feasible, but one feature, the omission of the word "women" from entry titles, is fairly consistent, since every article is about women.

This edition is arranged more simply than the last, in alphabetical order. In cases where it was thought that the grouping of entries would make locating them more convenient, individual entries will share a common heading (e.g., articles related to French women's history, such as the Code Napoleon, are listed under "France"; articles about dowry in Western Europe and in India are listed under "dowry").

Cross-references have been reduced to a minimum. When a word or phrase used as the heading of an entry appears as a noun in another entry, the cross-reference is indicated by an asterisk. When a major topic might be listed under several different headings, cross-references to the heading are given.

The names of the authors of entries follow the entries and are also listed under Consultants and Contributors. Those articles that are not signed were written by the editor.

Helen Tierney
October 1997

A

ABOLITIONISM is a comprehensive term that encompasses the diverse, complex movement to eliminate slavery from nineteenth-century society. In the United States, the movement divided into three fairly distinct periods: a conservative phase from the later eighteenth century through the 1820s, a "millennial" phase in the 1830s, and a period of political emphasis and compromise extending from the 1840s through the Civil War. Women's participation, though apparent through all three phases, proved most crucial in the second phase. The rhetoric and ideology of equality coupled with the effective grassroots organization adopted by women abolitionists during the 1830s helped form the foundation for the subsequent development of the woman's rights movement.*

Early abolitionism received only minimal direct support from women. Informed by currents of Enlightenment humanitarianism, evangelical religion, and the egalitarian ideals of the American and French Revolutions, abolitionism of this period was dominated by white, middle-class, well-read men, notably Quakers. Their conservative tactics embodied the belief that slavery should be abolished gradually, with minimum social and political dislocation: opposing views should be reconciled and racial anxieties diffused. Chances for success in this period dwindled as slavery became increasingly entrenched in the economic system of the South, and as anti-abolition opposition throughout the country strengthened.

The millennial 1830s imbued abolitionism with the emotional fervor and moral imperative of contemporary religious revivals, attracting legions of supporters who believed slavery was a sin and had to be eliminated immediately from American society. Women of diverse class, ethnic, religious, and racial backgrounds became involved during this period, with their auxiliaries promulgating the gospel of abolition on the local level. As they were excluded from "promiscuous assemblies" in which men and women might have worked together, women formed separate auxiliaries in which they gathered petitions and agitated the question in their neighborhoods through house-to-house visitations.

The mobilization of proabolition public opinion was highly successful: by 1830 there were 1,300 local antislavery auxiliaries, and membership in the American Anti-Slavery Society totaled one-quarter million. Many of these groups were radical in orientation and goals, provoking violent opposition in both North and South. Widespread antiabolition activity, including mob action and destruction of printing presses, responded to the spread of abolitionist fervor. Women's participation generated heated criticism: the well-publicized antislavery lecture tour of the Grimké sisters caused near-hysterical denunciations in North and South alike, particularly from the clergy.

In the late 1830s the antislavery movement in America divided in two. Radicals, embracing the root-and-branch moral reform philosophy of William Lloyd Garrison, vied for control of the national American Anti-Slavery Society with the moderate abolitionists who sought to pursue political remedies to slavery. Garrison and his radical supporters insisted that their comprehensive commitment to equality and justice led them to combine antislavery with other radical causes such as woman's rights. Opposed to the equal participation of women in the movement, the moderates split the abolition movement in two. From this time until the Civil War, abolitionists who remained loyal to Garrison pursued a range of radical activities, ranging from woman's rights to nonresistance, which complemented their focus on antislavery activity. Moderate, male, mainstream abolitionism underwent a period of reorganization and retrenchment, seeking to work within political and religious institutions rather than trying to reform them.

By the mid-1840s, the quest for a political solution to slavery replaced the moral, immediatist fervor of the previous phase as the cutting edge of the movement. In the 1840s, the abolitionist Liberty Party, followed by the Free Soil Party, positioned itself politically, as abolitionism became an issue that the major parties could no longer ignore. Concurrently, as the focus passed to the political arena from which women were excluded, leaders like Lucretia Mott and Elizabeth Cady Stanton began to channel their reform energies more exclusively to a movement for their own rights. Visions of social equality and justice dwindled as abolitionism increasingly accommodated white racism and fears of racial amalgamation. While abolitionists contributed to the battle that secured emancipation for the enslaved, they lost the war for obtaining equal rights and social justice for the African American.

The special attraction of antislavery for women became evident from the 1830s onward; abolitionism provided an important mechanism by which women's unexamined and disorganized discontents would be transformed into a genuine feminist movement. Through the extensive organization of the auxiliary movement and the network of female contacts, abolitionism provided women with the means to associate with one another and to focus their commitment on a common cause. This network was international in scope, as women abolitionists and feminists from the United States and Great Britain exchanged advice and encouragement. Abolitionism allowed women their first entry into formal political activity as they learned to petition Congress and canvass for antislavery candidates in general elections. These organizational skills coupled with the analysis of oppression women refined through their involvement in the abolition movement were directly applied to the woman's rights movement, devoted to securing their own equality in society.

References. Ellen Du Bois, "Women's Rights and Abolition: The Nature of the Connection," in Lewis Perry and Michael Fellman (eds.), *Antislavery Reconsidered* (Baton Rouge, La., 1979); Nancy Hewitt, *Women's Activism and Social Change: Rochester, New York, 1822–1872* (Ithaca, N.Y., 1984); Blanche Hersh, *The Slavery of Sex: Feminist-Abolitionists in America* (Urbana, Ill., 1978); Aileen Kraditor, *Means and Ends in American Abolitionism: Garrison and His Critics on Strategy and Tactics, 1834–1850* (New York, 1967). (See also ANTISLAVERY ASSOCIATIONS.)

KAREN I. HALBERSLEBEN

ABORTION. Definitions and Methods. Abortion is loss of a fetus* before the potentiality of independent life has been attained, legally in the United States before the twenty-eighth week of menstrual age (twenty-eight weeks after the last menstrual period). After the twenty-eighth week, the death of the fetus is called *premature* or *stillbirth*. *Fetal death* is death before the fetus is expelled or extracted from the mother, regardless of the length of the pregnancy.

Spontaneous abortion is the body's mechanism for expelling fetuses that, for a variety of causes, cannot complete the period of gestation.* The term *miscarriage* is usually limited to a spontaneous abortion before the third trimester (twenty-eighth week of menstrual age), although it is sometimes used of induced abortions as well. The great majority of spontaneous abortions occur early in gestation, due to abnormal development or death of the ovum or its membrane. They often occur before the woman realizes she is pregnant and are assumed to be menstrual irregularities.

Spontaneous abortions occur most frequently among the very young and those over thirty. A higher frequency among nonwhites may be the result of environmental factors. Causes usually stem from physical or physiological problems of the cervix or uterus, the great majority of which (around 90 percent) cannot be corrected medically. Common causes include congenital abnormalities, uterine fibroids, incompetence of the cervix (usually from its having been overstretched), and deficiency of progesterone. Other causes include uterine infections, radiation and chemotherapeutic drugs used in cancer treatment, and, although rarely, general diseases or infections that result in high body temperatures.

Induced abortion is the interruption of a pregnancy, by the mother or some other person, under conditions that are not spontaneous. Where induced abortions are illegal, exceptions are sometimes allowed for *therapeutic abortions*, to save the life or the health of the mother.

Evidence of induced abortion exists in every society with written records and in nearly all contemporary primitive societies. Although various methods have been used and advocated to induce abortion, ranging from the completely worthless, such as eating raspberries or applying sympathetic magic, to the extremely dangerous, the technique remained basically unchanged from ancient times until the latter nineteenth century, when industrialization and urbanization made efforts to control human fertility a major social problem in all Western nations.

The two basic methods can be traced back to ancient medical texts. The *herbal method* is the ingestion of substances toxic to the cell nucleus. The fetus will be killed, but the woman, hopefully, will recover. The best-known, most commonly used substance is oil of juniper: savin (*Juniperus sabina*) was used by the Greeks and Romans and its use spread from the Mediterranean to Northern Europe. Its use is mentioned in seventeenth-century English writings, including Nicolas Culpepper's *The Complete Herbal*. It is the main ingredient in Buchanan's Pills, best known of the nineteenth-century cures for "women's ailments." "Female correctives" sold everywhere, but especially in poorer countries, still contain oil of juniper. The most common time for administering it is within a few days of the missed period.

The *mechanical method* is relatively simple: to enter the uterus and completely remove the products of conception by the use of probes and instruments. The cervix must be dilated to pass the instruments into the uterus. The fetal membrane is then ruptured and natural expulsion of the conceptus invariably follows. The fifth-century B.C. Hippocratic Corpus describes a graduated set of dilators, and probes and instruments that have remained basically unchanged were found in the ruins of Herculaneum and Pompeii (destroyed A.D. 79). Great care is needed, and risks are serious. Dilation of the cervix by inserting unsterilized plant material that will absorb moisture and swell, causing a slow and even dilation, can cause infection. The position of the uterus and its extremely soft wall when pregnant make perforation and severe bleeding very easy. Raw areas, especially any placental material not expelled, form ideal sites for infection.

As the demand for abortions greatly increased in the nineteenth century, and before social-purity laws drove physicians and more or less open advertisements from the scene in many Western countries, the kind of abortion probably varied with the income level of the woman. Physicians and midwives probably used mechanical techniques. Products were advertised and sold as emmenagogues, correctives to bring on delayed menstruation. Herbalists sold their remedies to the poor.

Some progress in methods began to appear in the nineteenth century. The curette, a spoon-shaped instrument for scraping a wound clean, developed by the French in the eighteenth century, in the nineteenth began to be used for inducing or treating incomplete abortions. Bleeding and infection are reduced by curettage to remove all products of conception. Dilation and curettage (D&C) remains a basic technique.

The chief advances in dilation were laminaria tents, dried, compressed seaweed that can be sterilized, and the use of anesthesia to block the pain of cervical dilation.

"Drycupping," the forerunner of vacuum aspiration, was known as early as 1863. However, progress in acceptance was slow—the technique was known in Russia in 1927 and in China during World War II. By the late 1950s and early 1960s it had spread to Japan and Eastern Europe. Czech glassmakers were able to make excellent suction curettes, but the West did not adopt drycupping until the late 1960s. After it was combined with local anesthetic in Yugoslavia in 1966, it began to be used in England in 1967 and after this spread rapidly.

In 1961 Harvey Karman, an illegal abortionist who could not use anesthesia, developed a very small-bore tube so that the cervix would not need dilation for it to be passed into the uterus. With soft, flexible tubing this simple abortion catheter (about 4 mm diameter), which needs no or only local anesthesia, reduced the costs of abortion and was simple and safe. It can be used for pregnancies of up to six or eight weeks.

Today vacuum aspiration is most common for first-trimester abortions. A thin tube, or cannula, with openings on one end and attached to an aspirator, is introduced into the uterus. As suction is applied, the cannula is rotated and drawn in and out of the uterus, drawing out the products of conception. The diameter of the cannula depends upon the age of the fetus. D&C, once the standard method for first-trimester abortions, today is still used for treating all incomplete abortions. The cervix is dilated, a preliminary curettage is performed, then the placental tissue is detached by forceps.

Induction methods, which became the most widely used techniques for later abortions until the mid–1980s, began to be developed in the 1920s and 1930s. Special soaps or pastes were introduced in Germany in the 1920s and used, particularly in Germany and Denmark, in the interwar period. Medicated soap is introduced through the vagina into the extra-ovular space (between uterine wall and membrane). The soap spreads around the fetal sac and normally induces an abortion within 48 hours. Cases of infection led to decline in its use in Europe, but it is still used in developing countries.

After abortion was legalized in the United States in 1973, the common procedure for late abortions was the two-step method: first, the cervix was dilated and the normal reproductive process interrupted; hours later contractions began and the conceptus was expelled. A D&C was usually performed to make sure that all the products of conception were removed.

The most used two-step induction abortion method was by injection, under local anesthetic, of a liquid into the amniotic sac to kill the placenta and thus induce an abortion. The first steps in developing the method date to the 1930s, when liquids were injected into the amniotic cavity or into the fetal membrane. When abortion laws were liberalized, interest in the use of injection led to experiments with different substances: formalin, glucose, saline solution, urea, prostaglandins. (Prostaglandins are a family of long-chain fatty acids found in men and women. They play an important role in menstruation, spontaneous abortions, and labor.) Prostaglandin or prostaglandin and urea solutions were most commonly used in Europe, but saline solutions, or saline with urea and/or prostaglandins, continued to be preferred in the United States. However, injection carries risks to the mother. Saline solutions introduced into the mother's system, for instance, can be fatal. And this method is more traumatic than is evacuation.

Since the mid–1980s, dilation and evacuation (D&E) has replaced injection. After dilation, vacuum aspiration and forceps and curettage are used to remove the products of conception. The method is safer and takes much less time than the introamniotic injection technique. Today it is the method used for late first-trimester and second-trimester abortions.

For later abortions, hysterotomy (also called miniature cesarean section), dating from the nineteenth century, was the usual method for therapeutic abortions before the development of the two-step technique. It is now rarely used except in conjunction with sterilization. Through an abdominal incision the uterus is opened and emptied.

A hysterectomy, totally removing uterus and pregnancy, is used when uterine disease is present. Abdominal entrance is made in the presence of fibroids; vaginal, in cases of prolapse.

Menstrual regulation (menstrual aspiration, menstrual interruption, preemptive abortion) is the name given to surgical evacuation of uterine contents shortly after the first missed period (usually within 14 days). Vacuum aspiration with a Karman curette is the common method. Certain feminist groups use menstrual regulation monthly for fertility regulation and personal hygiene. (The long-range effects of this practice are not yet known.) Emptying the uterus before one knows for certain whether or not she is pregnant can help to avoid the negative emotional response that sometimes accompanies abortion. It can also change the legal rules (e.g., abortion is illegal in Argentina, but menstrual regulation is not considered a crime).

The first "morning-after pill" was synthetic estrogen, diethylstilbesterol (DES), taken over five days beginning no later than 72 hours after intercourse, to prevent the fertilized ovum from implanting on the uterus. However, it was found that, in addition to unpleasant side effects and increased incidence of ectopic pregnancies* (pregnancies outside the uterus), there were serious health risks to mothers and offspring when taken by women who were already pregnant. Ovral, combined pills with high progestional activity, taken within 72 hours of intercourse and repeated in 12 hours, has proved to be much safer. Use of Ovral to interrupt a possible pregnancy has been approved by the federal Food and Drug Administration (FDA) and is marketed by other trade names.

RU 486 or mifepristone is a drug that counters progesterone, a hormone needed to maintain pregnancy. Thirty-six to 48 hours after taking mifepristone, another drug, misoprostol, is taken to contract the uterus, thus expelling the fetus. When taken within the first seven weeks of pregnancy, it was found to be 95.5 percent successful. Mifepristone has been widely used in Europe since the 1980s but was approved by an advisory committee of the FDA only in 1996. It had not received final FDA approval by the time this entry was written.

ABORTION HISTORY. United States. Historically, abortion has been both persistent and prevalent. Since ancient times women have attempted to control their fertility through contraception and abortion. The doctrine of the early Christian church followed the practice of most early cultures in distinguishing pregnancy before and after "quickening," the time when the pregnant woman first perceived fetal movement. Since, under church doctrine, the fetus did not acquire a soul until quickening, abortion before then was neither a sin nor a crime. Abortion after quickening was denounced by the early church as interference with procreation but was rarely punished.

Under English common law, women who sought abortions before quickening committed no offense. Even later abortions were prosecuted infrequently. English common law prevailed in the American colonies, where abortion was not uncommon. There was no legal or moral condemnation of the act during the colonial period. Herbal abortifacients were advertised, and their use by midwives was known and accepted. Home medical manuals provided ready access to abortifacient information.

Prior to the mid-nineteenth century, women were not considered pregnant before quickening; instead, they were termed "irregular," and herbal potions, purgatives, and other "natural" strategies were often used to bring on "suppressed menses." Women took abortifacients not to abort but rather to restore the menses and saw this in the same light as preventing conception. Advertisements for clinics where menstrual irregularities "from whatever cause" could be treated appeared even in church newspapers.

The English Parliament adopted a statute in 1803 making abortion before quickening criminal, but American states rejected such broad prohibitions and continued to follow earlier common law. In 1821 Connecticut enacted a statute forbidding the administration of poison to produce an abortion *after* quickening, but it did not forbid abortion before quickening until 1860.

Despite the later adoption of criminal laws, abortions were common in the nineteenth century and were relatively easy for all classes of women to obtain.

The total white fertility rate decreased by half during the century, from an average of 7 children born to each married white woman to 3.5 children; this was due in part to abortion. Estimates in the mid- to late-nineteenth century range from 1 abortion for every 2 live births to 1 in every 5. In 1871, New York City, with a population of less than 1 million, supported 200 full-time abortionists. Doctors estimated that 2 million abortions a year were performed in the 1890s.

For most of the nineteenth century abortion was accepted as a matter of fact. By 1890, however, it had become illegal throughout the United States. This sudden reversal was not due to a religious or moral movement. Despite the 1869 papal bull declaring abortion at any stage of pregnancy to be a mortal sin, neither Catholic nor Protestant church leaders were prominent in the nineteenth-century crusade against abortion.

Instead, the campaign was led by the American Medical Association (AMA), which became the single most important factor in altering legal policies toward abortion. The change in policy was part of a larger effort by "regular" (AMA-affiliated) physicians to eliminate competition and to control the practice of medicine. Criminalization of abortion coincided with the "gynecological crescendo," which replaced midwives with male physicians and enabled men to take control of the procreative function.

The antiabortion movement was characterized by nativist prejudice against immigrants. Medical tracts of the period argued that the "wrong women" (white, married, Protestant, and middle-class) were seeking abortions and that consequently, "respectable" women would soon be outbred by "the ignorant, the low lived and the alien." Limiting access to abortion was presented as a necessary means to prevent "race suicide."

The antiabortion movement fed on anxieties about changing gender roles. The nineteenth century embraced the idea that woman's true nature is found in maternal domesticity. Abortion was a symbolic threat to social order and male authority. Physicians condemned abortion by the married woman as a disgusting self-indulgence, a sign that she had succumbed to male sensualism and abandoned the responsibilities of motherhood for "selfish and personal ends." Both abortion and contraception were associated by the medical profession with lewdness and rebellion against the idea of chastity and subservience.

By 1900 every state had adopted criminal statutes restricting or forbidding abortion. The movement led by the AMA successfully redefined the abortion decision as a question for professional medical judgment. Opposition to abortion became national policy. American women in substantial numbers continued to obtain abortions despite this legislation, but abortion became a socially invisible event. An upper-income woman with some plausible physical reason to avoid childbirth and motives that did not offend her doctor's values generally had little difficulty in obtaining a "therapeutic" abortion. Other women, however, had recourse only to illegal abortions, which were generally performed by unlicensed and sometimes untrained persons. By the 1960s, estimates of annual illegal abortions ranged from 200,000 to over 1 million.

Abortion did not become a significant political issue until the 1960s, when a strong movement for reform—and later, repeal—began to develop. In 1959 the American Law Institute proposed a change in its Model Penal Code to permit abortion when the life or health of the pregnant woman was threatened, if pregnancy resulted from rape or incest, or if permanent mental or physical defects in the child were likely. A bill modeled on this proposal was introduced in California in 1961 and adopted in 1967. Between 1967 and 1972, 16 states liberalized their abortion laws, but most of the others retained extensive procedural requirements that restricted the availability of abortion.

The medical and legal professions challenged existing laws as being unconstitutionally vague or interfering with legitimate medical judgment. Between 1969 and 1973, courts in seven states and the District of Columbia either declared existing abortion laws unconstitutional or greatly modified them through interpretation.

This same period saw the rise of the "second wave" of the women's movement and its involvement in this debate. In 1967 the National Organization for Women voted to include reproductive freedom, including the right to abortion, in its Women's Bill of Rights. The National Association for the Repeal of Abortion Laws (NARAL) was founded at this time; it is still active 30 years later as the National Abortion and Reproductive Rights Action League. Feminist groups consistently distinguished between reform, which implied acceptance of some state regulation, and repeal, which defined abortion as a woman's right and not subject to state control. They also rejected the categories of "therapeutic" ("medically necessary") and "elective" abortions common to reform proposals. As early as 1964, women in California testified that the state should repeal its abortion law altogether rather than reform it.

Women also carried the campaign for the repeal of abortion laws beyond the legal arena, organizing demonstrations and establishing self-help groups to provide needed information on reproduction and abortion through pamphlets and workshops. Feminists created abortion referral and counseling networks, often in cooperation with religious groups. JANE, an organization that operated in Chicago from 1969 to 1973, began as such a service and eventually provided low-cost abortions to an estimated 11,000 women without a single reported death.

In practice, California's 1967 abortion reform law came close to permitting abortion on request. By 1971, one in three pregnancies in California ended in abortion and over 99 percent of women seeking abortions had their requests granted. Abortion was covered as a routine medical procedure under Medi-Cal, the state's medical assistance program, and private insurance plans also provided coverage. When New York adopted a "near-repeal" statute in 1970, abortion became readily available to any woman with the financial ability to travel. By 1973, 3 states had joined New York in adopting statutes that rejected the Model Penal Code's restrictions. However, at least 25 states retained laws that permitted abortion only when necessary to preserve the woman's life.

The current legal status of abortion has been defined by the Supreme Court. In the landmark case of *Roe v. Wade* (decided on January 22, 1973), the Court concluded that the "right of privacy . . . is broad enough to encompass a woman's decision whether or not to terminate her pregnancy." The constitutional principles stated in the decision appeared to give broad protection to a woman's right to choose abortion, but the decision also provided for these rights to be limited when the state had a "compelling interest." Legitimate state interests in preserving and protecting the health of the pregnant woman and in protecting the potentiality of human life could each rise to the level of a "compelling" interest as the pregnancy progressed, thus justifying state regulation of abortion.

The number of reported abortions increased sharply after *Roe*, leveling off 10 years later at about 1.6 million abortions each year. The percentage of pregnant women who legally terminated a pregnancy rose from 19 percent in 1973 to 30 percent in 1979 and has remained at approximately that level, declining slightly in the 1990s. These women are primarily young (two-thirds are under 25) and unmarried (approximately 75 percent), in contrast to the older, married women who accounted for many of the abortions in the nineteenth century.

Rather than bringing their laws into agreement with the principles of *Roe*, many states made minimal changes in existing statutes, enacted patently unconstitutional laws, or imposed new restrictions to deter abortions. In the 1970s the Supreme Court struck down laws imposing absolute parental and spousal consent requirements but eventually upheld legislation requiring a minor to obtain either parental consent or judicial authorization (see *Ohio v. Akron Center for Reproductive Health*, 1990, and *Hodgson v. Minnesota*, 1990.)

In *Beal v. Doe* (1977) the Supreme Court upheld laws that drastically reduced the availability of abortion for poor women by denying coverage for most abortions under state and federal medical assistance programs. In 1980 (*Harris v. MacRae*) the Court upheld even more restrictive federal legislation, ruling that lack of funding places "no governmental obstacle in the path of a woman who chooses to terminate her pregnancy."

Although some states, including California and New York, provide state funding for abortions, most follow the federal standards. These policies significantly reduce the choices available to low-income women, yet the total number of abortions performed has not decreased substantially, due in part to the rise of freestanding abortion clinics. In 1973 the majority of abortions were performed in hospitals, but by 1982 many hospitals no longer provided abortion services for the general public. In 1982 over 80 percent of reported abortions were provided in clinics, rising to over 86 percent in 1988, while the number performed in hospitals dropped to 10 percent. The reliance on clinics limits abortion services to urban areas with large populations, leaving some rural states with virtually no services. State legislation regulating abortion clinics has been more concerned with discouraging abortions than with ensuring their safety (see *City of Akron v. Akron Center for Reproductive Health*, 1983), resulting in a very uneven level of services.

In *Webster v. Reproductive Health Services* (1989), the Supreme Court refused an invitation to reverse *Roe v. Wade* but did uphold a Missouri statute that banned the use of public facilities and public employees to perform abortions. Chief Justice William Rehnquist criticized *Roe*'s trimester approach to the constitutional right to abortion, but the Supreme Court as a whole remained divided on the issues.

In 1992 a still-divided Court reaffirmed the right to abortion by a 5–4 decision in *Planned Parenthood v. Casey*, holding that *Roe* had acquired "rare precedental power." The majority opinion, coauthored by three justices, recognized that a generation had grown up "free to assume *Roe*'s concept of liberty in defining the capacity of women to act in society, and to make reproductive decisions" and concluded that overturning *Roe* under political pressure would "damage . . . the nation's commitment to the rule of law." The opinion developed a new standard of constitutionality based on whether state regulation imposed an "undue burden" on the right to abortion. While this decision permitted more restrictions on abortion, including waiting periods, "informed consent," and parental consent requirements, it strongly affirmed the constitutionally protected status of abortion in the face of pressure to overrule *Roe v. Wade* entirely.

While the legal right to abortion was thus preserved in the 1990s, practical access to abortion continued to be eroded. Only half as many hospitals performed abortions in 1992 as in 1977. By 1992, 18 states, primarily in the Midwest, Great Plains, and South, had abortion providers in less than 10 percent of their counties. Eighty-three percent of all counties in the United States had no clinic or hospital that provided abortion.

Although the right to choose abortion is constitutionally protected, only 13 percent of the obstetric and gynecology residency programs in the United States required training in first-trimester abortions in 1991. Thirty percent provided no training in abortions, even on an elective basis, compared to 8 percent in 1976. In response to this trend the Accreditation Council for Graduate Medical Education announced that all accredited obstetrics programs would be required to teach abortion skills starting in 1996.

The 1990s also saw new progress toward the availability of pharmaceutical alternatives to surgical abortion in the United States. RU 486, or mifepristone, a drug that causes abortion by blocking essential progesterone in the uterus, had been used safely by women in Europe since the 1980s. Although its import had been banned under earlier Republican presidencies, Democratic President Clinton directed federal regulators to reassess whether RU 486 should be available in the United States. Clinical tests were completed in 1995, but the Food and Drug Administration had not released a final recommendation as this entry was written. A 1995 article in the *New England Journal of Medicine* discussed the use of methotrexate, which interferes with cell growth, as an abortifacient. In 1996 the National Abortion Federation endorsed this approach to abortion and began to develop a treatment protocol. There is debate in the feminist community as to the overall safety of both these drugs and the danger of incomplete abortions when using them.

Abortion clinics came under increasing pressure in the 1980s from blockades, harassment and threats, with over 1,000 documented attacks, including bombings and arson, in the decade after 1984. Representatives of several national groups went to the Federal Bureau of Investigation (FBI) after a series of clinic firebombings in the 1980s, but it declined to investigate. The blockades organized by Operation Rescue peaked in the early 1990s, when judges began to issue injunctions to control demonstrations and maintain access to clinics. In 1995 close to one-third of all clinics were protected by civil injunctions. The Freedom of Access to Clinic Entrances Act, adopted in 1994, authorized civil and criminal actions in federal court against those using force to attack or obstruct a clinic or its staff or clients.

In 1993 violence against abortion providers escalated to murder with the shooting of Dr. David Gunn in Florida, followed by the 1994 murder of Dr. John Britton (who succeeded Dr. Gunn at several Florida clinics) and escort James Barrett and the Massachusetts shootings that killed clinic workers Lee Ann Nichols and Shannon Lowney and seriously wounded five workers and escorts in 1995. In each case the shooter was convicted of first-degree, premeditated murder. Paul Hill defended himself, arguing that his killing of Britton and Barrett was morally and legally justified as necessary to defend the unborn. On the recommendation of the convicting jury, he was sentenced to death.

References. Laura Kaplan, *The Story of Jane: The Legendary Underground Feminist Abortion Service* (New York, 1995); Eva R. Rubin (ed.), *The Abortion Controversy: A Documentary History* (Westport, Conn., 1993); Carole Jaffe, *Doctors of Conscience: The Struggle to Provide Abortion before and after Roe v. Wade*

(Boston, 1995); Ellen Messer and Kathryn E. May, *Back Rooms: An Oral History of the Illegal Abortion Era* (New York, 1989); Patricia G. Miller, *The Worst of Times: Illegal Abortion—Survivors, Practitioners, Coroners, Cops, and Children of Women Who Died Talk about Its Horrors* (New York, 1993).

BARBARA J. HAYLER

ABSENTEE RATES. Sex Differentials in. Among women in 1979 the incidence of absenteeism was significantly higher than that among men. About 8.6 percent of women experienced an absence during a workweek compared to 5.5 percent of men. About 3.4 percent of hours worked by full-time wage and salary workers in the United States is lost due to absences resulting from illness, injury, and personal reasons. About 1 in 15 workers experienced one or more absences in a week for one or more of these reasons. Women lost 4.3 percent of their usual work time in May 1979 compared to 3.0 percent for men (D. Taylor, 1981, 68–70).

Exactly why the absentee rate of women is higher than that of men has been the subject of recent research. Some economists have attributed the higher absence rates of women to their role as family caregivers. Women miss work not only to care for their own illnesses but to care for family members as well. Other economists have attributed the differences to the occupational and wage distribution of the sexes. Women may be more heavily concentrated in those occupations that experience high absentee rates for both men and women.

Table 1 shows the proportion of time lost from work by race, sex, and marital status in May 1979. It is interesting to note that married men with spouses and never-married men have the same absentee rates, while married women have significantly higher rates than never-married women. This suggests that the presence of family responsibilities may affect the probability that women miss work for ill health and personal reasons. This could result for two reasons. First, women may serve as caregivers so that when a spouse, child, or older family member is ill, the wife or mother may miss work to care for the needs of the family member. Second, to the extent that women assume more household production responsibilities than men, they may be less willing to continue to work while ill and risk getting an even more serious illness.

Black women miss significantly more time from work than white women, and there is little variation in work loss by marital status among black women. The lack of variation in absentee rates by marital status may reflect the fact that single black women are more likely to be heads of households than single white women. Consequently, the family responsibilities assumed by single black women may not be significantly different from those faced by their married counterparts.

Carol Leon examined the incidence of weeklong absences among labor force participants in 1980. She found that during an average week 1.5

Table 1
Percent of Time Lost from Work for Illness and Personal Reasons

	Total	Married Spouse Present	Never Married
Women	4.3	4.5	3.4
White			
Men	2.8	2.9	2.8
Women	4.0	4.3	3.0
Black			
Men	4.6	4.3	5.0
Women	6.0	6.3	6.3

Source: D. Taylor, "Absences from Work among Full-Time Employees," *Monthly Labor Review*, March 1981, 68–70.

percent of women missed the entire week of work for health reasons compared to 1.4 percent of men ("Employed But Not at Work," 18–21). However, women were twice as likely as men (.9 percent compared to .5 percent) to miss work for reasons other than vacation, illness, bad weather, or a labor dispute. This finding further supports the idea that the higher absentee rates of women are due primarily to their role as family caregivers.

Leon also found that men were much more likely to be paid for weeks missed from work than were women. In 1980, men received pay for two-thirds of their weeklong absences. In contrast women were paid for about half of their full-week absences.

The National Health Interview Survey collects annual data on the number of work-loss days associated with short-term illness. The number of loss days for males and females by major diagnostic category is shown in Table 2.

Women workers miss an average of 3.7 days from work every year for ill health compared to 2.7 for men. For both sexes the number of work-loss days is lower for workers over 45 than for those age 18 to 44. Women miss more days from work for respiratory conditions and infective diseases, and men miss more for injuries and diseases of the digestive system. Among women under age 45, about .52 days per year of work loss can be attributed to pregnancy. Thus, excluding pregnancy considerably narrows the difference in work-loss days between men and women.

This evidence suggests that women experience more illness-related absences than men. However, the tables do not take into account earnings differences between males and females, differences in the occupational dis-

Table 2
Work-loss Days per Person Resulting from Acute Health Conditions—1985

Condition	Males All	Males 18–44	45+	Females All	Females 18–44	45+
All Acute	2.62	2.73	2.36	3.70	4.00	2.94
Infective & Parasitic Diseases	.17	.22	.06	.34	.40	.19
Respiratory Conditions	.85	.90	.72	1.38	1.37	1.38
Digestive Conditions	.17	.09	.34	.20	.18	.25
Injuries	1.22	1.37	.85	.83	.94	.5

Source: National Center for Health Statistics, U.S. Department of Health and Human Services, "Current Estimates from the National Health Interview Survey, United States, 1985," *Vital and Health Statistics*, Series 10, No. 160, DHHS Pub. No. (PHS) 86–1588.

tribution of the sexes, and the availability of fringe benefits such as sick leave that reduce the cost to an employee of missing a day from work for health reasons.

Steve Allen found that once he controlled for the wage rate, the availability of sick leave, the availability of income from other sources, and union membership, there were no significant differences in unscheduled absence rates between men and women ("An Empirical Model," 77–87). He also found that while women were more likely than men to miss a day of work for illness, the amount of time lost per absent worker was lower for women. He attributes this to the possibility that women may recognize and treat health problems at an earlier stage than men. Supporting this idea is the fact that while women miss more days from work at early ages, after age 55, absentee rates for women are lower than they are for men. Women may thus be making early investments in their health that they recapture over their working lives. By staying home and taking care of their illnesses when they first occur, women may increase their productive work lives.

Lynn Paringer examined work-loss differences between men and women for specific illnesses. She also found that once earnings, sick leave, occupation, age, and health status of a worker were controlled, there were no significant differences between the sexes in terms of work loss. Paringer found that days of work loss for a given illness increased with age, but that the increase was significantly higher for men than for women ("Women and Absenteeism," 123–127).

These research findings suggest that while women experience significantly higher absentee rates than men, most of the differential can be explained by occupation and earnings variables. A worker's sex is not a determining factor in work loss. This is an important finding since an employer looking at summary absentee data may conclude that women workers, by virtue of their higher absentee rates, are less dependable than their male counterparts. Research simply does not support this conclusion. Absentee rates are dependent on earnings, occupation, and age. They are not affected by a worker's sex.

References. "An Empirical Model of Work Attendance," *Review of Economics and Statistics* 63 (1981): 77–78; "Employed But Not at Work: A Review of Unpaid Absences," *Monthly Labor Review*, November 1981, 18–21; J. Hedges, "Absence from Work—Measuring the Hours Lost," *Monthly Labor Review*, October 1977, 16–23; J. Sindelar, "Differential Use of Medical Care by Sex," *Journal of Political Economy* 90 (1982): 1003–1019; D. Taylor, "Absences from Work among Full-Time Employees," *Monthly Labor Review*, March 1981, 68–70; D. Taylor, "Absent Workers and Lost Work Hours, May 1978," *Monthly Labor Review*, August 1979, 49–52; D. Wingard, "The Sex Differential in Mortality Rates: Demographic and Behavioral Factors," paper presented at the annual meeting of the Society for Epidemiologic Research, Minneapolis, Minn., June 1980. "Women and Absenteeism: Health of Economics?" *American Economic Review* 73 (1983): 123–127.

LYNN PARINGER

ACQUIRED IMMUNODEFICIENCY SYNDROME (AIDS). See HIV DISEASE

ADDICTION refers to a physiological dependence on a substance that involves both a physical process and a behavioral component. Addiction, which is often referred to as substance dependence, is also considered the end point on a continuum that begins with abstinence, continues to substance abuse, and ends with dependence. Drugs that people most often become addicted to are caffeine and tobacco but also include substances such as sedatives and narcotics.

As a physical process, addiction involves both tolerance of a drug and withdrawal symptoms. Individuals who develop a tolerance to a drug require increasing amounts of that drug in order to achieve the same desired effect. Withdrawal symptoms occur when a drug upon which the body has become physiologically dependent is removed and can be fairly mild to severe. For example, withdrawal symptoms from caffeine include headaches and agitation, whereas withdrawal from alcohol or narcotics can result in convulsions, delirium tremors (DTs), and even death. The more significant withdrawal symptoms require medical supervision, also known as detoxification. Experiencing these symptoms also produces a craving for the drug (both physical and psychological) that, when satisfied, forestalls the onset of the withdrawal process. Once any individual becomes physiologically dependent on a drug, he or she will experience withdrawal symptoms once the drug is no longer being used.

As a behavioral process, addiction is identified by an inability to control one's behavior regardless of repeated negative family, social, educational/vocational, legal, and medical consequences. The general population has often referred to many types of behaviors, such as drug and alcohol abuse, food, gambling, sex, and sometimes even relationships, as being addictions when they appear to become compulsive. While compulsive actions do not meet the definition of "addiction," the inability to control or stop a behavior and continuing that behavior despite serious negative consequences are easily recognized. Addictive behaviors are also marked by a preoccupation with the behavior that often causes a buildup of anxiety that can be remedied only through engaging in the behavior.

Women are more significantly linked to some behavioral addictions, such as spending, food (i.e., compulsive overeating or other eating disorders), and exercise (often associated with eating disorders), while they are typically less recognized as being involved with addictions such as gambling or sex. Very little research on these compulsive behaviors takes gender into account. Further, individuals who engage in these compulsive behaviors are difficult to identify and often become known only when they present for treatment services, and/or their behaviors have created multiple problems. However, there do appear to be some consistent psychological variables present in women with compulsive behaviors, regardless of their form. Women who have been identified with behavioral addictions seem to have symptoms of depression, anxiety, and low self-esteem. Women with behavioral addictions have experienced significant family disruptions such as physical abuse, incest, or parental alcoholism. Further, as adults, women exhibiting compulsive behaviors are often survivors of physical and/or sexual abuse and frequently present with multiple compulsive behaviors. Substance abuse is often present in women with eating disorders or gambling addictions, and substituting one addictive behavior for another is common.

DINA WILKE

ADDITIONAL WORKER EFFECT/DISCOURAGED WORKER EFFECT. The neo-classical model of women's labor force participation* implies that women may respond to an increase in the unemployment rate in one of two ways. They may increase their labor force participation to compensate for the fact that male breadwinners are out of work. This is termed the Additional Worker Effect. Alternatively, they may decrease their labor force participation because the higher unemployment rate makes finding a job more difficult. This is termed the Discouraged Worker Effect. Empirical studies find that for women the Discouraged Worker Effect dominates the Additional Worker Effect. This is one reason women's unemployment rates fall relative to men's during recessions.

SUSAN B. CARTER

ADULTERY is voluntary extramarital intercourse with a person of the opposite sex, whether unmarried (single adultery) or married (double adultery). Ancient patriarchal societies (e.g., Amorite, Assyrian, Hebrew, Greek, Roman) did not consider extramarital intercourse adultery unless a married woman (or a concubine) was the offender. In some societies no distinction was made between seduction of a woman and rape* (laws of Middle Assyria, Athens). In Rome, after adultery was made a crime at law (lex Julia de adulteris, 17 B.C.), the married woman's offense was adultery; the married man's, the lesser crime of vice.

The double standard,* that only the woman's infidelity deserves serious punishment, has permeated thinking in all patriarchal societies. It rests in large part on the idea of woman as property. The male's property right in the female is an important factor in completely forbidding extramarital intercourse for females in about half of all human societies. In others, extramarital sexual activities may be allowed, or even required, in certain instances (e.g., in fertility rites or with guests as a sign of hospitality). In few has extramarital sex been freely permitted for women, although there have been periods when women's adultery in the upper levels of society, if discreet, has been quietly tolerated (e.g., eighteenth-century Western Europe).

In most patriarchal societies, a couple caught in the act of adultery could be killed with impunity by the offended husband or the woman's relatives (in Assyria and Rome the man could not be killed unless the wife were also). In fact, juries have refused to convict "wronged husbands" in some U.S. jurisdictions into the twentieth century. Legal punishment varied, but, when not capital, usually involved some form of public humiliation for the woman.

The Christian church officially insisted that adultery was as wrong for a husband as for a wife and that a wife's adultery could not be used as grounds for divorce.* However, the idea that married men should be subjected to the same restrictions as married women was never translated into the general consciousness of the Christian community or into the laws of medieval jurisdictions. As grounds for legal separation, one instance of a wife's adultery was usually sufficient, but a husband's adultery was grounds only if it created a public scandal. In fourteenth-century Perugia, an adulterous wife was flogged out of town and exiled; an adulterous husband was fined £50 if the adultery was committed in his own house and was public knowledge. In thirteenth-century Spain a married man's sleeping with a Moslem or Jewish woman was not considered an offense. For a woman, adultery with a Moslem or Jew was the most disgraceful, most harshly punished act she could commit.

The Protestant emphasis on the patriarchal family tended to strengthen the emphasis on the need for female purity. Wherever divorce was allowed, adultery was a cause. And for a century after the Reformation, laws against adultery were tightened up in both Protestant and Catholic countries, with severe flogging or death frequent penalties for female offenders. Afterward, the laws were generally relaxed and seldom enforced. However, adultery was still a crime. In the United States after World War II only three states had no criminal penalties for it. In other states, the penalties ranged from a $10 fine to imprisonment for one offense.

In the twentieth century, with more openness about sexual matters, extramarital intercourse (EMI) has become a subject of serious study. The Kinsey reports (A. Kinsey et al., *Sexual Behavior in the Human Male* [Philadelphia, 1948] and A. Kinsey et al., *Sexual Behavior in the Human Female* [Philadelphia, 1953]) laid the groundwork for all subsequent study of EMI. Morton Hunt, in his follow-up study *Sexual Behavior in the 1970s* (Chicago, 1974), proposed an estimate of the incidence of EMI that indicated little change since the Kinsey studies: that the percentage of men who have ever engaged in EMI is close to, but not over, 50 percent; that of women, 18 percent. For men, he found little overall increase since 1948 and only a modest increase in the youngest (18- to 24-year-old) cohort of his sample. For women in the under 25-year-old group, however, he found an increase from 8 to 24 percent, a change of "historic dimensions." This approach toward equality in extramarital activity by young men and women would indicate a radical repudiation of the double standard by young women. Studies since Hunt's (e.g., C. Tavris and S. Sadd, *The Redbook Report on Female Sexuality* [New York, 1977] and P. Blumstein and P. Schwartz, *American Couples* [New York, 1983]) indicate that the trend toward equal participation in extramarital affairs between men and women has continued: EMI rates among women continue to increase slightly, especially among the college-educated. Husbands' rates are still higher than wives' but have remained fairly constant.

Despite the assault on the double standard, however, wives were still more often accepting of the extramarital activity of husbands than were husbands of extramarital activity by wives. Men were more likely to engage in relationships that they label as purely sexual than were women and to approve of extramarital affairs than were women. They reported more desire for extramarital sex and engaged in it earlier in their marriages, had more partners, and were more likely to consider their actions justified and to feel less guilt than were women. Women more often reported that their extramarital affairs stemmed from emotional involvement or grew out of marital dissatisfaction. They also reported more guilt feelings (S. P. Glass and T. L. Wright, "Sex Differences in Type of Extramarital Involvement and Marital Dissatisfaction," *Sex Roles* 12 [1985]: 1101–1120).

Despite the explosion of literature and talk advocating sexual freedom of marriage partners, group sex, mate-swapping, and so on, the "permissiveness" of the 1970s was much more in evidence among the single than among the married (Hunt, 270–274). The spread of herpes and the fear of AIDS brought a change of atmosphere in the 1980s, with "permissiveness" giving place to caution, "swinging" to talk of "safe sex."

Nearly all those engaging in extramarital intercourse still attempt to keep it secret from their marriage partner. If discovered, it can be devastating. To the marriage partner it may cause feelings of intense anger,* profound hurt, loss of self-esteem, trust, and confidence. In the perpetrator, it can cause inner conflict, guilt, and, if revealed, shame and sometimes relief. It often either destroys or irreparably damages the marriage. The modern marriage, unlike most marriages in previous ages, is based on emotional involvement. The discovery of marital infidelity can destroy the emotional cement that keeps this important human relationship together.

AESTHETICS, FEMININE (also known as female aesthetics or feminist aesthetics). Debates continue as to whether there is such a thing, what it is or might be, and what it might do. Of central importance to such debates are the questions of what "woman" is and what happens to traditional notions of art when women become subjects and creators as well as objects of artistic expression. In addition, once feminine aesthetics is claimed and given shape, there arises the question of whether it pertains exclusively to women or whether it incorporates those concerns and practices shared by any group of people marked "other" and marginal by dominant culture.

Aesthetics is what provides a theory of the beautiful and of art. In Western patriarchal culture, it is assumed that art and beauty are universal categories of truth. Feminist theory, however, reveals the extent to which such universals are actually androcentric (man-centered) specifics coded as the norm and thus not accessible to women within the system of cultural expectation. This fact holds true in parallel fashion for identifications of race and class (among others) as well as gender. Woman marks the sexual category of Man; it is a culturally produced image bearing little resemblance to, though powerfully influential for, actual women. As muse, primordial origin, eternal mystery, object of desire and loathing, Woman constitutes the enabling inspiration as well as the raw material of art; beauty can scarcely be encountered without evoking Woman. Feminist theory demystifies this Woman-image to reveal her existence as myth or ideological construct and to enable women to enact themselves as subjects and artists. Such enactments are variously described as nonlinear processes based on subjectivity, as shifting and multiple rather than stable and monolithic, as prepatriarchal ideals of female-centered experience, or as invisible and unspoken realities breaking through barriers of repression and silence. Important to the debate over feminine aesthetics is the argument between essentialism (woman by nature is . . .) and production (culture assigns and teaches gender), with most current feminist theory eschewing the all-too-familiar traps of essentialism.

Feminine aesthetics is a problematic term precisely because, in a male-dominant culture, anything feminine is understood as "other" and inferior. Many current female artists and writers, therefore—especially if they are avant-garde or feminist—purposely call attention to Woman in order to unmask the myth. Women's performance art and *"écriture féminine"* (a means to female-centered language through "writing the body") are but two examples of women using the female body, for instance, to claim female subjectivity while disrupting the androcentric codes. Because so much of women's art and writing, purposely or not, functions in the world to change the world, the term perhaps most appropriate to its accompanying theory is feminist aesthetics.

References. Gisela Ecker (ed.), *Feminist Aesthetics*, trans. Harriet Anderson (Boston, 1985); Teresa de Lauretis, *Alice Doesn't: Feminism, Semiotics, Cinema* (Bloomington, Ind., 1984); Rachel Blau Du Plessis and Members of Workshop 9, "For the Etruscans: Sexual Difference and Artistic Production—The Debate over a Female Aesthetic," in Hester Eisenstein and Alice Jardine (eds.), *The Future of Difference* (Boston, 1980).

NANCY GRAY

AFFIRMATIVE ACTION is a term first officially used in a 1961 executive order, issued by President Kennedy, requiring a nondiscrimination statement in all federal contracts. Title VII* of the Civil Rights Act of 1964 authorized the courts to "order such affirmative action as may be appropriate" in order to remedy the results of discrimination.* Executive Order 11246* (1965) and the associated regulations of Revised Order Number 4 (1971) identified for the first time specific actions to be taken by federal contractors to eliminate the effects of present and past discrimination.

Generally, affirmative action is considered to be an active form of nondiscrimination that comprises identifying the underrepresentation in all conditions of employment of qualified women, racial/ethnic minorities, and other protected groups and then taking specific actions to enable an employer to utilize the protected groups according to their availability (that is, to achieve affirmative action goals). These actions may include, for example, additional recruitment and advertising for qualified members of protected groups as well as developing, implementing, and monitoring employment policies that are designed to encourage increased protected group representation. Affirmative action does *not* involve the setting of quotas, which are illegal unless assigned by the courts when discrimination is found; nor does it mean the hiring of less qualified women, racial/ethnic minorities, or other members of protected groups. The person most qualified for a position should be hired, promoted, and so on without regard to race, sex, national origin, or other non–job-related characteristic; however, the employer must be able to document that good faith efforts were made to recruit qualified women, racial/ethnic minorities, or others.

References. Emily B. Kirby, *Yes You Can: The Working Woman's Guide to Her Legal Rights, Fair Employment, and Equal Pay* (Englewood Cliffs, N.J., 1984); J. Ralph Lindgren, *The Law of Sex Discrimination* (St. Paul, Minn., 1993); U.S. Department of Labor Women's Bureau, *A Working Woman's Guide to Her Job Rights* (Washington, D.C., 1992); Women's Bureau single-sheet *Know Your Rights* publications: *Age Discrimination* (1995); *Pregnancy Discrimination* (1994); *Sexual Harassment* (1994); *Family and Medical Leave* (1994); *Wage Discrimination* (1994); World Wide Web: Department of Labor Women's Bureau, http://www.dol.gov/dol/wb/University of Maryland InforM, http://www.inform.umd.edu:8080 / Educational__Resources /AcademicResourcesByTopic / WomensStudies/ GenderIssues/WomenInWorkforce

DAYLE MANDELSON

AFRICA. Historical Overview. No generalization can adequately capture the varied conditions of women in Africa. Living in a land area three times the size of the United States, with roughly 450 million inhabitants spread in widely different geographical, climatic, historical, and cultural settings, African women cannot be neatly characterized in a few paragraphs.

The existence of hundreds of differing ethnic groupings, mixed and altered by extensive migratory movements over thousands of years, renders meaningful generalization difficult, if not impossible. Widely varying customary attitudes and practices have shaped widely differing experiences for women. In farming communities the division of labor has commonly followed sex and age lines, with women typically caring for children and food farming while men hunted, prepared the land for farming, built houses, and fashioned tools and equipment. In nomadic communities the sexual division of labor was different: women typically cared for the children and prepared the food as well as housekeeping. A few kinship groups fostered matriarchy, while more tended toward patriarchy; most usually permitted polygamy.

Varied indigenous religions have typically helped to maintain a woman's status in her family and community. Predating European colonial rule, Islam imposed its own constraints on women's life roles in North Africa and, through missionaries, migratory movements, long-distance land trade, and Arab shipping, reinforced various degrees of male dominance over women throughout much of West, East, and Southern Africa. Primarily introduced by missionaries accompanying European colonists, Christianity brought notions of monogamy and, for some women, Western education; the latter, however, was seldom as extensive as for men and made few improvements in the status of the majority.

Nevertheless, over 100 years of direct European colonial rule did introduce fundamental changes in the conditions of life of both women and men throughout Africa. The several colonial governments introduced laws and exercised state power to coerce Africans in Eastern, Central, and Southern Africa to work for colonial mining companies and settler farms, producing raw materials for export to their home-based factories. Some used outright force, while others imposed hut and poll taxes that required African families to earn cash. Simultaneously, the colonial governments pushed Africans off the best lands and onto infertile, poorly watered reserves; denied them credit for farm inputs; imported mass-produced manufactured goods that squeezed out the local handicrafts; and discriminated against Africans in the marketplace—leaving them no way to obtain cash to pay the taxes (or later, to buy the imported manufactured goods) except by working for the colonists.

The preexisting sexual division of labor stimulated men—hundreds of thousands of them—to migrate to earn wages in the mines and on the big settler commercial farms. In most regions, men even worked for the colonialists as domestic servants. Most women, children, and old people stayed home in the "reserves," using age-old techniques to scratch a living out of infertile soils. Despite the reserves' overcrowded, unproductive conditions, on the unrealistic presumption that the women really could support themselves and their families, the colonialists claimed they needed pay wages only sufficient to support the individual men—well below the minimum that Karl Marx suggested capitalists must pay to cover the costs of the next generation of labor power.

In West Africa, the colonial system worked somewhat differently. Some scholars argue that the colonialists feared mosquito-borne malaria, while others believed that the stubborn resistance of the heavily populated western areas thwarted colonial settlement. Whatever the reason, instead of farming themselves, the colonialists used taxes to pressure Africans to cultivate their own land, to grow cash crops for sale at low prices to big colonial companies that shipped them abroad. Forced labor and taxes pushed hundreds of thousands of migrants—initially men and later their families—down from the savanna to work as sharecroppers. Typically, the African landowners kept for themselves two-thirds of the price the companies paid for the export crop; the migrants received only one-third but could also grow their own foodstuffs. Thousands more migrants—mostly men—worked for below–poverty-line wages in colonial mines, leaving the women to care for the rest of their families as best they could on the savanna.

Regardless of these differences, throughout the continent colonial systems of production disrupted the preexisting self-sufficient communities, chaining their economies to the vagaries of the world markets for their crude exports. They incorporated African men primarily as low-cost, unskilled labor, and they built a truncated socioeconomic infrastructure designed to facilitate the process. Missionary and government schools, mostly at a primary level, taught the "three Rs" primarily to a few boys, frequently the sons of chiefs or wealthier families; even fewer children went on to secondary school to learn the low-level clerical skills needed under the colonial rule. In West Africa, colonial governments introduced extension education, credit, and marketing institutions to help men expand export crop cultivation. For the most part, however, these colonial institutions altogether neglected the health, education, and productive activities of women. They actually undermined production of the largely women-cultivated, domestically consumed food crops. For many women, bearing numerous children seemed the only way of gaining status as well as of producing more income-generating labor and perhaps a degree of security in their old age.

After independence in many countries, the institutions and practices inherited from colonialism persisted. In a few countries, however, several countertendencies supported efforts to end the exclusion of women from the development process. Some governments, starting with Kwame Nkrumah's Ghana, created women's ministries and bureaus in an effort to ensure that women enjoyed equal access to education, property rights, and development programs. Realizing the importance of women's potential contribution to their ongoing liberation struggles, some nationalist movements—in countries as different as Guinea-Bissau, Zimbabwe, and South Africa—brought women into their leadership. The 1986 United Nations–sponsored International Women's Conference in Nairobi, Kenya, symbolized the growing numbers of women across the African continent who, even without the support of their governments, were beginning to mobilize and join the global movement to press for full participation in the development process.

By the 1980s the African economies' continued dependence on the export of crude minerals and agricultural produce had led to a crisis that engulfed the entire continent. The falling real value of their exports and mounting foreign debts forced many African governments to abandon their efforts to meet the poor majority of their populations' basic needs. Their austerity measures, often imposed as conditions for International Monetary Fund assistance, have particularly cut back programs designed to assist women and women-headed households. Stirred by competitive struggles for survival, ethnic violence has further undermined women's efforts to improve their own and their families' lives. Persisting into the 1990s, all this served to underscore the need for restructuring inherited government and economic institutions. Only that will enable women to participate creatively, together with men, in developing the continent's rich natural resources to provide productive employment opportunities and rising living standards for all.

Reference. For a full bibliography relating to gender and development, see Ann Seidman and Frederick Anag (eds.), *Towards a New Vision of Self-Sustainable Development* (Trenton and Atlanta, 1992), esp. ch. 7.

ANN SEIDMAN

AFRICA. Central (Zambia, Zimbabwe, and Malawi). Women in Central Africa have had three major turning points in their history. Before the introduction of colonialism in 1885, societies in this area were predominantly agricultural. Work was organized by sex and age, with women in charge of producing and processing the family's food, child care, and housework. Men usually cleared the fields, performed heavy agricultural labor, cared for large animals, and engaged in warfare and politics. Both matrilineal and patrilineal systems of inheritance developed in this region. Patrilineal societies, such as the Shona and Ndebele in Zimbabwe and the Ngoni in Zambia and Malawi, were characterized by the inheritance of property through the male line, large bride-wealth payments, and paternal rights over children. Wives resided in their husbands' village, and divorce was rare. In contrast, matrilineal societies were characterized by inheritance through the female line. Husbands often lived in their wives' villages, had no rights to children, and paid a much lower bride-price. While not endemic, divorce did occur, and marriages were relatively brittle. However, while women in matrilineal societies had more access to land and more control over their children, males dominated both matrilineal and patrilineal societies. In one system husbands and fathers dominated, while in another, brothers and uncles had control. Neither system gave much power or authority to women. Control over women's reproductive and productive labor remained crucial to men in all Central African societies.

British colonial rule transformed Central Africa into colonial states known as Northern Rhodesia, Southern Rhodesia, and Nyasaland (now Zambia, Zimbabwe, and Malawi, respectively). Colonialism and the introduction of colonial capitalism changed the traditional sexual division of labor. As European-dominated mining and agricultural production expanded, the need for African labor grew. In order to procure this labor, the colonial governments taxed African males, limited African access to land (especially in Zimbabwe), and bullied chiefs for labor recruits. As a result, Africans, especially young men, were drawn into wage labor in the towns, at the mines, and on the European farms. Women and children were encouraged to remain in the rural areas where they could reproduce the labor force and provide a place for returning workers, thus replenishing labor at little cost to the employers. This system functioned well for colonial officials, European settlers, and African men, especially rural chiefs. But it increased the workload of rural African women, who continued to perform their own work while doing much of the work formerly carried out by men. Not surprisingly, women began to look to the towns as a means to escape this burden, and many African women flocked to the new colonial towns, where they survived by selling their domestic skills, often including their bodies. By the 1920s, both African and European men believed that these new "independent" women must be brought under control, and new regulations were enacted to do just that. By the 1940s, independent women were finding it increasingly difficult to survive in town. Urban female migration slowed, and urban marriages stabilized.

As individual opportunities declined, women began to adopt more collective solutions. They joined male-dominated organizations such as trade unions and political parties and provided strong support for strikes and political rallies. Both rural and urban women participated actively in the nationalist political campaigns during the Federal period (1953–1964, when the three nations were joined in a federation). This activism was an important factor in the ultimate success of the nationalist movements in Zambia and Malawi, which won independence from Britain in 1964. Zimbabwean women fought for independence, but, like their men, they fell afoul of the white settlers' determined resistance. In all three countries it appears women realized that collective and political solutions were necessary before their lives could improve.

In Zambia and Malawi, independence brought some gains to women, many of whom moved to the cities, where they have better access to education and waged work. A few women have joined the very male inner circle; they work in ministries, universities, and businesses. But most women are less fortunate. Less than 10 percent of the waged workers are women, and they usually hold poorly paid, part-time, unskilled jobs. Most women in Zambia and Malawi eke out a living by petty commodity production and sales in the informal sector or by farming. Zambia, with over 50 percent urbanization, has more women than has Malawi who survive on the margins of urban life, pooling household resources and enduring low standards of living in order to make ends meet. Women participate in farming in both countries, but farms run by female household heads are usually poor, and most women work on their husbands' or brothers' land. Some women receive adequate compensation, but most have little or no control over family income. They find it difficult to obtain the credit, training, and land required to succeed on their own in agriculture. This situation is made worse by Zambia's current economic crisis, which limits national growth and opportunities for both sexes; and while Malawi's more buoyant economy provides women with some opportunities, the commanding heights of the economy and the state are still largely dominated by men.

In Zimbabwe, the liberation struggle between 1964 and 1980 preoccupied most African men and women. The settlers declared unilateral independence from Britain in 1964 and waged a bitter war to maintain their authority over the black majority. During the war women carried heavy burdens, often taking care of children and the elderly while also feeding the liberation army. Many fought in combat as well. The victory of these forces in 1980 and the election of Prime Minister Robert Mugabe has brought great changes in the lives of both African men and women in Zimbabwe. Women have been given new legal rights, and opportunities for education and jobs have expanded. Nonetheless, much remains to be done. Patriarchal traditions from both precolonial and settler periods still hamper women, and progress has been slower than anticipated. Women still occupy the lowest economic levels of society and have limited access to training and better jobs. Official support is often neutralized by patriarchal forces surfacing at all levels of society.

However, the women of Central Africa are determined to improve their lives and are becoming increasingly vocal about women's issues. Women's organizations are lobbying governments for improvements; some are even carrying out development projects for women. Pressures for positive change will continue: the women of Zambia, Zimbabwe, and Malawi will press on until they become equal partners in their societies.

References. Teresa Barnes, "The Fight for Control of African Women's Mobility in Colonial Zimbabwe, 1900–1939," *Signs* 17, 3 (1992): 586–608; Martin Chanock, *Law, Custom and Social Order: The Colonial Experience in Malawi and Zambia* (Cambridge, 1985); Rudo Gaidzanwa, *Images of Women in Zimbabwean Literature* (Harare, Zimbabwe, 1985); Elizabeth Schmidt, *Peasants, Traders and Wives: Shona Women in the History of Zimbabwe, 1870–1939* (Portsmouth, N.H., 1992); Ilsa Schuster, *New Women of Lusaka* (Palo Alto, Calif., 1979); A.K.H. Weinrich, *African Marriage in Zimbabwe* (Harare, Zimbabwe, 1982).

JANE L. PARPART

AFRICA. East. The states in East Africa are, with the exception of Djibouti, primarily rural and poor. Prior to colonialism, women had been responsible for nearly all subsistence cultivation. Colonialism's imposition of Western ideas altered the status of women, reducing their power. Since independence, most East African states have been wracked by ethnic, religious, or ideological conflicts that have destroyed many of the efforts at industrialization and development. The setbacks experienced by women during colonialism continued under early independence (best documented for Kenya) by registering and consolidating land and grants of titles to men, substantially weakening women's autonomy in economic opportunities.

Ethiopia. For centuries in Ethiopia, queen mothers were able to wield considerable powers, and women at court were visible in unusual ways. The queen, all the ladies of the court, and wives of important men stayed in the army camps and occasionally fought. More recently, Muslim ideologies concerning women have taken root along the east coast, gradually segregating women and requiring male mediators in any dealings outside the home.

Sudan and Uganda. Historically, in the interior states of East Africa, there were popular, female fertility religions that in some areas enhanced women's power. More contemporary examples of organizational power for women in the Sudan include worker unionization, such as *ayahaa* (child nurses) in Mombassa and teachers and nurses in Nairobi. The local Communist Party and later the larger national movement attracted large numbers of women. In the Sudan, women's groups have achieved legal reforms regarding economic and family position, but in the Muslim area of northern Sudan, seclusion and sex segregation continue. Zaar spirit possession cer-

emonies offer emotional release and a wide range of contacts through dancing and healing.

Kenya and Mozambique. During the postwar period, modern cities from
Cape Town to Nairobi grew to become principal centers for African workers and cultural and political innovation. Prior to this time, the majority
of urban dwellers were migrants who always returned to the preferred rural
way of life. The vast majority of urban women worked in the informal
sector as petty traders, beer brewers, prostitutes. They worked in food and
tobacco processing and the manufacture of cloth. Increasing numbers went
into domestic service. Land shortages increased the number of African
women occupying domestic jobs and drew Kikuyu women into Kenya. In
some parts of East Africa, women employed for wages faced jail sentences.
In Mozambique, they faced up to a year of forced labor.

During the Mau Mau revolt in Kenya, women took part in the armed
forces. maintained supply lines, and delivered medicine, food, and communications. In Kenya, during the Emergency of 1952–1956, large numbers of women obtained industrial jobs, only to lose them when the men
returned. Numerous legal and political barriers existed to women's ownership. In Kenya all but a minute number of women were deprived of
independent access to land. A small number of Western-educated women
entered suitably feminine professions like teaching, nursing, and social welfare. In Muslim communities there was a need for women professionals to
care for women's needs. In small Christian circles, a culture of domestic
dependency was fostered by the growth of elite girls' boarding schools.

To many, the presence of urban women was associated with declining
morality and the social ills of the day—prostitution, venereal disease, adultery, alcoholism, and so on. Urban or rural, the majority of independent
states continued to express ambivalence about women's equality. Mozambique consciously sought to improve women's situation, whereas the
Kenya National Assembly in 1969 repealed the act requiring men to contribute to the support of their illegitimate children.

Women's Organizations and National Politics. Women gained prominence in the anticolonial protests and the nationalist movements of the
1940s and 1950s. The Women's League and its successor, the Women's
Movement, began among the educated urban women and spread to workers and peasants. In the absence of political power, women formed associations to protect themselves and their children and to take part in
nationalist and revolutionary struggles.

National independence, however, failed to benefit women, and formal
independence brought little change save an increase in educational opportunities for girls at all levels. Development projects, on the other hand,
accepted the existing sexual division of labor as inalienable and ignored
women until after the mid-1970s, the United Nations (UN) Decade of
Women and the food crisis. As a result of redevelopment policies, women

controlled less land, their land was of poorer quality with lower yield, and they had little access to credit or extension services. Projects to register and consolidate land were especially detrimental. In the initial Tananian settlement scheme, land went to husbands.

For most women, the need for an independent source of income remains the main fact of life. With an increased number of educated professional women, most still enter stereotypically female fields. In some countries the increase in women's opportunities are largely in the field of domestic service. An increasing, but limited, number of low-paying, semiskilled factory jobs are held by women in the food and clothing industries, but they are replaced by men when mechanization occurs.

Conflicting demands for modernization and tradition, where tradition is seen as the patriarchal model, abound in family policy and religious practice. Pressure to bear children remains strong. Women consider a large family central to economic and emotional well-being. Abortion is illegal in most states, and contraception is a contentious subject. Reform attitudes are complex, combining efforts to increase woman's rights with the reluctance to upset the traditional—including bridewealth,* polygamy, clitoridectomy. Moasai women of Kenya unite in solidarity to protect women who commit adultery. Kenyans publicly attack traditional women's roles, and self-help groups in Tugen seek information on family planning and question clitoridectomy for daughters. The Tanania Marriage Act of 1971 enhanced the security of wives in some respects but cost them the custody of their older children in event of divorce. Ethiopian Civil Code affirms man as head of family, thereby meriting the wife's obedience.

The independence movement in Mozambique, FREIMO, voiced strong support for liberating women from customary practices (polygamy and bridewealth) and colonial heritage. The Somali Women's Democratic Organization, founded in 1977, has gained the support of women and the government against infibulation rituals. Muslim women have not challenged circumcision. "Only a few highly educated career women and those too old and too poor are able to escape increasing rigor of Islamic practice" (Berger, 32).

Many women's organizations purporting to speak for all speak only for interests of the elite. Leadership of Maedelso (main national women's organization of Kenya) changed in 1970 from a militant group to an elitist organization that alienated rural members. Yet from these elite have come prominent writers, artists, physicians, and others who have worked for a wide range of women's goals.

In Eritrea's continuing struggle, women were incorporated into armed units. Their concerns have entered public discourse. Underrepresented in leadership, the Eritrean Peoples' Liberation Front (EPLF) struggles for autonomy from Ethiopia while promoting gender-based land reform, education for girls and women, and more egalitarian marriage relations.

Rapid changes of the twentieth century have dramatically transformed the prospects of East African women. Their remarkable ability to adapt and to struggle against difficult conditions will be critical to reconstructing gender relations in the future.

References. Iris Berger, "Women of Eastern and Southern Africa," in Margaret Jean Hay and Shain Steihter (eds.), *African Women South of the Sahara*, 2d ed. (Harlow, U.K., 1995); Catherine Coquery-Vediovitch, *African Women: A Modern History* (Boulder, Colo., 1995).

GLORIA STEPHENSON

AFRICA. North. The lives of women in the African states bordering the Mediterranean Sea have been adversely affected by the modernization of their economy, by state intervention in that economy, and by the rise of Islamic fundamentalism.

Official statistics indicate that the economic activity rate for women in North Africa is the lowest in the world, but official statistics tend to undervalue women's economic activities, either not including or undervaluing the unpaid family labor of wives and daughters. Women's economic activity increased from 8 percent in 1970 to 21 percent in 1990. From 1985 to 1994, urban rates were higher than rural, nearly 20 percent compared to 12 percent. Distribution of the labor force was 25 percent in agriculture, 29 percent industry, 46 percent service.

In urban areas, the expansion of higher education has opened professional opportunities for men and women. Pressure from the Egyptian Feminist Union brought increased opportunities for professional education to Egypt in 1928. Middle-class Egyptian women entered professions in numbers sufficient to feminize many professions during the 1970s. Nasser and Sadat guaranteed jobs to all university graduates. As men went into the military or employment in other Arab countries, women went into traditional professions, but also engineering and other "male" professions.

In Egypt, a slowing of economic growth eventually produced a surfeit of professionals as education outstripped the pace of economic development. The resulting underemployment set the stage for the "back to the home" movement apparent in the popular press of the 1980s. Women were portrayed as supplemental workers whose primary role was as wife and mother.

Choice of occupations is narrower for lower-class women. In the early twentieth century they were sometimes recruited for factory labor, but overall participation was minimal. Generally, the woman who works outside the home loses status. If she must work the most acceptable occupations are home-based and are performed out of the view of unrelated men. Examples include spinning, weaving, clothes making, and the raising of small animals. A different attitude existed in Egypt, where women were well integrated into economic life. They didn't lose status and were highly regarded if they had to support a family. In the latter part of the twentieth century, rural migrant men went into wage labor, and women went into subsistence production in the home. Lower-class women's participation changed in the 1970s as new labor demands by oil-producing states drew men from Egypt, Jordan, and the Occupied Territories. Women entered factories as replacement workers. Economic imperatives overrode social constraints. Women's wages as a percentage of men's in Egypt were 64 percent in 1970, 62 percent in 1980, and 68 percent in 1990.

Conditions for women in rural areas have been affected negatively by the spread of the modern economy. Pastoral nomadism, the way of life for many women of the area, has been in gradual decline for various reasons, including population pressures and government efforts to settle the nomads. The growth of the state and market economy draws nomadic groups closer to society outside the tribe. As they are integrated into national life, the need of cash and economic specialization pushes men to seek outside income as shepherds, sharecroppers, or wage laborers in towns. Women's work falls more and more into the category of subsistence activities, while men earn money to purchase an ever larger proportion of the tribe's needs. The camel is being replaced by the truck, a sign of the times. Men monopolize the new technology, and women lose many of their former activities associated with the tribe's animals. As women shift to full-time subsistence activities, women's economic activities are reduced or eliminated. Their importance in caring for a herd, their voice in the choice of migration routes, and in the manufacture of woven objects to be sold for cash disappears.

Capitalization of agriculture has tended to exclude women from production, transforming them into consumers. In 1994, the distribution of women in agriculture was Algeria, 19 percent, 6 percent unpaid family workers; Egypt, 8 percent, 62 percent unpaid family workers; Morocco, 27 percent, with 31 percent unpaid; Libya, 32 percent, no figures for unpaid; Tunisia, 47 percent, with 49 percent unpaid.

Nationalist Movements. Women participated actively in political agitation, even in violent confrontations surrounding national liberation, but didn't necessarily reap rewards of increased political participation in formal politics of postindependence states. The Egyptian revolution of 1919 and the Algerian War of Independence, 1954–1962, both depended on mobilization of women in demonstrations as organizers, speech makers, and even fighters. Egyptian women of all backgrounds took part in street demonstrations protesting the arrest of nationalist leaders by the British in 1919. Wafdist Women's Central Committee, founded in 1920, began to play an important role in the nationalist movement. They organized a boycott of British goods, banks, and personnel. In Algeria, cadres of FLN (Algerian Front for National Liberation) acted as messengers, intelligence gatherers, combatants in guerrilla wars. Palestine mobilized women for civilian and military roles. In all cases traditional views of women eroded but didn't necessarily make any permanent difference in women's position of power.

Between 1969 and 1982, barriers were down. Unmarried daughters attended mixed-gender political meetings, worked in unsupervised settings (such as clinics), and stood guard duty alone at night. Yet there were no basic changes in the power structure. Women continued as bearers of cultural continuity through emphasis on traditional roles. "Mother of martyrs" remains a central symbol. But by engaging so many women in the political arena, some traditional restraints were relaxed.

Reforms such as repudiation of polygamy occurred in Egypt and Tunisia in the 1950s through the 1970s; however, the 1980s saw a period of re-Islamization of legal structures in Egypt, Sudan, and Algeria.

Feminist Movements. Egyptian feminist movement had legal reform as central to its agenda. Upper and middle eclipses women formed the Egyptian Feminist Union (EFU), headed by Huda Sharawi, who on coming home from an international conference in Rome in 1923, removed her veil and dropped it into the sea, causing consternation among officials meeting her at the dock and a divorce from her husband. Within a few years most women of her class in Cairo unveiled.

The EFU succeeded in getting the first women into the university in 1929. They lobbied for reform of personal status laws, especially divorce, polygamy, restrictions on age of marriage, child custody, and inheritance in the 1920s and 1930s. They argued within the framework of Islamic modernization for laws that would preserve the laws' intent but remove repression. They opened educational and work opportunities, but it took 50 years to effect legal changes.

EFU joined Women's Suffrage Alliance and emphasized commonality with European women. Gradually, in the 1930s, they moved out of alliance with European feminists and began to develop an Arab nationalist context. In 1945, members helped found the All Arab Feminist Union, which sought to develop Arab feminism with nationalist resonance. Elsewhere, women's organizations of the 1930s and 1940s were primarily charitable, with nationalist overtones. Literacy, day care, and jobs for the poor were basic goals. Pre-1948, the Palestine Women's Union was involved with orphans and emergency relief work. In 1946 the League of Sudanese Women had similar involvements. Many also associated with the Communist Party. Egypt in the 1940s had a new emphasis on reaching out; Daughters of the Nile Union, 1948, emphasized literacy and hygiene for poor women. EFU came to incorporate a left-wing focus on concerns of working-class women.

The 1950s and 1960s saw women's organizations brought to heel as states expanded their power. Egypt banned independent political organizations.

Morocco tested the hypothesis that the real cost of hiring women was higher because of high turnover and lack of work skills. Results found that women stay on the job longer and have higher educational levels than men. Mernissi, a prominent Moroccan woman writer, places legal constraints on females within a wider belief system that emphasizes power of sexuality, the active sexuality of women, the sexual vulnerability of men, and the consequent clash of heterosexual love with religious involvement. Women and men are separated because heterosexual love is deemed too dangerous to the order of Allah.

Tension is engendered by Islamic ideology of sexuality's confrontation with the Westernized model of modernization. Modernization decrees that women enter the marketplace to satisfy profit-maximization imperatives, but Islam decrees separation and dependency so humankind might better focus on God.

Education. Ratios of children enrolled in primary and secondary education in relation to the total population of elementary and secondary school-aged children rose from 50 percent in 1970 to 67 percent in 1990. For individual countries the increase was Algeria, 54 percent for girls, 75 percent for boys, to 72 percent and 86 percent, respectively; Egypt, 54 percent and 79 percent, to 81 percent and 98 percent; Morocco, 39 percent and 65 percent, to 41 percent and 59 percent; and Tunisia, 53 percent and 75 percent, to 74 percent and 86 percent. Girls' enrollment still lags substantially behind that of boys.

Overall literacy for men and women rose to 44 percent, but illiteracy remains high. The illiteracy rate in Egypt is 25 percent for women 15 to 24 years of age. In rural areas it is 61 percent. In Algeria, Egypt, Libya, Morocco, and Tunisia the difference in illiteracy rates between men and women in the 15-to-24-year range is greater than 10 percent overall—in Algeria, 24 percent, Egypt, 17 percent, Libya, 18 percent, Morocco, 27 percent, and Tunisia, 20 percent.

Enrollment in higher education increased from around 25 women for every 100 men in 1970 to over 60 per 100 men in 1990. The highest increase was in Libya, with 84 women per 100 men; the lowest was Algeria, with 50 per 100. Egypt had 59, and Morocco 57.

Health. Early marriage (ages 15–19) has declined considerably, from 38 percent to 10 percent, but teenage fertility is still fairly high. Fertility in general has declined significantly in the past 20 years. Only Tunisia allows abortion, but use of contraceptive devices rose between 1980 and 1990.

Infant and maternal mortality rates are high, but improving. Infant mortality fell significantly, from about 125 per 1,000 live births in the early 1970s to 40 per 1,000 in the early 1990s. Maternal mortality fell from 500 per 100,000 live births in 1983 to 360 per 100,000 live births in the early 1990s (in developed countries the rate is 26 per 100,000). Stunting, an indication of poor nutritional status, is higher in Tunisia for girls than boys.

Anemia among women is high—among pregnant women, 53 percent, and among the nonpregnant, 43 percent. In Morocco 5 percent of the population were in polygamous unions between 1986 and 1992.

Clitoridectomy,* a form of female circumcision, has long been practiced in Egypt, Sudan, and some Red Sea coastal districts but is not much practiced outside Egypt today.

Political. Women in Parliament: in Algeria, 2 percent in 1987 and 7 percent in 1994; Egypt, 4 percent and 2 percent; Morocco, 0 percent and 1 percent; Tunisia, 6 percent and 7 percent in the lower house. In 1994, women at the ministerial level in Algeria were 3.6 percent of 28 posts; Egypt, 3.6 percent of 18; Tunisia, 3.6 percent of 28. There are no women heads of state in the area and no women ministers or subministers in Morocco.

Fundamentalism has been curbed in Tunisia but is growing in Egypt and Algeria. It has affected laws, going back to Shira. Fundamentalists are very critical of Muslim feminists, claiming they aid foreign powers in the sabotage of Muslim society. Their views gained importance in the 1970s and 1980s as disillusionment with Arab socialism grew, and secular strategies failed. As conservatism swelled, many young women, especially of the lower middle class, have been drawn to the style of dress and behavior prescribed by conservatives. Others join fundamentalists, feeling more secure and comfortable in public and conducting their work and school life according to tradition.

AFRICA. South Africa and Namibia. The 1990s have seen a period of long-anticipated and dramatic political change in both South Africa and Namibia. In 1990, following a protracted armed struggle, Namibia attained political independence from South Africa, which had administered the territory since World War I. National multiparty elections for both the presidency and the national assembly in 1989 and 1994 were dominated by the South West African People's Organization (SWAPO), the former liberation movement, now turned political party. In 1994, after decades of political struggle, South Africa held universal multiparty elections that brought the African National Congress (ANC) to power in a government that also included the Inkatha Freedom Party and the National Party. During the long struggle in Namibia African women were armed combatants and also put themselves at great risk to provide more informal kinds of support—hiding and carrying supplies, withholding information from the South African army, concealing knowledge about the activities and movements of the liberation armies. In South Africa women, primarily, although not exclusively, African women, figured prominently in the antiapartheid movement in numerous ways that not only contributed to the end of white minority rule in South Africa but also forcefully inserted gender-specific concerns into the political struggle and the transitional process. But the experiences of political independence have been mixed for women in both countries, for while they now have political representation in the new governments, the remnants of the apartheid system ensure that there are many barriers yet to overcome.

In many ways, life in South Africa and Namibia is still shaped by the system of institutionalized racial separation known as "apartheid." Under apartheid, racial separation, white supremacy, and access to plentiful and cheap black labor were the top priorities in political processes and social relations. During apartheid's zenith following the election of the National Party in 1948 state policy institutionalized numerous discriminatory and violent practices. For example, the entire population was classified according to a system of officially sanctioned racial and ethnic categories. White South Africans controlled approximately 83 percent of the territory, even though they made up only 7 percent of the population. Africans, on the other hand, were assigned to officially designated rural "homelands," which were economically unviable and denied South African citizenship. Urban areas were also divided on the basis of white, African, Asian, and a mixed-race population officially known as "colored" categories, with the quality of accommodation, amenities, and education available to each group reflecting the ideology of white racial superiority. Additionally, the frequent reclassification of areas meant that Africans, coloreds, and Asians were routinely forced to move from their homes and reassigned to other urban areas or homelands. Africans were officially permitted access to "white" South Africa only to provide labor, and their mobility was regulated by a system of "influx control" that required them to carry passes. Political activity for "nonwhites" was severely circumscribed into powerless "official" channels, and broader protest efforts were met with harsh responses from the state.

Years of living under this system certainly took an incredible human toll in both South Africa and Namibia. Apartheid created a harsh system of inequality where Africans were relegated to poor living conditions, an inferior educational system, few economic opportunities, and no meaningful political participation, while whites lived in posh suburbs with access to high-quality, albeit segregated, education, economic resources, and a monopoly over political power. The migrant labor system quite literally tore African families apart. Initially, primarily male migrants left their families in rural homelands to work in mines or urban factories, but eventually, severe rural impoverishment drove women to leave their children in the care of parents or friends to find work in urban industries or the large domestic service sector. Across these wide divisions it remains difficult to talk about "women's politics" or "women's interests" without specifying the circumstances of particular women. White women have privileged access to education and economic resources, including access to the domestic labor of African women, while many African women do not have access to those economic or educational resources and cope with separation from families and state-sanctioned violence in ways that do not affect white women. These great divisions make it difficult for women to find common ground for collective organizing.

Women figure quite prominently in the long political struggle against the apartheid system. From African women's protesting government attempts to issue them passes, to women factory workers in the trade union movement, to the Women's League within the ANC, to women's involvement in the military wing of the ANC, *Umkhonto we Sizwe*, women have been highly visible within the antiapartheid struggle. Both the form and content of women's political activities transformed over time. In their early efforts, women were involved in auxiliary branches of political organizations, as well as in trade unions and women's organizations that sought to end or curtail apartheid policies. Some attempts at multiracial organizing were made, such as the Federation of South African Women, which was founded in the 1950s, but it was difficult for women to find lasting common ground across the racial and economic divisions created by apartheid. During the broad political mobilization of the 1980s women's collective organizing proliferated both within organizations such as the ANC and the Congress of South African Trade Unions and in autonomous groups such as Cape Town United Women's Organization in ways that were multiracial (reflecting the broader mass mobilization) and that raised gender-specific concerns. In the early 1990s during the period in which constitutional guidelines were being debated in South Africa, it became clear that women were not willing to subsume their gender-specific interests to the broader struggle. Indeed, the Constitutions in Namibia and South Africa are noteworthy precisely because they do contain provisions to guarantee freedom from discrimination based on gender (and sexual orientation in South Africa).

In many respects women's long and multifaceted history of political involvement sets the South African case apart from other cases of nationalist struggle. Whereas nationalist movements often highlight women's political participation and women's issues prior to gaining political power, it is common for women and women's concerns to be relegated to the margins during periods of political consolidation. But, by the mid-1980s in South Africa feminists were actively shaping the agenda of nationalist politics. Years of apartheid contributed to high rates of female labor force participation and high numbers of women-headed households, while years of antiapartheid struggle had given women the voices to articulate gender-specific demands and highly developed organizational frameworks. The combination of these factors suggests that the new government in South Africa will not easily be able to follow the usual pattern of nationalist movements and dismiss the political demands of women.

In South Africa and Namibia women have, in some respects, fared well in the processes of political transitions. In South Africa almost a quarter of the Parliament are women, and two women sit on the Constitutional Court. Women are also well represented at the local level. In Namibia, the percentages of women represented at the ministerial, subministerial, and parliamentary levels are much lower. But in neither case has political representation provided a panacea for long-established patterns of inequality that continue to disadvantage women, particularly African women. For example, issues such as housing and rural development remain profoundly gendered in the postapartheid era. Moreover, in the struggle to establish political power and social boundaries, patriarchal authorities are challenging women's demands for legal reform in the name of "African custom" or "African tradition."

Popular expectations surrounding the elections in 1994 were very high as the many previously disfranchised looked to their new voting rights to be quickly translated into real material gains. For example, housing was and continues to be one of the most pressing problems confronting the new ANC government. The new government set a target of building 350,000 houses annually, but 18 months after the election only 10,163 new houses had been built. The availability of affordable housing is of particular concern to women since they head two out of three households in urban areas, and they are turning their dissatisfaction into political action. The South African Homeless Peoples Federation (HPF) represents the poorest segment of the population. Women make up 80 percent of the membership of the HPF and are working to secure affordable and accessible housing for the poor. Women's political organizing is also prominent in numerous other issues confronting the government that range from land tenure, to health care, to affirmative action.

In both Namibia and South Africa processes of political consolidation have brought out gender conflicts in the area of legal reform as the new governments have grappled with women's legal status, property rights, marriage rights, and domestic violence. Women's gender-specific demands for political and economic rights have come under scrutiny by "traditional" African male authorities who fear losing the basis of their own power under the new governments. Practices associated with African customary marriages such as polygamy, the denial of property inheritance to women, and the payment of *lobola*, or "bride-price," are being contested in the legal systems of both countries. Recognizing African customary unions under common law would mean sanctioning practices that many women feel put them at a serious economic and personal disadvantage. (Both South Africa and Namibia maintain dual systems of marriage recognizing civil marriages, or marriages under common law, and customary marriages.) The problem of domestic violence has also been raised in connection with these debates as women's groups press the state for legal protections and services against those who assert the rights of men to control "their" women. Too often violence against women is overlooked or dismissed as part of the "tradition" involving the subordination of women, but women continue to press for change. In Namibia, the Namibian Women's Organization praised a 1996 decision by the High Court to sentence a convicted rapist to life imprisonment, an apparent break from the low bail and light sentences that encouraged repeat offenders.

While women in both South Africa and Namibia have yet to realize the many tangible benefits from their relatively new governments, their long histories of political involvement and collective organizing would suggest that struggles to achieve full political inclusion and a better life will continue in new forms and on many fronts.

References. Susan Bazilli (ed.), *Putting Women on the Agenda* (Johannesburg, 1993); Heike Becker, *Namibia Women's Movement 1980 to 1992: From Anti-Colonial Resistance to Reconstruction* (1995); Belinda Bozzoli, *Women of Phokeng* (Portsmouth, N.H., 1991); Binaifer Nowrojee, *Violence against Women in South Africa* (New York, 1995).

SITA RANCHOD-NILSSON

AFRICA. West Africa. Women play very diverse roles in their societies, from lawyers, doctors, and wealthy market women, to poor subsistence farmers. As in many Third World countries, class plays an important role in determining the extent to which patriarchy limits the opportunities for women in West Africa today. Rural and uneducated women experience the greatest restrictions on their ability to earn an income, power within the marriage, and access to a variety of resources. Nevertheless, it can be said that nowhere in the region do women enjoy equality of status and opportunity with their respective male counterparts. In recent years, an indigenous feminist movement has developed within the region and within the continent as a whole that is likely to make important challenges to the subordinate status of women.

Women play a vital role in the economies of West African countries. They are the backbone of the rural agricultural economy. Their labor produces nearly all subsistence crops consumed by their families and the bulk of food crops consumed in urban centers and cash crops destined for world markets. The latter include coffee, cocoa, groundnuts, cotton, rice, palm products, rubber, bananas, and pineapples. Oftentimes, due to inferior legal rights to land, women do not reap the benefits of their labor. This is particularly so for export crops, the incomes from which are often controlled by fathers, husbands, and brothers. In addition to farming, rural women engage in the processing of raw materials. They are also engaged in the production of a number of important industrial crafts, the products of which find their way to local, regional, and international markets. Certain parts of West Africa are well known for their dyed and stamped cloth, pottery, and baskets, largely produced by women and girls. Incomes from these sources are generally the property of the woman craftsperson or entrepreneur.

In urban areas, women play key roles in the informal sector. They control the sale of most of the farm produce, seafood, and cloth and the sale of much of the clothing, hardware, and utensils sold in open-air central and neighborhood markets. Again, income from these sources is usually the property of the woman in business. Many "market women" are wealthy, indeed. They invest in retail shops, urban and rural transportation, real estate, credit provision, and the import-export trade. Their business takes them not only to other parts of their own countries but to other countries in the region as well.

Urban women sell prepared foods during the day and evening on street corners, their stalls constituting informal restaurants. Other urban women own and run businesses such as travel agencies, boutiques selling local and imported clothing, and hair salons. Urban women, particularly in the coastal countries, can also be found at all levels of white-collar employment: secretaries in government bureaucracies, bank tellers, lawyers, judges, doctors, teachers, university professors, and heads of local and international nongovernmental organizations.

In spite of the central role women play in the economies of West Africa, they do not always share equally in the benefits of economic growth. Moreover, in times of economic downturn, women, along with children, are affected the most severely. During the colonial period, wage sector employment overwhelmingly favored men. Women remained behind in agricultural production, while men migrated to other areas of the colony or to other colonies in the region in search of wage labor. This was particularly the case in the savanna (the northern parts of the Ivory Coast, Ghana, Togo, Benin, and Nigeria) and the Sahel (Burkina Faso, Mali, and Niger). Though women constituted the majority of the agricultural labor force, colonial officials targeted men for training and credit when they sought to improve local food production or increase the production of export crops. Educational opportunities were also biased in favor of boys and men, as were employment opportunities in the lower levels of the colonial civil service. Independence has brought important changes, but women still lag behind men in access to jobs in the formal sector (particularly at the higher skill and salary levels) and access to development resources and advanced education.

Beginning in the early 1970s, with the Arab oil boycott, the economies of West Africa began a precipitous decline. World market prices for cash crops could not keep pace with inflation. A more general trend towards deteriorating terms of trade between West Africa's traditional exports and imports from industrialized nations took hold. This picture was complicated by periodic drought, declining production, the smuggling out of export crops to avoid fixed government prices, and large-scale rural exodus. Women, who are more dependent than men on incomes from the rural sector, experienced increased levels of poverty. By the early to mid-1980s, most West African countries had come under World Bank structural adjustment programs whose aims were to increase exports, reduce government expenditure and involvement in the economy, and encourage market principles. "Conditionalities," such as the devaluation of local currencies, the privatization of state-owned enterprises, the removal of government subsidies for food and fuel, the reduction of social welfare spending, and the retrenchment of government workers, increased the level of hardship for women. Cutbacks in government spending have reduced access to inoculations against childhood diseases, prenatal and neonatal care, birth control, and education in the rural areas.

In the social sphere, women in West Africa face numerous challenges. Customary law still determines the legal rights of most women, particularly those in rural areas. Customary law is a legal system that is supposedly based on precolonial African law. However, many scholars have noted that customary law is, in reality, those laws and procedures that were rewritten by colonial officials, often in consultation with male elders, to serve the interests of colonial rule. The law overwhelmingly favors men in marriage, divorce, child custody, inheritance, and property and land rights. Muslim women also face legal barriers to equality as religious men have dominated the interpretation of the Koran and legal rights within the family. Rights within polygamous marriages, arranged child marriage, divorce, inheritance, and female circumcision are also of concern to many rural and urban women. Increasingly, women's groups in Ghana, Nigeria, Senegal, Niger, and elsewhere are organizing and speaking out about their concerns. Attempts to introduce a "Family Code," which would transform women's rights within the family, have been successful in some Francophone countries but not in others. However, even where women have, in theory, gained equal rights under new national laws, local courts, where most family disputes are adjudicated, continue to be controlled by traditional male elders and Muslim clerics who resist change.

In recent decades, West African countries have been experiencing political turmoil and change: civil wars in Liberia and Sierra Leone, state repression of popular movements to return Nigeria to civilian rule, and national conferences and demands for democratization in Francophone countries. These political events have been generated by a number of internal and external forces such as economic crisis, loss of state legitimacy, and pressures ("political conditionalities") from the International Monetary Fund and other aid donors. Scholars have noted that African women have used the space created by these forces to organize and put their concerns on the national agenda. In Liberia and Sierra Leone, the rape of women and girls by soldiers on all sides of the civil wars and economic disruption and dislocation have brought out women in these two countries to press for an end to the armed conflicts. In Nigeria, women have participated as journalists, human rights lawyers and advocates, and spouses of political prisoners in the struggle for democracy. In Niger in 1991, 2,000 women, mostly urban and Muslim, staged a first-of-its-kind march and demonstration to protest their near-total exclusion from talks about the political future of the country (only 1 out of the 68 delegates to the talks was female). Efforts by Nigerian and other women, particularly those in other heavily Muslim countries, to organize politically, to run for political office, and to get the Family Code enacted have been met by a backlash from conservative Islamic groups that have sought to brand the women as anti-Muslim, immoral, and tools of Western imperialism. In a few cases, women have been physically assaulted for challenging long-established norms of female public invisibility. In Niger, where more than 95 percent of the population is Muslim, Western-educated, elite women have sought to form alliances with more conservative women in Muslim organizations in an effort to reinterpret the Koran in ways that are not patriarchal. By seizing the moral high ground, they have sought to take away one important weapon in the hands of those who oppose the Family Code.

In spite of the explosion of women's groups and women's activism, women in West Africa remain marginalized from the political process and centers of political power. However, over the past 15 years, West African women have gained a wealth of experience in organizing themselves and in identifying key concerns and strategies for change. The next stage in the development of "African feminism" is likely to be the making of more successful inroads into national policies affecting not only women but society as a whole.

References. Barbara Callaway and Lucy Creevey, *The Heritage of Islam: Women, Religion, and Politics in West Africa* (Boulder, Colo., 1994); Margaret Jean Hay and Sharon Stichter (eds.), *African Women South of the Sahara* (Essex, England, 1984); Gwendolyn Mikell, "African Feminism: Toward a New Politics of Representation," *Feminist Studies* 21, 2 (Summer 1995): 405–424; Eileen M. Reynolds, "The Democratic Transition in Niger, 1991–1996: Women Leaders' Theories and Organizational Strategies for the Empowerment of Women," M.A. thesis, International Development, Clark University, April 1997; Claire Robertson and Iris Berger (eds.), *Women and Class in Africa* (New York, 1986); Sharon Stichter and Jane Parpart (eds.), *Patriarchy and Class: African Women in the Home and the Workforce* (Boulder, Colo., 1988).

BEVERLY GRIER

AFRICA. Women in Development. The extractive model of development being followed by most African countries has not solved the critical development problems of poverty, ignorance, disease, and injustice. It favors commercialization, assuming that wealth and its benefits will trickle down to the masses, thus raising the general standard of living. However, even proponents of large-scale commercialization admit that the trickle-down approach has failed to meet basic human needs. African development poses a fourfold problem: there can be no development without equity; equity cannot be achieved without addressing gender inequalities within the household and the community; the dichotomized household/community approach is inappropriate in analyzing women's work; and equitable development must result in economic, physical, and social well-being.

Development is currently measured by the growth of the gross national product (GNP) and the impact of population growth on GNP. Statistics on African women consequently reflect the obsession of governments and development planners with rates of production and reproduction. These planners perceive population in terms of labor force participation, levels of education, and life expectancy. These mechanistic measures of development render women invisible by statistically underrepresenting their labor force participation rates and ignoring the impact of their labor power on domestic and wage productivity. Household and subsistence production is treated as marginal to commodity production for growth and accumulation.

The dominant tendencies in African development reflect the impact of Western economic, social, and political domination (colonialism). The extraction of resources from the colonies depended on the creation of export enclaves in agriculture and mining and the promotion of a private land-tenure system. These structural changes, which were aimed at stimulating production and accumulation, transformed self-provisioning communities through forced commercialization. Colonial development eroded women's traditional economic and social bases and increased their work as emphasis shifted from the extended family (a network of socially and economically cooperating conjugal families) to the autonomous, male-headed nuclear family as the unit of production. Colonial policies promoted "cash crop" agriculture and neglected subsistence farming as conservative and backward. Women farmers were officially ignored, and their contributions and interests were disregarded. Agriculture is still under-remunerated and undervalued. Women contribute two-thirds of the labor hours in agriculture, and small farms produce 90 percent of the food.

Most women's options and effectiveness are limited by the inequitable resource distribution within the household and the lack of access to information, labor, and credit in the community. The promotion of monogamous marriages, nuclear families, and private land tenure made women into unremunerated laborers dependent on their husbands for land and livestock. Agricultural and veterinary experts continue to bypass women with vital information, rationalizing their actions by citing women's conservatism or social codes prohibiting women from talking alone to men they don't know. The experts tacitly assume that women's work is secondary and avoid any apparent violation of men's rights. Women's limited resources hinder their utilization of paid laborers, and the banks' requirement of landed property as collateral excludes women from credit.

An equally pressing development problem is over-urbanization. This occurs when migration to the cities is not stimulated by the demands of cheap labor and forced saving that are characteristic of industrialization. Cities cannot meet the needs of the rapidly growing populations for basic services such as housing and transportation or reasonable job opportunities to ensure subsistence and survival. Most urban migrants are self-employed—their entrepreneurial endeavors are officially branded as unemployment. A relative lack of education makes women predominant among the self-employed. Issues of land ownership and food reappear in urban areas where unoccupied space between buildings, in river valleys, and on the outskirts of cities is used mainly by women for growing food both for subsistence and for income generation.

Entrepreneurial women, who control almost 80 percent of the food and petty trade in some African cities, are generally overlooked by planners but are legally harassed. Government officials would do better to concentrate on protecting the consumers by ensuring the availability of clean water and proper sanitation rather than interfering with the vendors, who provide an invaluable service.

Dissatisfaction with the existing model of development has led to the promotion of "Another Development" using integrative models offering multiple economic and social arrangements. They advocate structural transformation as a challenge to the economic, political, and institutional forms of domination at the international level, where imperialism treats Africa as a source of raw materials, food, and labor and as a market for industrial products; and at the national level, where forces of cultural, religious, and nationalistic fundamentalism use women as pawns in the struggle against international capitalism and imperialism, thereby reinstating obsolete patriarchal systems and practices even at the household level. The national rhetoric of self-reliance promotes control over women's productive and reproductive labor, and the resulting physical and mental demoralization of women hinders real development.

The integrative models thus insist on addressing the persistent gender inequalities at the household, national, and international levels. They stress the necessity of building genuinely democratic institutions as part of the development cooperative venture and assert that women will be integrated into the development process when their skills and knowledge are not treated as expendable. As proof, advocates point to the women's enthusiastic adoption of the appropriate (and efficient) technologies of fish smokers in coastal West Africa, wood-burning stoves in the Sahel, and grain mills throughout Africa. The acquisition of managerial, administrative, and commercial skills is actively promoted to empower women and to ensure, for instance, that women's income-generating activities create incomes for women rather than for male experts.

Integrative models also focus on the long-term impact of development programs and insist that well-being (economic, social, and physical) is development and that aspects of well-being can be evaluated. Hitherto, economic well-being—access to, enjoyment of, and control over income, credit technology, land, water, and other assets—has been the target of analysis and advocacy. The food, water, and fuel aspects of physical well-being have been examined, but housing, medical care, personal safety, and leisure have received only cursory attention. Social well-being—knowledge, power, and prestige—have been ignored. Integrative well-being models see the long-term goal of development as the promotion of the quality of life.

References. Lourdes Beneria, "Conceptualizing the Labor Force: The Underestimation of Women's Economic Activities," in Nici Nelson (ed.), *African Women in the Development Process* (London, 1981), 10–28; R. L. Blumberg, "Females, Farming and Food: Rural Development and Women's Participation in Agricultural Production Systems," in Barbara Lewis (ed.), *Invisible Farmers and the Crisis in Agriculture* (Washington, D.C., 1981); Elise Boulding, "Measurement of Women's Work in the Third World: Problems and Suggestions," in M. Buvinic, M. A. Lycette, and W. P. McGreevey (eds.), *Women and Poverty in the Third World* (Baltimore, 1983), 286–299; Barbara Rogers, *The Domestication of Women* (London, 1979).

CHRISTINE OBBO

AFRICAN AMERICAN ARTISTS. The earliest known artworks by African American women are crafted objects produced by anonymous slave women during the antebellum period. Crafted art production continued after the emancipation of slaves and remains a vital component of African American culture today. Predominant techniques are textile and basket-making traditions, which are directly linked to artworks in African societies, especially to those located in West and Central Africa, where the American slave population originated.

In accordance with American colonial practices, which maintained gender divisions in art production, slave women created works in materials and techniques that were prescribed to female artistry, such as weaving, embroidery, quilt making, and basket making, functional art creating objects specifically designed for household purposes. There is substantial evidence that some of these skills were brought from Africa to America (e.g., coiled basket-making techniques of South Carolina and Georgia). Although African American female and male art production differed (men employing techniques in blacksmithing, wood carving, pottery, and architecture, among others), a complementary pattern functioned to sustain the rich cultural memory of the African heritage.

Luiza Combs (1853–1947) and Harriet Powers (1837–1911) are the earliest identified women artisans. Combs, born in Guinea (West Africa), was taken as a child into slavery to Hazard, Kentucky. Powers was born into slavery in Athens, Georgia. Both produced works that significantly link African heritage to American experience in women's creative expression. Little is known about their lives and works: only a woven blanket dated

c. 1890 remains of Combs' work; two quilts appliquéd with biblical, social, and personal imagery and dated c. 1886 and c. 1895–1898 are attributed to Powers. Combs' blanket demonstrates technical expertise in dyeing and weaving that is directly connected to Guinea. Strip weaving, earth colors, and polyrhythmic broken line motifs convey particular aesthetic modes of that African continuum. Similar characteristics are present in Powers' quilts; however, more of an African and European blend in aesthetic canon and technique is apparent. Particular influences of appliqué textiles of Fon people in the Republic of Benin (formerly Dahomey) are recognizable in the color scheme, stylized figuration, technique, and narrative character that merges religious, social, and personal histories. European influences are evident in the technique and in the type of religious and social history depicted.

While crafted artworks by African American slave women are valued for their preservation of the African heritage and for their distinctive African and European mixture, they are also important because they explicitly demonstrate that African American women ingeniously engaged in aesthetic evaluation and creative expression as they met domestic responsibility.

Freeborn Edmonia Lewis (c. 1843–1900), of African American and Native American parentage, began to make her mark prior to emancipation and later became the first African American sculptor to gain recognition. Her style was neo-classical, but her subject matter often departed from neo-classical references in favor of people and circumstances relevant to her dual heritage. *Forever Free* (1867) and *Hagar* (1875) are two of her best-known works. Of marble (as are most of her works), both project statements about struggles and triumphs over slavery and oppression. Although she expatriated to Rome in 1865 and associated with the White Mamorean flock (American women sculptors who lived in Rome and worked in marble), Lewis remained conscious of her personal identity while producing a body of thematically diverse sculpture. Exhibitions, reviews, commissions, and an honorable mention in the 1876 Centennial Exhibition in Philadelphia attest to her achievement. Her works can be found in various collections, including those of the National Museum of American Art, Howard University, and Harvard University.

African American women artists emerged in significant numbers during the twentieth century. Their art production encompasses a variety of styles and media, and their professional experience is diverse. In general, their lives and works are best understood within the matrix of the cultural, social, and political experience of two major epochs particularly significant for African American artistic expression, the new negro of the 1920s and 1930s (also known as the Harlem Renaissance) and the civil rights/black power of the 1950s and 1960s. Both periods were charged with a social and political fervor that reaffirmed African American cultural pride and spirit of self-determination. The post-1960s period might be considered as a third era that marked a significant stage of development, particularly for African American women artists. Works of these later decades suggest that many women artists were more cognizant of womanist experience. While their works do not fall into Euro-American feminist paradigms, an interesting Afrifemcentrist (African-female-centered) mode is prevalent that has yet to be examined. (*Afrifemcentrist* is a term that was coined by the writer and presented as *Afrofemcentrist* in 1984.)

Meta Vaux Warrick Fuller (1877–1967), May Howard Jackson (1877–1931), Annie Walker (1855–1929), and Laura Wheeler Waring (1887–1968) were artists who worked just prior to and during the new negro movement. Sculptors Fuller and Jackson produced forms enlivened with feelings of strength and pride, while Waring and Walker presented a similar consciousness in painting. Little is known about Walker, but Waring is noted for her mastery of portraiture, especially of prominent figures of the Harlem Renaissance. Fuller has the highest reputation of the women artists of the period. Her imagery, in Romantic and impressionist styles, is infused with racial uplift, cultural identity, and Pan-American politics, all of which foreshadowed major ideological developments in the African American art of her time and influenced that of successive generations.

Elizabeth Prophet (1890–1960), Alma Thomas (1894–1978), Augusta Savage (1900–1962), Selma Burke (b. 1901), Delilah Pierce (b. 1904), Lois Jones (b. 1905), Elizabeth Catlett (b. 1915), and Margaret Burroughs (b. 1917) are prominent among the artists who followed. Prophet, Savage, Burke, and Catlett were/are sculptors; the others, painters. In addition, Catlett has mastered various printmaking processes, and Burroughs also produces prints. Much like their predecessors, each artist created works that reaffirmed a commitment to African American life. (It is important to say at this point that, although themes of African American art centered on African American life and experience, the artworks often present universal emotions, i.e., celebration, grief, anger, pride, etc.) Foremost, artists sought to master their medium while expressing ideas about social, cultural, political, and/or personal issues in styles that ranged from realism to abstraction. Their success is implicit in their exhibits, awards, and general ability to achieve in spite of the Euroethnic pallocratic slant of the art establishment. Invariably, these women created challenges, not only for themselves but also for their successors, who gained strength through their triumphs. Interestingly, several founded art institutions: Savage established the Savage School of Arts and Crafts in New York in 1932; Burroughs, the DuSable Museum of African-American History in Chicago in 1961; and Burke, the Selma Burke Art Center in Pittsburgh in 1968.

Artists without formal art education are also important in African American art. Prominent are Clementine Hunter (1885–1988), Minnie Evans (1892–1987), and Gertrude Morgan (1900–1980). Hunter and Evans were domestics, while Morgan was a preacher. All turned to painting late in life and command great respect as visionary artists.

The most prominent of these artists is Catlett, who began to emerge in the 1940s. Catlett's sculpture and prints have long sustained a vision of women's diversity, activism, and strength and thus stand on the cutting edge of Afrifemcentrist and general feminist orientations. *Homage to My Young Black Sisters* (1968) is one of her most popular works. A stylized, organically robust female form sculpted in wood, *Homage* depicts woman's powerful presence in the struggle against oppression, emphasized by its upwardly thrusting clenched fist. Celebrating the involvement of women of color in the battle for human rights, it exemplifies Catlett's commitment to the working class and her ability to speak universally for women in an idiom influenced by African and Mexican aesthetics.

Many artists have become visible since Catlett, some of her generation and far greater numbers of later generations. While their technical approaches to creativity have broadened to include video, performance, and multimedia installations, their struggles for success do not differ much from those of their predecessors. Their styles, however, are more acceptable within the art establishment, partly because of general postmodernist trends that overlap with ongoing African American social consciousness and artistic variation. Among the many artists who have or are developing national and international reputations are Marie Johnson-Calloway (b. 1920), Samella Lewis (b. 1924), Betye Saar (b. 1926), Barbara Chase Riboud (b. 1930), Faith Ringgold (b. 1934), Camille Billops (b. 1934), Mildred Thompson (b. 1936), Margo Humphrey (b. 1924), Mary O'Neal (b. 1924), Howardina Pindell (b. 1943), Evelyn Terry (b. 1946), Freida High W. Tesfagiorgis (b. 1946), Winnie Owens (b. 1949), Martha Jackson-Jarvis (b. 1952), Adrian Piper (b. c. 1950s), Virginia Meek (b. 1950), and Allison Saar (b. 1956). Samella Lewis is particularly significant as a painter who has placed her painting in the background of art historical discourse and curatorial practice. Through her research, publications (a journal, *International Review of African-American Art*, and book [see References]), and Museum of African-American Art in California, founded in 1976, the art of African American women and men has been documented and exhibited. Like Savage, Burke, and Burroughs, she has become an institution. Billops, too, is significant in the preservation of art and culture through the Hatch-Billops Collection, which she and her husband, James Hatch, officially established in New York in 1974.

Altogether, these artists are producing some very exciting works that are largely autobiographical, sociological, cultural, political, and psychological. While the artists vary in style and technique, an impressive common strand is evident in their self-defined, self-directed visual statements about life as they know it, statements about identity that defy any feminine stereotype.

Equally as impressive are their dynamic sense of color and dramatic manipulation of rhythm, which, however abstract, build upon long-established principles in African American culture.

References. David Driskell, *Two Hundred Years of African-American Art* (New York, 1976); Jacqueline Fonvielle-Bontemps and Arna A. Bontemps, *Forever Free: Art by African-American Women 1862–1980* (Normal, Ill., 1980); Samella Lewis, *Art: African-American* (rev. ed. Miami, Fla., 1978); John Vlach, *The Decorative Tradition in Afro-American Art* (Cleveland, 1978).

FREIDA HIGH TESFAGIORGIS

AFRICAN AMERICAN POETS. Women poets are significant in numbers and are leaders in the African American literary tradition. The earliest extant writing by an American black, "Bars Fight," is a short poem in tetrameter couplets by Lucy Terry, describing an Indian raid on an English settlement near Deerfield, Massachusetts, in 1746. Today, Terry's verse is important as a historical document, not for its aesthetic value. In 1773, Phillis Wheatley's *Poems on Various Subjects, Religious and Moral* was published in London, making her the first black living in America to author a book. The American edition appeared in 1786. Wheatley, a Senegalese slave woman, was brought to America as a child. She benefited from living with a Boston family that encouraged her literary interests. Her poetry, eighteenth-century neo-classical in style, belongs to the tradition of Alexander Pope.

Prominent eighteenth- and nineteenth-century black writers included approximately a dozen black women poets. The most important was Frances Watkins Harper, who lived from 1825 to 1911. Between 1854 and 1901 Harper published at least five volumes of poetry, one novel, and political essays. A teacher and abolitionist lecturer with strong religious beliefs, she was a staunch feminist and vigorously supported the temperance movement. Her writings reflect these concerns. Nineteenth-century black women also published poetry anonymously in religious journals, magazines, and newspapers, most of which are lost.

Black women poets of the twentieth century extend and enrich the earlier tradition. The writings of Alice Dunbar Nelson, Georgia Johnson, Anne Spencer, Jessie Redmon Fauset, Angelina Weld Gimke, and Helene Johnson represent the period between the early part of the century and the Harlem Renaissance of the 1920s, a stimulating time of artistic and cultural expression. These well-educated women wrote conventional poetry, less on racial themes and the social protest than their predecessors.

A second group of black women poets emerged between the end of the 1930s and the beginning of the 1960s. They, too, wrote mainly in traditional forms, but they chose the black experience for their theme. Gwendolyn Brooks, who has earned numerous awards for her work, is the most widely celebrated of them. In 1950 she received the Pulitzer Prize for *Annie Allen*, the first black American to be so honored. Others in this group include Margaret Alexander Walker, also the recipient of several awards, Margaret Burroughs, and Pauli Murray.

Influenced by the civil rights movement in America and simultaneous political upheavals in other parts of the world, a younger generation of women and men changed black writing drastically from the end of the 1950s through the 1960s. Combining political activity, racial consciousness, and creative expression, they produced a race-conscious literature that was visionary, immediate, nationalistic, and extremely energetic. For the poets, the symbol of the revolution became the rejection of traditional white poetic forms for the blues, jazz rhythms, and other manifestations of black vernacular speech. The oral folk tradition provided them usable patterns that expressed black pride, beauty, and strength. Deviations from traditional Western poetry such as musical accompaniments to spoken texts, the typographical variations in the uses of punctuation, the lengthening or shortening of words, and other visual changes in written texts were quickly incorporated into their style. Earlier black poets had experimented with blues and jazz rhythms, but the power of the shift in racial sensibility in the 1950s and 1960s led to what became known as the "new black poetry." Some older poets, including Gwendolyn Brooks, discarded the forms that had brought them fame in the white world and joined their younger colleagues in the search for a distinct black aesthetic.

The number of published black women poets has dramatically increased since the beginning of the new literary movement in the late 1950s. While many appear primarily in anthologies, magazines, and journals, others have several individual collections. Some are also outstanding for their fiction, autobiographies, and drama. Among the most prominent with multiple volumes of poetry and works in other genres are Maya Angelou, Nikki Giovanni, June Jordan, Audre Lorde, Ntozake Shange, Alice Walker, and Sherley Anne Williams.

References. Gloria T. Hull, "Black Women Poets from Wheatley to Walker," in Roseann P. Bell et al., *Sturdy Black Bridges: Visions of Black Women in Literature* (New York, 1979), 69–86; Erlene Stetson (ed.), *Black Sister: Poetry by Black American Women, 1746–1980* (Bloomington, Ind., 1981).

NELLIE McKAY

AFRICAN AMERICAN PROSE WRITERS. The first published works by black women prose writers were religious autobiographies, slave narratives, and essays and speeches condemning slavery in the early part of the nineteenth century. Religious autobiography was launched with the 1836 publication of *The Life and Religious Experiences of Jarena Lee*, an evangelist, while the first black female slave narrative was Harriet Jacobs' *Incidents in* *the Life of a Slave Girl* in 1861. Lee spoke for the spiritual authority of black women, Jacobs for resistance to, and triumph over, slavery. Autobiographies and nonfiction prose condemning slavery, lynching, and other racial injustices dominated black women's writings in the nineteenth century.

In contrast, twentieth-century African American women's autobiography is a disparate body of works characterized by careful selectivity in self-revelations. These works range from childhood remembrances of slavery, written in the early 1900s, to the conscious novel that emphasizes growth and development. Women in all walks of life write about themselves, including teachers, nurses, social workers, ministers, politicians, sports figures, entertainers, and writers. Excluding writers, who author few autobiographies and who are less self-revelatory in this genre than in others in which they write, most texts represent model lives. Writer Maya Angelou is unique in having written five volumes of her life story.

In the early 1830s, the publication of an antislavery tract by Maria W. Stuart, the first American woman to make a profession of the lecture circuit, launched the essay tradition in black women's writings. For many decades, the essay was relegated to magazines and newspapers. Since the late 1970s changes have occurred as collections of essays by individual writers such as June Jordan and Audre Lorde have appeared.

An early printed drama by a black woman was Alice Dunbar Nelson's *Mine Eyes Have Seen*, published in *Crisis* in 1918. This publication occurred at the beginning of the Harlem Renaissance, a period of intense black artistic and cultural activity that lasted until 1930. *Mine Eyes* examined black men's military obligations to America in times of war. By 1930, 10 additional black women had published 20 one-act plays, mainly in journals and magazines. Several won prizes. Themes range from folk drama, to comedy, to lynching, birth control for poor women, and women's social roles. Contemporary critics consider Marita Bonner, a Radcliffe graduate and prizewinning essayist, the most impressive of these playwrights, especially for her expert use of expressionist techniques in *The Purple Flower*, published in 1929. As dramatists, black women came of age with the Broadway debut of Lorraine Hansberry's acclaimed *A Raisin in the Sun* in 1959. In the wake of the civil rights movement of the 1960s and 1970s and the search for a distinctive black aesthetic, contemporary black women's drama reflects avant-garde experimental techniques, black theater history, spiritual sensibilities, and the celebration of black heritage and black women's heritage. The best-known dramatists include Alice Childress, Adrienne Kennedy, Sonia Sanchez, Maya Angelou, and Ntozake Shange.

In 1859, *Our Nig*, the first novel by a black woman, Harriet Wilson, was published in Boston. By 1900, four novels by black women had been published. The most important were *Our Nig* and Frances Watkins Harper's *Iola Leroy, or Shadows Up-lifted*. Both addressed white racism. For most of the twentieth century, short stories and novels have been the primary literary forms to engage black women writers. Most of the former continue to be published in anthologies, journals, and magazines, and few black women have collections of their own. Women's magazines that target black women audiences and anthologies published by small and/or feminist presses since the 1970s have significantly increased the number of stories that black women publish.

Between 1900 and 1920 two novels were published by black women. Between 1920 and 1930 the number was eight, reflecting the increase in black women's literary production during the Harlem Renaissance. Zora Neale Hurston, one of the most important black women novelists of the century, wrote short fiction during the 1920s. Jessie Fauset, who wrote four novels, and Nella Larsen who wrote two, concentrated on urban, black, middle-class women's lives and wrote two novels each. They were among the most productive members of the Renaissance. Their works, neglected for many years as products of the "genteel tradition," now receive wide critical appraisal.

Between the early 1930s and the mid-1950s, Hurston, Dorothy West, Gwendolyn Brooks, and Ann Petry were the most successful black women novelists. Hurston, who published four novels, rejected themes of racial oppression then popular in black writing in favor of exploring the internal strengths and weaknesses of the black folk culture. Critically ignored for decades, Hurston's work underwent a dramatic revival in the 1970s as the voices of black women critics joined the literary discourse. Janie, in Hurston's most celebrated work, *Their Eyes Were Watching God* (1937), a black woman in search of independent love and personal wholeness, is the first fictional black feminist heroine. West, a journalist, wrote short stories and one novel, *The Living Is Easy* (1948), examining black, middle-class aspirations in early twentieth-century Boston. In 1953, Brooks, better known for her poetry, published a novel, *Maud Martha*, in which an "ordinary" young woman in Chicago discovers her positive self. Petry, also a journalist, wrote stories for children, three novels, and short fiction. *The Street* (1946), her first novel, received wider critical attention in its time than any previous black woman's novel. Her protagonist, a black, working-class, single mother, struggles unsuccessfully against urban ghetto deterioration.

Black American writing changed drastically in the 1960s, a time now called the Second Renaissance. The civil rights movement at home, the liberation of several formerly colonized African nations, and the struggle for freedom by oppressed peoples in different parts of the world had a pronounced effect on the life and literature of African Americans. Black militancy, black nationalism, and the search for dignity penetrated all areas of black endeavor. Poetry and drama responded immediately to the political situation; fiction assumed a reflective role in expressing the hopes and aspirations of a people who had suffered long because of their race. Black women's fiction since then has thoroughly explored black women's lives in relationship to race, gender, sexuality, and class. Writers consistently convey pride in black female selfhood while exploring the impact of racism, sexism, homophobia, and economic oppression on the lives of black women. Models come from the lives of foremothers who had no opportunity to write fiction but were nevertheless artists in other ways. The number of contemporary black women novelists and short story writers grows impressively, and includes Nobel laureate Toni Morrison, Pulitzer Prize winner Alice Walker, Gloria Naylor, Jewelle Gomez, and Jamaica Kincaid. Black women writers have produced some of the most exciting American fiction of the last two decades.

References. Hazel Carby, *Reconstructing Womanhood, the Emergence of the Afro-American Woman Novelist* (New York, 1987); Barbara Christian, *Black Women Novelists* (Westport, Conn., 1980); Mari Evans, *Black Women Writers (1950–1980): A Critical Evaluation* (New York, 1984); Frances Smith Foster, *Written by Herself, Literary Productions by African American Women, 1746–1892* (Bloomington Ind., 1993); Marjorie Pryse and Hortense Spillers, *Conjuring, Black Women, Fiction, and Literary Tradition* (Bloomington, Ind., 1985); Cheryl Wall (ed.), *Changing Our Own Words, Essays and Criticism, Theory and Writing by Black Women* (New Brunswick, N.J., 1989).

NELLIE McKAY and TRACY McCABE

AFRICAN AMERICAN WOMEN (SINCE 1865) have had their social, political, and economic experiences shaped by triple discrimination: racism, sexism, and classism. However, black women have responded vigorously, engendering in the process a number of significant social movements and struggles: the club movement, the civil rights movement, and the raising of black feminist consciousness.

The discrimination of the antebellum period remained pervasive for southern blacks after the Civil War. Their political, social, and economic opportunities were circumscribed by the black codes that replaced the slave codes and by an exploitative economic system, of which sharecropping is the best-known feature. Occupationally, African American women in particular were victimized and relegated to a life of poverty. Unlike poor white women, who could work in textile mills and factories, African American women were forced by sexual and class codes to work as servants in the houses or as farm laborers in the fields where they had previously toiled as slaves. Moreover, often the sexual and racial complaints of white women, rather than of the white male employers, prevented African American women's access to better-paid employment.

Such social and economic restrictions did not, however, deter African

American women from continuing to etch out a place for their families in this new southern society. Among the first and perhaps most urgent decisions made after emancipation was the reestablishment of family ties. Considering the family a sacred institution, thousands of freedmen and -women advertised through newspapers for lost family members and participated in mass marriage ceremonies, which were often performed in open fields by black ministers. Another decision made by thousands of African Americans was to migrate. Frustrated with their plight, they opted to move north in search of a better life.

This mass exodus in the late nineteenth and early twentieth centuries resulted in a loss of about 200,000 blacks, the majority of whom were women, from the South. The women soon discovered that their northern experience was comparable to their southern experience: racial, sexual, and class oppression continued. They were destined to work in the jobs that white women left behind in their upward economic climb. Their employment areas were classified as "negro work"—the worst jobs, characterized by segregated and unhealthy conditions. In the 1920 and 1930 censuses, 97 percent of African American women were classified as maids, dishwashers, domestics, and unskilled factory workers. Working conditions were poor: long hours, poorly ventilated rooms, low wages, and frequent sexual harassment. Many working-class white women suffered the same abysmal conditions, but racism precluded the possibility of any gender bonds developing between blacks and whites.

An additional result of the rapid migration to northern cities was the rupture of the black family. Low-paying jobs for African American women, high unemployment among African American men, few recreational centers for black children, and the transformation of black communities into ghettos and havens for drugs, crime, and prostitution put familial relationships under constant strain. As the self-respect and authority of African American men foundered under a discriminatory system that provided few jobs for them and no welfare to low-income families whose fathers were present, many men deserted their homes, leaving the women as the sole providers.

These conditions galvanized a group of educated, leisured, middle-class women to reform activity through associations and clubs. These activists, the New African American women, advocated a black self-help theory paralleling the theoretical underpinnings of the Progressive Era social-justice movement.

Like the African American women activists of the Civil War period (women such as Sojourner Truth, Harriet Tubman, Frances Ellen Watkins, and Charlotte Forten, who had fought injustice through speeches and writing, through conducting slaves to freedom via the Underground Railway, and through establishing schools), the New African American Women were determined that through their efforts the race could be elevated.

Numerous African American women met the challenge to change society.

In 1909, Nannie Burroughs established the National Training School for Women and Girls in Washington, D.C. Ida B. Wells led an antilynching campaign in the 1880s and 1890s and continued her attack on discrimination through lectures and writings. Mary Church Terrell and Mary McLeod Bethune organized women's clubs, the National Association of Colored Women (NACW)* and the National Council of Negro Women (NCNW),* respectively. The poems and novels of Zora Neale Hurston, written during the Harlem Renaissance, promoted racial self-worth through maintenance of the African tradition. Madame C. J. Walker created black economic self-help by establishing a million-dollar hairdressing business.

The African American women's clubs, especially the NACW and the NCNW, established programs and trained new leaders, providing them with confidence as a group and instilling in them a sense of worthiness as women and of racial pride as black women. This training produced a feminism that allowed some black women to view themselves not as mere biological entities destined only to give birth and be mothers but as political organizers for social change as well. The psychological transition was inherent in their demand for rights of full citizenship—economic, political, and social—for all blacks, both women and men. Realizing that maximum effort was needed, the New African American Women aligned themselves with the National Association for the Advancement of Colored People (NAACP) in the frontal attack on discrimination.

In the late nineteenth and early twentieth centuries there was some interest in the woman suffrage movement among middle-class African American women who hoped that by joining in the effort to get votes for women, they could not only get the vote for themselves but also reenfranchise black men. When white suffragists followed the path of political expediency in their campaign for southern votes, by campaigning for votes for white women only, black club members and the NAACP tried to undermine their attempt, an experience that convinced black women that the battle for sexual and racial freedom would have to be waged solely by themselves.

World War II allowed greater participation by black women in the mainstream labor force. They worked in such positions as trained nurses, drillers in metal industries, clerks, elevator operators, and machine operators in war factories. Although there was a significant decline in the percentage of women in domestic services, from 60 percent to 45 percent, African American women were still victims of low wages and limited advancement. The government remained indifferent to this problem until forced to address it by the activism of the NACW and NAACP. The threat of 100,000 militant African Americans marching on Washington, D.C., in 1941, a march suggested by a black woman, according to Harvard Sitkoff, pressured President Franklin D. Roosevelt to issue Executive Order 8802 to forestall the march. This groundbreaking order established the Fair Employment Practices Commission (FEPC), which outlawed discrimination in the nation's defense industries on the basis of race, color, and national origin. African American women's optimism that this policy also protected them soon dissipated, however, as sexual discrimination remained rampant in war industries. The majority of complaints received by the FEPC were from black women.

However, the 1940s led to some participation of African American women in organized labor. The Congress of Industrial Organizations, established by John L. Lewis, attracted not only workers from mass industries such as steel, iron, and garment manufacturing but also workers in industries such as laundry and tobacco, who were primarily African American women. African American women later began to enter jobs once restricted to men and to gain positions in the labor union infrastructure. Further, as more African American women graduated from college, the percentage of women entering professional areas increased as much as, or more than, their increase in the workplace. By 1940, 3,244 African American women had received B.A. degrees from black colleges, compared to 2,463 African American males. Within a decade, the percentage of African American women who were professionals such as teachers, social workers, and nurses rose from 4 percent to 6 percent.

In the years after World War II, continued civil and political discrimination, threats to economic gains made during the war, the lessons of the earlier woman suffrage movement, and the issues surrounding the *Brown v. Board of Education* decision and other Court rulings created an atmosphere that catapulted some working-class and middle-class African American women into leadership roles in the civil rights struggle. Rosa Parks' decision not to give up her seat on the bus was a radical act of defiance that led to the successful 365-day bus boycott in Montgomery, Alabama, the first act in the growing onslaught against racism. Ella Baker was instrumental in building structures to sustain the attack. She helped to establish the organizational structure for the Student Non-Violent Coordinating Committee (SNCC) and the Southern Christian Leadership Conference (SCLC). Daisy Bates led the desegregation movement in the public schools at Central High School, Little Rock, Arkansas, in 1957. In 1964, Fannie Lou Hamer transformed the civil rights struggle from social and political theorizing to political applicability by establishing the Mississippi Freedom Democratic Party (MFDP). (See CIVIL RIGHTS MOVEMENT, BLACK WOMEN IN.)

Though Parks, Baker, Bates, and Hamer were older women whose feminism had been nurtured for many years, some young African American women of the civil rights movement were relegated to female support roles, either taking telephone calls or preparing coffee. Paradoxically, although the civil rights movement was vital for the beginnings of the women's rights movement,* initially, the latter movement addressed the special interest of white, middle-class women who had entered the workforce. Very few African American women joined their ranks, as race, sex, and class issues were excluded from Equal Rights Amendment (ERA) and the National Organization of Women (NOW) rhetoric.

Important to the lives of African American women in the 1970s and 1980s were issues of high unemployment among African Americans, the "feminization of poverty," and the educational needs of children. The primacy of these issues enhanced feminism among African American women of all classes and led to a call for dialogue between African American and white women. The woman's rights movement of the 1980s must have been a collaborative effort of all races, classes, and sexes. Historically, African American women have been especially effective in addressing and generating changes that are much needed for all involved.

The elevation of the African American race through political, social, and economic activism has been the paramount goal of African American women since 1865. They have viewed their role as nurturers who transcend the home to reach into the community and the political arena. Because their history has been one of oppression from all sides and angles, African American women are well equipped to work with white women, white men, and people of all classes. The African American woman activist of today must view social issues as human and international in scope. She must continue the African American feminine tradition of including the dynamics of race, class, and sex in the search for solutions to the problems that all human beings will continue to face.

The 1990s have elevated African American women's involvement in the political arena. On the local, state, and national level, African American elected officials have doubled since the 1940s. The recent elections and the polemical welfare reform agenda have forced female elected officials such as Eva Clayton, Eleanor Norton Holmes, and Maxine Waters to voice alarm and opposition for fear that these measures will promote family dissolution and the continuous feminization of poverty. The 1996 Stand for Children sponsored by the Children's Defense Fund in Washington, D.C., represented a rainbow coalition of advocates against the pending reform agenda. On the local level, African American women and others have organized focus groups to educate all women, particularly women of color and poor women.

References. Angela Davis, *Woman, Race and Class* (New York, 1981); Paula Giddings, *When and Where I Enter: The Impact of Black Women on Race and Sex in America* (New York, 1984); Sharon Harley and Rosalyn Terborg-Penn (eds.), *The Afro-American Woman: Struggles and Images* (New York, 1978); Joyce Ladner, *Tomorrow's Tomorrow: The Black Woman* (New York, 1971); Jeanne Noble, *Beautiful, Also, Are the Souls of My Black Sisters: A History of the Black Woman in America* (Englewood Cliffs, N.J., 1978); Harvard Sitkoff, *A New Deal for Blacks* (New York, 1978).

BEVERLY W. JONES

AFRICAN ARTISTS. Women artists assume an important role in art production throughout Africa. They create artworks in a wide range of techniques including weaving, pottery, basketry, mural painting, fabric dyeing, beadwork, body decoration, and, more recently, metalwork and wood carving. In general, African women artists can be divided into two broad categories: traditional and modern. Traditional artists work within the limitations of gender proscriptions and prototypes that are imposed by society, while modern artists produce works within and outside such structural boundaries and are far more flexible in their selection of materials and personal expression. Both groups constitute the historical continuum in the art of African women. The first group sustains artistic traditions that are centuries old, while the second intervenes in society to add modern dimension to culture indicative of social transformation. Women artists, whether traditional or modern, complement male artists in formulating the essential female–male duality that has long been established in African art and life.

Within their particular societies, traditional women artists produce functional artworks that are highly valued. Their creativity centers around their own household responsibilities and is, therefore, primarily produced within domestic settings, where they acquire their skills from older women, usually relatives. Functionally, however, artworks serve both domestic and public spheres. For example, pottery is used in the home for cooking and storage, yet it is also used in ceremonies of the larger community. Public demands for such works, which meet religious, social, and political needs, provide women with some degree of economic independence. Additionally, such demands emphasize their value as participants in the life-sustaining practices of their society.

Modern African women artists work in contexts and systems that are radically different from those of the traditional artists. They develop their artistic skills through formal education in institutions controlled by men, including foreigners. As in most modern societies, their artworks are not central to everyday life and, therefore, fall to the periphery of life's activities. Consequently, modern women artists, like their male counterparts, must create a place for themselves in their various societies as they confront the global arena of exhibitions, reviews, and so on. Some preparation to meet this challenge is made in the educational institutions, where the artists interact in a social climate that is characterized by competitiveness in teacher–student roles and in peer associations. Perhaps the primary compensation for the artist's marginal status and competitive lifestyle is her "freedom" to choose materials, forms, and themes to produce artworks according to the dictates of her intellect.

In general, African women artists remain virtually unknown to the Western world. Indeed, few traditional women artists have become recognized outside their indigenous societies; however, a number of modern women artists are beginning to develop reputations in African and European countries. Those who are achieving recognition are artists of the current generation, although some are known to have been active in and outside Africa for several decades. Suzanna Ogunjami, a Nigerian, for example, is listed in a 1935 Harmon Foundation catalog as having an exhibition at Delphic Studio in New York during the same year. Artists' works are commanding more attention today because artists are more active on the European art scene. At this point, it would be premature to suggest the most significant modern African artists because of the dearth of scholarship in this area of contemporary art. It is appropriate, however, to identify some who are periodically presented in the literature. They are Miranda Burney-Nicol of Sierra Leone (b. 1928), E. Betty Manyolo of Uganda (b. 1938), Kamala Ishag of Sudan (b. 1939), Clara Ugbodaga of Nigeria, Afi Ekong of Nigeria, Rosemary Karuga of Uganda, Helen Sebidi of South Africa (b. 1943), Theresa Musoke of Uganda (b. 1944), Assa Djionne of Senegal/France, Oyenike Olaniyi (Nike) of Nigeria, Sokari Douglas Camp of Nigeria (b. 1957), and Kate Appiah of Ghana (b. 1962).

These artists work in a wide range of materials and styles that defy traditional restrictions. Metal sculpture, oil, and batik painting are among their various techniques. It is difficult to classify their styles since they do not fall into Western established categories. Many works, however, are figurative and share a common thread—a thematic focus on humanity in its various manifestations. Images, ranging from aspects of traditional life to urban political unrest, suggest the diversity in their social consciousness. Although the artists themselves tend to reject the notion of a feminist quality in their works, many compositions, oppositionally, exhibit some element of womanist interpretations. Women subjects, for example, assume active, positive, and multiple roles that significantly transform the prevailing nurturing prototype of women in the works of men. Another characteristic in these works is the influence of traditional African art that emerges in stylized figuration, patterning, and color.

Historically, African women artists have met the demands of social change in both traditional and modern contexts. Whether these artists remain central or marginal to society, they give shape to ideas that illuminate their own psychological, cultural, social, and political situation, as well as their assessment of global issues. While they do not profess a feminist perspective, their works are enlivened with knowledge gained from women's personal experience. They present to the world an exciting new dimension in contemporary art that expands its pluralist character and challenges the modern scholar to de-Europeanize and demasculinize the pervasive territorial boundaries of art historical inquiry.

References. Lisa Aronson, "Women in the Arts," in Margaret S. Hay and Sharon Stichter (eds.), *African Women South of the Sahara* (London, 1984); Kojo Fosu, *Twentieth Century Art in Africa* (Zaria, Nigeria, 1986).

FREIDA HIGH TESFAGIORGIS

AFRICAN WRITERS. Since 1960, publications by *black African women writers* have experienced rapid increase and accelerating respect within and beyond the African continent. The most prominent sub-Saharan and Sahelian nations and their writers in this flourishing of black African women's writing are Cameroon (Werewere Liking), Congo (Cécile-Ivelse Diamoneka, Amelica, Néné, Marie-Léontine Tsibinda), Ghana (Christiana Ama Ata Aidoo, Asare Konadu, Efua Theodora Sutherland), Kenya (Micere Githae Mugo, Rebeka Njau, Grace Ogot), Mozambique (Noémia de Sousa), Nigeria (Buchi Emecheta, Flora Nwapa, Zulu Sofola, Adaora Lily Ulasi), Senegal (Mariama Bâ, Annette M'baye d'Erneville, Aminata Maïga Ka, Aminata Sow Fall), South Africa (Jane Chifamba, Bessie Head, Miriam Tlali), Tanzania (Martha Mvungi), and Zaire (Ikole Bolumbo, Marie-Eugénie Mpongo, Tol'Ande Myeya, Madiya Nzuji). These novelists, poets, and dramatists write and publish their work primarily in French and English, although some, such as Efua Theodora Sutherland in the Akan language and Martha Mvungi in Swahili, also publish in African languages. Writers working primarily in African languages include Jane Chifamba (South Africa) in Shona and Beverly B. Mack (United States), who has edited a volume of Hausa women's poetry. Very little African women's writing is available in Portuguese, although respect for the widely anthologized poetry of Noémia de Sousa has been well established since 1960.

The life and work of Mariama Bâ of Senegal have become emblematic of the power and creativity of black African women writers. When her *Une si longue lettre* (So Long a Letter) was published in 1979, she achieved almost instantaneous audience and respect for her work, which was awarded the Noma Prize at the 1980 Frankfurt Book Fair. This first novel focuses on acts of cultural independence by a Senegalese woman, Ramatoulaye, who suffers from the effects of polygamy and who, upon widowhood, refuses to marry her brother-in-law, Tamsir, as is dictated by tradition. Bâ died in 1981, prior to the publication of her second novel, *Un chant écarlate* (A Scarlet Cry).

The literary concern with the choices available to black African women as well as the depiction of African intracultural, colonial, and postcolonial conflict are also powerfully present in the writings of Buchi Emecheta, Aminata Sow Fall, Flora Nwapa, and Grace Ogot. Emecheta's *The Bride Price* and *The Slave Girl* are concerned both with gender conflicts and with tensions of intracultural influence and change. The tensions of such changes are also emphasized in Aminata Sow Fall's *Le Revenant* (The Spector), in which a young African man chooses to fake his own death in response to local pressure. Nwapa and Ogot, while giving acute attention to the details of women's lives in their novels, focus thematically on the effects of cross-cultural change on individuals, male and female, within local African communities. Bessie Head, a South African who wrote from exile in Botswana until her death in 1986, has written novels of intense artistic power that focus on themes of exile, racial mixture, racism, cultural exclusion, insanity, African oral tradition, and love.

Black African women dramatists such as Aidoo, Micere Mugo, Sutherland, and Liking have focused primarily on political and cultural issues. Christiana Ama Ata Aidoo's *The Dilemma of a Ghost* details conflicts between African and African American heritage for the protagonist. Efua Sutherland's *Edufa*, on the other hand, is meticulously circumscribed within the local African community.

Alongside the rapid growth of imaginative literature by black African women there has been a surge in the publication of oral narrative and autobiography. Such works as *Nisa*, edited by Marjorie Shostak, *Three Swahili Women*, edited by Sarah Mirza and Margaret Strobel, and *Die Swerfjare van Poppie Nongema (Poppie*, in Eng. trans.), a collaboration between a black South African woman Else Joubert and Sandra Kotze, are examples not only of interest in autobiography but of focus on native African languages.

The most prominent *North African women writers* are Fatima Mernissi (Morocco), Alifa Rifaat (Egypt), Nawal el Saadawi (Egypt), and Fettouma Touati (Algeria). All of these women have elaborated and analyzed problems of male–female conflict in Muslim society. El Saadawi is highly prolific in fiction and nonfiction and is dedicated to depicting, analyzing, and helping to correct the problems of Arab women. Mernissi has published several works of nonfiction concerned primarily with women's issues. Autobiography is also rapidly developing in North African countries as evidenced by the work of Fadhma Amrouche and Wédád Zenié-Ziegler and Fatima Mernissi's own edition of interviews with Moroccan women (*Doing Daily Battle*).

Among *white African women writers living in Africa* Nadine Gordimer is the most prominent. Her South African tales and novels, which focus thematically on the tensions and dire prophecies evoked by apartheid, provide imaginative, provocative, creative, and complex renderings of her country's racial and personal tensions. Her insistence upon examining racial and social problems in literary form separates Gordimer dramatically from earlier white African women writers such as Beryl Markham and Isak Dinesen, who rarely depicted racial tensions explicitly. Olive Schreiner (1855–1920) is the earliest internationally recognized white African woman novelist, and her work focuses thematically on issues of race and cultural conflict. White African women writers living outside Africa include Doris Lessing, who is treated more fully under NOVELISTS, BRITISH (TWENTIETH-CENTURY).

Several *diaspora African women writers* living in Africa are contributing to the rapidly developing canon of African literature. Among these are Peggy Appiah (England/Ghana), Maryse Conde (Guadeloupe/Sahelian Africa), Elizabeth Delaygue (France/Comores), and Myriam Warner-Vieyra (Guadeloupe/Senegal).

Reference. Beverly B. Mack, "Walcokin Mata: Hausa Women's Oral Poetry" (diss., University of Wisconsin–Madison, 1981).

CAROLIVIA HERRON

AGE-EARNINGS PROFILES are plots of workers' earnings over their lifetimes. Men's age-earnings profiles tend to rise steeply from their labor force entry until about age 55 and then decline slightly. Women's age-earnings profiles tend to be flat.

SUSAN B. CARTER

AGE OF CONSENT is the age fixed by law at which one's consent to certain acts, such as sexual intercourse and marriage,* is valid. The age of consent for females has generally been younger than that for males, but in the United States all except two states now have the same age for both. Over time the age of consent has risen, from 12 for women and 14 for men in the Middle Ages to 18 in most states of the United States today (exceptions: in Louisiana it is 21, and in Mississippi 15 for women, 17 for men).

AGING women are increasingly important as more people in industrialized societies can expect to live longer lives. Reflecting the greater female life expectancy, the average American woman can expect to live seven years longer than her male counterpart. American women 65 and over now outnumber their male age peers 3:2—a dramatic increase from 1900, when the ratio was almost equal. Clearly, old age today is a territory pioneered and inhabited by women for longer periods. Given present patterns of life expectancy, women will continue to constitute most of the elders in industrialized nations in the future.

Race, social class, religion, ethnicity, and sexual identity shape how women age. Now-old women born in the United States, however, share common slices of history: technological changes (air travel, television, computers, superhighways, frozen food, microwave ovens); social changes (the Great Depression, several wars, the civil rights movement, the second women's movement); and changes in women's roles. Immigrant women are less likely to have such commonly shared experiences; their immigration histories, race and ethnic identity, and cultural traditions vary as widely as do their countries of origin. They represent differences in patterns of gender roles, intergenerational family structures, occupational skills, languages, and socioeconomic backgrounds.

Whatever one's ethnicity or race, being married has different consequences for men and women throughout life. Marriage is apparently a more successful guarantee for social interaction, life expectancy, and mental well-being among men than women. Belying the notion of the traumatic effect of either the menopause or the empty nest on women, postmenopausal women often experience renewed vitality, self-esteem, and a greater sense of power and independence. Moreover, aging women are more likely than women in their childbearing years to experience greater sharing and companionship in marriage.

Widowhood, however, is a predictable crisis for women. Females are far more likely to be widowed in old age than males, and widowers are more likely to remarry—often to younger women. Given the high rates of widowhood and low probability of remarriage, it is not surprising that, of the approximately 9.8 million older Americans living alone, women constitute the majority. Many elderly women living alone have no surviving children, a situation more common among African Americans than whites. Among widows with living children, African American, Asian and Pacific Island, and Latina women are more likely to live with other family members and widowed white females to maintain separate households: differences reflecting both cultural tradition and high rates of poverty. Current evidence indicates that while white, non-Latina women are most likely to live with their children due to mental or physical disability, African American and Latina women do so primarily as a result of economic necessity.

Although young and middle-aged women have benefited from challenges to male authority and stereotypes by the new women's movement, older women have largely been ignored. As Barbara MacDonald, an older woman activist, commented: "From the beginning of this wave of the women's movement . . . the message has gone out to those of us over sixty that your sisterhood does not include us. . . . You do not see us in our present lives, you do not identify with our issues, you exploit us, you patronize us, you stereotype us. Mainly you ignore us" (p. 6). Despite recent gains in employment opportunities for younger women and increases in career reentry among the middle-aged, aging women when employed are concentrated in a few low-paying jobs. Women between 40 and 65 remain disadvantaged in the labor force; they encounter more overt sex discrimination, less opportunity for on-the-job training, and more age discrimination than men or younger women.

Consequently, aging and old women of every marital status have lower money incomes than their male counterparts due to lower wages, inadequate pension coverage, economic dependency on men, and widowhood or divorce. Widowhood or divorce can mean financial disaster. Women 65+ constitute almost three-fourths of the elderly poor. Most vulnerable to poverty are widows who are very old and members of minorities. Elderly women living alone are generally the most vulnerable to poverty, both in the United States and elsewhere. In the United States, over half the elderly African American and Latina women not living with family members have incomes below the poverty level; half of all women aged 75 or over living alone exist on incomes below 150 percent of the poverty level. Moreover, while elderly women's economic status in industrialized European nations has improved over the last few decades, American women have not kept pace. That more American older women have lower incomes reflects the lack of universal pensions, policies to divide pension credits equally between spouses, and adequate, means-tested supplemental benefit levels: all policies benefiting women in many other nations.

An additional hazard for aging women is the likelihood that they will be the primary caregiver for an infirm family member. Approximately three-quarters of all long-term care is provided by women to a family member, with wives and daughters far more likely than husbands or sons to be the caregivers. An often-overlooked area of caregiving is the recent trend toward grandmothers as primary caregivers for one or more grandchildren under the age of 18. That grandmothers find themselves parenting young children echoes many social issues, including increases in drug use, AIDS, teen pregnancy, and marital breakups. Despite the age of the care recipient, caregiving takes a toll: female caregivers are likely to assess their physical health as poorer than women of the same age not providing care.

Most disabled elderly in the community are also women, many widowed after tending an impaired spouse. Less frequently recognized than caregiver stress is the stress felt by older women themselves when they receive care. Although expectations for care from adult children vary by ethnicity, religion, social class, and race, women living in the homes of adult children or grandchildren are more likely to have lower morale and satisfaction than those living in their own homes. Although their higher rates of discontent are no doubt influenced by their disabilities, their lost autonomy should not be belittled. Elderly women are also likely to enter a nursing home after their families can no longer provide care. That older women are at greater risk for illness and disabilities in late life than men is due not only to their greater longevity but to the lifelong association between feminine poverty and poor health throughout life.

It seems unlikely that public policies truly benefiting and enhancing aging women will emerge until there is a broader focus on the vulnerability of females in all age groups. Policy debates designed to create false dichotomies, such as the rights of unborn infants, children, and young adults versus the old, obscure the continuing realities of economic inequality. Females, who at all adult ages are more likely to be poor than men, are pitted against their own self-interests. If we care about people of all ages, issues of poverty and structural inequality must be addressed. Racial, gender, and age discrimination; pay equity for women; job training and retraining for both genders; adequate income maintenance throughout life, including old age; sensitive solutions to caregiving; and a universal health care system for people of all ages: these are issues affecting not only the mental health and quality of life of aging women but the life chances of everyone. To neglect the problems of aging women negates their past contribution both to the present and to the future that they have made possible. Surely, they, their children, and grandchildren who will one day be old deserve better. Herein lies a task for feminism, for social policy, and for everyone.

References. Jessie Allen and Alan Pifer (eds.), *Women on the Front Lines: Meeting the Challenge of an Aging America* (Washington, D.C., 1993); Sara Arber and Jay Ginn (eds.), *Connecting Gender and Ageing* (Bristol, Pa., 1995); Nancy D. Davis, Ellen Cole, and Esther D. Rothblum (eds.), *Faces of Women and Aging* (New York, 1993); Sarah Delany and A. Elizabeth Delany, *Having Our Say: The Delany Sisters' First 100 Years* (New York, 1993); Beth Hess and Elizabeth Markson (eds.), *Growing Old in America*, 4th ed. (New Brunswick, N.J., 1990); Barbara MacDonald, "Outside the Sisterhood: Ageism in Women's Studies," *Women's Studies Quarterly* 17 (1989): 6–11.

ELIZABETH WARREN MARKSON

AGNATE/COGNATE. *Agnate* is a relation by descent in the father's line. *Cognate* is a relation by descent from either the mother or the father. *Cognate* is often popularly used, however, as the opposite of *agnate* and in such cases would refer to relation by descent through the mother's line.

In early patriarchal societies succession usually gave preference to agnates over descendants in the mother's line. In Athens, for instance, descendants of the deceased's father had preferences before relations of the mother down to a certain point. In Rome, other cognates succeeded only in default of agnates.

AGORAPHOBIA is the most frequently occurring clinical phobia, with a high prevalence rate for females (65 to 85 percent female). The American Psychiatric Association (1980, 226–230) defines agoraphobics as showing "A marked fear of being in public places. . . . Normal activities are increasingly restricted as the fears or avoidance behaviors dominate the individual's life . . . behaviors may occur with or without panic attacks." Clinical symptoms include (1) "fear of fear": worry about physical symptoms that escalates to panic attacks; (2) avoidance behaviors (the phobias); (3) self-sufficiency problems (needing others to be with them); (4) unassertiveness; and (5) depression* (Chambless and Goldstein, 1982).

For many women, agoraphobia begins in the late teens or soon after marriage* or motherhood and may last a lifetime (mean age of onset is mid-20s). Agoraphobic symptoms appear to be related to stress associated with marital or interpersonal conflict.

In the past 10 years, with the advent of behavior therapy and the documented success of exposure treatment and the use of psychopharmacological drugs for alleviating the major symptoms of agoraphobia, there has been an enormous increase in the research and clinical literature on agoraphobia and anxiety disorders.

The major treatments can be categorized as the biological versus the more sociocultural and the psychodynamic versus the behavioral. There have been attempts recently to integrate the various approaches. On one end of the spectrum are (1) biological theories that stress constitutional factors that predispose individuals to panic disorders and anxiety attacks. One popular theory, which has no research support, is that women have an inborn constitutional deficit (mitral valve prolapse [MVP]) that lowers their threshold for panic attacks. (2) Psychopharmacological theories, which consider physiological arousal deficits as primary, are gaining in popularity as more positive research findings are reported. On the other end of the spectrum are (1) psychodynamic theories that consider early attachment problems, conflict, and/or sexual repression as primary, (2) learning theories that favor a conditioning model, and (3) social/cultural feminist theories that stress familial learning and societal factors.

Most theorists agree that agoraphobia runs in families, although they differ on the attention paid to familial factors in treatment. Agoraphobics are typically found to have mothers and even grandmothers who are classified as having agoraphobia or anxiety disorders themselves. (In one study 34 percent had a phobic mother, whereas only 6 percent had a phobic father.)

Phobic symptoms are reported to coexist with personality patterns of dependency and avoidance. Generally, mothers have been blamed for the presumed childhood overprotection linked to the symptoms, with little attention directed toward fathers. Feminist writers and therapists who addressed the issue of why agoraphobics are predominantly female argue against a constitutional factor. They stress that both parents create a climate for the inculcation and continued fostering of an agoraphobic ideology of extreme helplessness and dependency that results from overtraining in the stereotypic aspects of the female role. Researchers on female agoraphobics report low scores on sex-role stereotyping scales that measure instrumentality, activity, and assertiveness. The low scores support the link between phobias and stereotypic feminine behavior.

Whereas agoraphobia has been characterized as a high-prevalence disorder for women and linked to a stereotypic female socialization pattern, the most popular treatments have been some variant of behavior therapy that generally do not put women's issues in the foreground. While psychoanalysts have been interested in treating agoraphobics, such treatment stresses the lifting of sexual repressions and/or conflict resolution. These traditional therapies have not been demonstrated to be effective. Instead, the majority of female agoraphobics seek treatments at behaviorally oriented anxiety disorder clinics and self-help programs. The main features of such programs are variants of behavioral treatment entailing assessment and treatment for the fear of fear, anxiety, or panic attack. The client is taught anxiety management techniques, that is, relaxation and breathing exercises. Sometimes antianxiety drugs are used. Next there is treatment for phobic avoidance through exposure to feared situations. This may involve imaginal or real-life exposure treatment that teaches the client to confront rather than avoid the feared situation. (In imagination she constructs a hierarchy of her fears, from least to most frightening, and then works out a program of assignments to confront these feared situations in real life.) A key goal is the acquisition of coping, problem solving, and assertiveness skills. Most behavioral programs also feature some variant of cognitive therapy; that is, the client is enabled to get in touch with irrational or unproductive thinking about her anxieties and phobias (e.g., "I can't handle myself when anxious") and taught to either combat it or substitute more productive thinking (e.g., "I can learn how to cope with anxiety").

For the most part, behavior therapists have been somewhat successful in designing short-term treatments that feature exposure to the feared stimuli as primary. In most studies, 60 to 70 percent of the cases are reported to be improved. Yet for some agoraphobics such programs may not be as helpful as promised. There are reports of high dropout rates, resistance, and dissatisfaction with behavioral treatment.

Since feminists have argued that agoraphobics were socialized to be "stereotypically female," behavior therapy can be construed as a model therapy for remediation of the avoidant, dependent behaviors through the development of more independent coping strategies. However, given the high dropout rate and the resistance of many agoraphobics to behavioral treatment, there is need for an expanded cognitive/behavioral treatment for agoraphobics that takes account of ongoing interpersonal stresses, for example, being in the wife role. Consequently, increasing attention is being paid to interpersonal variables through work with couples in phobic treatment programs. Given the importance of the therapist in teaching the female agoraphobic client new ways of behaving, feminist therapists have also focused on the therapist–client process as an additional ingredient for fostering change.

References. American Psychiatric Association, *Diagnostic and Statistical Manual of Mental Disorders*, 3d ed. (Washington, D.C., 1980); K. A. Brehony, "Women and Agoraphobia: A Case for the Etiological Significance of the Feminine Sex Role Stereotype," in V. Franks and E. Rothblum (eds.), *The Stereotyping of Women: Its Effects on Mental Health* (New York, 1983); D. Chambless and A. Goldstein (eds.), *Agoraphobia: Multiple Perspectives on Theory and Treatment* (New York, 1982); I. G. Fodor, "The Phobic Syndrome in Women," in V. Franks and V. Burtle (eds.), *Women in Therapy* (New York, 1974); I. G. Fodor, "Cognitive/Behavior Therapy for Agoraphobic Women: Toward Utilizing Psychodynamic Understanding to Address Family Belief Systems and Enhance Behavior Change," in M. Braude (ed.), *Women, Power and Therapy* (New York, 1987); G. Thorpe and I. Burns, *The Agoraphobic Syndrome* (New York, 1983).

IRIS G. FODOR

AGRICULTURE. Women have worked in agriculture since they first domesticated plants and animals 8,000 to 10,000 years ago. As farm operators, family workers, or paid laborers, they have performed the same jobs as men or worked in gender-segregated tasks. As operators they have raised the same crops and animals and paid the same rents, dues, and fines. As paid workers, laboring alongside men or in gender-segregated jobs, they have usually been paid one-half to two-thirds as much as men.

In nineteenth-century United States a large proportion of farm operators were tenants. In the South after the Civil War many of the farms were rented on a sharecrop basis; in other areas cash rents were more common. Much of the work was gender-specific. In general women were responsible for child and household care and for producing much of the food and other products consumed in the household. Many other items needed in the home were bought with profits from the sale of goods produced by the women: butter, eggs, poultry, or produce from the garden. Women could also be expected to work in the fields when extra hands were needed, as during soil preparation and harvest or in emergencies. When record keeping became necessary (for many, not until they became liable for income taxes in the twentieth century), bookkeeping became part of "women's work."

The major functions in soil preparation; purchase, care, and use of the team and machinery; production and marketing of the cash crop; and transactions involving the sale or rental of land were the man's domain. Profits from the cash crop were used for major expenses in keeping up or improving the farm, such as machinery or additional land.

The needs of the farm were primary, so farm equipment was considered more important than household improvements. In emergencies, women would be expected to give up their "butter and egg money" to help pay for needed farm repairs or machinery. Women (primarily daughters) also contributed directly to farm income by going off-farm to work and sending a large part of their earnings home. Most of the earliest employees of the New England textile mills were young farm women. In the South daughters of white small farmers went into the textile mills; the daughters of black farmers, into domestic service or field work for pay. Women's activities in sustaining the family were vital, but men's activities took them into the public sphere and were more prestigious.

As technological development and improved transportation brought the farm family within easy access of markets where food and manufactured goods sold for less than it would cost to produce them in the home, women's role in providing for the household changed from producer to buyer. Profits from the cash crop now supplied family consumption needs as well as farm needs.

As machines replaced human labor, women did less field work. Machinery, part of man's domain, was designed for men, and most women were cut out of any jobs requiring handling of the equipment. As families became smaller, and hired labor was reduced, less time would be spent in cooking, child care, and caring for needs of employees. Technological development, then, reduced women's visible economic role in the family farm enterprise and thus their status.

This change can be seen in women's declining participation in farm organizations. Women joined and were active members of nineteenth-century farm organizations such as the Grange and the Farmers' Alliance. But at the turn of the century they began to be excluded. In the twentieth century when women participated in farm organizations, it was usually in their auxiliaries. Auxiliaries could be important in public education and lobbying efforts, but the organizational apparatus, its direction, and decision making were in the hands of the men. Public policy, which regarded farm operators as white males, ignored women as well as minority farmers. When extension services were organized, they were generally sex-segregated; child care and homemaking for women, farm management for men.

The Great Depression, government policy, and technological advances accelerated the movement toward larger and fewer farms, a movement that continues. However, from 1974 to the mid-1980s, the number of small farms (less than 50 acres) increased, then began to decline again. In 1974, there were 508,000 small farms; in 1982, 637,000, and by 1992, 554,000. There are few tenant farms (only 11.3 percent of all farms in 1992), but many of the small farms are part-time farms, held by operators whose principal occupation is in off-farm work.

Women remain vital to farming. They are only a small percentage of farm owners and farm managers, but as the total number of farms has decreased, the proportion of women owners and managers and the proportion of farmland owned by women have increased. In 1950, 3 percent of farm owners and managers were women; by 1995, that figure had grown to 25.3 percent but most of the women-operated farms are small. In 1992, of the 145,000 farms operated by women, only 50,000 (34.5 percent) had annual sales of over $10,000.

The majority of farm women are farm operators' wives engaged in unpaid house- and farmwork. At some stage of their lives they may also engage in child rearing and, increasingly, in off-farm work. In 1984, 30.9 percent of the female farm population was in nonagricultural employment.

The farm wife continues to be involved in the work of running the farm. From the fairly simple bookkeeping of midcentury she now often tracks farm operations in complex computer programs. As the costs of labor rise, her involvement in production jobs increases—some machinery has even been redesigned so that the average-size woman can operate it. Women still help support the farm by off-farm work, but now the wife, not the daughter, does so.

The 1980 Farm Women's Survey (see Rosenfeld, 1985) showed that, in general, women on large farms spend more time in farmwork than women on small farms and that women in dairy and livestock operations spend more time in farmwork than women on farms where work is more seasonal. Also, as farm size increases, the variety of women's work narrows, and the work falls more along traditional gender lines. However, on the part-time farm, where more men than women work off-farm, most of the farm operation is often left to the women.

Rosenfeld also found that woman's part in decision making, while varying according to the size, type, and complexity of the farm operation and according to whether she has a share in ownership or lease arrangement, has increased in matters concerning production. Where outside agents such as banks and government agencies are concerned, however, the woman seems less involved.

Farm women themselves have become more vocal. They are again active in farm organizations and have started organizations of their own, such as American Agri-Women and Women Involved in Farm Economics. Both were founded in the mid-1970s and are organizations of farm wives interested in protecting family farming and the rights of women in family farm businesses. As well as increasing activity on behalf of the family farm, farm women are also developing interests beyond it, taking a more active role in community volunteer and political activities.

Very few women are paid agricultural workers. Over the period from 1950 to 1995, the percentage of women in the labor force who were in agriculture fell from 6.3 percent to 0.95 percent. Although corporate farming offers some well-paying, highly skilled jobs as managers and specialists, women hold almost none of these. Most of the waged work of women is in low-paying, low-skill "stoop labor," in harvesting fruits and vegetables where few of the protections mandated for industrial workers (e.g., unemployment insurance) are available for farmworkers, except on the largest farms. Women's role as a reserve army of labor is clearly evident. Most of the women are seasonal or occasional (less than 25 days a year) workers. In 1983 approximately 85 percent of the women in agricultural and related occupations were not full-time workers.

Since the 1970s the number of migrant laborers has declined sharply. Many of the migrants settled in one spot and have either gotten out of farm labor completely or do not depend on it for the major part of their income. Some, including some women, still follow the harvest or, like the "fruit tramps" in California, are part of husband–wife teams that do skilled "tree work" on regular yearly circuits of fruit ranches.

The majority of women in paid farmwork, then, are neither full-time nor migratory workers but local women, often housewives and students from neighboring towns or small farms who work for less than two and a half months a year in fruit and vegetable harvesting. As mechanical harvesting has spread from one crop to another, the average days worked a year and the total number engaged in paid farmwork have continued to decline. As the earning possibilities in farm labor decreased, both the numbers and percentage of women workers increased up to the mid-1980s, then began to fall. In 1995 the percentage of paid agricultural workers who were women was 18.1 percent.

All statistics in this entry can be found in U.S. Bureau of the Census, *Statistical Abstracts of the United States, 1996*, 116th edition (Washington, D.C., 1997).

References. C. B. Flora and S. Johnson, "Discarding the Distaff: New Roles for Rural Women," in *Rural U.S.A.: Persistence and Change* (Ames, Iowa, 1978); Wana G. Haney and Jane B. Knowles (eds.), *Women and Farming: Changing Roles, Changing Structure* (Boulder, Colo., 1988); R. A. Rosenfeld, *Farm Women: Work, Farm, and Family in the United States* (Chapel Hill, N.C., 1985).

ALGERIA. Historical Background. The history of contemporary Algerian women is intimately linked to the history of the colonization of their country by the French beginning on July 3, 1830. Prior to this date, women's status was shaped by the agrarian nature of the society, where the family and community played a significant role in gender relations. In addition, social class determined women's access to education and the division of labor within the family. Well-to-do women had servants and slaves to help them with domestic tasks and child rearing, whereas poorer women were free to work as purveyors of services such as selling goods door-to-door. Family law, or *shari'a*, was predominantly based on the Maliki school of law, which is relatively moderate, but its application varied widely. Women's freedom of movement, the practice of veiling, and attitudes toward marriage varied from region to region and according to the rural/urban axis, with women in the town of Bou Saada in the southwest being the freest. They typically danced in cafés and often chose their husbands before retiring. The veil was shorter in cities such as Algiers and nonexistent in rural areas.

The colonial encounter had long-lasting impacts on women. First, French authorities singled out religion, women, and politics as the symbolic markers of the difference between the West qua Christian and the East qua Muslim. Natives were defined solely in terms of their religion in such a way that being a Muslim became a legal category of social, economic, and political discrimination. To be classified a "native-Muslim" meant until 1958 to have fewer rights than a French citizen. By politicizing Islam, French authorities also politicized identity and laid the groundwork for present-day Islamists' insistence on religion as the only foundation of identity for women and men. Second, French legislators attempted to amend the *shari'a* primarily in order to curtail men's freedom to divorce and to protect women from early marriage. In so doing, colonial authorities established a link between colonialism, religion, and gender, which native men resisted. Third, French novelists, chroniclers, painters, and travelers focused on what they perceived as women's "oppression," creating fictitious stories of secluded, passive women awaiting their liberation by benevolent Frenchmen. Finally, during the war of decolonization (1954–1962), the colonial government targeted women for political propaganda aimed at winning their support. This culminated in an official unveiling ceremony on the steps of the Governor's Palace on May 16, 1958. These policies made it difficult for women, during the colonial era, to address their own needs independently of their menfolk's without seeming to side with the colonial definition of their situation. They also created possible conditions for an Islamist movement that claimed to save women from colonial acculturation.

After the independence of their country in 1962, women made significant strides in education and began to enter the professions, especially medicine and law, although their general participation in the labor force remained low (6 percent to 9 percent). However, women's perception of themselves changed just as the family changed from extended to conjugal, and the country started on the road of industrialization.

Women in Postindependent Algeria. The most important issue facing women today is the rise of Islamism. In 1989 the government initiated reforms aimed at democratizing the political process. As a result, the Front of Islamic Salvation (FIS) party was formed and soon emerged as the most serious opposition to a government deemed corrupt because it was "secular." In December 1991, the party won the first round of parliamentary elections, prompting the government to cancel runoff elections. Banned, the FIS began an armed insurrection that split the Islamist movement and spawned a radical group known as the Armed Islamic Group (AIG), which has, among other things, targeted women for death.

Although the FIS was perceived as "moderate," its leaders' attitude toward women was conservative. Thus, its coleaders, Ali Benadj and Abassi Madani, conceived of women as homemakers and mothers. They advocated paying women to stay home, retiring those who work, and they emphasized the veil as a woman's prime duty to God. At the same time, they opened up feminine sections in their party to educate women about their religious obligations as defined by the FIS and sought their support in building the future Islamic republic. Such agitation among women was not without success, since many joined the ranks of the FIS before its demise. Most importantly, the FIS defined women as the keepers of cultural authenticity, symbols of a pristine way of life deemed compromised by colonialism and the "secular" policies of the state.

The Armed Islamic Group's attitude toward women may be seen as the direct consequence of the FIS' redefinition of women's roles in society. The AIG has killed women for not wearing the veil; for refusing to marry its members according to a distorted version of the Iranian custom of temporary marriage (or *mut'a*), which enables a man to marry a woman for as little as a few days in a warped legalization of rape; for working as journalists, hairdressers, beauticians, or fortune-tellers. Between 1992 and

1995, over 400 women were either killed or wounded. The AIG also uses women as symbols of cultural authenticity who must be saved from the damaging influence of the "West."

The rise of the Islamist movement threatens to jeopardize the gains women made during the first two decades after the independence of their country. Coeducation is no longer the norm as it was in the 1970s. Outside big urban centers, female teachers feel obligated to wear a *hijab* (veil) in the classroom. Fear of rape and physical harm compels women to stay home after work and travel less freely than they used to. Finally, the general climate of uncertainty and insecurity created by acts of terrorism in public places and armed assaults on city neighborhoods and small towns has made it difficult for women to engage in concerted action to defend their interests.

Nevertheless, the liberalization of politics in 1989 enabled women to create a number of associations aimed at promoting their rights. Most have demanded the repeal of the 1984 Family Code based on the *shari'a*, which legalized gender inequality in matters of marriage, divorce, and child custody. The most vocal critics of Islamism have been women, some of whom live under the threat of death for their being outspoken.

Although it has generally benefited from female activists opposed to Islamism, the government has done little to defend them from attacks or to initiate affirmative action policies in favor of women. Despite the votes they gave President Liamine Zeroual in 1995, women were not adequately represented in his cabinet. Nor did the amendments to the constitution approved in November 1996 address women's plight. Islamist violence against women is portrayed graphically on the state-controlled television, yet no commission was appointed to identify the perpetrators, just as no special security measures have been taken to protect women. They are seen as civil war casualties, like men, regardless of their greater vulnerability. There have been reports that the state police and security apparatus have committed atrocities on individuals accused of Islamist sympathies, some of whom were women.

The impact of Islamism on women is compounded by a deteriorating economy that has seriously affected women's position in society and threatens to limit the prospects for an improvement in gender relations. Since the early 1980s the government has proceeded to roll back its socialist policies that provided medical, food, educational, and transportation subsidies. The change to a market economy has been accompanied by the implementation of structural adjustment measures initiated at the request of the International Monetary Fund, to which Algeria owes $26 billion. The resulting inflation, devaluation of currency, layoffs, and cuts in social subsidies have caused an increasing number of women to become managers of poverty. Endemic housing and water shortages have burdened women who continue to have large families (an average of five children per woman). In the face of chronic unemployment, women find it harder to work outside their home except in menial positions. The socially conservative mood fostered by the Islamist movement makes it more difficult for women to secure positions of responsibility. More importantly, the destruction of over 800 schools by Islamists and the lack of security may affect the education of girls in the future. The state lacks the necessary funds to rebuild so many schools. As is customary, when resources are scarce, boys rather than girls are sent to school.

Despite the determination of women to defend their interests in the wake of the emergence of the Islamist movement, they cannot be heard by a government too busy keeping afloat to be concerned with their problems. Women's associations need funds, equipment, and international support. However, only when security is restored will they have a chance to a fair struggle. Theirs will be an uphill battle against an indifferent government, an allegedly "moderate" Islamist opposition as represented by the Hamas party (renamed "party of Peace in Society"), and the changes that the FIS' agitation has wrought on Algerian culture now infused with a new religiosity based more on selective *Hadith* (oral utterances attributed to Prophet Muhammad and his companions) than on the Koran.

References. Lahouari Addi, *L'Algérie et la Démocratie* (Paris, 1994); Frantz Fanon, *A Dying Colonialism* (New York, 1967); Smail Goumeziane, *Le Mal Algérien* (Paris, 1994); Kamel Hamdi, *Ali Benhadj, Abassi Madani, Mahfoud Nahnah, Abdellah Djaballah. Différents ou Différends?* (Alger, 1991); Djedjiga Imache and Ines Nour, *Les Algériennes Entre Islam et Islamisme* (Aix-en-Provence, 1994); Marnia Lazreg, *The Eloquence of Silence: Algerian Women in Question* (New York, 1994); Amine Touati, *Algérie, les Islamistes à l'Assaut du Pouvoir* (Paris, 1995).

MARNIA LAZREG

ALIMONY (SPOUSAL SUPPORT) is an allowance for support or maintenance. The use of the term is now confined almost exclusively to payments made to support one party to a marriage* after the dissolution of the marriage by separation or divorce.* Alimony may be granted for a term of years or until the death of one of the parties or the remarriage or cohabitation with a member of the opposite sex by the recipient.

By the eleventh century the medieval church had succeeded in making marriage indissoluble, but in a few instances it permitted separation. Since the couple were still legally married, and the husband continued to control the wife's property, maintenance for the wife had to be provided. The husband, unless the wife was living openly in adultery, had to provide the wife's necessaries, which would vary according to the status and wealth of the erstwhile partners.

With the Reformation, in all Protestant countries marriage became a civil contract, and except in England, divorce became possible on very restricted grounds (chiefly adultery and impotence). Since the divorce proceedings were adversarial, alimony became tied to the idea of guilt and innocence.

In the United States marriage was regulated by the colonies, then by the individual states. After the American Revolution, grounds for divorce were expanded in many states by the legislatures and/or by judicial interpretation of "cruelty." By the opening of the twentieth century women were receiving far more divorces than men, but few were granted alimony, and even fewer actually received it—a pattern that persists.

Through the nineteenth and early twentieth centuries a welter of laws that differed widely and a rising divorce rate were the subjects of concern and debate among liberal and conservative reformers, but little change was made in the granting of alimony (by World War II three states allowed alimony to husbands under certain circumstances). The movement for divorce reform that began in the late 1960s, however, did address this issue, and a new standard, "rehabilitation," was adopted as the goal of alimony in the Uniform Marriage and Divorce Act of 1974, a model law approved for state adoption. Since the late 1960s almost every state has made some changes in its divorce laws. About one-third have moved in the direction of "rehabilitative" alimony.

With rehabilitative alimony, if the dependent partner, whether male or female (in 1979 the Supreme Court struck down gender-based alimony laws), is deemed capable of becoming economically self-sufficient, alimony is provided for a limited time period and includes, in addition to maintenance, a sum sufficient to pay for education or training* that is supposed to allow for earnings that will approximate the person's economic status during marriage.

In 1986, all states made provision for alimony except Texas. Many states had eliminated consideration of fault, but two, Louisiana and Idaho, specifically limit the possibility of alimony to the innocent party, while 14 others take misconduct into account. Florida, Georgia, North Carolina, South Carolina, and Virginia prohibit the granting of alimony to anyone guilty of adultery.*

Fourteen states had, with varying degrees of explicitness, moved in the direction of temporary alimony. For example, in Delaware, for anyone married less than 20 years, alimony is limited to 2 years. In New Hampshire, if there are no minor children, alimony is limited to 3 years and will cease three years after the youngest child reaches its majority.

Although rehabilitative alimony has, at least to some extent, reduced the fraud and cheating that pervade the whole system of child support and alimony payment, it has not been entirely successful, especially from the viewpoint of the dependent (with few exceptions, the female) partner. The premise that after a few years of training the ex-wife will be able to find entry-level employment allowing her a standard of living in any way comparable to her ex-husband's is ludicrous. Older women, in particular full-time homemakers, are especially left high and dry. Those without other income and marketable skills have little likelihood of earning enough to stay above the poverty level. The need has led to displaced homemaker laws in many states, but the quantity and quality of the services provided vary widely.

ALTERNATIVE LIFE-STYLES. See SEXUAL ORIENTATION

AMERICAN CLASSICAL CANON. This term refers to writers whom the critical, publishing, and scholarly communities establish as the most significant in the national literature. As taste and critical standards are educated through the canon, it defines literary merit and promotes what it finds meritorious.

The American, or more rightly, the United States, canon has been driven by nationalist urges to assert a native literature distinct and separate from the British. While changing national identity and critical standards continually reshape the canon, it has generally been a list of Great Books by Great Men, selected and organized through chronological periods and associated with particular sociophilosophic worldviews, for example, romanticism, realism, modernism. Women writers seldom neatly fit such categories, and the canon's selection of representative writers has tended to privilege males in defining the works, authors, subject matter, and techniques that are kept in print, anthologized, taught, and discussed in journals. Despite occasional brief spurts of attention to women writers, the proportion of women represented in standard anthologies of American literature hovered around 10 percent until the 1960s–1970s. Women's representation gradually increased to near 15 percent and sometimes reached 25 percent, occasionally more, in the 1980s. Across the anthologies, course syllabi, and established critical journals, however, the consensus on classic American women writers revolves around a very few names: Anne Bradstreet and often Phillis Wheatley (for the colonial era), Emily Dickinson (for the nineteenth century), and (for the twentieth century) Willa Cather, Edith Wharton, Edna St. Vincent Millay, and a sampling of poets—typically, Elizabeth Bishop, H. D., Amy Lowell, Marianne Moore, Sara Teasdale, and Elinor Wylie. Women writers who were major figures in the nineteenth-century canons—Harriet Beecher Stowe, Sarah Orne Jewett, Helen Hunt Jackson, and Mary Wilkins Freeman—have essentially disappeared from the establishment lists. Only recently has critical consideration turned to assessing whether the classical canon accurately represents the history and diversity of American literature in terms of writers or readers.

From the beginnings of the United States to about 1825, the primary impetus in canon formation was defining a native literature. Early U.S. literary journals, like the *North American Review*, were established specifically to identify and advance American writing. Women writers who represented unique native contributions were included.

Anne Bradstreet was the first woman with a place in the canon, perhaps ironically because British reviewers acknowledged her as one of the first North American poets. Phillis Wheatley, the black slave poet, enjoyed international celebrity in the eighteenth century and intermittent canonization. While American critics saw her poetry as largely derivative, British attention and her singular social role ensured Wheatley's prominence. In the early period, canonization had an ambiguous relationship with literary merit and with American critics. Many early American writers were identified and developed by British reviewers and accepted because they fit the vaunted goal of a native literature.

In the mid-nineteenth century, other women moved into the canon when they represented distinctive features in the developing literature. Harriet Beecher Stowe was granted temporary inclusion because of her association with defining national social and political issues. Initially recognized for the national influence and international reception of her antislavery novels, *Uncle Tom's Cabin* and *Dred*, Stowe retained continuous popularity and status with her New England local color fiction. In the elite circles of nineteenth-century eastern publishing, Stowe was often the only female face. Despite Stowe's standing, editors and reviewers never treated her works with the respect generally accorded a canonical author. Her magazine editors considered themselves free to rewrite, usually without consultation. Critics have treated her works more as sociological artifact than as literature.

Later nineteenth-century women writers continued Stowe's attention to national issues and local color. In the 1870s and 1880s, new regional subjects and technical innovations brought Sarah Orne Jewett, Helen Hunt Jackson, and Mary Wilkins Freeman into the canon. Jewett, first published in the *Atlantic Monthly*, revealed rural New England deserted by young males gone west in search of opportunity. Helen Hunt Jackson (who often published under the pseudonym Saxe Holm) opened new social issues, especially mistreatment of Native Americans. Mary Wilkins Freeman displayed the dialect and repression of poor rural New England. Nineteenth-century popular and critical interest focused on their contributions of novel characters and subjects and on their realism, but they were not promoted with the force devoted to now-classic male writers. Then, as now, literary reputation was established not only by acceptance and publication but by critical reviews and essays. *The Century Illustrated Monthly Magazine* solicited extended critical treatments of Henry James and Mark Twain to bolster and enlarge their reception, but no similar reputation building was devoted to their women contemporaries.

Throughout the nineteenth century, women, especially women fiction writers, held the popular audience in volume publication, while now-classic male writers found selling their work extremely difficult. Nathaniel Hawthorne even complained to his publisher that "scribbling women" monopolized the American audience. The perception that the American popular audience dismissed, or at least failed to buy, books lauded by the growing critical establishment led to the development of magazines specifically designed to promote and to provide a market for American writers. *Harper's Monthly*, the *Atlantic Monthly*, and the *Century Illustrated Monthly Magazine* provided income, markets, audience, and prestige for the writers who would constitute the classical canon. The magazines' impetus to educate the popular taste brought a firm and continuing distinction between great literature and popular literature, a distinction that would prove damning to the majority of women writers.

Magazine editors acknowledged that they promoted writers who had not succeeded with the larger reading public. Recognizing that women were the primary readers of literature, the magazines set out to educate their taste. The national magazines' power to award canonical acceptance was generally reserved for a small nucleus of male writers with strong personal and professional liaisons to each other and to the major magazines and their editors. Initially, sustained attention to writers like Henry James and Nathaniel Hawthorne came from editors' feeling the need to sell and explain these less popular writers. The liability of women writers' popularity thus became a two-edged sword. The separation between popular and critical acceptance ensured that popular writers were less likely to be ranked as classic and to be promoted through solicited reviews and essays. Decisions regarding promotion, unfortunately, were often decisions regarding prestige and status, as affected by reception as they were by critical standards.

In the last half of the nineteenth century, the editors and reviewers of literary magazines, a small group of eastern publishers, and the growing literature departments of northeastern universities effectively became the canon's arbiters. On the eastern seaboard, with the majority of publishers, presses, and journals, social factors impacted canon formation. Writers, critics, editors, and publishers constituted a sort of brotherhood, from which women were largely excluded. Quasi-institutionalized networks of old boys published and reviewed, and novices came to worship at the seats of power. While William Dean Howells and a few others became supporters of women writers, they worked within the restraints of an entrenched insider tradition of literary practice. When editors and critics groomed in the New England tradition found a place for women colleagues, that place was defined by distinctive subject matter or approaches, which established a separate place from that reserved for the male pantheon.

While the women writers of the 1870s–1890s lacked full acceptance in the canon-established male literary circles, they formed for themselves a strong and effective community. Though often geographically separated and hampered by the difficulties of travel and lack of funds, they supported each other, aesthetically, personally, and professionally.

Resentment of the popularity of women writers remained a continuing problem. The habit of decrying the American audience's tastes died hard, in part because of the general understanding that the majority of American readers were women. After 1870, as the literary marketplace failed to support growing numbers of male writers, traditionalist writers and critics grew especially misogynist in their critical preferences.

The male network of friendship and authority, tied to the national journals and major universities, did lead to the promotion of Emily Dickinson. While Dickinson's life was notably sequestered, she responded to an *Atlantic* column, "Advice to the Young Contributor." Its author, Thomas Wentworth Higginson, wielded considerable influence in promoting the fortunes of new writers, and Dickinson asked not for publication but for Higginson's response to her poetry. While Higginson hardly knew what to do with Dickinson's untraditional metrics, he recognized her genius. When volumes of Dickinson's verse were eventually published, Higginson promoted her singular voice through a series of critical articles, placing Dickinson before the canon's arbiters and pointing to qualities that made her a unique voice in American literature.

Encouraged by George Santayana's 1917 indictment of a feminine literary "genteel tradition," critics of the 1920s and 1930s redefined the canon. Women's writing on regional subjects was rejected as nostalgic, delicate, unworthy of a striving nation. Castigating the American audience who had rejected robust masculine writers, this criticism canonized masculine innovators. Walt Whitman and Samuel Clemens came into the canon; women, by and large, went out.

Despite deletions from the historical canon, the twentieth century's less centralized literary marketplace created openings for new women writers, although again women were admitted into the canon primarily because of distinctive subject matter. Willa Cather's regional subjects—Nebraska pioneers, frontier heroism, Roman Catholicism in New Mexico—placed her squarely in the tradition of her predecessors. Her early magazine writing and editing served as traditional means to belonging and recognition. *My Antonia* (1918) and *Death Comes to the Archbishop* (1927) became early classics, though Cather's inclusion in the canon lagged far behind that of her male contemporaries.

Edna St. Vincent Millay, like Emily Dickinson, wrote her first poems separate from the tradition and without echoes of imitation. Though her emotionally charged verse and drama were noticed for originality and technical skill, Millay was also distinctive for her cynicism, her surprising turns on expectation.

Edith Wharton broke new ground when her highly detailed portraits of society met the spirit of twentieth-century arbiters while also selling well and garnering international attention. Wharton quickly joined the American literary pantheon, even becoming, in 1920, the first woman to win the Pulitzer Prize. Along with St. Vincent Millay and Wharton, a number of women poets represent the canon's modern period. The six most frequently included—Elizabeth Bishop, H. D., Amy Lowell, Marianne Moore, Sara Teasdale, and Elinor Wylie—are all significant for technical innovation and virtuosity. Lowell and H. D. are practically synonymous with imagism, and all are masters of unconventional and unduplicated poetic systems.

While open to Wharton's portraits of society life, the canon's sense of universality and defining American subjects excluded black and other minority writers. Black women actively published and won prizes throughout the twentieth century, but only Gwendolyn Brooks has enjoyed some peripheral inclusion in the classical canon. Brooks established black life as a subject for traditional literary audiences. Brooks' status derives from her subject matter, her technical virtuosity in traditional forms, and the overwhelming number and prestige of the literary prizes she has won.

Since widely available anthologies, required reading lists, and library purchases tend to reproduce the classical canon, lack of canon status has made women's writing less available. The classical canon's concepts of a representative national literature and disdain for popular literature often belie the experiences and preferences of women readers.

Women's studies scholars of the 1970s and 1980s have focused on reconstructing the canon, rediscovering lost women writers, or creating a countercanon of women writers. While this scholarship has abated the canon's exclusiveness and increased the numbers of women writers in standard courses and texts, women remain distinctly underrepresented in the classical canon. Some feminist scholars also are concerned that reconstructing the canon or establishing alternative canons reifies the values of traditional canonical exclusion, buying into a process by which a few writers are elevated and established, to the exclusion of multiple voices.

References. Robert von Hallberg (ed.), *Canons* (Chicago, 1984); Paul Lauter, *Canons and Contexts* (New York, 1991); Lillian S. Robinson, *Treason Our Text: Feminist Challenges to the Literary Canon* (Wellesley, Mass., 1983).

CAROL KLIMICK CYGANOWSKI

AMERICAN INDIAN AND ALASKAN NATIVE WOMEN. "Indian" was formerly used to refer to the indigenous worlds of North and South America, until the 1970s, when "Native American" came into popular use. Soon, the latter term came to designate Native Hawaiians, Pacific Islanders, and some immigrant Europeans who claimed to have been "born here, too." Thus, the political organizations of tribal peoples resumed the use of the terms "American Indian" and "Alaskan Native." However, these all-encompassing terms cover a wide range of tribal peoples of over 300 extant cultural groups in the United States. Here tribal enclaves range from the largest, the Navajo, to small, scattered groups in the East, to the Inuit (formerly called Eskimo) in Alaska. Each tribal group views itself in terms of the native linguistic designation for its people, such as *Dene* for Navajo and *Lakota* for Sioux, and the designation of Pueblos as *Toas* and rancherias as *Covelo* in California. Each group is an entity with its own culture, language, worldview, social structures, and gender views, and each has maintained a residual culture of "nativeness" that has persisted despite centuries of coerced change. This unique cultural background colors women's perception of self and social group.

Many tribal peoples believe that the significant role of women as the primary socializers of children has allowed for the persistence of culture, worldview, and identity. This belief is often articulated in women's statements that "We are the carriers of culture" and the fact that many culture "heroes," or bringers of cultural form, ritual, belief, proper behavior, and rules for living, have been female. Examples of these "culture bearers" are Changing Women among the Navajo (a matrilineal society) and the White Buffalo Calf Women among the Lakota (often referred to as a "warrior society"). Other groups present various cultural heroines.

Roles of women in North American Indian societies must be understood in the context of the tribe. Aboriginal beliefs persist to varying degrees in contemporary attitudes. The internalization of the cultural rules, values, and behaviors of the society is an important aspect of the "identity" and self-image of American Indian or Alaskan Native females. Matrilineal societies, such as the Iroquoian groups or the Pueblos, have a different orientation from that of societies that are patrilineal or bilateral.

In the social universe of Native women in North America, Canadian Native women are not to be slighted. Categories that pertain to them are status (treaty), nonstatus (nontreaty), and Metis (mixed-blood). This is complicated even further by the enactment of a law in 1984 that allows Native nonstatus women to become reinstated within their groups. This is presently a prominent issue in Canada.

Generalizations about the roles of Indian women in present-day society are difficult. Roles vary according to the value orientations of each tribal group and the adjustments that have resulted through the experiences of Native women as they have attempted to achieve a satisfactory life. Some individuals seem to embody all the expectations of their tribal group; others are but white women in brown encasements; and still others may be called truly bicultural, as they are adept at identifying cultural clues and views from both societies and at making contextual adjustments.

Women fulfill their roles as daughters, sisters, wives, and mothers in accordance with the residual tribal culture as it is learned. Role fulfillment can vary widely. Indian women are found in suburbs of larger cities, in professional categories of all sorts, and in such ongoing bureaucratic structures as the U.S. Bureau of Indian Affairs and Public Health Service. They can also be seen on the skid rows of the major cities in North America in various capacities, such as the homeless; in off-reservation border towns; and in "Indian bars" throughout "Indian country."

Ways of living, then, are diverse. Child raising varies from white, middle-class standards, to neglect and abandonment of children in urban ghettos and on reservations. The entire range from two-parent families to one-parent or one-parent surrogate (grandmothers, aunts) domestic units is evident. Problems such as women raising children alone, spouse and child abuse, and the fosterage and adoption of Indian children into white families, about which there is a great furor, are concerns of Native women.

The quality of education that North American Indian girls receive and the level of education they attain vary as widely as their living conditions. However, the overall trend is that more North American Indian women are obtaining advanced educational degrees than ever before. Master's and doctor's of education degrees in counseling and guidance, education, and special education are especially prominent, while doctorates are fewer in fields such as the social sciences, social work, and the natural sciences. Many Indian women have completed medical and law degrees.

As in any analysis of feminine roles, the interactions of females and males must also be charted. The entire social fabric must be understood to isolate gender variation.

Indian women have established their own organizations in the United States and Canada. In summer 1970, the North American Indian Women's Association (NAIWA) was organized with a strong tribal base and sponsorship by the U.S. Bureau of Indian Affairs. NAIWA still continues and for over a decade had a strong contingent of Canadian Natives in attendance. The Native Women's Association of Canada was formed in 1971. Most provinces and U.S. reservations have women's sodalities.

Few Indian women are involved in the feminist movement of the larger society. The issues that sparked the feminist movement in the larger society seem unimportant to Indian women, who are concerned with the sheer survival of self, family, and tribe. Some consider it a middle-class movement for white women, while others have never heard of it. Many Indian women insist that they have always been liberated.

After a long history of education away from tribal lifestyles, women of Indian ancestry have made adaptations. One experience that has been common to all Indians is the superimposition of a "civilized" and "superior" lifestyle. Women have been the socializers of children into languages and ways of behavior that determine the style of living they follow: Indian-oriented or white-directed.

Published life histories of Indian women show they have utilized strategies that both allow them to remain native and help them adapt into a new society. Indian women have maintained some mechanisms that have allowed for the continuity of Indian cultures and assured that continuity in a changing society.

References. Patricia Albers and Beatrice Medicine, *The Hidden Half: Studies of Plains Indian Women* (Washington, D.C., 1983); Gretchen M. Bataille and Kathleen Mullen Sands, *American Indian Women Telling Their Lives* (Lincoln, Nebr.,

1984); Rayna Green, *Native American Women: A Contextual Bibliography* (Bloomington, Ind., 1983).

                                                        BEATRICE MEDICINE

AMERICAN REVOLUTION. While throughout the eighteenth century most women's influence was confined to the household, the Revolution brought politics and war into the home and women out into the public arena to express their political views. In addition, the republican ideologies that fed the Revolution had a significant impact on the image of womanhood and on female roles in the new country. Wartime emergencies and ideologies produced complex circumstances that affected women in a wide variety of ways and set in motion a series of changes that would revolutionize women's status.

Some women experienced the throes of war directly. Women like Deborah Sampson Gannett, who impersonated a man and fought with the Fourth Massachusetts regiment, and "Molly Pitcher" (Mary Hays), who carried buckets of water, nursed the wounded, and even took her wounded husband's place at the cannons, are often mentioned. Few women, however, actually fought in battle. The majority of women who became part of the Continental army were camp followers who traveled with the soldiers, cooking, laundering, and tending to the sick and wounded. Army leaders regarded camp followers as nuisances and granted provisions only to those who earned their keep. Officially, the army recognized and paid salaries to female nurses.

Women expressed their patriotism in ways that brought them out of the private domain. General George Washington recognized the efforts of the Ladies Association of Philadelphia, which went door-to-door raising money for the war effort. This group's success inspired women's organizations throughout the colonies to launch similar campaigns. As producers and purchasers for the household, women also participated in boycotts against English goods, producing their own "homespun" cloth, making their own clothes, and refusing to buy English tea. Community members gathered in sewing circles and spinning meetings to make blankets and other supplies for the army. Bolder groups organized in mobs to protest against merchants who hoarded goods in short supply.

Though men did not regard most of these efforts as overtly political or as a threat to the haven of the home, fund-raisers and boycotts had definite political connotations, and the Revolution inspired a lasting interest in politics in some. Mercy Otis Warren, daughter and wife of prominent men, and Abigail Adams, wife of patriot John Adams, corresponded extensively on women's political rights during the war. Warren later wrote an extensive history of the American Revolution. Women's participation in wartime efforts established a tradition of female public political behavior for the first time.

Most commonly, the American Revolution forced women to endure hardships and take on challenging new responsibilities. Many took over the day-to-day running of businesses and farms. Even though women's household production had long contributed to the family income, most wives were ill prepared to handle business transactions. The war gave them a unique opportunity to prove to their husbands and themselves that they could take on new roles. Most, however, were glad to return to normal life after the war. The predominant image of female patriotism was the passive, long-suffering wife and mother who sacrificed her husband and son to the army. Women admirably rose to the challenges of wartime, but many likely would have traded the knowledge and experience they gained for a guarantee that their loved ones would not be killed or injured.

The Revolution was an unwelcome intrusion into most women's lives, but Revolutionary ideology created new and powerful roles for women. At the same time that it celebrated equality, republican thought excluded men without property, slaves, and women from positions of political influence. Despite women's patriotic activity and their role in maintaining their households during wartime, they were not considered citizens under the Constitution and were not given the right to vote. American male leaders recognized that government affected women's lives within the domestic sphere, but they did not believe the Revolution created a public role for women. One of the ways in which the Founding Fathers attempted to justify the exclusion of women from political life was to impart a new meaning to public virtue, changing it from masculine courage and heroism to feminine morality and self-discipline. As the keepers of civic virtue, women could find satisfaction in boycotts, fund-raisers, and petition campaigns and did not feel the need for the full rights of citizens. Joan Hoff Wilson asserts that women deserved a full role in public life and characterizes women's status as a result of the Revolution as "unrequited patriotism."

Linda Kerber and Mary Beth Norton point to the new, glorified role of republican mother, as well as women's fund-raising and petition efforts during the Revolution, as precursors to women's political movements in the mid-nineteenth century. Republican motherhood infused women's domestic roles with political significance; it was not a fully public role but one that placed women on the edges of political life for the first time. Women's new responsibility was to raise and educate the virtuous citizens on whom the republic depended. Mothers, then, acted as the intermediary between the public and private sphere. Women took advantage of this idea, becoming more politically aware, enjoying improved educational opportunities, and becoming more competent and confident individuals. While this new role kept women within the domestic sphere, republican motherhood represented a "revolutionary" step toward women's acceptance into civic life.

Republican ideals had other implications for women as well. Just as the colonists sought liberty from their mother country, women like Abigail

Adams hoped to limit husbands' absolute power over their wives. The ideal of the republican wife offered wives a greater measure of equality within the marital bond. Theoretically, with greater equality between husband and wife, the marriage of two virtuous people became the paradigm for political life in the new republic. True marital equality, however, rarely existed. Jan Lewis argues (1987, 689–721) that the concept of republican marriage helped to legitimate women's legal subjection to the will of their husbands, excluded women from participation in politics by making the husband the voice of his wife, and ultimately demanded that wives defer to their husbands on all issues. Thus, while Kerber and Norton assert that republican ideology was modified to include and elevate women, Lewis claims republicanism provided only an empty, transient model of womanhood.

At the same time that relationships between husbands and wives became more equal, the hierarchical character of parent–child relations declined as well. Daughters began exercising more independence in courtship and marriage, demanding power over their marriage choice, deciding not to marry, and even seeking divorce. This transformation resulted, in part, from a decline in the number of marriageable men. This, combined with the need to provide a solid education for the girls who would become republican mothers, led to the formation of female academies. Though this kind of education was available mostly to wealthy daughters, these women were the first to aspire to real equality with men. With knowledge and an improved sense of self-esteem, they became teachers, missionaries, and founders of female associations. Whether intended or not, these changes constituted real gains for women.

Most women, however, experienced no real change or gain in status as a result of the Revolution. The American Revolution was fought to secure rights and privileges for white men, who continued to deny the most basic rights to black men and women. The most painful result of the American Revolution for female slaves, though, was the constitutional provision that ended the import of slaves, placing the perpetuation of the institution on the transference of slave status from mother to child. Not until after the Civil War would slaves benefit from the legacy of the Revolution.

Ultimately, the American Revolution had mixed results for women. As far as tangible or material gains such as improved legal status and economic position are concerned, the Revolution failed the women of America. If scholars consider women's self-conceptions, though, such as the satisfaction they gained from boycotting against the British, keeping their farms running, or raising successful sons, the war takes on a different meaning. In this light, the idealized roles that society attributed to women allowed them to expand their influence in both public and private life. Based on this premise, it is possible to see the war take on a different meaning and to see the Revolutionary era as the beginning of women's movement toward a higher status and legal position that would begin to be realized almost a century later.

References. Joy Day Buel and Richard Buel, Jr., *The Way of Duty: A Woman and Her Family in Revolutionary America* (New York, 1984); Ronald Hoffman and Peter J. Albert (eds.), *Women in the Age of the American Revolution* (Charlottesville, Va., 1989) (see especially articles by Jacqueline Jones, Mary Beth Norton, and Laurel Thatcher Ulrich); Linda K. Kerber, *Women of the Republic: Intellect and Ideology in Revolutionary America* (Chapel Hill, N.C., 1980); Jan Lewis, "The Republican Wife," *William and Mary Quarterly* 44, 4 (October 1987): 689–721; Mary Beth Norton, *Liberty's Daughters: The Revolutionary Experience of American Women, 1750–1800* (Glenview, Ill., 1980); Joan Hoff Wilson, "The Illusion of Change: Women and the American Revolution," in Alfred F. Young (ed.), *The American Revolution* (Dekalb, Ill., 1976).

JENIFER GRINDLE DOLDE

AMERICANS WITH DISABILITIES ACT OF 1990 prohibits discrimination against individuals with disabilities in the areas of employment, transportation, public accommodations, state and local government, and telecommunications. For the purpose of this law a disability is defined as a physical or mental impairment that substantially limits one or more of an individual's major life activities, a record of such impairment, or being regarded as having such impairment. Private employers with 15 or more employees, state and local governments, employment agencies, and labor unions may not discriminate against *qualified* individuals with disabilities in regard to job application procedures; the hiring, advancement, or discharge of employees; employee compensation; job training; or other terms, conditions, and privileges of employment. Employers are required to make *reasonable* accommodations for *known* disabilities in order to enable qualified applicants or employees with disabilities to participate in the application process or to perform essential job functions. Reasonable accommodations may include such elements as improving accessibility of employee facilities, job restructuring, schedule modification, provision of qualified readers or interpreters, and acquisition or modification of equipment. Title I of the law regarding employment is enforced by the Equal Employment Opportunity Commission. Titles II and III regarding state and local governments, public accommodations, and commercial facilities are enforced by the Civil Rights Division of the U.S. Department of Justice.

Americans with Disabilities Act (ADA) Information Files, updated periodically, is available in the reference sections of 15,000 libraries across the United States. It provides a comprehensive resource on the ADA, including, among other things, the law and regulations, technical assistance, manuals, status reports, questions and answers for persons with disabilities and employers, and design guides.

References. *ADA Information Line*, voice and automated telephone assistance maintained by the U.S. government to allow people to obtain general information, order free materials, or ask about filing a complaint. Phone numbers: 800–514–0301 (voice—English/Spanish), 800–514–0383 (automated—English/Spanish). Internet: http://gopher.usdoj.crt/ada/

DAYLE MANDELSON

AMNIOCENTESIS is a procedure that can be used to detect fetal health problems, both genetic and environmental, through tests performed on amniotic fluid. By the early 1980s amniocentesis could be used to assess the sex and maturity of the fetus* and to diagnose around 90 prenatal health problems through a variety of biochemical tests on, and the karotyping of fetal cells in the fluid. Among the anomalies that can be detected or diagnosed are Down's syndrome, Tay-Sachs disease, and neural tube defects. Anomalies such as cleft palate and clubfoot cannot be detected. Women should recognize the potential for abuse of amniocentesis, especially in its use in determining the sex of the fetus. (See also REPRODUCTION, ETHICAL ISSUES IN.)

ANDROCENTRISM places man in the center and woman on the periphery. In 1903 Lester F. Ward defined androcentric theory as "the view that man is primary and woman secondary, that all things center, as it were, about man, and that woman, though necessary to the work of reproduction, is only a means of continuing the human race, but is otherwise an unimportant accessory" (292). Feminists picked up the word from Charlotte Perkins Gilman's use of it (1911) and use it as a term signifying man's assumption of superiority over females and other "defective" beings and man's biases in conflating and confusing the masculine with the generic. Other words meaning essentially the same thing are "masculinist," "masculist," "phallism," and "male chauvinist."

References. Charlotte Perkins Gilman, *The Man-Made World: Our Androcentric Culture* (New York, 1970, c. 1911); Lester F. Ward, *Pure Sociology* (Paris, 1906), 292.

ANDROGYNY is the combination of masculine and feminine characteristics within a person. The idea of androgyny is an ancient one rooted in classical mythology and literature. Since the early 1970s it has been widely adopted as a new sex-role alternative to the dichotomous psychological characteristics and roles traditionally prescribed for the sexes. In its most generic sense, androgyny signifies an absence of any sex-based differentiation, including unisex dress styles, bisexuality,* and hermaphroditism. Social scientists generally restrict usage of "psychological androgyny" to describe an individual who manifests in personality or behavior a combination of characteristics labeled as masculine and feminine in our society.

The concept of psychological androgyny is based in previous ideas about the nature of psychological differences between the sexes but reflects tolerance of a much broader range of sex-role options for men and women. Traditional notions of sex differentiation held that the sexes were or ideally ought to be as different psychologically as they were physically. The core of those characteristics stereotypically associated with women (femininity*) is sensitivity, emotionality, selflessness, and interrelationships with others (expressive/communal). Characteristics associated with men (masculinity) center around goal orientation, assertiveness, self-development, and separation from others (instrumental/agentic). The association of these instrumental/agentic characteristics exclusively with men and expressive/communal characteristics with women was considered typical, expected, and psychologically healthy. Individual deviation either through failure to exhibit attributes typical of one's sex or through endorsement of some characteristics atypical of one's sex implied psychological maladjustment of some sort.

This traditional model did not account for the presence of similarities across the sexes or differences within the sexes in feminine and masculine characteristics. Also with the resurgence of the feminist movement, the sex-role values embodied within this model increasingly appeared to be overly restrictive and outdated. The concept of psychological androgyny provided a way to frame sex-role alternatives in terms of masculinity and femininity without the prescriptive, sex-specific values of more traditional views.

Proponents of psychological androgyny generally assume that masculinity and femininity are independent but not mutually exclusive groups of characteristics existing in everyone to varying degrees. Individuals can be meaningfully described by the extent to which they endorse each group as self-descriptive. Both masculinity and femininity have a unique and positive but not sex-specific impact upon a person's psychological functioning (e.g., both sexes benefit from being feminine). Thus, possession of high levels of both sets of characteristics, or androgyny, should represent the most desirable, even ideal, sex-role alternative.

Descriptions of psychological androgyny differ considerably according to what types of psychological characteristics are emphasized. All of the descriptions portray a blending or an ultimate transcendence of sex-linked dichotomies of personality characteristics and behavior. Androgynous persons have been frequently defined as those who possess both masculine and feminine personality traits. Other descriptions have emphasized possession of socially appropriate, observable behaviors or thought processes that do not rely upon sex-related cues or meanings. The manner in which masculinity and femininity might work together to produce androgyny has also been variously explained. Androgyny may mean the balancing or moderating of masculinity and femininity by each other, a beneficial summation of the positive qualities of femininity and masculinity, the emergence of new qualities, of elimination of sex-stereotypic standards in an individual's perceptions and decisions, thus making masculine/feminine distinctions irrelevant.

An especially influential early description of androgynous persons proposed by Sandra Bem portrays them as flexible and adaptable, with an ability and willingness to engage in either masculine or feminine behavior as the situation warrants. In contrast, predominantly feminine or masculine (sex-typed) individuals presumably use sex-based standards to guide their behaviors, resulting in a seriously limited repertoire of options.

Research on psychological androgyny indicates that researchers have somewhat succeeded in capturing the expressive/communal and instrumental/agentic nature of femininity and masculinity through their newly developed femininity and masculinity measures. However, individuals' masculinity and femininity self-descriptions often do not strongly relate to other aspects of sex roles (e.g., attitudes or behaviors). Masculinity has proven to be much more closely related to individuals' self-esteem and psychological adjustment than is femininity. Masculinity's greater strength in this area probably stems from the more positive valuing of masculine characteristics in American society.

Numerous studies have attempted to demonstrate that androgynous individuals enjoy mental health benefits not shared with those who are sex-typed or those who see neither set of characteristics as particularly self-descriptive. Androgynous persons do tend to score as the best adjusted on a variety of measures, although the data are not conclusive. Contrary to researchers' early expectations, individuals who are high in masculinity (and low in femininity) often appear to be as well off as androgynous persons. However, individuals low in both masculinity and femininity are clearly disadvantaged. Evidence for sex differences in the androgyny literature suggests that the process, likelihood, and implications of becoming androgynous may be different for men and women. Finally, sex-role related characteristics are probably very complex and affected by a variety of factors. For example, an individual who is androgynous in self-description could appear to be quite traditional in attitudes, behavioral preferences, actual behaviors, and so on, depending on the person and the situation. Today, because of the nature of the research results and new refinements in sex-role theory, researchers are less likely to consider androgyny to represent a particular type of person who can be expected to behave in a consistent, predictable manner across a variety of situations.

Despite ambiguities suggested by research, mental health practitioners have found androgyny to be useful in naming new personality and behavioral alternatives for individuals coping with widespread social changes in how the sexes view themselves and each other. As a value and goal in counseling and psychotherapy, androgyny represents the desirability of

moving away from prescriptions based on biological sex alone toward enhancing of individual adaptability and choice.
Reference. E. P. Cook, *Psychological Androgyny* (Elmsford, N.Y., 1985).

ELLEN PIEL COOK

ANGER was viewed by Freud as an outgrowth of the destructive drive.
Accordingly, traditional psychiatric and psychological formulations have
regarded anger as an unruly emotion that must be subdued, as a problem
that resides within the individual. This approach has, however, ignored
some other important considerations about anger: the social context of
anger and anger expression as an instrument for social change. Anger is a
justifiable reaction to oppression and is a common experience among disfranchised persons. The failure to recognize the anger of disfranchised
groups in the context of oppressive societal conditions has serious ramifications. If anger is viewed as a problem within the individual, then it becomes the domain of mental health professionals, who can then treat angry
persons for their "personal" problem.

The experience of anger and societal reactions to it have special significance for disfranchised persons. Any individual who is frequently subjected
to oppression and subjugation is likely to react with anger. When the traditional Freudian model is applied to analyze this anger, the culturally instigated anger comes to be viewed as an inherently dangerous drive that
should be controlled and suppressed. For disfranchised individuals and
groups the traditional perspective of anger has translated into a denial of
the anger experience. This invalidation of anger can be viewed as a subtle
means of social control in that there is no attempt to consider the social
context in which anger arises. The focus is not on addressing the *source* of
the anger—which may be injustice—but on removal or suppression of the
individual's anger.

Further, anger expression is not considered acceptable behavior for
women, and, in fact, women experience higher levels of anxiety and guilt
over the experience and expression of anger and aggression than do men.
Thus, women may be more likely to experience and to give in to the pressure to suppress their anger.

Some contend that even if anger is a justifiable reaction to oppression, it
is a destructive emotion. Anger can, however, be experienced and expressed
without being destructive; in fact, it can be a force for constructive change.
For instance, if one person in a relationship feels anger over a sense of
unfair treatment, an assertion of this anger that is designed to inform the
other and to introduce an atmosphere of cooperative problem solving is
more likely to lead to fruitful discussion than is either a stormy accusation
or an attempt to suppress the anger.

On the other hand, anger that is expressed with the intent of injuring or insulting another is likely to have a destructive effect on interpersonal relationships since it may affect the capability of each person to trust the other. This instrumental anger manifests itself in attempts to control another, as in instances of intimidation. When the purpose of anger is to control another, the intimidator tends to evidence a lack of respect for others, presuming a right to control them. Typically, there is confusion over personal boundaries, such that the intimidator does not take personal responsibility for his or her reactions and refuses to understand and respect the rights of other persons.

For many, however, the concern is not how to express anger but whether to express it. Persons who are not aware of their oppression are not likely to experience anger over it. Women and other disfranchised persons are especially vulnerable to pressures to suppress their anger—pressures that may be imposed by themselves as well as by others. The cost of this suppression may, however, be lowered self-esteem, a sense of powerlessness, and fear of responding to, or of even recognizing, oppressive conditions. It must be recognized that anger may be a justifiable response to social-political injustice and, as such, may represent an individual or group attempt to challenge that injustice. An important contribution of the feminist analysis is an examination of the broader social context in which anger arises and the validation of anger as a justifiable response to oppressive social-political conditions.

References. V. Burtle, "Therapeutic Anger in Women," in L. B. Rosewater and L.E.A. Walker (eds.), *Handbook of Feminist Therapy: Women's Issues in Psychotherapy* (New York, 1985), 71–79; B. A. Kopper and D. L. Epperson, "Women and Anger: Sex and Sex-Role Comparisons in the Expression of Anger," *Psychology of Women Quarterly* 15 (1991): 7–14; Harriet G. Lerner, *The Dance of Anger: A Woman's Guide to Changing the Patterns of Intimate Relationships* (New York, 1986).

MARY KAY BIAGGIO

ANNULMENT is a judicial decision voiding a marriage on the grounds that, because of some defect or impediment, it was not a valid marriage. In the United States, specific grounds for annulment vary in each state, but, in general, marriages may be nullified because of a defect in mental or physical capacity (e.g., unsound mind, minor marrying without consent), in intent (e.g., consent obtained by fraud, bigamy), or in the procedural formalities (e.g., failure to comply with licensing or witness requirements).

Since the declaration of nullity means that no valid marriage ever existed, any children of the union would be illegitimate. Some states, to protect the rights of any children involved, have stipulated that the offspring of voided marriages are legitimate. Georgia forbids annulment if there are children or will be children from the marriage. Also unlike a suit for divorce, which must be brought by one of the parties to the marriage, an application for annulment may be brought by a third party and may even be brought after the death of one of the marriage partners.

Applications to civil courts for annulments have declined since divorce laws have been liberalized, but applications to ecclesiastical courts have risen sharply. Since the Catholic Church does not recognize complete divorce from the marriage bond, separated or divorced Catholics who wish to remarry and remain practicing members of the faith may resort to the diocesan marriage court to seek an annulment under canon law. Canon law recognizes defective consent, an impediment existing prior to the marriage, and lack of canonical form as grounds for nullity. The Catholic Church in the United States requires that the partners to the marriage have a civil divorce before it will consider a request for nullification. It does not consider offspring of the marriage to be illegitimate.

As the number of American separated or divorced Catholics grew, diocesan marriage courts became clogged with cases, which sometimes took years to be settled. In the late 1960s only several hundred annulments were granted a year. However, the number of annulments has risen sharply since the early 1970s, as more liberal interpretations of grounds such as "conditional consent" have been applied. In the 1990s American diocesan courts were granting more annulments than all the rest of the church combined, over 50,000 a year.

ANOREXIA NERVOSA AND BULIMIA NERVOSA are two eating disorders found primarily among young, white, affluent women in modern, industrialized countries. Anorexia nervosa is purposeful starvation alone or in combination with excessive exercising, occasional binge-eating, vomiting, and/or laxative abuse. Body weight is less than 85 percent of that expected for age and height. Bulimia nervosa denotes a recurrent pattern of binge-eating followed by such behavior as fasting, self-induced vomiting, or misuse of laxatives. Bulimics' weight tends to be normal or close to normal for age and height. Both eating disorders often involve a fear of fatness and a distorted body image. These eating disorders are major health problems. Six to 20 percent of anorexics die, with bulimia nervosa being less life-threatening. Physical effects of anorexia nervosa include cardiac arrhythmias, hypothermia, anemia, and edema. Bulimia nervosa entails such physical consequences as cardiac arrhythmias, esophageal tears, gastric rupture, and loss of dental enamel. Elements of socialization relating to culture, family,* and gender roles* clarify why anorexia nervosa and bulimia nervosa are most prevalent in certain groups.

Cultural Socialization. In developing countries, fatness can be seen as a symbol of wealth and a desirable aspect of body shape. However, in modern, industrialized nations, fatness no longer signifies affluence because people generally have an adequate supply of food. In fact, it is possible to eat too much. Slimness therefore symbolizes discretionary eating, and appearance norms shift from plumpness to thinness.

The affluent tend to value slimness more and be thinner than other individuals. With whites composing most of the upper strata, eating disorders are more prevalent among whites. As other ethnic groups become more upwardly mobile, eating disorders among them are increasing. The slim body ideal is often accompanied by a fear of fatness and an urgent pursuit of slimness.

The prevalence of anorexia nervosa and bulimia nervosa among women can be explained by the emphasis society places on women's appearance. Role models portrayed in movies and television, as well as in magazines and television advertisements, are uniformly slender. Traditional beauty standards also reflect the slimness norm. Available analyses indicate that from 1959 into the 1980s, *Playboy* centerfolds and Miss America became progressively thinner; from 1970 to 1978, Miss America was slimmer than the average contestant. Because women are viewed as visual objects, they try to fulfill society's expectations about their appearance by conforming to the thinness orientation. Although a slimness norm for men exists, it is overridden by a strength/muscularity norm.

One indication of how urgently women pursue the thin body ideal is the national obsession with dieting. Over the last two decades, there has been a vast increase in weight-reducing centers and diet plans, aids, and books. Diet articles and advertisements routinely appear in women's magazines. In a survey of women aged 24 to 54, more than half had dieted at least once in the previous year; three-quarters dieted for cosmetic rather than health reasons. A history of dieting, beginning in one's teens, is common among anorexics and bulimics. Individuals who develop eating disorders are responding to the cultural norm of thinness and can be seen as extensions of the slim body ideal.

Family Socialization. Anorexics and bulimics are also socialized by their families to value thinness. Their siblings and parents are often preoccupied with eating, exercising, and body weight and shape. These issues become matters of rivalry among family members. In addition, parents of anorexics and bulimics emphasize achievement and perfection. Many individuals with eating disorders maintain near-perfect grades and fulfill high expectations. However, their accomplishments are not recognized by their family because such achievements are considered normal.

Another element of socialization within these families is the valuing of conformity. Anorexics and bulimics are negatively sanctioned for not adhering to parents' expectations of attractive appearance, diligence, and obedience. However, especially in anorexics' families, emotions are often not verbalized; family members rarely express antagonism or anger. Although families with eating-disordered individuals appear to be close and supportive, their underlying interaction is impaired due to a lack of meaningful communication.

Families of individuals with eating disorders also exhibit excessive interdependency. Anorexics and bulimics are reluctant to make decisions without consulting their parents, especially their same-sex parent. This parent, in turn, reinforces dependency by encouraging the child's need for approval and discouraging efforts toward independence. Dependency and the desire to satisfy others' expectations maintain low self-esteem among individuals with eating disorders.

Anorexics and bulimics perceive their bodies and eating behavior as areas of autonomy. To cope with their families' enforced dependency and extreme emphasis on appearance, achievement, and conformity, anorexics starve, and bulimics binge and vomit/purge. For females, dependency, conformity, and concern for appearance are compounded by cultural and gender-role socialization.

Gender-Role Socialization. With divergent adaptations, individuals who have eating disorders are responding to gender-role expectations. Anorexics' girlish appearance is interpreted as a rejection of femininity and womanhood. In contrast, bulimics are characterized as overconforming to traditional female roles.

By becoming progressively slimmer, anorexics lose breast and hip development, stop menstruating, and assume the body of prepubescence. In their reversion to a childlike appearance, anorexics remove themselves from the sexual arena and postpone adulthood. Through denial of hunger, adolescent females, those most likely to be anorexic, regain a feeling of control in the upheaval and powerlessness caused by changing bodily processes and social roles.

Despite their quest for power and control, anorexics actually become more dependent because of their weakness and frailty. Their extreme slimness parodies feminine appearance norms of delicacy and petiteness. Paradoxically, while anorexics reject female sexuality with their asexual bodies, they epitomize the idealized feminine traits of fragility and smallness.

Bulimics conform more thoroughly than anorexics to stereotyped femininity. Overidentifying with traditional female gender roles, bulimics have an intense need for validation from males. They seek approval from men and are often exceedingly compliant to their partners' wishes. Dependent and passive, bulimics have a minimal sense of control in their lives.

Striving to fulfill the idealized feminine role, bulimics expect to be rewarded by males' wanting and pursuing them. When they perceive rejection, bulimics blame the appearance of their bodies. Believing that they are not thin enough to please men, they begin to diet. When dieting fails to result in male companionship, bulimics use bingeing as a release from frus-

trations and from their strictly controlled lives. However, the fear of becoming fat from bingeing leads to vomiting or purging. The use of bingeing
for a release and vomiting/purging for weight control and purification becomes a self-perpetuating cycle. Thus, through different processes, bulimics
and anorexics embody gender-role socialization.

References. M. Macsween, *Anorexic Bodies: A Feminist and Sociological Per-*
spective on Anorexia Nervosa (London, 1993); E. Stice, "Review of the Evidence
for a Sociocultural Model of Bulimia Nervosa and an Exploration of the Mechanisms of Action," *Clinical Psychology Review* 14 (1994): 633–661.

DIANE E. TAUB and PENELOPE A. McLORG

ANTIFEMINIST MOVEMENTS are organized opposition to feminist demands for equality of treatment under the law. Antifeminist movements
have a largely female constituency, although males appear to provide considerable financial support. Their major ideological theme is the defense of
the traditional family, consisting of a breadwinning husband and nonem-
ployed wife. This sexual division of labor is perceived as the basis of family
stability and female privilege. According to the antifeminist argument, universalistic laws will deny women the special protections they have always
enjoyed: the right to be exempt from military service,* to be financially
supported by their husbands, and especially to be a full-time homemaker.

There have been two major waves of antifeminist activity in the United
States: opposition to woman suffrage and more recently to the proposed
Equal Rights Amendment (ERA).* Antisuffrage organizations existed before the twentieth century, but the founding of the National Association
Opposed to Woman Suffrage in 1911 marked the heyday of the counter-
movement. This organization claimed 350,000 members and 25 state chapters, mostly in the northern and midwestern states. Between 1912 and
1916, they helped defeat 15 of the 21 state woman suffrage referenda before the male electorate. By 1917, however, antisuffrage momentum was
lost as New York, long considered a key state by both sides, added a
woman suffrage amendment to its state constitution; this event was quickly
followed by presidential endorsement, congressional passage, and state ratification of the Nineteenth Amendment enfranchising 26 million American
women in 1920.

The anti-ERA movement was more successful than its predecessor. It
began to coalesce in 1972, the first year of the ERA ratification process.
Twenty-two states ratified the ERA in that year, and 8 more followed in
1973; in most states, there was strong consensus on the amendment, and
political observers predicted that ratification by the required 38 states
would occur long before the March 1979 deadline. But this did not happen.
Despite a congressional extension to June 1982, the Equal Rights Amendment lapsed three states short of ratification. Significantly, no additional

states ratified the ERA after January 1977, and several states attempted to rescind their ratification.

The credit for reversing the momentum of the amendment goes to Phyllis Schlafly and her STOP ERA organization. While there have been other contemporary antifeminist organizations with such eye-catching names as Eve Reborn, HOT DOG (Humanitarians Opposed to Degrading Our Girls), and HOW (Happiness of Womanhood), STOP ERA overshadows all others in political influence. Schlafly founded STOP ERA in October 1972 and operated it with no paid staff, no membership dues, and minimal bureaucratic structure. But it had a charismatic leader who could mobilize her loyal constituency on a moment's notice and who proved adept at turning the liabilities of a housebound constituency into a strategic advantage.

Phyllis Schlafly is an accomplished woman with extensive political experience. She put herself through college, did graduate work at Radcliffe, and, after raising six children, earned a law degree. Long active in the Republican Party, Schlafly served as speechwriter for presidential candidate Barry Goldwater, several times ran unsuccessfully for Congress, and before the ERA issue was best known for her writings in favor of a strong U.S. defense policy. After being defeated in a bitter contest for the presidency of the National Federation of Republican Women in 1967, she launched *The Phyllis Schlafly Report* to communicate with her loyal followers and the Eagle Trust Fund to receive donations for the support of conservative causes. Since 1968, Schlafly has held annual training conferences for her top lieutenants; in 1975, she began publication of the *Eagle Forum Newsletter*, which provides detailed instructions on antifeminist strategy. This includes emphasizing the differences between "libbers" and themselves by appearing in ladylike attire, holding bake sales, and lobbying state legislators with gifts of homemade jam. Telephone trees and letter-writing campaigns maximized the resources of homemakers who were difficult to mobilize for collective action. Schlafly also orchestrated clever media events, including skits, original songs, props such as caskets for burying the ERA, and colorful quotes to keep the issue before the public.

The success of STOP ERA derives also from its coalition building. Schlafly capitalized on her broad political network to forge links with such conservative organizations as the Moral Majority, the American Farm Bureau Association, and the John Birch Society, as well as single-issue groups against abortion,* pornography,* gun control, and unions. The strategy of integrating STOP ERA with the so-called New Right increased its available resources and enabled the adoption of more sophisticated tactics, such as the use of computer-generated mailing lists, political action committees, and highly coordinated campaign strategies targeting pro-feminist candidates for defeat.

Compared to feminist activists, anti-ERA women were older, less educated, more religious, more likely to be married, and less likely to be married to professionals or to be in professional occupations themselves. These background characteristics were more weakly associated with ERA opposition among the general population, who were more influenced by the anticipated consequences of the amendment: those who thought the ERA would harm male employment opportunities and lower family incomes were more likely to oppose it. Such findings suggest that the defeat of the Equal Rights Amendment was effected in part by the economic downturn of the 1970s, which may have increased its perceived threat.

References. J. K. Boles, *The Politics of the Equal Rights Amendment: Conflict and the Decision Process* (New York, 1979); S. E. Marshall and A. M. Orum, "Opposition Then and Now: Countering Feminism in the Twentieth Century," in Gwen Moore and Glenna D. Spitze (eds.), *Research in Politics and Society* (Greenwich, Conn., 1986), 2, 13–34; G. D. Spitze and J. Huber, "Effects of Anticipated Consequences on ERA Opinion," *Social Science Quarterly* 63 (1982): 323–331.

SUSAN E. MARSHALL

ANTI-SEMITISM. Before National Socialism. Throughout the centuries, the most virulent manifestations of European anti-Semitism were usually aimed at men rather than women. Unlike Jewish females, Jewish males were distinguishable from the rest of the population by circumcision and were viewed as being "maimed in both spirit and body." Anti-Semitic literature, painting, sculpture, and cartoons, religious as well as secular, were therefore particularly vehement in their negative depictions of men. Jewish women, by contrast, were much more sympathetically portrayed. In Strasbourg Cathedral, for example, the synagogue is represented as a blindfolded, graceful young maiden with delicate features. This portrayal has none of the physical distortions commonly used in male depictions, whether individual or collective, of Jews and Judaism.

In Western literature, Jewish women tended to be shown as exotic beauties who were wise, charming, compassionate, and frequently the objects of love for handsome young Christians. Among the best known of the literary Jewish heroines are Jessica in William Shakespeare's *The Merchant of Venice*, Abigail in Christopher Marlowe's *The Jew of Malta*, and Rebecca in Sir Walter Scott's *Ivanhoe*. (Upon the advice of his American friend Washington Irving, Scott modeled his Rebecca after Irving's great friend Rebecca Gratz, a prominent Philadelphia socialite.) All three beautiful young women are the daughters of fathers who are portrayed in archetypically negative, anti-Semitic terms. The positive image of the Jewish woman, however, continued to be perpetuated by the popular conception of the vivacious, gracious, Jewish intellectual hostesses who presided over many of the nineteenth-century cultural salons of Vienna. That image, in turn, gradually gave way to the early twentieth-century version of the young Jewish female as social reformer and revolutionary, with Rosa Lux-emburg as the real-life prototype. The way in which Rosa Luxemburg came to be viewed, however, was a signal of the change that began to occur in the twentieth-century depiction of Jewish women.

In European anti-Semitic material in the interwar years, there is a steady increase in the numbers of Jewish women appearing alongside Jewish men, most noticeably in cartoon caricatures. Rosa Luxemburg herself, although she was a victim rather than a perpetrator of violence, was to become a popular symbol of the evils thought to be threatening German society and womanhood. She and other women activists, Jewish and non-Jewish alike, were remembered with fear and loathing as examples of what national socialism was pledged to prevent.

Status of Jewish and Non-Jewish Women under National Socialism. The Nazi revolution aimed to restore German women to the "idyllic" destiny from which they were "diverted" in the years leading up to World War I. Germany was going to rid itself of Marxist internationalists, liberals, and feminists. Women could not participate actively in this Nazi revolution; allowing them to do so would be to deny what the revolution stood for. According to Nazi ideology, women were to be "wives, mothers, and home-makers," as in the old three-K formulation of *kinder, kuche, kirche* (chil-dren, kitchen, church). Women were to be left out of all aspects of public life—the legislature, the executive, the judiciary, and the armed forces—thus virtually excluding them from playing any significant role in the Final Solution.

While a growing number of German women were eager to be active participants in the national socialist movement, they were encouraged to take supporting roles, as wives to the party's "fighting menfolk" and moth-ers to the blond, blue-eyed children it was hoped they would conceive with their husbands or even with selected male partners on special "breeding farms" established for this purpose. Despite the obstacles there were some Nazi organizations for women, but they were marginal in importance and played little part in the implementation of the Final Solution. All the top Nazi officials were men.

While the status of the Aryan woman in Nazi Germany was distinctly second-class, Jewish women were inferior not just to men but to the entire Aryan race. There, as elsewhere, the traditional preferred status of Jewish women was disappearing. "Sara" had to be added to the name of each Jewish female residing in Nazi Germany. In the anti-Jewish legislation known as the Nuremberg Laws, which took effect September 1, 1935, cer-tain statutes were especially pertinent to women, such as the Law for the Protection of German Blood, which prohibited marriages and extramarital intercourse between Jews and Germans, and the law forbidding the em-ployment of German maids under the age of 45 in Jewish households.

Jewish women, however, were still exempt from the worst brutalities.

During *Kristallnacht* (Night of the Broken Glass), the first of the Nazis' organized pogroms, which occurred November 9 through 10, 1938, and involved outbreaks of anti-Semitic violence throughout Germany and Austria, close to 100 Jewish men were murdered, while many others were beaten up, and about 30,000 were arrested and deported to the concentration camps of Dachau, Buchenwald, and Sachsenhausen. Jewish women, however, were spared both deportation and death during the first pogrom, though a number were beaten and raped.

References. Livia Bitton-Jackson, *Madonna or Courtesan?* (New York, 1982); Jill Stephenson, *The Nazi Organization of Women* (Totowa, N.J., 1981).

YAFFA ELIACH

ANTISLAVERY ASSOCIATIONS. Activity in antislavery associations was an important part of the process by which nineteenth-century women widened their sphere of social and political activity. These women formed auxiliaries that made significant contributions to the antislavery crusade: major auxiliaries in Boston and Philadelphia were founded in 1833 and functioned until after the American Civil War. Smaller organizations rose, flourished, declined, and died, involving countless women at the grassroots level and creating a network of activity that covered the North. Most auxiliaries were allied to the radical, Garrisonian branch of American abolitionism, as William Lloyd Garrison preached equal rights for all—woman as well as slave—and women had more potential for meaningful activity within this branch of the movement.

Women's auxiliaries originally functioned to raise funds for the men's local organizations and the national American Anti-Slavery Association. They also exerted influence in their homes and neighborhoods, winning converts to the cause. Exerting their power as consumers, women worked to limit the purchase and use of slave-grown products. By midcentury they had also become very adept at gathering petitions and flooding Congress with their appeals on behalf of the slaves. Their range of acceptable activity increased as the movement matured, and the country moved toward the Civil War.

Auxiliaries in Boston; Rochester, New York; and Philadelphia annually held large bazaars to raise funds, displaying great amounts of ingenuity and effort in planning these successful endeavors. They formed strong alliances with women's organizations in England, exchanging views on both the antislavery crusade and the emerging position of women within each society. Lucretia Mott and Maria Weston Chapman, among others, visited their sisters in Great Britain to advance the cause of Garrisonian abolitionism. This interaction helped spread the recognition of women's important role in the crusade as well as their potential within society.

Women became involved in these auxiliaries out of a strong sense of Christian and feminine duty, honoring their perceived roles as the guardians of both the nation's ethical and religious purity. By identifying slavery primarily as a religious issue, they assured themselves a ready-made part in the crusade. Moreover, as a consequence of leaving their homes and banding together with other women to agitate against slavery, they measurably increased their sphere of influence and activity within society.

The knowledge women gained as they formed and maintained their auxiliaries—raising funds, gathering petitions, and forming networks with other women—contributed to the effective organization of the women's rights movement* after the Civil War. Through their antislavery work they carved out new spheres of respectable activity, ultimately enlarging the foundation for future agitation on their own behalf. (See also ABOLITIONISM and WORLD'S ANTI-SLAVERY CONVENTION OF 1840.)

KAREN I. HALBERSLEBEN

ARAB WOMEN. Arab women's history is currently the focus of an unprecedented number of studies that promise to challenge assumptions about the subject in fundamental ways.

The term "Arab" as used today is a quasi–political-national definition based on linguistic boundaries. Countries or territories defined as Arab are (proceeding from West Africa eastward): Morocco, Algeria, Tunisia, Libya, Egypt, Sudan, Palestine, Jordan, Saudi Arabia, Yemen, Oman, United Arab Emirates, Qatar, Kuwait, Bahrain, Iraq, and Syria. These areas include populations that are urban, rural, and nomadic. As a national-political definition, the term "Arab" is of relatively recent origin, emerging only in the twentieth century as a result of, and also a response to, the nationalisms of European states and their colonialist activities in the Middle East. All the Arab areas just mentioned are predominantly Muslim, although most states also have significant minority populations, which are primarily Christian. Before the twentieth century the region defined itself on the basis not of language but of the religion of the state and the majority, that is, as part of the world of Islam. A complexity of reasons, including European nationalism and colonialism as well as the breakup, around the time of World War I, of the Muslim Ottoman empire, of which the Arab countries had been a part, led to the emergence of a political identity transcending religious differences and based on a common language.

Historically, the term "Arab" referred to natives of the Arabian Peninsula. From this land, in the seventh century of the Christian Era, the Arabic language and the monotheist religion of Islam spread to the Middle East and North Africa. Immediately prior to the Arab conquest these regions had been successively under the rule of the Hellenistic, Roman, and Byzantine empires. At the time of the Arab conquest the population was predominantly Christian but also included Jews and Zoroastrians. Religious conversion to Islam and linguistic conversion to Arabic, the religion and language of the ruling class, occurred gradually over the following two or three centuries. A minority, however, clung to the older faiths indigenous to the region, Judaism and Christianity.

By the time of the Arab conquest, the region had already known several cycles of civilization and had a complex and sophisticated lettered heritage, best articulated in the religious and legal traditions of Judaism and Christianity, and by no means matched by the incoming Arabs, whose contribution to the written heritage was paramountly the Koran. At the core of the elaborate scriptural traditions of the two older religions were clearly articulated beliefs about the nature and meaning of gender (beliefs that some scholars trace back to Mesopotamian civilization) and the proper subordination, in the cosmic and the human order, of women. This older, sophisticated population of converts to Islam played a vital role in fleshing out the Koran into a legal and religious system that, among other things, encapsulated the social and religious views and attitudes about gender of the indigenous pre-Arab population and transferred them to Islam. Crystallized into the edifice of Islamic law, these attitudes form part of a legal system in force (at least in matters of family law) to this day.

Thus, the customs popularly thought of as intrinsically Islamic, such as veiling and seclusion, are actually accretions to Islam with roots in both Mediterranean and Mesopotamian-Iranian pre-Islamic practice. Prior to the Arab conquests and during the lifetime of Muhammad (570–632), women of the Muslim community of Arabia did not veil and were not secluded. On the contrary, they played an active role in the community and are known to have participated not only in poetry competitions but also in warfare, on both the Muslim and the opposing sides. In battles, they acted, for the most part, as nurses going onto the battlefield to tend the wounded or to chant encouragement to their men, but occasionally they also engaged in combat.

Only following the conquests did the customs of veiling and seclusion, which were already in practice among the upper classes in the Mediterranean and elsewhere, spread through the Muslim community. Previously, only Muhammad's wives (and only toward the end of his life) were required to seclude and veil themselves. This requirement was imposed on them to guard them, it is thought, from the constant importunity of the throngs of Muhammad's followers as he became famous.

It would obviously be impossible to give an account of Middle Eastern women's history in the space available here. The following notes, therefore, aim at pointing out some of the salient findings of current research with respect, first, to women of this region in the premodern era and then with respect to the modern era. The majority of Muslims in Arab countries are Sunni (as distinct from Shiite) Muslims. The laws referred to in the following are therefore Sunni laws.

The Premodern Era

The Family

1. Polygamy: Studies for all periods suggest that the practice (up to four wives were legally permitted) was generally confined to rulers and the wealthiest elite.

2. Concubines (slave women serving sexual purposes): Again, the practice of keeping concubines was essentially confined to royalty and the extremely wealthy. Children fathered by the owner/master and acknowledged by him were legally free and entitled to share in the paternal inheritance, and slave women bearing such children became legally free on the master's death (if not before).

3. Divorce: Research suggests that this was quite common at all class levels and in the different Arabic societies apparently throughout the Islamic era. Examples of frequent divorce and remarriage for women are known for upper-class women of the early Islamic era, middle-class women in the medieval period, and middle-and lower-class women in the nineteenth century. Most commonly, divorce was initiated by the man. Women could obtain divorces if their marriage contract stipulated that they had the right to do so. Although the law permits this clause, generally only upper-class women had the leverage to demand its inclusion. They could also obtain a divorce through private negotiations with the spouse, possibly by forfeiting payments to which they were entitled or, although the conditions for this were stringent, by petitioning the courts. Custody of the children was the mother's during the "tender years" (different law schools set different ages as the limit), during which time the father was obliged to support them. After this time they came under the custody of the father.

4. Sexuality, contraception, and abortion: Sexual satisfaction was considered to be a woman's right in marriage. Most schools of classical Sunni Islamic law permitted contraception and, although with less unanimity, generally permitted abortion. Some schools debated whether a woman needed the permission of her husband to resort to either type of fertility control, with several ruling that she did not. (In today's societies, state policies on contraception and abortion differ from state to state.)

Economic and Other Activities. By law women had the right to inherit and to retain exclusive control of their property even after marriage. Consequently, independently wealthy women were a feature of all Islamic societies. Some women were active as merchants, working often through a male agent, or ran great estates. Throughout history Arab women have endowed universities, mosques, and benevolent institutions. Spinning and weaving, sewing, and embroidery of textiles were occupations practiced by women of all classes and served, for middle- and lower-class women, as sources of additional income. Scholarship also occupied upper- and middle-class women, though rarely serving as a source of income. A fifteenth-century biographical dictionary lists 1,763 notable women of its century, noting of a fair number of them that they were reputed to be learned. Occasionally, a woman achieved such fame as a scholar that she was sought out by male students. The upper-class custom of seclusion required women to service the women's quarters; therefore, lower-class urban women worked as midwives, peddlers, entertainers, bath attendants, and so forth, to *harim* women. Some women worked as street vendors of foodstuffs and domestic servants. They could also be members of religious and mystic orders, although convents in the Christian manner were rare. Rural women were crucial to the economy; they worked in the fields, often at different tasks from men. For instance, the men tended to plowing and irrigation, and the women to seed sowing, harvesting, animal husbandry, and textile production.

The Modern Era. Radical change began to occur following the economic and, subsequently, the colonial encroachment of European states. The beginning of the nineteenth century is the period during which this encroachment began, at least in some areas of the Middle East, particularly Egypt and the eastern Mediterranean. The subsequent course of the history of the Middle East to our own day is inextricably bound up with the area's integration into the world economy.

For women the impact of European encroachment was largely negative in economic terms. The pattern of production and export of raw materials (e.g., Egyptian cotton) for European factories and the importing of machine-made textiles into which the area was forced led to the decline of local textile production, sharply affecting the employment of lower- and middle-class women. Wealthy women traders also suffered as trade patterns shifted from the old routes within the Islamic world to new routes with Europe. In the countryside, agricultural estates were consolidated to supply exports to Europe. Rural working families lost their precarious hold on land, and women as well as men were forced to migrate to urban areas. On the positive side, the shock of European dominance and encroachment as well as exposure to European ideas prompted a drive to emulate Europe, in particular in the pursuit of education and social renovation. Education for women as well as men became a goal, and some intellectuals began to assert that women's participation was essential to the society's advancement.

By the end of the nineteenth century education for women was making significant advances. A teacher-training college for women was founded in Egypt in 1890. Women's magazines flourished, and feminist women writers and activists, mainly of the upper class, took up the causes of furthering women's education and of legal reform in family law. In 1928 the first Egyptian/Arab women were admitted to the Egyptian National University in Cairo.

Education and the entry of women into professional and white-collar employment have been the major areas of achievement for Arab women in the twentieth century. In the wake of the socialist-inclined revolutions of the 1950s and 1960s in Egypt, Syria, Iraq, and Algeria, free education at all levels, including higher education, became available to both women and men. Thereafter it became available in most Arab countries. Oil wealth made it possible for the countries of the Arabian Peninsula to follow those of North Africa and western Asia in offering free education. Although studies have indicated that women in Arab countries are behind women in many other Third World countries in entering factory work, the pursuit of education and of jobs requiring some education has been avid. Women have made enormous inroads into white-collar work and the professions: they are engineers and doctors as well as academics, teachers, nurses, social and clerical workers, and workers in service industries.

Economic shrinkage and increasing male unemployment, however, are elements fueling the "back to the home" wave that has recently made its appearance. It is an important element in the Islamic fundamentalist movement, which gained ground during the 1980s.

Reform in family law (including women's right to divorce and the banning of polygamy), a feminist cause in Muslim countries since the beginning of this century, has made almost no headway in the Arab countries with the exception of Tunisia.

Women have the vote in Morocco, Algeria, Tunisia, Libya, Egypt, Sudan, Jordan, the Yemen People's Republic, Iraq, and Syria.

LEILA AHMED

ARCHETYPAL CRITICISM, FEMINIST, engages literary critics in the analysis of texts to determine the impact of gender upon the way archetypes structure literary works. Archetypes are images, symbols, and narrative patterns that recur over hundreds of years, in art and religion as well as in literature, with certain constant features. They are not rigid "givens," however, but complex variables modified by the personal and cultural signature of the author. For example, the Aphrodite/Venus archetype always retains the connotation of a powerful feminine sensuality as a constant, but this characteristic will be interwoven with attitudes toward it varying according to gender and culture. In the period before 1700, for example, women were considered as sensual as men, though lacking in control; after that time men and women were defined as essentially different, men experiencing strong sexuality and women ideally sexless. Thus, a male poet's structuring of a poem on the Aphrodite archetype during the Renaissance would be determined, in part, by his culture's definition of women's sensuality; in the nineteenth century he would be more likely to value sexlessness in women and consider sensual women deviant. Correspondingly, a woman poet writing in the nineteenth century would punish herself for "monstrous" sexual desires more readily than her Renaissance counterpart. The archetypal experience of authentic feminine sensuality is interwoven in each text with overlays of cultural and gender determinants.

The feminist archetypal theory that emerges from this criticism is not dependent on the archetypal theories of Carl Gustav Jung and his followers, nor does it conform rigidly to the theory of literary archetypes of Northrop

Frye. Although aspects of Frye's and Jung's theories prove useful to feminist archetypal methods, other aspects have been critiqued and discarded. Thus, when examining an archetypal narrative like the quest pattern (the journey of self-discovery undertaken by a young hero), feminist archetypal critics have noted significant differences between the quests of women and the quests of men heroes.

Some feminist archetypal critics define women writers' use of archetypes as a process of "revisioning" materials understood as basically masculine in origin, a process of usurpation of nonfeminine images and symbols and reworking them in manners appropriate to women's psychological experiences. Some of these critics assume that not only myths but language itself are masculine products. Other critics define Western European culture and its mythologies as only the most recent layer of archetypal materials in a long series of layers, tracing Aphrodite, for example, back to the literature of Inanna in Sumeria of 2000 B.C. These critics approach the use of the archetype in a single text as the product of a dialectical relationship between recent responses and earlier responses to it, taking into consideration such mythic systems as that of Old Europe as a factor in classical mythology.

Feminist archetypal criticism draws upon the rich field of feminist theology and upon women's studies scholarship in psychology and anthropology as well as in history and the arts. Since archetypes can be understood as recurrent ways that the psyche responds to such key life experiences as sexuality, they form a useful basis for classroom discussions appropriate to women's studies emphasis on experiential pedagogy.

References. Estella Lauter, *Women as Mythmakers: Poetry and Visual Art by Twentieth-Century Women* (Bloomington, Ind., 1984); Estella Lauter and Carol Rupprecht, *Feminist Archetypal Theory* (Knoxville, Tenn., 1985); Annis Pratt, *Archetypal Patterns in Women's Fiction* (Bloomington, Ind., 1981).

ANNIS PRATT

ARCHITECTURE and women have always been closely linked, although one may not realize it at first glance. Throughout history and around the world, women have always assumed significant roles in architecture as consumers, critics, and creators of the built environment. Women constitute over one-half of the world's population and as such are among the major users of all works of architecture. Women have always had opinions about the buildings in which they live and work and as such are architectural critics. Women clients have long been key sponsors of architectural works, and as women have slowly entered the profession of architecture, they have increasingly assumed roles as creators and designers of architectural work.

Yet until recently, most of their contributions have gone unnoticed. Only in the past few decades, as more women have become educators, researchers, and scholars of architecture, have women's contributions begun to be properly acknowledged.

Ironically, often the foresight of women clients—progressive, upper-class consumers—provided opportunities for white male architects to flourish in their careers. For example, the Dana Thomas house in Springfield, Illinois, an architectural masterpiece designed by Frank Lloyd Wright, would not have been possible had not Susan Lawrence Dana (1862–1946), later known simply as Susan Lawrence, been willing to pay the bill for Wright's services back in 1902. In the early 1900s, women across the country established many clubs that provided centers for recreational, educational, and civic activities and often hired women architects to design them.

Not surprisingly, the public is largely unaware of the pioneering roles that women have played in historic preservation movements across the United States. Many women's clubs engaged in preservation interests. The Daughters of the American Revolution, organized in 1890, became the first national organization to protect historic sites. In 1916, the National Association of Colored Women vowed to preserve the home of Frederick Douglass in Anacostia, outside Washington, D.C. Some of the United States' most architecturally significant historic districts have been preserved largely due to the efforts of women. Examples include such memorable places as Rainbow Row and environs in Charleston, South Carolina; Olvera Street in Los Angeles; and the French Quarter in New Orleans. In the early 1960s, First Lady Jacqueline Kennedy took the lead in restoring the White House to its original early nineteenth-century design and helped spearhead today's historic preservation movement. Her successor, Lady Bird Johnson, lent her public support to the National Trust for Historic Preservation, providing a favorable climate that led to passage of the National Historic Preservation Act in 1966. She also led an effective campaign to improve the monuments, parks, and public vistas of Washington, D.C.

What about women architects? In ancient Egypt, Queen Hatshepsut planned many monuments, including her own funeral complex at Deir el-Bahari. It is reported that in ancient Mesopotamia, a woman named Semiramis designed Babylon's hanging gardens. Native American women played a major role in fabricating tepees and other designs. Another early trace of a woman architect can be found as far back as fifteenth-century Florence, Italy, when a woman submitted a model for the lantern of the cupola of the Duomo.

In most countries, women were not allowed into architectural schools until the late nineteenth and early twentieth centuries. In the 1890s, Finland was most likely the first European country to graduate women architects from the university. In Russia, the first private design school for girls, the "Women's Architectural Classes," opened around 1899 in Odessa; in Moscow, the "Women's Construction Courses" offered training in design and construction since about 1906. Yet neither school offered an academic degree. Not until the Revolution of 1917 were Russian women allowed to enroll in coed architectural schools.

In the United States, Cornell and Syracuse Universities opened their doors to both genders in architecture in 1871, and the University of Illinois did so in 1873. Margaret Hicks was the first woman to graduate from architectural school, receiving her degree from Cornell in 1880. Yet other Ivy League schools were not as liberated. From 1916 to 1942, while Harvard University did not allow women into its architectural program, the Cambridge School provided an alternative for aspiring women architects.

In 1888, Louise Bethune, who entered the male-dominated profession through an apprenticeship at a Buffalo, New York, architectural office, became the first female member of the American Institute of Architects. Another of her contemporaries was Sophia Hayden (1869–1953), the first woman to graduate in architecture from the Massachusetts Institute of Technology and designer of the Woman's Building at the Chicago World's Columbian Exposition of 1893. Marion Mahony Griffin (1871–1961), an accomplished designer in Frank Lloyd Wright's studio, later with her husband and partner Walter Burley Griffin, designed numerous projects in Australia. One of her best early works is the Adolph Mueller house in Decatur, Illinois, built in 1910.

In 1898, Julia Morgan (1872–1957) became the first woman to enroll at the Ecole des Beaux Arts in Paris, and in 1904, she became the first woman architect registered in the state of California. Her prolific career was largely made possible through her association with a network of women clients. First and foremost among them was Phoebe Apperson Hearst, mother of William Randolph Hearst, who built an empire in newspaper, radio, and film. Morgan is best remembered for her design of the outstanding Hearst Castle in San Simeon, on the coast of central California. One of that state's most popular tourist attractions, the Hearst Castle (1920–1938) is often compared to the Palace of Versailles in France. It was one of the most important architectural commissions in the United States in that era. Throughout her career, which spanned 47 years, Morgan designed approximately 700 buildings in California and elsewhere.

Another architect whose talented career is only now being rediscovered is Mary Colter (1869–1958). Her most visible works are those along the South Rim of Grand Canyon National Park, including Hopi House, Desert View Watchtower, and Bright Angel Lodge.

During both World War I and World War II, increasing numbers of women enrolled in architectural schools, particularly throughout Eastern Europe. The first significant wave of women to enter such schools in the United States came in the 1960s and 1970s, following the women's liberation movement. A number of books written by women architectural scholars began to emerge in the 1970s and afterward, highlighting women architects and their work.

Some of the most accomplished contemporary women architects in the United States include Carol Ross Barney, Denise Scott Brown, Kate Diamond, Diane Legge Kemp, Susan Maxman, Cathy Simon, Norma Sklarek, and Cynthia Weese. A more comprehensive list is simply too long to include here. They have produced a wide range of significant buildings, such as the Sainsbury Wing of the National Gallery in London and the Art Museum of Seattle (Denise Scott Brown, with her partner and husband Robert Venturi); the air traffic control tower at Los Angeles International Airport (Kate Diamond); and the San Francisco Main Library (Cathy Simon, with James Freed).

Many scholars have called for increasing recognition of women in architecture. Others call for an end to "discrimination by design," how the built environment has reflected society's attitudes toward men and women, often relegating women to the role of second-class citizens. The "potty parity' " issue is one such example. Long lines outside women's rest rooms at theaters, airports, stadiums, and elsewhere often place women in discomfort and can lead to bladder infections; yet rarely does one see such lines outside men's rest rooms. In 1987, California passed the first "potty parity" law, and 10 years later, approximately 10 states had similar laws. These specify that new construction or substantially remodeled facilities must have either equal numbers or a 2:1 ratio of women's to men's toilet stalls. As more women become architects and serve in related professions, issues like these will continue to come to light, and eventually the built environment will reflect greater sensitivity to the needs of women.

Despite the progress made during the 1970s, 1980s, and 1990s, women continue to be sorely underrepresented in the architectural profession. According to the U.S. Bureau of Labor Statistics, in the late 1990s women constituted 15 percent of all architects. Yet at the same time, only about 10 percent of the members of the American Institute of Architects, the major professional organization in the field, were women. Research by Anthony (forthcoming), including surveys and interviews of over 400 architects nationwide, identified several barriers to women's professional advancement in architecture. Nonetheless, the same study confirmed that many women in architecture have an almost magnetic attraction to the field, one that helps them survive and thrive and continue to design spaces that enrich our environment in countless ways.

References. Kathryn H. Anthony, *Designing for Diversity: A Gender, Racial, and Ethnic Critique of the Architectural Profession* (Urbana, Ill., forthcoming); Ellen Perry Berkeley and Matilda McQuaid (eds.), *Architecture: A Place for Women* (Washington, D.C., 1989); Sara Holmes Boutelle, *Julia Morgan Architect*, rev. and updated ed. (New York, 1995); C. Lorenz, *Women in Architecture: A Contemporary Perspective* (New York, 1990); Susanna Torre (ed.), *Women in American Ar-*

chitecture: A Historic and Contemporary Perspective (New York, 1977); Leslie
Kanes Weisman, *Discrimination by Design: A Feminist Critique of the Man-Made
Environment* (Urbana, Ill., 1992).

KATHRYN H. ANTHONY

ARISTOTLE ON WOMEN. This is a topic that the vast majority of the
world's influential thinkers, from the period of the ancient Greek philosopher's own lifetime, 384–322 B.C., to our own, would probably consider
too unremarkable to include in any encyclopedia. The reason for this perception can be found in Aristotle's central idea concerning women, which
is that women are by nature inferior to men and must therefore be subordinate to, and ruled by, men.

The tenacity with which this key sexist concept has been held by historically acclaimed thinkers and writers testifies to the appalling ease with
which ignorance can pose as knowledge and with which the self-
aggrandizing prejudices of those who wield intellectual and social power
can pass as rational judgment.

The parallel between ways of justifying sexism and racism is noteworthy.
One recurring feature is that persons of prominence, experts in various
fields, describe in wondrous detail what is called "nature" (the counterpart
of this in the religious realm is usually "the divine will"). Some of the most
respected scientists of the eighteenth and nineteenth centuries thus promoted racism. Believing in the inherent superiority of their own "white"
race, these scientists, not unsurprisingly, discovered all sorts of putative
evidence to confirm the assumptions that governed their investigation of
nature. These same scientists would have likely scoffed at the suggestion
that their basic methodology was not all that different from Aristotle's.
Had not modern science so superseded anything called science in premodern times that it was clear that such a title was appropriate only for what
was modern? However, when it came to examining living beings, humans
in particular, these Enlightenment thinkers and their heirs had much in
common with the ancient Athenian, who had a passion for collecting, preserving, and scrutinizing data.

Like any good scientist, Aristotle was fond of appealing to facts. But if
Aristotle did not invent the habit of interpreting facts both in terms and in
justification of the cultural milieu and political relationships of his own
society, he certainly perfected it long before the renowned eighteenth-
century French naturalist George-Louis Buffon compared the Hottentots to
monkeys or the nineteenth-century naturalist Charles Darwin speculated,
in light of his Malthusian-inspired principle of natural selection, that in the
not too distant future, "an endless number of the lower races will have
been eliminated by the higher civilized races throughout the world" (416).

Anticipating by centuries the kind of inept reasoning currently flourishing
among proponents of biological determinism, Aristotle looked at the status

of women in his own slaveholding class and wrote solemnly of how natural it is for a woman to lead a quiet, sedentary life, staying indoors to nurture children and preserve possessions acquired by her "natural ruler," man (33), who is well constituted for activities outside the home. What today's sociobiologist proclaims as genetically determined characteristics predisposing male and female humans for distinctive roles (of domination and subordination) in the powerist, sexist, racist, xenophobic, and militarist relationships conspicuous in societies producing sociobiologists, Aristotle simply called "nature." The words are different, but the music is the same.

Clearly, though, the first major composer of this music on a grand scale for Western consciousness was Aristotle. Thinkers before him in his own culture had written chords (light and rationality are male; darkness and irrationality are female) and even themes ("Silence is a woman's glory"), but Aristotle integrated fragments from his predecessors with the work of his own inventive genius to create the first symphony of sexism. Combining his ontological judgment that the nature of something is what it is "when fully developed" (*Politics*, 1252b. 32–34) with his biological assumption that the fully developed human is male, he concluded that woman "is as it were a deformed male" (*Generation of Animals*, 737a. 28). What makes woman a physically defective human is her inability to produce semen, which, according to Aristotle, is the only active principle in conception. In procreation, therefore, *passive* woman provides only material, which *active* man fashions into a new human.

While Aristotle's ideas on reproduction, which were accepted in Western intellectual circles for at least 15 centuries, can be easily dismissed today, his correlative ideas in the psychological, moral, and political realms qualify him to be the patron saint of contemporary sociobiologists. Aristotle believed that nature ordained not only physical differences between male and female but mental differences as well. His followers may even take many items in his list of sex-specific "mental characteristics" as fine examples of his observational powers. By comparison to man, he argued, woman is "more mischievous, less simple, more impulsive . . . more compassionate[,] . . . more easily moved to tears[,] . . . more jealous, more querulous, more apt to scold and to strike[,] . . . more prone to despondency and less hopeful[,] . . . more void of shame or self-respect, more false of speech, more deceptive, of more retentive memory [and] . . . also more wakeful; more shrinking [and] more difficult to rouse to action" (*History of Animals*, 608b. 1–14). Moreover, in accord with his society's custom of allowing girls and women to eat only half as much as boys and men, he added that woman "requires a smaller quantity of nutriment" (*History of Animals*, 608b. 14).

Prescinding from his talent as a nutritionist, if one looks again at the traits Aristotle attributed to woman, what stands out in most of them is what he apparently considered the empirical manifestation of what nature intended, namely, that a woman always requires the guidance of a free, adult man. Every woman requires such outside authority because nature has made her not only physically deficient but also intellectually and morally so. The principle of life for woman, as for man, Aristotle argued, is a soul with capacities for both rational faculties (deliberation and decision) and irrational faculties (emotions and appetites); however, in the soul of woman, unlike that of man, the rational power is not strong enough to govern the irrational one. This explains the need for woman to be subject to the being that "the order of nature" itself has made her ruler, man. From the "permanent inequality" that exists between woman and man, moreover, it follows that the virtues of each must be different. For example, "The courage of man is shown in commanding, of a woman in obeying" (*Politics*, 1259b. 1, 1260a. 24). Such reasoning so impressed the thirteenth-century philosopher/theologian Thomas Aquinas that he made it the keystone of his argument on why women could not be priests, an argument that, in turn, impressed officials of the Catholic Church into the twentieth century.

Aristotle did not believe that in his depiction of women as subordinate to men he was simply describing the status quo of his own society. Like today's sociobiologists, he was convinced that he had detected principles of nature that explained the kind of relationships prevailing between the sexes. The fact that he spoke of "corrupted natures" or of people in an "unnatural condition" shows that he did not believe that whatever people did was necessarily in accord with their true nature (*Politics*, 1254b. 1–2). However, by defining the human as a rational animal and then by taking the male of the species as the paragon of humans, the first professional logician in the Western world created a problem that his androcentrism apparently prevented him from perceiving. The problem resides in this fact: Aristotle held that it is the very constitution of the human soul that the rational part should naturally rule the irrational part or, in other words, that the deliberative faculty should have authority over the nondeliberative faculty, and not vice versa; however, he also held that the deliberate faculty does not have authority in the souls of women and that because of this lack, women are by nature subject to the rule of men. Given what Aristotle said about the natural condition of the human soul, it is difficult to see how he could have reconciled that belief with what he had to say about the nature of women. Three options present themselves: he might have denied that women are human, but that would have wrought havoc with both his biological and ontological classifications; he might have proposed that women are by nature evil or corrupted beings, but that would have put him at odds with the ideas of freedom and responsibility that are central to his ethical teachings; or, finally, he simply might have said that women are naturally unnatural, and that statement, however philosophically embarrassing, might have proved the most illuminating decision he could have made.

Fittingly, Aristotle may be the perfect example of his own idea of the protagonist of a tragedy. He argued that such a person, who is neither extremely bad nor "preeminently virtuous and just" (*Poetics*, 1453a. 6–9), suffers grave misfortune not because of vice or depravity but because of some "great error of judgment." In the last quarter of the twentieth century, Aristotle for the first time has come under the scrutiny of feminist scholars. The result, which is similar to that in other fields where feminists have been planting land mines, is nothing short of momentous. Even critics who for the last century took exception to Aristotle's belief that some people are by nature slaves have not made so noticeable an impact. After all, most academicians have no difficulty seeing Aristotle's mistake on that issue. If the idea that some people are innately slaves is not accepted in polite circles these days, however, the same cannot be said about the idea that women are innately what a dominant culture says they are. That is why the feminist critique of Aristotle is both informative and liberating. Still with us are many of his ideas on issues addressed in nearly every social science. To meet Aristotle, then, is to meet something of our cultural selves, and to be able to recognize his great error of judgment in assuming that in the study of humans he could remove the clothes of culture to find a naked nature is to be freed to see the same error in its various guises today.

References. Quotations from the *Politics* were taken from Richard McKeon (ed. and trans.), *The Basic Works of Aristotle* (New York, 1941). Quotations from *Generation of Animals* and *History of Animals* are from the Loeb Classical Library editions, *Aristotle: Generation of Animals* (Cambridge, Mass., 1963) and *Aristotle: Historia Animalium*, 3 vols. (Cambridge, Mass., 1965), ed. and trans. A. L. Peck. Ruth Bleier, *Science and Gender* (New York, 1984); Charles Darwin, letter to W. Graham, July 3, 1881, quoted in Gertrude Hemmelfarb, *Darwin and the Darwinian Revolution* (New York, 1962), 416; Lynda Lange, "Woman Is Not a Rational Animal: On Aristotle's Biology of Reproduction," and Elizabeth V. Spelman, "Aristotle and the Politicization of the Soul," in Sandra Harding and Merrill B. Hintikka (eds.), *Discovering Reality* (Dordrecht, The Netherlands, 1983), 1–15, 17–30.

BARBARA A. PARSONS

ART EDUCATION. Europe in the Nineteenth Century underwent progressive changes, allowing women for the first time to receive professional artistic training comparable to men's. Throughout the century middle- and upper-class families supported their daughters' efforts to learn to draw and paint, as these aesthetic accomplishments were considered suitable for a role as guardian of culture and domestic affairs. Until the closing decades, however, male artists were protected from serious female competition by the belief that women lacked the intellectual and physical qualities neces-

sary to excel beyond the amateur level and by the social stigma attached
to women earning incomes outside the home. Equally important, women
were denied admittance to the prestigious art academies and study from
the life model, a prerequisite for figure drawing and the high-status historical and religious genres. Before 1900 the majority of females who obtained
recognition continued to come from artistically oriented bourgeois and
upper-class families or were connected by birth or association with a male
artist. Some exceptional women artists, for example, Anna Lea Merritt,
Camille Claudel, and Suzanne Valadon, taught themselves. Others received
instruction from family members or private instructors. Yet, after midcentury, newly established art schools figured prominently in the history of
women's art education, traditionally male schools were forced to change
their admission policies, and the number of professional female artists vis-
ibly increased.

Until 1860, when Laura Hertford's admission to the Royal Academy
(RA) Schools opened the door for others of her sex, Englishwomen's options were limited. As in France, most schools, including the National Art
Training School, South Kensington, trained women for commercial work
and teaching. Only Henry Sass' School of Art and Mr. Dickinson's Academy (founded 1845) specifically catered to those wishing to paint professionally. The curriculum at Dickinson's (later Leigh's and then
Heatherley's) was particularly progressive: Kate Greenaway, Louise Jopling, and Anna Blunden all studied there. Other schools that were popular
with serious women artists and served as good training grounds for the RA
Schools were the Lambeth School of Art (founded 1853) and St. John's
Wood Art School (founded 1880). By the 1890s mixed classes were available to women, as was study from the nude model. However, the Royal
Academy and St. John's Wood were typical in maintaining segregated life
classes in which the males posed with covered loins. Even at the Slade
School (founded 1871), which prided itself on offering equal opportunities
to both sexes, women worked from a draped male model probably until
the late 1890s.

The Metropolitan School of Art, Dublin, accepted women by the 1870s
and was the most important school for Irishwomen, though many continued their studies in London and Paris. The continental art centers attracted
students from all over the world. At the Royal Academy, Antwerp, Charles
Verlat's classes included a large international contingent, but women do
not appear to have been accepted. Native and foreign female students did
attend the German Verein der Kunstlerinnen, which were established in
Berlin, Munich, and Karlsruhe in 1869. Since women were excluded from
the state-sponsored art academies, Käthe Kollwitz and Paula Becker sought
art instruction at the Berlin branch in the mid-1880s and late 1890s, respectively. The only other alternative to the Verein der Kunstlerinnen was
to rent a studio and pay for private lessons. Elizabeth Forbes, a Canadian,

found this alternative an isolating experience, appropriate only for advanced students, and left for France after only five months.

By 1880 Paris was acknowledged to be the art student's mecca, for its atelier system (private studio instruction) was considered the exemplary method of training. For women the ateliers offered an opportunity to be taken seriously and have their particular talents and interests encouraged. They could study with reputable artists either individually or in one of the popular and cheaper academies, like Julian's or Colarossi's. By 1877 Julian's expanding student population induced him to create separate ateliers for men and women, yet the course of instruction remained the same for both, and in later years he instituted joint competitions. Frenchwomen achieved important, if belated, victories when in 1896 the Union des Femmes Peintres et Sculpteurs succeeded in integrating the life classes at Colarossi's and, more critically, in gaining women's admittance into the École des Beaux Arts.

Serious women art students had to possess considerable ambition, confidence, and independence. Even these qualities did not allow them to escape their dependence on male role models and the social constrictions dictated by their sex. In France, particularly, students felt their true education resulted from the ability to travel freely, experience cultural life fully, and share the companionship of like-minded peers. This view is the reason the comparatively egalitarian atmosphere of the art colonies in Grez-sur-Loing, Brittany, Normandy, and Worpswede was so important to female students like Becker, Armstrong, Helen Trevor, and Cecilia Beaux.

Major institutional barriers did crumble for women in the late nineteenth century. Nevertheless, important psychological and social ones remained.

References. Marie Bashkirtseff, *Marie Bashkirtseff: The Journal of a Young Artist (1860–1884)*, trans. Mary J. Serrano (New York, 1889); Deborah Cherry, *Painting Women: Victorian Women Artists* (London, 1993); Paula Modersohn-Becker, *The Letters and Journals of Paula Modersohn-Becker*, trans. and annot. J. Diane Radycki (Metuchen, N.J., 1980); Pamela Gerrish Nunn, *Victorian Women Artists* (London, 1987); Charlotte Yeldham, *Women Artists in Nineteenth-Century France and England*, 2 vols. (New York, 1984).

BETSY COGGER REZELMAN

ART STUDENTS LEAGUE. This league is a New York institution that has been encouraging both men and women students to explore a broad range of stylistic and technical approaches to the visual arts for more than 100 years and a pioneer in the field of arts education for women. The league was established in 1875 by pupils from the National Academy of Design who were tired of the latter's rigid, conservative policies—in particular, its emphasis on drawing the human body from plaster casts of noted ancient sculptures (for centuries, the standard method in both European and American academies). Instead, the students wanted to be able to work from the living model, and they did—under Lemuel E. Wilmarth, a noted painter of his time—beginning that fall. The league's life classes were the first ones available to women students (who were restricted until the mid-1920s to their own, gender-segregated sessions) in New York City and only the second in the United States (after those offered at Philadelphia's Pennsylvania Academy of Fine Arts; other schools, notably the Cooper Union in lower Manhattan, had provided earlier art classes—but not life classes—for women).

Today, as in 1875, the Art Students League (ASL) remains a highly democratic organization, emphasizing flexibility and accessibility to students from a variety of academic and economic backgrounds. There are no entrance requirements or examinations, no prescribed courses of study, and no semesters; students may enter or withdraw from the league whenever they like, and the modest tuition is paid on a month-by-month basis.

From the start, women have played an important role in the league's administration, faculty, and student body. Women have generally formed the majority of the Board of Control, the 12-member body (one-third of whom must be current ASL students) that governs the league, and there has always been both a men's and a women's vice president. Whereas, during the nineteenth century, female art teachers tended to be assigned only those subjects considered appropriate for their sex (fashion illustration, miniature painting, and classes for young children), early women teachers at the league—such as sculptor Mary Lawrence Tonetti—taught their specialties. Today, roughly one-sixth of the league's 65 teachers and more than one-half of its 2,000 students are women.

As one of New York's longtime artistic landmarks, the league counts an impressive list of well-known professional artists among its alumni. Prominent painters and sculptors who have studied and/or taught at the league include Thomas Hart Benton, Isabel Bishop, Alexander Calder, Thomas Eakins, Audrey Flack, Helen Frankenthaler, Red Grooms, Lee Krasner, Jacob Lawrence, Roy Lichtenstein, Marisol, Louise Nevelson, Georgia O'Keeffe, Jackson Pollock, Ben Shahn, John Sloan, and David Smith.

References. Kennedy Galleries, *The Hundredth Anniversary Exhibition of Paintings and Sculptures by 100 Artists Associated with the Art Students League of New York* (New York, 1975); Ronald G. Pisano, *The Art Students League, Selections from the Permanent Collection* (Hamilton, N.Y., 1987).

NANCY G. HELLER

ARTISAN is a worker skilled in handicraft manufacturing, originally distinguished from "artist" by the degree of intelligence required by the specific "mechanical art" practiced. Hence, a saddle maker might be termed an artisan, while a jewelry maker was called an artist. Traditionally, artisans belonged to guilds, or corporations, of workers, which established and enforced rules governing the labor and life of all members, including the organization of work processes, the employment of labor, specifications for manufactured articles, market prices, and even conditions of marriage and family life. Although in the twelfth and thirteenth centuries some girls served as apprentices in craft guilds, particularly where manufacturing required highly delicate and dextrous work, by the fourteenth and fifteenth centuries females no longer became apprentices but continued to work in guild shops only as family members (sometimes they were adopted by masters who needed additional labor). In a few exclusively female corporations in the clothing trades, however, recent research shows that some women, even as single adults (*filles majeures*) exercised well-defined legal rights and privileges, negotiating contracts and controlling guild finances. These "merchant mistresses" at best enjoyed fewer opportunities than their male counterparts; and most women participated in the guild system through relationships to men. As wives, women played an essential role in artisanal production. Some corporations even required marriage as a condition of membership, for the standard division of labor required a wife to perform certain steps in the manufacturing process—often detailing or finishing work. For instance, cobblers' wives sewed the upper parts of a shoe after men cut the leather and nailed on the soles. Women also purchased raw materials, sold finished products, kept shop accounts, and, during their husbands' absence or often after their death, supervised the shop. Widows' rights to inherit guild shops, however, were restricted, and their participation in most guild activities was severely limited. By the late eighteenth century, women's roles were further diminished, even in female corporations such as the spinners' guild of Rouen, France, by the process of fiscalization, which increased costs and allowed men increasingly to purchase masterships. While strict corporative control of production gave way to laissez-faire capitalism, artisanal organizations persisted well into the nineteenth century, and artisans, including cabinetmakers, metalworkers, printers, tailors, and watchmakers, played an important role in industrial and political conflicts that accompanied socioeconomic transformations. When male workers organized into trade unions, women were generally excluded from their ranks and, by virtue of their marginalization in the labor force, from consideration as skilled labor. Although many tasks in the female-dominated clothing trades, especially hand sewing, embroidery, artificial flower making, and the like, required considerable talent and training, women were rarely viewed as skilled labor or awarded commensurate distinction or pay. Because of their marginal role in the organized labor force and the prevalence of low pay in characteristically female work (and because as homework their labor could be identified as housework), women have rarely been designated as skilled workers or artisans.

References. M. J. Boxer, "Women in Industrial Homework: The Flowermakers of Paris in the Belle Epoque," *French Historical Studies 12* (1982): 401–423; N. Z. Davis, "Women in the Crafts in Sixteenth-Century Lyon," *Feminist Studies 8* (1981): 47–80; D. Hafter, "Gender Formation from a Working Class Viewpoint: Guildwomen in Eighteenth-Century Rouen," *Proceedings of the Annual Meeting of the Western Society for French History* 16 (1989): 415–422; J. Quataert, "The Shaping of Women's Work in Manufacturing: Guilds, Households, and the State in Central Europe, 1648–1870," *American Historical Review* 90 (1985): 1122–1148; C. Truant, "The Guildswomen of Paris: Gender, Power, and Sociability in the Old Regime," *Proceedings of the Annual Meeting of the Western Society for French History* 15 (1988): 130–138; M. Weisner, "Women's Work in the Changing City Economy, 1500–1650," in M. J. Boxer and J. H. Quataert (eds.), *Connecting Spheres, Women in the Western World, 1500 to the Present* (New York, 1987), 64–74.

MARILYN J. BOXER

ARTISTS AND PAINTERS. See ARTISTS under country or regions; PAINTERS

ASCETICISM. Ascetics, Recluses, and Mystics (Early and Medieval Christian) followed a mode of life idealized and pursued by Christians as early as the first century. Men and women both withdrew to the desert not to escape the wiles of the tempter but to engage him in spiritual warfare. Living in caves or solitary huts, early hermits dedicated themselves to prayer, performed spectacular feats of mortification, and thus gained power over demons. In fourth-century Egypt, the theory and practice of the ascetic life gave rise to monasticism; in Syria, Asia Minor, and Palestine, the solitary ideal developed further whereby hermits living on the fringes of organized society as permanent "outsiders" became figures of authority for surrounding farmers and townspeople and channels through which supernatural power was believed to flow into the world.

Many women were attracted to hermetic life. Palladius, a fifth-century historian of monasticism, mentioned almost 3,000 women living in the desert in Egypt. Stories concerning the most famous Desert Mothers, including St. Mary of Egypt, Apollonaria, Athanasia, Hilaria, and Theodora, were popular as early as the sixth century. These legends share with stories of the Desert Fathers an emphasis on the value of withdrawal and strict asceticism, but there are three distinctive motifs in stories about women: flight from the world occasioned either by impending marriage or a life of sin; assumption of male attire and subsequent seclusion; and discovery and recognition. Male disguise was once thought to express women's desire for androgynous perfection, but since these stories were written by and for monks, they are better explained as male fantasies. Disguised as men, holy women neutralized the threat of female temptation when they were discovered living within a male community as blessed companions.

Solitary life in the West was incorporated by monasticism. The Benedictine Rule acknowledges both the value and difficulty of solitary life, which it reserves for the few who "being well armed, are able to go forth . . . to the singlehanded combat of the desert . . . to fight with their own strength against the weaknesses of the flesh and their own evil thoughts, God alone aiding them." Only a small proportion of nuns and monks became solitaries, but hermetic life remained an alternative to regular religious life. It was also adopted by a few laypeople in the first stages of conversion. Beginning in the twelfth century, especially in England, it became a relatively popular choice for women. Recluses lived in isolated cells attached to chapels, village churches, or hospitals. Not bound by monastic routine, recluses spent their time in prayer and manual work (needlework for women). Some requested and received letters of instruction from spiritual authorities that guided them in the practice of virtue and contemplation.

Severe asceticism combined with solitude may seem inherently conducive to mystical experience, but we do not find a strong mystical tradition among women solitaries until after 1200, when there was a dramatic increase in the number of women mystics (not all of them solitaries). Women's turn to mysticism can be understood, at least in part, as a solution to the deprivation they experienced under the Gregorian reform movement, which enhanced the status and power of priestly office while depressing that of women religious. Nuns lost the few sacerdotal functions they had previously exercised, and the policy of enclosure, now strictly enforced, further limited their power. Excluded as well from the new life of apostolic poverty institutionalized in mendicant orders, which offered some men an alternative to the role of priest, women discovered a new route to power as contemplatives. In mystical contact with God, women found a source of authority not based on office that enabled them to assume the valued roles of teacher, preacher, and writer. Many of the best-known women saints of the later Middle Ages were mystics who played an important role in political events.

It would be mistaken, however, to see visions as rooted only in women's desire for authority. Visions were the mode in which medieval women expressed their spiritual insights. Some of the most distinctive and enduring features of late medieval piety were the innovations of women mystics. The Christmas crèche, which is generally attributed to St. Francis, actually originated with the Belgium Beguine Mary of Oignies. The mystical nuns of Helfta consolidated and elaborated the devotion to the Sacred Heart first evolved by St. Bernard of Clairvaux. The feast of Corpus Christi was the inspiration of Juliana of Cornillon. Julian of Norwich developed a powerful new theology of sin and redemption based on a vision of Jesus as Mother. Taught to associate female principle with matter and male principle with spirit, women identified with a supremely physical and human God in their visions, from which they

drew an understanding of salvation as the redemption of the whole human person, body and spirit together.

References. Caroline W. Bynum, *Jesus as Mother* (Berkeley, Calif., 1982); Ann
K. Warren, *Anchorites and their Patrons in Medieval England* (Berkeley, Calif.,
1985).

SUSAN DICKMAN

ASCETICISM. In India. Asceticism is found in the three main religions that
originated in the subcontinent: Jainism, Buddhism, and Hinduism. Jainism
and Buddhism, which grew as protest movements against the authority of
the Brahmans from within Brahmanism, were essentially monastic organizations. Nuns (*niganthi*) were allowed to join the Jaina Order from its
beginning, while the Buddhist Order of nuns (*bhikkuni*) was formed a little
after that of the monks. Both orders were organized according to precise
rules of life, which were the same for monks and nuns. However, nuns
were put under permanent control of the monks, although their association
was severely restricted.

Buddhism spread outside India to become a major religious force in the
whole of South Asia, but for a number of reasons it did not flourish in the
country of its origin after the twelfth century.

Jainism, which never knew the prosperity of Buddhism, was also spared
its downfall. It remained confined to the northwest and the south, but it
has maintained its identity in India down to this day. This identity rests on
a strong monastic tradition whose three main traits are inoffensiveness,
self-restraint, and penance. The Jaina nuns with their shaven heads, im-
maculate white robes, begging bowls, mouth masks and brooms (both to
avoid harming all forms of life), and strenuous lifestyle appear as the very
embodiment of these characteristics. They exist in a very limited number
and are found only within one of the two rival sections of the Jains, the
Svetambara ("those who are clad in white"). According to the other section, the Digambara ("sky-clad," i.e., naked) women cannot obtain Liberation.

Hinduism is the later stage of the religion of India that was earlier known
as Vedism, then as Brahmanism. Ascetics have existed in India since the
earliest times, but not much is known about the first woman ascetics. In
the Upanishads we come across the Brahmavadini, the "woman who holds
discourses on the Brahman" ("the Absolute"). Gargi is an example. Later,
however, the practice of asceticism was forbidden for women by the orthodox (Brahmanical) lawgivers, who ruled that they need not renounce
the world to obtain salvation from the endless cycle of birth and death but
could reach that goal by being dedicated to their husbands (e.g., *Manu* 2:
67). But sectarian movements arose, most of them founded by ascetics, in
which a few women were admitted, and some of the women's names appear in the religious literature (e.g., Akka Mahadevi and Lal Ded). Today

Hindu monasticism is formed by the ascetic branches of numerous sects and is characterized by its lack of unity. The Hindu women ascetics' status, role, and lifestyle depend on the particular ideology of each sect. According to their order they may be clad in white, yellow, or saffron robes; keep their hair shaven or very long and loose; bear different sectarian marks on their forehead; and carry specific utensils. They are known as Brahmacarini, Sannyasini, Bairagini, or Yogini. Some live independently, often as wandering mendicants; others stay in monastic communities under a guru (spiritual master). They have to survive within the framework of systems and institutions that are essentially male-oriented and were designed by males for males. As a rule, women remain largely unwanted in the sectarian orders that accept the orthodox institutions (like some orders of the Visnuite School) or whose discipline is extremely rigorous (like some orders of the Sivaite School), while orders presenting reformist tendencies are more open to them and to members of the low castes (e.g., the Ramanandi *sampradaya*). The contemporary reformist movements are also not opposed to feminine asceticism (e.g., the Svaminarayani *sampradaya*, the Ramakrishna Mission, and the Anandamayi *sangha*). However, even the oldest and most orthodox and important order, the Dasnami *sampradaya*, has fraternities that admit women. Actually, thanks to the loose structure of the sectarian organizations and the considerable freedom and power of the guru, women ascetics are present everywhere. In rare cases they may even rise to the status of guru and be held in the highest esteem. Feminine asceticism remains, however, an extremely marginal practice in Hinduism.

References. S. A. Altekar, *The Position of Women in Hindu Civilization: From Prehistoric Times to the Present Day* (Delhi, 1956); H. Chakraborti, *Asceticism in Ancient India in Brahmanical, Buddhist, Jaina and Ajivika Societies* (Calcutta, 1973); Catherine Clémentin-Ojha, *La Divinité conquise: carrière d'une sainte* (Nanterre, France, 1990); G. S. Ghurye, *Indian Sadhus* (Bombay, 1953); Robert L. Gross, *Hindu Asceticism, a Study of the Sadhus of North India* (Berkeley, Calif., 1979).

CATHERINE CLÉMENTIN-OJHA

ASCETICISM. In Western Antiquity. Women who intentionally and permanently abstain from heterosexual contact for religious reasons are relatively rare in Western antiquity before Christianity, the Vestal Virgins of Rome, who guarded the fires of the city, being the major exception. Temporary ritual asceticism was a feature of numerous cults in which women participated, including the rites of Isis and Demeter. Jewish law as set forth in Leviticus 15:19–24 and expanded in the Mishnah and Talmud deemed women to be ritually impure for a period of seven days following menstrual bleeding. As a result, married Jewish women were apparently expected to refrain from sexual intercourse with their husbands until they were ritually pure in order to avoid rendering their husbands impure. Regrettably, we have virtually no evidence about the extent to which Jewish women actually observed the menstrual purity regulations in the Greco-Roman period.

Other than the Vestals, the earliest evidence for permanent sexual asceticism by women occurs in Philo Judaeus' (d. c.50 C.E.) description of a small Jewish monastic community living on the shores of Lake Mareotis outside Alexandria. According to Philo, the women of the Therapeutae, as he called the community, were "aged virgins" who studied philosophy and the Scriptures with the same dedication as the men and who thus received a reward of "spiritual children" in place of the human children they had not had. The Jewish historian Flavius Josephus (fl. late first century C.E.) also described a branch of the Essene sect whose members married only for procreative purposes. Presumably, both the women and the men otherwise abstained from heterosexual activity.

Very early in the development of Christianity some Christians came to understand sexual asceticism as a crucial feature of their identity. Paul urged Christians at Corinth to imitate him in his sexual asceticism, if possible, but conceded that Christians who could not do so might legitimately express their sexuality in marriage. By the time I Timothy was written, probably in the early second century C.E., there were apparently orders of widows, Christian women who may have been married previously but no longer engaged in heterosexual activity.

The apocryphal *Acts of the Apostles* of the second and third centuries are replete with accounts of the conversion of women and men who adopted sexual abstinence as a way of life, reflecting forms of Christianity in Syria and elsewhere in which sexual asceticism was an integral, if not a definitional, part. The second-century *Acts of Thecla* may be the prototype of such accounts. In this work, a woman named Thecla, of Iconium in Asia Minor, breaks her engagement to a prominent man and permanently renounces marriage and sexuality in order to follow the apostle Paul, eventually becoming a prominent Christian teacher. Tertullian later denounced those who used the *Acts of Thecla* to legitimate women's teaching and baptizing.

By the mid-to-late fourth century, Christian asceticism appears to have become more prevalent and institutionalized. That this occurred only after the conversion of Constantine may not be accidental. The Christianization of Rome greatly reduced the opportunity for Christian suffering through persecution, so asceticism may have succeeded martyrdom as the favored form of Christian suffering and *imitatio*.

The earliest evidence for women's monastic communities comes from Egypt, where women's monasteries were founded in tandem with men's, such as the communities of Pachomius and his sister Maria. Collections of sayings of the Desert Fathers, Egyptian monastics who often lived alone in the desert, contain a handful of sayings attributed to Desert Mothers. From a similar provenance come literary accounts such as the *Life of St. Pelagia the Harlot,* in which women whose sexuality is described as extensive and offensive renounce their former ways and adopt an ascetic Christian life, often masquerading as men while living alone in the desert.

Egyptian monasticism may have found its way to Rome in the person of an aristocratic woman, Marcella, who established a small circle of ascetic Christian women. Jerome, who arrived in Rome in 382 C.E., developed such close ties with these women that he was forced to leave Rome three years later under suspicion of having had inappropriate relationships with them. Relocating in Bethlehem, he founded a monastery for men; his Roman friend Paula with her daughter Eustochium ran a nearby monastery for women. Jerome wrote many letters to women both known and unknown to him, urging an ascetic way of life.

Scholarly discussions of Christian asceticism through the fourth century have begun to consider whether sexual asceticism was more prominent among women than among men or whether an ascetic way of life meant something different for women than for men. Some scholars have observed that sexual asceticism freed women from conventional norms that value women primarily for their roles as daughter, wife, and mother. The question of why asceticism did not develop as a structured, permanent option for women in non-Christian communities has not been systematically addressed.

The relationship between asceticism and conversion also has not been considered fully. Since sexual asceticism in a closed community must lead rather rapidly to the community's extinction, asceticism can be the norm of (hetero)sexual behavior only in societies where the continuity of the community can be assured through the conversion of outsiders. Jerome surely understood this when he praised marriage for its ability to produce Christian virgins. At least one scholar has examined the economic ramifications of Christian women's asceticism in fourth-century Roman families, where for several generations most daughters were raised to be ascetic Christians while sons continued to practice paganism. Those daughters who did have children were encouraged to adopt ascetic practices as soon as they were finished bearing children.

In considering the functions of asceticism for women, whether asceticism is temporary or permanent becomes significant. Temporary asceticism, religiously legitimated, may afford women a measure of social control, whether in the Jewish ritual purity regulations or in spirit possession cults in Africa, the Caribbean, and modern-day Egypt. Permanent asceticism often allows a woman to adopt roles in the public sphere that would otherwise be closed to her. Thecla, having renounced sexuality, marriage, and children, became a wandering Christian teacher; Paula traveled from Rome to Jerusalem and ran a monastery there. Eventually, however, the development of ascetic communities may also represent attempts by male authorities to control and regulate the very power that accrues to ascetic women. Asceticism released women from male control: cloistering them in monasteries could bring them right back under it.

The religious underpinnings of Christian asceticism and their implications for women also deserve further study. When Paul urged first-century Christians to become and remain celibate, he offered several rationales. The imminent end of the world is one: those concerned with marriage and children cannot properly prepare for the coming cataclysm. Imitation of Paul himself was also offered, together with an implicit imitation of Jesus. Although the obvious paradigm for women's asceticism might be Mary, the mother of Jesus, such a model is not explicit in early Christian texts, although it is evident in later writers such as Jerome. Possibly, Christian asceticism reflects exegesis of Genesis 2:1ff., envisioning a return to the primordial condition of Paradise during which Adam and Eve were presumably not aware of, nor engaged in, sexual behavior. Few texts make this explicit, although some, like the *Acts of Andrew*, suggest a connection. Further study of religiously legitimated asceticism in antiquity must recognize that while Christian asceticism was not unique to women, it clearly had different social implications and consequences for women than for men.

References. Peter Brown, *The Body and Society: Men, Women, and Sexual Renunciation in Early Christianity* (New York, 1988); Virginia Burrus, *Chastity as Autonomy: Women in the Stories of the Apocryphal Acts* (Lewiston, N.Y., 1987); Elizabeth Clark, *Ascetic Piety and Women's Faith: Essays on Late Ancient Christianity* (Lewiston, N.Y., 1986); Stevan L. Davies, *The Revolt of the Widows: The Social World of the Apocryphal Acts* (Carbondale, Ill., 1980); Ross S. Kraemer, "The Conversion of Women to Ascetic Forms of Christianity," *Signs* 6 (1980): 298–307.

ROSS S. KRAEMER

ASIA. East Asia. See CHINA; JAPAN; TIBET

ASIA. South Asia. See INDIA

ASIA. Southeast Asia (Burma/Myanmar, Cambodia, Laos, Vietnam, and Thailand). Mainland Southeast Asia is an ethnically diverse region, with peoples of different religions, languages, cultures, and life situations within its borders. However, a few general outlines of history, culture, and politics can provide a beginning point for discussing women's situations. Southeast Asia was populated primarily by waves of immigrants from Tibet and southern China. Hindu and Buddhist missionaries from South Asia had an important impact on the religious and cultural development of these societies but did not have as great an impact on women's equal participation in political life, access to education, and personal autonomy.

Geography has been an important factor in its history and in the development of women's roles. High mountain ranges limited travel, reduced the availability of land suitable for agriculture, and also prevented warring groups from having easy access to one another. Tribal highland mountain groups practiced swidden (slash-and-burn agriculture), while valley-dwelling groups engaged in wet rice agriculture. Hill tribe people still live in their traditional patterns in the highlands, though legally their social and political rights are shaped by the nation-state that claims their territories. The larger, more powerful ethnic groups (the Lao, the Thai [Siamese], the Burmese, the Khmer, and others) tended to reside in the fertile river valleys.

Frequent raids and invasions by other groups made the organization of defensive military troops and raiding parties critical to the survival of the lowland peoples. The ruling elite (who became the royal and noble classes) specialized in the organization of men for defense and invasion, and the low population of the region meant women's work on the farms was important to the success of these societies. Because men were required to donate months of service each year to the king for defense and other tasks, women's labor was more reliable, and families tended to depend more on their daughters. Daughters were seen as "naturally" more competent and more loving and respectful than their brothers and also as having important economic responsibilities toward parents. Therefore, though men retained formal control over their families as fathers, women were the traditional inheritors of property and had many important political rights, such as the right to voice complaints about their treatment to the king.

Among the elite, women had special positions as upholders of cultural traditions and the arts, particularly dance, literature, and drama, and so were important to demonstrating the splendor and power of the elite through the production of court entertainments. Elite women received education, and some were highly literate, particularly in the Thai (Siamese) and Burmese courts as well as Cambodia and Laos. This led to an easy transition from private tutelage at home in the premodern period to modern schooling. In Thailand, never colonized directly by the West, plans for extending public education to women were in place almost from the very beginning. As early as 1930, women were employed in public schools as teachers.

Before being conquered by the Chinese in 111 B.C.E., Vietnam's society was traditional matrifocal and matrilineal; women proposed marriage and acted as judges, chiefs, and traders. After conquest, the Chinese imposed Confucian values and standards; women were forbidden education, forbidden to own land, and expected to live under strict male supervision. Reportedly, however, some daughters of wealthy families disguised themselves as men in order to study. Further, women have figured prominently in military history. The two sisters Trung Trai and Trung Nhi were said to have trained 36 female generals in 40 C.E. leading 80,000 troops in a successful war against the colonizers. They ruled for three years and committed suicide when China regained control. Trieu Thi Trinh, another female general, led more than 30 battles against the Chinese in 240 C.E., keeping Chinese troops at bay for six months.

In the nineteenth century, Southeast Asia fell under Western domination, and Western values and ideas about women's place were imposed in laws, education, and systems of political administration. Thailand (Siam) was the only Southeast Asian nation that was not directly colonized; however, it was forced to submit to significant changes in its national economy, government, and system of education by the threat of colonization. Systems of concubinage, slavery, and polygamy were swept away by this threat. Westerners were surprised with the lack of resistance to the idea of women's education, especially in Thailand. However, the educational systems and political structures that the colonial powers themselves established reflected the patriarchal, colonial values of the West.

During World War II, mainland Southeast Asia was occupied by the Japanese, who forced many Southeast Asians into military service and labor camps. Some women were forced into sexual slavery as "comfort women"* for the occupying Japanese troops. The colonial powers of Britain and France were forced out, fueling hopes on the part of many Southeast Asians for the creation of free and independent nations. However, after the defeat of the Japanese, the Western powers attempted to reestablish their colonial domination. The formerly colonized peoples vigorously contested this attempt, and a period of intense nationalism in Laos, Cambodia, Burma, and Vietnam followed.

Women's rights were specifically addressed in many nationalist contexts. In 1946, for example, the Democratic Republic of Vietnam's Constitution granted women equal rights, equal pay, and paid maternity leave. Literacy campaigns; military training for women; and campaigns against polygny, forced marriage, and child marriage followed. A Vietnamese general, Nguyen Thi Dinh, has reported that prostitutes acted as saboteurs and spies and were responsible for the destruction of nearly one-third of all the French posts destroyed by the Viet Minh. In the North, Nguyen asserts, women assumed control and administration of village agriculture and served as snipers, while in the South, 40 percent of the commanders of the People's Liberation Armed Forces were female. When the U.S. troops withdrew in 1975, over 1 million women were widowed and 800,000 children were orphaned by U.S. bombings. Since unification, the Women's Union has led literacy campaigns and has worked to draft legislation and submit it to the National Assembly, acting as an advocate for women at both the village and national levels.

Cambodia was significantly changed by the wars and military upheavals following World War II. Its fall to the Khmer Rouge resulted in a genocidal holocaust that significantly destroyed much of the cultural treasures, such as music and dance, where women's knowledge and talents were centered. The ratio of men to women was also knocked out of balance. As Cambodia attempts to build a democratic nation, the needs of the whole society for greater economic security, health, and sustainable development are significant issues for both men and women.

In Laos and Burma/Myanmar, the socialist regimes that took hold have attempted to promote certain kinds of political and social equality. Legally, women have many important rights, such as the right to education and the right to work. However, various ethnic groups within these nation-states have reacted to their marginalization by mounting guerrilla campaigns. In Myanmar, Aung San Suu Kyi, the daughter of a martyred nationalist hero, has emerged as a leader in the struggle for social and political change in that country.

While the other nations of mainland Southeast Asia suffered significant political and economic dislocation due to warfare and political unrest, Thailand has made steady and dramatic gains. Women have achieved increasing access to education and improved rights under the law, though not without periods of struggle. Despite startling improvement in professional employment, women still trail men in wages, and this situation has been an important factor in the serious problem of the growth of the sex industry in Thailand, a product of the unequal distribution of economic opportunities since the turn of the century. The increase in prostitution was exacerbated by the Vietnam War, when American troops flooded Bangkok, significantly raising the incomes of sex workers, which remained higher than for many other unskilled jobs. With the close of the Vietnam War, local demand for prostitution climbed, along with men's wages. While women who worked as prostitutes did suffer some social stigma, on the whole, Thai culture was more accepting of prostitution as a sacrifice that enabled the very poor woman to help her to fulfill her obligations to help provide for her parents and siblings. The widespread acceptance of prostitution (even though it has been technically illegal since 1908) led to the AIDS epidemic that rages in Thailand and other parts of Southeast Asia. The AIDS epidemic has changed many attitudes about prostitution as well as men's and women's relationships, generally. Since the early 1990s, Thai women have become even more active politically, making significant changes in many laws that affect women, such as marital laws. However, women still lag behind men in wages, opportunities, and education.

In mainland Southeast Asia, women leaders are numerous, and women's access to education and political rights has made tremendous strides in the past half century. However, health issues, warfare, and general economic issues complicate any discussion of women's status in any of these nation-states. This region is in a situation of change, and as women are increasingly able to make their own decisions and get access to greater resources, they have the potential to make a tremendous impact on their social worlds. (See also INDONESIA; PHILIPPINES.)

References. Nguyen Tri Dinh, "The Braided Army," in Robin Morgan (ed.), *Sisterhood Is Global* (New York, Anchor Books, 1984); David M. Engel, *Code and Custom in a Thai Provincial Court* (Tucson, AZ, 1978); Rebecca L. Goolsby, "Women, Work and Family in a Northeastern Thai Provincial Capital," diss., University of Washington, 1994; Aung San Suu Kyi, *Freedom from Fear: Aung San Suu Kyi* (London, 1991, 1995).

REBECCA L. GOOLSBY

ASIAN AMERICAN WOMEN are immigrant women and their U.S.-born female descendants whose ancestry is traced to Asia. In contemporary America most Asian American women are first-generation because of the series of Asian exclusion laws, passed between 1882 and 1952, that prevented Asian women from immigrating to the United States.

The Asian immigrant population in the late nineteenth and early twentieth centuries, particularly among Chinese and Filipinos, was predominantly males, and the sexual imbalance remained the predominant demographic characteristic among Chinese, Koreans, and Filipinos until 1970. Between 1907 and 1924, about 45,000 Japanese and Okinawan and 1,000 Korean "picture brides" came to Hawaii and California to marry their "picture grooms," who were plantation and farm laborers. (See PICTURE BRIDES.) Between 1945 and 1952, in the aftermath of World War II and as a result of a series of laws and the Korean War, approximately 100,000 Asian women from the Philippines, Japan, and Korea entered this country as nonquota immigrant war brides of U.S. military personnel. The stereotypic image of Asian women as exotic sexual objects and accommodating, passive domestics contributed toward their reputation as perfect wives.

Political and economic conditions in their homelands created by international power relations, combined with liberal immigration law introduced in 1965, have resulted in profound changes in the United States in the demographic characteristics of the immigrant population, including Asian American communities in the United States during the late twentieth century. The majority of the newcomers are now women. As a result of the Vietnam War and its aftermath, thousands of Vietnamese and Cambodian women, both war brides and refugees, have joined women from other Asian countries in the United States. Moreover, many woman arrive annually as mail-order picture brides from the Philippines, Malaysia, Korea, Japan, and other Asian countries. Accordingly, the Asian female population has been growing at a faster rate than the Asian male population. Among Chinese, Japanese, Filipino, and Korean adults in the 20-to-40 age group, there are more women than men.

Besides those coming as a result of U.S. involvement in Vietnam, Asian women immigrants come predominantly from South Korea, the Philippines, Taiwan, and Hong Kong and consist mainly of urban, middle-class, educated wives and other female relatives who came primarily to join their families, and women professionals and students who immigrate independently. In comparison to earlier immigrant women, who relied more heavily on multiple wages earned by family members and on family-operated businesses, the most recent Asian war brides, refugees, and mail-order picture brides are more likely to be either unemployed or, as single mothers and female heads of households, working to support themselves and their dependents, who may include parents and siblings. For those who seek employment out of economic necessity, a lack of education or employable skills forces them to find work as unskilled agricultural workers in rural areas or as low-paid cannery workers, hotel maids, waitresses, and bar hostesses in urban areas.

Asian American women draw heavily on their own history, culture, and contemporary reality to devise political and economic strategies for survival. There have been two major economic adaptive strategies developed by both early and recent Asian immigrant women: entering into wage labor and engaging in unpaid labor in family farms and businesses. When the sexual imbalance among Japanese and Chinese immigrants was at its greatest during the late 1800s and early 1900s, with men far outnumbering women, most of the Chinese and Japanese women were prostitutes brought into the country by Asian importers and brothel owners. The average Chinese prostitute was indentured for four to five years without wages. Because of the economic structure; the double burden of home and paid work; the low level of training, education, and skills; and racial and ethnic discrimination, most of the Chinese and Japanese females immigrating after 1907 entered into low-paying service jobs such as seamstress, domestic, laundress, cook, and rooming-house operator. Those who worked with their husbands in family businesses, such as laundries, restaurants, and boardinghouses, did so as unpaid family laborers. The great majority of pineapple and sugar field workers in Hawaii and domestics in California were Japanese immigrant women. Besides those who engaged in wage work, many Japanese and Korean picture brides were self-employed; they operated kitchen services and did laundry for the single male laborers of the community. Filipino women in Hawaii contributed to their families' financial support by offering daily bathhouse services for male agricultural laborers or by keeping house for single male boarders, washing their clothes, or cooking their meals. Some women made men's underwear, embroidered pillowcases, or baked Filipino pastries and other delicacies that were sold to single male workers.

Today, due to the discrimination experienced by recent Asian immigrant men and their resultant low wages and frequent changes of employment, approximately 75 percent of all adult Asian American women are in the labor force as compared to about 50 percent of white women. Asian immigrant women often work 10 to 16 hours a day for low wages under difficult work conditions, experiencing occupationally related health problems and the pressures of the double burden of wage and family work. Although Asian American women, especially Filipino women, are better educated than males or females from any other ethnic group in America, the discrepancy between education and income is greater for them than for white women. The majority of recent Asian immigrant women are employed in garment, grocery, food, and laundry services; as jewelry, cannery, and electronic-assembly factory workers; or as domestic servants, hotel maids, nurses' aides, and clerks. Native-born Asian American women are also crowded into the least visible, low-status, and low-paying occupations, mostly in sales and clerical jobs. Employers usually perceive Asian American women according to the racial and sexual stereotypes: as quiet, submissive, hardworking, and minutely detail-minded subordinates. Asian immigrant women with professional or technical training and occupational experience find it difficult to transfer their credentials to the United States because of licensing, local training, and experience requirements.

The tradition of family businesses is still attractive to many recent immigrants. They prefer the longer hours of unpaid family labor in independent businesses because of the flexible hours and informal structure and supervision. Those with sufficient capital to start family businesses have opened restaurants, laundry facilities, grocery stores, and gift shops in which husbands and wives work together.

Despite their differing backgrounds, professional training, and experience, the majority of both early and recent Asian immigrant women have engaged in similar kinds of service jobs. Both groups have been affected by the sexually segregated job market, the sexual division of domestic labor, and the economic exploitation prompted by both sexual and racial stereotyping and discrimination. In addition to discrimination in the labor market, for both groups the burdens of housework and child-rearing responsibilities have made it difficult for them to work and have restricted the types of jobs they could seek.

In light of this contemporary reality, the image of Asian American women as the model minority group should be rejected as a myth. The multiple oppressions of gender, class, and race experienced by early Asian immigrant women are also faced by recent immigrants despite their higher educational attainments and urban, middle-class origins. Their experiences should be understood in their multidimensional complexity in relation to gender, class, and racial and ethnic identities. While they have been subject to multiple forms of oppression, Asian immigrant women have been active political strategists and have struggled to achieve their goals through hard work, strong religious faith, utilizing their mothers' and grandmothers' strengths, and forming female solidarity groups. By analyzing the experiences of average Asian American women whose everyday, ordinary actions have helped their people survive, we can hope to formulate a conceptual framework for understanding the lives of all women.

References. Asian Women United of California, *Making Waves, Writings about Asian American Women* (Boston, 1989); Alice Yun Chai, "The Struggle of Asian and Asian American Women toward a Total Liberation," in Rosemary Skinner Keller (ed.), *Spirituality and Social Responsibility* (Nashville, Tenn., 1993), 219–263, 327–328; Bok Lim C. Kim, *Women in Shadows: A Handbook for Service Providers Working with Asian Wives of U.S. Military Personnel* (La Jolla, Calif., 1981).

ALICE YUN CHAI

ASIAN AMERICAN WRITERS are American writers of Asian ancestry creating and publishing fiction, memoir or autobiography, poetry, and drama in the United States. In exceptional cases (most notably, Joy Kogawa and Sky Lee), Asian Canadian authors are also included in this grouping, with the justification that the term "America" refers to more than the United States. Although the western borders of geographical Asia fall along the Ural Mountains and include all of what is known as the Middle East, the term "Asian American" or "Asian Pacific American" commonly refers to people whose ancestry is East Asian (Chinese, Japanese, Korean), Southeast Asian (Vietnamese, Cambodian, Laotian, Hmong, Burmese or Myanmar, Filipino, Indonesian), South Asian (Indian, Sri Lankan, Pakistani, Bangladeshi, Nepali), and Hawaiian or South Pacific Islander. The wide geographical scope of the Asian half of the term thus covers an enormous diversity of races, cultures, customs, languages, and religions.

Since immigration from Asia is ongoing, the spectrum of Asian Americans ranges across a century and a half, from Chinese who came to California in the mid-nineteenth century as merchants' wives or slaves and prostitutes, to the Southeast Asians who flocked here in the wake of the Vietnam War, to Tibetan refugees of the 1990s. What binds such diversity together is the common experience of life in the United States as a paradoxical combination of welcome and exclusion, opportunity and glass ceilings, freedom and internment, free speech and silencing. For many dominant Americans, a sixth-generation Chinese American is indistinguishable from a recent Laotian immigrant because Asian facial features signal "foreigner" or "alien." Thus, it is a common experience for Asian American Ph.D.'s in literature and for major Asian American writers, like Maxine Hong Kingston, to be complimented by strangers on their "good English." In fact, Asians were the last minority group to receive the franchise in the United States, for they were permitted to become naturalized American citizens only in 1954. The lateness of this date underlines the persistence of the belief that Asians are "foreign" and "unassimilable."

Since nearly all Asian societies have traditionally been patriarchal, Asian

American women suffer a double oppression: racism from the dominant culture and sexism within the Asian culture. In traditional Asian societies, women are taught obedience to men: as girls to their fathers, as wives to their husbands, and as widows to their eldest son. Furthermore, since the writings of Marco Polo and promulgated continuously through the figure of Madame Butterfly, Asian women have been represented in Western story, opera, and film as exotic, fragile, sexually desirable but expendable "playthings." The contemporary incarnation of Butterfly is *Miss Saigon*, with over six years on Broadway. This, in brief, is the social context against which Asian American women must struggle in order to write.

To organize such a diverse topic as Asian American women writers, I break it down along ethnic and chronological lines. Constrained by length limitations, this entry can only scratch the surface of this large and continually growing subject.

The first writers of Asian ancestry to publish fiction in the United States were two Eurasian sisters, Edith and Winnifred Eaton (their mother was Chinese; their father English), whose work appeared at the turn of the last century. Countering the Sinophobia of the day, which culminated in the Chinese Exclusion Act of 1882, English-born Edith Maud Eaton took the pen name Sui Sin Far and published short stories, bold for their day, that introduced such new topics as the between-worlds plight of the Eurasian, the humanity of Chinese immigrants, and the dignity of unmarried, self-made, working-class women. These stories were collected in one volume, *Mrs. Spring Fragrance* (1912, republished by University of Illinois Press, 1995). Winnifred Eaton, born in Montreal, chose a Japanese persona and, between 1899 and 1924, published more than 100 short stories and nearly two dozen novels in the United States under the pen name Onoto Watanna. A skilled storyteller, though often catering to Orientalist fantasies, Winnifred Eaton created best-selling romances between Japanese or Japanese Eurasian heroines and Anglo men. The most popular, *A Japanese Nightingale* (1901), was translated into several European languages and adapted for Broadway in 1903 to compete with David Belasco's production of the John Luther Long short story "Madame Butterfly," the basis of Puccini's opera.

After the Eaton sisters, the few Chinese American women living in the United States fell into silence until *Fifth Chinese Daughter* (1945), an autobiography by 24-year-old Jade Snow Wong. With traditional Chinese politeness and restraint, Wong detailed her childhood in San Francisco's Chinatown in an entrepreneurial family governed strictly by Confucian rules. *Fifth Chinese Daughter* inspired young Maxine Hong Kingston, whose brilliant, award-winning books *The Woman Warrior* (1976), *China Men* (1980), and *Tripmaster Monkey* (1988) have garnered international attention. In 1989, Amy Tan expanded on the mother–daughter tensions of Kingston's *The Woman Warrior* in her best-selling novel *The Joy Luck*

Club, which was produced as a feature-length film in 1993. Tan's second novel, *The Kitchen God's Wife* (1991), continued the mother's stories of war-torn China and was followed by a third novel, *One Hundred Secret Senses* (1995). In elegantly spare and vigorous language, *Bone* (1993) by Fae Myenne Ng spirals around the story of a family coping with the suicide of one of three sisters in San Francisco's Chinatown. Humor and lightness of tone characterize the writing of Gish Jen, whose two novels, *Typical American* (1991) and *Mona in the Promised Land* (1996), further explore the fluidity and multiplicity of ethnic identity. In *Mona*, Jen's Chinese American heroine, Mona Chang converts to Judaism and is known by her Scarshill friends as "Changowitz"; her Jewish boyfriend wears dashikis, and an African American roommate at Harvard teaches her sister how to be more "Chinese."

Japanese American women have excelled in the genres of poetry, short story, and drama, although among the earliest texts are two memoirs of the relocation experience: Monica Sone's *Nisei Daughter* (1953) and Jeanne Wakatsuki Houston and James D. Houston's collaboration, *Farewell to Manzanar* (1973). Mitsuye Yamada's chapbook, *Camp Notes* (1979), was one of the earliest poetic treatments of the relocation experience; in her recent volume, *Desert Run* (1993), Yamada finds beauty in the desert to which she had been confined as a teenager. Activist Janice Mirikatani has written several volumes of poetry, some insistent in its protest; the latest is *We, the Dangerous* (1995). Hisaye Yamamoto's *Seventeen Syllables and Other Stories* (1988) and Wakako Yamauchi's stories, plays, and memoirs, *Songs My Mother Taught Me* (1994), beautifully evoke the heroic struggles and quiet tragedies of Japanese American families in California before and during World War II. Written in the 1940s and 1950s, these stories were published many decades later. Both writers focus on women caught between personal desires and familial duties. Yamauchi's *And the Soul Shall Dance* and *The Music Lesson*, set in the farming community of the Imperial Valley, California, are her best-known and most frequently produced plays. Velina Hasu Houston, a prolific playwright, drew from her parents' experiences for her trilogy: *Asa Ga Kimashita* (Morning Has Broken) is the story of her African American father's courtship of her Japanese mother; *American Dreams* sets the hapless couple in Harlem, where his family objects to his marriage with "the enemy"; and in *Tea* the suicide of one of their members brings together three other Japanese "war brides" after years of isolation and loneliness on the army base in Kansas to which they had all been relegated.

Among Korean American women writers, the most notable are Theresa Hak Kyung Cha, Kim Ronyoung, and Sook Nyul Choi. Theresa Cha's *Dictee* (1982) is an experimental volume combining poetry, history, images, diagrams, and text in many languages in an attempt to capture faithfully the author's fractured, multilingual identity set amid a war-torn Korea and multiple geographical transplantations. Kim Ronyoung's novel *Clay Walls* (1987), set in the 1930s, presents a Korean American family's struggle to make a living in the greengrocery business in Los Angeles. Sook Nyul Choi has authored a trilogy for young adults—*The Year of Impossible Goodbyes* (1991), *Echoes of the White Giraffe* (1993), and *A Gathering of Pearls* (1994)—tracing the life of a Korean girl, Sookan, from multiply colonized North Korea to university studies in the United States.

Bharati Mukherjee, author of four novels and two collections of short stories, is the oldest and best known among South Asian American women writers. Her collection *The Middleman and Other Stories* (1988) won the National Book Critic's Circle Award. Of all her novels, *Jasmine* (1989) is the most centrally concerned with the immigrant South Asian woman's experience of fighting traditional gender constraints and adjusting to the quick transformations that characterize life in the United States. Sara Suleri, a professor at Yale, published a memoir, *Meatless Days* (1989), that stretches the English language through extraordinary verbal portraits of close friends and family members from childhood days in Pakistan with a Pakistani journalist father and a Welsh mother. Meena Alexander, a professor at Hunter College, has written a poetic memoir of her cosmopolitan life, *Fault Lines* (1991); she has also authored several books of poetry and a novel, *Nampally Road* (1991). Kirin Narayan, professor of anthropology at the University of Wisconsin, Madison, sounds a lively and humorous note in her novel of a young Indian woman student at Berkeley looking for Mr. Right in *Love, Stars and All That* (1994). The struggle between conflicting codes of behavior, Indian and American, is the central theme of a poignant collection of short stories, *Arranged Marriage* (1995) by Chitra Bannerjee Divakaruni, who has also written several volumes of poetry and a novel, *The Mistress of Spices* (1997).

As the most recently arrived, Southeast Asians have produced somewhat fewer writings, and these are generally coauthored. In 1986, Wendy Wilder Larsen and Tran Thi Nga produced a collection of narrative poems, entitled *Shallow Graves: Two Women and Vietnam*. Le ly Hayslip, with Jay Wurts, wrote *When Heaven and Earth Changed Places* (1990), an account of her life in Vietnam during the war years; her son James Hayslip with Jenny Wurts produced a sequel, *Child of War, Woman of Peace* (1994), recounting Le ly's attempts to bring health care to her native land in the aftermath of war and in the face of American political sanctions. Barbara J. Rolland and Houa Vue Moua have described the Hmong experience in Laos in *Trail Through the Mists* (1994). Out of Burma, or Myanmar, has come *The Coffin Tree* (1983) by Wendy Law-Yone, the disturbing story of the life-and-death struggles of a brother and sister adjusting to a new life in the United States bereft of all emotional and familiar supports. Law-Yone's second novel, *Irawaddy Tango* (1993), follows the adventures of a feisty young woman in Myanmar dancing between two factions at war. Philippine American Jessica Hagedorn's hip, pop novel *Dogeaters* (1990) and Ninotchka Rosca's novels *State of War* (1989) and *Twice Blessed* (1992) paint the complex social and political scene in the Philippines, while a recent collection of short stories, *Her Wild American Self* (1996) by M. Evelina Galang, focuses, with humor and satire, on the experience of Filipinos in the United States.

In a climate hospitable to new perspectives, made possible by the civil rights and feminist movements of the 1960s and 1970s, Asian American women writers and scholars have been flourishing for the past three decades. They have outnumbered male Asian American writers and have maintained an impressive presence on the contemporary literary scene. In the 1980s, Maxine Hong Kingston's first two books, *The Woman Warrior* and *China Men*, were the texts most widely taught on American college campuses by any living author. In 1995 these two books were transformed into a theater piece and performed in several cities across the United States. In the past decade, the filming of three books (Tan's *The Joy Luck Club*; Hayslip's *Heaven and Earth*, McCunn's *Thousand Pieces of Gold*) has helped to bring the Asian American experience into the dominant consciousness, making a small dent in the stereotypes that still prevail. But much still remains to be done.

References. King-Kok Cheung, *Articulate Silences: Hisaye Yamamoto, Maxine Hong Kingston, Joy Kogawa* (Ithaca, N.Y., 1993); Elaine Kim, *Asian American Literature: An Introduction to the Writings and Their Social Context* (Philadelphia, 1982); Shirley Geok-lin Lim and Amy Ling, *Reading the Literatures of Asian America* (Philadelphia, 1992); Amy Ling, *Between Worlds: Women Writers of Chinese Ancestry* (New York, 1990); Cynthia Sau-ling Wong, *Reading Asian American Literature: From Necessity to Extravagance* (Princeton, 1993).

AMY LING

ASSERTIVENESS TRAINING, when popularized as part of the self-help movement for women, tended to be regarded as a means for women to "act like men" or "become aggressive," and as a result some people lamented the loss of "femininity."* The theoretical and clinical basis for assertiveness training rests on the assumption not that women (or men) should be more aggressive but rather that being assertive is different from being either passive or aggressive.

People's beliefs about a psychologically "healthy adult," "healthy man" and "healthy woman" reveal some striking contradictions. Most people describe a "healthy adult" and a "healthy man" in similar terms, saying they are strong, independent, capable of being a leader. By contrast, a "healthy woman" is described as weak, dependent, a better follower than leader. Being a "healthy woman" means not being a "healthy adult" (Boverman et al., 1–7).

Assertiveness training addresses these contradictions. It provides training* in some of the attributes previously associated with being a "healthy adult."

How assertive behaviors are taught differs from one trainer to another, but the foundation is similar. Learning to be assertive involves recognizing what one's feelings and wishes are, developing insight into what one would like to say or do, and learning to express one's wishes directly and clearly. Assertive behavior is not intended to harm others, though it may include expressing anger and other negative feelings. It also includes setting limits and saying "no."

Assertiveness trainers often present their trainees with a "Bill of Rights," which includes such items as (1) you have a right to make your wants known to others and (2) you have a right to say "no" and to set limits on what you will permit.

Assertiveness training has focused more on women than men, in part because women need to counteract their traditional upbringing. Women have traditionally been taught to pay attention to other people's needs and feelings rather than their own. As wives, mothers, and even daughters, women and girls are expected to nurture others and "be nice." Many of the problems women bring to assertiveness training concern their inability to express some of their own wishes—to ask someone else to do something for them or to refuse someone else's request. Unassertive behavior—not knowing how to make requests of others and not being able to say "no" to others—does not create good social or interpersonal relations if the woman subsequently feels resentful.

In assertiveness training women learn to distinguish among several kinds of behavior: (1) unassertive, (2) indirect aggressive, (3) direct aggressive, and (4) assertive.

Unassertive behaviors are accessions to another person's wishes, often against one's will and without a clear expression of one's own wishes. The unassertive person does what she's told, but grudgingly and perhaps ineffectively. An office worker who repeatedly works late against her will might put in time but not the necessary care and attention. Her unassertive accession undermines both her own and the other person's wishes.

Indirect aggressive behaviors are refusals to go along with another's wishes by offering an excuse or in some way deflecting the responsibility for one's choice. A woman asked to work overtime against her will might say she can't because her husband or members of the car pool would be inconvenienced and upset. "If you make me stay late again, all those other people will be upset, and it will be your fault" is an example of indirect aggression if the woman does not assume responsibility for her own preferences, and it is direct aggression if she accuses the other persons of acting to harm her.

Direct aggressive responses impugn the other's motives or character:

"You treat me like a servant . . . you seem to think I don't have anything better to do than stay late every day."

In contrast to the preceding modes of reacting, a woman behaving assertively acknowledges the wishes of the other person but also states her own needs and wishes: "I understand that you need someone to work overtime, but I count on being able to leave at 5:00 and do not want to work later than that." By assertively setting her own limits, she might hurt or anger the other person, even though that is not her intention. She can be prepared for that consequence without assuming responsibility for the other person's reactions.

In the examples chosen here, the woman faces different types of risks. By complying unassertively, she risks feeling unworthy in her own estimation and appearing unworthy in the other's eyes. She appears to be cooperative but unenthusiastic and ungenuine. By refusing in an indirect aggressive manner, she risks angering the other person both because she did not comply and because she did not assume responsibility for her noncompliance. By refusing in a direct aggressive manner, she risks seeming hostile and provoking a hostile counterresponse. An assertive refusal is also risky if the other person is her boss. The worker might appear noncompliant and uncooperative and could risk losing a job or promotion. Assertiveness training does not change those power imbalances, but it does provide practice in the direct expression of one's needs and wishes without hostile accusations.

In these examples, the woman's position of power vis-à-vis the person making the request affects the objective risk she faces by making an assertive statement. If the woman is dependent on the other person for financial or other resources, she encounters greater risks for whatever actions she chooses. Assertiveness training does not encourage women to risk their jobs or other relationships at all costs. It rather provides alternatives to the other three modes of acting.

Scholars have studied the effects of assertiveness training to understand how it affects a woman's subsequent actions and feelings and how it affects other people's perceptions of the woman. Assertive women are often evaluated more negatively than assertive men. Being assertive, therefore, creates greater risks for women than for men. On the other hand, being unassertive or passive means not acting like a "healthy adult." Assertive women contradict the traditional sex-role stereotype, and that is part of the goal of assertiveness training.

References. I. K. Boverman, D. M. Broverman, F. E. Clarkson, P. S. Rosenkrantz, and S. R. Vogel, "Sex Role Stereotypes and Clinical Judgments of Mental Health," *Journal of Consulting and Clinical Psychology* 34 (1970): 1–7; N. Costrich, J. Feinstein, L. H. Kidder, J. Marecek, and L. Pascale, "When Stereotypes Hurt: Three Studies of Penalties for Sex-Role Reversals," *Journal of Experimental Social Psychology* 11 (1975): 520–530; M. Crawford, "Gender, Age, and the Social Evaluation of Assertion," *Behavior Modification* 11 (1987): 8–87; L. S. Kahn, "Group Process and Sex Differences," *Psychology of Women Quarterly* 8 (1984): 261–281; J. A. Kelly, J. M. Kern, B. G. Kirkley, and J. N. Paterson, "Reactions to Assertive versus Unassertive Behavior: Differential Effects for Males and Females and Implications for Assertiveness Training," *Behavior Therapy* 11 (1980): 670–682.

LOUISE H. KIDDER

AUSTRALIA is a country with cultures both ancient and modern. The status of women today reflects this fact. Indigenous women live with the consequences of colonization—the loss of their land and languages. They have had to cope with more recent government policies such as that of the removal of children from their Aboriginal mothers into white families and institutions. Their communities face high unemployment and greater dislocation, which manifest in alcohol abuse and a high level of violence, especially against Aboriginal women. They experience higher infant mortality rates and shorter life expectancies than the population as a whole: 64 years for Aboriginal women compared with 81 years for Australian women as a whole; 57 years for Aboriginal men compared with 75 years for Australian men as a whole. Indigenous Australians experience higher levels of imprisonment and subsequent deaths in custody than the rest of the population. They struggle to combat these problems and to reconnect dispersed family members, as they simultaneously campaign for reconciliation, native title to their lands, and pride in their Aboriginal heritage.

Non-Aboriginal women live with the consequences of an immigration history. Having been settled as a convict colony (1788), the majority of this colonial population throughout the nineteenth century was male. Convict men outnumbered convict women by a staggering 7:1. A high ratio of men continued as the demand for heavy physical labor in a primarily agricultural and pastoral economy left little room for women except as domestic servants or wives. Only by 1900 was the male:female ratio approaching equal proportions, and this only really in the towns and cities. This was because the colonial birthrate was very high, higher than in other Western countries. Natural increase slowed, however, as Australian women from the 1870s onward began reducing their family sizes. By 1900 family sizes had halved: from an average at mid-century of nine children per family, there were now four. Aboriginal people were never counted in these censuses of population.

Once the six separate colonies federated into the nation of Australia (1901), government concerns about strengthening the size and caliber of the white population led to innovative welfare measures (e.g., maternity allowance, 1912) directed specifically at women as mothers and to further immigration programs. Until 1945 the population was predominantly from the United Kingdom, with only a sprinkling of immigrants from other European countries. A White Australia Policy, implemented with the Constitution and in place until 1967, kept most Asians and other non-Europeans out. The Anglo-Celtic Culture began to break down after World War II, however, when Australia embarked on a massive immigration program to build up the labor force through population growth. Asian immigration increased following the Vietnam War.

Therefore, like the convicts of an earlier period, immigrants were expected to settle and form families. Although the demand at first was for male labor, women were also encouraged, and they swelled the ranks of the unskilled factory workforce. While Australia's immigration program has been very successful for Australia, the advantages to non–English-speaking backgrounds (NESB) women have yet to be established. Australia prides itself on being multicultural; NESB women seek to have their voices heard. Some now sit in Parliament; others have led strong feminist campaigns, occasionally at odds with the dominant Anglo-Celtic culture. Tensions along these lines have sometimes surfaced within the women's movement.

A women's movement began in Australia (1869) before the establishment (late 1880s) of state organizations of the Women's Christian Temperance Union (WCTU), which campaigned for woman suffrage* and women's economic independence as well as against the liquor trade, but the WCTU quickly grew in strength and numbers. Australian women were enfranchised early, at first in the states of South Australia (1894) and Western Australia (1899) and then federally with the first commonwealth franchise (1902). It took until 1943 for a woman to be elected to the Commonwealth Parliament, although women had more success at the state-level elections. Still, few women have been elected to Parliament (only 37 to the national Parliament in the years from 1943 to 1987), and none have been prime minister. A woman leads the smallest of the three main political parties, the Australian Democrats; for a short time in the 1980s women were leaders of state (Victoria and Western Australia) branches of the Australian Labor Party and therefore briefly became state premiers. In 1997 there were 46 women out of a total of 176 members of federal Parliament. That's approximately 20 percent and is equivalent to the proportion (19 percent) of women in state Parliaments. Seven of the 55 federal ministers and shadow ministers were women. The first woman state governor was appointed in 1991, and in 1997 of the six state governors, one was a woman.

Australia has a strong laborist tradition. Powerful trade unions and the formation of the first Labor Party in the world (1890s) led to very progressive advances for the working class that had contradictory consequences for women. The establishment of a compulsory arbitration tribunal (1904), which set mandatory award wages and conditions, strengthened the position of weaker workers in relation to their employers. But it also advantaged male workers by establishing (Harvester judgment, 1907) a family wage as the minimum for men, with women to be paid 54 percent of that. Consequently, by the 1930s Australian women's status lagged behind that of women in other Western countries. Despite Australian women's long (from the 1890s) and continuous history of demands for equal pay, it was not until 1969 that the Arbitration Commission finally granted the principle of equal pay for equal work. This covered so few women workers that subsequent decisions had to be granted in 1972 and 1974 to accede to the principle of equal pay for work of equal value. Only after 1972 and the election of Gough Whitlam as prime minister did the Australian Labor Party begin to advance the cause of women. The appointment of an adviser to the prime minister and the establishment of an Office of Women's Affairs led to the appointment of many women working in government positions (called "femocrats") to advance the causes feminists had identified. Current reforms of the industrial relations system and the replacement of a central wage-setting tribunal with enterprise bargaining do not augur well for the future status of women workers.

Throughout the twentieth century Australian women's participation in paid labor has grown steadily. In 1980, of 12 Organization for Economic Cooperation and Development countries Australia had the highest level of occupational segregation. In the 1990s women remain concentrated in two occupational groups, clerks and sales and personal service workers. In 1996 women were 43 percent of the labor force, and 52 percent of married women were employed for wages. The majority (53 percent) of women are employed, 28 percent of these full-time, and 38 percent of single women and 46 percent of married women work part-time. Seventy-three percent of men are employed, 12 percent of them part-time.

These rates vary for different age groups. Women of childbearing age are less likely to be in the workforce. As unemployment and part-time work continue to increase, women's participation in the paid labor force similarly grows: in the past decade women's participation grew by 30 percent, while men's grew by 14 percent, but men's unemployment rate increased more than women's. Women of all ages earn less than their male counterparts—the greatest gap is for those aged 45–54, where women's earnings are 73 percent of men's. Overall, women earn 83 percent of men's earnings. Those occupations where women are most concentrated also have the biggest gap (69 percent of men's wages) in earnings.

From 1872 onward Australian states began requiring compulsory schooling until the age of 15. This state-provided education was made available to boys and girls, although curricula could differ. Historians are just beginning to assess its significance for the status of women in the subsequent decades. State-provided secondary schooling was much slower to develop. Universities began to allow women to enroll in 1880. In 1997 more girls (78 percent) were completing secondary education than boys (67 percent), and more were enrolling in higher education. Yet fewer women than men are undertaking doctoral dissertations.

Sports are a major part of Australian culture, but women's sports generally get less attention and media coverage. There have, however, been some conspicuous stars, for example, Dawn Fraser, who won gold medals for swimming in three separate Olympics. Women athletes made up 40 percent of Australia's representation at the 1996 Atlanta Olympics and won 44 percent of the medals. Usually, however, they have had a harder time getting sponsorship or financial support, despite taking a larger percentage of the medals. While Aboriginal athlete Cathy Freeman excelled in the Atlanta Olympics by taking an individual medal in her track event, a member of the women's hockey team was the first Aboriginal person to win Olympic gold. Further success is anticipated in Sydney 2000 when the Games return to Australia.

References. Heather Goodall, *Invasion to Embassy: Land in Aboriginal Politics in New South Wales 1770–1972* (Sydney, 1996); Patricia Grimshaw et al. (eds.), *Creating a Nation* (Ringwood, Victoria, 1994); Diane Kirkby (ed.), *Sex, Power and Justice: Historical Perspectives on Law in Australia* (Melbourne, 1995); Diane Kirkby, *Barmaids: A History of Women's Work in Pubs* (Cambridge, U.K., 1997); Jill Matthews, *Good and Mad Women* (Sydney, 1984); Marjorie Theobald, *Knowing Women: Origins of Women's Education in Nineteenth-Century Australia* (Cambridge, U.K., 1996); Wray Vamplew (ed.), *Australians: Historical Statistics* (Broadway, Fairfax, Syme, and Welden, 1987) and Australian Bureau of Statistics, Office for the Status of Women, *Australian Women's Year Book 1997* (Canberra: AGPS, 1997).

DIANE KIRKBY

AUSTRALIAN AND NEW ZEALAND WRITERS. Women have made notable contributions to their country's literatures, though these have not always received full recognition. Writing was introduced to both countries with European settlement: from 1788 in Australia, a few decades later in New Zealand. The Australian Aborigines and the New Zealand Maoris both had oral literatures to which women contributed. White invasion destroyed much of this literature, particularly in Australia, where there were many different tribes with their own languages and cultures. There have been recent attempts to revive the indigenous languages and literary traditions. In New Zealand Maori is now taught in schools, and many Maori writers are choosing to write in their own language or jointly in English and Maori. A work in the latter category, Keri Hulme's (b. 1947) *the bone people* (1983), won the prestigious Booker Prize for Fiction in 1985.

In the early days of white settlement, most writing was functional or descriptive. Letters sent to maintain the links with relatives and friends sometimes found their way into the columns of newspapers or even between the covers of a book. Diaries or journals might eventually also be sent "home" to England and occasionally published. Many unpublished letters and diaries have been printed more recently, especially since the 1970s and the increasing interest in both social history and women's writing. Notable letter writers and diarists from Australia include Elizabeth Macarthur (1769–1850), Annie Baxter (1816–1905), Georgiana McCrae (1804–1890), and Rachel Henning (1826–1914); from New Zealand, Sarah Selwyn (1809–1867), Mary Taylor (1817–1893), and Charlotte Godley (1821–1907). Some of these women also wrote books based on their pioneering experiences, as did Australia's Louisa Anne Meredith (1812–1895) and New Zealand's Mary Anne Barker (1831–1911).

Women began contributing to local newspapers and magazines as they became established. Since most of these contributions were made anonymously or under a pseudonym, and little detailed research has yet been undertaken in this area, many nineteenth-century women writers remain to be discovered. Most women in this period contributed fiction or poetry, though a few, like South Australia's Catherine Helen Spence (1825–1910), made the breakthrough into journalism, writing lead and political articles as well as criticism and reviews.

There was almost no commercial book publishing in either Australia or New Zealand until the twentieth century. Authors or their friends and relations paid to have a book printed and hoped to recover expenses through sales. The first novel by a woman to be written and published in Australia, Anna Maria Bunn's *The Guardian* (1838), was, however, intended only for private circulation. Spence's *Clara Morison* (1854), the first novel by a woman to be written and set in Australia, was published in Britain. She was writing to earn money and did make a few pounds from the novel, despite being charged for its abridgment, without her consent, to fit into a series. Like Spence, most later women writers from Australia and New Zealand published abroad from financial necessity. Many others, such as Miles Franklin (1879–1954) with *My Brilliant Career* (1901), found that the published novel was substantially different from what they had intended.

The fact that so many women writers became expatriates, particularly in the period from 1880 to 1950, is, then, hardly surprising. Nor is it surprising that expatriate writers were the first to achieve international reputations. Rosa Praed (1851–1935) moved from Queensland to London before publishing her first novel, *An Australian Heroine* (1880). She went on to produce over 40 more, besides plays, stories, and autobiography. Melbourne's Henry Handel Richardson (Ethel Florence Richardson, 1870–1946) traveled to Germany in 1888 to study music; after many years writing in relative obscurity, she wrote a best-seller, *Ultima Thule* (1929), final volume of the trilogy *The Fortunes of Richard Mahony* (1930). Katherine Mansfield (Kathleen Beauchamp, 1888–1923) was sent from Wellington to London for her education; determined to become a writer, she realized that London was the only place for her. Despite her fairly small output of stories and tragically early death, Mansfield is probably still the woman writer best known to those outside New Zealand and Australia, increasingly acknowledged as a pioneer of the modern short story. Later notable expatriate writers include the Australians Christina Stead (1902–1983), Shirley Hazzard (b. 1931), and Germaine Greer (b. 1939) and the New Zealanders Ngaio Marsh (1899–1920) and Fleur Adcock (b. 1934).

Many of the writers who remained at home became involved in the fight for women's rights and other types of social reform. Louisa Lawson (1848–1920) published *Dawn* (1888–1905), the first feminist journal in Australia, and was a leading suffragette. In 1893, New Zealand became the first country to give women the vote; Australia followed suit in 1902. There was, however, still much to criticize. Australian novelists Catherine Martin (1847–1937) and Jessie Couvreur ("Tasma," 1848–1897) and the poet and novelist Ada Cambridge (1844–1926) queried the institution of marriage. So did Jane Mander (1877–1949) in *The Story of a New Zealand River* (1920). Mander, like her compatriot Edith Searle Grossman (1863–1931), also brought a woman's perspective to bear on pioneering life, as did the Australians Barbara Baynton (1857–1929) and Miles Franklin. Women writers, particularly Mary Gilmore (1864–1962), Katharine Prichard (1883–1969), and Eleanor Dark (1901–1985) in Australia and Blanche Baughan (1870–1958) in New Zealand, were in the vanguard of attempts to write sympathetically about Aborigines and Maoris and to expose the effects on them of white settlement of their lands. These same writers and others, such as New Zealanders Jean Devanny (1892–1962) and Robin Hyde (Iris Wilkinson, 1906–1939) and Australians Lesbia Harford (1891–1927), Marjorie Barnard (1897–1987), Dymphna Cusack (1902–1981), and Kylie Tennant (b. 1912), kept alive the radical critique of society's treatment of other marginalized groups, especially women and workers.

In the post–World War II period the major women novelists have undoubtedly been Christina Stead and New Zealand's Janet Frame (b. 1924). Though Stead began publishing in the 1920s, her reputation did not consolidate until the 1960s and the rediscovery of her *The Man Who Loved Children* (1940). Frame's reputation as the greatest living New Zealand writer, which had been steadily growing since the 1950s, was fully established in the 1980s by her three volumes of autobiography. Other important novelists who began writing during this period include, in New Zealand, Sylvia Ashton-Warner (b. 1908), Marilyn Duckworth (b. 1935), Joy Cowley (b. 1936), and Margaret Sutherland (b. 1941) and, in Australia, Thea Astley (b. 1925) and Elizabeth Harrower (b. 1928). Since 1975 women have been major producers of new fiction in both countries. In Australia, Jessica Anderson, Elizabeth Jolley (b. 1923), Olga Masters (1919–1986), Barbara Hanrahan (b. 1939), Beverley Farmer (b. 1941), Helen Garner (b. 1942), and Kate Grenville (b. 1950) have won many local awards and seen their books increasingly distributed in Europe and the

United States. Colleen McCullough (b. 1937) had a major international success with *The Thorn Birds* (1977). While Keri Hulme is the only contemporary New Zealand writer to be well known overseas, another Maori novelist and story writer, Patricia Grace (b. 1937), has been widely published in New Zealand, and Sue McCauley's *Other Halves* (1982) was a local best-seller.

Women are also becoming increasingly prominent in the poetry of both countries. There has, indeed, always been a strong tradition of women poets in New Zealand, from Jessie Mackay (1864–1938), Blanche Baughan, and Mary Ursula Bethel (1874–1945), through Eileen Duggan (1894–1972), Robin Hyde, and Ruth Dallas (b. 1919), to present-day writers. Lauris Edmond (b. 1924), who began publishing only in 1975, won the Commonwealth Poetry Prize in 1985. Among her contemporaries are Rachel McAlpine (b. 1940), Elizabeth Smither (b. 1942), and Cilla McQueen (b. 1949). Judith Wright (b. 1915) has long been the leading Australian woman poet, though both Rosemary Dobson (b. 1920) and Gwen Harwood (b. 1920) have increased their reputations with each new collection. *We Are Going* (1964) by Kath Walker (b. 1920), the first collection of poems by an Aboriginal, was a national best-seller. A significant group of younger poets come from non-English backgrounds: Antigone Kefala (b. 1936), Anna Couani (b. 1948), and Ania Walwicz (b. 1951).

Since 1975 poet Dorothy Hewett (b. 1923) has also become the first Australian woman to win widespread recognition as a dramatist, though many earlier women wrote for amateur and fringe companies. Plays by the New Zealand expatriate Alma de Groen (b. 1941) are also increasingly being performed by mainstream companies in Australia. In New Zealand, where the development of local drama has taken even longer than in Australia, women have been making a mark only since the 1980s, most notably the Maori feminist Renée (b. 1929).

Specialist feminist presses, journals, and magazines have been established in both countries since the 1970s, with varying degrees of success. In Australia, the most prominent are *Hecate* (1975–), *Refractory Girl* (1979–), and *Australian Feminist Studies* (1985–); in New Zealand, *Spiral* (1976–), *Broadsheet* (1971–) and *Women's Studies Journal* 1985–). Melbourne's Sybylla Press (named after Miles Franklin's heroine) and the now defunct Sisters, along with Sydney's Redress Press, have concentrated on publishing contemporary writing. Auckland's New Women's Press has also reprinted works by earlier women writers. Interestingly, the major English feminist presses were founded by expatriates from Australia and New Zealand: Virago by Carmen Callil, Pandora by Dale Spender, and Women's Press by Stephanie Dowrick. All have reprinted works by Australian and New Zealand women; Penguin Australia has also recently begun a reprint program.

References. Carole Ferrier (ed.), *Gender, Politics and Fiction: Twentieth Century Australian Women's Novels* (St. Lucia, Queensland, 1985); Drusilla Modjeska, *Exiles at Home: Australian Women Writers, 1925–1945* (Sydney, 1981).

ELIZABETH WEBBY

AUTOBIOGRAPHIES AND DIARIES, BRITISH, are as diverse as British women themselves. Therefore, it is hard to characterize this vast and ever-growing area of study. In the past 30 years, as literary critics began to embrace works formerly considered outside literature, feminist scholars have promoted what some categorize as personal prose, pieces perhaps not originally intended for publication. Despite some obvious differences, it is difficult to distinguish among autobiography, memoir, journal, diary, and personal essay. Many authors mix the forms within their works, placing segments of journals in their autobiographies or addressing their diaries to particular readers. The autobiography is the most consciously literary form; it requires plotting out a discrete part of the author's life, selecting events to present a consistent character and having an awareness of the reader. However, besides the public figures who expect a large readership, many women wrote for only their immediate families; other texts are discovered in attics, presumably unread except by the writer. On the other hand, journals and diaries, supposedly composed with the self as audience, either to record events or provide an outlet for speculation or simply to keep the writer company, have in the twentieth century become a popular form of publication for novelists and poets.

Women's studies scholars have been in the forefront of the movement to study personal prose, frequently characterizing it as an especially feminine form; it certainly is an outlet for authors barred from traditional publication and discouraged from "serious writing." Women's studies scholars have worked in two directions. The first has been to recover lost and forgotten works. Many autobiographies and journals have been resurrected from attics, historical societies, library stacks, and general obscurity to be published, promoted, and studied. Feminist scholars point out that literary critics have focused on autobiographies written by men, ignoring many important works by women. Other scholars have looked for gender differences, claiming that women are more likely to combine forms of personal prose into nonlinear works or to emphasize others rather than themselves in their autobiographies. However, differences in life histories by men and by women seem slight and may be related to how well the author fits into the mainstream of the culture rather than to gender; characteristics of women's self-writing can be found in works by the working class and other excluded groups. However, since women who wanted to write for publication or for themselves were frequently blocked from other literary outlets, a study of women's autobiographies, journals, and diaries provides an especially fruitful look at women's lives and women's prose.

What follows is not a comprehensive bibliography of British autobiographies and published diaries and journals. This field is constantly growing, with more works rediscovered and added to bibliographies every year. Only the best known are noted. Although autobiographies and diaries have been separated, following traditional distinctions between books that appear to be overviews of lives and works that consist of daily or sporadic entries, the distinction is fuzzy.

Some scholars have claimed that the first autobiography written in English was by a woman, Margery Kempe, in 1438. Other medieval and mystical texts, besides *The Book of Margery Kempe*, include *Showing of God's Love* by Julian of Norwich and St. Brigitta's *Revelations*.

Because dissenting religions emphasized a close, personal relationship with God and the importance of conversion, many Quakers and Puritans wrote spiritual autobiographies, stressing religious belief and minimizing daily life.

By the seventeenth century, women were writing secular autobiographies as well. From the upper class, most of these women held traditional views. Although some delayed marriage, nearly all eventually married and treated domestic matters as the focus of their lives. Unusual among the predominantly male diarists of the century, Celia Fiennes describes the English countryside in her diary, *Through England on a Side-Saddle in the Time of William and Mary* (1888).

The authors and so their works in the eighteenth century show more social, economic, and occupational diversity. These women were not always fulfilled by domestic or religious concerns alone. Although some worked as novelists or actresses, social and economic factors pressured most into marriages, frequently uncongenial. Paralleling scenes from contemporary sentimental novels, women portrayed themselves besieged by unscrupulous and treacherous men and complained about the disparity of power. Spiritual autobiographies, secular autobiographies by upper-class women, and gossipy social diaries were still composed. More influential in the development of autobiography were the "apologies" by women of questionable reputation, Laetitia Pilkington, Frances Anne Vane, Con Phillips, and actresses George Anne Bellamy and Charlotte Clarke. Fanny Burney and Hester Thrale, who established themselves as part of the eighteenth-century literary scene, kept extensive journals.

A central work of the nineteenth century is Harriet Martineau's *Autobiography* (1855), in which she details her intellectual and personal development. Margaret Oliphant, Mrs. Humphrey Ward, and Mary Mitford were minor novelists whose autobiographies display the tensions between the expected Victorian woman's role and their profession. Of the many diarists, the most famous was Queen Victoria herself. Other diarists of note include Caroline Fox, friend of Thomas and Jane Welsh Carlyle and John Stuart and Harriet Taylor Mill; Elizabeth Fry, prison reform worker; Fanny Kemble, actress probably best known in the United States for the 1863 volume of her diary criticizing southern plantation life, *Journal of a Residence on a Georgian Plantation*; Mary Shelley, novelist; Elizabeth Barrett Browning, poet; George Eliot, novelist; Dorothy Wordsworth, sister of the poet; and a transplanted American, Alice James.

Women who were politically active in the late nineteenth and early twentieth centuries such as Annie Besant, Hannah Mitchell, Annie Kenney, and Emmeline Pankhurst championed a variety of social causes, including woman's rights, in their autobiographies. Beatrice Webb published a multivolumed diary: *My Apprenticeship* (1926), *Our Partnership* (1945), *Beatrice Webb's Diaries, 1912–1924* (1952), *Beatrice Webb's Diaries, 1924–1936* (1956).

Texts proliferate in the twentieth century. Virginia Woolf's and Katherine Mansfield's diaries (*The Diary of Virginia Woolf*, 4 vols. [1877–1982]; Mansfield's *Journal* [1927; rev. and enl. ed. 1954]) are prototypes for literary notebook-journals. The turn of the century and, later, World War II produced a spate of nostalgic looks at bygone times. These autobiographies and reminiscences usually focus on childhood, especially in rural and working-class areas. One of the most extensive is Flora Thompson's trilogy *Lark Rise to Candleford*.

Interest in British women's autobiographies and diaries no doubt will continue to grow. Autobiographies and diaries have remained a popular form of expression for women writers, popular reading for the public, and a popular area of study for feminist scholars.

References. Shari Benstock (ed.), *The Private Self: Theory and Practice of Women's Autobiography* (Chapel Hill, N.C., 1988); Mary Jean Corbett, *Representing Femininity: Middle-Class Subjectivity in Victorian and Edwardian Women's Autobiographies* (New York, 1992); Carolyn Heilbrun, *Writing a Woman's Life* (New York, 1988); Estelle C. Jelinek, *Women's Autobiography* (Bloomington, Ind., 1980); Personal Narratives Group (ed.), *Interpreting Women's Lives: Feminist Theory and Personal Narratives* (Bloomington, Ind., 1989); Sidonie Smith, *A Poetics of Women's Autobiography: Marginality and the Fictions of Self-Representation* (Bloomington, Ind., 1987); Domna C. Stanton (ed.), *The Female Autograph* (New York, 1984).

NAN HACKETT

AUTOBIOGRAPHIES AND DIARIES, U.S., are nonfiction narratives that record the personal lives and the historical significance of their authors. Genres closely related include letters, journals, memoirs, reminiscences, travel accounts, and fictionalized diaries and autobiographies. The female and, at times, feminist perspective is clearly present.

The motivating factor in these writings is the impetus toward claiming and proclaiming one's identity. For women, as for men, this process means a restating of the eternal "I am," but for women, more often than for men, it also means "I am in relation to you."

Autobiographies. Women's autobiographies have such purposes as self-revelation, self-justification, propaganda, apologia, self-knowledge, and historical record. Closely related to the interest in psychology and the women's movement, women's autobiographies have proliferated in the latter part of the twentieth century. The writer's translation of subjective, introspective experience into a public text provides a language for, and a substantiation of, the reader's private experience. Thus, women's autobiographies become a source of political feminist power. They contribute dramatically to an understanding of the history, psychology, and sociology of American women. Women's autobiographies emphasize human relations, the personal, the domestic, and inner, rather than outer, reality, and action.

Autobiographies have several major content emphases: (1) personal, spiritual, psychological; (2) political; (3) minority; and (4) career.

1. Personal, spiritual, psychological. Some autobiographies emphasize more than others the development of the self, the growth of an identity. *The Living of Charlotte Perkins Gilman* (1935) chronicles Gilman's personal and emotional life within the context of political and social activities. Mary McCarthy's *Memoirs of a Catholic Girlhood* (1957) is a series of analytic memoirs about her past and her family. *The Long Loneliness* (1972) by Dorothy Day is a philosophical and spiritual autobiography. Kate Millet's *Flying* (1974) is representative of the personalization of contemporary feminist issues.

2. Political. Political autobiographies often have a persuasive as well as a personal tone. They function as propaganda, reminiscence, or charismatic message. See *Living My Life* (1931) by anarchist Emma Goldman, *This I Remember* (1949) and *On My Own* (1958) by president's wife and United Nations representative Eleanor Roosevelt, *With My Mind of Freedom* (1975) by black activist Angela Davis, and *Bella! Ms. Abzug Goes to Washington* (1972) by hatted congressional representative Bella Abzug.

3. Minority. Autobiography is an effective medium for the minority voice because the genre can personalize and individualize her larger concern. Maya Angelou's four-volume autobiography begun by *I Know Why the Caged Bird Sings* (1970), Zora Neale Hurston's *Dust Tracks on a Road* (c. 1942), and Anne Moody's *Coming of Age in Mississippi* (1968) are significant texts by black women.

   The Asian American woman's voice is heard in *The Woman Warrior* (1976) by Maxine Hong Kingston. The American Indian woman is found in the autobiography of Mountain Wolf Woman, Helen Sekaquaptewa's *Me and Mine* (1969), and Louise Abeita's *I am a Pueblo Indian Girl* (1939).

   Joan Baez's, *Daybreak* (1968), and *And a Voice to Sing with: A Memoir* (1987) and *The Education of the Woman Golfer* (1979) by Nancy Lopez are three popular texts written by women of Mexican background.

4. Career. Career autobiographies are interesting because the autobiographer is

typically more interested in telling about her personal and emotional life than about her professional achievements and successes. A popular enterprise, career autobiographies are as varied as the careers of their authors, from actress to zoologist. A sampler includes *Blackberry Winter* (1972) by anthropologist Margaret Mead, *Pentimento* (1973) by playwright Lillian Hellman, *The Story of My Life* (1903) by the blind and deaf scholar and writer Helen Keller, and *The Fabric of My Life* (1946) by Hannah Solomon, Jewish and feminist activist.

Diaries. Diaries may be classified as either private or public. They are usually chronological and episodic. Private diaries record women's daily lives and private thoughts and feelings. Public diaries provide historical records, pass on family traditions, or justify one's life and actions.

Women's diaries may document both American history and female experience. In general, diaries can be organized into five major categories of experience: (1) pioneering and travel; (2) personal, spiritual, psychological; (3) political; (4) minority; and (5) career.

1. Pioneering and travel. Colonial and pioneer women's diaries provide an invaluable account of largely ignored aspects of American history. Not typically introspective, the diarists keep records of domestic life. They occasionally reflect an awareness of the historical significance of their lives. The diaries are substitutes for the writers' absent female network. The travel diaries of the westward movement appear in multiple collections. Other travel diaries are accounts of pleasure or adventure trips. Some have historical significance. In others, overtones of "innocents abroad" or "the ugly American" appear. The first known travel diary by a woman was written by Madam Sarah Knight, who traveled on horseback from Boston to New York in 1704. The feminist perspective is well represented in Julia Holmes' *A Bloomer Girl on Pike's Peak, 1858* (1949) and in Eslanda Robeson's *African Journey* (1945).

2. Personal, spiritual, psychological. As society recognized the value of the individual, and women saw themselves as more than adjuncts to their fathers, husbands, and sons, the diary as a form of personal ratification gained importance. For many women the diary was an outlet for their private thoughts, since they were not free to enter into the larger world occupied by men. Important texts here include the *Journal and Correspondence of Miss Adams* (1841) by Abigail Adams, *Pilgrim at Tinker Creek* (1974) by Annie Dillard, *The Diary of Alice James* (1964), *I, Mary MacLane* (1917), *The Diaries of Sylvia Plath* (1982), and May Sarton's *Journal of a Solitude* (1973).

3. Political. The diaries of such well-known political women as Elizabeth Cady Stanton, Dorothy Day, Lucretia Coffin Mott, Angela Davis, and Barbara Deming are important as both personal narrations and political argument.

The texts evidence their authors' consciousness of participating in history and their desire to interpret and explain the events in which they are involved. Political diaries also include works by women who kept records of a period with a consciously historical intention, for example, Mary Lydia Daly, whose *Diary of a Union Lady, 1861–1865* had as its purpose "to preserve, for rereading in the future, the immediate impressions of a coming national emergency." Mary

Chesnut, Fanny Kemble, and Miss Emma Holmes all produced diaries detailing the painful loss of a way of life.

4. Minority. Minority women's diaries trace the experience of being both female and a member of a minority group in white male America. Important texts include *The Journal of Charlotte L. Forten* (1953), *The Cancer Journals* (1980) by Audre Lorde, and *Give Us Each Day: The Diary of Alice Dunbar-Nelson* (1985).

5. Career. Career diaries generally chronicle the rise of women successful in a certain profession. Many of these are written on the popular level. Some are primarily anecdotal, even gossipy. Others are more reflective and philosophical, sometimes serving as notes for further work.

Interesting career diaries include *The Notebooks of Martha Graham* (1973), writer Janet Flanner's *Paris Journal* (1965, 1971), *The Adolescent Diaries of Karen Horney* (1980), *Dear Josephine: The Theatrical Career of Josephine Hull* (1963), *Katherine Dunham's Journey to Accompong* (1946), and *Stay with It, Van: From the Diary of Mississippi's First Lady Mayor* (1958) by Dorothy Crawford.

References. Cheryl Cline, *Women's Diaries, Journals, and Letters: An Annotated Bibliography* (New York, 1989); Margo Culley (ed.), *A Day at a Time: The Diary Literature of American Women from 1764 to the Present* (New York, 1985); Estelle Jelinek (ed.), *Women's Autobiography: Essays in Criticism* (Bloomington, Ind., 1980); Mary Jane Moffat and Charlotte Painter (eds.), *Revelations: Diaries of Women* (New York, 1974); Lillian Schlissel, *Women's Diaries of the Westward Journey* (New York, 1982).

CAROLE GANIM

B

BACKLASH refers to the antagonistic counterassault on woman's rights that attempts to reverse the achievements of the feminist movement. Such reactions against woman's rights historically have been triggered by the perception that the status of women is rapidly improving.

As described by journalist Susan Faludi, the backlash is rooted in popular culture and fueled by media that uncritically accept inaccurate statistical information about women in society. The agents of this backlash are numerous: purveyors of high fashion, lingerie, cosmetics, and plastic surgery; television shows, movies, and self-help books featuring love-addicted single women and cocooning mommy trackers; the Republican New Right; and male critics such as George Gilder, Allan Bloom, Warren Farrell, and Robert Bly.

The very influential analysis of Faludi does not address the contemporary backlash in its entirety. Another important component is "postfeminism," a term used to describe the more conservative environment of the 1980s and the decline of the women's movement. It is argued that gender equity has been achieved and that feminism has become an anachronism, irrelevant to, and even reviled by, women. Recent public opinion polls clearly reflect the demonization of "feminism"; feminist ideals are supported, but the label and movement are rejected. According to a 1986 Gallup poll, 56 percent of U.S. women considered themselves feminists. By 1992, a *Time*/ CNN poll found that only 29 percent were willing to call themselves feminists, and that figure was even lower among young women.

Today's young women have little personal experience with traditional sex-role behavior and may see little need for a feminist movement to combat these roles. Women today are employed, attend college, and are delaying marriage and motherhood. Instead, a media-driven definition of the feminist movement as man-hating, antifamily, and extremist may underlie the current disinterest and alienation of women. Young and working-class women in particular can least afford to be seen as deviant; open support for feminism and career success may be inversely related.

A final dimension of the backlash is the popular attention now given to long-running intellectual debate among feminists themselves. In the tradition of the academy, the fault lines involve theory, methods and measurements, and pedagogy. While some critics charge that feminists today demand a doctrinaire, monolithic, politically correct way of thinking, in violation of a free marketplace of ideas, feminist theory has always had many varieties and varying positions on contemporary issues.

One prevalent theme is discomfort with, or rejection of, the "difference" or "gender" feminism of Carol Gilligan, Sara Ruddick, and Deborah Tannen. Such critics fear that this belief that the sexes differ in significant ways and that women's "different voice" and "ethic of care" are superior signals a return to gender stereotypes, separate spheres, and the moral and spiritual crusades of earlier temperance and suffrage campaigns.

Strongly libertarian feminists see deep conflicts between free speech and some feminist analyses of pornography, hate-speech, sexual harassment, and sex work such as prostitution and exotic dancing. An associated concern was voiced by journalist Midge Dector in the early 1970s (and more recently by Katie Roiphe, Rene Denfeld, and Camille Paglia) that feminism currently represents a return to chastity, Victorianism, and repressive antisexuality. These authors argue that the creation of a "rape culture" has made women fearful of sex, denied them agency to handle dating situations, verbal harassment, and domestic violence, and valorized the victimization of women.

In contrast, other feminists score the individualism of liberal or equity feminism for uncritically adopting the male model of formal equality and ignoring the importance of gender differences, the claims of a collective social life, and the role of love, motherhood, and home in women's lives. Without differential treatment of women and without policy accommodation for childbirth, child care, divorce,* and health care, authors such as Betty Friedan, Sylvia Ann Hewlett, and Elizabeth Fox-Genovese have argued that women can never be equal in society.

Having identified problems faced by women, the new feminist movement has also attempted to measure their prevalence and to suggest likely policy solutions. In a version of the "losing ground" argument, the movement has been portrayed as having seriously harmed women by supporting no-fault divorce,* gender-neutral alimony and child custody laws, and greater labor force participation for women in advance of an available family leave and child care support network.

The writings of Susan Faludi and Christina Hoff Sommers have shown the inherent inability of social scientists to rigorously define and measure the incidence of rape,* sexual harassment,* domestic violence,* the wage gap,* self-esteem, and gender bias in education. These methodological debates rage within every discipline, but, because of their link with a large social movement, the softness of these social statistics has attracted much greater public scrutiny. Such definitions are political. An inclusive definition of domestic violence, for example, may promote greater spending on solutions but also produce roughly equal victimization rates for men and women, obscuring the fact that women are at much greater risk for serious physical injury.

The backlash* against women's studies by professors of those courses comes closest to echoing the organized antifeminist movement that has long charged these programs with bias, indoctrination, and encouraging illiteracy in the standard canon of Western civilization. But if, as some women's studies scholars have urged, knowledge about women were mainstreamed into the general curriculum, critics fear the problem may then become one of "filler feminism," or the forced inclusion of minor characters and events.

In a field of study that is multidisciplinary, it is predictable that those trained in the hard sciences will recoil from a feminist pedagogy that introduces the personal and self-disclosure into classroom discussions and sometimes resembles pop-psychology therapy. Literary techniques such as postmodernism and the rejection of logic, objectivity, and quantitative methods are questioned by feminist scientists who view many of their colleagues as engaging in nonscholarly, anti-intellectual enterprises.

The answer to "who stole feminism" is often "women's studies scholars" who dominate curriculum transformation projects and tenure, promotion, and recruitment decisions and bring feminist activists with few or no educational credentials into the academy. Women's studies scholars are now the primary sources for media stories about feminism. What they say either may be inaccessible or, when translated into lay terms, seem silly or simplistic (e.g., all men are potential rapists). But there are excesses in every movement. Many feminists probably long for the enforced consensus and singular focus of the suffrage and Equal Rights Amendment* campaigns. Even so, this dialogue is helpful in that it permits self-criticism. Although a mass movement is not easily sustained by a debate monopolized by intellectuals, this feminist backlash, in part, confirms the membership of women's studies in an often rancorous academic community.

References. Rene Denfeld, *The New Victorians* (New York, 1995); Susan Faludi, *Backlash: The Undeclared War against American Women* (New York, 1991); Daphne Patai and Noretta Koertge, *Professing Feminism: Cautionary Tales from the Strange World of Women's Studies* (New York, 1994); Katie Roiphe, *The Morning After: Sex, Fear, and Feminism* (Boston, 1993); Christina H. Sommers, *Who Stole Feminism?* (New York, 1994).

JANET K. BOLES

BANGLADESH. Living in a predominantly Muslim country, Bangladeshi women are most often caricatured in the media and in academic literature as shy and dependent observers of purdah,* or female seclusion. Indeed, a rigid division of labor and social space had shaped the lives of many Bangladeshi women, particularly the rural majority, who depend on agriculture for their daily sustenance. But, since independence and increasingly with the mid-1980s trend toward the global reorganization of production and finance, Bangladeshi women have forged new opportunities and patterns of behavior. While dramatically altering everyday life, changes in behavior and expectations do not find either their source or expression solely in processes of global economic restructuring. Instead, experiences and new traditions have taken shape within a context of nationally constituted reforms embodied in the politicization of Islamic fundamentalism and the increasing individuation of everyday life.

These changes have taken place in concert with two broad trends in the rural economy: the reorganization of agricultural production and the increased demand for employment brought on by declines in subsistence production. For women, this meant a transformation of their household strategies to diversify income sources in response to the decline in the demand for agricultural workers, for crop processing and home-based production. It also meant a new openness among women to credit opportunities and development initiatives that offered them ways to meet household needs that increasingly depended on the sale and purchase of goods and services.

Thus, seeds of transformation can be partially traced to women's development programs introduced in the mid-1970s. Concerned with poverty reduction, these programs extended credit to support agricultural projects as well as consciousness-raising, literacy training, and handicraft work (e.g., BRAC [Bangladesh Rural Advancement Committee]). Yet, because they assumed that women could not, and would not, find work in rural nonfarm production and services, these early initiatives often focused on activities that could be undertaken within the purview of women's household responsibilities.

Importantly, these initiatives recognized the need for employment among families increasingly dependent on diverse income sources to meet household needs. However, the ability of poor and marginal households to earn sufficient income requires the employment of increasing numbers of family members, including women in the nonfarm sector, where both daughters and wives have become part of a growing female labor force. Hence, while most women previously worked as unpaid laborers in home-based enterprises, by the early 1980s, they participated outside the household compound in irrigation and water management programs and road maintenance and building schemes and received credit for agricultural activities such as animal rearing and silk production. During the past decade, there have been dramatic growth and diversification of government and private support for women's credit, including support for such activities as microenterprise development and petty trade. Perhaps the most notable of these efforts is the Grameen Bank Project, which distributes credit to women for nonfarm as well as farm activities.

Together, the changes brought about by new credit and employment opportunities means that fewer women now work in the privacy of the household compound, where they could maintain forms of seclusion and limit their physical mobility and interaction with men. Women, particularly from land-poor and marginally productive farm households, have increasingly had to secure off-farm and nonfarm daily and seasonal work that requires new forms of social interaction with non-kin men. These women, as well as those from landless families, are among those most vulnerable to exploitative labor exchanges as well as physical harassment or abuse from their village kin.

In urban areas women's demand for, and access to, work has expanded. Service work, including sales, is increasingly performed by women, usually from educated middle-class families, who must chart new modes of interaction with men unfamiliar with their new status in the labor market. The economic position of upper-class women, in contrast, provides both access to most public resources and protection from the harassment and abuse commonly experienced by their poorer urban and rural counterparts.

Dramatic economic reforms of the 1980s, expressed initially in 1982 as the "new industrial policy," opened the economy to export production, the development of export enclaves, investments in an urban workforce, and a new demand for women workers. These reforms provided even greater, if less direct, access to credit and training through continually expanding nongovernmental resources. By the mid-1980s, women were employed as teachers and health workers, public and private service employees, owners and workers in an expanding number of microenterprises, as well as in export manufacturing.

For women who previously had been excluded from recognized wage employment, these changes dramatically altered the potential for economic and social independence. These new forms of social engagement drew on women's need and willingness to work as well as on their increased access to credit and training to expand petty trade, production, and service activities. While low when compared to other southern countries, women's total employment has more than doubled, from a female labor force participation rate of 4.0 percent to 10.6 percent between 1974 and 1989. Moreover, although agriculture still provides employment for the majority of workingwomen, export manufacturing has significantly increased the number of female wage workers. In the industrial sector, including export production, about 28 percent of women workers find employment, and in garment manufacturing alone women account for between 80 and 90 percent of those employed.

Thus, while women's total employment remains relatively low, women's economic and social position in the contemporary period is constructed through their greater participation in nonsubsistence employment. This stands in stark contrast to the immediate postindependence period, when families were less mobile, when production was organized primarily among extended family members and village communities, and when gender relations and female status were constituted according to the organization of the household. Notable, too, is the fact that while in the past families with working daughters suffered reduced status because of their assumed inability to maintain their daughters in purdah, today a daughter's employment may be an asset on the marriage market.

Despite these important trends, women's future participation in the labor force and the conditions of their employment are difficult to calculate. Several factors contribute to this difficulty: women are likely to engage in "informal" household and commodity production and wage exchanges; they have limited rights and protection as workers, often receiving less than the national minimal wage; and they are less often counted than are men among those employed part-time. Moreover, notwithstanding declines in agricultural subsistence production, women continue to hold responsibility for seasonal activities such as grain processing and spice and vegetable production on home plots. During the nonharvest season, for example, some women work as animal herders, house cleaners, and fuel gatherers as well as petty producers and traders; others secure income as contract laborers for middlemen who provide the raw materials for such activities as fishnet making and silk spinning. Thus, household production, whether for in-kind or cash remuneration, remains a significant source of rural employment and income but continues to be underestimated in analyses of the labor force and labor market dynamics.

While women's participation in the labor market has increased, literacy rates remained relatively unchanged between 1974 and 1981. Preliminary results of the 1991 census suggest that girls continue to attend school at a much lower rate than boys, and although there has been a significant increase in those entering primary school, dropout rates remain above 50 percent. Even with the introduction of a private system of higher education in the mid-1990s, postsecondary education remains limited to a small proportion of the national population, with significantly fewer women than men in attendance.

Perhaps the most dramatic change in women's place in Bangladesh is their active engagement in social and political movements. Women in rural communities have played key roles in mobilizing resources from government and nongovernmental organizations, are increasingly active in struggles for legal and social rights, and have been recognized as important stakeholders in political decision making in the national bureaucracy. The success of these efforts is reflected in the demands of fundamentalist political parties, most notably the Jamaati-Islami, which mark women as the emblem of what is problematic with the economic direction of the country. Indeed, challenges to economic liberalization and the political and economic security of the rural elite evoke abuses against women that range from public embarrassment and rebuke to stone throwing and even murder. But despite the backlash against women's increasing participation in public life and the activities of development organizations, women continue to forge new spaces for social engagement, redefining their experience and its meaning as they reconstitute gender relations in their everyday lives.

References. Shelley Feldman, "Contradictions of Gender Inequality: Urban Class Formation in Contemporary Bangladesh," in Alice Clark (ed.), *Gender and Political Economy: Explorations of South Asian Systems*) (Delhi, 1993); Shelley Feldman, "(Re)presenting Islam: Manipulating Gender, Shifting State Practices and Class Frustrations," in Amrita Basu and Patricia Jeffery (eds.), *Appropriating Gender: Women's Activism and the Politicization of Religion in South Asia* (London and New York, 1998); Shelley Feldman and Florence E. McCarthy, *Rural Women and Development in Bangladesh: Selected Issues* (Oslo, 1984); Naila Kabeer, *Reversed Realities* (London, 1994); S. C. White, *Arguing with the Crocodile: Gender and Class in Bangladesh* (London, 1992).

SHELLEY FELDMAN

BATTERED HUSBAND SYNDROME (and Other Tall Tales). The role of men as perpetrators of crime (white-collar, assaultive, property) has been highlighted in the written and visual media. According to June Stephenson in her book *Men Are Not Cost-Effective*: "Thirty-one percent of people arrested and sent to prison are men between the ages of eighteen and twenty-four, and another 45% are men aged twenty-five to forty-four. Ninety-four percent of prisoners are male" (p. 2). Since the "discovery" of spouse abuse by the feminist movement in the early 1970s and the passing of legislation making it a crime in the early 1980s, data collectors once again point their collective fingers at men as the primary perpetrators of spousal violence. Approximately 90–95 percent of the victims of physical battering are female, and 5–10 percent are male, according to police arrest statistics, Federal Bureau of Investigation (FBI) Unified Crime Reports, and noncriminal justice surveys.

Shortly after the battered woman syndrome (BWS) was formulated by Lenore Walker, questions about the abuse of men in intimate (primarily heterosexual) relationships began to appear in articles, research, and occasionally on television. I have been asked about battered men and violent women since I began speaking on woman abuse in 1979. Dan Rather hosted a documentary on abused men in the 1980s, but the idea did not get much play. In fact, several of Rather's abused men were later discovered to have histories of wife assault.

To determine whether there is evidence for a battered husband syndrome, we would need to answer a significant question, What does it take to batter someone? More specifically, what would it take to batter a male? We would expect that a battered male would exhibit characteristics and behaviors present in an abused woman and described by the BWS. Indicators of battered women syndrome can be divided into three major categories:

1. traumatic effects of victimization by violence
2. learned helplessness deficits resulting from the interaction between repeated victimization by violence and others' reactions to it
3. self-destructive coping responses to the violence (Sonkin)

Specifically, we would be looking at levels of fear, chronic apprehension, symptoms of posttraumatic stress disorder (e.g., reexperiencing the trauma, numbed responsiveness, depression, anxiety), and injuries.

Level of fear is a critical feature characterizing violent relationships. Women, in general, develop over time a chronic level of fear for their personal safety that is not usually experienced by males. For example, a man walking down the street alone and at night would probably be unafraid if he saw three women approaching him (unless they were Mary Kay Commandos). A woman would already be tense because she was alone, and it was dark. The approach of one, two, or more male strangers would usually exacerbate her fear. A battered woman's fear is grounded in reality and compounded by experience.

What would it take to create a comparable level of fear in a man? When a man is attacked by a woman, he normally retains the ability to control or stop the aggressive act. A woman's aggression does not usually present a "survival problem" to a man unless she uses an equalizer (e.g., gun, knife). "The few truly battered men I have known have shown an incomplete reversal of roles, because men victims do not show the terrible fear that so characterizes women victims. Even though the men are receiving injuries, they seem to know they can be the ultimate winners any time they choose" (Jeanne Deschner in Stephenson, p. 49). Fear is a requisite in the development of BWS, and it is much more difficult for women to create that level of fear in men than the reverse.

This is not to say that women cannot be violent or abusive. It is simply to say that, for the most part, a woman's violence does not create a "battered husband syndrome." When men are abused, they are given assistance. For the most part, that aid has been in the form of counseling or legal advice. I have not met a man or spoken to one on the hot line who has needed emergency shelter.

Battering is not an equal opportunity employer. Study findings contradict any assumption of gender equity. Not only are wives more seriously injured than husbands, but they also less frequently use severe violence. A trauma syndrome is developed when a significant number of individuals are affected by a recognized and pervasive set of circumstances. We do not have evidence, either empirical or clinical, to support the conceptualization of a battered husband syndrome. The authors of the Spousal Assault Risk Assessment (SARA) sum it up very well. In writing their guide, they use a definition of spousal violence not limited by gender. They conclude, however, that husband-to-wife assault can be considered the more serious form of spousal abuse due to its prevalence, its repetitive nature, and its high risk of morbidity and mortality.

References. Ola Barnett and Alyce LaViolette, *It Could Happen to Anyone: Why Battered Women Stay* (Newbury Park, Calif., 1993); Donald Dutton, *The Batterer* (New York, 1995); Randall P. Kropp, Stephen D. Hart, Christopher D. Webster, and Derek Eaves, *Manual for the Spousal Assault Risk Assessment Guide* (Vancouver, 1995); Daniel Sonkin, *Domestic Violence on Trial* (New York, 1987); June Stephenson, *Men Are Not Cost-Effective* (New York, 1995); any of the books by Lenore Walker.

ALYCE LAVIOLETTE

BATTERED WOMEN are women who are beaten in a repeating pattern by their husbands or male companions. Lenore Walker has called this pattern the cycle of violence (55–77). This cycle encompasses the tension-building phase, the acute battering phase, and the phase of kindness and contrite loving behavior. While acts of violence against women are not historically new, awareness and concern have grown since the 1970s, when the women's movement brought the enormity of violence perpetrated by men against women out from behind closed doors. M. Koss et al. (p. 44) estimate that as many as 4 million women in the United States experience severe or life-threatening assault from a male partner. Women are more likely to be injured in their homes by violent attack than in any other place. Violence in the home is often seen as a private matter, and injuries to women are often minimized by those who do not wish to address the problem. Further, blame for violence has frequently been placed on the victim by the perpetrator and society. This blaming of the victim is an easier approach than addressing the multivariate issue of domestic violence and societal factors that foster its continuance.

In the early 1970s Erin Pizzey became aware that many of those seeking assistance at an advice center in London were battered women. Chiswick Women's Aid, the first battered women's shelter, grew from her awareness. In the United States, the interest of women's groups led to the formation of local self-help groups and subsequently to state and national coalitions working to end violence against women. In 1996, there were 11 National Domestic Violence organizations, 50 state coalitions, and approximately 1,755 community shelters and domestic violence service providers. Most of these raise money through private fund-raising endeavors, grant writing, and limited state and federal support. Though approaches to working with battered women may vary from professional interventions to peer advocacy, common principles are empowerment, the value of self-determination, and respect for the dignity of each individual. A typical domestic violence program provides a 24-hour hot line, safe shelter for women and their children, supportive advocacy during legal procedures, such as obtaining orders of protection, and networking with social services. Information is provided about the dynamics of battering and the cycle of violence. In daily shelter interaction and support groups women share their experiences, thus breaking their isolation. Counseling provides a safe, confidential place for women to express their feelings and to make choices about their lives. Child advocacy services emphasize the effect of violence on children and offer parenting skills, if necessary. Many domestic violence programs have counseling services for abusive men.

The experiences of shelter programs and research studies have contributed to a growing body of knowledge about violence between intimates. The problem of battering crosses all socioeconomic and racial boundaries; however, younger women and women living in poverty are at greater risk. Battering may be of a physical, psychological, or sexual nature. Physical abuse may be shoving, slapping, punching, choking, biting, injuring with an object or weapon. It can also include abandonment in an isolated area, throwing the victim from a moving vehicle, or holding her at knifepoint Physical abuse may include focused blows to the abdomen, especially if the victim is pregnant. Women seeking assistance may have sustained cuts, bruises, black eyes, broken bones, or internal injuries. These injuries can result in hospitalization and death. Psychological abuse takes the form of continual verbal degradation of women and their capabilities, threats to physically injure or kill, threats to withdraw financial support for her and any children, threats to take children away from her. Constant policing of her actions and questioning her behaviors and decisions all can have an incapacitating effect. Sexual abuse can be the forcing of participation in nondesired sexual acts, violence directed at genitals and breasts, and rape. In domestic violence where children are present, it is not uncommon for children to be forced to watch and listen to the abuse of their mothers. Children may also be physically or sexually abused. Children often witness their pets being killed.

Although research continues, some studies report that battering men may have low self-esteem. Those who batter tend to believe in the traditional role expectations that place men in a dominant position in the family. They may believe that they are justified and have permission to control their family by whatever means deemed necessary. Battering men tend to be jealous and blame others for their problems. They exhibit heightened levels of denial and minimization of abusive behaviors. These abusive behaviors are choices for which many battering men refuse to take responsibility. They may or may not abuse while drinking alcohol. Although alcohol and drugs may contribute to the level of violence, they may become convenient excuses to unleash violence or to later avoid responsibility for their actions. Battering men frequently have been raised in homes where they witnessed or experienced abuse themselves. Motivation to change is often not present in men who batter.

Battered women are victims of violent crime, yet many stay in, or return to, abusive relationships. This behavior has been grossly misunderstood, as clinicians in the past speculated that these women enjoyed the abuse. More is now known about the dynamics of abuse and reasons for the pattern of leaving and returning. The reasons can vary with the duration of the relationship. Early in the relationship it may be hopefulness and love; later it may become economic dependence, lack of housing and transportation, and lack of employment opportunities or job skills. Women may have limited support from family and friends who have become exhausted by the pattern of leaving and returning. They may fear loss of their children and retaliation for having dared to attempt to leave. They may know that the majority of women who are killed by their abusive partner are killed when attempting to leave. Women with financial resources may have different barriers to leaving. They may fear loss of status, style of life, or educational opportunities for their children. They may be able to flee to a hotel or relocate if abuse threatens or until injuries heal. Women are taught that they are responsible for their partner's behaviors and happiness. They believe their partner's judgment that the abuse is deserved and provoked by them. While many women victims come from families where manipulation, intimidation, and battering have been accepted patterns in relationships between men and women, many victims have not. Religious and cultural constraints may reinforce their belief that the marriage must be kept intact. Most women love their partners and hope that they will cease to abuse them. The loving and remorse-filled days that follow a violent attack reinforce the belief that change will occur and be lasting this time. Counseling may be sought as a means to end the violence.

Battered women experience several stages. Initially, they deny the abuse or its severity. When they acknowledge the abuse, women blame themselves and hope for change. At some point they may seek help by choice, following law enforcement intervention and referral, or after being forced to flee in the middle of the night. At this time, the woman may gain information and enhancement of survival skills. This can result in increased self-confidence. Safe from the abuser and his continual influence, she may learn that violence is a crime, that he is responsible for his own actions, and that she and her children deserve to be safe.

References. Howard Davidson, *The Impact of Domestic Violence on Children: A Report to the President of the American Bar Association* (Washington, D.C., 1994); E. W. Gondolf, "Who Are These Guys? Toward a Behavioral Typology of Batterers," *Violence and Victims* 3 (1988): 187–203; M. Koss, L. Goodman, A. Browne, L. Fitzgerald, G. Puryear Keita, and N. Russo, *No Safe Haven: Male Vi-*

olence against Women at Home, at Work and in the Community (Washington, D.C., 1994); M. D. Pagelow, *Family Violence* (New York, 1984); Erin Pizzey, *Scream Quietly or the Neighbors Will Hear* (London, 1974); Lenore Walker, *Battered Women* (New York, 1979).

KATHERINE ST. JOHN and SYLVIA ROBERTSON

BETROTHAL is a formal agreement of marriage* at a later date made between the parties whose consent is necessary for the marriage to take place. In many premodern societies the betrothal was legally necessary for a valid marriage and could be as binding. After the financial and other arrangements were decided upon by the husband-to-be or his guardian and the guardian of the wife-to-be, a public betrothal, involving ceremonial acts (e.g., pouring perfume over the girl's head in ancient Mesopotamia; placing an iron ring on her finger in ancient Rome), took place. The marriage, sometimes occurring without further formality, might follow within a few weeks or, in the case of infant betrothals, not for years.

In some societies the couple did not have the right to refuse marriage (e.g., India, Greece); in others, they could, at least theoretically, refuse consent (e.g., Hebrew, Roman). In Roman and medieval law generally the betrothed couple had to be old enough to understand what was being said (age 7) and could not be forced to marry without their consent. However, many infant betrothals are recorded, and young men could much more easily evade marriage than could young women. In Rome a girl could refuse marriage only if she could prove the young man morally unfit. Under Germanic law, a daughter could not escape from a betrothal entered into by a parent on her behalf.

Through the early modern period betrothal remained a binding contract. In rural areas in Europe and America and in other cultures throughout the world many young couples began sexual relations after betrothal, but generally this was not considered a serious offense. However, for a betrothed person to have relations with a third party could be considered adultery,* for which the penalty was severe.

Betrothal could be dissolved for cause or by mutual consent of the young man and the woman's guardian, but unilateral failure to honor the contract could have serious consequences. Even when betrothal was not legally required for a valid marriage, as in England, a suit for breach of promise could be brought against a man for defaulting on a betrothal. In the United States 28 states still recognize breach of promise suits, although some have limited the recovery of damages.

Where the arranged marriage has given way to the marriage of choice, and where dowry* or bridegift* is not a concern, the betrothal, with its signification of parental control and family alliances, has disappeared, sometimes being merged into the marriage ceremony (e.g., Russian Orthodox, Judaic), generally leaving behind a residue of customs and informal practices.

BIOLOGICAL DETERMINISM. See SOCIOBIOLOGY

BIOPSY. A biopsy is removing living tissue from the body and subjecting sections of it to microscopic examination. Biopsies can be performed on almost any tissue and are done whenever there is a possibility that cancer* might be present. In women tissue from the breast, cervix, cervical canal, vulva, and endometrium, along with skin growths, are most frequently subject to biopsy. The procedure is used whenever an abnormal Pap smear* or the discovery of a lump in the breast indicates the need for examination. It is used during cancer operations to try to determine whether the cancer has spread beyond the area known to be involved. Endometrial biopsies are also useful in diagnosing menstrual and infertility problems.

Methods include, among others, scraping cells with a spoonlike curette (as in endocervical and endometrial curettage), inserting a needle into a lump in the breast and aspirating the fluid, or, with hard lumps, using a hollow needle to withdraw the core of the tumor (needle biopsy) or by surgical procedure. Tissue is sent to a pathology laboratory, where it is sectioned and examined. Most procedures can be performed in the doctor's office under local anesthesia.

Formerly, when breast cancer was suspected, a one-step procedure was used. The woman was prepared for surgery and given a general anesthesia; the biopsy was performed; the excised material was sent to the laboratory, where it was sectioned, and one or more sections quick-frozen and examined. Within 10 to 15 minutes word was sent back to the operating room, and if cancer was present, an immediate operation was performed. The woman did not know when she went under anesthesia whether she would wake up with one breast or two.

A two-step procedure is preferable and can be used for almost all biopsies unless the tissue is so deep that major surgery is necessary to get to the tissue (e.g., in ovarian biopsies). There should be no need for a one-step procedure in breast cancer. With the two-step method, biopsy is an outpatient procedure. A permanent section, which takes several days, is done. It is more accurate and yields more information. With more time and information, the woman can better make informed decisions about the need for further tests or for getting a second opinion and about the type of treatment to be used.

BIRTH CONTROL. See CONTRACEPTIVES

BIRTHING ALTERNATIVES (ALTERNATIVE BIRTH MOVEMENT).

The development in the United States of a range of choices in childbearing services and techniques in contrast to, and as a critique of, an essentially monolithic, highly mechanized Western health care system has largely shaped prevailing patterns of childbirth.* Many choices are based on evaluation of nonmedical traditions for management of childbirth in the United States as well as on identification and examination of management modalities in non-Western cultures. In general, alternatives are to (1) hospital-based birth, insofar as that implies loss of maternal autonomy in the childbearing experience; (2) escalating costs of childbirth; and (3) what can be perceived as an inadequate response to the universal sense of physical and psychosocial vulnerability experienced by mothers and significant others at the time of childbirth.

In the last 20 years, this movement has precipitated, and continues to precipitate, major changes in the management of childbirth. Major categories of choice, or alternatives, while not discrete, are birth setting, childbirth attendants, birth position, and pharmacologic and technologic support.

Setting. The model is the home, rather than the hospital; the rationale, that childbearing is best experienced in a setting that is, or approximates, the context of the childbearing woman's life and that maintains nonseparation of the infant from the mother and significant others. Alternatives range from home birth through birth centers and birthing rooms. Birth centers are freestanding or hospital-affiliated. The model and demonstration project for freestanding birth centers, the Maternity Center Association, New York, has demonstrated that safety can be maintained and cost-effectiveness accomplished for healthy women and infants attended by certified nurse-midwives. Hospital-based birth alternatives may be autonomous, though contiguous, birth centers but in some settings may be birthing rooms in labor and delivery suites. In the former, essentially the same principles apply as in freestanding centers; in the latter, labor, birth, and immediate recovery take place in one room, after which time mothers and infants may be moved to separate hospital areas (postpartum suites for mothers and newborn nurseries for infants). In some settings mothers and infants are not moved from the room of birth; in these instances the birth setting is usually referred to as a single-unit delivery system (SUDS).

Childbirth Attendants. A case can be made for differing emphases between nursing/midwifery and medicine relative to childbirth. Because the tradition and science of nursing and midwifery* emphasize holism and health as characteristic of human reproductive phenomena, therapeutics is based on maintenance and enhancement of the social, cultural, and physiologic protective mechanisms surrounding childbearing. By contrast, because emphases in the tradition and science of Western medicine have been on detection and treatment of disease, therapeutics is based on employment of diagnostic methodologies and technologies to discover and correct instances of disease or dysfunction in mother and fetus/infant.

A third category of birth attendant is the lay midwife or attendant who acquires training* by experience and/or apprenticeship and who sees her role as "standing by" or being "with woman" (the generic meanings of obstetrics and midwifery, respectively). The rationale commonly employed by those selecting lay attendants is that there is, thereby, no influence of pathology-oriented training (which some perceive to extend to formally trained and licensed nurses and midwives) that can result in use of technologies judged to be nonphysiologic, invasive, unnecessary, inhumane, unsafe, or otherwise inconsistent with maternal autonomy in childbearing.

While birth attendants can function in a variety of settings, the usual pattern is that lay- or nurse-midwives attend home births and nurse-midwives and/or physicians, plus nurses, attend women in birth centers and birthing rooms.

Birth Position. Rather than adhering to a single standard position (i.e., dorsal lithotomy [lying prone with legs elevated]), alternative birth settings, by their lack of limitation of hospital equipment, facilitate the mother's use of whatever activity or position she perceives to be most beneficial for herself and her infant. Research indicates that maternal freedom of movement during labor and some variation of upright position for birth (e.g., standing, squatting, sitting) are safe for both mother and infant and produce the least risk of iatrogenic (therapy-induced) circulatory complications for both.

Pharmacologic and Technologic Support. Concern is with the routine, nondiscriminate employment of any or all anesthetic, analgesic, amnesic, or stimulant medications and routine use of attendant-dominated technologies (e.g., continuous or intermittent electronic fetal monitoring equipment, stirrups, high-technology infant care equipment) that interfere with spontaneous processes of labor, birth, and recovery; that shift control over the childbearing experience from the mother and significant others to the birth attendant(s); and/or that pose a threat to the safety of the mother and infant. Although some kind of technology, however simple, is a concomitant of most birth settings worldwide, the general approach in alternative birth settings is to employ minimum, or no, medication and simple technologies.

VBAC. An emerging development that might be considered under the aegis of birthing alternatives is vaginal birth after previous cesarean birth (VBAC). The rationale for VBAC, in addition to the philosophic bases for other birthing alternatives, is threefold:

1. Surgical technique for cesarean birth that involves cutting the uterus in the lower, noncontractile portion does not jeopardize contractile activity in subsequent labors.

2. Frequently, reasons for cesarean management of childbirth are not necessarily repeatable (e.g., breech presentation; "failure to progress" as a diagnosis). "Failure to progress," in particular, reflects the fact that the etiology of the onset and progress of labor remains incompletely understood, and there is little reason to presume that the conduct of one labor will be repeated in subsequent labors.

3. Vaginal birth after cesarean birth, other things being equal, is safer than repeat cesarean birth for both mother and infant.

Criticism. Negative criticism of the alternative birth movement usually proceeds from the premise that advances in Western medical science have decreased maternal and infant morbidity and mortality, that issues of maternal and infant safety cannot be adequately addressed outside the hospital setting, and that not all women enter childbearing in a healthy state. Each of these issues (including the last, which may seem the most incontrovertible) requires reexamination and clarification to determine its accuracy, validity, and applicability. For those reasons most responsible practitioners in the United States view the alternative birth movement as an opportunity to engage in ongoing evaluation of the premises on which the care of childbearing women and their infants is based.

References. B. Jordan, *Birth in Four Cultures* (Montreal, 1983); J. W. Mold and H. F. Stein, "The Cascade Effect in the Clinical Care of Patients," *New England Journal of Medicine* 314 (1986): 512–514; National Association of Childbearing Centers, Box 1, RD #1, Perkiomenville, Pa. 18074.

MARY ANN ZETTELMAIER

BISEXUALITY within the feminist community is often defined as the sexual orientation* of women who devote their primary energy to other women but whose affectional and sexual preference includes both women and men.

Bisexuality was recognized in the early sex research of Alfred Kinsey at Indiana University as including more persons than homosexuality. Kinsey viewed sexual orientation on a continuum from those who preferred exclusively same-sex partners to those who preferred exclusively opposite-sex partners, with most persons falling along the range rather than at the poles. Other views of sexuality recognize the complexity of sexual identity and expression. Rather than polar models, concrete boundaries, and fixed identity through time, it may be more helpful to acknowledge seeming contradictions, change throughout the life span, and the effects of oppression, privilege, social constraints, and political movements on sexuality.

Women who name themselves bisexual often get criticism from both the community-at-large and the lesbian community. Homophobia (fear of homosexuality) and especially the threat that lesbian relationships present to male dominance affect bisexual women as well as lesbian women. Lesbian women sometimes criticize bisexual women for being in transition and not yet accepting their "true" sexuality (assumed to be lesbian by the lesbian community), for being unable to decide between men and women, for stealing energy from the lesbian community, for seducing lesbian women without exclusive commitment to women, for exploiting heterosexual privilege.

Support groups for bisexual women are often well attended but cloistered because of the vulnerability women feel about the issues surrounding bisexuality.

During the era of HIV disease (human immunosuppressive virus), the term "bisexual" has come to be associated with people who provide a conduit of HIV virus between the gay and larger communities. If they engage in unsafe sexual practices, bisexual men are in a position to transmit the HIV virus to women in heterosexual interactions. However, bisexual women are at greater risk themselves because of their interactions with men.

ELAINE WHEELER

BLACK ARTISTS. See AFRICAN AMERICAN ARTISTS

BLACK WOMEN AND FEMINISM. A long tradition of black female competence, leadership, and self-determination forms the bases of black women's relationship to feminism. Black women have shared many of the general concerns of the women's movement such as suffrage and education in the nineteenth century and equal pay and child care* in the twentieth. Yet they have not readily identified with a movement defined in terms of the experiences of white, middle-class women, nor have they participated en masse in its organizations and activities. Their absence is not, as often mistakenly assumed, from a lack of feminist consciousness* but rather from their invisibility within, and the racism of, the movement's ideology and politics. Black feminist thought, organizations, and activism have existed and continue to exist independent of the women's movement. Black feminism is an active commitment to struggle against the multiple and simultaneous oppressions black women face and is articulated through the perspectives of African American women's cultural heritage.

Patricia Hill Collins (S14-S32) has identified three recurring themes in black feminist thought: (1) the affirmation of self-definitions and self-valuations; (2) attention to the interlocking nature of race, gender, and class oppressions; and (3) an awareness of the cultural heritage that has enabled generations of black women to resist these discriminations. The first theme stresses the importance of black women's establishing positive individual and collective images; discovering their own perspective on their life circumstances; and applying their own standards of beauty, thought, and action. In asserting self-determination, a single black female perspective, image, or feminism is not presumed. Just as the realities of black women's lives differ, so, too, does the acceptable range of their political and social expression. Maria Stewart, perhaps the first woman to speak publicly in this nation, wrote in 1831 of the importance of black women describing and naming themselves (see 183–200).

The second persistent theme in black feminism is the recognition of the multiple jeopardies of race, class, gender, and sexuality that circumscribe black women's lives. Anna Julia Cooper, who was born in slavery in 1858 and became a noted educator, earning a Ph.D. at the age of 63, spoke of black women's being "doubly enslaved" and of their confronting both "the women question and a race problem" (see selections from her writings in Loewenberg and Bogin and in Lerner). Today, black female scholars and writers still examine the issue of these dual discriminations. (See DOUBLE JEOPARDY.) This acknowledgment of simultaneous oppressions necessitates a more encompassing, humanist vision in their feminist theorizing. Black women have continually insisted that their liberation must entail the liberation of all black people. At the First National Conference of Colored Women in 1895, activist Josephine St. Pierre Ruffin stated, "Our woman's movement is a woman's movement that is led and directed by women for the good of women and men, for the benefit of all humanity, which is more than any one branch or section of it" (see Lerner, 440–443).

This note of universalism is heard in the voices of contemporary black feminists such as bell hooks, who states that "feminism . . . is a commitment to eradicating the ideology of domination that permeates Western culture on various levels—sex, race, and class, to name a few—and a commitment to reorganizing U.S. society so that the self-development of people can take precedence over imperialism, economic expansion, and material desires" (194).

Black feminism always entails a recognition of community. Feminist concerns are manifest in work for religious, health, educational, cultural, and other community institutions through such organizations as the National Association of Colored Women and the National Council of Negro Women. In the economic arena, black women have organized mutual benefit associations like the Independent Order of Saint Luke, which founded the longest continuously operating black bank in the country, labor unions such as the Tobacco Workers Union, and community development foundations.

A recognition of black feminism's historical origins in African American women's culture is the third theme. Black females learn skills, values, and attitudes for maintaining collective efforts and perpetuating positive self-concepts. The wisdom born of resistance has encouraged the development of dignity, strength, independence, and imagination, which have continued through generations (see Davis). Through informal work, local service groups, and a national club movement, black women labor together seeking emancipation. Their political activism and savvy were developed in such groups as the Women's Era Club of Boston, founded in the 1890s, which, through its newsletter, *The Women's Era*, denounced lynching and advocated woman suffrage; the Combahee River Collective (1974); the National Black Feminist Organization (1973); the National Political Congress of Black Women (1984); and the Black Women's Liberation Committee of the Student Non-Violent Coordinating Committee.

This collective consciousness is preserved, studied, and shared through the scholarship of black feminists. There are black women's courses, programs, and conferences; research centers such as the Center for Research on Women at Memphis State University or the National Institute on Women of Color in Washington, D.C.; journals such as *Sage: A Scholarly Journal on Black Women*; and publishing companies such as Kitchen Table: Women of Color Press. A decidedly pro-woman culture enriches and empowers black women to create choices even in the face of external constraints.

The historical continuity of black feminist expressions can be traced from the 1833 address of Maria Stewart, "What If I Am a Woman," to Sojourner Truth's famous "Ain't I a Woman?" speech in 1851, to Amy Garvey's 1925 editorial "Women as Leaders," to Alice Walker's "womanist,"* a concept that comes closest to encompassing the range of ideologies and praxis of black women's feminism: "A womanist acknowledges the particularistic experiences and cultural heritage of black women, resists systems of domination, and insists on the liberty and self-determination of all people" (quoted from Womanist, Womanism, Womanish, *infra*).

References. Patricia Hill Collins, "Learning from the Outside Within: The Sociological Significance of Black Women's Feminist Thought," *Social Problems* 33 (1986); Angela Davis, *Women, Race and Class* (New York, 1983); bell hooks, *Ain't I a Woman: Black Women and Feminism* (Boston, 1981); G. I. Joseph and J. Lewis, *Common Differences: Conflicts in Black and White Feminist Perspectives* (New York, 1982); Gerda Lerner, *Black Women in White America: A Documentary History* (New York, 1972); Bert James Loewenberg and Ruth Bogin (eds.), *Black Women in Nineteenth-Century American Life* (University Park, Pa., 1976); B. Smith (ed.), *Home Girls: A Black Feminist Anthology* (New York, 1983); Alice Walker, *In Search of Our Mothers' Gardens: Womanist Prose* (San Diego, 1983).

DEBORAH K. KING

BLACK WRITERS. See AFRICAN AMERICAN POETS; AFRICAN AMERICAN PROSE WRITERS

BLOOMSBURY GROUP. A loose association based on close friendship, of writers, painters, critics, and economic and political theorists in London's Bloomsbury; its women members included the sisters Virginia Woolf (1882–1941) and Vanessa Bell (1879–1961). Although its own participants and later historians all disagree about its exact nature, time span, and very membership, the Bloomsbury group strongly influenced British fiction, biography, art, criticism, economics, and politics in the 1920s and 1930s.

While its members insisted that they gathered for conviviality and conversation and that they embraced no single philosophy or aesthetic, their ideas and attitudes overlapped in complex patterns. Detractors of the group saw its members as snobbish intellectuals who scoffed at artistic, social, and sexual conventions.

The group, mostly children of eminent Victorians, began in 1904 around the four children of Julia and Leslie Stephen, Vanessa, Thoby, Virginia, and Adrian. Thoby welcomed his Cambridge friends, especially Lytton Strachey, Clive Bell, Desmond MacCarthy, and Saxon Sydney-Turner; slightly later, Molly MacCarthy, Duncan Grant, Roger Fry, Leonard Woolf, and Maynard Keynes completed the stable core.

Friendship was highly valued and became accepted as possible between men and women. Eroticism never permanently damaged friendship, although openly acknowledged heterosexual and homosexual liaisons recombined often over the years. Of the women, Virginia Woolf was closest to Vanessa Bell, Lytton Strachey, and Leonard Woolf, to whom she was happily married, although she was in love at different times with women such as Violet Dickinson and Vita Sackville-West. Vanessa Bell married Clive and had two sons. She then had an intense affair with Roger Fry before settling permanently with Duncan Grant, who was primarily homosexual and with whom she had one daughter. Bell and Fry remained her loyal friends.

The individual achievements of the Bloomsbury Group are impressive, and Virginia Woolf was one of its most brilliant members. Her best-known novels were written in her middle period. *Mrs. Dalloway* (1925) follows a day in Clarissa Dalloway's life while shifting among characters' minds and memories to elicit the whole beneath the surface. *To the Lighthouse* (1927) is both critical portrait of Woolf's stifling patriarchal family and lyrical tribute to an angelically giving mother and a gifted father. Woolf then romped through English history in *Orlando* (1928), which celebrated Woolf's love for Vita Sackville-West. *The Waves* (1931) presented phases from the lives of six consciousnesses in a stylized, dramatic form. In these novels Woolf experimented with narrative form, voice, and style. Her recurrent themes include the importance of androgyny; absence, decay, and death, which are barely opposed by human creativity and love; and the opposition of fact and truth, the latter being attainable through art and during mystical moments of vision or being or unity. She often used the imagery of houses, the ocean and flora, and the structure of natural cycles.

Woolf's other novels include *The Voyage Out* (1915) and *Night and Day* (1919), which are now attracting feminist criticism for their biographical implications and their submerged feminist agendas; *Jacob's Room* (1922), Woolf's first experiment with form; *The Years* (1937), a historical novel; and *Between the Acts* (1941).

Besides her novels, Woolf also wrote several short stories, two biographies, and volumes of diaries and letters. She regularly reviewed books for the *Times Literary Supplement* and wrote elegant essays on subjects ranging from the Greeks to contemporary fiction.

Although Woolf never considered herself a political activist, because she believed that as an artist she was unable to influence society directly, she did over the years work quietly for the Women's Co-operative Guild and the woman suffrage* cause. Her major direct contribution to feminism, however, came in two essays. *A Room of One's Own* (1929), an essay on "women and fiction," calls for androgynous, enriched writing from both sexes, while pointing out that women will require what men have had, income, privacy, and education, to release the "Shakespeare's sister" within them. *Three Guineas* (1938) is more direct, more strident. Woolf links the patriarchal oppression of women with the black threat of Hitler's fascism.

The strain of the war that followed added to profound unhappiness with her current fiction writing, and fear of another bout of madness, which had plagued her intermittently since her mother's death in 1895, drove her to suicide in the River Ouse in March 1941.

Vanessa Bell was as dedicated and prolific a painter and designer as her sister was a writer, although Bell never achieved similar fame and is not now considered a major talent. Having studied briefly with Sir Arthur Cope and then with John Singer Sargent at the Royal Academy Schools from 1901 to 1904, she came in 1910 under the influence of Picasso, Derain, and especially Matisse, whose color, curvilinear shapes, and decorative approach to painting appealed to her.

From 1910 to 1920, Bell was at the forefront of English postimpressionism. She exhibited four paintings at the Second Post-Impressionist Exhibition (1912), which stormed London. In her landscapes, still lifes, and portraits, with subjects drawn from her own surroundings, experience, and friends, she concentrated on flat color areas and on the formal relationships within each picture.

Design also interested her. She decorated Virginia Woolf's books and others at the Woolfs' Hogarth Press. In 1913, she became codirector of Roger Fry's Omega Workshops and decorated furniture, textiles, pottery, murals, and interiors, often in collaboration with Duncan Grant. After 1920, Bell's work returned to a more conventional impressionism, but she remained concerned with formal relationships and color. In the 1920s she exhibited with the London group and later at the Anthony d'Offay Gallery and the Lefevre Gallery. Posthumous shows include those at the Adams Gallery, London (1961), the Arts Council Gallery, London (1964), and Davis and Long Company, New York (1980).

Vanessa Bell was not an active feminist, but, having totally rejected conventional society, she led a radically free personal life. Strachey considered her the most complete human being of the Bloomsbury Group.

The last woman member of Bloomsbury was Molly (Mary Warre-

Cornish) MacCarthy (1882–1953), married to Desmond; she who wrote the popular book *A Nineteenth-Century Childhood* (1924) and who founded for Bloomsbury the highly successful Memoir Club, devoted to frank, personal reminiscence.

Three other women were peripheral to Bloomsbury. Karin Costelloe Stephen (1889–1953), married to Adrian Stephen, practiced psychoanalysis and published *The Wish to Fall Ill: A Study of Psychoanalysis and Medicine* (1933, 1960). Dora Carrington (1893–1932) was a promising Slade School–trained painter. She worshiped Lytton Strachey from 1915 and relinquished her own identity to become his platonic companion until his death and her subsequent suicide in 1932. Lydia Lopokova (1892–1981) was a Russian-born ballerina with the Imperial Russian Ballet and Diaghilev's company; she married Maynard Keynes in 1925.

Many non-Bloomsbury people are now associated in the public mind with some Bloomsbury member. These include Lady Ottoline Morrell (1873–1938), a wealthy patron of the arts who ran a salon; Vita Sackville-West (1892–1962), a poet, novelist, and gardener; and Dame Ethel Smyth (1858–1944), composer, conductor, feminist, memorialist, and ardent admirer of Virginia Woolf in the 1930s. Smyth, imprisoned in 1911 for militant suffrage activities, composed the campaign song "The March of the Women."

References. Elizabeth Abel, "Narrative Structure(s) and Female Development: The Case of *Mrs. Dalloway*," in Elizabeth Abel, Marianne Hirsch, and Elizabeth Langland (eds.), *The Voyage In: Fictions of Female Development* (Hanover, N.H., 1983), 161–185; Quentin Bell, *Virginia Woolf: A Biography* (New York, 1972); Jane Marcus (ed.), *New Feminist Essays on Virginia Woolf* (Lincoln, Neb., 1981); Frances Spalding, *Vanessa Bell* (New Haven, Conn., 1983).

ANNE S. HIGHAM

BLUES. A solo black folk music (contrasting to the group music of the spiritual) that developed after the Civil War out of male southern field-workers' hollers and street cries and spread throughout the South and Midwest by male itinerant musicians. By the 1900s traveling tent and vaudeville shows included acts featuring young, black, female blues singers. The blues, with their plaintive melodies using flatted thirds and sevenths, were taken up by brass bands and orchestras in New Orleans, which were already playing syncopated rag tunes, and became an essential element of jazz. (See JAZZ: THROUGH THE 1950s.) Southern women dominated blues performance and recording in the decade of the 1920s, the classic blues era.

Gertrude Pridgett ("Ma") Rainey, the "Mother of the Blues," stayed close to country blues style, even though, on tours with the Theater Owners' Booking Agency (TOBA) ("tough on black ass," as the entertainers called it), she wore flamboyant satin gowns and jewelry of real gold coins. She recorded 92 sides.

Bessie Smith, the greatest of the early blues and vaudeville singers, traveled like Rainey in tent shows and with TOBA. Writing many songs herself, Smith, the highest-paid black entertainer of her time, soon headed her stage shows as the "Empress of the Blues," carrying Rainey's country blues and her own humorous vaudeville tunes into the big theaters of Atlanta, New York, Philadelphia, and Chicago. She made 160 records for Columbia (all reissued in 1970), accompanied by such jazz greats as Louis Armstrong, Don Redman, and James P. Johnson.

Ida Cox ranks third among the classic blues singers because of her unique style and impressive career: composer of almost 100 songs and performer in road shows for nearly 50 years.

Other important vocalists of this blues decade include Mamie Smith, the first black vocalist to record a blues; Clara Smith, "The World's Champion Moaner" (there were 13 Smiths who recorded blues, all unrelated); Sara Martin, who recorded more than 130 songs; Sippie Wallace, the "Texas Nightingale," wailing high C blues; Victoria Spivey, the "Texas Moaner," playing organ, piano, and ukulele, briefly owning her own club, establishing her own jazz/blues label, and performing until the year of her death; Alberta Hunter, first black singer to record with a white band, not restricted to singing blues and jazz, performing in New York nightclubs and European cabarets; Edith Wilson, appealing to white patrons in Broadway houses more than to blacks, popular on both sides of the Atlantic; Ethel Waters, "Sweet Mama Stringbean," singing popular music as well as vaudeville tunes and the blues, with an enduring career on stage and screen; Memphis Minnie and Lucille Bogan, country blues; Lizzie Miles, Creole songs and vaudeville ballads as well as blues; Lucille Hegamin and her Blue Flame Syncopaters.

Performers strongly influenced by the blues though not generally considered blues or jazz singers include Sophie Tucker, Mae West, Helen Morgan, and Ruth Etting.

Carrying the blues into the 1940s were Bertha ("Chippie") Hill, Blue Lu Barker, and Lil Green.

Rhythm and Blues (R&B). R&B was a new name announced in *Billboard* in 1949 for "race" records (blues and jazz intended for sale in black communities). R&B music offers more 16- than 12-bar blues and more varied harmonies and uses new electrical instruments to emphasize bass lines. Julia Lee and Dinah Washington were rhythm and blues stars. Lee reigned over the blues in Kansas City for 40 years with numerous Top Ten hits on the R&B charts, accompanying herself on piano, often with a boogie beat. Washington, "Miss D," the "Queen of the Blues," recorded 450 songs in 20 years of singing, with numerous R&B Top Ten hits and unique interpretations of pop songs. In the 1960s and 1970s Willie Mae ("Big Mama") Thornton, dancer, comedian, singer, and composer, brought new life to the blues, inspiring Janis Lyn Joplin (as did Leadbelly, Odetta, and

Bessie Smith) to her fiery, intensely emotional delivery. In the 1970s and 1980s Linda Hopkins toured with her *Me and Bessie* show, based on Bessie Smith songs, and Koko Taylor reached audiences in clubs, on radio, and in U.S. and European concerts.

Blues Lyrics Sung by Women. Written by women and men to express sorrow caused by poverty, frustrating work, imprisonment, unfaithful lovers, and natural disasters such as floods, boll weevils, tuberculosis, old age, death; the majority concerned mistreatment by lovers. Many of Ma Rainey's earliest lyrics describe the misery of a passive, suffering woman, accepting any kind of treatment from a man, with no hope to change her life; or the desperation of a woman deserted by her man, obsessed with the need to get another one, any kind of man. By the 1920s, many blues lyrics exhibit a woman's awakening to the possibility of different responses to a man's mistreatment, a change from passive acceptance to active resistance. The focus remains, however, on male–female relationships. A woman whose man is unfaithful may return to her family, seek a fortune-teller to help her reclaim her man, stay with him but take on another lover, or give him up completely and move on to a new man. She may become aggressive, kill her female rivals, or, the ultimate revenge, kill him. Whatever choice she makes, her realistic, resilient humor underlies her complaints, enabling the singer to laugh ironically at herself and her desire for a man.

The blues queens of the 1920s enlarged the themes of the blues, in non-blues vaudeville tunes that they often wrote themselves, to declare a woman's hard-won freedom from a man's mistreatment, based on her new financial independence. Now able to pay her own household bills, she requires two actions of any man she allows to be around: to share his money with her and to be faithful to her; otherwise, she kicks him out. If the man cannot perform sexually on cue, she may cruelly taunt him with being nothing but a good old wagon that's broken down and needs an overhaul. This frank new woman does not promise faithfulness to male or female friends. If she wants a friend's beau, she may go after him, take him part-time when she can get him, and try to make him all hers. Or she may adopt infidelity as a way of life and keep several men around. By not getting too emotionally involved with any one man, she has no blues if one misbehaves. A few independent women kick all men out of their lives and exult in their freedom from the ball and chain of marriage, from the male demand for a maid, nurse, mama, and lover in one. Some even suggest a preference for another woman.

The realistic depiction of male–female relationships and the independent attitudes of women expressed in blues and vaudeville lyrics of the 1920s contrast sharply with the romanticized expressions of happy fidelity and uncomplicated love in the popular music of the period, where female submissiveness to mistreatment remains a constant theme. A wife begs her wandering husband to please come home, accepts all blame for his leaving, and hopes he won't be mean to her, because she loves him, even when he beats her. By the 1930s and 1940s some popular music and Broadway songs reduce the adult female in love to a simpering, whimpering, childlike person whose heart belongs to her Daddy dear in exchange for the financial and emotional support he provides. This arrangement contrasts vividly with the straightforward sexual pleasure anticipated, indeed demanded, by the lyrics of the lusty blues.

References. Daphne Duval Harrison, *Black Pearls: Blues Queens of the 1920s* (New Brunswick, N.J., 1988); Sandra Lieb, *Mother of the Blues: A Study of Ma Rainey* (Amherst, Mass., 1981); Rosetta Reitz, Liner Notes for Records in Women's Heritage Series, Rosetta Records (New York, 1980–1987).

JEAN KITTRELL

BLUESTOCKINGS. This is a name applied, for about a century (c. 1750–c. 1850), to Englishwomen who had, or who affected to have, literary and other intellectual interests. The term implied that such women were unfeminine, careless of their appearance, and neglectful of their proper domestic role.

The term itself refers to men's plain worsted stockings, usually blue or gray, and was first used to deride men who wore worsted instead of black silk stockings in public. The Little Parliament (aka Barebones Parliament) of 1653, made up of 140 Puritan worthies nominated by the independent churches, was also referred to as the Bluestocking Parliament.

"Bluestocking" came to be applied to women, apparently because Mr. Benjamin Stillingfleet, one of the scholars who attended Mrs. Elizabeth Montagu's "conversation parties," often showed up not in proper evening attire. From 1750, Mrs. Elizabeth Montagu (1720–1800), in her bid to be London's social leader, began giving evening assemblies at which card playing, the usual entertainment, was replaced by conversations on literary topics. Other hostesses followed her lead, and some say Admiral Boscawen, husband of one of them, derisively dubbed the "conversation party" the Bluestocking Society. The name was proudly taken up by the women who attended these salons, and "bluestocking ladies," "bluestockingers," or simply "blues" came to be used to designate, first, female habitués of the literary salons, then, any woman who dared to show interest in other than trivial subjects outside her proper domestic sphere.

In her 50 years as undisputed leader of intellectual society, Mrs. Montagu is credited with helping to introduce a healthier note into London society by breaking the grip of card playing (and its attendant gambling) on social occasions. Regular guests at her evenings included Horace Walpole, Samuel Johnson, Sir Joshua Reynolds, and Edmund Burke. Women writers Elizabeth Carter (1717–1806), Hester Chapone (1727–1801) and younger contemporaries Fanny Burney (1732–1840) and Hannah More (1745–1833), leading bluestocking of the next generation, were members of her circle. Among other bluestocking hostesses were the Mesdames Boscawen, Vesey,

Ord, and Greville and Dorothy Bentwick, duchess of Portland. Hannah
More celebrated Mrs. Montagu's beneficent effect on society in her 1781
poem "Bas Blue."

In the early nineteenth century the term was used with frequency and
condescension by reviewers of women writers. Lord Byron's satire "The
Blues: A Literary Epilogue" (1821) pours ridicule on bluestocking hostesses
and the male writers who frequented their salons.

BOARDINGHOUSE KEEPING has been an important income-producing
occupation for women who did not wish to or could not work outside the
home. It became particularly significant in the period between 1840 and
1940 in industrializing nations. In this period, when married and widowed
women found working outside the home both difficult and distasteful,
boardinghouse keeping permitted them to make money by the production
of household goods and services (cooking, cleaning, washing, etc.) for nonfamily members within the confines of their own homes.

Although women had traditionally cared for nonfamily members in their
households (indentured servants, apprentices and journeymen, orphans and
the aged of the community, etc.), before the early nineteenth century this
work had seldom been paid. As the importance of boarding rose with urbanization and industrialization, the opportunities for women to make
money doing this job rose as well. Because nineteenth-century boardinghouse keeping actually generated income, albeit through traditional female
activities done within a family context and for the family good, this occupation represented an important transitional stage for women between a
preindustrial household economy and modern wage labor. Women's willingness to engage in this occupation was of crucial importance in amelio-
rating a number of negative effects of rapid population growth and
urbanization (such as housing shortages, high rents, and the large number
of young people living away from parental discipline) that accompanied
industrialization in the nineteenth and early twentieth centuries.

Studies show that by the mid-1880s, in most industrializing cities in the
United States around 20 percent of families took in boarders or lodgers,
and in most of these households either the wife of the household head or
a widowed woman cared for them. Mining boom towns, industrial cities
that attracted a large percentage of young single men or women, and the
port cities through which most European immigrants passed offered even
greater opportunities for boardinghouse keeping. Boardinghouse keepers
presided over residences that ranged in size from very large hotel-like enterprises, where the husband and wife might both be engaged in running
the business, and several servants would help with the domestic tasks, to
small private households where one or two boarders would occupy spare
bedrooms. In Portland, Oregon, a rapidly growing western town in 1880,

the average number of boarders and lodgers served by female boarding-house keepers was seven.

Although census reports consistently undercounted this form of employ-ment for women, the importance of boarding- and lodginghouse keeping for married women can be seen in the fact that in 1855 in a working-class ward of New York City, 22 percent of all Irish married women kept one or more boarders, and 84 percent of the Irish married women who worked were boardinghouse keepers. In addition, a study of major West Coast cities found that in 1880 between 53 percent and 60 percent of all married working women were boarding- or lodginghouse keepers. The income that women could bring into the family by taking in boarders was equivalent to the income they could make in the jobs that were available outside the home to women in this period. Moreover, strong evidence from one study indicates that the income produced by women who took in boarders made up nearly one-third of their gross family incomes.

Boardinghouse keeping began to decline in importance as an occupation for women in the 1930s as the migration to cities began to slow, new residential alternatives like apartment buildings appeared, and housing con-struction began to catch up to population growth. Perhaps more important, middle-class reformers' strong belief in the importance of family privacy and the detrimental effects of permitting "strangers" into the household had gained acceptance throughout American society. The decreasing de-mand for the sort of service that boarding house keepers had provided and the growing unwillingness of families to take in boarders were accompanied by the expansion of other job opportunities for women during and after World War II. As a result, married and widowed women increasingly started to contribute to the family income by working outside the home.

References. J. M. Jensen, "Cloth, Butter and Boarders: Women's Household Pro-duction for the Market," *The Review of Radical Political Economics* 12 (1980): 14–24; J. Modell and T. K. Hareven, "Urbanization and the Malleable Household: An Examination of Boarding and Lodging in American Families," *Journal of Marriage and the Family* 35 (1973): 467–479.

MARY LOU LOCKE

BONA FIDE OCCUPATIONAL QUALIFICATION (BFOQ). In inter-
preting Title VII* of the Civil Rights Act of 1964, the Equal Employment Opportunity Commission (EEOC) has determined the extent to which sex can be considered a bona fide occupational qualification (BFOQ). Sex is a BFOQ if the employer can prove business necessity, but it is not to satisfy customer or employee preference. Neither marital status, existence of pre-school children, nor general assumptions about women's capabilities or commitment to the labor force may be a basis for failure to employ on the basis of sex.

A major problem in nondiscriminatory hiring was state protective legislation.* The EEOC Guidelines of 1968 affirmed the belief that Title VII did not overturn state differential legislation but refused to recognize a protective legislation BFOQ that was discriminatory rather than protective in effect. After the *Rosenfeld v. Southern Pacific Company* (293 F. Supp. 1219 CD Cal. 1968) decision struck down most state sex-specific laws, the guidelines read that when protective legislation conflicts with EEOC regulations, the regulations supersede. According to the 1972 guidelines, protective legislation must not be sex-specific but must cover all workers.

Without the EEOC's stringent interpretation of sex as a BFOQ, Title VII would have been meaningless insofar as combating discrimination* in the hiring of women is concerned.

DAYLE MANDELSON

BRAZIL WOMEN'S MOVEMENT developed by the early twentieth century, following scattered feminist activities dating to the mid-nineteenth century. Largely through the newspapers they edited, beginning with *O Jornal das Senhoras* (The Journal for Ladies), in the 1850s a small group of urban women endeavored to awaken other women to their potential for self-advancement and to raise their level of aspirations. They attempted to spur changes in the economic, social, and legal status of women in Brazil. Members of the growing minority of literate females, these early feminists emphasized education as a source of both increased options for economic independence and societal improvement. The end of the empire and the establishment of a republic in 1889 strengthened desires for political rights. However, the first serious effort to achieve women's suffrage, by inserting this right into the new republican constitution drafted in 1891, proved unsuccessful. Neither the handful of pioneer feminists nor their supporters in the Constituent Congress could counter male resistance or fears for the fate of the family and the home.

By the beginning of the twentieth century, increasing numbers of women were receiving education, although large segments of the population still remained illiterate. More urban, middle-class women began to find employment outside the home, especially in the classrooms, government offices, and commercial establishments. By 1920, they were competing for high-level positions in government service. The women who succeeded in entering the traditional, prestigious professions like law—the doors of Brazil's institutions of higher learning, which prepared people for the professions, had opened to women in 1879, as feminists had demanded—represented only a tiny fraction of the total female labor force, and the professions remained overwhelmingly male-dominated. Nonetheless, from the ranks of these professional women came most of the minority of Brazilian women who are consciously working to change their social and political status in the twentieth century.

A moderate women's rights movement became acceptable in Brazil by the 1920s. The achievement of the vote by women in several major European countries after World War I aided the cause. Not only the examples but also the personal links established between Brazilian feminists and international suffrage leaders spurred the formation of formal women's rights organizations in Brazil. The Federação Brasileira pelo Progresso Feminino (Brazilian Federation for the Advancement of Women), founded in 1922 by Bertha Lutz, a biologist and one of the first women to successfully compete for a high-level position in public service, became Brazil's preeminent suffragist and feminist organization in the 1920s and 1930s. The professional women prominent in the federation, including lawyers, doctors, and engineers both in and outside government service, possessed the necessary organizational skills and determination, as well as the personal contacts, to lead an effective and well-publicized suffrage campaign. In 1932, only a decade after the founding of the federation, Brazil became the fourth country in the Western Hemisphere to grant the vote to women (subject to the same literacy qualifications as men). This victory was confirmed by the constitution of 1934. Although their movement lacked the widespread following of the movement in the United States, it proved to be larger and better organized than most subsequent movements in Latin America. Bertha Lutz was appointed to the commission drafting the constitution of 1934; one woman, Dr. Carlota Pereira de Queiroz, was elected to the Constituent Congress, which approved the constitution, while other women achieved state and local office or served on government commissions. The Brazilian suffragists tackled problems of concern to the working class, such as salaries, shorter working hours, working conditions, and maternity leaves, but interclass linkages proved very difficult.

With the establishment of Getúlio Vargas' *Estado Novo* (New State) in 1937 and the elimination of elections and congresses, the first small wave of feminine political activism in Brazil was smashed. Women's organizations that were formed after the demise of the *Estado Novo* in 1945, such as the Women's Committee for Amnesty, the Housewives' Association against the High Cost of Living, and the Brazilian Federation of Women, lacked a specifically feminist orientation. But a small number of well-educated, upper-middle-class professionals continued to work for women's rights. In 1962 they secured a major modification of the civil code, theoretically ending the husband's virtually complete control over decisions affecting the family. Moreover, married women were no longer considered permanent minors under the law. In 1977, legalized divorce finally came to Brazil, although people were limited to one divorce in a lifetime, a restriction that would be lifted by the 1988 constitution.

During the mid-1970s, a new feminist movement emerged in Brazil. The International Women's Year of 1975 marked the appearance of several small feminist groups in Rio de Janeiro and São Paulo, beginning with the Centro da Mulher Brasileira (Brazilian Women's Center), as well as the founding of the Movimento Feminino pela Anistia (Women's Movement for Amnesty), which was not a feminist organization but rather a women's amnesty movement seeking to loosen the grip of the military dictatorship that had been imposed in 1964. United Nations sponsorship of the International Women's Year permitted the creation of women's groups in Brazil when other political activity was discouraged or repressed. The well-educated, middle-class women (some of whom were experienced political activists) participating in the new women's organizations attempted to place so-called specific women's issues within a broader struggle for a democratic, just society and to give priority to the needs and demands of working-class and poor women. Some sought interclass linkages with the more numerous neighborhood women's associations now forming in working-class districts of major manufacturing centers, some under the sponsorship of the church or the (banned) parties. These women's associations, which resisted the feminist label, focused on neighborhood services, especially day care, the high cost of living, and political participation.

By 1979, as the country slowly moved back toward liberal democratic rule, and political exiles began to return to Brazil after more than a decade abroad, the nation's small feminist movement was displaying increasing vigor as it was infused by women who had become feminists in Europe. Groups grew, proliferated, and splintered. Some sought less formal hierarchical structures free from party alliances that hindered efforts to deal with issues of personal politics such as sexuality, violence against women, reproduction, and abortion rights (abortion is legal only in cases of extreme danger to the woman's life or if the pregnancy resulted from rape or incest). With the return to full elective government, more feminist energies were devoted to party politics, while such feminist concerns as violence against women, as well as individual feminists, became part of government efforts and organizations, beginning with the first State Commission on the Status of Women (Conselho Estadual da Condição Feminina), created in 1983 by the government of São Paulo, Brazil's most industrialized state, which also pioneered the establishment of all-female police precincts to deal with such problems as domestic violence. In 1985, the federal government created a similar commission on women (Conselho Nacional dos Direitos da Mulher), which also sought to increase women's participation in the Constituent Assembly that drafted a new constitution for Brazil in 1987 and 1988. The following decade, nationwide preparations for the United Nations Fourth World Conference on Women, held in Beijing in 1995, served as another focus for female energies, as women in Brazil drew attention to the need to construct a just and egalitarian society and to conquer full citizenship for women. New laws were passed, ranging from extensions of maternity benefits to a requirement that 20 percent of the candidates to municipal office be women. Such issues as reproductive rights, health care, and violence against women continued to occupy women's rights advocates after the Beijing Conference, as before.

In the 1980s and 1990s, ever more women won election to office on both the local and national levels, although they did not all embrace the contemporary women's movement. By 1996, 6 female senators (out of 81) and 34 female deputies (out of 513) held seats in the national congress. Despite the problems and obstacles feminists have faced, the women's movement in Brazil has demonstrated more successes than is common in Latin America, raising a broad range of issues, creating new institutions, and promoting changes in government structures.

References. Sonia E. Alvarez, *Engendering Democracy in Brazil, Women's Movements in Transition Politics* (Princeton, 1990); June E. Hahner, *Emancipating the Female Sex: The Struggle for Women's Rights in Brazil, 1850–1940* (Durham, N.C., 1990).

JUNE E. HAHNER

BRAZILIAN WRITERS. Brazilian literature traces its origins to the highly literate and descriptive letter written to the king of Portugal by the scribe Pêro Vaz de Cominha, who chronicled the discovery of Brazil by Pedro Álvares Cabral in 1500. The subsequent 400 years of maturation of letters in the New World were the exclusive domain of men writers, with the notable exception of *As aventuras de Diófanes* (1725; The Adventures of Diophanes), considered by some scholars to be the first Brazilian novel. The author, Teresa Margarida de Silva e Orta, by using an anagrammatic pseudonym (Dorothea Engrassia Tavareda Dalmira), confused the issue of authorship. The editor of the third edition erroneously attributed the work to Alexandre de Gusmão. In general, women, until the twentieth century, had had scant opportunity for higher education and were, thereby, precluded from participating in the intellectual and public life of the country in general. However, this century has brought a profound change and a vindication of women's roles in society.

The turning point in the status of women may be placed in the first 30 years of the twentieth century, which were marked by social and political unrest. Specifically, the pressure for change was manifest in the arts, as evidenced by a series of concerts, exhibits, and lectures collectively called *The Week of Modern Art* held in São Paulo in February 1922. This event gave rise to an artistic and literary movement best known as modernism. European artistic ideas and literary vanguard currents, such as cubism, dadaism, and surrealism, as well as the new psychoanalytical Freudian and Jungian insights, provided a new dimension and direction for the arts. These concepts were incorporated into the resurgence of nationalism, which emphasized Brazilian character, values, and themes. For the first time in Brazilian intellectual history, women were to play a highly visible and sig-

nificant part. Modernism made possible the emergence of two women painters, Anita Malfatti and Tarsila do Amaral, and an internationally
recognized pianist, Guiomar Novaes, all of whom became influential in
artistic circles in Brazil. This first phase of modernism (1922–1930) was
characterized by conflicting and competing literary, political, and ideological debate.

The second phase of modernism (1930–1945) focused its attention on a
socially conscious literary "regionalist" current that utilized the novel as
the primary vehicle to transport ideas. Its themes were derived from social
ills and maladjustment of a region in decline and consequent psychological
trauma. Among a clearly defined northeastern regionalist group we find a
woman writer, the initiator of the modernist novel, Rachel de Queiroz,
whose plays, novels, and journalism have exerted a powerful influence on
Brazilian ideas. Some of her novels are O quinze (1930; The Fifteen), João
Miguel (1932), The Three Marias (1939; Eng., 1985). Her plays include
Lampião (1953) and A beata Maria do Eqito (1950; The Pious Mary of
Egypt). She portrayed legendary characters, some extracted from local folklore, with intense interest in ethical concerns such as good and evil, honor
and duty. The local settings often serve as points of departure into the
universal. Her works illustrate individual adaptation to the environment,
the relativity of truth, and the tragedy of life itself.

The 1930s witnessed the appearance of Lúcia Miguel-Pereira, who for
two decades was the country's foremost woman literary critic. In poetry
there were two noteworthy women, Adalgisa Nery and Henriqueta Lisboa.
However, of all the poets of this time period, Cecília Meireles (1921–1964)
is the best known and most critically acclaimed, having been named for
the Nobel Prize twice. Meireles' poetry is timeless, as she was concerned
with the problem of fleeting time, the abstraction of the moment that had
meaning only as it faded into memory. This introspective poetry led to
doubt and cynicism, a melancholy verse almost mystical in character. Her
principal works include Espectros (1919; Specters), Viagem (1939; Voyage), Vaga música (1942; Vague Music), Romanceiro da inconfidência
(1953; Collection of Poems of the Inconfidência). In English a bilingual
selection of her poetry is available: Cecília Meireles: Poems in Translation
(1977).

The third phase of modernism (1945–1964) was oriented toward the
search for the universal in the human condition, and the themes stressed
existential anguish in contemporary society. Several major women writers
emerged during this third generation. In 1944, Clarice Lispector (1925–
1977) began her literary career with Perto do coração selvagem (Close to
the Untamed Heart), and Lygia Fagundes Telles began hers with Praia viva
(Living Beach). Both authors describe characters in their introspective intimacy. Lispector, through her novels, develops a psychoanalytic study of
human behavior and emotional states in an attempt to decipher the meta-

physical reason for existence. Her heroes suffer the existential anguish caused by the freedom that each has to choose in a universe that is at the same time absurd and indifferent. The metaphysical and psychological concerns are evident in *Alguns contos* (1952; A Few Stories), *Family Ties* (1960; Eng., 1984), *The Apple in the Dark* (1961; Eng., 1986), *Foreign Legion* (1964; Eng., 1986), *The Passion according to G. H.* (1968; Eng., 1988), *An Apprenticeship or the Book of Delights* (1969; Eng., 1986), and *The Hour of the Star* (1977; Eng., 1986). Lygia Fagundes Telles in her short stories and novels elaborates her characters' futile attempts to live authentically only to be doomed by memories or some obscure remorse from the past. Themes of extreme futility and frustration bordering on the morbid and even the macabre abound in *Marble Dance* (1954; Eng., 1986), *Verão no aquario* (1963; Summer in the Aquarium), *O jardin selvagem* (1965; Savage Garden), *Antes do baile verde* (1970; Before the Green Masquerade), *The Girl in the Photograph* (1973; Eng., 1986), and *Tigrela: And Other Stories* (1977; Eng., 1986). Both women have secured their position among the ranks of major Brazilian writers. Many of Lispector's works are widely available in the United States.

Nélida Piñon is another talented woman writer who began her career in the 1950s. Her more recent works are notable for the creation of an almost surreal atmosphere that rivets the reader's interest in tales that are at the same time allegorical and fablelike. Illustrative works include *Sala de armas* (1973; Weapons Room), *O calor das coisas* (1980; The Heat of Things), and *A república dos sonhos* (1984; The Republic of Dreams).

Each succeeding generation of writers has produced an increasing number of women among its ranks. The increase of women writers has brought the development of feminist themes to the forefront along with a wide experimentation in literary techniques, topics, and styles in general. Of particular interest is the appearance of a highly vocal and articulate feminism. It seems that at last women are expressing their concerns and experiences of what it is to be a woman in a conservative, male-dominated society. In this new wave of women writers are Maria Alice Barroso, Maura Lopes Cançado, Sônia Coutinho, Marina Colasanti, Márcia Denser, Tânia Jamardo Faillace, Lélia Coelho Frota, Yone Gianetti Fonseca, Judith Grossman, Hilda Hilst, Lya Luft, Ana Maria Martins, Maria Geralda do Amaral Mello, Adalgisa Nery, Marly de Oliveira, Adélia Prado, Diná Silveira de Queiróz, Edla Van Steen, Socorro Trindade, and Dinorath do Valle.

With the exception of Hilda Hilst, who has been writing since the 1950s and has produced 28 works, the last group of women writers has not been critically studied. However, these are names that merit further scrutiny, and perhaps many will permanently enrich Brazilian cultural and intellectual life.

References. Assis Brasil, *A nova literatura*, 4 vols. (Rio de Janeiro, 1973–1976); Wilson Martins, *The Modernist Idea: A Critical Survey of Brazilian Writing in the*

Twentieth Century (New York, 1970); Massaud Moisés, *História da literatura Brasileira*, 4 vols. (São Paulo, 1983); Samuel Putnam, *A Marvelous Journey: A Survey of Four Centuries of Brazilian Writing* (New York, 1971).

LASSE T. TIIHONEN

BREASTS. See MAMMARY GLANDS (BREASTS)

BRIDEGIFT/BRIDEWEALTH is a form of marriage payment in which wealth in the form of property, money, goods, or services is given by the groom or his family* or kin group to the bride or her family or kin group. Anthropologists no longer use the term "brideprice" because of its connotation of buying a wife. A distinction may be made between bridewealth and bridegift, using bridewealth to refer to gifts to the bride's family or kin group and bridegift to refer to gifts part or all of which are given to the bride.

This form of marriage payment has been found in many societies throughout history but is more characteristic of small, preindustrial, egalitarian or polygamous societies than of highly stratified or monogamous ones.

BRIDESERVICE. A term used by some feminist anthropologists for a type of sex-gender system found among many foragers and hunter-horticulturists. Because marriage* organizes relations of privilege and obligation in societies where labor is divided only by sex, age, and kinship position, not by caste or class, a classification scheme that distinguishes different ways of validating marriages can highlight relationships among gender, productive relations, political processes, and cultural representations. In "brideservice" societies, where grooms are expected to work for their in-laws or provide gifts the groom obtains with his own labor, marriages do not create long-term relations of debt among adults. All adults control the distribution of their produce; ongoing relationships depend on the continued willing exchange of goods and services through which people organize the distribution of food. In less egalitarian "bridewealth" societies, where grooms are expected to present in-laws with gifts obtained through the labor of someone other than the groom himself, the acquisition of gifts puts young men in debt to the elders who help them marry. Elders who have helped many youths marry control the distribution of many people's products. They become political leaders who help less fortunate elders, organize trade and warfare, and sponsor public ceremonies.

In common anthropological usage, "brideservice" refers not to a type of society but to a mode of marriage found in many types of societies, including complex, archaic civilizations. It is defined as a mode of obtaining a wife in which the groom works for the bride's kinsfolk. The term belongs to a contrast set that includes bridewealth (in which the groom or his relatives provide substantial gifts for the bride's kin), token bridewealth, gift exchange, dowry* (in which the bride's relatives transfer property to the bride, the groom, or the groom's kinsmen), the direct exchange of one woman for another, and the absence of exchange.

Reference. J. Collier and M. Rosaldo, "Politics and Gender in Simple Societies," in S. Ortner and H. Whitehead (eds.), *Sexual Meanings* (New York, 1981).

JANE F. COLLIER

BRITAIN. Contagious Diseases Acts were instituted in England in 1864 and extended in 1866 and 1869. They were designed to protect military and naval personnel from venereal disease by providing for the registration of prostitutes in 17 garrison towns. Women, led by Josephine Butler (1828–1906) and her Ladies' National Association, objected because the acts "violated women's purity" while men were neither examined nor punished. Because of their efforts, the acts were finally repealed in 1885.

The acts were instituted during the Crimean War, though the possibility of government control of prostitution had been argued ever since 1843, when the *Lancet* reviewed Dr. H. Prater's *The Action of Preventives of Venereal Disease*. The admiralty and War Office oversaw the acts, while metropolitan police identified prostitutes, ensured their attendance at periodic examinations, and escorted infected women to the hospital, where they could be held as long as nine months.

The acts were a subject of controversy during their 20-year history. The Association for the Extension of the Contagious Diseases Act to the Civil Population of the United Kingdom was formed in 1866, while Butler's Ladies National Association for the Repeal of the Contagious Diseases Acts was organized in 1869. Opponents published more than 500 books and pamphlets, presented petitions to Parliament, and held more than 900 public meetings; proponents were equally busy.

Butler, who believed that men and women should adopt the same high moral standard before marriage and after, argued that the acts did not discourage prostitution, that they interfered with civil liberty, that evidence in favor of intervention was inadequate, and that innocent women could be subjected to degrading medical examinations. The suicide of an innocent woman, Mrs. Percy, in 1875, seemed to confirm the latter charge. In addition, doctors raised specifically medical objections, including the difficulty of distinguishing venereal disease from other conditions and the danger of contaminating healthy women with infected instruments.

Ultimately, the acts were repealed partially because of Butler and her followers and partially because extending them would have been too expensive. However, the campaign to repeal the acts acquainted middle-class feminists with political organizing as well as with conditions that affected other women.

References. J. A. Banks and Olive Banks, *Feminism and Family Planning in Victorian England* (New York, 1964); R. L. Blanco, "The Attempted Control of Venereal Disease in the Army of Mid-Victorian England," *Journal of the Society of*

Army Historical Research 45 (1967); E. M. Sigsworth and T. J. Wyke, "A Study of Victorian Prostitution and Venereal Disease," in Martha Vicinus (ed.), *Suffer and Be Still* (Bloomington, Ind., 1972), 77–99; Judith Walkowitz, "Male Vice and Feminist Virtue: Feminism and the Politics of Prostitution in Nineteenth Century Britain," *History Workshop Journal* 13 (1982).

CAROL A. SENF

BRITAIN. Married Women's Property Law in England has been the subject of two theoretical debates since the mid-nineteenth century, one establishing a married woman's right to hold property in her own name and the other developing the concept of "marital property" to which both spouses have claims.

Prior to the passage of the Married Women's Property Acts of 1870 and 1882, the common-law doctrine of "coverture" held that upon marriage, a woman's legal personality was absorbed in that of her husband. William Blackstone's *Commentaries on the Laws of England* (1765–1769) gave the rationale for this rule: if husband and wife were "one body" before God, then they were "one person" in the law, and that person was represented by the husband. A married woman was under coverture (she was a *feme couvert*) and could not hold property in her own name, enter into contracts, sue or be sued, or make a valid will unless her husband joined her.

A wealthy woman could avoid the consequences of coverture by having property placed in trust for her. Such trusts were governed by equity rather than the common law and were known as a married woman's "separate estate" or "separate property." She could receive income, sue and be sued, and will such property as if she were unmarried (a *feme sole*).

The Married Woman's Property Act of 1870 gave a married woman possession of her earnings, and the act of 1882 gave her possession of all other property that she held before and after her marriage; such property was henceforth her "separate estate."

The Law Reform (Married Women and Tortfeasors) Act of 1935, which eliminated a husband's liability for his wife's debts and her torts, completed the process of giving married women and men essentially the same property rights.

The Matrimonial Proceedings and Property Act of 1970 and the Matrimonial Causes Act of 1973 worked a second major change in the laws governing the property of married women by recognizing the principle of "matrimonial property" or "family assets." "Matrimonial property" is property to which both spouses have a claim regardless of who earned it or held title to it. Reformers pressed for these measures at the time when Parliament was passing a no-fault divorce law. They were worried that without such a measure to recognize the economic value of unpaid work in the home, divorced women would suffer severe economic hardships. The new property stipulation allowed the courts wide discretion in distributing "family assets" between a husband and wife on divorce, thus giving spouses (mainly women) rights to property that would not pertain under general property law. The Matrimonial and Family Proceedings Act of 1984 provided that if there were children of a marriage, the main financial obligation of either spouse after divorce was to provide for the welfare of the children and the person who takes care of them. The act gives judges a great deal of discretion concerning how to divide marital property. In future years, legislators and judges will have to decide whether equity between husband and wife with respect to property is best served by separate title, by the concept of "marital property," or by obligations to provide maintenance payments to one's ex-spouse and children. Issues of married women's property raise deep questions about what kind of partnership marriage is and what marriage might be in a more just society.

References. Susan Atkins and Brenda Hoggett, *Women and the Law* (Oxford, England, 1984); William Blackstone, *Commentaries on the Laws of England* (1765–1769); Lee Holcombe, *Wives and Property: Reform of the Married Women's Property Law in Nineteenth Century England* (Toronto, 1983); Carol Smart, *The Ties That Bind: Law, Marriage and the Reproduction of Patriarchal Relations* (London, 1984).

MARY LYNDON SHANLEY

BRITAIN. Nineteenth and Twentieth Centuries.

Before World War II. In Great Britain (England, Wales, and Scotland) from the end of the eighteenth century the growth of an industrial middle class resulted in a wealthy, leisured class of women, many of whom, impelled by a religious revival (the Great Awakening) and the growing awareness of the problems of early industrial society, became dedicated to good works, philanthropy, and, increasingly under the expanding concept of the domestic sphere, causes that would improve all of society. As helping poor women and children moved from parish charity work to a wider arena, women became active in prison and insane asylum reform, temperance, and the social purity movement. They worked to remove the double standard, for example, the repeal of the Contagious Diseases Act* (1864–1885) and to help working-class women, for example, through the Women's Protection and Provident League (1873; in 1890 the Women's Trade Union League). (See BRITAIN, Contagious Diseases Acts.) They worked for married women's rights to their own wages (1870) and other property (1882) and guardianship of their children under 7 and access to their children under 16 (1839). They won a divorce law in 1873, albeit one that allowed divorce on narrow grounds more restrictive for women than for men and so expensive that few could afford it. Women were also successful in gaining access to higher education, the professions, and the electoral franchise. (See BRITAIN, Woman Suffrage Movement.) After the suffrage success in 1928, other movements, for birth control, divorce reform, peace, and trade unionism, continued until World War II brought a hiatus in feminist activity that continued under the resurgent domesticity of the postwar years.

For impoverished members of the upper classes who had to find employment, opportunities were very limited in the nineteenth century: governess, school mistress, upper servant. The better-educated might earn a bare living translating literature, and late in the century a few women began to enter the professions. In 1871 there were 8 women medical doctors in Britain; by 1911, there were 477.

The majority of employed women were domestic servants, but many also worked in factories. Although some of the worst excesses of the textile mill sweatshops were curbed in a series of reforms beginning in the 1830s, sweated conditions remained in dressmaking, tailoring, and nail and match making. Home industry* employed many in very low-paying piecework such as tinting Christmas cards and book illustrations. At midcentury, when about 25 percent of all adult women were in paid employment, the numbers declined as a period of prosperity and the success of male workers in pushing for a "family wage" meant that women could leave paid employment upon marriage. By the early twentieth century female employment was around 10 percent, and by 1921 married women made up only 4 percent of the workforce.

Single women continued to work until they married, and widows and some married women returned to work from economic necessity, but fewer worked in factories. More were now entering white-collar jobs. Clerical occupations* opened to women with the invention of the typewriter, and by World War I most clerical workers were women. Women were also entering teaching and the postal service, and nursing had become a respectable women's occupation even earlier. Whatever their job, however, they were paid less than men. In the early twentieth century it was common for women to get one-third to two-thirds of men's wages.

Britain lagged behind many countries in Western and Central Europe in providing for the education of its children. Tutors and private schools (called public schools) provided education for the male scions of the privileged, but daughters of the elite were educated at home by governesses and sometimes by visiting language and music teachers. There were also some "schools" purporting to train young ladies in religion and the social graces and perhaps some "accomplishments" (music, art, French), but until Cheltenham Ladies College in 1853 there was no girls' school comparable to boys' better public schools.

For the lower classes, educational opportunity was very limited. In 1815 about a quarter of British children had some sort of schooling. Village "dame schools" might teach reading and writing, but little else. Charity schools of varying competence offered some limited opportunities; Sunday schools, the least competent, were founded to teach the rudiments to the children of the new industrial classes. By 1850 about half of English children had some kind of schooling, but the government did not begin to develop a primary school system on a systematic basis until after 1870, and secondary education was neglected until the twentieth century. As late as 1920, only 9.2 percent of English and Welsh children were still in school at age 13. Local authorities were not compelled to provide secondary education until 1944; then a three-tier system of unequal secondary education was established with attendance along class lines.

Queens College in London accepted women in 1854, and they could take degrees at the University of London in 1880. Although women's colleges were established in Cambridge in 1869 and Oxford in 1879, both universities withheld degrees until 1920–1921.

Post–World War II. Married women moved back into the workforce to stay during World War II. In 1993 a higher percentage of women worked in Britain and Germany than in any other European Union country except Denmark. They have an economic activity rate of 46 percent in the United Kingdom (which includes Northern Ireland), and they make up 39 percent of the labor force The proportion of married women at work had grown to almost 61 percent of all women ages 16 to 60 by 1988. However, about 44 percent of women workers, most of them married, work part-time.

Despite regular proposals from women, there was no equal pay act until 1970, and it did not go into effect until 1975. In 1983 the act was reluctantly amended by the Thatcher government to include work of equal value, thus bringing Britain into minimal compliance with European Union (EU) Law.* As a result, women's earnings have risen to about 74 percent of men's.

The Sex Discrimination Act of 1975 was also necessary to comply with the equal pay and equal treatment directives of the EU. However, the Equal Opportunities Commission, dominated by nominees from management and the trade unions, has made little use of its wide powers to implement and enforce its provisions.

The impetus for second-wave feminism in the late 1960s came from worker militancy, anti–Vietnam War and New Left activism; and the works of feminist writers such as Juliet Mitchell, Sheila Rowbotham, and, from the United States, Germaine Greer and Shulamith Firestone. Unlike the movements in the United States and Canada, traditional and New Wave women's groups did not generally work together. The absence of the political clout that mainline women's organizations could command has been noticeable in the limited response of the government to women's concerns.

From 1968 through the 1970s, consciousness-raising and single-action groups, women's health centers, publishing collectives, organizations in professions and political parties, and a small, but significant, women's studies movement were established. Women's groups tended to be small, with diverse interests, but there was general agreement on basic demands and, despite the small membership and the splits and reformations of groups, they were able to mobilize much larger numbers of women for specific actions.

One of the most successful feminist efforts was in aiding victims of violence. Erin Pizzey began the first refuge for battered women in 1972; by 1980 there were 200 refuges and a national Women's Aid Federation. The first rape crisis center was set up in North London in 1976; by 1981 there were 16 centers and telephone hot lines. Women Against Violence and Reclaim the Night Marches brought attention to the problem of violence against women. Parliament passed the Domestic Violence Act and the Sex Offenses Amendment Act in 1976.

Through the efforts of the well-organized Abortion Law Reform Association the abortion law was liberalized in 1967, and the National Abortion Campaign (NAC), which supports abortion on demand, has mobilized support to prevent changes in the law.

The class basis of education began to be reduced in the 1950s with the establishment of comprehensive schools. By 1994, 86 percent of students in the United Kingdom attended comprehensive schools. The expansion of higher education followed in the 1960s, with new universities and the upgrading of the polytechnic schools. A binary system of higher education resulted, with more men attending universities than did women, who were more likely to pursue careers in teaching, nursing, and so on through the polytechnic and other tertiary educational institutions. In 1990–1991, women made up 43 percent of the students at universities in England and Wales and 44 percent in Scotland. In 1992 the polytechnics and some other higher education institutions became universities, automatically increasing the percentage of women in universities.

As one of the few parliamentary governments to use single-member districts rather than candidate lists, the United Kingdom has one of the lowest proportions of women legislators of any country in Europe, until 1997 below 5 percent. Margaret Thatcher was Britain's first woman prime minister (1979–1990). However, in the year she became prime minister (1979), fewer women were elected than at any time since 1951 (19 of 635 members, or 3 percent of Parliament). Also, only 2 women besides Thatcher had ever served in cabinet posts other than education, health, and women's affairs.

Women did even less well in appointive than in elective posts. The bar against married women working in civil service was not removed until 1946, equal pay was not instituted until 1955, and there have been very few women at the highest levels of civil service. In 1994 there were only 4 women (7.1 percent) in subministerial positions.

In the overwhelming Labor Party victory in 1997, however, 120 women were elected to Parliament, nearly doubling their numbers, and 5 women were named to cabinet posts, including a woman as Northern Ireland secretary.

The conservative Thatcher government eroded some of women's gains under the British "welfare state." Reductions made in social services and benefits as part of a government policy to shed some of its welfare functions, combined with decreased employment opportunities in the declining economy of the late 1980s, have increased the burdens of women in their role as family caregivers. The new "centrist" Labor Party is not likely to reverse the Thatcher policies.

BRITAIN. Woman Suffrage Movement was an organized effort to gain the parliamentary franchise for women. It was founded in the mid-nineteenth century but did not achieve complete success until 1928. While voting for women was only one of the goals of early British feminism, the suffrage struggle eclipsed other issues and achieved international prominence in the early years of the twentieth century.

The women's suffrage movement reflected both the gradual acceptance of democratic principles in nineteenth-century Britain and also the small, but growing, pressure for equal rights for women. Though there had been isolated demands for votes for women earlier in the century, in the 1860s a small group of London women formed a committee to press for the parliamentary franchise. The time seemed ripe for such a demand since Parliament was considering legislation to widen the male suffrage. The committee persuaded John Stuart Mill to propose that any franchise reform should include votes for women. Though Mill's proposal was defeated, the issue was now on the public agenda. Local women's suffrage committees sprang up throughout the country.

For the rest of the century these societies labored in a constitutional manner for their cause. They held meetings, drafted bills, wrote propaganda, and lobbied members of Parliament. In 1897 the various local societies joined together in one national organization, the National Union of Women's Suffrage Societies (NUWSS). At first, most of the women who joined these societies were middle-class. However, by the turn of the century, many working-class women, particularly in industrialized northwest England, joined the struggle because they had come to believe that only with the vote could they pressure the national government to address their economic and social problems.

In 1903 a new element entered the struggle with the formation of the Women's Social and Political Union (WSPU). The WSPU was founded by the women of the Pankhurst family. Discouraged by the moderation of the suffragists, as the members of the NUWSS were known, Emmeline and Christobel Pankhurst, whose followers soon acquired the nickname of "suffragettes," were determined to try more dramatic methods. "Deeds, not words" was their motto. From the beginning the suffragettes sought public attention by the use of militant tactics. Members of the WSPU disrupted political meetings, staged huge outdoor rallies, and engaged in acts of civil disobedience. At times they deliberately courted arrest for the publicity engendered by the spectacle of respectable women being jailed for their beliefs. This publicity, in turn, increased financial support and attracted new members for both the suffragist and the suffragette wings of the movement.

However, despite the growing attention to, and support for, the women's cause, the Liberal government of the day refused to grant women the vote. Frustrated by official opposition, the WSPU escalated its tactics, resorting to the destruction of property. As a result, many more women ended up in jail, where they demanded to be given the status of political prisoners. When the government continued to treat the suffragettes as ordinary criminals, some of the women went on hunger strikes. The government responded by force-feeding the prisoners, causing a public outcry. Reacting to public indignation and also fearing that one of the hunger strikers might die and thus create a martyr for the women's cause, the government enacted the infamous "Cat and Mouse Act" (the Prisoner's Temporary Discharge for Ill Health Act). This legislation allowed the government to free a fasting prisoner and then rearrest her when her health improved, a process that continued until she had served her full sentence.

The situation had reached an impasse. Neither the government nor the WSPU was willing to compromise. In 1914, however, suffrage activity virtually ceased with the coming of war. Women in both wings of the suffrage movement suspended their agitation and threw themselves into war work. Millions of women joined the labor force for the first time. By 1918 even old opponents agreed that women had earned the right to vote through their support of the war effort. The government was also worried that the suffragettes might resume their militancy once peace was declared. Consequently, the Representation of the People Act of 1918 granted the franchise to most British women over the age of 30. The age limit reflected the politicians' fear that if women, like men, could vote at the age of 21, they would outnumber men in the electorate.

This obvious gender inequality kept the issue of votes for women alive in the 1920s. Though British feminists turned much of their attention to other matters concerning women, they continued to press for the full franchise. At last, in 1928, with little opposition, Parliament granted all British women over 21 the right to vote. Three-quarters of a century after British women began to agitate for suffrage, their cause had triumphed.

References. Jil Liddington and Jill Norris, *One Hand Tied behind Us: The Rise of the Women's Movement* (London, 1978); Andrew Rosen, *Rise Up Women: The Militant Campaign of the WSPU, 1903–1914* (London, 1974); Ray Strachey, *The Cause: A Short History of the Women's Movement in Great Britain* (London, 1928; repr., London, 1978).

DIANE WORZALA

BRITISH ARTISTS. Victorian Artists and the wider society they were part of are often perceived as having been rigidly divided into separate spheres, masculinity defined around the public and professional, while femininity was completely confined within the domestic and amateur. Recent feminist work has challenged this idea and sought to uncover how Victorian women artists were able to negotiate and sustain professional artistic careers and actively redefine the relationship between femininity and artistic practice and identity.

By the end of the nineteenth century unprecedented numbers of women from the middle and upper classes were training and practicing as fine artists, while working-class women were steered toward vocational design-based study and work. For women artists, gaining access to the professional training long enjoyed by men, which both nurtured creative development and also importantly introduced the student to artistic circles and contacts, was the cause of struggle throughout the Victorian period. During the early part of the nineteenth century most women's art training was limited to private schools for women or, if they were wealthy and ambitious enough, to lessons from artists. These provided instruction in art as an accomplishment rather than serious training for the would-be artist. However, from midcentury onward women fought to gain access to formal art training as part of their wider battle for higher education. In 1860, the Royal Academy schools, exclusively male and regarded as the stepping-stone for artistic success, bowed to women's pressure following a campaign of letters and a petition and agreed to admit women students; even so, it forbade them entry to its life rooms and attempted later, albeit unsuccessfully, to exclude women once more. By contrast the Slade School of Fine Art at University College, founded in 1871, admitted women from its inception, allowed them to study from the life-model (although in a separate room from the male students), and became extremely popular. By the 1890s not only was the Slade seen as the most progressive of all the art schools, but approximately two-thirds of its students were women.

There was no one style of art produced by Victorian women artists; they used diverse mediums and tackled many subjects in their work. Hundreds of women worked in pencil and watercolor, drawing and painting for pleasure as a leisure activity and making images of landscapes, domestic life and spaces, and portraits of family and friends. In addition some professional artists worked exclusively in watercolor, such as Helen Paterson Allingham, who painted rural, working-class women and cottages; Marie Spartali and Elizabeth Siddall, who painted figure subjects often with historical or literary references; and Kate Greenaway, watercolorist and illustrator. Women artists also worked in oils, painting a variety of subjects. These included the monumental scenes of army life painted by Elizabeth Thompson (later Lady Butler) throughout her career, Henrietta Rae's and Evelyn Pickering de Morgan's large canvases of classical figures, and Edith and Jessica Hayllar's paintings of domestic life and social rituals. Portraiture was also undertaken by many women. Mary Severn made a successful career from commissions and sales of her portraits; her clients included members of the royal family, the aristocracy, and the upper middle classes. In addition self-portraits were an important way of representing women's artistic identity. Mary Severn exhibited her own self-portrait at the Royal Academy in 1863, and Emma Richards, a successful painter of religious pictures, also painted and exhibited pictures of herself, proclaiming her presence as an artist. Other women painters included Laura Epps (Lady Alma Tadema); Louise Jopling; Emily Mary Osborn; Eloise Harriet, Anna Maria, and Emily Coppin Stannard; Charlotte, Eliza, Louisa, and Mary Ann Sharpe; and Fanny and Louisa Corbeaux.

Although women's progress was not as great within the field of sculpture, often more resistant to women as the large scale of the work and the necessity of using unwieldy tools and messy materials could be defined as masculine, women did become better represented as the nineteenth century progressed. This was partly due to the shift during the late Victorian period toward smaller-scale sculptures, as well as the wider influx of women into art training and practice. Victorian women sculptors included Mary Thornycroft, Margaret Giles, Ruby Levick, Ellen Mary Rope, and Florence Steele.

The history of Victorian women artists is not one of unalloyed and unimpeded progress. Although women were increasingly admitted to art schools, they were segregated within these institutions, which were organized in terms of sexual difference, creating a separate category of women students and thus attempting to preserve the privileges of their male colleagues. This sexual differentiation also occurred when artists set up in professional practice and attempted to establish a reputation and make a living from their work. Women were barred from some of the social spaces where male artists networked, met clients, and secured commissions and sales, such as the London clubs. Exhibiting organizations, dealers, and galleries also often discriminated against women; even by the late nineteenth century only 10 percent of the work at major exhibitions was created by women. Women were also subject to different economic status. Until the Married Woman's Property Act of 1882 a wife's property and earnings belonged to her spouse, and, given bourgeois definitions of femininity as dependent, their work often fetched lower prices than did men's. However, in opposition to this discrimination women developed different strategies of resistance and mutual support. Their cool reception by the art establishment led them, in some instances, to develop their own networks of exhibiting organizations, audiences, and buyers for their work, a Victorian phenomenon that Deborah Cherry has termed the "culture of matronage." At the forefront of this development was Queen Victoria herself, who collected and commissioned work from women artists, including Emily Mary Osborn, Henrietta Ward, and Elizabeth Thompson. Women artists also managed some successful forays into men-dominated exhibitions, the most notable of which was Elizabeth Thompson's exhibit at the Royal Academy show in 1874. The painting *Calling the Roll Call after an Engagement, Crimea*, which was bought by the Queen from its first owner, was one of the three most popular Academy pictures of the century and became hugely successful in reproduction.

Despite the fact that the increasing number of women practicing as fine artists during the Victorian period met with some resistance to their work and careers and that moves were made to limit their success, such as the sexual division of art education and the ongoing discrimination of the art market, women artists were not necessarily caught in, or held by, masculine definitions of women artists and their work. Access to art training meant that women could carve out their own niche for cultural production and engage in the politics of representation themselves. Changing images of femininity also helped women to redefine themselves and lay claim to artistic identities. They could model themselves on the cultural representations of creative women, from the woman painter who is the heroine of Anne Brontë's *The Tenant of Wildfell Hall*, to the "New Woman" of the 1890s with her independent life and intellectual interests. The rising importance of travel and study abroad for artists completing their training from the midcentury onward did not exclude women. On the contrary, many women traveled to European cities, particularly Paris and Rome, in order to train in the ateliers. This not only offered them the opportunity of pursuing their own work and seeing the art housed in the great European collections firsthand (extremely important in an age in which reproductions of artwork were not good) but also gave women the chance to build independent lives based on communality of work rather than family ties and duties. By the turn of the century large communities of expatriate women artists had formed in cultural centers such as Paris, and the work they produced into the early twentieth century is now being uncovered and discussed, thus revising established views of modernism.

References. Deborah Cherry, *Painting Women: Victorian Women Artists* (London, 1993); Ellen Clayton, *English Female Artists* (London, 1876); Pamela Gerrish Nunn, *Canvassing: Recollections by Six Victorian Women Artists* (London, 1986), and *Victorian Women Artists* (London, 1987); Roszika Parker and Griselda Pollock, *Old Mistresses: Women, Art and Ideology* (New York, 1981); Charlotte Yeldham, *Women Artists in Nineteenth-Century France and England*, 2 vols. (New York, 1984).

ALICIA FOSTER

BUDDHISM. Women are endowed with the same potential for making progress on the Buddhist path to its goal of enlightenment as are men. In the sixth century B.C.E. the Buddha granted the request of his aunt Mahāprajāpati for the foundation of a nuns' order and freed women from the demands of family life, giving them the same opportunities as men for serious religious practice. However, while he affirmed women's equal potential for spiritual development, he did not challenge societal practices of subordinating women to men.

Women's abilities for pursuing the religious life were never called into question, but in deference to social norms, Buddhism preserved male control over nuns through the imposition of special disciplinary rules. These rules required that nuns live under the supervision of monks and that monks participate in the ordination of nuns, determine the dates for the bimonthly confessional meetings, participate in the interrogation of nuns who transgress the rules, help decide penalties, and stipulate that all nuns treat even junior monks with the respect due a senior member. These rules institutionalized the social norm of female inequality and made nuns subordinate to men, regardless of their religious experience. However, these rules did not impede a nun's religious practice, and spiritual development is the ultimate determinant of religious status in Buddhism.

The *Therīgāthā*, a collection of verses in the Theravādin canon of Sri Lankan and Southeast Asian Buddhists, celebrates the achievements of nuns who attained the enlightened status of an *arahant* (saint). Monks, however, wrote and compiled virtually all the texts included in this early Buddhist canon. Much of this material reflects their ambivalent attitudes toward women. The negative images of women as evil temptresses suggest that monks saw women's sexuality as a potential threat to both individual monks' spiritual growth and the stability of the monastic community. On the other hand, the economic survival of the Buddhist community often depended on the generosity of laywomen; and in early works we find positive images of women as nurturers and almsgivers. Female lay patronage from the merchant and royal classes helped Buddhism prosper first in India and in the Central, East, and Southeast Asian regions into which it later spread.

Increased participation by the laity, by laywomen in particular, may have influenced the rise of the Mahāyāna movement circa 100 B.C.E. through 100 C.E. and contributed to the generally more positive views of women in Mahāyāna scriptures. Although Mahāyāna, which is associated today with Central and East Asia, recognized the spiritual potential of nuns and laywomen, the Mahāyāna scriptures were written primarily as guides for monks training to become *bodhisattvas*, the idealized Buddhist practitioners. On the question of female *bodhisattvas* the Mahāyāna scriptures differ. Some texts, such as the *Pure Land Scriptures*, mandate a change of sex from female to male, a transformation from carnal to spiritual, before entrance into the Pure Land. Other texts, in which *bodhisattvas* and Buddhas are asexual beings, consider the motif of sexual transformation as incompatible with the Buddhist teaching that the dualistic thinking exemplified in the discrimination of maleness and femaleness must be transcended. Although scriptures that identify the feminine with the sacred are rare, representations of the *bodhisattva* Avalokiteśvara (Guanyin) in female form became a favorite subject of East Asian Buddhist art. This popular *bodhisattva* manifests the infinite compassion of an enlightened being for the suffering of all creatures and fulfills all their wishes, especially the desire for children.

The Vajrayāna or Tantric tradition of Buddhism, which was introduced into Tibet from India in the seventh century C.E., gives prominence both to female symbolism and to women practitioners. The hagiographies of accomplished Tantric practitioners (*siddha*) show women as men's companions on the Tantric path and as skilled spiritual guides. Yeshey Tsogyal, who was born in the late eighth century C.E., exemplifies the successful practitioner who overcomes the dualism inherent in such discriminations as male–female, active–passive, and sacred–profane; and for some later generations' liturgical and meditational practices, as the "Great Bliss Queen" (*dDe chen rgyal mo*), she symbolizes nondualistic wisdom in female form.

Laywomen continue to be active in the Buddhist community, but the unbroken transmission of full ordination (*bhiksunī*) for nuns disappeared in the last millennium in all regions except China, and only novice ordination (*śramanera*) remains. Theravādin and Tibetan Buddhist nuns who are interested in the restoration of full ordination in their respective traditions must receive this ordination from Chinese orders now in Hong Kong and Taiwan.

References. Tsultrim Allione, *Women of Wisdom* (London, 1984); Rita Gross, *Buddhism after Patriarchy: A Feminist History, Analysis and Reconstruction of Buddhism* (Albany, N.Y., 1993); I. B. Horner, *Women in Primitive Buddhism* (Delhi, 1975); Anne C. Klein, *Meeting the Great Bliss Queen: Buddhists, Feminists and the Art of the Self* (Boston, 1995); Diana Y. Paul, *Women in Buddhism* (Berkeley, Calif., 1985); Miranda Shaw, *Passionate Enlightenment: Women in Tantric Buddhism* (Princeton, 1994); Karma Lekshe Tsomo (ed.), *Sakyadhita: Daughters of the Buddha* (Ithaca, N.Y., 1988).

KAREN C. LANG

C

CANADA (SINCE 1945). Women constitute just over half of Canada's 28 million people.

During World War II the government of Canada encouraged women, both single and married, to enter the workforce as part of the war effort. After the war, government and industries pressured these same women to "return" to their homes and take up a "normal" life. Certainly, participation rates of women in the labor force in 1946 indicated a drastic reduction. In 1945 women were 31.4 percent of the workforce, but in 1946 they were 22.7 percent. That reduction, however, proved to be only temporary. Woman's participation in paid work increased during the 1950s, and especially significant was the increase in married women workers. In 1951 only 30 percent of women workers were married; by 1961 over 47 percent were.

The workingwoman of the 1960s had become a reality that many Canadians could not ignore, no matter how much they may have wanted to. By 1971, women were over one-third of the workforce, by 1983 over 40 percent, and by the mid-1990s they were almost 50 percent. Young women entering the workforce stayed in it longer, even after they married and, by the mid-1980s, even when they had young children. By 1981, the majority of married women were in the paid labor force doing double duty working both inside and outside the home. Day-care facilities had expanded but nowhere met the demand, forcing many women to make their own arrangements for the care of their children. The situation has not changed.

Despite the phenomenon of women's entering the workforce in unprecedented numbers, the cruel reality of Canada was and is that the poor are largely women and children. In 1970 two-thirds of all welfare recipients were women, and two-thirds of these were widowed, separated, or divorced. More than 50 percent had small children. Throughout the 1980s, women never went below being 55 percent of the total poor of *any* age in Canada. Part of this is accounted for by the wage differential between men and women, even though the gap decreased from about 60 percent in 1970 to 72 percent in 1994. The situation of the late 1980s and the 1990s has not been kind to women. Economic dislocation as a result of the restructuring of the economy that occurred in the wake of an increasing global economic network and the Free Trade Agreement negotiated with the United States has hurt many workers.

The personal lives of women have changed drastically over the last several decades as well. The age of first marriage for women decreased from the pre- and postwar period so that by 1961 it was 22.9 years. This was accompanied by a significant increase in the birthrate, accounting for the so-called baby boom, which reached its peak in 1956. Marriage age continued to decrease, but at the same time so, too, did the birthrate. By the end of the 1980s, new, albeit slight, trends emerged. The birthrate increased slightly, and marriage age increased to 26.2 years in 1992. Not all groups of women experienced these trends in the same way. Especially significant was the decline by 50 percent in the birthrate of Quebec women between 1959 and 1969. As a result, Quebec began to feel that its future in the Confederation was not assured. On the other hand, native women's increased fertility ran counter to the general decline for most of the modern period. It underlay a resurgence in native strength and demands on the largely white community to recognize native reality. However, the birthrate of native women could not hide the fact that their lives and those of their children were often lived in squalor, and while their babies might have a better chance of survival than previously, the native infant mortality rate was still significantly higher than that of other Canadians, and the life expectancy rate much lower.

The law clearly needed to be changed to catch up to the personal reality of women's lives, and in 1969 this finally occurred when the law was changed with respect to both birth control and divorce. Birth control and abortion were legalized, although abortion was carefully controlled by the medical profession, and access was difficult except for medical reasons and for women who had access to doctors who would support them in their requests. These women tended to be married, white, and middle-class. In 1969, the divorce law of Canada was made more open in recognition of the changing nature of marriage and the number of people who were divorcing. This law essentially recognized marital breakdown with no blame attached to either partner. Further legal gains for women came in the 1980s. The Supreme Court recognized the inequities of the abortion law and in 1988 struck it down. The law with respect to native women also changed. In the Indian Act of 1869 a native woman marrying a white man lost her right to be a status Indian, as did her children. Various native women's groups and organizations agitated for change in this law, and finally in 1985 this part of the Indian Act was repealed.

Native women were not the only ones who were agitating for change. Other women from the majority and minority streams had long been involved in reform activities and in 1918 had been successful in achieving the federal vote for most women. However, while women have long had the vote, they have not been particularly successful in getting elected at the national level. Nonetheless, in 1993 Kim Campbell's succession to the leadership of the Conservative Party and consequently to the prime ministership of Canada for a short time led to her becoming the first woman prime minister of the country.

If women's organizations had been the driving force behind the suffrage movement, in the post–World War II period many of the same organizations continued to press for reform to meet the changing realities of women's lives. They were the link between the first and second wave of the women's movement. One of the more significant groups to form in the early 1960s was the Voice of Women, an organization concerned about the escalation of the Cold War. Quebec women organized to lessen the legal restrictions on wives so they could participate in a profession on their own and sign contracts. In 1966, the Committee for the Equality of Women in Canada formed to press successfully for a Royal Commission on the Status of Women (RCSW). The commission reported in 1970, and its 167 recommendations became the platform of the feminist movement. To put pressure on the government to implement the recommendations, a National Ad Hoc Committee on the Status of Women was formed and eventually transformed itself into the National Action Committee on the Status of Women, an umbrella organization of many women's groups, eventually representing over 5 million women in the country. At the same time that the RCSW was being set up, many young educated women who came out of the student movement and the counterculture of the 1960s joined the feminist cause. Referring to their efforts as "women's liberation" in identification with the liberation of other colonized peoples and nations, they aligned themselves with the rhetoric and analysis of Marxism and socialism. For their part, radical feminists maintained that the economic system was not at the root of the inequities faced by women but rather the oppression of women by men. These radical groups had a separatist orientation taken even further by the lesbian movement, which, through the women's movement, found a public voice.

This first generation of modern feminists tended to be white and middle-class women. They overemphasized the benefits of being in the labor force and the oppression felt by many women in the home. In doing so, they often antagonized homemakers who rightly felt proud of what they were doing. This first generation was also not as sympathetic as they might have been to working-class women and women of color. Until the mid- to late 1980s, they ignored the problems of disabled women and lesbian women. They had an inclusive ideology but one that was not always practiced.

Women are much more visible in Canadian society than they have been. They earn more than 50 percent of the B.A.'s in the country, although they are underrepresented in the earning of graduate degrees. They are more than 50 percent of the law students and almost 50 percent of the medical students. Women have increased their representation in the judiciary, and in 1982 the first woman was appointed to the Supreme Court of Canada. Due to their activism, women have been more visible in the major political issues of the day. Many commentators have argued that in the crucial 1980 Quebec referendum on the Constitution women were instrumental in the victory of the yes side, that is, the side that supported continued participation with Confederation. In the revamping of the Canadian Constitution with its Charter of Rights and Freedoms in 1980–1981 women were able to ensure that the equality clause against gender discrimination was not weakened.

References. Micheline Dumont et al., *Quebec Women: A History* (Toronto, 1987); Diana Pedersen, *Changing Women, Changing History: A Bibliography of the History of Women in Canada* (Toronto, 1996); Paul Phillips and Erin Phillips, *Woman and Work: Inequality in the Canadian Labor Market* (Toronto, 1993); Alison Prentice, Paula Bourne, Gail Cuthbert Brandt, Beth Light, Wendy Mitchinson, and Naomi Black, *Canadian Women: A History* (Toronto, 1996).

WENDY MITCHINSON

CANADIAN WRITERS. Anglophone. Women writers are prominent in Canadian Anglophone letters, particularly in fiction and poetry. A woman novelist, Frances Brooke, wrote *The History of Emily Montague* (1769), the first novel about Canadian life. In the nineteenth century, the sisters Susanna Moodie and Catherine Parr Traill documented the adventures of British gentlewomen in the wilds of Upper Canada. At the turn of the century, the social realist Sara Jeanette Duncan wrote *The Imperialist* (1904), a novel that dramatizes political and economic tensions between Canada and the United States from the perspective of a passionate, independent female hero. Twentieth-century women writers have relied on these literary precursors to portray women in various kinds of crises. Martha Ostenso, in *Wild Geese* (1925), uses the main female character to expose a patriarchal misanthrope whose daughter demonstrates how female wildness and independence can free a family from male tyranny. Ethel Wilson, in both short stories and novels, explores twentieth-century women's social and spiritual values.

From the mid-1950s on, women writers have dominated Canadian fiction. Because Canadian literature and the women's movement blossomed simultaneously in the 1960s, women writers often use female identity quests to parallel Canada's quests for identity. Many have gained international followings. Margaret Laurence, probably Canada's major twentieth-century novelist, in such novels as *The Stone Angel* (1964), *Rachel, Rachel* (1966), and *The Diviners* (1974), centers on strong prairie women whose roots are deeply Canadian and who are beginning to produce a distinctive Canadian literary mythology. Like other women writers, Laurence dramatizes female development from various chronological perspectives and in different classes.

Five other fiction writers deserve special mention: Sheila Watson, Mavis Gallant, Marian Engel, Audrey Thomas, and Alice Munro. Sheila Watson's *The Double Hook* (1959), considered by many to be Canada's first contemporary novel, presents, cryptically and poetically, Canada's West as a wasteland controlled in many ways by female characters. Mavis Gallant, best known for her many *New Yorker* short stories, although resident for years in Paris, frequently describes Canadian landscapes. Two novels, *Green Water, Green Sky* (1959) and *A Fairly Good Time* (1970), illustrate female characters struggling to emerge whole from cultural patterns designed to defeat them. The novellas (*Its Image on the Mirror* and *The Pegnitz Junction*) and the autobiographical Linnet Muir stories (*Home Truths*, 1981) emphasize the development of the female artist from various perspectives. Marian Engel is best known for her novel *Bear* (1976), an ironic commentary on such male-centered stories as Faulkner's "The Bear." In this poetic, mythic novel, the female narrator gradually learns about the world through her intense relationship with a male bear. Somewhat more realistic, but also marked by Engel's frequently bizarre imagination, are the domestic novels, *The Honeymoon Festival* (1970) and *Lunatic Villas* (1981). In each of these and in many of her short stories, Engel focuses on women whose considerable wit allows them to survive crises with style. Audrey Thomas, the most stylistically experimental of this group, dramatizes, in the connected novels *Mrs. Blood* (1970), *Songs My Mother Taught Me* (1973), and *Blown Figures* (1974), unconscious fantasies and delusions, not only by realistic description but by interrupted narrative, fragmented by interjections from newspapers, unattached voices, and floating memories. The content of her fiction is profoundly female, emphasizing relationships between mothers and daughters and demonstrating women's thoughts as they experience pregnancy. Finally, Alice Munro, in short story collections like *The Moons of Jupiter* (1982) and *The Progress of Love* (1986), as well as in the connected stories of *Lives of Girls and Women* (1971), dramatically illustrates female desire in narrative plot and structure. Munro's stories are intricately detailed, evoking the specificity of particular times and spaces while also ironically questioning the nature of realism.

Margaret Atwood is Canada's best-known writer. Novelist, short story writer, poet, essayist, and critic, she has been concerned, throughout her career, in clarifying national literary characteristics. Her 1972 guide to Canadian literature, *Survival*, emphasizes victimization (with survival) as distinctively Canadian; this theme is reflected particularly in women's writing and through female characters. In *Surfacing* (1972), the unnamed narrator passes through various victim positions in an epic quest designed to teach her what it means to be a Canadian woman. Increasingly political, later Atwood novels like *Bodily Harm* (1981) and *The Handmaid's Tale* (1986) are radical, subversive analyses of patriarchal cultures that can damage women physically and spiritually.

Atwood is also Canada's major poet. Like her novels, her poetry is political. *Power Politics* (1971) dramatically correlates American imperialism with patriarchal power, situating Canada in a female position. *You Are Happy* (1974), *Two-Headed Poems* (1978), *True Stories* (1981), and *Interlunar* (1984) metaphorically present border disputes (between Canada and the United States and between French Canada and English Canada) as battles between the sexes, demonstrating, in a world on the verge of extinction, the dangers of rigid gender terminology.

Other important women poets are Dorothy Livesay, Gwen MacEwen, Margaret Avison, and Phyllis Webb. Dorothy Livesay's interest has moved from historically focused political poetry to poetry directed toward women's issues. *The Unquiet Bed* (1967) and *Plainsongs* (1969) demonstrate this interest, while she celebrates aging in *Ice Age* (1975) and *The Woman I Am* (1977). She has edited a collection of poetry by women, *Forty Women Poets of Canada* (1972). MacEwen's work is marked by history and myth. Her latest poetry, *The T. E. Lawrence Poems* (1982), in which Lawrence's voice is vividly evoked, and *Earthlight* (1982) use fantasy to create subtle images. Phyllis Webb continues to publish work of remarkable technical virtuosity, particularly notable in *Wilson's Bowl* (1980) and *The Vision Tree* (1982). Margaret Avison's second collection, *The Dumbfounding* (1966), established her as a major poet. *Sunblue* (1978) further demonstrates an intense religious conviction as well as considerable social sensitivity.

Canadian drama is less advanced than either fiction or poetry. Nonetheless, several important Canadian playwrights are women. Gwen Ringwood, author of more than 60 plays, has influenced the development of Canadian drama. *The Collected Plays of Gwen Pharis Ringwood* (1982) reveals her skill in establishing place. Five other women dramatists pay particular attention to women: Carol Bolt, Joanna M. Glass, Sharon Pollock, Erica Ritter, and Margaret Hollingsworth. In *Red Emma* (1974), Bolt examines Emma Goldman's Marxist politics and her concern with woman's rights. *Shelter* (1975) and *One Night Stand* (1977) dramatize issues of particular concern to women. Joanna M. Glass frequently explores male–female relationships in contemporary society. *Canadian Gothic* and *American Modern* (1977) concentrate on domestic despair, while *To Grandmother's House We Go* (1981) explores often frightening connections among three generations. Sharon Pollock began by satirizing specific political problems in British Columbia but, as *Blood Relations and Other Plays* (1981) demonstrates, has become increasingly broader in dealing with the effects of public events on private lives. Best known for *Automatic Pilot* (1980), Erica Ritter often writes of female characters in comic situations. Like other plays of hers, *The Passing Scene* (1982), an exposé of journalism, is a satire. Margaret Hollingsworth, in plays like *Ever Loving* (1980) and *Mother Country* (1980), demonstrates the difficulties that face women who attempt to speak out. Her plays treat women's voices symbolically.

References. Lorna Irvine, *Sub/Version* (Toronto, 1986); M. G. McClung, *Women in Canadian Life and Literature* (Toronto, 1977).

LORNA IRVINE

CANADIAN WRITERS. Francophone. Women's contributions to the development of French Canadian literature, particularly since the latter part of the nineteenth century, have been substantial and influential. Contemporary women writers in Quebec are well aware of the formidable accomplishments of their literary foremothers and often remember them publicly and in their own writings.

The novel became the preferred medium of artistic expression for many French Canadian women writers until the late 1960s. The popularity and literary merit of novels by Laure Conan (Félicité Angers; 1845–1924), Germaine Guèvremont (1893–1968), Gabrielle Roy (1909–1983), Anne Hébert (b. 1916), and Marie-Claire Blais (b. 1939) are well established. More recently, Acadian writer Antonine Maillet (b. 1929) has attracted international attention for her imaginative historical novels about the epic struggles of the Acadian people dispersed by the English between 1755 and 1762 from the original French settlements of L'Arcadie.

Women novelists have often critiqued the culturally acceptable ideals of womanhood and the ideological forces that dominated Quebec culture until the "Quiet Revolution" of the 1960s. Laure Conan's *Angéline de Montbrun* (1882), commonly considered the first important psychological novel in French Canada, explores the emotional strength, idealism, and psychological complexity of a young woman who suffers disfigurement and subsequently decides to break her engagement to a man who no longer loves her. Themes of marriage, solitude, and autonomy are central to Conan's feminine characterization. In *Le Survenant* (1945), a best-seller in the 1940s and a radio series from 1953 to 1955, Germaine Guèvremont examines the lingering force of rural values in Quebec society, especially the patriarchal nature of familial relations and the pervasive authority of the Catholic Church. Her rebellious male protagonist subverts the existing order by rejecting the conventional wisdom that happiness flourishes only in the traditional family unit and in an agrarian landscape that never changes.

Equally recognized for her contributions to the short story and the novel,

Gabrielle Roy is most widely known for her realistic portrayal of working-class life in *Bonheur d'occasion* (1945), a novel that depicts the effects of urban poverty, particularly on women who, as mothers of large families in dismal urban dwellings, become the double victims of urbanization and rural patriarchal values. Marie-Claire Blais, whose novel *Une saison dans la vie d'Emmanuel* (1965) has been translated into 16 languages, has used both urban and rural Quebec landscapes for her haunting portraits of impoverished children, social outcasts, lesbians, and a seemingly lost generation of adolescents, all of whom fall prey to the disapproving gaze of a patriarchal and wantonly self-destructive society. Virtually all of Blais' protagonists—primarily young women—are engaged in various stages of subconscious or conscious revolt against the repressive structures and moral hypocrisy of the dominant culture.

Anne Hébert, whose works span five decades and mark four genres, has distinguished herself as Quebec's poet-novelist par excellence. The troubled young women in her fictional works are tormented by both sexual yearnings and the fear of punishment. In the claustrophobic and decaying worlds of *Les Chambres de bois* (1958), *Kamouraska* (1970), and *Les Fous de Bassan* (1982), women are brutalized, raped, and closeted away or murdered so as to prevent any undermining of the precarious social order, a patriarchal and heavily masculine order that will crumble nevertheless because of its rigidity and hypocrisy, its inherent taste for violence, and the sexual repression of women. Hébert's novels have enjoyed a wide reading public in Quebec and France, and both *Kamouraska* and *Les fous de bassan* have been adapted to the cinema.

In the late 1960s, the Quebec novel began to yield its position of influence to more open-ended forms of literary expression, which appeared to coincide with a new era of political awareness and artistic experimentation, an era of particularly rapid changes in the legal, social, and cultural status of women in Quebec. During the 1960s and early 1970s, postmodern writers (women and men alike) were challenging the intent and efficacy of representational art as well as the restrictive categories of literature. Feminist writers began to produce new literary forms, creating a growing number of "mixed texts" that combined fiction, autobiography, poetic fragments, theory, and political reflections.

The new generation of self-consciously feminist writers that emerged in the mid-1970s includes many writers who, despite differing attitudes regarding the wide range of political issues facing contemporary women, are attempting to incorporate feminist political concerns and recent theories of women's place in language, culture, and history into their writing. Nicole Brossard, Madeleine Gagnon, Louky Bersianik, France Théoret, Yolande Villemaire, and Jovette Marchessault are among the most critically acclaimed writers in the 1970s, although their reading public is relatively small because of the highly experimental nature of their works.

The most widely read of recent feminist texts in Quebec, Louky Bersianik's *L'Euguélionne* (1976) is a humorous, woman-centered antibible that recounts the arrival of an extraterrestrial female being who, dissatisfied with the sexual politics on her own distant planet, has come to earth in search of a more "positive planet" and a male species that is more feminist in outlook. She is greatly troubled and disappointed by what she discovers on earth.

Two other groundbreaking texts are Nicole Brossard's *L'Amèr ou le chapitre effrité* (1977), a poetic search for the lost warmth, regenerative power, and repressed speech of the mute mother, and Madeleine Gagnon's *Lueur* (1979), which combines Gagnon's own personal quest for origins with a psychoanalytic journey back to the mother's womb in search of a lost female language, a language that Gagnon links to the historically silenced maternal body and primeval forms of life.

During the 1970s and 1980s, women writers also gravitated toward the theater in increasing numbers. Denise Boucher's controversial *Les Fées ont soif* (1976) sent a shock wave through Quebec's theatrical establishment for its "disrespectful" and all-too-human representation of the Virgin Mary. The collaborative feminist play *La Nef des sorcières* (1978) also broke new ground with its six female monologues in which women denounce various male myths about who they are and struggle to construct an identity on their own terms. The feminist plays of Jovette Marchessault, particularly *La Saga des poules mouillées* (1981), have been well received by the critics and general public, no doubt because of their unusually creative mixture of poetry, history, and sexual politics. In *La Saga*, Marchessault brings four of Quebec's most influential women writers together—Laure Conan, Germaine Guèvremont, Gabrielle Roy, and Anne Hébert—to discuss their accomplishments and collective dreams as artists and to mourn the censorship of their works and the oppression they suffered as women.

Women writers in Quebec today have a solid feminine literary tradition behind them. In their current experimental efforts to rename and rewrite women's experience they continue to carve new paths for women writers in general and for French Canadian literature.

References. Mary Jean Green, Paula Gilbert Lewis, and Karen Gould, "Inscriptions of the Feminine: A Century of Women Writing in Quebec," *American Review of Canadian Studies* 15 (1985): 363–388; Paula Gilbert Lewis (ed.), *Traditionalism, Nationalism, and Feminism: Women Writers of Quebec* (Westport, Conn., 1985).

KAREN GOULD

CANCER is one of the leading causes of death in adult women, being responsible for more deaths now than in our grandmothers' day, largely because deaths from complications of childbearing have been reduced significantly. Changes in the environment, especially in the work environment, as well as the consequences of cigarette smoking put women at greater risk of cancer now than earlier.

Women of color* have a greater incidence of cancer and are more likely to die of it than are white women. Nor have reductions in cancer mortality benefited women of color as much as white women; for example, black women continue to have twice the rate of cervical cancer as white women, even though the rate of cervical cancer for all women has dropped substantially, approximately 2 percent per year since 1988. Rates for esophageal cancer are over three times higher among blacks than among whites (American Cancer Society, 1996).

Among the reasons for a higher incidence of cancer in women of color is their lower likelihood of having regular Pap smears taken. The Pap smear* does an effective job of detecting cervical cancer early enough for it to be successfully treated, but 50 percent of women who develop cervical cancer have never had a Pap smear. Another factor is environmental racism. To the extent that environmental racism has been described, people of color are being exposed to environmental carcinogens (cancer-producing substances), known and unknown, in greater number and to a greater degree than are whites.

Cancer treatment has been controversial for women. Hysterectomy (removal of the uterus) has been used to treat uterine cancer but has also been done in situations in which, in fact, cancer was not found to be present. Radical surgery of the breast has been done for decades when more conservative treatment produces the same life expectancy.

Women should know that the American Cancer Society defines "survival rates" as being alive five years after diagnosis. The survival rate for women with breast cancer is calculated at 83 percent, but at 10 years after diagnosis 65% of women survive, and at 15 years only 56 percent of affected women are still alive (American Cancer Society, *Cancer Facts and Figures,* 1996).

Lung Cancer. During the decade of the 1980s, a 50-year trend changed when lung cancer overtook breast cancer as the leading cause of cancer deaths in women. This change resulted not from lower incidence or fewer deaths from breast cancer but largely from the effects of increased cigarette smoking by women that began in the 1940s and led to increased lung cancer many years later. (Rates peaked for men in 1984 and continue to decline, while the rate continues to increase for women.)

Although more men and women continue to become ex-smokers, it is clear that women find it more difficult to quit and that teen women are the group with the greatest increase in cigarette smoking. This can be expected to have devastating effects on women's health in 20 years, not only from lung cancer but also from cervical, ovarian, pancreatic, and bladder cancer.

Lung cancer has no early symptoms, and survival rates are not improving significantly. Prevention is the best defense. Prevention measures include avoiding cigarette smoking, avoiding passive smoking (inhaling the second-hand smoke of family or coworkers), and avoiding occupational exposure to chemicals and dust. Environmental exposure plus cigarette smoking multiplies the risk of lung cancer.

Cigarette advertising has been successful at targeting women, especially young women, by using tactics such as camaraderie among women and even women's liberation to sell the product. Images of women in the media continue to portray cigarette smoking as glamorous and sophisticated. There is also evidence that women in the Western world continue to smoke to limit eating in an effort to stay thin. Interestingly, young black women in the United States seem to be more successful in resisting the advertising and start to smoke less than other teen women.

Although a number of groups within the women's community have taken up the cause of reducing breast cancer in women, organizing against the cause of lung cancer is not as popular, in part, because of the more controversial behavioral component of lung cancer risk. Smoking cigarettes has been linked with the independent woman for decades. Breaking that association is the challenge.

It is important that women not be deluded into thinking that a risk-free cigarette exists. The impetus is to create a product that is more, rather than less, addicting, thus ensuring a steadfast consumer. Products portrayed as having low tar and nicotine may be misrepresented and are not a safeguard against lung and other cancers.

As social and work settings become less tolerant of smoking behavior, women can take the initiative in breaking the association between smoking, sophistication, and rebellion that advertising promotes and many teen women, lesbian women, and low-income women buy.

Breast Cancer. Until 1987 breast cancer was the number one cause of cancer deaths in women. Since then the increase in smoking among women has been the main factor causing lung cancer to surpass breast cancer in its effect on cancer mortality. The incidence of breast cancer increased 4 percent per year between 1982 and 1987 and has had lesser increases since that time. The American Cancer Society cites increased use of mammography for increased detection, but one should also consider the effects of higher levels of exposure to environmental contamination. Deaths have not been reduced in spite of better education (e.g., campaigns to encourage mammography and breast self-examination) and in spite of aggressive surgical intervention.

Overall, 1 in 9 or 10 women is expected to develop breast cancer in her lifetime. A number of factors have been identified as increasing a woman's risk of breast cancer. Increasing age is the most important factor; three-quarters of breast cancer occurs after the age of 50. Women with a mother or sister who had breast cancer before menopause are at greater risk. A genetic marker has been identified for women with a risk of premenopausal breast cancer. Eighty percent of women who develop breast cancer, however, have no family history of the disease.

Additional risk factors for women include (1) fibrocystic changes in breast tissue that make detection of cancerous changes difficult; (2) exposure to diethylstilbestrol (DES) as an attempt at "morning-after" contraception, to "dry up" breasts of a birthing woman who did not intend to breast-feed, or in the belief that it would preserve a pregnancy (since disproven); (3) increased number of menstrual cycles (resulting from early onset of menses, late menopause, having no children, delaying childbearing until later in life).

Regular examination of the breast by the woman herself or by her spouse/lover is important in detecting changes such as a lump or thickening, nipple discharge, or breast skin changes. These signs need to be investigated by a physician skilled in detection and management of breast disease.

Mammography, low-dose X-ray of the breast tissue, is more sensitive than manual examination in the detection of breast changes, especially in women over 40, the age at which breast cancer risk increases greatly. Before that age the density of the breast tissue makes imagery less effective. When "dedicated" X-ray machines (machines used only for mammography and never adjusted upward to greater doses of X-ray) are used, the risk of exposure to X-ray is outweighed in women past menopause.

The American Cancer Society recommends the following schedule for the use of mammography:

Age 40: one baseline mammography (for comparison)

Age 41–49: mammography every 1–2 years

Age 50+: mammography every year

Women who find they have an early localized breast cancer (under 5 mm in size) should insist on surgical removal of the lump only (which may or may not need to be supplemented by radiation therapy). For many years surgeons have continued to perform radical mastectomies (removal of the entire breast, lymph nodes under the arm, and sometimes muscle from the chest wall), leaving the woman disfigured and, at times, disabled. Research in Europe and later in the United States confirmed that women with localized disease do not live longer with the radical procedure than if the lump alone is excised (lumpectomy) and radiation is used when indicated. Women's knowledge and demands as well as cost containment efforts will change this practice.

Women whose breast tumors are larger when detected or whose cancer has spread face more complicated choices. Women need to focus on detection of early changes in breast tissue and on treatment choices.

Treatment philosophy has recently emphasized reconstructive procedures aimed at cosmetic improvement for women undergoing breast surgery.

Women are interested not only in cosmetic appearance but in discovery of substantial, preventable risk factors of breast cancer, making early detection measures accessible to all women, and in treatment options that control disease without causing disfigurement and disability.

Cervical and Uterine Cancer. Cervical and uterine cancer are often considered together because the cervix is the lower portion of the uterus (womb), but the two cancers present different risk patterns. The cervix, which can be felt at the back of the vagina, is more susceptible to cancerous changes in women who have early exposure to sperm (before 18 years of age). Young women in early puberty (13 years) and younger girls who are subjected to repeated sexual abuse involving exposure to sperm are especially at risk of developing cervical cancer 20 years later. When young girls and women have sex with a number of men, their risk of cervical cancer is increased as well.

Women who have had herpes genitalis or human papilloma virus (HPV) are also at increased risk of developing cancerous changes on the cervix. Smoking cigarettes is associated with increased risk; in fact, nicotine can be recovered from the cells of the cervix in women who smoke.

Use of barrier methods of birth control, especially the male and female condom and the diaphragm, reduces the risk of cervical cancer. Young teen women having consensual sex with men are less likely to use barrier methods for birth control and prevention of sexually transmitted disease, and in fact they need it for an additional reason: the prevention of cervical cancer.

The Pap smear is highly effective in detecting early cervical cell changes. Recommendations regarding the frequency of Pap smear testing vary from every year to every three years after three normal annual results. It makes sense that women at higher risk get Pap smears more often. Lesbian and celibate women often mistake their risk of cervical cancer as zero and get Pap smears rarely or never, which is unwise. Women without identified risk factors also need periodic Pap smears as part of a well woman examination.

Cervical cell changes that are detected early can be treated by removal of a localized area on the cervix, avoiding the need for hysterectomy while preserving childbearing ability, if valued.

Uterine cancer, or cancer of the endometrium, the lining of the uterus, occurs more often in women over 40 years of age, women who are significantly overweight (20 percent above weight range for height), women who have taken sequential birth control pills (estrogen-only pills for part of the month, estrogen and progesterone pills for the remainder of the month), women who have taken estrogen replacement for long periods without also taking a progesterone product, and women with irregular or absent ovulation, with diabetes, or with high blood pressure.

The Pap smear is not a good method of detecting uterine cancer. Women over 45 years who have irregular or unexplained uterine bleeding (vaginal bleeding, similar to menses) should have an endometrial biopsy or endometrial wash. If cancer cells are found, a second opinion regarding the advisability of hysterectomy is essential and even required by some insurance companies or health maintenance organizations because of the frequency of removal of normal uteri in the past.

Women sometimes discontinue regular health care visits after the "childbearing years," when the risks of uterine, breast, and colon cancer, as well as cardiovascular risk, increase. It is important to continue health care visits throughout the later years of life.

Ovarian Cancer. Ovarian cancer is the fourth leading cause of cancer deaths in women. The challenge is perplexing because there are no early symptoms and no techniques for early detection of this deadly disease. Ovarian cancer occurs most often in women after age 55; therefore an ovarian mass felt on pelvic examination can be watched in younger women; any enlargement in a woman past menopause needs further investigation.

Risk of ovarian cancer increases with age, with childlessness, with a family history of the disease, and with personal history of breast cancer. Use of oral contraceptives appears to have a protective effect.

Use of talcum powder on the genitals or on sanitary napkins should be avoided because of a link with ovarian cancer.

Treatment involves surgery, radiation, and chemotherapy. Women who have a number of close relatives with ovarian cancer may be encouraged by physicians to have their ovaries removed prophylactically, but the risks of abdominal surgery and the effects of loss of ovaries without known disease make the practice highly questionable.

Colon and Rectal Cancer. Deaths from colon and rectal cancer have been reduced substantially in women in the last 30 years. Even so, colon and rectal cancer continues to be the third leading cause of cancer deaths in both women and men.

People at risk of colon and rectal cancer are those with a personal or family history of such cancer or a history of intestinal polyps or of inflammatory bowel disease. Persons who eat a diet high in processed foods and low in fiber may be at greater risk. High-fat diets have also been suggested as a risk factor for colon cancer.

The American Cancer Society recommends the following schedule for early detection: (1) a digital rectal exam as part of an annual checkup after age 40; (2) a test done at home for blood in the stool every year after age 50; and (3) a flexible sigmoidoscopy, a visual exam of the lower bowel, done in a physician's office every 3–5 years after age 50.

Reference. American Cancer Society Inc., *Cancer Facts and Figures* (Atlanta, 1996).

ELAINE WHEELER

CARDIOVASCULAR DISEASE refers to deficits in the function of the heart, lungs, and blood vessels throughout the body. Some of the health problems resulting are heart attack, stroke, high blood pressure, varicose veins, peripheral vascular disease, and coronary artery disease.

Cardiovascular disease (CVD) has been decreasing steadily in the United States since 1960 and especially since 1980. In spite of these decreases, CVD remains the most frequent cause of death in adult women and men. Most of the research done and the media attention have been focused on men. As a result, many women think CVD is a man's health problem.

Women have particular cardiovascular risks. Women are more likely to start smoking and slower to quit than men. Women report less exercise than men; fewer than 20 percent of women report exercise, while one-third of men report being active. Women who have a heart attack are more likely to die as a result than are men. Even women who have surgical intervention for coronary heart disease are more likely to die than men who have the same surgery, especially in older age groups. Women develop CVD later in life, possibly as the protectant effects of estrogen recede. Women at 60 years have comparable risk to 50-year-old men. At 75 years the risk is similar for women and men.

Women are also at risk due to the stress associated with oppression: racism, sexism, homophobia, poverty. Women are concentrated in jobs characterized by lack of control over one's time, space, and activities, a factor associated with increased risk of heart attack and high blood pressure. Even when such risk factors as age, race, education, and smoking are statistically eliminated from the equation, people in the bottom 10 percent of the job echelon have four to five times the risk of heart attack as those at the top 10 percent of the ladder (University of California-Berkeley, *Wellness Letter*, May 1994).

Some risk factors for CVD cannot be controlled. These include aging, gender, ethnic group (those with a significant proportion of heritage from Africa have twice the risk of high blood pressure), and family history. Women can pay closer attention to lifestyle changes when they know that their age, ethnic group, or family history makes CVD a particular risk for them.

Risk factors that can be impacted are smoking, high blood pressure, overweight, diabetes. Women who smoke are two to six times more likely to have a heart attack than nonsmoking women. The damage done to blood vessels by smoking (reduction in elasticity) can be reversed after 5–10 years without cigarettes. Low-tar and-nicotine cigarettes, often marketed to women, do not reduce risk of CVD.

High blood pressure is a risk for stroke and heart attack. It can be controlled through diet (lowering salt helps some groups), exercise (walking is the best), and medication. Antihypertensive medication often has difficult side effects; women should report problems with medicine to the prescriber so that a different medicine can be tried, rather than not taking the medicine altogether. One side effect not often spoken about with women is interference with sexual response. Some antihypertensive medication is less likely to cause this problem than others.

Weight control is a major issue for women. Some may rebel against the unreasonable social standard for thinness in women. However, maintaining reasonable weight reduces risk of a number of health problems, including CVD. Exercise is a critical factor in controlling weight.

Diabetes increases risk of hypertension and coronary artery disease in men, but more so in women. Weight control and exercise can improve the utilization of blood sugar and prevent or slow the onset of diabetes.

Other changes that can reduce risk of CVD include (1) reducing blood cholesterol through diet changes and exercise. (2) taking one-half aspirin each day, with food to avoid stomach irritation. Aspirin can reduce risk of heart attack by reducing the ability of platelets in the blood to form clots. (3) drinking a *small* amount of alcohol (one serving). Large amounts of alcohol produce the opposite effect of aggravating other risk factors. (4) taking hormone replacement therapy after menopause. Estrogen (and progestin) therapy raises "good" cholesterol and lowers risk of heart disease in other ways. Research is in progress to learn more about the impact of hormone replacement therapy.

Reference. University of California-Berkeley, *Wellness Letter*, May 1994.

ELAINE WHEELER

CARIBBEAN WRITERS IN ENGLISH (TWENTIETH-CENTURY). Women writers of the former British West Indies live in a society of extreme diversity and cultural fragmentation. The insecurity of human relationships, particularly between man and woman and mother and daughter, and uneasiness about personal identity are the most common concerns of the prominent writers: Phyllis Shand Allfrey (Dominica), Zee Edgell (Belize), Merle Hodge (Trinidad), Jamaica Kincaid (Antigua), Paule Marshall (Barbados), Jean Rhys (Dominica), and Sylvia Wynter (Jamaica).

Although these women come from different countries, their writing explores the shared problem of establishing personal and cultural identity within a small community that has suffered the conquest and genocide of its aboriginal people, the enslavement of Africans, absentee landlordism and imperialistic control, racism, isolation, claustrophobia, and tension between indigenous African and imported European cultural elements. During the colonial era, Caribbean literature was based on models derived from European, particularly British, attitudes. However, with independence there was an increasing consciousness of the African and distinctively Creole elements in West Indian culture. A new literature that reflected this great awakening was needed. Many writers questioned the importance of European literary models, but no easy solutions have been found as the area struggles to find a new language and a new literature that genuinely express a Caribbean sense of reality. In the last 10 years, only an ambivalent balancing of European and African cultures has been achieved.

Women sometimes write with great anxiety, since their models are usually male, and their societies emphasize that women's vocation lies in nurturing relationships with men and with children. Nevertheless, these writers have created characters who are self-supporting, often single parents of great strength and endurance. They struggle and survive because of their basic respect for life, and they depend on no man for success in their fight for basic survival.

Women writers have investigated the problems women experience in growing up in the West Indies. Jean Rhys' best novel, *Wide Sargasso Sea* (1966), and Phyllis Shand Allfrey's first novel, *The Orchid House* (1953), examine the identity problems that destroy the descendants of white Creole families, disliked by blacks as the descendants of slave owners and patronized by the British as colonials, not genuine Europeans. Rhys shows that the lack of a sense of identity with the West Indian community, combined with tenuous relationships within the family, leads to despair, alcoholism, and suicide. Novels focusing on the African-Caribbean woman's passage into maturity are more positive. The adolescent Beka in Zee Edgell's *Beka Lamb* (1982) learns to survive rejection by males, while her pregnant friend Toycie disintegrates when her Mexican boyfriend rejects her because she is not light-skinned. Beka's survival shows a strength similar to that of Télumée Miracle in Guadeloupean Simone Schwarz-Bart's *Bridge of Beyond* (1972). Télumée survives desertion because the Toussine women teach each generation the endurance and self-reliance needed for survival.

Paule Marshall and Jamaica Kincaid, who have lived for long periods in the United States, have examined both the problems of a young woman's adolescence and the tension she experiences between life in the United States and life in the West Indies. In Paule Marshall's *Brown Girl, Brownstones* (1959), Selina Boyce, who grows up in Brooklyn, rejects the coldness of the other Barbadian exiles who have embraced the worst of North American values and decides to return to Barbados, her parents' birthplace, to seek the human values they have lost through their emigration. Jamaica Kincaid's characters move in the opposite direction in *At the Bottom of the River* (1978) and *Annie John* (1983). Both explore the close, but alternatively suffocating, relationship between a daughter and her mother. In the latter book, Annie John as a child adores her mother but during adolescence comes to hate the older woman and, finally, after near death, leaves the island to start a career.

Both Sylvia Wynter, whose *The Hills of Hebron: A Jamaican Novel* (1962) explores the culture of Afro-Jamaicanism, and Merle Hodge, in *Crick Crack Monkey* (1981), examine the tension between the African-Caribbean and metropolitan cultures. In Hodge's novel, Tee must choose between Aunt Beatrice's attempts to imitate British upper-class society and language and Tantie's more honest acceptance of Creole manners and dialect. Although Tee feels more comfortable with Tantie, her earlier contact with Beatrice's values makes it impossible for her ever to identify completely with the black Creole culture. Hodge deals with this traditional theme of male writers, the problem of cultural identification, perhaps best of all the women writers. Although the women do not, anymore than the men, offer a convincing alternative to the present ambivalent balancing of the two cultures, they do offer many more positive models of strength and endurance. Their women characters who survive, physically and psychologically, do so because they have formed strong and supporting bonds with other women in their families and communities.

References. Edward Kamau Brathwaite (ed.), *Savacou: Caribbean Woman* (Washington, D.C., 1977); Barbara Comissing and Marjorie Thorpe, "A Select Bibliography of Women Writers in the Eastern Caribbean (excluding Guyana)," *World Literature Written in English* 17 (1978): 274–304; Donald E. Herdeck, Maurice A. Lubin, and John Figeroa (eds.), *Caribbean Writers: A Bio-Bibliographical Critical Encyclopedia* (Washington, D.C., 1979); Leota S. Lawrence, "Women in Caribbean Literature: The African Presence," *Phylon* 44 (1983): 1–11.

LAURA NIESEN DE ABRUÑA

CHAUCER'S WOMEN derive from the religious, classical, and continental chivalric traditions yet create a native English tradition less tied to stereotypically opposed roles. The tradition of biblical exegesis poses an opposition between the Old Testament Eve and the New Testament Mary. The classical tradition opposes Philosophia and Fortuna. The continental tradition opposes the courtly love lady, Fin Amour, and the fabliau lady, False Amour. In Chaucer's work, such figures as Dame Alisoun, the Wife of Bath, and Criseyde of *Troilus and Criseyde* expose the limitations of those stereotypical roles to suggest a richer sense of women's lives.

The Wife of Bath's prologue opens with an examination of terms from the medieval debate on knowledge: "Experience, though noon auctoritee/ Were in this world, is right ynogh for me/ To speke of wo that is in marriage" (ll. 1–3). The Wife of Bath, however, soon demonstrates that the dichotomy between the patriarchy's authority found in books and women's experience does not contain the complexity of feeling and awareness of human knowledge. She is able, through challenging Jankyn's learning and using her experience, to dissolve simple distinctions. Her achievement of "maistrye," like that of the old wife in her tale of a callow Arthurian knight's education, provides a model for heroic womanhood. Neither Eve nor Mary, neither Lady Philosophy nor Lady Fortune, neither Fin Amour nor False Amour, the Wife of Bath epitomizes the complexity of Chaucer's representation of women.

In *Troilus and Criseyde*, Chaucer's debt to Boethius' *Consolation of Philosophy* is revealed in the tension between Lady Philosophy's and Lady Fortune's control of the fates of the characters. Yet in Criseyde's fate as a political pawn in the Trojan War, abandoned by her father, torn from her lover, and then reconciled to life in the Greek camp with Diomede, a new lover, only men seem to wield effective power. Here her representation derives from the passive role of the Fin Amour love object of the chivalric tradition. Yet just as Chaucer reevaluates that tradition, so he reexamines the women's role in it. Criseyde, a widow, not without experience, declares, "I am myn owene woman, wel at ese" (1. 750). Although Pandarus violates her independence through manipulating his niece into an amorous relationship with Troilus, Criseyde retains sufficient resourcefulness in difficult circumstances to survive and perhaps thrive.

In every instance, Chaucer's women reevaluate the limiting roles to which their lives have traditionally been ascribed. In "The Clerk's Tale," Griselde triumphs over, and questions the part of, the "patient Grissel." Alison, the wife of "The Miller's Tale," alone of all her community escapes punishment, apparently beyond judgment in her vitality. The poor widow and her two daughters in "The Nun's Priest's Tale" preside like a kind of communal female divinity over their paradisal barnyard, a universe marred only by Chaunticleer's male pride and folly.

Yet the darker side of women's position in late medieval England remains a subject of Chaucer's poetry. In both "The Franklin's Tale" and "The Physician's Tale" virtuous women become the sacrificial victims of male allegiance to false vows. Dorigen of "The Franklin's Tale" submits to her husband, Arveragus', inflexible conception of "trouthe." In "The Physician's Tale," Virginia, like Jephthah's daughter, to whom Chaucer alludes, is sacrificed to her father's false justice. Chaucer's treatment of these traditional views of women as victim leads to a vigorous reevaluation of the patriarchal structure that perpetuates them.

References. Ruth M. Ames, "The Feminist Connections of Chaucer's *Legend of Good Women*," in J. N. Wasserman and Robert N. Blanch (eds.), *Chaucer in the Eighties* (Syracuse, 1986), 57–74; Robert W. Hanning, "From *Eva* and *Ave* to Eglentyne and Alisoun: Chaucer's Insight into the Roles Women Play," *Signs* 2 (1977): 580–599; H. P. Weissman, "Antifeminism and Chaucer's Characterization of Women," in G. Economou (ed.), *Geoffrey Chaucer: A Collection of Criticism* (New York, 1975), 93–110.

NONA FIENBERG

CHICANA. See LATINA

CHICANA WRITERS are women of Mexican descent who live in the United States and write from that perspective. Among the most recent arrivals to the American literary world, they made their first appearance as part of the Chicano literary outburst of the early 1970s, the peak of the Chicano movement. Thus, writings by Chicanas are best understood if read in the same historical, societal, and cultural contexts as those of their male counterparts. However, since Estela Portillo Trambley published her first play (*The Day of the Swallows*) in 1971, it has been clear that sexism was to be an important theme among Chicana writers.

Chicanas' experiences are unique in that they have been subjected to a threefold oppression. First, the Chicana has been victimized by racism, since she is of mixed Indian and Spanish blood in a society dominated by Anglo-Americans. She has also been the victim of economic exploitation as a member of an ethnic group historically relegated to poor, working-class status. Finally, she has been subjected to a double dose of discrimination against women by both American and Mexican traditions of male domination.

However, there is a positive side to this threefold experience. Cordelia Candelaria shows this in *Chicano Poetry: A Critical Introduction* by not only explaining the Chicana's "triple jeopardy" but also stressing her "triple joy," namely, the advantages of her Spanish/English bilingualism, the three cultures she has at her disposal (Indian, Spanish, and American), and the traditions of feminism in Mexican and, even more, in American history (172). Chicana writers draw from all aspects of this "triple jeopardy/triple joy," giving the best Chicana writing distinctiveness and freshness.

According to Tey Diana Rebolledo, Chicana writers began to express themselves in much the same manner as male Chicano movement poets, in angry protest. Much of their poetry in the 1970s was an explosion aimed primarily at males in the Chicano movement who pressed for liberation but denied Chicanas equal status. They also expressed frustration with, and alienation from, middle-class feminism, which they felt excluded them. Their anger gave rise to protest, says Rebolledo, but much of the poetry it generated paid little heed to the craft itself and did not express a full range of Chicana experience.

Since the initial outburst of the 1970s, Chicana writers have waged what Rebolledo calls a "quiet revolution." Although this historical summary overlooks two poets of the 1970s, Bernice Zamora and Marina Rivera, who were writing much more than angry protest, it provides a generally valid description of Chicana writers' evolution from the beginning of the movement to the present. Rebolledo also offers a good overview of major themes found in Chicana writing: growing, identity, reflection and creation of self through female family members, especially mothers and grandmothers, the search for, and adaption of, myth and tradition, the depiction of everyday life, love and passion, the craft and function of writing, and, of course, social criticism. One should also add the philosophical themes commonly found in literature: reflections on nature, life, death, and the supernatural.

Many themes developed by Chicanas are common to all Chicano writing: cultural conflicts, suppression of the Spanish language, the exploitation and struggles of Chicano workers, the immigration authorities, social mobility, conditions in the barrios (Chicano neighborhoods), and the effects of U.S. society on barrios, families, and traditions. Some writers also express resentment toward Anglo-Americans' expropriation of Mexican lands after the Mexican-American War.

However, unlike Chicanos, Chicanas are often critical of traditional Mexican patriarchy and its suppression of women. Perhaps one theme Chicana writers have in common is the assertion of self against sexism. Chicana literature is often a necessary response to rape, sexual exploitation, domestic violence, rigid gender roles, suppression of sexual desires, and other injustices against women.

The first published Chicana writer and the most prolific is Estela Portillo Trambley. Her lyrical play *The Day of the Swallows*, vivid and rich in metaphor, stirred much controversy because of its depiction of lesbianism and denunciation of traditional Mexican male domination. Her book of short stories, *Rain of Scorpions* (1976), also has feminist themes, whose dimensions are deepened by tapping Greek, Catholic, and ancient Mexican Indian myths and worldviews. Her other drama includes *Sun Images* (1976) and *Sor Juana and Other Plays* (1983). Her first novel, *Trini*, was published in 1986.

Other fiction writers have emerged. Most notable is Sandra Cisneros, whose *House on Mango Street*, an American Book Award winner, is a finely wrought, poetic collection of sketches narrated by, and revolving around, a young Chicana coming of age in an urban barrio. With humor and moving sensitivity, Cisneros depicts the hopes, joys, and often sad realities of barrio people, especially women. Other Chicana fiction includes *There Are No Madmen Here*, a novel by Gina Valdés, *The Last of the Menu Girls*, a collection of memoirs by Denise Chávez, and *The Moths and Other Stories*, by Helena Viramontes.

Although recent trends show Chicana writers moving into other genres, most are poets. Among the most important are Lorna Dee Cervantes, Evangelina Vigil, Bernice Zamora, Lucha Corpi, Angela de Hoyos, Inés Tovar, and Pat Mora. Cervantes' *Emplumada* stands out as the only Chicana book of poems published by mainstream academe, the University of Pittsburgh's Pitt Poetry Series. Bernice Zamora's *Restless Serpents*, Corpi's *Palabras de Mediodia/Noon Words*, Inés Tovar's *Con razon corazon*, Evangelina Vigil's *Thirty an' Seen a Lot*, De Hoyos' *Arise, Chicano, Selected Poems*, and *Woman, Woman*, and Pat Mora's *Chants and Borders* are also noteworthy.

Summarizing Chicana writers' themes is impossible, for theirs are multifaceted expressions of women who are, as Pat Mora says in *Chants*, "sliding back and forth/between the fringes of both worlds" (52). Portillo Trambley urges a personal and societal balance and wholeness. Zamora seeks an alternative to greed and racial purity, a "deeper, wider mind" that "knows itself to be muddy with adobe" (*Restless Serpents*, 58). Marginalized by both American and Chicano societies, Chicanas have learned, to paraphrase Cervantes, to trust only what they have built with their own hands (*Emplumada*, 14). Perhaps Cisneros sums up the Chicana writer's perspective when she tells of her desire to have her own house. "Not a man's house. Not a daddy's. A house all my own . . . quiet as now . . . clean as paper before the poem" (*House on Mango Street*, 100).

References. Cordelia Candelaria, *Chicano Poetry: A Critical Introduction* (Westport, Conn., 1986); Roberto J. Garza, *Contemporary Chicano Theatre* (Notre Dame, Ind., 1976); Tey Diana Rebolledo, "The Maturing of Chicana Poetry: The Quiet Revolution of the 1980s," in Paula A. Treichler et al., *Alma Mater: Theory and Practice in Feminist Scholarship* (Chicago, 1985); Marta E. Sanchez, *Contemporary Chicana Poetry: A Critical Approach to an Emerging Literature* (Berkeley, Calif., 1985).

TOMÁS VALLEJOS

CHILD ABUSE. See DOMESTIC VIOLENCE; INCEST

CHILD CARE is the "looking after" of children. With urbanization and industrialization old ways of tending the children of working mothers were no longer always possible, as residential and work patterns changed, and employment no longer centered in the home. As a result, in the eighteenth and nineteenth centuries, private and public services were created to help parents who worked outside the home care for their children.

Child care policy refers to various public and private sector benefits and programs, actual or desired, to influence the care of young children. Most familiar are group and family day care programs provided by either the government or the employer. But child care programs may also encompass tax policies, such as child care deductions and credits, or direct cash grants to facilitate and encourage childrearing. Employment-related policies include not only the place and number of day nurseries but also the option of paid maternity and parent leave with job protection and seniority and medical benefits. Flexible work hours and job-sharing opportunities for parents also come within the contemporary understanding of child care policies.

The nature of child care reflects societal attitudes toward families, parenting, and, in particular, women. Although the number of women working in paid employment outside the home has increased dramatically in the past several decades, childrearing has remained primarily the mother's responsibility. Curiously, however, societal responses to child care needs have turned less on service to women and children than on concerns over decreasing population and labor needs, especially in wartime.

Families need child care for many reasons, the most familiar being to enable parents to work. But parents might also need day care while they complete their education, if they become chronically ill, or when they need

what psychologists call "quality" adult time. Increased labor force participation* of women has stimulated the demand for day care and other child
care policies that permit families to care well for their children. In countries
like the United States, the larger number of single women raising children
alone has drawn attention to the inadequacies of child care benefits. So
have the needs of an increasing number of homeless families whose children
would benefit from the services that are often part of a good day care
program.

Child care benefits and services vary widely from country to country. For
a number of reasons, including the tremendous loss of population in World
Wars I and II and the influence of social democratic parties, European
governments have far more extensive child care policies than the United
States. In Europe it is far more common to find public crèche and nursery
school programs open to children regardless of family income. Paid maternity leave is also part of the European agenda. The average leave is five
months at full pay. In Sweden fathers as well as mothers may elect to take
paid parent leave. Parents may also adopt a six-hour workday until a child
is 8 years old. West Germany offers a monthly housework day. Italian
women receive substantial credit toward job seniority with the birth of each
child.

The situation in the United States is sharply different. With population
steady through much of the twentieth century, neither employers nor government has perceived a need to encourage a higher birthrate or higher
workforce participation through child care policies. Until major changes in
tax policy, introducing first a child care tax deduction and then, in the mid-
1970s, a tax credit, most child care policy consisted of income-tested day
care programs. Families not considered "needy" were thought properly beyond receiving aid for child care. Indeed, President Nixon in his 1971 veto
of comprehensive child care legislation described this kind of government
intervention as "family weakening."

Influenced by the women's movement, the realities of female employment, and a birthrate now below replacement level, employers and government in the United States are beginning to discuss "adaptation" to
feminization of the workforce. Alarmed at the weakening of the family,
officials now speak of child care as "something that supports family life."
There is considerable argument, however, about the nature of such supportive policies. Contention centers on whether tax policies or a family
wage to encourage women with children to stay home should prevail over
freely available day care centers that permit women to work out of the
house after bearing children. Child care policy is, and will be, as it has
been, a means of influencing not only children's but women's lives and
well-being.

References. S. B. Kamerman and A. J. Kahn, *Child Care, Family Benefits and
Working Parents* (New York, 1981); J. Norgren, "Child Care," in Jo Freeman (ed.),

Women: A Feminist Perspective, 3d ed. (Palo Alto, 1984); J. Norgren, "The Voteless Constituency: Children and Child Care," in J. K. Boles (ed.), *The Egalitarian City: Issues of Rights, Distribution, Access, and Power* (Westport, Conn., 1986).
                                                                                    JILL NORGREN

CHILDBIRTH cross-culturally is an event of enormous personal and societal significance. It is, after all, the process through which new members are recruited into a society. Apart from the changes the birth of a child engenders in the lives of a couple, birth also constitutes a rite of passage that transforms their status within the family and the community. Indeed in many societies a female is not considered a woman until she has borne a child, and a union is not considered a legitimate marriage* until a child has been produced.

It is useful to draw a distinction between "parturition,"* the physiological aspects of birthing, and "childbirth," the ways in which this process is experienced, endowed with meaning, and behaviorally managed. Parturition, determined by human anatomy and physiology, is universal. The growth of the fetus,* the beginning of uterine contractions at the end of the pregnancy, the opening up of the birth canal, the eventual expulsion of baby and placenta, and finally lactation happen for all women no matter where they give birth, in a hut in jungles of South America or in a modern hospital.

It would be reasonable to expect that these panhuman characteristics of parturition would have led, in the course of evolution, to some optimal way of bringing a baby into the world and that this method would have spread to all human groups because of its survival value. However, this is not the case. What we find, instead, is tremendous cross-cultural variation in birth practices, attitudes, and beliefs.

Cross-cultural variation begins with ideas about conception. For example, there are societies where the baby is thought not to be conceived at one time but rather as "built up" during the pregnancy through the joint efforts of the couple. The mother contributes the red parts of blood (which explains why it no longer flows during pregnancy), while the father contributes the white parts, for example, skin, bones, and intestines, through his semen. In such societies, continued intercourse is considered necessary for building a healthy baby. In other cultures, particularly where people believe in the reincarnation of ancestors, conception is thought to occur because a "spirit child" wants to be born and finds itself a mother. Australian Aborigines believe that the child may enter the woman either through the vagina (e.g., if she squats at certain springs frequented by spirit babies) or through the mouth (e.g., if she eats a fish prepared by the father into which a spirit child has entered because it wants to be born). Conception, then, occurs on the agency of the baby, not the parents. In such societies, our Western birth control methods make little sense. Similar cross-cultural differences can be traced for all aspects of pregnancy, birth, and the postpartum period.

Because of the universally acknowledged significance of birth, people everywhere have regulated its conduct: each culture, each subculture has developed a distinct set of beliefs and practices that constitute a "birthing system." These practices and beliefs are grounded in the culture in which they arose and are congruent with people's ideas about the world, the supernatural, their attitudes toward their bodies, their view of women's roles and competencies, and their concept of what constitutes a human being. What happens in birth has to make sense in the society at large, so that if, for example, a society is highly technologized, we are likely to find technologized birth. If the society treats women as important and autonomously functioning members, it is also likely that women get treated that way during birth. Thus, birth both reflects and reinforces the shared values that people hold.

In the United States and most other industrialized countries birth has come to be defined as a medicotechnological event and has passed from the women's domain into the realm of specialist medicine. This comparatively recent view sees birth as (at least potentially) pathological and makes pregnant women into patients requiring treatment by physicians in hospitals, where the resources of biomedical technology, pharmacology, and surgery are available. In most industrialized countries the biomedical model of birth has supplanted the traditional view of birth as a marked, but common, life cycle event that women are competent to manage. Increasingly, however, countermovements to the pathological view of birth are emerging in industrial societies.

Everywhere in the industrialized world birthing is currently the subject of intense debate. This debate is generated, in part, by the often harmful outcomes of overly technologized birth but also, especially in the United States, by the women's health movement. Increasingly, women now insist that they can and should be active participants in the birth process rather than passive patients who give their care to technical specialists. This has resulted, in the last decades, in the rise of the natural childbirth movement; the reemergence of lay and nurse-midwifery and home birth; and the growing popularity of hospital birthing rooms, freestanding birthing centers, and family-centered perinatal care. In the last few years some of the methods used by traditional practitioners have been revived in the West. Some practitioners now recommend walking and upright position during labor, physical and emotional support by family and friends, and sometimes even the use of the technique of external cephalic version, by which a baby in the wrong position for birth is turned around before labor begins.

In developing countries modernization efforts overwhelmingly rely on the biomedical model of birth, in spite of the fact that in the impoverished Third World the practice of hospital-based, physician-dependent, technology-intensive perinatal management is severely hampered by insufficient supplies of drugs, inadequately trained staff, nonrepairable machinery, and the like. This endemic lack of resources, coupled with culturally motivated resistance to hospital birth by indigenous communities, has prevented Western-style obstetrics from replacing traditional ways of birthing. Today, outside the frame of Western medicine, the birth of children is still seen as a normal (rather than a pathological) life cycle event that should be handled by the family and the women's community. Where indigenous ethnoobstetrics has not been replaced by biomedical obstetrics, the conduct of birth relies on an empirically grounded and often supernaturally sanctioned repertoire of practices and a network of traditional birth attendants who subscribe to a body of beliefs about the nature of birth that they share with childbearing women (and often with men).

In spite of the extensive cross-cultural variation in birthing practices and beliefs, there are some general principles to which traditional birthing systems tend to adhere. These emerge from the view that birth is a normal, physiologic life cycle event and thus stand in contrast to routine obstetric management in technologized birth.

The first of these is that birth is women's business. Until recently, the conduct of normal birth has been almost exclusively in the hands of childbearing women themselves, assisted by women of the family and community midwives. Outside Western medicine, male specialists (curers, shamans, medicine men) are consulted only in severely pathological cases. The categorical exclusion of males from the birth chamber (sometimes with the exception of the father of the child) has been nearly universal. While there are a few societies where men can become birth attendants, only in the United States and similarly technologized countries are men considered the most appropriate decision makers at normal births.

Cross-culturally, most births take place on the woman's territory, either her own house or hut or, on occasion, the house of her mother. Most people believe it is important that the woman give birth in a familiar place, where she feels comfortable and protected. Even today, 60 to 80 percent of all births around the world are attended by midwives in the home.

Another cross-cultural regularity is that women do not give birth alone or with strangers but are attended by other experienced women who provide physical and emotional support. Biomedical research in hospitals in Guatemala and the United States has shown that the presence of other women (*doulas*) not only influences the experience of birth but also shortens labor and positively affects neonatal mortality and morbidity. This "*doula* effect" may be one reason midwife-attended births tend to produce better outcomes than births attended by physicians under similar conditions.

Decisions about the management of labor, which the biomedical model locates in the physician, are, in ethnomedical systems, made collaboratively by the woman and her attendants. In nontechnologized birth, information about the progress and nature of labor comes primarily from the wisdom of experienced women who have themselves successfully borne children. By contrast, medical decision making is based on test results, machine output, and conformity of the labor pattern to a preestablished ideal norm, which only medical specialists are thought to be competent to interpret.

Cross-culturally, women are mobile during the early stages of labor. In most societies it is the rule that they carry out their normal activities until labor is well established. Almost everywhere women are free to assume whatever position they feel most comfortable in during the period when the baby descends and the birth canal opens up. During full labor, women tend to assume a great variety of positions, such as walking, standing, kneeling, and sitting. During the second (pushing) stage as well, vertical, rather than horizontal, positions are most common, and these not only provide the aid of gravity in the descent of the fetus but also lead to active involvement of the woman in the birthing of her baby. The passive on-the-back position with legs immobilized, which is common in technologized birth, was unknown before Western obstetrics. It increases the control of the physician in the active management of labor but leads to a series of negative effects, such as lower oxygen saturation, circulatory problems, slowing down of labor, and lack of participation by the woman.

In most societies, the baby is cleaned, wrapped, and otherwise made presentable before being given to the mother. The afterbirth is almost universally treated with great care and is often thought to hold some mystical connection to the baby. It may be buried or burned with some ritual. Universally, it is thought important that mother and baby undergo a period of rest and seclusion, most typically lasting from a week to a month. During this time breast-feeding is established, mother–infant attachment takes place, and the mother recuperates from the exertions of giving birth. The mother adheres to a special diet and observes culturally determined rules of behavior, which often focus on replacing "heat" lost during childbirth. The seclusion period is often terminated by a coming-out event, during which the mother in her new status and the newborn baby are introduced to the community. Naming of the baby and according it full human status may take place at this time or may be delayed even longer.

A cross-cultural approach to birth outlines the range of variation as well as important unifying principles in the management of parturition. Exploring the range of options that different cultures have taken up can provide important alternatives to an overly narrow biomedical view of childbirth.

References. Robbie Davis-Floyd, *Birth as an American Rite of Passage* (Berkeley, Calif., 1991); Robbie Davis-Floyd and Carolyn Sargent (eds.), *Childbirth and Authoritative Knowledge: Cross-Cultural Perspectives* (Berkeley, Calif., 1996); Brigitte Jordan, *Birth in Four Cultures: A Crosscultural Investigation of Childbirth in Yu-*

catan, Holland, Sweden and the United States, 4th ed. (Prospect Heights, Ill., 1992); M. Mead and N. Newton, "The Cultural Patterning of Perinatal Behavior," in S. Richardson and A. Guttmacher (eds.), *Childbearing—Its Social and Psychological Aspects* (Baltimore, 1967).

BRIGITTE JORDAN

CHILDREN. Their Effect on Labor Supply. With few exceptions, the presence of children reduces the amount of paid labor supplied by women; and at the same time, workingwomen* have fewer children. This complex relationship makes it difficult to estimate the exact impact of children on paid labor supply.

The presence of children can alter labor supply in two ways—labor force participation* and hours of work. First, women with children less than 6 years old are less likely to be "in the labor force" (defined as employed for pay for at least one hour in the last week or actively seeking employment), although much of the recent growth in female labor force participation has been due to the entrance of married women with young children. Second, women with young children reduce employment through hours worked. In fact, the largest group of part-time workers is women of childbearing years (aged 25 to 54).

As well, employment decreases the number of children a woman has since women devoting time to labor market activities may substitute, first, education and, later, market work for children. Since investing in, and maintaining, market skills often requires continuous labor force attachment, women specializing in labor market activities reduce childbearing to facilitate labor market work. Employed women are more likely to be childless or to have only one child than women who are not engaged in labor market activities.

While aggregate trends portray work habits of females with children, they mask varying patterns among sociodemographic groups. African American women have higher fertility rates than white women, and Hispanic women have higher fertility rates than either African American or white women. African American women bear an average of 2.47 children, white women 1.97, and Hispanic women 2.90 over a lifetime. Educated women are more labor force-committed, have fewer children, and work more hours than women with lower levels of education.

Employment, fertility, and their interrelationship change over time. While females have increased labor market activities since 1900, they have decreased their fertility. At the turn of the century, the average woman had nearly four children over her lifetime. While fertility rates fell for generations, around 1921 the decline quickened, and fertility fell by more than a third in the next 12 years, with birthrates reaching historic lows during the Depression. In 1947, birthrates jumped and continued to rise until 1957 (the baby boom). At this time, birthrates began to fall again through 1978, when they bottomed out at 1.76 children per woman. Today the average woman has about 2.07 children, below the population replacement rate of 2.2.

Four principal hypotheses, each with some empirical support, explain these phenomena. First, the presence of children makes women less able or willing to take employment outside the home. Employment and motherhood are inherently incompatible because of the time and emotional energy needed for both. Child care outside the household becomes the (partial) solution to undertaking both activities, with employment decisions of women currently influenced by the cost of child care that they face. Unfortunately, there is a lack of available, affordable, quality child care, and this reduces employment for women with children.

Second, women restrict childbearing to be more actively involved in paid employment. Because labor market employment requires investing time and training* (e.g., education) as opposed to child raising and because dropping out of the labor force to raise and/or bear children depreciates a woman's skills, women specializing in labor market employment reduce the number of children that they have or forgo childbearing.

Third, outside or antecedent factors (e.g., child care, education, family background, or attitudes) explain both employment and the number of children a woman bears, with the decision changing when these factors change. Child care (e.g., availability, quality), attitudes (e.g., views toward sex roles, work, children, or religion), family background (e.g., socioeconomic status of family of origin, mother's employment status, parental encouragement in school), and personal family characteristics (e.g., woman's wages, education, spouse's income, marital duration) all independently affect both the fertility and employment decision, with the outcome determining the number of children and hours of paid employment that a woman undertakes. Increasing child care availability, changing attitudes toward women, work, and education, and changing relative wages in the market will alter both employment and fertility.

Fourth, couples (or the single woman) decide about employment and children at the same time, based on antecedent/outside factors; however, once a decision is made, it is followed throughout their lifetime. For example, a couple decides to have two children and have the female drop out of the labor force during childbearing years (or the couple may decide to forgo children so that both partners can work). This decision becomes the basis for action in the marriage and workplace, and, as such, changes in child care, attitudes, or employment have little impact on the fertility decision of those women currently of childbearing age but will impact future generations of women.

While empirical and theoretical explanations for the inverse employment–fertility relations differ, a few generalizations can be made. First, changing social attitudes toward women's working facilitated employment and education of females and thereby made it costly (in terms of market wages forgone) for a woman to engage exclusively in household production. Thus, over time both social and economic forces operated to increase women's paid labor market activities and to decrease the number of children that a woman bears.

Second, the inverse relationship between fertility and paid labor market activity suggests that historically, women specialized in childbearing or labor market work. This specialization is no longer the case, however. Married women with young children participate in paid employment at the same rate as all women, yet they still bear the primary responsibility for child care and raising. Instead of specializing their work within the labor market or in the household, women today face dual shifts of responsibilities in paid employment and in the home. Studies have shown that, while women have increased their total time spent both in work at home and in the labor market (primarily in the latter), men have not experienced a concurrent increase in work at home.

Furthermore, the workplace needs to respond by increasing adequate child care facilities, by expanding the number of part-time positions, and by creating flexibility in employment opportunities (e.g., job sharing, flextime). Females need to respond by investing in labor market skills. Both children and female employment are here to stay, and women, men, and employers need to respond accordingly.

References. Susanne M. Bianchi and Daphne Spain, *American Women in Transition* (New York, 1986); David M. Blau (ed.), *The Economics of Child Care* (New York, 1991); Arlie Hohschild, *The Second Shift: Working Parents and the Revolution at Home* (New York, 1989).

NAN L. MAXWELL

CHINA. Ancient China includes four preimperial eras: the Neolithic (8000–2500 B.C.E.), the Shang (2500–1056 B.C.E.), the Western Zhou (1056–771 B.C.E.), and the Eastern Zhou (770–221 B.C.E.). Historical documents date from the late Eastern Zhou period but include sections that may represent earlier traditions. Paleographic evidence is available beginning from the Shang period. Historical documents, subject to generations of editing and annotation at the hands of Confucian scholars, tend to reflect Confucian social concerns, such as the establishment of *zongfa*, "law of the patriarch." (See CONFUCIANISM.)

Antiquity was characterized in texts dating to the third century B.C.E. as a time when "people knew their mothers but not their fathers." However, mortuary evidence for the Neolithic cultures, particularly later cultures, generally indicates a patrilineal-patrilocal society with perhaps some regional exceptions. Women overall seemed to have had a lower social status than men, as they died earlier, received fewer grave goods, and were given formal burial less often. In an effort to establish a matrilineal stage of social evolution, some archaeologists point to the arrangement of large and small residence foundations (presumably emblematic of grouped males and individualized females) in the early Neolithic villages. Generally, Chinese scholars associate the rise of agriculture with the shift to patrilineal society.

During the Shang and Zhou periods, the most powerful position, *wang*, "big man" or "king," was held by a man and passed on to male kin. Scholars generally assume that any record of a politically powerful female must be understood within the context of *zongfa*, that is, she must have been a stand-in for an absent or dead husband of high status. Although literary tradition links female influence upon male rule with calamity and the fall of the ruling house (Shang, Zhou, etc.), myth preserved in the Confucian *Analects* admits the existence of a woman (*furen*) among the sage rulers of "antiquity." (In fact, a number of the mythical hero-founders may have been goddesses [see Cook].)

The referent for an elite women was *fu*. It is typically read as "wife" or "consort." During the Shang period, all the *fu* recorded in the oracle bones dated to the reign of a particular *wang* are assumed to have been his wives. This interpretation supports the existence of polygamy (evident by the Eastern Zhou period) and an early *zongfa* social structure. However, these *fu*—whatever their relation to the king—were politically active. They presented tribute from outlying areas where they most likely lived and ruled; they held office in the Shang court, led armies, concerned themselves with the regulation of agriculture, and supervised religious activities. They were also the objects of cult worship in *zong*, a word that referred to a lineage temple in ancient China. In the only large Shang tomb excavated intact in the Anyang mortuary complex of Yinxu, archaeologists have discovered numerous bronzes, including weapons and ritual vessels, dedicated to a Fu Hao (the name Hao could also be read Zi, the lineage name or *xing* associated with the Shang people in later historical texts) and a number of female ancestors. If the tomb belonged to Fu Hao (no skeleton remained), then the extreme wealth of the tomb and the existence of a *zong* over the tomb reflect the high status and power of a woman who, according to the oracle bones, assembled large armies to attack various border peoples during her lifetime and received repeated sacrifices after her death. Despite her obvious power, scholars, who assume she was a consort of the king Wuding, highlight a line from an oracle bone inscription concerned with her birth of a girl as inauspicious.

Bronze inscriptions support the continued participation of women in religious and political life. They participated in Zhou gift-giving rituals, in positions of authority as gift-givers and as recipients of awards for their military, ritual, or civil merit. These awards symbolized their participation in the Zhou ritual economy and the right to use bronze vessels to present mortuary feasts to their ancestors (male and female), to their deceased husbands, and possibly to display bridewealth at the marriage of female kin.

They performed state sacrifices, authorized, and likely participated in, military campaigns. One female ruler of the Jin nation (northwest China, eighth century B.C.E.) noted that she had inherited the rule from an older woman, possibly a member of her natal kin group.

Cult worship of goddesses and ancestresses may have been associated with fertility rites performed by *wu*, "female shamans," in temples (referred to later as Gaomei or Bigong). In northeastern China, pregnant goddess figurines have been excavated from a number of Neolithic sites, most spectacularly those found in the context of a circular stone temple, dating to c. 3500 B.C.E. Lineage songs in the historical *Shijing* text celebrate the union of the mythical birth-mother of the Zhou people, Jiang Yuan, with the "High God" through the shamanistic dance of stepping on his "footprint."

Gender separation is a clear concern expressed in the Eastern Zhou period by Confucian and non-Confucian political thinkers alike. They advised that dividing walls be built to keep girls and boys physically apart until formal marriage could be contracted by the parents through an official go-between. Confucians were concerned that ritual offerings—symbolic of rank and prestige—be different for women and men. Gender distinctions were encouraged in the workplace as well: while men plowed, the women spun, although common women not only worked as artisans but were conscripted into the military as well. The production of cloth, particularly of silk and hemp cloths used in ritual and trade, is associated with women.

Confucians did not discourage a little sexual indulgence by men, but women were to obey their husbands. Tales of women who formed their own sexual liaisons inevitably describe an unfortunate end. The sexual potency of women was termed *gu*, understood as either a poison or a love potion concocted by *wu* out of stinging insects and snakes or a natural toxin affecting men after overindulgence in sexual relations with women. The association of female sexuality with death may represent an early form of the yin (darkness) and yang (light) dichotomy of cosmic forces developed more fully during the imperial age. (See YIN AND YANG.)

Eastern Zhou period texts confirm that marriage was generally patrilocal (customs to the contrary were condemned as improper), but only women carried the lineage marker (*xing*) in their names. Scholars have assumed that offspring carried the father's *xing*, but the contradictory evidence found in both historical and paleographical sources suggests a more complex system of descent in which the female's lineage continued to play a role after marriage, particularly as marriage bonds were often formed as part of political "covenants." It is not clear how old the *xing* system was or even how it operated (many scholars claim it was a remnant from the "primitive" matrilineal period), but terms such as "the many mothers" and "the many fathers" found in Shang and early Zhou inscriptions do indicate a kinship system for ancient China quite different from the *zongfa* model of imperial times.

References. E. Childs-Johnson (ed.), "Excavation of Tomb No. 5 at Yinxu, Anyang," *Chinese Sociology and Anthropology* (Spring 1983); T. T. Chow, "The Childbirth Myth and Ancient Chinese Medicine: A Study of Aspects of the Wu Tradition," *Ancient China: Studies in Early Civilization*, (Hong Kong, 1978); C. A. Cook, "Three High Gods of Chu," *Journal of Chinese Religions* 22 (Fall 1994): 1–22; Wang Ningsheng, "Yangshao Burial Customs and Social Organization: A Comment on the Theory of Yangshao Matrilineal Society and Its Methodology," *Early China* 11–12 (1985–1987): 6–32.

CONSTANCE A. COOK

CHINA. Cultural Revolution (1966–1976) is the period from 1966 to 1976 in China, when leftist factions controlled the Communist Party and various government organizations and institutions. Great stress was placed on class struggle and on rooting out any remaining elements of feudal or capitalist culture.

The All-China Women's Federation was branded as reactionary and was disbanded, as was its magazine, *Women of China*. Feminism as such was seen as "rightist" and divisive for failing to take class struggle as the key issue. However, some feminist critiques emerged briefly in the 1973 campaign to criticize Confucius, when traditional ideas about women's abilities and proper social roles were attacked.

Throughout the decade, many women intellectuals and leaders were targeted as "class enemies" and, like their male counterparts, were subject to public humiliations, physical abuse, imprisonment or house arrest, labor camp detention, and exile to the countryside. Educated young women who spent those years in internal exile were rarely able to find compatible marriage partners there and, when eventually allowed to return home, were seen as too old or unmarriageable: stories circulated that many of the young women had been raped or forced to trade sexual favors for easier work assignments or even for food while in the countryside or work camps, which further lessened their chances for marriage. As for women already married at the start of the turmoil, many were separated from their children and divorced by their husbands.

Despite these negative aspects of what is now referred to as "the 10 years of disorder," women in general made some gains. In the cities, newly organized neighborhood factories offered work to unemployed women. Neighborhood and factory child care facilities eased some of the domestic burden. Street clinics, staffed by local women who had been given some basic training, dealt with common ailments, made referrals to local hospitals, and dispensed detailed information about family planning, prenatal care, and infant health. Women were highly visible in neighborhood committees and study groups.

Rural women also benefited, even though they continued to be viewed as less useful in basic agricultural work and were paid less than men. In the more successful rural collectives, where the slogan of "self-reliance" had led to the development of new agricultural sidelines and small industries, women found new lines of employment that were seen as more suitable for women, since they were less physically demanding than field labor. Young women were recruited and trained as "barefoot doctors" and midwives for village and commune health stations, and their work in public health and family planning did much to raise the health levels of rural women and children. The growth of collectively funded primary schools at the village level increased girls' chances for basic education, and the new commune middle schools gave some an opportunity for higher schooling. Young women also participated in the local militia forces. Women's enhanced earning abilities strengthened their position within their families.

Nationwide there was a conscious effort to bring women into positions of leadership, particularly at the lower cadre levels, where close to one-third were women. The numbers, of course, included primary school teachers, barefoot doctors, and those in charge of women's work groups, but some had a wider authority. Membership in both the Youth League and the Communist Party itself seems to have opened up for women during those years when a truly peasant or proletarian background was more crucial for political success than high levels of education or political sophistication. Some women rose to national prominence, most notably, Jiang Qing (the wife of Chairman Mao), who had a strong hand in the reshaping of opera, theater, and films.

In the search for creating a proletarian culture, women were strongly urged to forgo feudal and capitalist practices such as cosmetics, jewelry, brightly colored clothing, and Western fashions. Drab, unisex, loose trousers and jackets became the norm, along with short, bobbed hairstyles. Folksongs and romantic popular songs were banned because of their sexual content. Most literature, whether Chinese or foreign, disappeared from the bookstores, replaced by new fiction with patriotic, proletarian themes. In these works, as in the theater, women often figured as guerrilla fighters and soldiers, as sturdy peasants and workers, and as dedicated revolutionaries who put class struggle ahead of petty domestic concerns. Women were encouraged to postpone marriage until their late 20s (though it appears relatively few took that risk), to engage in production, study, and political work, and to still find time to do a good job of looking after the household.

References. Phyllis Andors, *The Unfinished Liberation of Chinese Women, 1949–1980* (Bloomington, Ind., 1983); Elizabeth Croll, *Feminism and Socialism in China* (London, 1978); Jung Chang, *Wild Swans* (New York, 1991).

NORMA DIAMOND

CHINA. Han Through Song Dynasties. From the third century B.C. to the twelfth century A.D., China's characteristic form of government, the imperial bureaucracy, was created. During this time, China's principal ideology, Confucianism* was formed, its two major religions, a native faith called Taoism,* and a belief system of foreign origin known as Buddhism,* were introduced and reached maturity, and the typical Chinese family system developed. These systems of political, religious, and social belief and behavior provided the context for women's lives and history during this long period.

Throughout this 1,500-year period, sources for women's history are difficult to find. Most historical works provide information only if we read between the lines. However, literary and religious texts as well as works of art do reveal Chinese assumptions about women and their roles.

During the Han dynasty (206 B.C. to A.D. 220), the place of women in the mainstream of Confucian thought was set, and the normative role models of filial daughter, obedient wife, self-sacrificing mother, and dutiful widow took shape. For women, family virtues and domestic skills were emphasized, as can be seen in instructional literature, biographies of exemplary women, and art. Women's economic contributions, which were mainly limited to work within the household, formed an essential part of the Chinese economy. (China's economy was overwhelmingly agricultural, and its population predominantly rural during the Han through the Song dynasties.) Silk production is the archetypal woman's work in China, but women also engaged in crop raising and animal husbandry. There were probably always class distinctions in women's roles, with women of the literati class coming under the strictest control. Some alternatives to the limited roles allowed women in early Chinese society appeared in the lives of women of great families and those living under extraordinary circumstances: the Han dynasty gives us women rulers, religious leaders, poets, historians, warriors, and merchants. But the normative roles and constraints, with these few exceptions, remained in effect for almost 2,000 years, until the beginning of the twentieth century.

In the Six Dynasties period (220–589), traditional roles for women persisted. Some women found new alternatives in the religious life, as Taoist or Buddhist nuns or church officials. Among the northern and western minorities, whose organization was tribal and whose economy was nomadic, women had more scope for power and prestige than they did in upper-class China. The Chinese had more contact with their foreign neighbors during this era, and the hardier customs of the border regions had some impact on roles of Chinese women. Nonetheless, poetry of this period depicts upper-class women as fragile beauties languishing in the boudoir, while short stories sometimes present a more frightening aspect of women as thirsty vampires who suck the life force from men.

The brief Sui dynasty (589–618), in addition to continuing old models of behavior for women, contributed two new images: the great patroness of religion and the powerful mother. Each had existed before, but both received new strength when they occurred together in the person of the mother of the first emperor.

The Tang dynasty (618–907) saw an increase of power and prestige for women in royal, aristocratic, and official families. During this time, one woman—Wu Zitian—ruled as emperor of all of China and did the job as effectively as it has ever been done. Imperial concubines enjoyed increased influence in the capital. One famous concubine, a beautiful dancer and actress known by the title "Precious Consort Yang," was the beloved mate of the emperor Xuan Zong. Lady Yang helped her family achieve wealth and government position. Both Wu and Yang have been reviled since the Tang as examples of the negative effects of allowing women access to political power. At the same time, however, they have been celebrated in literature as great heroines.

The Tang was the period in Chinese history that allowed the greatest autonomy, freedom of choice, and influence to women before the modern era. Taoist and Buddhist nuns, religious officials, and hermits found a path of life outside the family circle. Laywomen engaged in religious activities without leaving their families. Women's chances for education and literacy increased, and they entered many professions and crafts, becoming courtesans, musicians, dancers, prostitutes, doctors, and artisans. Women also engaged in traditionally male forms of recreation such as calligraphy, painting, poetry, chess, polo, and hunting. They entered the economy as both producers and consumers in a wider range than before. The influence of foreign and minority women, with their greater freedom of movement, continued. As portrayed in poetry and fiction, women's roles became more complex and broader in scope.

The Song dynasty (960–1279) was characterized by great social, technical, economic, and ideological changes. Urbanization and the rise of the merchant class transformed society. Printing and new chemical processes altered technology. The rise of a money economy along with new systems of landholding and taxation that arose in the middle Song changed the Chinese economy forever, and Neo-Confucianism became the dominant political ideology for nearly 1,000 years to come. These changes ultimately constrained women and reduced their sphere of activity.

During the Song, the severe restrictions on women that typify late imperial China began to appear. With the rise of the philosophy of Neo-Confucianism, women's roles began to diminish and to receive strict definition. The family became the boundary of a woman's activities, and chastity became the most important virtue. One of the great Neo-Confucian thinkers, Zhang I, commented, in forbidding widow remarriage, that it was a small thing to lose one's life but a serious matter to lose one's virtue. Foot-binding, a symbol of women's crippled potential and restricted status, becomes fashionable among the elite. (See FOOT-BINDING.) Not until modern times, with the great social reform movements of the late nineteenth and early twentieth centuries, have the trends toward confining and limiting women started to reverse.

References. Suzanne Cahill, *Transcendence and Divine Passion: The Queen Mother of the West in Medieval China* (Stanford, Calif., 1993); Richard W. Guisso and Stanley Johannesen (eds.), "Women in China," *Historical Reflections* 8, 3 (Fall, 1981); Margery Wolf and Roxanne Witke (eds.), *Women in Chinese Society* (Stanford, Calif., 1975).

SUZANNE CAHILL

CHINA. People's Republic of China. Women were given new legal rights and a wider opportunity to participate in all aspects of life under the socialist government of the People's Republic. New laws relating to marriage* and the family* were promulgated in 1950, shortly after the establishment of the new regime. Child betrothals and forced, arranged marriages were outlawed, as were concubinage,* female infanticide,* and interference in the rights of divorced or widowed women to remarry. Women were granted the right to participate in work and social activities, to seek a divorce, to own and inherit property, and to retain the use of their own names after marriage. Marriage was redefined as a partnership of equal status bound by love and respect. Minor revisions to the legal code in 1980 raised the minimum age of marriage for women from 18 to 20 and stressed the responsibility of the couple to practice family planning. There were widespread educational campaigns to acquaint the public with the provisions of the new laws through the media, meetings organized by the All-China Women's Federation chapters, as well as through the efforts of special "work teams" that toured the countryside publicizing the new laws and organizing discussion groups.

Slogans such as "Women hold up half the sky" and "Times have changed: anything male comrades can do, women comrades can also do" reflect the state's concern with moving toward gender equality. Although the state did not take measures to assure equal pay for equal work, there was recognition of women's "special conditions." State-managed factories, shops, and organizations are required to provide a paid 56-day maternity leave, and state enterprises with large numbers of female workers are likely to include crèches and nursery schools. Women in state employment usually retire at 55, five years earlier than men, and receive a pension. Save for a brief period in the 1950s and again in the early 1980s, women have been strongly encouraged to participate in the workforce and repeatedly told that full social equality comes through contribution to social production and service to the society. However, the state has been less vocal in encouraging men to share in housework and child care; most writings on the subject suggest that women are expected to shoulder the domestic burden and also earn an income. This continues to be true under the free market reforms that have come into play since 1979.

Women have entered all sectors of the workforce in large numbers since 1949. In the rural areas, where 80 percent of the population still lives, the organization of collective agriculture and collective sideline enterprises brought most women into the full-time labor force after 1956, while shifting some of the domestic responsibilities to teenage children or mothers-in-law. Since access to cash income, grain rations, fuel, and purchase-coupons for scarce commodities could be obtained only through work in the collectives, traditional ideas about women's work roles changed fairly rapidly. However, women were usually paid fewer work points for their daily labor, and many had to work reduced hours in order to meet new household responsibilities. These now included labor on the households' private plots, which produced most of the vegetables that a family consumed. In some rural collectives there were attempts to improve women's image by the formation of special all-women work groups calling themselves "Iron Maidens" or "March Eight Teams," which took on heavy agricultural tasks or other jobs considered suited only for men (such as deep-sea fishing or reforestation work) and competed successfully against men.

However, since 1979, the rural collectives have gradually disbanded, returning almost all agricultural production and management to the household level and privatizing most subsidiary agricultural occupations. Rural industrial enterprises run by the villages and townships hire relatively few women. As a result of the reforms, women are overrepresented in basic agriculture. Although over 100 million new jobs have been created within the new or reorganized village and township enterprises, rural women make up only 22 percent of that sector of the workforce.

For young rural women the best work opportunities may be factory and service work as contract laborers in the new Special Economic Zones (SEZ) funded heavily by joint-venture capital. In the Shenzhen SEZ 70 percent of the workers are female and earn wages higher than those in state factories. Others have joined the flow of rural job seekers to the large cities; for example, some 60,000 young peasant women from Anhui province have found work in Beijing as servants in the households of urban cadres and the nouveau-riche entrepreneurs. Those who remain in the countryside are encouraged to augment household income by raising rabbits and pigs or doing piecework knitting and embroidery work in their "spare time." Some have become active as producers and sellers for the "free markets" that were allowed to reopen under the reform agenda.

Urban women entered the workforce at all levels after 1949. Generally, urban women workers were assigned to light industry, particularly textile and clothing manufacture, and to retail and service occupations. Some entered the workforce at managerial and technical levels; close to one-third of college and technical school graduates are women. Since the reforms, a significant number have moved into the private sector, providing goods and services of all sorts (small restaurants, day-care centers, tailor shops, market stalls for fresh produce, and the like). Inflation and a growing consumerism make two incomes a necessity for most urban households. But urban women, too, carry the added burden of housework, albeit simplified today by the rising purchases of refrigerators and washing machines, and their chances for job advancement and higher wages do not match those of men. Women also enter the military, sometimes rising to officer rank, which would have been unthinkable in the old society, and they are also represented among the ranks of government administrators and cadres, though not yet in proportionate numbers.

All women are expected to follow government family planning regulations. Generally, over the past two decades, urban couples are allowed to have one child. Rural couples may have two. Failure to comply with the policy can lead to forced abortion or to heavy financial penalties. Only in special cases, such as the birth of a handicapped child, are couples allowed to exceed the ideal quota. However, the importance of having a son to carry on the family name and support the parents in their old age continues. As a result, there has been a startling increase in the number of female infants who are abandoned or killed at birth, in hopes that the next child will be a boy. There has also been a rise in divorce, many instigated by men who hope that their next wife will be able to provide a son.

Since 1950, except for a break during the years of the Cultural Revolution,* women's interests have been advanced by the All-China Women's Federation, an organization with branches in all work units, neighborhoods, and rural townships. It has provided literacy classes, vocational training, and political education and has kept women informed of their legal rights. Local leaders intervene as mediators in domestic conflicts, and in recent years the federation has played a major role in encouraging birth control and family planning. However, it does not directly address feminist issues; mainly it encourages women to fulfill their dual role as housewives and workers.

Women have gained considerable social freedom since the revolution, in part due to increased access to education for everyone. Though women's enrollments lag behind those of men at the secondary and college levels, primary schooling is almost universal, and all schools are now coeducational. Friendships outside the family and across gender lines are now possible and permitted. Increasingly, engagements and marriage are decisions made by consenting couples, although family approval and assistance are still very important. However, sexual relations outside marriage are strongly disapproved and in some cases punishable by law. Birth control technology is not available to unmarried women.

Among China's various minority peoples (some 8 percent of the population) women have traditionally held a more equal status and participated more in production and in community life. For them, the main gain from the revolution has been access to schooling, but it is possible that some of their former social freedoms have been curtailed by Sinicization.

References. Delia Davin, *Woman-Work* (Oxford, 1976); Christina K. Gilmartin et al. (eds.), *Engendering China* (Cambridge, 1994); Ellen Judd, *Gender and Power in Rural North China* (Stanford, Calif., 1994); Judith Stacey, *Patriarchy and Socialist Revolution in China* (Berkeley, Calif., 1983).

NORMA DIAMOND

CHINA. Republican Period (1912–1949) was the time when feminist issues gained widespread currency in China, and the struggle for gender equality achieved its first noteworthy results. The groundwork for these advances had been laid in the first decade of the twentieth century, when Chinese women, particularly those educated in the newly founded girls' schools, took their first steps toward a wider participation in the public sphere. The more radical members of the coterie of Chinese feminists joined the revolutionary groups that, in 1911, participated in the overthrow of the Qing dynasty and the establishment of a republic. Throughout this initial period of development, feminism was conceived narrowly as a subset of nationalism; women's energies had to be liberated and their talents utilized in order to strengthen the country.

During the iconoclastic May Fourth movement (1915–1921), feminism assumed a new dimension as educated women turned their gaze inward to analyze their own psyches and the possibilities of freeing the true female self from the shackles of Confucian patriarchy. The May Fourth writings of famous women authors such as Ding Ling tended to be narrowly introspective and lacking in any trenchant social critique, yet they nevertheless represented the beginnings of a feminist literature that over time became increasingly political.

The fortunes of women in the Republican period were linked to the battle between the Nationalist Party (KMT) and the Chinese Communist Party (CCP), each of which controlled significant portions of the country by the 1940s. The KMT's commitment to gender equality was tenuous at best. Its most notable achievement was the promulgation from 1929 to 1931 of a new civil code that granted women unprecedented legal rights. They could own and inherit property, initiate divorce proceedings, and bring suit against unfaithful or polygamous husbands. The legal reform had little impact on rural women, but their urban sisters exercised the new rights to gain a larger measure of control over their lives and, by doing so, furthered an incipient transformation in family structure in cities in KMT territory. After this bold legal revision, however, the KMT grew progressively more conservative in its attitude toward sexual equality.

The CCP was much more overtly feminist than the KMT, but its record on women's issues during the Republican era was similarly mixed. While Communist rule brought greatly expanded opportunities and responsibilities to women in their base areas, the reality of most women's lives tended to lag behind party rhetoric. At the heart of the CCP's feminist agenda lay the Marxist dictum that liberation depends on the engagement of women in socially productive labor. The party leadership launched a series of campaigns to bring women into production outside the home, efforts that, not incidentally, also served to replenish a labor force that had been depleted by continual warfare. At the same time, the party encouraged women's participation in politics by recruiting female members into its ranks and by insisting that women representatives be elected to the newly created village assemblies and associations. Finally, to ensure that women would be able to engage in activities outside the confines of their households, the CCP sought to equalize gender relationships within the family through its radical marriage regulations of 1931. The more liberal provisions of this law later underwent modification as the communists became concerned lest they might alienate poor peasant men, the vanguard of the socialist revolution in the countryside.

This retreat from radicalism also characterized the party's policies on land reform. CCP pronouncements, arguing that property ownership would provide the material basis for emancipation, promised women equal rights to land. However, during redistribution, communist cadres allotted land on a family (not an individual) basis, thus enabling male heads of household to consolidate their economic dominance. Feminism remained subordinate to socialism, an ordering of priorities that continued after the communist victory in 1949.

References. Kay Ann Johnson, *Women, the Family and Peasant Revolution in China* (Chicago, 1983); Judith Stacey, *Patriarchy and Socialist Revolution in China* (Berkeley, 1983); Marilyn B. Young (ed.), *Women in China: Studies in Social Change and Feminism* (Ann Arbor, Mich., 1973).

KATHRYN BERNHARDT

CHINA. Yuan, Ming, and Qing Dynasties. The roles available to women in late traditional China were more restricted than they had been during the earlier traditional period. The proper role of women was domestic, but Chinese social theory ascribed great significance to harmony within that sphere. Thus, despite significant restrictions on behavior, the contributions of women as wives, mothers, and participants in the household economy were explicitly valued by the larger society.

The Chinese Song dynasty fell to the Mongols in 1279. The Mongols, a northern nomadic people, adopted Chinese governmental techniques to rule China and selected the dynastic name of Yuan (1279–1368). The Mongols were followed by the Chinese Ming dynasty (1368–1644), which was in turn followed by the Manchu Qing dynasty (1644–1911). Mongol women had occupied an important place in preconquest society. Bortei, the mother of Genghis Khan, was a forceful and influential woman. However, despite being conquerors of an empire, the Mongols seem to have had little impact on the social life of the Chinese. During the Yuan, the practice of footbinding introduced during the Song became so widespread that Taizu, the first emperor of the native Chinese Ming (1368–1644) dynasty, forbade crude jokes about big feet because he felt that they reflected on the unbound feet of his wife. Other trends begun in Song times saw their full fruition under the Ming and Qing. Widow chastity, conceived of as a virtue in the Song, had become a veritable cult during the Ming and Qing, though it must be noted that widows frequently remarried nonetheless. Under the Yuan, Ming, and Qing, a woman who was widowed before she was 30 and remained unmarried until the age of 50 would be honored by the state with a memorial arch. These arches conferred prestige on her locale and on both her family of birth and of marriage. During the Ming, a widow who committed suicide at the death of her husband (frequently, though not always, resisting pressure to remarry) was honored with a memorial arch. Under the Qing the state did not reward widow suicides as extensively as it had under the Ming, partly out of humanitarian motives and partly because suicide, especially in the early Qing, carried overtones of loyalty to the overthrown Ming dynasty, overtones the Qing were not likely to encourage.

Chinese women occupied a protected status within the legal system. For most crimes women (and the very young, the very old, and the infirm) could commute corporal punishment with cash payment. The only exception was a kind of sorcery (*qu*) involving the collecting of poison from scorpions and other venomous insects, which seems to have been regarded as a particularly female crime. Rape was regarded as a crime, more serious than, but not qualitatively different from, ordinary illicit sexual intercourse. Never easy to prove, under the Qing proof of rape became even more difficult: both witnesses and physical evidence of struggle were required.

Control and protection are two sides of the same coin: foot-binding, concern with chastity, and preferential legal treatment can all be seen as attempts to restrict the sphere of women's activity to the family. What of the family during this period? Marriage was a compact between two families rather than an agreement between two individuals. The bride usually resided with her husband's family, frequently in another village. A man might have only one principal wife, but he might have as many concubines as he could afford. Children of a concubine were not generally disadvantaged as heirs; in fact, they were regarded legally as the children of their father's principal wife. Marriage was nearly universal for women. Clerical celibacy, though it did exist on a small scale, did not play the same demographic role as it did in the West. Marriage was accompanied by both dowry and bride-price. The relative expense of marriage for the family of the bride and groom varied according to region, social class, and time. Property in traditional China was held collectively by the family unit and was administered by the patriarch and his adult sons. A widow could hold property as a kind of trustee until her sons reached maturity. If she had no son, a widow could accept a male to serve as heir. The ideological center of the Chinese family was the cult of the ancestors, which demanded male heirs in order to continue sacrifices to the spirits of the deceased. The need for male heirs (and for labor) seems to have produced pronatalist attitudes in general. However, there does seem to have been infanticide in China, and baby girls were more vulnerable than baby boys.

During the sixteenth and seventeenth centuries, especially in South China, lineages (corporate kinship groups claiming descent from a common patrilineal ancestor) strengthened their position. At the same time, there was a growth in literature prescribing proper female behavior, the most famous example of which is Lu Kun's *Guifan*. As in earlier periods, the proper sphere of women was the home, and within that sphere they exercised considerable influence. Two of their most important tasks were management of the household budget and the education of children. Epitaphs of women, like those by the late Ming writer Gui Youguang, praise qualities such as intelligence and resourcefulness in managing these tasks as well as loyalty and chastity. That a mother was in charge of the early childhood education of her sons meant that a woman, especially a woman of the upper classes, would receive some education.

Women participated in income-earning activities, especially textile production; in some areas, such as the Yangtse delta in the sixteenth century, a woman could earn as much in a day's work in sericulture as a man could in the rice fields. Domestic production of handicrafts was the dominant income-producing activity of Chinese women, but women also pursued a variety of occupations outside the household. Some of those were created by the gender separation of Chinese society. It was virtually impossible, for example, for a male doctor to examine the body of a female patient. Women thus found work as midwives, wisewomen, and coroners. Others became wet nurses (who typically resided in the home of the infant they nursed) or prostitutes. Not all occupations were gender-bound; for example, we read of female peddlers, shopkeepers, and storytellers.

Women of the upper classes, the wives and daughters of the Confucian literati, led a more restricted existence than women of the peasantry. The role of a woman was bound by certain universals—the hierarchy of the

Confucian family system, for example—but, equally important, determined by social class, economic position, and local culture as well.

References. Victoria Cass, "Female Healers in the Ming and the Lodge of Ritual and Ceremony," *Journal of the American Oriental Society* 106 (1986): 233–240; Mark Elvin, "Female Virtue and the State in China," *Past and Present* 104 (1984): 111–152; Joanna Handlin, "Lu K'un's New Audience," in Margery Wolf and Roxanne Witke (eds.), *Women in Chinese Society* (Stanford, Calif., 1975), 13–38; Ann Waltner, "Widows and Remarriage in Ming and Early Ch'ing China," *Historical Reflections* 8 (1981): 129–146.

ANN WALTNER

CHINESE ARTISTS (BEFORE 1912). In premodern China some of the daughters and wives of professional artists painted, but only a few became famous enough to attract the attention of leading collectors and connoisseurs. Most of the Chinese women painters known through textual accounts and extant works either belonged to scholar-official families, China's gentry, or were courtesans who served gentlemen of this class. They were counterparts to the male scholar-amateur painters whose theories and practices came to dominate Chinese painting in the Ming (1368–1644) and Qing (1644–1912) dynasties. The story of these women belongs to the history of the scholar-amateur tradition that modern writers have characterized as almost exclusively male.

Recognizing the calligraphic roots of their art, Chinese scholar-painters, men and women, counted calligraphers among their artistic ancestors. A model for women was Madame Wei (272–349), an early teacher of China's most celebrated calligraphy master, Wang Xizhi. During the Song period (960–1279), when the theoretical foundation for scholar-amateur painting was established, a number of leading literati families boasted artistically gifted ladies. These women painted the same subjects and employed the same styles as their male relations. The younger sister of Li Chang (1027–1090) made excellent copies of paintings of pines, bamboo, and rocks; the third daughter of the bamboo painter Wen Tong (1019–1079) learned her father's methods and transmitted them to her son. The foremost female poets of Song, Li Qingzhao (1084–c. 1151), and Zhu Shuzhen (twelfth century) are said to have sketched blossoming plum and "ink bamboo." Ink-monochrome bamboo was a staple of the scholar-amateur tradition, and, according to one account, it originated with a tenth-century woman. Sitting alone in a garden pavilion one moonlit night, she noticed the shadows cast by the bamboo and used her writing brush to trace them on the paper window.

The full flowering of scholar-amateur or literati painting came in the Yuan dynasty (1279–1368) with the revolutionary achievements of the "Four Great Masters" and their predecessor, the statesman, calligrapher, and painter Zhao Mengfu (1254–1322). Artists of later times constantly looked to the works of these men for inspiration, producing countless imitations of their compositions and brush styles. They also revered the work of Zhao Mengfu's wife, Guan Daosheng (1262–1319), the most famous female artist in Chinese history. Like her husband, Guan was known as a calligrapher as well as a painter, and their son Zhao Yong (c. 1289–c. 1362) was similarly accomplished. Their talent was recognized by an emperor who proclaimed that he wished later generations to know that his reign "not only had an expert female calligrapher, but a whole family capable in calligraphy—an extraordinary circumstance."

In painting, Guan Daosheng excelled at various subjects, including Buddhist figures and landscape, but she is remembered especially for her ink bamboo. In this genre she contributed a variation—the depiction of bamboo groves in mist after rain. This depiction is the subject of one of the best paintings today attributed to her, *Bamboo Groves in Mist and Rain*, a horizontal composition mounted in a collective hand scroll of Yuan works, now in the National Palace Museum, Taipei. Guan Daosheng's reputation continued to grow through the centuries, and both men and women frequently painted bamboo in her manner. As a bamboo painter she was as highly regarded as any male artist except the Song master Wen Tong.

Other women artists were active during the Yuan period, but women began to enter the Chinese art-historical record in significant numbers only in the Ming dynasty (1368–1644). This timing was due to a combination of social developments, especially the growth of female literacy. Women increasingly acquired the education prerequisite to scholarly artistic activities. They went from reading "improving" literature, their primary course of study, to composing poetry and pursuing the sister arts of calligraphy and painting. They exchanged poems and paintings, formed poetry clubs, and were encouraged by fathers, husbands, and lovers.

Most of the celebrated female painters of the Ming resided in the coastal provinces of the Yangzi River region, China's cultural heartland, and were active in the sixteenth and early seventeenth centuries. Compared to the women artists of earlier and subsequent times, they were a socially diverse group. The daughter of the professional artist Qiu Ying (c. 1492–c. 1552) was one of the few women of the artisan class to achieve enduring fame for her painting. Like her father she specialized in figures, especially Buddhist deities and palace women. Wen Shu (1595–1634), on the other hand, was the descendant of the literati luminary Wen Zhengming and married into an old Suzhou gentry family. Wen Shu depicted scenes from the residential gardens of Suzhou. Typically, she created restrained compositions of eroded garden rocks, flowers, and butterflies in cool colors on paper. Handsome examples are in the Freer Gallery and the Metropolitan Museum. Like Guan Daosheng, Wen Shu had a substantial following in later times, but unlike Guan's it was primarily female. Critics even suggested that the refinement of Wen's style could be imitated only by women.

Equally well known in the seventeenth century was Li Yin (1616–1685), the concubine of a respected scholar of Haining. After her husband died in 1645, Li supported herself by selling her decorative flower-and-bird compositions. Most were boldly brushed in ink on satin. Her work was so popular that some 40 local artists found it profitable to turn out paintings under her name.

Lower on the social ladder, yet still within the literati cultural sphere, were the courtesan-painters, most notably Ma Shouzhen (1548–1604) and Xue Susu (Wu) (c. 1565–1635). Both were romantic figures, and painting was just one of the entertainments they offered their clients. Xue Susu, for instance, was also skilled in poetry, calligraphy, embroidery, and archery; upon occasion she performed crossbow stunts on horseback. In painting, her subjects included landscapes, Buddhist figures, plants, insects, and flowers—especially orchids. Her works can be seen in the Honolulu Academy of Arts and the Asian Art Museum of San Francisco. Ma Shouzhen painted orchids in delicate ink monochrome and colored styles. The Metropolitan Museum has a fine ink study, *Orchid and Rock*, by Ma. Orchids were a popular theme long treated by male and female artists alike, but they were especially favored by courtesan-painters, no doubt because courtesans were likened to these fragrant plants that blossom in seclusion.

The Ming-Qing transition period of the seventeenth century was a great age in the history of the women painters of China, and many more individuals might be introduced, such as the landscape painters Lin Xue (early seventeenth century) and Huang Yuanjie (mid-seventeenth century); the literatus Mao Xiang's painter-concubines Dong Bai (1625–1651), Jin Yue (later seventeenth century), and Cai Han (1647–1686); the famous concubines Gu Mei (1619–1664) and Liu Shi (1618–1664); and the sister teams of Chai Jingyi and Zhenyi, Zhou Xi and Hu (mid-seventeenth century). Their works were well received by contemporary scholars, and their biographies testify to the widespread acceptance of female participation in the scholarly artistic life of the period.

Chen Shu (1660–1736) was one of the leading women artists of the early Qing dynasty. Another was Wang Zheng, and the two invite comparison because, unlike so many female painters, neither was born into a prominent family of artists. Their artistic development seems to have been self-motivated. Moreover, their flower paintings suggest that their taste was similar. Both left impressionistic sketches of the sort popular with the literati, as well as tightly executed, detailed nature studies. Chen Shu also painted figures and landscapes. In landscape, she aligned herself with the "orthodox school" and imitated the styles of the Yuan masters. This position was a popular, but conservative, one for the period. On the whole, Chinese women painters did not pursue the individualistic paths opened by some of their male contemporaries.

Because of the efforts of her son, who presented her paintings at court,

Chen Shu became the woman artist best represented in the Qing dynasty imperial collection. (Most of her extant works are in the National Palace Museum.) She also instructed men who became well-known artists, accepted female pupils, and, through her art, touched painters of subsequent generations.

The famous eighteenth-century artists Yun Bing, Jiang Jixi, and Ma Quan all came from celebrated scholarly families of painters who specialized in floral subjects. These families were, moreover, closely associated socially and artistically. Yun Bing was a descendant of the master Yun Shouping (1633–1690); Jiang Jixi was the younger sister of the master Jiang Tingxi (1669–1732), a Yun Shouping follower; Ma Quan was the daughter of Ma Yuanyu (1669–1722). The painters of the Jiang and Ma families were greatly influenced by Yun Shouping, so works of these three women have much in common. They all bring garden flowers to life in rich, shimmering colors and fine detail, in a manner reminiscent of the realistic courtly traditions of the Song dynasty. An outstanding example is Yun Bing's flower album of flowers and insects in the Musée Guimet.

The late eighteenth century saw the continued growth of women's participation in the poetic and visual arts. Fang Wanyi, Luo Qilan, and Wang Yuyan, to cite just three examples, were accomplished in both arts. By the nineteenth century noteworthy female painters were active all over the country, from the art circles of Guangdong in the south, to the court at Beijing in the north. Miao Jiahui, a lady of southwestern China, for instance, was summoned to the court to serve as a painting instructor and "substitute brush" for the empress dowager Cixi (1835–1908). The empress dowager had some artistic ability and a genuine enthusiasm for painting and calligraphy. Many of the works that bear her name, however, were actually the work of Miao and other court ladies.

The paintings produced at the late Qing court, although entertaining, were determinedly backward-looking. The foundation of modern Chinese painting was laid not in official circles but in the thriving commercial centers of Guangdong and Shanghai. Prominent in the former were Wu Shangxi, the daughter of a famous art collector; Yu Ling, the concubine of the painter Su Liupeng (c. 1814–1860); and Ju Qing, a descendant of a distinguished family of flower-and-bird painters. In Shanghai, Wu Shujuan (1853–1930) was considered the equal of the leading male flower painter of the city, and Ren Xia (1876–1920) carried on the figure, bird, and animal painting methods of her enormously influential father, Ren Yi (Bonian, 1840–1896), occasionally signing his name to her own works to make them sell better.

The Rens were professional artists who painted for the affluent merchants of Shanghai, but by the nineteenth century commercialism had long been a reality in literati painting circles as well. Not a few of the women mentioned before, after learning to paint as amateurs, went on to use their art, as their male relatives did, to contribute to the support of their families. In sum, the amateurism of Chinese women painters must be understood in its peculiarly Chinese art-historical context, where it was esteemed far more than professionalism yet was often more posture than fact.

References. Ch'en Pao-chen, "Kuan Tao-sheng and the National Palace Museum 'Bamboo and Rock,' " in *Ku-kung chi-k'an* (National Palace Museum Quarterly) 11, 4 (Summer 1977); 51–84 (English summary: 39); Marsha Weidner (ed.) *Flowering in the Shadows: Women in the History of Chinese and Japanese Painting* (Honolulu, 1990); Marsha Weidner and Ellen Laing (eds.), *Views from Jade Terrace: Chinese Women Painters, 1300–1912* (Indianapolis, 1988); Tseng Yu-ho, "Hsüeh Wu and Her Orchids in the Collection of the Honolulu Academy of Arts," *Ars Asiatiques* 2 (1955): 197–208.

MARSHA WEIDNER

CHINESE ARTISTS (MODERN). Women have achieved considerable recognition, both in traditional-style Chinese painting and in new Western-inspired art forms, but none have been accorded the status given the most famous twentieth-century masters.

This fact is somewhat paradoxical in view of the emphasis on sexual equality in the ideology of the Chinese revolution and the fame of such women writers as the novelist Ding Ling. Moreover, in traditional Chinese society women had already established their ability to use the brush, usually in what was considered the more appropriately feminine genre of flower-and-bird painting. But neither this secure, if minor, niche in the art of old China nor the transvaluation of sexual attitudes that has marked the birth of new China has been sufficient to lift women to a position approaching equality in the Chinese art world.

The reasons for this situation lie partly in the general failure to achieve sexual equality after the success of the communist revolution and partly in the particular social and cultural conditions surrounding modern Chinese art. The decline of the traditional ideal of the upper-class amateur scholar-painter by the beginning of the twentieth century and the rise of neoliterati professional painters in the major urban centers affected women artists in two ways. First, women had more opportunity to study with famous masters, usually as personal disciples but sometimes in the new art school environment. Yet, at the same time, even the most talented of the new women artists encountered serious social obstacles to pursuing the kind of professional artistic career that brought maximum recognition. For most women artists in the first half of the twentieth century, painting was a polite accomplishment but not a full-time career.

This description was particularly true for the numerous upper- and middle-class women who painted in the traditional style and usually painted the traditional feminine subjects, but it can also be seen among the young urban women who entered the more radical world of Western-style painting. The careers of two of the most prominent women oil painters of the precommunist period illustrate this point.

Pan Yuliang (1905–1979) was a "kept woman" in Shanghai who happened into the first coeducational school for Western art and became a star pupil of its founder, Liu Haisu. At his urging, she studied in Paris and took up the position of instructor in oil painting in the Art Department at the National Central University in Nanking. A superb draftsperson, she was in the forefront of the small group of "modernists" in urban China. But her career in China was short-lived. Hounded by scandal over her personal life as a "second wife," caught in factional rivalries within art circles, and hampered by the lack of a market for modern, European-style paintings, she returned to France and lived the rest of her life there in relative obscurity.

Fang Junbi (b. c. 1908), another Paris-trained oil painter, came from a more respectable social background and did not have the same economic problems. But, although she had some rather minor teaching positions in Canton in the 1930s, she failed to receive the kind of teaching and administrative appointments that could have made her a major force in modern Chinese art. She, too, withdrew from China to live in the West. In other words, the diploma from L'École des Beaux Arts, which was a ticket to fame and sometimes fortune for male artists, did not open the same doors for women painters.

With the founding of the People's Republic of China in 1949, the social basis of art changed, and supposedly the obstacles facing women artists disappeared. In the new government-sponsored art colleges, women formed a significant portion of the student body, continuing a trend started in the progressive private schools before the revolution. However, women were less numerous in the nationwide Chinese Artists Association or in the academies for recognized artists that were set up in most major cities. The prestigious Shanghai Academy of Traditional Painting, for instance, as of 1981 had only 13 women among its 81 full members. This underrepresentation becomes even more striking at the very top of the Chinese art world—the artists in key administrative teaching posts and those who have been honored with individual exhibitions and reproduction volumes by the state-controlled art institutions.

He Xiangning (1878–1972) is certainly the most widely publicized woman artist in the People's Republic, before and after her death. Associated with the revolutionary Cantonese School of Painting, she was an unusually vigorous painter in the traditional style, painting fierce lions, soaring pines, and lofty landscapes in addition to the more standard female subjects of birds and flowers. But the acclaim for her had political overtones, for she was widow of the martyred revolutionary leader Liao Zhongkai. She is the only woman in the modern painters section of the *Dictionary of Chinese Art* (Peking, 1984), but the spotlight on her is partly reflected glory.

Xiao Shufang (b. 1911) is another well-known artist, married to a better-known man, the artist and art administrator Wu Zuoren. She combines her prerevolutionary training in English watercolor technique with traditional Chinese flower painting to produce some of modern China's freshest and most vigorous painting in that genre. But she is usually linked to her more famous husband.

In the post-Mao era, women artists have been somewhat more prominent in the freer artistic atmosphere that has generally prevailed since the late 1970s. Some, still working with flower-and-bird or female figure painting, have pushed these traditional female genres into new directions. In Shanghi, Chen Peiqiu (b. 1923) does bold and lyrical bird painting. At the Peking Painting Academy, Zhou Sicong (b. 1939) has given the often insipidly treated subject of national minority women more substance and dignity, while her younger colleague, Zhao Xiuhuan (b. 1946), has attracted attention with her marvelously detailed nature studies.

Perhaps most significant, however, are the women painters such as Yang Yenping (b. 1934), Nie Ou (b. 1948), and Shao Fei (b. 1954), who go beyond the traditional feminine genres to do powerfully innovative landscapes and figure paintings. They are expanding the scope of women's art in China, but it remains to be seen how far they will rise in the strict and seniority-conscious hierarchy of the Chinese art world.

Since at least the 1920s, the talent, the promise, and the positive example of female success in the literary world have been there for Chinese women artists. But, to date, even through revolutionary periods, social and cultural conservatism has been too strong for that promise to be realized.

References. Joan Lebold Cohen, *The New Chinese Art, 1949–1986* (New York, 1987); Ellen Johnston Laing, *The Winking Owl: Essays on Art in the People's Republic of China* (Berkeley, Calif., 1988); Cao Xingyuan, "Nine Women Artists," *Chinese Literature* (Winter 1987): 165–167.

RALPH CROIZIER

CHINESE LITERATURE. Chinese Traditional Fiction constitutes a massive written resource for the study of the cultural ideals, popular images, and actual lives of women throughout China's long history. In portraying women, Chinese storytellers were far more curious and comprehensive than Confucian historians and far less bound by Confucian stereotypes of vice and virtue. Most authors, including patriarchal conservatives, wrote works that vividly illustrate the social and psychological pressures on women in traditional China. Their image of women is extremely complex and diverse; the following brief survey only suggests some of this diversity.

Water Margin (Outlaws of the March [Beijing and Bloomington, 1981]), written in the fifteenth century, is a loosely structured Robin-Hood-style adventure tale. Women are only minor characters, but their portrayal illuminates some of the negative stereotypes of women in Chinese popular culture. Although usually weak and dependent on men, the women are also seen as potentially very dangerous in their cunningness and sexuality. Often criticized as a thoroughly misogynist work, *Water Margin* contains chilling descriptions of brutality toward women without exhibiting very much sympathy for their plight.

A much more detailed description of ordinary women's lives is found in *Jin ping mei (The Golden Lotus*, 4 vols., repr., London, 1972; abridged trans.: *Chin P'ing Mei* [Toms River, N.J., 1960]), a late sixteenth-century novel of manners and one of the most graphically erotic works in the Chinese tradition. A work of sophisticated social and psychological realism, *Jin ping mei* chronicles the rise and fall of a wealthy merchant, Ximen Ching, his six wives, and their house full of servants and maids. Totally dependent on their playboy husband's whims and insecure unless they produce him a male heir, the women in this household must use sex as a major weapon in their struggle for survival. Much more than a simple work of pornography, this novel is the most complex and intimate portrait of women's lives in China (and perhaps in any country except for Japan's *Tale of Genji*) before the eighteenth century.

Jin ping mei is surpassed in both psychological realism and feminist concerns by China's greatest novel, *Dream of the Red Chamber (A Dream of Red Mansions*, 3 vols. [Beijing, 1978–1980]; *The Story of the Stone*, 5 vols. [New York, 1973–1986]), written in the mid-eighteenth century by Cao Xueqin. Although framed as a Buddhist allegory, the bulk of *Dream of the Red Chamber*'s 120 chapters describes in meticulous detail the long, painful decline of a very prominent aristocratic family. Featured are the young male protagonist (a partial self-portrait of the author) and dozens of his female relatives, friends, and servants, all described in a leisurely, realistic, almost Proustian style. Nearly all the major female characters meet a tragic end: some commit suicide to escape and protest their mistreatment by the family; some live in quiet desperation with unloving and unlovable husbands; some seek solace in joining Buddhist nunneries and renouncing earthly ties; and some strive to submit to the authority of their elders and to serve the family through Confucian self-sacrifice. Despite the novel's occasional bow to Confucianism and the Buddhist proclamations of its narrative framework, none of these strategies appear to succeed in saving the family or in providing individuals with much meaning or satisfaction in life. No other novel in the Chinese tradition is as encyclopedic in its theme, as sympathetic and insightful in its portrayal of women, or as sharp in its social criticism as *Dream of the Red Chamber*.

In the early nineteenth century, a little-known amateur painter and poet, Shen Fu, wrote *Six Chapters of a Floating Life (Six Records of a Floating*

Life [New York, 1983]), a poignant autobiographical memoir detailing, among other things, Shen's intense lifelong love affair with his wife, Yun. Although technically not fiction, Shen's memoir is so self-consciously artful that its truth, like the truth of fiction, depends far more on its plausibility than on its facticity. Because they are romantics and in love, Shen and his wife are ostracized by his family, and she eventually dies in poverty and despair. Among her chief sins, Yun had fallen in love with a singing girl, with Shen Fu's sympathetic consent! Shen Fu is no modern-style feminist— he has an open affair with a singing girl himself—but his memoir beautifully illuminates the dilemmas of romantic conjugal love in a pragmatic, hierarchical, Confucian, family-centered society.

A more famous and also more conventional, early nineteenth-century work is *Flowers in the Mirror* by Li Ruzhen (abridged trans. [Berkeley, 1965]). An inventive travelogue-style fantasy designed to show off Li's encyclopedic knowledge, *Flowers in the Mirror* is a clever satire of many facets of traditional Chinese society. Its most famous part portrays a Kingdom of Women where traditional Chinese sex roles are completely reversed. When a Chinese merchant visits the Kingdom of Women to sell cosmetics, he is captured and properly "feminized" (complete with the most painful binding of his feet), so that he can be a concubine for the female emperor. Li Ruzhen's feminism is easily overstated (e.g., he approved of widow suicide), but he does illustrate that some traditional Chinese males could be both Confucians and staunch critics of such practices as concubinage and foot-binding.

The preceding are only the most famous traditional Chinese works that serve to illuminate the lives of women from the fifteenth to the nineteenth century. Thousands of other works from this time and earlier are equally revealing. Use of these sources promises to provide a much fuller understanding of the evolution of women's lives, expectations, roles, and status in China over the centuries.

References. Louise P. Edwards, *Men and Women in Qing China: Gender in "The Red Chamber Dream"* (Leiden, 1944); Anna Gerstlacher et al. (eds.), *Women and Literature in China* (Bochum, FRG, 1985); Wai-yi Li, *Enchantment and Disenchantment: Love and Illusion in Chinese Literature* (Princeton, 1993); Tonglin Lu, *Rose and Lotus: Narrative of Desire in France and China* (Albany, N.Y., 1991); Keith McMahon, *Misers, Shrews, and Polygamists: Sexuality and Male–Female Relations in Eighteenth-Century Chinese Fiction* (Durham, N.C., 1995); Yenna Wu, *The Chinese Virago: A Literary Theme* (Cambridge, 1995).

PAUL S. ROPP

CHINESE LITERATURE. Writers of the Classical Period. Women have played a less important role in Chinese literature than the far more numerous male writers. This difference may be attributed largely to restrictions that the Confucian-based Chinese society imposed on women.

Confucianism, which emphasized social order and relations, defined women's role as the fulfillment of three major responsibilities, that is, performing household duties, attending to the needs and comfort of the husband and elders, and raising children. The activities of women were generally confined to the home. Though Confucianism advocated female education, this was mainly to prepare women for their prescribed familial responsibilities. Reading or writing literary works was discouraged, for imagination and spontaneity stood against the Confucian doctrine of restraint and decorum as moral correctives. Thus, Chinese women writers generally regarded literature as a mere amusement or distraction. Many even destroyed their own manuscripts, a practice that resulted in a serious loss of women's literature.

Few works dated before the Han period (206 B.C.–A.D. 220) can be ascribed to female authorship with certainty. Among women writers of the Han, Zhuo Wenjun (fl. 150–115 B.C.), Ban Zhao (?–c. A.D. 116), and Cai Yan (fl. A.D. 162–239) were the most noteworthy. Zhuo achieved distinction in literature through a single poem entitled "Baitou yin" (A Song of White Hair), written in protest against her husband's intention to take a concubine. For centuries, this poem has been a symbol for wives abandoned because of old age and waning beauty. Ban was renowned for her accomplishments in both historical scholarship and literary creation. Erudite and well informed, she had a share in the completion of *Han shu* (History of the Han). She was also a skillful writer in the prose and *fu*, or rhyme-prose, forms. Cai's fame arose from her extraordinary personal experience, powerfully embodied in three poems attributed to her, "Huqie shiba pai" (Eighteen Verses Sung to a Barbarian Reed Whistle) and "Beifen shi" (Poems [two] of Lament and Resentment). In a tone of wrath and agony, each poem chronicles her abduction by the Huns, then China's most threatening enemies, life among the barbarians, and return to China.

The most celebrated woman writer during the Jin period (265–420) was Zuo Fen (fl.275). Her writings include poetry, prose, and *fu*.

Women's literature of the southern dynasties (420–589) is best represented by *yuefu*, a type of song poetry. These songs deal almost exclusively with love. Couched in characteristically fluent and conversational language, feelings are usually expressed with little restraint. The most notable of the *yuefu* is "Ziye ge," a group of 42 poems attributed to a girl named Ziye (fl.third and fourth centuries). These poems were emulated by later generations.

During the Tang period (618–907), usually considered the golden age of Chinese poetry, many court ladies, upper-class women, courtesans, and Taoist nuns wrote poetry. Most renowed were Xue Tao (768–831) and Yu Xuanji (fl.844–871). Xue favored such conventional subjects as friendship, lovesickness, the passage of time, and the vicissitudes of history. The overall tone of her poetry was one of resignation and acquiescence. In poetic talent and skill, Yu was the equal of Xue. Yu, however, demonstrated in her works an awareness, rarely seen among other women poets, of the sexual inequality in society. In some poems, she clearly demanded that women be allowed to take more than one lover and to participate in state examinations leading to officialdom.

In the Song period (960–1279), many women composed *ci*, a type of poetry with a musical origin. The most celebrated was Li Qingzhao (1081–c.1141), generally recognized as China's greatest woman poet. In accordance with two distinct stages in her life, Li describes in her poetry one of two contrary moods: either that of a happily married young woman or that of a distressed, aging widow. In either mood her poetry had an intimacy, accuracy, and immediacy rarely surpassed by China's other writers. She was especially skillful in experimenting with difficult prosodic devices.

During the Yuan (1234–1368) and Ming (1368–1644) periods, *sangu* poetry, a variation of the *ci*, became the dominant form. Women poets of this time were noted for their successful exploration of the female mind. Huang E (fl.1535) was especially remarkable because of her undisguised descriptions of love and sex.

The multiplicity of women's literature in the Qing period (1644–1911) is reflected by the presence of both elite forms, such as poetry and drama of the literati, and those of folk origin, such as *tanci*, stories put into rhyme for chanting with musical accompaniments. In poetry, Gu Taiqing (1799–1876?) was the most noteworthy. She was skillful in the employment of simple language to create an atmosphere of sublimity and the manipulation of rhymes to achieve desired sound effects. Famous female dramatists include Ye Xiaowan (1613–?), Liang Yisu (fl.1644), and Wang Yun (dates unknown). Their works concern separation, lovesickness, and the vicissitudes of life. In *tanci* literature, of greatest renown was Chen Duansheng (fl.1785), whose work reveals strong feminist thought in demanding equal career opportunities for women.

Considered as a whole, Chinese women's literature of the classical period consisted of poetry as the major genre and fiction, drama, and prose as minor ones. Works written in the literary language outnumbered those in the vernacular, and the focus of creative attention was on the individuality of the writers, rather than their surrounding society.

References. Marián Galik, "On the Literature Written by Chinese Women Prior to 1917" in Ivan Dolezal (ed.), *Asian and African Studies* 15 (1979): 65–100; Sharon Shih-jiuan Hou, "Women's Literature," in William H. Nienhauser, Jr. (ed.), *The Indiana Companion to Traditional Chinese Literature* (Bloomington, Ind., 1986), 176–195; Kenneth Rexroth and Ling Chung (trans. and eds.), *The Orchid Boat: Women Poets of China* (New York, 1972).

SHARON SHIH-JIUAN HOU

CHINESE LITERATURE. Writers of the Modern Period. The first significant women writers of modern China appeared during the 1920s in connection with the May Fourth Movement (named after the widespread demonstration on May 4, 1919, protesting concessions given to Japan by the victorious Western Allies at the Versailles Peace Conference). The movement witnessed the upsurge of antitraditionalism and political consciousness among Chinese intellectuals, as well as the adaptation of vernacular language as a literary medium and the introduction of Western literature with its techniques and sentiments. Amid the male-dominated literary scene, there emerged a small number of women writers (Lu Yin [Huang Ying, 1896–1934], Bing Xin [Xie Wanying, b. 1900], Ling Shuhua [1904–1994], Ding Ling [Jiang Bingzhi, 1907–1986], Xie Bingying [b. 1906], Xiao Hong [Zhang Naiying, 1911–1942], Cao Ming [Wu Xuanwen, b. 1913], and Yang Jiang [b. 1911]) who were mostly from the elite class, some even educated abroad. Their works were mainly short stories and novellas that were characteristically autobiographical and often written from the woman's perspective. Besides revealing the psychology of the frustrated, lonely, and love-seeking urban intellectual female (such as Ding Ling's "The Diary of Miss Sophie"), they also deal with the plight of Chinese women in the overwhelmingly oppressive social milieu (such as Ling Shuhua's "The Embroidered Pillow"). There were very few women poets, and those who did write poetry (such as Bing Xin and Lin Huiyin [1905–1955]) produced mainly poems of love and nature. Playwriting was rarely attempted by women writers, perhaps with the exception of Yang Jiang.

In the late 1920s and early 1930s, the increasing influence of Marxism led to different groupings of Chinese writers. Of the women writers, Ding Ling was the most conspicuous in her drastic change to include themes of class struggle (as shown in the novella *Water* [1931]). During the Sino-Japanese War (1937–1945), many patriotic and communist-oriented intellectuals from the coastal cities made their way to Yan'an, then the revolutionary base of the Communist Party led by Mao Zedong. Mao's Yan'an Forum on Literature and Art (1942) laid down the rules for Chinese writers for the following several decades (among these rules are "literature and art serve politics" and "literature and art serve the workers, peasants, and soldiers"). Ding Ling was the most outstanding woman writer in Yan'an, and because of her artistic conscience and social obsession, she was among the earliest to be criticized during the Rectification Campaign (1942). She was sent to "experience" life and later came up with the novel *The Sun Shines over the Sanggan River* (1953), which won her a Stalin Prize.

While some women writers turned to the communists during the Sino-Japanese War, others continued to produce works of nonpolitical content, stressing instead their personal artistic sensibility. Among them, Zhang Ailing (Eileen Chang, 1921–1995), Xiao Hong, and Yang Jiang were representatives. Zhang Ailing, who left China in 1952 for Hong Kong and then went to the United States in 1955, remained one of the most sophisticated

Chinese writers of the twentieth century in terms of her striking imagery, powerful depiction of characters, and unparalleled insight into life and human nature.

After the communist takeover in 1949, women writers (e.g., Yang Mo [b. 1914], Liu Zhen [b. 1930], Ru Zhijuan [b. 1925], and Ke Yan [b. 1929]) nurtured by the communists wrote mainly within the confines of party ideology. During the 1950s, the party's successive campaigns for ideological conformity among intellectuals brought criticism to at least two female writers, Yang Mo and Ding Ling. Yang Mo was criticized because of her novel *The Song of Youth* (1958), which focuses on urban intellectuals. Ding Ling, because of her allegedly "bourgeois" influence among young people, was condemned more severely than the first time and sent to labor reform in northeast China, to be "rehabilitated" only in 1979. She died in 1986.

During the Cultural Revolution (1966–1976), literature and art were reduced to a mere propaganda role. Most Chinese writers were silenced, purged, or forced to commit suicide. Chinese literature revived only in 1979 with the pragmatic government led by Deng Xiaoping. The literary thaw facilitated the emergence of an unprecedented number of women writers (prominent names include Chen Rong [b. 1936], Zhang Jie [b. 1937], Dai Houying [b. 1938], Cheng Naishan [b. 1946], Wang Xiaoying [b. 1947], Lu Xing'er [b. 1949], Zhu Lin [b. 1949] Zhang Kangkang [b. 1950], Zhang Xinxin [b. 1953], Wang Anyi [b. 1954], Liu Suola [b. 1955], Tie Ning [b. 1957]). The vigorous call for "writing with truth" and the rerecognition of the value of a human being in the post-Mao era have enabled Chinese women writers realistically and, to a considerable extent, artistically to depict various aspects of the life of Chinese women. The sensational appeal and psychological depiction in their works overshadow those of the male writers. These women writers reveal the vulnerability of women to exploitation and abuse by vicious and corrupt officials (as shown in many stories of young women sent to the countryside during the rustication movement from the late 1960s to the mid-1970s), the loss of female identity because of the dogmatism and extreme puritanism (as shown in many stories about female Red Guards), the search for romantic love and sexual equality (as shown in many stories on love), and the boredom and hopelessness of domestic life (as shown in many stories on marriage). All these themes were discouraged, if not banned, in Maoist literature. As far as poetry is concerned, it is no longer dominated by male poets as in the May Fourth Period. Prominent women poets (such as Shu Ting [b. 1952] and Wang Xiaoni) have produced modernistic poetry with profound individuality and artistry. On the whole, for Chinese women writers, this period is the most prosperous one in Chinese literary history.

Anthologies in English translations of works by modern Chinese women writers include R. A. Roberts and Angela Knox, *One Half the Sky: Stories from Contemporary Women Writers of China* (New York, 1987); Nienlng Liu et al., *The Rose Colored Dinner: New Works by Contemporary Chinese Women Writers* (Hong Kong, 1988); *Seven Contemporary Women Writers* (Beijing, 1982); *Contemporary Chinese Women Writers II* (Beijing, 1991); Zhu Hong (trans. and ed.), *The Serenity of Whiteness: Stories by and about Women in Contemporary China* (New York, 1991).

References. Tani E. Barlow (ed.), *Gender Politics in Modern China: Writing and Feminism* (Durham, N.C., 1993); Rey Chow, *Women and Chinese Modernity: The Politics of Reading between West and East* (Minneapolis, 1991); Michael Duke (ed.), *Modern Chinese Women Writers: Critical Appraisals* (Armonk, N.Y., 1989); Christine K. Gilmartin et al., *Engendering China: Women, Culture, and the State* (Cambridge, 1994); Laifong Leung, *Morning Sun: Interviews with Chinese Writers of the Lost Generation* (Armonk, N.Y., 1994); Lu Tonglin (ed.), *Gender and Sexuality in Twentieth Century Chinese Literature and Society* (Albany, N.Y., 1993).

LAIFONG LEUNG

CHINESE RELIGION. Religion in traditional China was pervasive but diffuse. No single religious institution had even remotely the impact that the Catholic Church had on European culture. Both Taoism* and Buddhism* had formal church structures, but, especially after the ninth century, those forms of Buddhism (Chan, more commonly known in the West by its Japanese name of Zen, and Pure Land) that dominated found their strength in lay piety. The absence of any single arbiter of orthodoxy meant, first, that the religious scene in China was rich and diverse, and second, that most forms of religion at most times could peacefully coexist. (The cardinal exception to this is sectarian religious sects in the late imperial period, which the government feared held the potential for rebellion.)

The multiplicity of the Chinese religious world found room for women as both devotees and deities. Women's religious activity tended to center around domestic cults, whether the cult activity was to honor the ancestors, the kitchen god, or other deities. A major theme of hagiography of female religious is the conflict between the demands of family life and religious life. Indeed, themes common to the life of Chinese female religious figures (such as Mazu, Miaoshan, and Tanyangzi) will strike the student of Western female saints as startlingly familiar—the refusal to marry, extreme fasting, and conflict with parents over the religious vocation seem to be universal attributes of female sanctity.

Women's religiosity occasionally found public expression: indeed, visits to temples and pilgrimage sites were among the rare outings allowed women of the upper classes. Moreover, public religiosity found another outlet during the Ming (1368–1644) and Qing (1644–1911) dynasties in sectarian religion whose leaders were occasionally female and that often advocated gender equality.

Early goddesses (prior to the Song dynasty [960–1279]) seem to have been powerful, even aggressive, figures. Nu Gua is a powerful creator; the Queen Mother of the West is the Taoist deity who controls access to immortality; and there are countless lesser goddesses and intermediaries between the world of the gods and that of mortals. The sexual power of the Queen Mother and of other early Taoist figures is conveyed directly, without prudery.

With the Song dynasty, as the role of mortal women became more circumscribed, so did the role of the goddesses. The Chinese saw the world of the gods in terms that largely mirrored their own world: like the mortal world, the immortal world was ordered in bureaucratic hierarchy. However, bureaucratic hierarchy was a more useful principle of organization for male deities than for the females: women are not bureaucrats. In the later imperial period, female deities increasingly deal with domestic concerns. (It should be stressed here that domesticity encompasses procreation, health, and long life, all issues that were central to the concerns of Chinese social thinkers.)

Guanyin, the Chinese transformation of the Indian Buddhist deity Avalokiteśvara, was male in India. His translation into Chinese entailed a gender transformation. Guanyin is associated with mercy and comes to be a patron of childbearing. The importance of the mother–son bond is given mythic recognition in the tale of Mulien, who rescues his mother from hell. Ma-tsu, a pirate-subduer and patron of fishermen, was a fertility goddess to women. Popular art, especially woodblock prints widespread from Ming times on, display a wide variety of female deities who are charged with enhancing fertility, aiding in childbirth, protecting from specific diseases, and so forth. Male deities were not unconcerned with matters of health and procreation, but Chinese women seem to have been more ready to appeal to female deities in regard to their health and sexual problems.

The most significant appearance of a female deity in traditional Chinese popular religion occurs in the sixteenth century, with a new deity, known as *wu sheng lao mu*—the Venerable Eternal Mother. The primary deity of salvational sectarian religion, she is a grandmotherly figure who wants to call back to heaven all of her children, the inhabitants of this world. The cults devoted to her were often explicitly egalitarian, and women played prominent roles as leaders.

Religion offered women in traditional China a wider variety of social roles than did any other realm, and perhaps as important as the social roles, religion (especially popular religion) presented to Chinese women a rich symbolic structure in which female gender was validated.

References. Suzanne Cahill, "Performers and Female Taoist Adepts: Hsi Wang Mu as the Patron Deity of Women in Medieval China," *Journal of the American Oriental Society* 106 (1986): 155–168; Glen Dudbridge, *The Legend of Miao-shan* (London, 1978); Steven Sangren, "Female Gender in Chinese Religious Symbols," *Signs* 9 (1983/1984): 4–25; Ann Waltner, "Visionary and Bureaucrat in the late

Ming: T'an Yang-teu and Wang Shih-chen T'an Yang-tzu and Wang Shih-chen: Late Ming," *Late Imperial China* 8, 1 (June 1987): 105–133.

ANN WALTNER

CHIVALRY permeated medieval culture and provided an aristocratic military regime for mounted warriors, a code of personal behavior, and a malleable literary theme. Paradoxically, it inspired both self-sacrifice and self-seeking, artifice and practicality. Its mutations mirrored changes in economics, technology, religion, politics, and social life.

Tenth- and eleventh-century France is the traditional provenance, but chivalry also drew on Germanic, Christian, and Roman precedents. The basic vocabulary is French: *cheval* (horse), *chevalier* (horseman). The collapse of the Carolingian empire impelled local noblemen to maintain cavalry to defend against foreign invaders such as Northmen and Magyars and to battle rival barons. Mutual feudal obligations bound the warrior-knight and his employer as vassal and lord, respectively. In return for military service the lord provided equipment, training, and often land (a fief).

Initially, chivalry concerned only actual warfare with military training through tournaments—the *mêlée*, the joust, the *pas d'armes*—which were unregulated, disorderly, and bloody. The church objected to tournaments because they caused violent chaos in the surrounding area, wasted money, and encouraged vainglory. Unable to curb the unfettered aggression of knights, the church countered by whipping up Crusade fervor (with a first call in 1095) and Christianized knighthood. Knights were expected to support the church, following the example of the militant archangel Michael. Ordination ceremonies accumulated religious symbolism with a vigil, mass, ritual bath, and blessing of weapons. Knights vowed to protect the helpless and oppressed, particularly clergy, women, orphans, and unarmed men.

Gradually, chivalry developed a general code of honorable conduct in which knights were to show generosity (*largesse*), courtesy, and mercy to all persons, including opponents, and to take no unfair advantage. However, taking booty and prisoners for ransom continued to be essential motives for warfare.

Another softening influence was "courtly love," which began in the twelfth century and drew on the Cult of the Virgin as well as Arabic and troubadour poetry. It encouraged knights to serve and idealize women and to be instructed by them in social behavior and morals. The noble lady as an exemplar of virtue inspired the knight to improve both his character and his military performance, and an adored lady might reward the valiant and successful knight with her erotic favors. The feudal model was adapted to courtly love relationships, with the lady as lord and the knight as her vassal.

The relationship of chivalric values to actual life is a complex and difficult question with sparse solid evidence. Undoubtedly, some knights did exhibit honor, courtesy, and refinement in their professional and private lives. However, the attempts to regulate military behavior argue strongly for its intractability, and historical examples of unchivalric conduct abound. For example, knights butchered St. Thomas à Becket in Canterbury Cathedral; some crusaders displayed savagery even to fellow Christians; and a knight rapes a young virgin in Geoffrey Chaucer's *Wife of Bath's Tale.*

The chivalric code applied only to the nobility, and common soldiers and ordinary, nonaristocratic men and women fell outside its bailiwick. The status of women did not significantly improve as a result of chivalry and courtly love. The Crusades at times augmented women's political and economic powers when a wife administered her absent husband's estates or inherited his fief upon his death, but chivalry remained essentially a masculine code that articulated male interests. Even the feminist Christine de Pisan's fifteenth-century *Book of Fayttes and Armes of Chyualrye* ignored women's issues and concentrated on purely military strategies and ethical problems of actual warfare.

The impact of chivalry on literature, however, was rich and diverse: chivalry informed chronicles, biographies, and treatises, but especially *chansons de geste* and romances. Epics such as the *Chanson de Roland* and the *Poem of the Cid* praised chivalric bravado in the first case and the financial advantage of loyalty to one's lord in the second. Women's interests were virtually absent from the epic, and female characters functioned mainly as marriageable commodities who seal an advantageous alliance and/or secure a fortune for their husbands. The brutal treatment of the Cid's daughters was seen as a violation of proper behavior by a vassal, not as inappropriate conduct toward women.

Chrétien de Troyes's twelfth-century romances formed the prototype of that genre, exploring not only glorious knightly achievement but also conflicts between love and duty. Gottfried von Strassbourg's *Tristan* (thirteenth century) and Thomas Malory's *Morte d'Arthur* (fifteenth century) presented the medieval tragic conflict of loyalties of knights caught between their love for their lords and their love for their lords' wives. *Sir Gawain and the Green Knight* (fourteenth century) revealed seriocomically the inadequacy of secular chivalry and courtly love as they are put to the test of life, death, and Christian grace. Edmund Spenser's *Faerie Queene* (sixteenth century) used knightly quests to promote patriotic, humanistic, and Christian doctrines, and the author exalted his lady-monarch Queen Elizabeth as the paragon of courtly, moral, and political virtues. Miguel de Cervantes brought the literature of medieval chivalry to a close with his affectionately ironic *Don Quixote* (1605), in which the courtly lady was cast now in the person of the prostitute Dulcinea.

Changes in chivalry reflected historical alterations of all sorts. The advent of the stirrup allowed the use of the lance, the mounted warrior's distinctive weapon. The long bow and gunpowder in the fifteenth century favored infantry over cavalry. Mercenaries increasingly replaced feudal knights; some knights themselves became hired soldiers. The rise of stable monarchs with standing armies, the growth of towns, and the power of the middle class all diminished the practicability of chivalry.

By the sixteenth century the knight had metamorphosed into the courtier and bourgeois gentleman, who was responsible for administrative, juristic, and political functions, not merely war. The gentleman had as his consort the Renaissance lady, who was expected to be a chaste and obedient helpmate as well as an epitome of Petrarchan beauty and idealism. Humanism and Protestantism helped undermine the remnants of medieval chivalry.

Ironically, however, as practical chivalry declined, ceremonies of knighthood flourished—emphasis on lineage and pageantry intensified, and knighthood became hereditary. Secular chivalric organizations like the orders of the Band, Garter, and Star flowered in the fourteenth century to maintain legal and social prestige for upper-class knights. Chivalry became more nostalgic and ritualistic as it also became more divorced from actual battle. A practical code of conduct for eleventh-century warriors became instead a litmus to distinguish the hereditary aristocrat from the common person.

Chivalric ideals still haunt the imagination of modern, industrial societies. Writers of the nineteenth century like Walter Scott, William Morris, and Alfred, Lord Tennyson re-created the Middle Ages through the prism of romanticism. The Pre-Raphaelite image of women in the arts and literature portrayed them as pallid, delicate, ethereal creatures, languishing in dreams and sorrow.

The twentieth century rendered chivalry even more bourgeois and democratized as the tournament metamorphosed into professional and college sports and the rodeo. The eighteenth/nineteenth-century version of the joust—the duel—modulated into the American western shoot-out. The most decayed reminiscences of the chivalric code of honor were found in the values of the Old South and the Ku Klux Klan. Today, chivalry has come to mean an archaic, though charming, pattern of manners in which men are polite to ladies, tip their hats, open doors, and shield them from distasteful language. The romantic hero is still called a "knight in shining armor," but he is a myth, not a reality.

References. Georges Duby, *The Chivalrous Society*, trans. Cynthia Postan (Berkeley, Calif., 1977); Léon Gautier, *Chivalry*, ed. Jacques Levron, trans. D.C. Dunning (London, 1965); Frances Gies, *The Knight in History* (New York, 1984); Maurice Keen, *Chivalry* (New Haven, Conn., 1984).

SUZANNE H. MACRAE

CHLAMYDIA INFECTION, a sexually transmitted disease, is caused by a bacterium, chlamydia trachomatis, which is a major threat to the health and fertility of women, especially in the age group 15–25. Chlamydia rates increased 106 percent in women from 1987 to 1991, with only a slight increase in men. Chlamydia is many times more prevalent than gonorrhea, but the two are similar because most women (70 percent) and many men (25 percent) have no symptoms and because they affect the cervix and the urethra, and at times the rectum.

Untreated chlamydia is the major cause of pelvic inflammatory disease (PID) in women. PID is an infection that can be life-threatening in its severe forms and can cause scarring of the fallopian tubes, resulting in infertility. Young women are more severely affected, and women who have repeated PID are more likely to become infertile.

Chlamydia is transmitted by contact with the body fluids of an infected person. Chlamydia does not live outside the body. Women can transmit chlamydia to other women, but it is generally found that the risk of chlamydia and other sexually transmitted diseases is more closely related to intimate sexual contact with men. Women with multiple partners, women whose partners have multiple partners, and women having sex with persons in the age group 15–25 are at greater risk than other women. Young women in the juvenile and adult corrections systems and women who have suffered unwanted sexual contact experience higher rates of chlamydia.

Chlamydia is so prevalent that many women's health centers routinely screen young women and those with multiple partners. The test is similar to a Pap smear and can be done at the same time. A woman whose partner has chlamydia should be treated. Sexual partners from the previous 60 days should be treated. Treatment is usually with tetracycline unless the woman is pregnant, when erythromycin is used. Alternative treatments have not been found to be effective.

Because chlamydia can be transmitted to the baby during birthing, pregnant women should be tested and treated for chlamydia. Chlamydia can cause eye infection in the infant; in fact, chlamydia is a major cause of blindness in newborns in countries without adequate health care. Antibiotic eye drops are routinely used in the United States to prevent eye infection in newborns. The drops may not be needed if the mother knows she is free from infection. Chlamydia can also result in pneumonia in the infant at a later time; the only signs may be a cough and lack of expected weight gain.

A woman who has burning on urination, bleeding or spotting between menses (even those on oral contraceptives), or bleeding or spotting after intravaginal sex, and women who have multiple (male) partners may want to request chlamydia testing. Symptoms of PID such as abdominal pain may be milder than those of PID caused by gonorrhea and therefore harder to recognize.

Chlamydia can be prevented by using male or female condoms or detected early by visualizing the cervix periodically to notice inflammation or bleeding with touch. Use of other barriers and spermicides during sexual interactions is likely to reduce the risk of getting chlamydia.

References. Boston Women's Health Collective, *The New Our Bodies, Ourselves* (New York, 1992); Montreal Health Press, *STD Handbook* (Quebec, Canada, 1995).

ELAINE WHEELER

CHRISTIAN CHURCH, EARLY. The first four Christian centuries show considerable variation in the roles assumed by women in the church. In general, the early centuries saw a gradual restriction of women's activities, a trajectory not expected from Jesus' open treatment of women and Paul's acknowledgment (Romans 16) of women's contributions to the upbuilding of Christianity. Later New Testament literature (from c. A.D. 80–150) rather praises women for conformity to traditional matronly standards. The author of Acts, writing about A.D. 85, does not imagine earlier Christian women as missionaries but rather as the providers of hospitality for male leaders (e.g., Lydia in Acts 16:15), although he credits Prisca/Priscilla (in conjunction with her husband) with assistance to Paul and with the conversion of Apollos (Acts 18). Where some Gospel evidence points to women's activity, the author of Acts attributes it to men: compare, for example, John 4, in which a woman is credited with beginning the Samaritan mission, to Acts 8:4–13, in which this mission is attributed to Philip.

Several later New Testament books (such as I Peter, I Timothy, and Titus) instruct women to be obedient and submissive to their husbands; gone is Paul's preference for celibacy (I Corinthians 7). Apparently, these writers feared that Christianity would be discredited among non-Christians if Christian women moved outside the boundaries of traditional wifely behavior. I Timothy 5:3–16 speaks of a group called "widows," but the author makes more difficult a woman's entrance to the group; in addition, he advises younger widows to remarry. Whether the "widows" here mentioned were yet part of a fixed order is not known. They were, however, an organized group according to second-, third-, and fourth-century literature (e.g., Tertullian's treatises, *Shepherd of Hermas, Apostolic Traditions, Didascalia Apostolorum*, and *Apostolic Constitutions*), where they are commended for their pious deeds and prayers but were not permitted to fulfill clerical duties. It appears that the "widows" lost ground as a group with the rise of deaconesses and virgins.

It is likewise unknown when deaconesses became an order within the church. Although Paul calls Phoebe a *diakonos* (Romans 16:1), the word may not yet connote an office. Nor is I Timothy 3:11 any more helpful: Are women deacons meant, or wives of male deacons? Pliny's letter to the emperor Trajan (c. A.D. 113) may refer to deaconesses as *"ministrae."* By the later third and early fourth centuries in Eastern Christianity, the office of deaconess was firmly recognized. Although the Council of Nicaea (A.D. 325) counts them among the laity, other texts speak of their ordination; *Apostolic Constitutions* 8:20 gives the prayer recited during their ordination service, and Canon 15 of the Council of Chalcedon (A.D. 451) also testifies to their ordination. Deaconesses visited sick women in their homes, anointed women's bodies below the head after their baptisms, instructed women, and accompanied women to conferences with bishops and deacons. Even in the East, however, deaconesses were not allowed to baptize; and in the West, we have no record of early deaconesses being ordained.

Traditions of women's fuller participation in Christian life were preserved in New Testament apocryphal literature, on one hand, and in schismatic and "unorthodox" groups, on the other. Thus, the late second-century *Acts of Paul and Thecla* credits the heroine with a self-baptism and with "enlightening many people with the word of God" before her death. In Montanism, a mid-second-century movement of prophetic enthusiasm, two prophetesses, Priscilla and Maximilla, were held to be direct vehicles for the revelations of the Holy Spirit. Moreover, in some second- and third-century Gnostic groups, women were encouraged to prophesy and were allowed to lead, teach, and even baptize. "Mainstream" church leaders, however, condemned such activities for women, although they praised women martyrs for their stalwart courage. Here, the *Martyrdom of Perpetua and Felicitas* is particularly notable since many scholars think that Perpetua herself wrote the first sections that describe her early experiences and visions.

In the fourth century, however, with the rapid development of Christian asceticism, new avenues were opened to women desiring nontraditional lives. (See ASCETICISM, Ascetics, Recluses, and Mystics [Early and Medieval Christian.]) By around A.D. 330, the first communal monastery for women (for which we have firm evidence) had been founded in Egypt. In the middle of the fourth century, the pattern of "familial asceticism," in which a woman adopted a life of ascetic renunciation within her family's home or with a few like-minded companions, was common. In the 370s and thereafter some Western aristocratic women (e.g., Melania the Elder and Paula) moved to Palestine, where they founded monasteries for women and for men. By the end of the fourth century, John Chrysostom's friend Olympias had founded a monastery for women in Constantinople. Other monasteries for women were established in Asia Minor, North Africa, Egypt, Europe, and elsewhere. These monasteries provided opportunities for female leadership as well as women's education and opportunities for service. Although women were not allowed to become priests, they thus had available an alternative mode of religious life that was to become extremely prominent in later Catholicism.

ELIZABETH A. CLARK

CIRCUMCISION (FEMALE) is a euphemistic, but widely used, term for several forms of genital cutting performed on girls and women, also now frequently referred to as "female genital mutilation," or FGM. The most frequently practiced form is clitoridectomy, or excision, which consists of amputation of the clitoris and removal of the surrounding tissues such as the prepuce (clitoral hood) and part of the labia minora. Partial removal of the clitoris or pricking or cutting of it is a modified form. The least harmful form consists of the removal of the prepuce only (analogous to male circumcision). The term *sunna* circumcision is often used for these variants of clitoridectomy or prepuce removal. Caution should be exercised in interpreting the label *sunna*, however, as it has many interpretations by different practitioners, ranging from prepuce removal only to even more drastic surgeries than excision, and it carries religious implications. The most severe form of the surgeries is commonly known as pharaonic circumcision, in which the entire clitoris, prepuce, and labia minora are removed, along with the adjacent parts of the labia majora, and the two sides of the vulva are stitched shut (infibulated), occluding the urethra and most of the vaginal opening but preserving a single tiny opening for the passage of urine and menses.

Although medically unnecessary and often very harmful, female genital cutting continues to be performed in many of the world's cultures, but the prevalence of, and rationales for, the practices vary a great deal. Until the 1950s, for example, clitoridectomies were sometimes performed on female mental patients in the United States if they were considered to masturbate too much. In other situations, the surgeries are more widespread, being done on large percentages of the female population simply because they are female. While some cultures practice it as a puberty rite or transition to marriage, it is more common for the operations to be performed on much younger girls, ages 4 to 9. In most cultures it is performed by older women, often midwives.

Where female circumcision is commonly performed, the practices are usually considered justified by customary and/or religious values concerning gender-role expectations, and they are therefore often referred to as "ritual" genital surgeries. There is no single religion or ethnic group through which these customs are perpetuated, and their goals, effects, and meanings are quite variable in different contexts. Forms of these practices are found in many countries of Africa and the Middle East, among Muslims, Christians, and followers of other religions. The practices have spread to certain areas of Asia and are found in Europe and the Americas as well, particularly among immigrant groups. Reasons given for the practice include ideas of purification and the protection of virginity through the reduction of sexual sensitivity and (in the case of infibulation) the creation of a barrier to intercourse, but the range of symbolic meanings in the various cultures cannot be generalized.

The shifting terminologies used by both practitioners and analysts cause some confusion. As people who practice one form are taught that another is preferable, they have been known to adopt the new term without changing the form of cutting. The term *sunna* circumcision, for example, is from the Arabic for "tradition," that is following the traditions of the Prophet Mohammed, who is supposed to have permitted his followers to "reduce but do not destroy." *Sunna* has therefore become the term preferred by those Muslims who practice it, and the unfortunate religious association of this term may serve to justify continuing a practice not specifically required and not practiced by most followers of Islam.

Common health consequences following the surgeries include hemorrhage (bleeding), shock, infections, septicemia (blood poisoning), injury to adjoining structures, and retention of urine, as well as psychological effects. These are exacerbated when the surgeries are performed, as they often are, in unhygienic circumstances—often in homes with dirt floors, by untrained midwives using unsterile instruments, and without antiseptics, anesthesia, or pain relievers—and deaths sometimes result. The infibulated state can also cause many health problems later, including scarring, abscesses and cysts, dysmenorrhea, chronic pelvic infections, recurrent urinary tract infections, infertility, difficulty with urination, and vasico-vaginal fistula. First intercourse is often painful and difficult, often requiring cutting or tearing. Childbirth can result in complications from obstructed labor and usually requires a long incision that is reinfibulated after delivery by the birth attendant.

Those who practice FGM often experience ambivalence about it, but in many cases it forms a strong element of national and gender identity for both women and men. Outsiders who criticize the surgeries have often been resented for their insensitivity to cultural self-determination. International activism against FGM led by African women has dramatically increased, and the Geneva-based Inter-African Committee on Traditional Practices Affecting the Health of Women and Children publicizes the harmful effects on health through local activities in more than 25 countries. Recent federal and state legislation in the United States has explicitly prohibited the practices. Where women experience social pressure to conform against their wishes, fundamental changes in the status of women may be necessary to allow women themselves to determine what changes they desire.

References. R.H.D. Abdalla, *Sisters in Affliction* (London, 1982); A. El-Dareer, *Woman, Why Do You Weep?* (London 1982); E. Gruenbaum, "The Cultural Debate over Female Circumcision," *Medical Anthropology Quarterly* 10,4 (1996): 1–21; N. Toubia, *Female Genital Mutilation: A Call for Global Action* (New York, 1993).

ELLEN GRUENBAUM

CIVIL RIGHTS ACT OF 1964. See TITLE VII

CIVIL RIGHTS MOVEMENT, BLACK WOMEN IN. Black women played important roles in provoking crises, organizing and running movement organizations, and serving as (and socializing with) the foot soldiers in the demonstrations that transformed the civil rights movement from limited to mass protest and the American South into a different world. Their roles in shaping and reshaping political behavior, in creating new groups, and in maintaining and transforming older groups for political protest have been obscured by the fact that civil rights organizations have been formally governed by male, charismatic religious leaders. In fact, Ella Baker, Septima Clark, Fannie Lou Hamer, Ruby Hurley, Anne Moody, Diane Nash, Rosa Parks, and many other black women, serving in both formal and informal leadership roles, were critical to every aspect of the civil rights movement.

The period from 1954 to 1966 was especially important in the struggle for civil rights. The National Association for the Advancement of Colored People (NAACP) and the NAACP Legal Defense and Educational Fund successfully challenged the constitutionality of segregation in a legal campaign culminating in the Supreme Court's decision in *Brown v. Topeka, Kansas, Board of Education* case in 1954. (The plaintiff in the Topeka case was elementary school pupil Linda Brown; there were also plaintiffs in four other cases in the states of South Carolina, Delaware, Virginia, and Washington, D.C., which, taken as a group, made up the cases now known as the *Brown* decision.) The decision changed the political environment, permitting broader attacks on the structure of racial segregation and political subordination and the development of a strategy of nonviolent direct action and civil disobedience, imposed by organized masses of African Americans.

That strategy began to develop in the early 1950s. Rosa Parks rode the bus each day to and from her work as a seamstress in Montgomery, Alabama; when she refused to give a white person her seat on December 1, 1955; Mrs. Parks was arrested and jailed. Her action sparked the yearlong boycott of the bus company that laid the foundation for the civil rights movement. Parks was not simply a woman who was tired at the end of a long day's work. She had been very active as a member and officer of the local and state NAACP and numerous other city, state, and regional organizations. She had also attended the Highlander Folk School, where nonviolent resistance was discussed.

The history of organized challenges to school segregation and of student protests shows that women were involved not only in planning but also on the battle lines. In Little Rock, Arkansas, the local NAACP head Daisy Bates helped shepherd a group of high school students, six girls and three boys, as they desegregated Little Rock Central High School. As regional director of the NAACP, Ruby Hurley escorted Autherine Lucy when she desegregated the University of Alabama at Tuscaloosa. The university suspended and expelled Lucy for insubordination because she had accused it of conspiring to bar her from classes. Massive statewide resistance efforts later forced Hurley to close the NAACP regional offices in Alabama. Charlayne Hunter and Hamilton Holmes were the first African Americans to attend the University of Georgia at Athens; Hunter was the first to graduate.

The quiet courage of black women and men, in the face of violent resistance and uncontrolled mobs intending to block attempts to integrate or protest racial segregation and voting discrimination, created the uncomfortable contrasts that forced the Eisenhower, Kennedy, and Johnson administrations to commit themselves simultaneously to integration and to protecting the students from violent attack.

Black women were also organizers and leaders in the civil rights and new mass movement organizations that brought about so much change (e.g., the Montgomery Improvement Association, Student Non-Violent Coordinating Committee, and the Southern Christian Leadership Conference). Perhaps the most important person in the civil rights movement was Ella Baker, a protest facilitator and organization woman who precipitated the creation of, and became the organizational liaison for, numerous civil rights groups.

In the late 1940s Baker helped build the NAACP at the local, regional, urban, and national levels. In the mid-1950s, after Baker and others suggested the creation of an organization that became the Southern Christian Leadership Conference (SCLC) to coordinate movement activities, Baker became the SCLC's first associate director and second executive director and built the procedures and infrastructure that made its later protest campaigns possible.

In 1960, as protest spread among black college students, Baker organized a meeting of the students and also blocked the efforts of the SCLC, the Congress of Racial Equality (CORE), and the NAACP to absorb them into their respective organizations. Thus, the Student Non-Violent Coordinating Committee (SNCC) was created and, with it, an organizational framework and structure quite different from that of the older civil rights groups. Baker had also maintained a focus on egalitarian rather than hierarchical decision making. "Ella Baker had become midwife to the two organizations that would have the most far reaching impact on the civil rights movement: SCLC and SNCC" (Giddings, 275).

For political protest to succeed, local organizations such as churches and political and civil rights groups, as well as important institutions like black colleges, had to be mobilized to challenge segregation and attack barriers to political participation. While these groups were led by men, their infrastructure was composed of, and constructed by, women. Convincing the "leadership" in a community to challenge the racial status quo therefore often meant converting black women to commit their organizations to the struggle.

This meant using local church buildings for rallies and planning meetings or for shelter when demonstrators were threatened by white mobs; raising money to support activities; hosting and feeding civil rights workers; accepting invitations to attempt to register and vote; joining in, and encouraging, husbands and older children to participate in protests, sit-ins, and freedom rides; and encouraging, or at least accepting participation in, protest by their children aged 13 and under.

African American women accepted and often welcomed these roles, even though they risked jobs, homes, churches and lives because of their protest. Septima Clark was fired as a teacher in Charleston, South Carolina, because she belonged to the NAACP, and Fannie Lou Hamer and her family were ordered off a Sunflower County, Mississippi, plantation after 18 years when she attempted to register to vote by taking a literacy test. Commitment to civil disobedience often meant jail and the certain consequences of physical and psychological violence and possibly death. Convincing the women of local black institutions sometimes made the difference in an organization's, and therefore a community's, commitment to change.

The internal units of most important African American institutions were controlled by women; the social and political norms and values of family and community life were produced, reproduced, communicated, maintained, and reinforced or transformed by women. As black women accepted or rejected existing norms, local black communities remade themselves and made the civil rights movement. (See AFRICAN AMERICAN WOMEN [SINCE 1865].)

References. Vicki L. Crawford, Jacqueline Anne Rouse, and Barbara Woods, *Women in the Civil Rights Movement: Trailblazers and Torchbearers, 1941–1965* (Bloomington, Ind., 1993); Marianna Davis (ed.), *Contributions of Black Women to America* (Columbia, S.C., 1982); David J. Garrow (ed.), *The Montgomery Bus Boycott and the Women Who Started It* (Knoxville, Tenn., 1987); Paula Giddings, *When and Where I Enter, the Impact of Black Women on Race and Sex in America* (New York; 1984); Aldon Morris, *The Origins of the Civil Rights Movement: Black Communities Organizing for Change* (New York, 1984); Charles M. Payne, *I've Got the Light of Freedom: The Organizing Tradition and the Mississippi Freedom Struggle* (Berkeley, Calif., 1995).

DIANNE M. PINDERHUGHES

CLERICAL OCCUPATIONS are the largest class of female-dominated occupations in the United States and in other Western countries. Currently, one out of every three employed American women is in a clerical job, and nearly 80 percent of all clerical workers are women.

In the middle of the nineteenth century clerical work was a man's job.

The first U.S. women hired into clerical positions were employed by the Treasury to clip currency because of the shortage of qualified male workers during the Civil War. The success of this experiment, in which women were paid half the male wage, led to the hiring of more female clerks by the federal government. In 1870, there were fewer than 2,000 female clerical workers, and under 3 percent of all U.S. clerical workers were women.

The situation changed rapidly in the 1870s with the invention and adoption of the typewriter. Use of the typewriter spread quickly, leading to a demand for trained operators. Perhaps because of similarities between the typewriter and the sewing machine, typewriter operation was early seen to be an appropriate job for women. Although there was considerable public debate about the suitability of office employment for women, women typists soon became common, and their employment increased rapidly as use of the writing machine spread. By 1890, women were 20 percent of the much larger clerical labor force, and nearly one-third of women clerical workers were employed as stenographers and typists, whereas only 4 percent of men were so employed.

As the economy grew and became more complex, clerical employment increased rapidly. In 1870, only 1 of every 100 nonagricultural workers was in a clerical job. By 1930, 1 of every 10 was so employed; and by 1980, 1 in 5 workers was in a clerical occupation. As clerical employment grew, women's share of the clerical labor force also grew from under 3 percent in 1870, to 53 percent in 1939, to nearly 80 percent in 1980.

The expansion of women's employment in clerical jobs was due to a number of factors. Technological change in the office created conditions that fostered the employment of more women. As new machines and organizational schemes were adopted, clerical operations were standardized and broken into smaller parts. Jobs in the larger, more technologically sophisticated offices required skills that were transferable between employers, could be learned in schools, and were therefore appropriate for women workers, who were expected to have short-term attachment to the firm. This differed markedly from the situation that prevailed in earlier days, when offices had a few male clerks who were trained by the firm and hoped to work their way up to a managerial position. Because of the extremely rapid growth of total clerical employment, there was very little actual displacement of male office workers by women. Both male and female clerical employment has increased over time, with substantial segregation by sex among the clerical occupations. Women found work in the new routinized and mechanized office jobs, while men's clerical employment was concentrated in supervisory positions and jobs, such as shipping clerk, with substantial manual components. Men continued to be able to use clerical jobs as the first rungs on the ladder to upward mobility long after most women in offices were confined to dead-end jobs.

Wars also played an important role in opening opportunities in office employment for women. Wartime labor shortages led employers to experiment with hiring women in jobs that they had not previously held. In clerical occupations, these remained women's jobs after the wars ended. During the Civil War the federal government hired the first female clerks. World War I saw the opening of many clerk positions to women. Bank telling became a woman's occupation during World War II.

As the demand for clerical workers increased, employers found women eager and able to take the new jobs. Women's educational levels increased as more and more attended and graduated from high schools. The number of private business schools grew rapidly, and public high schools began to offer instruction in clerical skills. Women enrolled in these courses in large numbers.

Women were attractive to employers because their lack of other opportunities meant that they worked for lower pay than did men. Clerical jobs were attractive to women because the pay and working conditions were superior to those in most other jobs available to women. In the nineteenth century, earnings of women clerical workers were higher than those of almost all other employed women. Over time the pay of women clerical workers fell relative to the pay of women in other occupations but generally remained above the pay of women in manufacturing jobs. Even as the relative pay of clerical workers fell, the jobs remained attractive to many women because of the better working conditions and higher social status of office jobs.

The women who went into clerical jobs prior to World War II were mostly young, single, native-born whites. Many were the unmarried daughters of the respectable middle class who eschewed blue-collar jobs. Employers commonly had regulations against the employment of married women clerical workers. As time went on, older women, married women, black women, and working-class women found jobs as clerical workers. However, as late as 1930, 82 percent of all female clerical jobholders were unmarried, and more than half were under age 25. Black women were not hired into clerical jobs in substantial numbers till the mid-1960s, when some racial barriers fell.

In the 1960s and 1970s, office work was changed by the introduction of computers, but employment continued to grow at a rapid pace. In the 1980s, office work was again transformed by the adoption of microcomputers, which may have as profound an impact as did the typewriter in the late nineteenth and early twentieth centuries.

References. M. W. Davies, *Woman's Place Is at the Typewriter: Office Work and Office Workers, 1870–1930* (Philadelphia, 1982); H. A. Hunt and T. L. Hunt, *Clerical Employment and Technological Change* (Kalamazoo, Mich., 1986); E. J. Rotella, *From Home to Office: U.S. Women at Work, 1870–1930* (Ann Arbor, Mich., 1981).

ELYCE J. ROTELLA

CLIMACTERIC is the gradual ending of ovarian activity until it completely ceases at menopause.* The process extends over a period that may last for

10 years or more, usually beginning in the early 40s and ending sometime between the ages of 45 and 55. The period of the climacteric is marked by menstrual irregularity, and as menopause nears, ovulation during the menstrual cycle* becomes less frequent.

CLITORIDECTOMY. See CIRCUMCISION (FEMALE)

COGNITIVE ABILITIES, SEX DIFFERENCES IN. There have been two quite different approaches to the study of sex differences in cognitive abilities. One approach has assessed sex differences in performance on various indicators of cognitive skills such as grades in school and scores on tests of mathematical, scientific, verbal, and spatial skills. The other approach has investigated sex differences in cognitive style (the ways males and females approach cognitive tasks and their response to challenge and difficulty).

Cognitive Abilities. In what is acknowledged as the most comprehensive review of sex differences,* Maccoby and Jacklin concluded that there are reliable sex differences in only four areas, three of which are cognitive: mathematical, spatial, and verbal skills. Since that date, several more sophisticated studies and research syntheses have been done. In general, these studies and reviews suggest the following conclusions. (1) Males outperform females, especially after the age of 14, most consistently on timed tests of spatial perception and mental manipulation of objects (measures of spatial skills), and on timed tests involving mathematical problem solving and proportional reasoning. (2) Sex differences (with females outperforming males) on timed tests of verbal skills are quite weak and, in most cases, insignificant and more likely to occur prior to age 17. (3) Females outperform males slightly in school grades for verbal skills, and there are no sex differences in grades for mathematics and science. (4) The general pattern of sex differences may emerge somewhat earlier and may be somewhat large among gifted and talented students.

It should be noted, however, that except for the sex differences on spatial skills, which account for as much as 8 percent of the variance, the obtained sex differences are not very large (accounting for only 1 to 4 percent of the variance). In addition, the magnitude of the differences is influenced by a variety of factors, including age, previous course enrollment patterns, ethnic background, maturational rate, the particular test given, the historical period in which the study was done (differences are much smaller in more recent studies than in earlier studies), test-taking strategies, and the domains in which the problems are couched. Finally, the variance within sex on all measures is much greater than the variance between the sexes.

Given that sex differences in quantitative and scientific reasoning occur most consistently on timed tests rather than on other indicators of achievement such as school grades, tests and test taking should be discussed in a bit more detail. Performance on tests of mathematical and proportional reasoning depends on the individual's familiarity with the domain in which the questions are couched. An individual's reasoning capacity can be assessed with problems from several different domains (e.g., biology, physics, population genetics, cooking, etc.). Since how well one does on a particular problem is influenced by the extent to which one is familiar with the domain in which the problem is couched, and since many reasoning problems are couched in domains more familiar to males than to females (e.g., physics), tests of mathematical reasoning may be biased in favor of demonstrating male superiority.

Sex differences in variables linked to test-taking behavior may also be important mediators of the sex differences that emerge on timed tests. Females are more likely to use the response option "I don't know" rather than guessing, especially on difficult items. Females also report higher levels of test anxiety than males and are less likely to be risk takers, especially in male sex-typed domains. Each of these differences could have a negative impact on females' test-taking behavior sufficiently large to account for the sex differences on tests of mathematical and scientific reasoning.

Origins of Sex Differences on Cognitive Tests. Several explanations have been provided for the obtained sex differences on tests of mathematical reasoning and spatial skills. These include a sex-linked recessive gene for spatial skills, differential patterns of brain lateralization, hormonal influences, differential social and educational experiences both at home and in school, and differences in psychological characteristics (such as achievement motivation, confidence, interest, anxiety, cognitive style, autonomous learning behaviors, and mastery orientation). The evidence is least consistent for the biological explanations and most consistent for the social factors: males receive more and perhaps better math and science instruction and more encouragement to develop these skills. Parents and teachers also have higher estimates of adolescent and adult males' mathematical and scientific talent, often in the face of contradictory information. Evidence regarding the psychological factors varies across the particular construct being considered, with the strongest evidence supporting the importance of stereotyped sex differences in confidence, interest, and anxiety. In each case, however, the relationship of these antecedents varies across outcome measures; thus, it is likely that performances on spatial, mathematical, verbal, and scientific reasoning tasks is differentially influenced by various antecedents. Biological factors, for example, may have their largest influence on tests of particular spatial skills, while social and psychological factors may be more influential on tests of knowledge.

Cognitive Styles/Orientation. Several investigators have suggested that males and females differ in a set of characteristics that influence their general orientation to cognitive tasks. For example, Block argues that males are more likely to exhibit an "accommodative" mode of interacting with the world, while females are more likely to exhibit an "assimilative" mode. The accommodative mode is characterized by cognitive efforts to create new mental structures and new strategies when confronted with new information or with disequilibrating experiences and by a general orientation to explore and exploit the environment. In contrast, the assimilative mode is characterized by efforts to fit new information into existing mental structures, by relying longer on familiar strategies, and by a generally conservative orientation to one's environment. A somewhat similar distinction has been offered by Dweck (1040–1048). She argues that females are less likely to seek out intellectual challenges and are more likely to resort to familiar strategies, to seek outside help, or to give up when faced with difficult intellectual problems. The evidence regarding these hypotheses is quite weak at present, but research in this area is just beginning. I suspect, however, that sex differences on these types of variables, as on sex differences on cognitive skills, will be quite small and that the overlap of males' and females' scores will be quite large.

References. J. H. Block, *Sex Role Identity and Ego Development* (San Francisco, 1984); C. S. Dweck, "Motivational Processes Affecting Learning," *American Psychologist* 41 (1986); J. S. Eccles, "Sex Differences in Achievement Patterns," in T. B. Sonderegger (ed.), *Psychology and Gender: Nebraska Symposium on Motivation, 1984* (Lincoln, 1985); D. F. Halpern, *Sex Differences in Cognitive Abilities* (Hillsdale, N.J., 1986), J. S. Hyde and M. C. Linn (eds.), *The Psychology of Gender: Advances through Meta-Analysis* (Baltimore, 1986); E. E. Maccoby and C. N. Jacklin, *The Psychology of Sex Differences* (Stanford, Calif., 1974).

JACQUELYNNE S. ECCLES

COLONIAL AMERICA. Settlers in what was later the United States brought different domestic and settlement patterns from the regions of their origins and settled in areas of differing climate and soil conditions. As they underwent the adjustments necessary to meet the new conditions, different lifestyles emerged in accordance with the background of the settlers and the resources of their areas of settlement.

Immigrants in New England and the middle colonies usually came as family groups and in New England settled in tight-knit agricultural communities. Those in the Chesapeake area often came singly and settled on scattered farms devoted to cash crop agriculture. Where migrants came mostly in family groups, there were probably about two women to three men; where they came singly, there were perhaps as few as one woman to three men.

Since native American women were not trained in the skills needed to run a European farm household, European women were essential to the success of the colonies and were actively recruited. In a few instances land was allocated to women, but usually when women were considered in land distribution, the male head of household was given additional allotments for his wife, children, and servants.

The first generation of immigrants (free, indentured servant, and slave) generally married late. Most single women came to the colony at a relatively late age and, if indentured, were unable to marry until freed. Their daughters married much younger. In New England, where conditions were especially favorable, women's fertility rates were very high, averaging eight children. By the mid-seventeenth century women's age at first marriage was usually in the early to mid-20s.

In the Chesapeake colonies the single women who migrated were mostly indentured servants who could not marry until their indenture was completed. The harsh conditions of labor on tobacco farms, the isolation, and new diseases such as malaria, influenza, and dysentery resulted in high mortality. The women who survived invariably married, but only one marriage in three lasted 10 years, with the surviving spouse frequently left with two or three children. The precariousness of marriage resulted in a weak and unstable family system.

Infant mortality was very high. White southerners did not reproduce themselves until the eighteenth century, but as immunity built up, southern women proved as fertile as those in New England, tended to marry at an even younger age, and, because of the weak family system, chose partners without parental supervision. In the North, arrangements preliminary to marriage continued much as they had in the mother country.

Society and family were patriarchal. In the Puritan ideal, woman is the "helpmate" complementary to her husband, doing work as necessary as his and sharing equal responsibility, but not equal authority, in the home. Outside the home in the early years women exercised a degree of informal power through their networks, which were used for the exchange of surplus domestic production, news, and information. There is evidence that some women attended town meetings and at least one report of their voting. Once things were settled, however, women were quickly barred from political activity.

Although religion recognized the equality of souls, equality did not apply within the church except among the Quakers, who held that women received the gift of the Holy Spirit as well as men. Women could speak at Quaker meetings and serve as ministers; women's meetings functioned as complete and autonomous units. Quaker missionaries, many of them women, went through New England from 1656 to 1664 seeking converts. Both the men and the women were persecuted, but the women endured particularly severe punishments, in part, because it was felt they had stepped outside their proper roles. Mary Dyer (d. 1660) was hanged in Massachusetts after being banished and returning three times.

Religious heresy was one means by which women vented their frustrations against the patriarchal Puritan theocracy. Women were the majority of followers of Roger Williams (1603–1683), who stressed freedom of conscience and religious toleration. Anne Hutchinson (1591–1643) was the leader of an antinomian heresy asserting an indwelling Holy Spirit in the Elect, which makes the evidence of good works superfluous as a sign of salvation. She and several other women were banished from Massachusetts Bay Colony in 1637 and 1638. (See RELIGIOUS DISSENT IN COLONIAL NEW ENGLAND.)

The frustrations endemic to women's role in the Puritan patriarchy may also be responsible for the last outburst of Europe's witchcraft mania in Salem in 1692. Accusations of witchcraft were brought by adolescent girls living in the home of the minister of Salem village. That the girls, who were reaching maturity at a time when Salem was faced with a shortage of marriageable young men, found themselves facing a future at odds with their appointed sex roles may have contributed to the adolescent hysteria that resulted ultimately in around 200 persons being jailed and 20 hanged. (See WITCHCRAFT CRAZE.)

During the initial settlement of an area, women worked in the fields, but thereafter, except for emergencies, wives and daughters did fieldwork only on the poorest farms. Women's work was to produce goods for domestic consumption. They raised vegetables and poultry, tended the dairy cattle, butchered livestock, and made beer, cider, clothing, and other items for household use. They usually bought cloth and candles and had their grain commercially ground. The South, where cash crop agriculture prevailed, bought more manufactured items from abroad than did the northern and middle colonies.

Women might earn extra money by spinning and were occasionally called on by the authorities to care for the sick, orphaned, widows, or poor in their homes. Wives of artisans and small merchants might tend vegetable plots and dairies but were more often occupied with helping in the family business. An increasing number of single women supported themselves by "women's trades" such as millinery or the trade of their husband or father, by going into domestic service, by running inns or taverns, or by setting up "dame schools." Quite a few ran printing presses. In the Brandywine Valley, farm women made butter that was sold in Philadelphia and the West Indies. In New Amsterdam, where women still knew mathematics, single Dutch women often hired themselves out to merchants and planters for their passage.

Indentured servants were found in all colonies. Many New England girls were indentured servants to the age of 18; some acquired a trade during servitude. In the Chesapeake colonies the great majority of single women migrants were indentured servants bound for four or, later, five years. Conditions were harsh—those working on small or midsized tobacco farms might be put to field labor as well as heavy household work—and mortality was high. The women were vulnerable to sexual abuse by their masters and male servants. One in five was taken to court for pregnancy, but very few named their master as responsible. Pregnant servants who could not buy out their terms faced a fine or a lashing and one to two additional years of servitude.

From the late seventeenth century African women were brought to the colonies as slaves. (See SLAVES, AFRICAN AMERICAN.) Many ended up on farms where they were the only servant or where none of the other slaves spoke their language. Slave women did fieldwork, except for a few who, once the demand for field labor was satisfied, might be spared for work in the "big kitchen." They lived in slave quarters where, in the early morning and late evening, they processed their own food from garden plots (when this was possible). In the slave quarters, African and European elements combined in distinctive patterns to create an African American community marked by extensive kinship networks, including "fictive" kin, and distinctive social and religious patterns.

Some of the intricacies of English common law disappeared in the colonies, but overall, the legal rights of married women continued to be minimal. Widows were assured of the usufruct of at least one-third of their husband's estate except in Pennsylvania, where creditors had first claim. Husbands demonstrated confidence in their wives' abilities by making them executors of their estates, and, as children of immigrants reached maturity, some female heirs who came into property concerned themselves in business and the buying and selling of real estate. However, widows and spinsters were not the only women engaging in business. Married and remarried women could keep control of their property through premarital agreements, trusts, and wills stipulating independent control. Court records in New Amsterdam show that married women engaged in all sorts of economic activities.

A few enterprising women were highly successful in business. Margaret Brent (c. 1601–c. 1671) had manorial rights over more than 1,000 acres in Maryland, engaged actively in business on her own behalf, and acted as executor for Governor Leonard Calvert and attorney for the Lord Proprietor (Cecilius Calvert, Lord Baltimore). Her actions at the time of Calvert's death in 1647 may have averted a very serious crisis. Margaret Hardenbrook Philipse (fl. 1659–1690) carried on mercantile activities in New Amsterdam. According to her prenuptial agreement, she continued her activities as merchant, trader, and shipowner during her marriage. Eliza Lucas Pinckney (1722?–1793) of South Carolina managed her father's estates, experimenting with different crops and successfully cultivating indigo. After her marriage she cultivated silkworms on one of her husband's plantations, and after his death she managed all his properties.

In the northern colonies single women could meet the property qualifications of "freemen." However, when Margaret Brent claimed a vote in the Maryland House of Burgesses on the basis of her freehold property and a vote as the Lord Proprietor's attorney, she was refused. The election laws were changed in 1699 specifically to exclude her and other propertied women from qualifying to vote.

By the middle of the eighteenth century the colonies had about equal numbers of males and females, but there could be serious imbalances in different areas. While men continued to predominate on the frontier, in some eastern cities the surplus of women was as high as 15 percent. There the age of first marriage rose, and the remarriage of widows declined. There, as well, the artifacts of upper-class European society could be acquired, and its manners emulated. In eastern cities and southern plantations, gentlewomen did not engage in business but rather cultivated an active social life and supervised servants, who came from a different class, in an increasingly complex household.

References. Sara M. Evans, *Born for Liberty: A History of Women in America* (New York, 1989), ch. 2; Mary P. Ryan, *Womanhood in America: From Colonial Times to the Present*, 3d ed. (New York, 1983), ch. 1.

COLONIAL SPANISH AMERICA. See SPANISH AMERICA. COLONIAL PERIOD

COLOR, WOMEN OF, are women in the United States who are of African, Asian, Hispanic, and American Indian heritage. These categories are umbrella terms that can be further broken down into finer divisions within each racial-ethnic category. Divisions within the African category include black Americans, Afro-Caribbeans, and other women from the African diaspora who now live in the United States. Asian women include Japanese, Chinese, South Asians, Pacific Islanders, and new immigrants from Southeast Asia. Hispanic women include Mexican Americans, Puerto Ricans, Cubans, and immigrants from South and Central America. American Indian women encompass over 300 tribal affiliations crosscutting reservation and urban Indian life.

Increasingly, scholars point out that black/white comparisons can no longer dominate the discussion of gender, race, and ethnicity in America. While discussions of race and ethnicity have focused on men, and discussions of gender have focused on white women, a third category, women of color, is emerging as a legitimate theoretical and conceptual framework for viewing a range of racial-ethnic women in America. The term has also been applied cross-culturally, but for purposes of this discussion the analysis is restricted to the American case.

While women of color are distinct from the white majority in terms of race and ethnicity, historical differences between the groups make them not strictly comparable. These differences are anchored in unique experiences involving culture, language, racism, and sexism.* Nonetheless, their common experiences of racial and sexual discrimination* in a society defined in terms of whiteness and maleness are the major unifying feature of their existence.

Thus, in this entry the focus is on contrasting and comparing two major dimensions in the lives of women of color. The first emphasis is on a shared theoretical lens through which to view their history and current-day status. This theoretical framework is the intersection of race, class, and gender in their lives. The second focus involves looking at women of color's deep embeddedness in family and work relations. They are central forces in the social construction of racial-ethnic family life, and their economic positioning in labor markets is a reflection of race and gender inequality.

The central theoretical theme in the analysis of women of color is race, gender, and class inequality. These inequalities are interconnected. This means that the ideology of racism, economic inequity, and gender inequality are distinctive, but interrelated, forces in their lives. Women of color often occupy unique economic, cultural, and gender niches. Hence, their evolution as women is somewhat separate from that of Anglo and other white ethnic women.

Regarding race, women of color suffer from the cultural and symbolic definitions and practices of white supremacy. Thus, in a related sense, the self, language, religion, and family practices of women of color have been stigmatized and treated as inferior. In addition, gender has been the basis of inequality in their lives. Women, generally, do not fare well in a society organized along patriarchal lines. Yet, in a society crosscut by racial inequality, women of color are doubly at risk. For example, in the economic sphere, even though all women are heavily ghettoized in clerical positions, when supervisory positions are held by women, white women tend to be in the supervisory positions, and women of color tend to be supervised. Another case in point is that while political, economic, and social power is monopolized by white males, women of color must rely largely on innovative political strategies and resistance. These tools have been part of the arsenal of black women's struggle since the time of the slave trade. Other women of color have been more submerged politically but are beginning to come into their own, defining their interests and organizing to achieve these goals.

In terms of class and economic relations, women of color are disproportionately poor. This is especially true for Mexican American, American Indian, and black women. It is somewhat less so for certain Asian women, such as the Japanese, but the new Southeast Asian immigrants, such as the Hmong, are often impoverished. Nevertheless, these women share in common gender experience with all women because of their connection to the range of gender inequality: distinctive gender socialization and gender discrimination.

Finally, crosscutting race, class, and gender issues are the domains of work and family. Family is essential in the lives of women of color. The feminist critique of the family as a site of oppression has been challenged by these women. Feminists from these groups argue that the family is central to their existence and often serves as a haven in a society which demeans them (Hooks). For example, black women have centered their lives in family and community as well as paid work. This tradition continues to the present. Historically, Hispanic women have not been as involved in paid work as black women have, but this is changing as a growing number of Hispanic women enter the paid labor force. Home, however, has been quite essential to them. Baca-Zinn and Eitzen note that Mexican-American women have been powerful forces within their homes. Family has also been central in the lives of Asian women. Furthermore, extensions and kin-shared family relations are also indicative of American Indian family life.

As workingwomen,* each group faces discrimination in the labor market. This discrimination has varied somewhat by group, since the women are rather differently located in the labor force. Yet, overall, women of color have been in sex/race categories with job ceilings and disproportionately occupy jobs at the bottom of the labor market, this positioning profoundly shaped by race, ethnicity, and sex. Only in the last 20 years have the labor market experiences of women of color increasingly converged with the experiences of white women. Now all groups of women are sex-segregated in the labor force, primarily in service and clerical work. Even so, white women are more likely to be employed in executive and managerial levels than are other groups.

More specifically, black women are still overrepresented in service and nonhousehold domestic work. Mexican women are involved more than others in seasonal work, and skilled Mexican American women are centered in the low-paying clerical, operative, and service occupations. American Indian women predominate in low-level service work but confront the dilemma of obtaining any kind of employment since unemployment rates tend to be high on reservations and in urban areas. Japanese, Filipino, and Cuban women are at the top of the professional work categories, but Asian women dominate in garment, piecemeal, and semiconductor work in this country (Almquist). Neither group is free from race and sex discrimination in the workplace.

In short, there is unity in diversity in the context of these women's work and family lives. For all, there remains the difficult struggle of maintaining a sense of self and a degree of personal integrity in hostile environments. Yet, through their innovations, struggles, and resistance, women of color are a positive and notable force in American society.

References. E. M. Almquist, *Minorities, Gender and Work* (Lexington, Mass., 1979); M. Baca-Zinn and D. S. Eitzen, *Diversity in American Families* (New York, 1987); b. hooks, *From Margin to Center* (Boston, 1984).

ROSE M. BREWER

"COMFORT WOMEN"/MILITARY SEXUAL SLAVERY. Throughout history, soldiers have used rape and sexual slavery of women as effective weapons to control, destroy, and humiliate the enemy by violating its "property": women. Violence against women was justified as a reward for the fighting troops and considered inevitable. The Japanese military sexual slavery system established during its colonial expansion into China in the 1930s and lasting until the end of World War II is the most extreme and blatant case of this practice.

In the 1930s and 1940s, the Japanese government mobilized women in colonized countries (e.g., Korea, Taiwan) and occupied areas (e.g., China, the Philippines) by force or deceit, for use as sex slaves for the Japanese Imperial Army. The combined term military "comfort women"/military sex slaves refers to 80,000 to 200,000 women drafted for military sexual slavery by Japan between the early 1930s and 1945.

Approximately 80 percent of the military "comfort women"/sex slaves were Korean, but there were also Chinese, Taiwanese, Filipino, Burmese, Indonesian, Papua New Guinean, Japanese, Okinawan, and even some Dutch women prisoners from Indonesia.

According to the personal testimonies of survivors and government documents discovered since 1991, the use of sexual slaves, euphemistically called "comfort women," was long-term, systematic, and institutionalized state rape planned, designed, and enforced by the supreme commander of the Japanese Imperial Army. Military sexual slavery camps were managed by the army's Recreation Division, and military "comfort women"/sex slaves, classified as military supplies, were transported by the military transportation system.

Military sexual slavery camps were set up wherever army personnel were stationed: in Taiwan, Sakhalin, Burma (Myanmar), China, Manchuria, the Philippines, Malaysia, Indonesia, Borneo, Papua New Guinea, Korea, Okinawa, and Japan. Camps could be found also on railroad and construction sites and at mines and war factories where large numbers of male laborers were working.

The system apparently began after the Manchuria Incident (1931) but was institutionalized after the Nanking Massacre (December 1937), in the hope that the army's providing a psychosexual outlet for its soldiers would prevent a repeat of the atrocity in which an estimated 115,000 Chinese civilians were killed, including 20,000 women who were reportedly raped and murdered.

In the beginning, the Japanese army drafted daughters of Korean coal miners in Kyushu, Japan. From 1938 onward, they recruited women from impoverished farm families in Kyungsang and Chulra provinces in the southern part of South Korea. As the war intensified and expanded, preteen and teenage women were drafted from factories and from middle and elementary schools all over Korea, and even married women and mothers with nursing infants were coerced into sexual slavery on Japan's battle-fronts. These women worked without monetary compensation, were promised savings accounts at the end of the war that they never saw, or were paid with military coupons that became worthless after the war.

According to testimony from survivors, they were conscripted (1) by promises of jobs such as factory work, cooking, laundry work, domestic help, or nursing; (2) by the possibility of earning large sums of money to send home to their families and obtaining meals with "polished white rice," which only elite Japanese had access to; (3) by promising opportunities for formal education and technical training; (4) by threatening the family with drafting their sons if daughters were not offered; and (5) by hunting them down in public areas such as farm fields, public wells, roads, market areas, or even kidnapping from private homes.

Military "comfort women"/sex slaves were provided as royal gifts from the Emperor (Tenno). However, they were classified by the Japanese Imperial Army as military supplies in the same way as ammunition and food rations and identified by item numbers, not as human beings with names. The women, then, were used and discarded as supplies, without documentation of entry and/or exit (death), while the records for dogs and horses used by the army were meticulously kept. The women were placed in tiny cubicles partitioned by curtains, in tents, or in buildings with temporarily constructed wooden panels, unused school buildings, regular civilian houses, even on the hills at battlefields. They were gang-raped by an average of 20 to 30 soldiers during weekdays and, on weekends, between 40 to 50 or even up to 100 soldiers a day.

In order to protect the Japanese soldiers, military "comfort women"/sex slaves were given regular medical examinations for venereal disease and received injections called Number 606, which was also an effective abortifacient. Even though the soldiers were required to use condoms, many of the sexual slaves contracted venereal disease, usually within 6 to 12 months of their enslavement, in part, through the soldiers' refusal to use condoms, in part, because of the poor quality of recycled condoms, which were washed and hung to dry every day by the sex slaves themselves.

Almost invariably, women who had been deceived or kidnapped attempted to escape or to resist sexual assaults, with dire consequences. They were severely beaten or, in extreme cases, slashed to death with a sword in front of other sexual slaves as a warning against attempting escape or resistance.

According to Aso Tetsuo, a former Japanese Imperial Army gynecologist, the sex slaves were subjected to continuous gang rape at an average frequency interval of 5 to 10 minutes rather than the officially designated 30 minutes per soldier. During weekdays when they were not used for sex, they were obliged to do housekeeping chores, nursing, carrying military supplies, or even fighting in Japanese military uniform. Moreover, they were often used as human shields during last-ditch battles.

The ordeals of survivors did not come to an end with Japan's defeat in 1945. It was almost impossible for the survivors to return to Korea because the Japanese Imperial Army provided transportation only for their soldiers and civilian personnel. When Japanese soldiers returned to Japan or went into hiding, they left the women behind without informing them of Japan's surrender. They were simply abandoned, left to fend for themselves, without knowledge of where they were and without any resources. In some instances, to hide the evidence of their existence, they were driven to mass suicide along with the soldiers or massacred by being shoved into tunnels or piled into dungeons.

For those in China, the only way to return to Korea was by foot, spending many months without material resources such as clothes, shoes, and food and almost all of them suffering from ill health and sexual assault trauma.

The Korean women had been socialized in a Confucian society where virginity and chastity were considered more important than life itself. Some women committed suicide aboard civilian ships carrying them toward Korea rather than face a homecoming of degradation or lifelong social isolation. Those military "comfort women"/sexual slavery survivors who did return to Korea were unable to go back to their own home villages or to their families. Most led miserable and difficult lives. Some were captured as prisoners of war and served the Allied Occupational Forces as military prostitutes. Most military "comfort women"/sexual slavery survivors, suffering from mental and physical ill health, poverty, and inability to live as ordinary women (e.g., to marry and bear children), wished that they had died in the war.

The full extent of the sexual slavery system from 1932 to 1945 will remain unknown since the Japanese government destroyed most of the documents after the war and killed or deserted almost all of the military "comfort women"/sex slaves. Moreover, both the women survivors and Japanese Imperial Army personnel have either died or kept silent until recently.

In 1991, a 50-year silence was broken when Kim Hak Soon, a Korean military "comfort women"/sexual slavery survivor, publicly told her story. Now, approximately 1,000 survivors have come forward from all over the Asian and Pacific region and the Netherlands. They are working with activist groups to make Japan accountable for this crime against humanity.

Approximately 180 military "comfort women"/sexual slavery survivors who responded to the Korean government's registration system and the hot lines set up by the Korean Council for the Women Drafted for Sexual Slavery by Japan since 1992 are still suffering from the effects of their sexual enslavement. Venereal disease and other gynecological abnormalities, various physical disabilities, and mental illnesses remain as a lifelong result of the atrocities they experienced.

Despite their poverty, old age, and ill health, they, along with human rights activist groups, are working diligently at the United Nations (UN) Commission on Human Rights demanding that the Japanese government recognize its military sexual slavery as a war crime and violation of international humanitarian laws. They are demanding that the Japanese government publicly make apologies to the individual survivors and pay reparations. The survivors are now working toward one common goal: to die with the knowledge that they have helped to bring a genuine peace with justice to the whole Asian and Pacific region and to the world.

References. Alice Yun Chai, "Asian Pacific Feminist Coalition Politics: The Chongshindae/Juguniaufu (Comfort Women) Movement," *Korean Studies, An Annual Publication of the Center for Korean Studies* (University of Hawaii) 17 (1993): 67–91, George Hicks, *Comfort Women: Sex Slaves of the Japanese Imperial Army* (London, 1995).

ALICE YUN CHAI

COMMON-LAW MARRIAGE is a union of husband and wife that is recognized as a valid marriage, even though state requirements of licensing and/or ceremony were not followed. Once accepted by all the common-law states in the United States, it is now invalid in most or recognized only if entered into many years before. When Florida ended recognition of common-law marriages entered into after 1985, it joined 9 other states that have cut off recognition since the 1920s. By 1987 only 13 states and the District of Columbia had statutory provision for common-law marriages. In general, in those states that still recognize common-law marriage, three things are necessary for validity: the capacity to enter into marriage, the present intent to be married, and reputation in the community as being married.

COMMUNICATION. The Impact of Gender. The disciplinary study of women and communication may be said to have begun with the examination of both women-specific communication and the search for communication styles and patterns unique to women. The new paradigm or model in the study of women and communications may be understood as the gender and communication paradigm or model.

This model is characterized by three approaches, including the study of women- and men-specific communication practices and styles; the study of the differences between the communication practices and styles of women and men; and the study of perceptions of, and communications about, women and men in society. This model shows greater theoretical and empirical complexity and sophistication than the previous model, even as it draws from, and extends, it. First, on the theoretical premise that biological sex is different from gender, the model does not assume that women are innately different from, or superior or inferior to, men. Rather, research examines how gender identities are constructed and enacted through communication in contexts by women and men. Second, the model includes the study of both women's and men's communication practices and styles. Third, the model examines perceptions and communication about women and men in society so as to understand how power relations are organized and may be transformed in society. Fourth, the model takes for its premise the ethical principle that if we are to create and live in a world of gender equality, then we ought to understand communication in relation to both women and men.

In this entry, I highlight five scholarly works that make significant contributions to the study of gender and communication. The essays illustrate the three approaches within the gender and communication paradigm. They collectively demonstrate the rich variety of research approaches within the paradigm. More specifically, the essays vary in their focus on communication phenomena ranging from small group, through family, interpersonal, and third party, to public communication. Also they focus on different media, including speech, writing, and symbolic media. Further, they draw from both social scientific and critical theory.

Women- and Men-Specific Communication. The review and critical essay (68–85) by Meyers and Brashers extends group communication research by theoretically emphasizing women's communication practices and gender-based communication goals as important topics in this subspecialty. The researchers found two knowledge gaps in current research on small-group communication. First, women-specific small groups and communication practices and styles were not studied in a substantial or satisfactory manner. Second, masculine goals of instrumental communication drove much of the research on small-group communication to the exclusion of feminine expressive goals, such as group continuity, connection, and co-operation. In a related fashion, research focused on task- and decision-making-related communication and did not pay attention to the use of narrative. On the basis of a feminist theoretical perspective the researchers make a compelling claim for the study of bona fide women's small groups and styles, feminine communication goals, and the study of narrative.

In the research article Sandra Petronio and Bradford (162–175) extend current research on children's adjustment in the context of divorce. Current social psychological and family development research on the impact of divorce on family members has examined the sense of loss and uncertainty experienced by children. It also examines how maintenance of relational bonds can facilitate the process of children's adjustment, with a particular emphasis on children's use of letter writing as a tool for expressing emotions and maintaining relational bonds.

The researchers extend current understandings of this important area of study by focusing on uncertainty, letter writing, absentee divorced fathers, and children's adjustment. They conducted a survey with absentee divorced fathers who were part of a nationwide writing program. The overall finding was that the greater the uncertainty with their roles as parents, the greater the writing apprehension and decreased feeling of writing competence experienced by fathers. The authors arrive at this valuable conclusion: "When they feel that they can predict their child's behavior and feel competent as writers, these fathers perceive that their ability to write effectively increases on several dimensions" (172).

Communication Differences between Women and Men. Dindia (345–371) argues that so far, much of the research on interruptions makes the erroneous claim that women are more prone to being interrupted by men than by women in conversational settings. Dindia also questions related findings: that men interrupt more than women and that women are interrupted more than men; that men–women relational settings (opposite-sex dyads) show greater asymmetry in interruptions compared to men–men or women–women relational settings (same-sex dyads), with men interrupting women with greater frequency; and that women interrupt less assertively and respond less assertively to interruptions in comparison with men.

Dindia uses complex statistical procedures and advances three results that refute current findings on women and interruptions. First, men did not interrupt more than women, and women did not get interrupted more in comparison with men. Second, the symmetry or asymmetry of interruptions was comparable in both opposite-sex and same-sex dyads. Third, women's interruptions were not less assertive than men's; neither were women less assertive in responding to interruptions.

Perceptions and Communications about Women and Men in Society. Burrell, Donohue, and Allen (447–469) extend current inquiry into the relations between dispute mediation and gender of the mediator. Current research suggests that sex/gender plays a significant role both in perception of the effectiveness of the dispute mediator and in the process of mediation. The researchers extend current understandings on this topic in the particular context of interventionist dispute mediation, an approach where the mediator actively intervenes and shapes the process and outcomes of the mediation.

The particular study that was conducted by researchers was mediation of a mock conflict situation in same-sex dyads where male and female subjects were trained as mediators within the interventionist dispute model. Statistical research yielded a very important and statistically significant overall finding "that gender stereotyping is alive and well" (463). Specific findings include the perception of female mediators as being less controlling, even though they may be said to have employed controlling styles. Similarly, male mediators were seen as being more controlling, even though they may be said to have employed less controlling styles of dispute mediation.

Olson and Goodnight (249–276) use the analytical genre of social controversies to examine the controversy over women's use of fur that raged in America during the 1980s. The authors argue that woman's symbolic practice—the practice of wearing fur—becomes the rhetorical site for the entanglements of consumption, cruelty, privacy, and fashion. The pro-fur groups, including women who wear fur, stake out their claims by appealing to conventional premises and arguments that generally assume a separation between public and private realms, while the antifur group does the opposite. In particular, both parties make opposing arguments about the "relationships between humans and animals, traditional meanings attached to buying and wearing fur garments, and the sanctity of consumption as a matter of private choice" (253). The authors conclude by conceptualizing human communication as a vehicle through which society can debate and decide how men and women may engage in ethical practice.

References. Nancy A. Burrell, William A. Donohue, and Mike Allen, "Gender-Based Perceptual Biases in Mediation," *Communication Research* 15 (1988); Kathryn Dindia, "The Effects of Sex of Subject and Sex of Partner on Interruptions," *Human Communication Research* 13 (1987); Renee A. Meyers and Dale Brashers, "Expanding the Boundaries of Small Group Communication Research: Exploring a Feminist Perspective," *Communication Studies* 45 (1994); Kathryn M. Olson and G. Thomas Goodnight, "Entanglements of Consumption, Cruelty, Privacy, and Fashion: The Social Controversy over Fur," *The Quarterly Journal of Speech* 80 (1994); Sandra Petronio and Lisa Bradford, "Issues Interfering with the Use of Written Communication as a Means of Relational Bonding between Absentee, Divorced Fathers and Their Children," *Applied Communication Research* 21 (1993); Julia T. Wood (ed.), *Gendered Relationships* (Mountain View, Calif., 1996).

K. E. SUPRIYA

COMMUNITY PROPERTY is a system of property ownership and control in which marriage* is treated as an economic partnership to which each spouse makes an equal, but different, contribution and in which each is entitled to an equal share of the assets.

Community property was introduced into the United States in territories formerly held by Spain and France: Arizona, California, Louisiana, New Mexico, and Texas. Idaho, Nevada, and Washington also use the system; some others adopted it briefly because of its income tax advantages but reverted to common law when the Revenue Act of 1948 ended the advantage.

In general, under the community property system, property brought to the marriage and property acquired by one of the spouses through gift, devise, or inheritance during the marriage remain under individual ownership. All other property belongs equally to both spouses. Originally, the husband controlled the common property and, in some cases, the wife's separate property as well. The wife's rights in the joint property, then, were of practical importance only at the dissolution of the marriage.

During the marital property reform movement of the late nineteenth century, the husband's absolute control was weakened. He could not encumber or sell real property without his wife's knowledge and consent or transfer any property to defraud his wife. Where she did not have it before, the wife gained the right to manage her own property and, in some states, to control her own wages.

In the reforms of the 1960s and 1970s, husbands lost the sole right of management of joint property. In 1967 Texas adopted a "gender-neutral" system of control according to which spouse held title, in effect leaving most husbands in control of most assets. The Washington reform in 1972, however, gave equal management and control to both parties. The other six states adopted the Washington pattern over the next seven years.

The community property system has decided advantages over a separate property system for most married women in matters of credit, contract, and management and control of property. In property settlements at the death of the husband or in cases of divorce,* community property's equal division contrasts with the widow's third that is usually the norm in cases of intestacy and is often used as a guideline in "equitable division" divorce settlements in common-law states.

Courts in common-law property states found community property rules helpful in determining property settlements at divorce. When in the 1970s and 1980s common-law states moved to erase sex discrimination in credit and contract and to reform divorce and inheritance laws, community property rules were again consulted. Feminists in common-law property states have worked for, and supported, the adoption of the community property (marital property*) concept.

COMPARABLE WORTH (also called "Pay Equity") is a wage policy requiring equal pay within a jurisdiction or firm for job classifications that are valued equally in terms of skill, effort, responsibility, and working conditions. In practice, implementing this policy requires the application of a *single* job evaluation system to all job classifications within the jurisdiction or firm. The job evaluation system measures in detail the skill, effort, responsibility, and working conditions of every job classification and combines the scores in each area to produce a *single* overall score for every classification. Job classifications with equal overall scores are considered to have equal value to the jurisdiction or firm. Under a comparable worth wage policy, classifications of equal value are paid equivalently. All individuals holding the same jobs within equal classifications would not be paid the same wages, however, because seniority, merit, or quantity or quality of work done would continue to differentiate individuals' wages within equivalent classifications.

Comparable worth became controversial when an analysis of the relationship between current wages and points revealed differences in compensation related to gender, race, and ethnicity. A large number of studies have shown that if two job classifications have the same value according to the job evaluation system, but one is held primarily by men and the other held primarily by women, or one is held primarily by whites and the other by people of color, the job held by men or whites usually pays more. For example, Minnesota used the results of a Hay Associates point-factor job evaluation to determine whether, at equivalent point levels, female-dominated and male-dominated jobs were paid equivalently. At equal Hay point values, jobs dominated by women paid less than those dominated by men. Minnesota's analysis did not extend to comparisons of race and ethnicity because Minnesota's workforce, like the state's population, has fewer than 3.5 percent people of color. Using a somewhat different methodology, the comparable worth analysis undertaken for New York State employees included race, ethnicity, and gender comparisons and showed parallel findings.

Opponents of comparable worth, relying on a neo-classical view of economics, believe that wages should be established not by the value of a job to the firm or jurisdiction but rather by what the marketplace pays for each type of job. Comparable worth supporters respond, in the tradition of institutional economics, that the market embodies the customs and practices that encourage low wages for jobs filled by women and minorities. The gender-, race- and ethnicity-based wage differences found within jurisdictions and firms for equally valued jobs are evidence that the market does not properly value the work traditionally done by women and minorities.

The movement for comparable worth arose from the persistence of wage differentials between women and men, differentials that were exacerbated for women of color.* In 1984, figures for full-time workers showed that white women earned 64¢, black women earned 58¢, and Hispanic women earned 54¢ for every dollar earned by white men. In that same year, black men earned 74¢ and Hispanic men 71¢ in comparison to the dollar earned by white men. While the earnings differentials between minority and white workers had become narrower after World War II, earnings differentials between women and men remained fairly stable. The Equal Pay Act of 1963 and Title VII* of the Civil Rights Act of 1964 did little to reduce the overall earnings differentials between women and men.

One of the major reasons the Equal Pay Act and Title VII did not change earnings differentials is that women and men do not, for the most part, hold the same kinds of jobs. According to 1980 census data, women workers, regardless of race or ethnicity, were likely to work in occupations that were two-thirds filled by women, and men were likely to work in jobs whose incumbents ranged from 69 to 79 percent male, depending on color. The more an occupation is filled by women or people of color, the lower its wage rate.

The history of comparable worth began soon after World War I, when the newly created International Labor Organization called for "equal pay for work of equal value." In the United States during World War II the War Labor Board created a policy of equal pay for equal work and very briefly supported a policy of equal pay for jobs of equal content, regardless of the sex of the worker. Sustained interest in equal pay and comparable pay did not survive the war years. Not until 1963, when Congress passed the Equal Pay Act, did the "equal pay for equal work" standard become law, eschewing the comparable worth standard proposed in earlier versions of the bill. In 1964, Title VII of the Civil Rights Act created a general national prohibition against employment discrimination.* Section (h) of Title VII, referred to as the Bennett Amendment, reconciled the provisions of the Equal Pay Act and Title VII with regard to women's wage discrimination claims. Title VII has become particularly important in the implementation of comparable worth because it prohibits not only intentional discrimination but also neutral policies having an adverse impact on protected groups.

One of the legal questions yet to be decided under the incorporation of the Equal Pay Act into Title VII of the Civil Rights Act of 1964 is whether Title VII accepts a comparable worth wage standard. In 1981, in *County of Washington v. Gunther*, the Supreme Court ruled that Title VII was not restricted to the equal work standard of the Equal Pay Act. Although the Court explicitly chose not to rule on the "controversial concept of 'comparable worth,' " advocates agreed that the Court had not precluded further consideration of comparable worth cases.

The *Gunther* opinion offered a boost to local, state, and national activists. Working from a base of several years of grassroots efforts, public employee unions, particularly the American Federation of State, County and Municipal Employees, joined women's organizations, minority groups, and others to form the National Committee on Pay Equity in 1979. Opponents also organized, primarily through business associations like the National Association of Manufacturers, to lobby against the policy.

Litigation, legislation, and collective bargaining have been used to achieve comparable worth. Like many equity reforms, the early efforts have focused on the public sector. A growing number of state and local governments use or plan to use pay equity as the basis for compensation of public employees. As of April 1987, 28 states had conducted job evaluation studies for state workers, and 17 states had begun to make some kind of comparable worth wage adjustments, using legislative appropriations. The cost has generally been in the range of 2 to 5 percent of total payroll. In 1984, Minnesota became the first state to require all local jurisdictions to prepare plans to implement comparable worth policies for their public employees. Some cities like Los Angeles and San Jose have approached comparable worth through collective bargaining. Since 1980, efforts to study or implement comparable worth for the federal workforce stalled due to partisan divisions.

SARA M. EVANS and BARBARA J. NELSON

COMPOSERS (TWENTIETH-CENTURY). The twentieth century has witnessed three distinct generations of women composers.

The first of these can be represented by the American Amy Marcy Cheney (later, Mrs. H.H.A. Beach), who was trained as a pianist by prominent teachers in Boston but was denied the study of composition because of her gender. She was educated in composition outside the system, as women would have to be in the United States until after World War II. Beach is known especially for her sensitive song settings and her instrumental works, including a Piano Trio and the *Gaelic* symphony. Like most of her generation, she aimed to work in the mainstream, establishing herself as a powerful exception to the rule but not committing herself to changing the rule.

In this group were a few spectacular successes, such as Lili Boulanger, whose fine music had a supreme spokesperson in her sister Nadia, who held a vital pulpit as the great seminal teacher at the American Conservatory at Fontainebleau. Boulanger is representative: no threat to any man because she was safely dead (at 25), and her music was advertised with persistent conviction by someone else. Exceptionally, Dame Ethel Smyth was more active in fighting for herself and for other women in music, but she worked in Great Britain, a land much more tolerant of eccentrics. These composers produced scores of unquestioned value but were granted limited (and insufficient) recognition.

The second generation can be represented by Ruth Crawford (later, Seeger), trained outside the system but having joined it by marriage (her husband was a professor of ethnomusicology) and latterly (and, to greatest effect, posthumously) accepted within it. Whereas earlier composers had seen themselves as working outside the system, this generation wanted to work inside and to be a part of it. Some women of this group, such as Marcelle de Manziarly, Dorothy James, Undine Smith Moore, Grazyna Bacewicz, Peggy Glanville-Hicks, Rebecca Clarke, and Miriam Gideon, have commanded universal respect. Their music is vibrant and strong: one thinks of the String Quartet of Crawford; the Song Cycles and Piano Trio of Manziarly; the operas of Glanville-Hicks, Moore, and James; and the choral and orchestral works of Gideon.

But with this generation, even genuine success as a composer could not open the door to positions as professor of composition, still reserved exclusively for males. The success of the women in this group is not to be measured in their own careers but in the careers of the women who followed them, for whom they had won their victories.

The third generation can be represented by Ellen Taaffe Zwillich, educated within the system and therefore eligible for recognition (she won the Pulitzer Prize) within the system. Her graduation in composition, from Juilliard in 1975, was the first anywhere for a female. She joins a growing cadre of women already working for the first time within the system, though trained outside it, fine composers such as Joan Tower, Thea Musgrave, Dorothy Rudd Moore, Jean Eichelberger Ivey, and Nancy Van de Vate. This generation may contain women who will breach the fastness of university professorships of composition and bring women into full citizenship as composers.

References. Jane Bowers and Judith Tick, *Women Making Music: The Western Art Tradition, 1150–1950* (Urbana, Ill., 1986); Aaron I. Cohen, *International Encyclopedia of Women Composers* and *International Discography of Women Composers* (Westport, Conn., 1982 and 1984); Jane Frasier, *Women Composers—A Discography* (Detroit, Mich., 1983); Judith Lang Zaimont, *The Musical Woman*, 2 vols. (Westport, Conn., 1984, 1987).

EDITH BORROFF

CONCERT ARTISTS. Among beginning piano students, girls outnumber boys about 25 to 1. From then on, the ratio changes radically: by the time students reach large regional piano competitions, the ratio is perhaps 6 women to 4 men; in major international competitions, about 1 woman to 15 men. New York management companies usually have only a token number of women to 20–30 men.

The larger number of girls and their much higher attrition rate compared with boys in the early years of study attest to the fact that the tradition of women's "accomplishments" lives on. Parents think that playing the piano is a "nice" thing for girls to learn how to do. The relatively few who continue study may attend a conservatory, enter competitions, win prizes, and give public concerts, but they find the career possibilities so daunting that they turn to teaching. They usually marry. If they become mothers, they discover that it is extremely difficult to combine motherhood and career as a concert artist.

Women concert artists, like women in other professions, have to try harder. In the conservatory, teachers take boys more seriously than they do girls. It is easier for young men to find patrons to support them in international competitions, to secure their first recording contract, and to find a good manager. Managers let females know that in their experience women are less dependable, less reliable, less dedicated, and much harder to sell. The same kinds of discrimination that are found in the business world operate in the music world. Women who complain are weak, fussy, aggressive, "bitchy," in the same situations in which men are assertive or "true artists." Women who have careers in music manage to grit their teeth, never cancel, never change their minds, are consistently reliable, and don't get fussy and balk at playing on bad instruments.

There is another factor unique to the arts: women more frequently than men foster the arts, are the major force in fund-raising, sell tickets, arrange benefit performances, actually attend concerts—and generally prefer a male performer. Further, the bulk of the concert repertoire was composed by men and originally played by men; the male tradition is well rooted and familiar.

The women performers who are the role models for the concert artists of the late twentieth century coped with the problem of a career usually with the help of supportive husbands or other family members. Alicia de Larrocha's husband (also a pianist) took care of the children while she was on tour. Myra Hess and Gina Bachauer had no children, but Bachauer's husband, conductor Alec Sherman, left his career to manage hers and travel with her. Erica Morini's brother was her agent. A number of women musicians today have close relatives who manage their careers; most, however, are doing it on their own.

Trying to juggle family needs and a concert career is a special problem for women with children. The most careful planning cannot take childhood diseases, which seem to come at the worst possible times, into account. Another hindrance is competition juries who still believe that since a long career is less likely for a woman, when big prizes are awarded, it is better to give them to men.

The scarcity of concert opportunities is a serious problem for the careers of both women and men. Men complain that in the competition for concert dates, women have an advantage they do not—there are only a few women concert artists, whereas male artists tend to be swamped by other men.

The great tradition of solo concert artists probably peaked in the 1920s. By the 1930s radio broadcasts and musical recordings were already affecting the market for touring artists. Hoffmann, Rachmaninoff, and Paderewski traveled with a retinue in private railway cars. Today the soloist hangs out alone in desolate airports, waiting for the weather to break to make connections to the next concert date.

A woman preparing for a career as a concert pianist needs to be ready for any opportunity to play, to be able to sight-read accurately and artistically, to be diligent about learning the chamber music repertoire, and to be ready to accompany or be part of an ensemble. Conservatories would do well to teach a course in the business aspects of music. It helps to work part-time for a recording company or concert management. Otherwise, it comes as a shock to a pianist to find herself a "product" to be sold. There are relatively few concert dates and crowds of competent men and women eager to fill them.

What keeps serious pianists going is the sheer love of playing. The satisfaction derived from the beauty of the music and the ability to share this beauty is basic. There has to be a belief in performance as a vocation or calling that cannot be refused or denied. Students should think of themselves as sharing and serving when they perform and think of music as a tool for life.

The material in this article was abstracted from concert pianist Virginia Eskin's article "Why Should a Woman Play Like a Man?" (*Keynote* 10, 9 [November 1986]: 14–17), with permission from the author and the publisher.

VIRGINIA ESKIN and HELEN TIERNEY

CONCUBINAGE is a legally and socially recognized union of a man with a woman who does not have the full status of a wife. In many monogamous societies, although a man could have only one wife, he might have one or more concubines of inferior status. Ancient Rome differed in that, although concubinage was recognized, a man could not have a wife and a concubine at the same time. Areas recognizing legal concubinage have slowly dwindled: Eastern Europe ceased recognition with the spread of orthodox Christianity, Western Europe in the sixteenth century, China in the early twentieth.

Concubines or secondary wives might be procured for various reasons. Princes and aristocrats might take secondary wives or might be offered concubines to form family alliances. If a marriage was childless, the husband might take a concubine rather than divorce and remarry. Young concubines were taken for pleasure, especially as the wife got older. Widowers, instead of remarrying, might take a concubine so as not to produce new heirs.

The concubine is usually of much lower social status than the husband. She is often a slave or a freedwoman but could be an alien whose marriage with a citizen was not legal, a freewoman in a union with a member of the nobility or from a family* too poor to pay a dowry.* The concubine and her husband might live together in all respects as a married couple, or she might live in the same household with a wife and possibly other concubines as well. In the latter case, she would be in an inferior position and would have to show proper respect to the legal wife. Her inferior position did not prevent her being subject to the same punishment as a legal wife for sexual misconduct.

There are usually few or no guarantees of permanency for the union or for the concubines' future maintenance. The fate of a slave concubine was likely to be sale to a brothel. The fate of a freewoman dismissed without maintenance, even if she had a family to grudgingly receive her, would not be enviable. In Athens a daughter given in concubinage might bring a gift, similar to a dowry, which, since the gift would have to be returned if the woman were dismissed, helped to assure the stability of the union. In medieval Spain the *barragania* was protected by a contract. If dismissed, she had the right to maintenance for life and sometimes the right to inheritance.

Children of the union were usually considered illegitimate and inherited their mother's status. They did, however, have some legal rights and might inherit in the absence of children by the wife. In Rome the father had to maintain them, and in the absence of legitimate heirs, they inherited one-sixth of his estate. In China, the children of concubines were accounted children of the principal wife and shared equally. The children of a *barragania* inherited their father's status.

Although considered very improper, some freewomen lived in concubinage with slaves. In Rome from the mid-first century A.D. a woman who did so could be reduced to the status of freedwoman or even enslaved. Her children, until the time of Hadrian (d. 138), were slaves.

In Roman law only a thin line separated marriage and concubinage, the *affectio maritalis* (the intention of being married). A dowry was a sign of intent to marry. Many people who could not marry (e.g., Roman soldiers until A.D. 197, members of the senatorial class with freedpersons) lived together permanently in all respects as man and wife. Soldiers commonly married their concubines upon retirement.

The Eastern, or Byzantine, empire ceased to recognize concubinage under Leo the Philosopher (d. 911), but it remained legal in the West. The position taken by the Council of Toledo (c. 400), that a married man who kept a concubine was subject to ecclesiastical punishment but an unmarried man who did so was not (canon 17), was restated, in full or by implication, in councils and synods through the mid-eleventh century.

By the ninth century, after the church had gained ground in its fight against multiple wives and/or concubines and repudiation of wives, it attacked quasi marriages by portraying concubines as loose women and seductresses. However, its general acceptance of concubinage for single laymen remained the same. Civil law in various areas of thirteenth-century Europe also attest to the legality of the institution.

In fact, as long as "word of mouth" marriages, vows exchanged without witnesses, were accepted, there could be no sharp distinction between marriage and concubinage. It was not until the Reformation in the sixteenth century, when, in both Protestant and Catholic areas, strict conditions for a lawful marriage were imposed and enforced, that concubinage ceased to be a legally recognized form of union in Western Europe.

CONDUCTORS. In the late nineteenth and early twentieth centuries, women, to play in professional orchestras, had to form their own orchestra, thereby allowing a few women the chance to conduct. Among the best known were founder/conductors Caroline B. Nicholas, Women's Fadette Orchestra in Boston, 1888–1920; Ethel Leginska (Ethel Liggins), Women's Symphony of Boston, 1920s–1930s; Frederique Petrides, Orchestrette Classique (later Orchestrette of New York), 1933–1945; and Antonia Brico, New York Women's Symphony Orchestra, 1934.

The heyday of all-woman orchestras was from 1925 to 1945, but after

World War II most disappeared and, with them, their women directors. The number of women conductors began to grow slowly in the 1970s. In 1971, 1.4 percent of the orchestras registered in *The Musicians Guide* were led by women. In 1981, 32 of 737 (4.3 percent) orchestras in the annual American Orchestra League Directory published by *Symphony Magazine* had women directors; in 1988, the number was 56 out of 845 (6.6 percent). But no woman headed any of the 35 major United States symphonies, and only 7 (12.5 percent) led larger ensembles (3 urban, 2 metropolitan, 2 regional orchestras). The rest directed community/college (27) or youth/training (22) orchestras. A few women who have gained national or international recognition also appear as guest conductors with major orchestras.

Although the attitude toward women conductors is more favorable than it once was, forces working against hiring women have not disappeared. The dominating, European-trained male is still part of the American image of the conductor. Boards of directors and women's committees have been charged with considering qualities such as stamina, which women are sometimes thought to lack, and male sex appeal (the "Leonard Bernstein Syndrome"), which they do lack, in choosing conductors. Attractive women, on the other hand, may not be considered seriously—the more attractive, the less seriously—by hiring agencies or by players. The assertiveness that is expected of the male conductor tends to be translated as aggressiveness in a woman (Lawson, 47–49). Whatever the initial response to the conductor, once she has proven herself, prejudice among players disappears. If, however, the woman conductor does not succeed, sex figures prominently in discussions of her failure.

Several women conductors gained national and international recognition during the 1970s. Antonia Brico (1902–1988) ties women conductors of the 1930s with those of the 1970s. In the early 1930s she was a successful guest conductor, but by 1937 the novelty of a woman's conducting men had worn off, and job offers had dried up. Then in 1975, at age 72, she began a second career as a result of the documentary *Antonia: A Portrait of a Woman*. Appearances as conductor of major orchestras included a concert at the Hollywood Bowl, where she had made her American debut in 1930.

Sarah Caldwell (b. 1924) has reinvigorated American opera through her Opera Company of Boston, founded in 1957 as the Boston Opera Group. In the early years of struggle her refusal to be other than herself, despite abundant advice to the contrary, helped build her legend. In 1970 she became the first woman to conduct the Metropolitan Opera Orchestra, and she has also directed the Central Opera Company of Peking.

Eve Queler (b. 1930) founded the Opera Orchestra in 1967 and developed it into a highly acclaimed orchestra that presents seldom performed operas in concert, giving singers and instrumentalists experience with operatic repertoire and expanding audience knowledge beyond the standard U.S. operatic fare.

Judith Somogi (b. 1937), like Eve Queler, has remained primarily interested in opera. In 1982 she was named first conductor of the Frankfurt Opera. Other successful operatic conductors include Paulette Haupt-Nolan, the first woman to receive an Affiliate Artists Exxon/Arts Endowment residency, and Doris Lang Kosloff, named musical director of the Connecticut Opera in 1983.

Margaret Hillis (b. 1921), one of the world's premier choral conductors, in the latter 1950s organized the Chicago Symphony Chorus, the best of its kind in the world, then added orchestral conducting to her repertoire (Kenosha [Wisconsin] Symphony Orchestra [1961–1968] and Elgin [Illinois] Symphony [1971–1985]). In 1977 she directed the Chicago Symphony Choir, the Elgin Symphony Orchestra, the Civic Orchestra of Chicago, and the Department of Choral Activities at Northwestern University. That same year she won a Grammy for her recording of Verdi's Requiem and rave reviews when she stepped in to conduct the Chicago Symphony's New York performance of Mahler's Symphony no. 8 on a few hours' notice.

In the 1960s both Sylvia Caduff (b. 1933) of Switzerland and Delia Atlas of Israel chose international competitions as the route to recognition and employment. Sylvia Caduff was a winner in the Guido Cantelli Competition in Novarro, Italy and in 1966 won first prize in the Dimitri Mitropolis International Conducting Competition in New York—the rules had to be changed to allow a woman to enter. In 1977 she was appointed Generalmusikdirektor of the orchestra of Soligen, Germany. Delia Atlas' prizes in the Guido Cantelli Competition (1963), the Royal Liverpool Philharmonic Competition (1964), the Dimitri Mitropolis Competition (1964), and the Villa-Lobos Competition (1978) opened up conducting opportunities worldwide.

The rising women conductors of the 1980s include Iona Brown, who in 1986 became one of two women to lead regional U.S. orchestras (Los Angeles Chamber Orchestra); Jo Ann Falletta (b. 1954), who in 1985 won the Leopold Stokowski Conducting Competition and became musical director and conductor of the Denver Chamber Orchestra in 1983 and musical director in 1986 of the Bay Area Women's Philharmonic Orchestra; and five women recipients of Affiliate Artists conducting residencies between 1977 (the first year of the program) and 1986.

The Affiliate Artists Exxon/Arts Endowment Program, established in 1973, funded a residency of up to three years with a cooperating orchestra. By 1986 three women had been chosen to participate in this highly competitive program: Victoria Bond, 1979–1980; Paulette Haupt-Nolan, 1978; and Catherine Comet, 1982–1984. In 1980 Affiliate Artists also established a one-to-two-year program for promising candidates with little or no experience. In its first five years, two of the conducting assistants in the program were women: Antonia Joy Wilson, 1982–1983, and Rachael Worby, 1983.

Victoria Bond (b. 1949), the first woman to earn a doctorate in conducting from the Juilliard School of Music, is a composer as well as a conductor. In 1986 she was named music director and conductor of the Roanoke Symphony Orchestra. Catherine Comet, born in France, had her first professional experience in the orchestra pit of the Paris Opera's National Ballet Company. In 1986 she became the first woman conductor of a regional U.S. symphony orchestra, the Grand Rapids Symphony. After her Artists Affiliate experience Antonia Joy Wilson returned to formal training for a year, then became musical director of the Johnson City (Tennessee) Symphony. Rachael Worby in 1986 was named music director/conductor of the Wheeling (West Virginia) Symphony Orchestra.

References. Kay D. Lawson, "A Woman's Place Is at the Podium," *Music Educators Journal* 70, 9 (May 1984): 49; Jane Weiner LePage, *Women Composers, Conductors, and Musicians of the Twentieth Century*, 3 vols. (Metuchen, N.J., 1980–1988); Judith Lang Zaimont et al. (eds.), *The Musical Woman*, 2 vols. (Westport, Conn., 1984–1987).

CONFUCIANISM is the dominant religious-political tradition of China, which accorded women a central, though subordinate, role in its teachings. Confucianism saw all human beings, male and female, as operating in a highly contextual world of hierarchical relationships with behavior dictated according to the demands of ritual propriety. The human order was to model itself on the cosmic order, which ran smoothly and harmoniously as long as each of the parts occupied its proper position. Gender roles were to follow the primal division of the cosmic order into heaven, the superior yang (masculine) principle, and earth, the inferior yin (feminine) principle, with men assuming the dominant role of heaven, and women the subservient role of earth. (See YIN AND YANG.)

These roles were especially important in the context of the family, which Confucians reverenced as the nexus of the life-generating activity of humans and as the custodian of the chain of life. Since Confucianism was without a priesthood or special houses of worship, men and women in their roles as spouses and parents in the family took on a sacerdotal character. Marriage was the vocation of all, and its purpose for both man and woman was to serve the interests of the family at large: to honor the family's ancestors with periodic sacrifices, to obey and care for the husband's living parents, and to produce new life to keep the family's bloodline going. Because none of these primary functions of the family could be done without her, a woman commanded a certain degree of honor and respect. At the same time, a woman's effort and dedication were geared toward honoring and perpetuating the male, not the female, bloodline, and she was seen as subject to some form of male authority at every stage of her life. As a daughter, she was subject to her father; as a wife, to her husband; and as a widow, to her son.

All childhood education for girls was for the purpose of preparing them for their future roles as wives, mothers, and daughters-in-law. They were to apply themselves to four areas: womanly virtue, womanly speech, womanly comportment, and womanly work. At age 15, they received the hairpin in a coming-of-age ceremony, and by the age of 20, they should be married. Since Chinese marriage was patrilocal, the wedding ceremony gave attention first to the severing of a woman's ties with her natal family and then to her ceremonial introduction to the husband's parents and to their ancestors. She now had an ancestral altar on which a tablet for her would stand. (Daughters cannot have a tablet on their natal families' altar.) Once married, the couple was advised to treat each other with the formality and reserve they would extend to a guest and to observe a degree of sexual segregation in the household, except when sleeping. That is, the man was to occupy the outer quarters of the household, while the woman was to remain in the inner quarters.

Once formed, the marriage bond should not be broken. However, if the wife was guilty of certain behavior, the husband could divorce her. The seven traditional grounds for divorce were disobedience to his parents, failure to bear a male heir, promiscuity, jealousy, contracting an incurable disease, talking too much, and stealing. The wife could never initiate a divorce against her husband and even upon his death was expected not to remarry. Her marriage bond was not just with him but with his family as well, and her obligations to them remained (to maintain the ancestral sacrifices, to serve his parents if they were still alive, and to raise her children). Women were advised that just as a loyal minister does not serve two rulers, a chaste woman does not have two husbands.

When Confucianism became the state ideology during the Han dynasty (206 B.C.E.–220 C.E.), specific literature for and about women began to appear. The two most important texts were Liu Hsiang's collection of women's biographies, the *Lienu Zhuan* (see *LIENU ZHUAN*), and Ban Zhao's *Instructions for Women*. Ban Zhao was a noted female court scholar who wrote this primer for her unmarried daughters to prepare them for their duties in marriage. The text, though short in length, exerted a tremendous influence over the lives of Chinese women. It began a tradition of instructional literature written by women for women, and Ban Zhao became the archetypal female instructress, so much so that later female authors often adopted her voice in their works rather than using their own. Some of the important later texts by women include the *Classic of Filial Piety for Women* by Ms. Cheng of the eighth century, the *Analects for Women* by Sung Ruozhao of the ninth century, *Instructions for the Inner Quarters* by Empress Xu of the fifteenth century, and *A Handy Record of Rules for Women* by Ms. Liu of the seventeenth century. While all of these were addressed to an audience of elite women, many of their teachings filtered down to a broader audience in the form of popular primers set to rhyme, such as the *Three-Character Classic for Girls*.

With the fall of the Han dynasty, Confucianism was eclipsed by Buddhism and Taoism as the dominant religious traditions for the next 800 years. (See BUDDHISM and TAOISM.) Only with the advent of the Song dynasty (960–1279) did Confucianism reassert itself, in the form of Neo-Confucianism. While Neo-Confucianism saw itself as having triumphed over Buddhism, it was not without Buddhist influence in its teachings, especially in its greater wariness about the body and human feelings and in its concern for control over these. Consequently, it developed new and stricter programs for self-discipline. The program it articulated for women emphasized to a new degree the importance of chastity, and special attention was given to the chastity of women whose husbands had died. Women who refused to remarry and, when pressured to do so by their parents, either committed suicide or disfigured themselves by physical mutilation (such as cutting off their ears or nose) were singled out for praise. Those women who did remarry were criticized. When one Neo-Confucian leader was asked whether, in the extenuating circumstance that a woman was poor, all alone, and about to starve to death, she might remarry, he replied that to starve to death was not a big issue, while losing one's integrity was (and for the woman to remarry would be to lose her integrity). Whereas in earlier Confucianism women had been honored for a wide variety of reasons, in later times they were honored almost exclusively for the maintenance of their chastity (and such related heroics as a widow's unstinting care for her mother-in-law). Later emperors promoted the chastity cult by publicly honoring chaste widows with special arches built in their honor.

Late Imperial China found Neo-Confucian males polarized over the issue of women. Conservatives saw their mission as preserving the purity of women by keeping them unschooled and secluded from worldly contact. Liberal thinkers, on the other hand, expressing concern for the plight of women, advocated women's education and denounced such practices as foot-binding, widow suicides, and female seclusion. (See FOOT-BINDING.) Changes of any significance and scope, however, were not realized until the various reform and revolutionary movements of the twentieth century that included women among their participants. Confucianism today is viewed with ambivalence: at its best, as having contributed to the ennobling of women, and at its worst, to their subjugation and oppression.

References: B. Birge, "Chu Hsi and Women's Education," in W. T. deBary and J. Chaffee (eds.), *Neo-Confucian Education: The Formative Stage* (Berkeley, Calif., 1989); Patricia B. Ebrey, *The Inner Quarters: Marriage and the Lives of Chinese Women in the Sung Period* (Berkeley, Calif., 1993); M. Elvin, "Female Virtue and the State in China," *Past and Present* 104 (1984): 111–152; Richard W. Guisso and Stanley Johannesen (eds.), *Women in China* (New York, 1981); T. Kelleher,

"Confucianism," in A. Sharma (ed.), *Women in World Religions* (Albany, N.Y., 1986): 135–159; D. Ko, "Pursuing Talent and Virtue: Education and Women's Culture in 17th- and 18th-Century China," *Late Imperial China* 13 (1992): 9–39; Margery Wolf and Roxane Witke (eds.), *Women in Chinese Society* (Stanford, Calif., 1975).

M. THERESA KELLEHER

CONSCIOUSNESS-RAISING is the process of transforming the personal problems of women into a shared awareness of their meaning as social problems and political concerns. Through consciousness-raising (CR), women come to understand the intricate relationships between the individual aspects of their experience and public, systemic conditions; that is, the personal become political. For feminists, changed consciousness is a fundamental component of social change.

Consciousness-raising is the cornerstone of feminist theory* and practice. It is a core component of feminist activities and organizations, including the large national women's organizations; women's caucuses and political action groups; women's studies courses and scholarship; feminist service agencies; feminist music, theater, art, and literature; and women's CR and support groups.

Through consciousness-raising, feminist theorists and activists redefine and reinterpret the meaning of women's social experience. In women's organizations, understanding the nature of female oppression is essential for assessing needs, establishing goals, providing alternative programs and services, and working toward social change. Also, significant personal change occurs for women through understanding themselves as part of a larger social group and through viewing personal problems within the context of common social roles and social conditions.

The primary mechanism for consciousness-raising in the contemporary feminist movement has been the CR group. In their early stages, mid-1960s to the early 1970s, CR groups consisted primarily of radical feminists, and group discussions focused on political analyses and the development of feminist ideology. Also, these early CR group members educated themselves and others through projects such as writing pamphlets and newsletters, serving as a "speakers' bureau," planning demonstrations and protests, and organizing other women's CR groups. Proliferation of CR groups during this period and public awareness of feminist thought can be largely attributed to their efforts. These early groups served as mechanisms for educating and radicalizing women and for creating a broad-based social concern with women's issues.

By the mid-1970s, the political education functions of activists in these groups became less salient. The presence of gender bias and discrimination* and the principles and goals of the feminist movement were increasingly discussed in society at large. At the same time, the appeal of the personal growth and support aspects of CR groups became prevalent. CR became widely identified as a way for women to examine issues in their own lives in terms of their social conditioning. By altering women's perception of themselves and of society at large, CR groups were seen as effective mechanisms for personal and social change.

In CR groups, institutional structures and social norms, as well as individual attitudes and behaviors, provide the framework for analysis. Through sharing, CR groups help women understand and deal with personal problems as they are related to their gender-role conditioning and to their experiences with bias, discrimination, and victimization. Through this process, personal attitudes, behaviors, roles, and relationships, as well as social policies and practices, become targets for change. Although literature may be used to provide additional information, the personal experiences of group members are the central ingredients for understanding problems and for devising solutions, both private and public.

CR groups epitomize feminist theory and method. Based on equal sharing of resources, power, and responsibility, they are generally leaderless and stress principles of sisterhood and the authority of personal experience. There is an assumption of shared experience and shared difficulties. CR groups emphasize being supportive and nonjudgmental toward members' behaviors and attitudes but critically examine social values and political beliefs.

Studies indicate that CR group outcomes include (1) increased self-awareness, self-respect, and self-esteem; (2) increased awareness of the effects of traditional gender roles* and sexism*; (3) increased awareness of a commonality with other women; (4) improved relationships and a sense of solidarity with other women; (5) development of a sociopolitical analysis of female experience and the nature of female oppression and the development of a feminist identity; (6) changes in interpersonal relationships and roles; and (7) participation in a range of activities designed to change women's political and social circumstances. The most prevalent findings concern changed perceptions, attitudes, and beliefs in a pro-feminist direction.

By the late 1970s, with women having multiple sources for heightening their awareness of female subordination, many CR groups emerged as a result of women's feminist identity. These groups (often referred to as women's support groups) provide women with support, validation, and assistance as they work to incorporate feminism into their everyday lives. In these groups, women continue to explore the social structural nature of their problems and share strategies for dealing with them; they develop feminist alternatives to apply in their work and in their personal relationships. For women who are not actively involved in the movement, CR groups continue primarily as a means for personal growth through shared understandings of problems common to women.

Consciousness-raising is an integral part of the services offered by feminist agencies, including women's counseling centers, rape crisis centers, and shelters for battered women.* Also, feminist workers in traditional agencies design programs and services to help female offenders,* women who abuse alcohol and drugs, women with eating disorders, incest victims, and so on and include consciousness-raising as an important part of their overall efforts. The goal is to help women understand how traditional gender roles and gender inequality have contributed to their distress and victimization.

Also, consciousness-raising is a central component of feminist approaches to therapy. Feminist therapists believe that it is growth-producing for women to evaluate the ways in which cultural ideology and structural realities shape female experience. Feminist therapists often use all-women groups, which facilitate the consciousness-raising aspects of their work. These groups de-emphasize the authority of the therapist and help the group members share and understand the experiences that have influenced them collectively as women.

For many women, redefinition of gender roles* and new attitudes toward women have translated into political activism. For all women, personal change from consciousness-raising has political significance. Female oppression is supported by women's internalizing cultural views that devalue women and legitimate women's powerlessness and victimization. By helping women understand the multifaceted ways in which their personal difficulties are inextricably linked to their subordinate social status, consciousness-raising significantly alters how women view themselves, women as a group, and their social circumstances. By altering these internalized views, consciousness-raising challenges one of the primary ways in which oppression is maintained.

Similarly, many of the changes that occur in women's values, attitudes, and behaviors are in opposition to the dominant cultural ideology. When the nature of personal change conflicts with the dominant values of society, personal change becomes political and holds broad social implications. The transformation of the meaning of personal experience through consciousness-raising creates feminist supporters and activists and thereby remains the core of feminist approaches to social change.

References. M. L. Carden, *The New Feminist Movement* (New York, 1974); Hester Eisenstein, *Contemporary Feminist Thought*, "Consciousness Raising: The Personal as Political" (Boston, 1983), 35–41; M. M. Ferree and B. B. Hess, *Controversy and Coalition: The New Feminist Movement* (Boston, 1985); D. Kravetz, "The Benefits of Consciousness-Raising Groups for Women," in Claire Brody (ed.), *Women's Therapy Groups: Paradigms of Feminist Treatment* (New York, 1987).

DIANE KRAVETZ

CONTRACEPTION is at least as old as civilization. Evidence of techniques is found in Egyptian papyri (1900–1100 B.C.) and Greek and Roman scientific literature (sixth century B.C. to second century A.D.). Other practices, of varying degrees of worth and harm, were passed down orally. How widely contraception was actually practiced is unknown, but its use is inferred; for instance, in Roman concern over falling birthrates in the first century A.D.

Christian doctrine condemning contraception was shaped by the battle against rival Gnostic, Manichaean, and, later, Cathar belief in the evil of material creation. For Christians who posited procreation as the purpose of marriage, the use of any material or technique to contravene that purpose was considered sinful. The basic view in the Eastern Church that such interference was homicide passed to the West through St. Jerome. St. Augustine's conclusion that contraception sins against marriage because it destroys the good of marriage (offspring) was determinant, but both views became part of Christian teaching and entered medieval canon law collections.

Between 1450 and 1750 theological writings broadened the purpose of marital intercourse and reflected a rising interest in limiting fertility. There were a range of opinions on the lawfulness of *amplexus reservatus (coitus reservatus)* and some indication of its use. There was also an attitude that penitents acting in good faith should not be disturbed by questioning.

The eighteenth century saw a phenomenal increase in Europe's population. In England problems caused by rapid industrialization and urbanization led to concerns about the relations between population and poverty, most notably by Thomas Malthus (*Essays on the Principles of Population* [1798]). Since Malthus opposed any "preventive check," those favoring contraceptive measures were called Neo-Malthusians.

Contraception was first publicly advocated in the 1820s by radical reformers and freethinkers, but their advocacy met with little success. It not only preceded the vulcanization of rubber (1843), which was necessary for cheap and effective barriers but came when working-class children still contributed to family income.

In the 1870s interest in fertility control increased when a long period of prosperity gave way to depression, and legislation limiting child labor (1867) and introducing compulsory education (1870) changed working-class children from assets to liabilities. Then, in the early 1880s, a means became available that women could control, the diaphragm, developed by Dr. Mensinga in Holland. In 60 years the birthrate was halved.

Social Purity advocates opposed contraception as encouraging immorality. The publicity from their unsuccessful attempt in 1877 to prosecute the publishers of contraceptive literature resulted not only in increased sales of such literature but in the founding of the Malthusian League (1877–1927) by Dr. George Drysdale to promote acceptance of contraception as a weapon against poverty. With a tiny membership and little income, the league published *The Malthusian* (1879–1921), gave lectures, canvassed in poor districts, and in 1913 began to hold mass meetings. As audiences asked for practical information, the league issued a leaflet with specific information on preventive methods.

Success came in the 1920s and 1930s. In 1921 Dr. Marie Stopes founded the Mothers' Clinic, the first birth control clinic in Britain. A second, the Malthusian League's Walworth Clinic, followed in eight months; by 1932 there were 16. Success led to the league's demise in 1927 and in 1930 the founding of the National Birth Control Council (later, the Family Planning Association), a coordinating body.

Medical opinion slowly changed from opposition to acceptance, and the Ministry of Health, pressured by the Women's Conference of the Labour party, moved to approve and support family limitation. In 1930 government clinics were allowed to, and by 1934 they had the duty to, give contraceptive information to married women if pregnancy would be detrimental to their health. In 1949 the Royal Commission on Population approved giving birth control information to any married woman, and since 1967 the National Health Service has provided free contraceptive advice and materials.

In Western Europe contraceptive methods were widely used by the end of the nineteenth century. In 1882 George Drysdale helped found a Neo-Malthusian society in Holland, and Dr. Alleta Jacobs established the world's first birth control clinic in Amsterdam. In France, where family limitation was widespread by the early nineteenth century, Paul Rolin organized the first international conference of Neo-Malthusians, which was held clandestinely in 1900. Birthrates began to fall in Belgium from c. 1880; in Germany, Austria, and Italy from c. 1890. Before World War I Neo-Malthusian societies existed in France, Germany, Bohemia, Belgium, Switzerland, Spain, Sweden, Italy, the British dominions, and Cuba and Brazil.

By the 1930s birth control societies had been established in Eastern Europe, and legal restraints on contraception had been overcome in most Western European countries except Catholic Belgium, Spain, and Ireland. After the papacy of Leo XIII (1878–1903) the Catholic Church assumed a more active stance, culminating in Pius XI's *Casti connubii* (1930), which again condemned contraception but allowed the rhythm method. Also, concern about low birthrates led France, after its huge population losses in World War I, to stiffen the law, but to no avail, and the fascist regimes in Germany and Italy during the depression similarly instituted repressive legislation.

In the United States, although the birthrate fell consistently throughout the nineteenth century, the fight for legalized contraception was longer and harder than in England. The earliest advocates of fertility control were often utopian communitarians, either socialist, such as Frances Wright, or religious, such as John Humphrey Noyes. Their emphasis was not on curing poverty but on improving the lives of women.

Contraception was seldom mentioned. Noyes advocated, and his Oneida* Community successfully practiced, *coitus reservatus*, as did others (e.g., Alice Stockham, *Karezza* [1896]). Champions of "Voluntary Motherhood" advocated family limitation by restraint and generally opposed contraception as encouraging promiscuity.

Social Purists, who were concerned with prostitution, pushed for strict obscenity laws that banned information about, and sale of, contraceptive material. Anthony Comstock (1844–1915), secretary of the New York Society for the Prevention of Vice, was instrumental in passage of the 1873 federal statute (Comstock Law) that banned sales of contraceptive materials in federal areas and the importation or mailing of written material, drugs, medicines, or articles for the prevention of conception. Comstock, as special inspector for the Postal Service, for 42 years dedicated himself to enforcing the law, and most of the medical community, whether out of fear or conviction, supported him.

However, in the first decades of the twentieth century, radical groups and individuals (e.g., Helen Gurley Flynn, Dr. Antoinette Konikow, and Emma Goldman), for whom fertility control was one aspect of sexual freedom and working-class reform, were openly advocating contraception. Anarchist-feminist Emma Goldman (1869–1940) spoke on fertility control from c. 1910. After Margaret Sanger (1883–1966) was indicted for violation of the Comstock Law (1914) and fled to England, Goldman toured the country (early 1915 to early 1917) discussing methods and distributing pamphlets. She and others were arrested and jailed for doing so, but by the time she turned to other matters that were to her more pressing, she had helped to found a movement.

For liberal advocates, birth control was a civil liberties issue. Mary Ware Dennett's (1872–1947) National Birth Control League (1915–1919), the first birth control society in the United States, and the Voluntary Parenthood League (1919–1927) worked to legalize the dissemination of birth control information and materials.

Sanger, who became the leading champion of birth control, a term she first used in 1914, was attracted to radical activism in pre–World War I Greenwich Village, New York City. Her interest in birth control was strengthened on a visit to Paris in 1913, but it was not until after her stay in England to avoid (or put off) her trial for obscenity, and her association there with Havelock Ellis, that she restricted herself to just the one cause. As a result of her associations and study in England, when she returned to the United States, she was convinced that only those with expert knowledge should instruct women in contraceptive use. She now needed acceptance by the medical community.

Back in the United States Sanger gained publicity and support for her case (the indictment was dropped in 1916) and her cause, especially at times when she was arrested or barred from speaking. In 1916 she and her sister Ethel Byrne opened the Brownsville clinic in Brooklyn, the first birth control clinic in the United States, but without an attending physician—none would join them. Their subsequent arrests and imprisonments and especially Byrne's hunger strike, forced-feeding, and near death aroused public opinion. Sanger published the first issue of *Birth Control Review* (1917–1940) while in jail.

In the 1920s Sanger became a leading influence in the United States and international movements. In 1921 she began the American Birth Control League (ABCL, 1921–1938), the first birth control organization of national scope. The ABCL won respectability by recruiting affiliates through middle- and upper-middle-class women's organizations and eschewing such overtly illegal tactics as mass meetings and the distribution of contraceptive literature in poor districts. During the late 1920s and 1930s, through ABCL's affiliates, clinics were set up across the country.

In 1923 Sanger founded the Clinical Research Bureau (CRB), but lack of physician support prevented it from becoming much more than a clinic for the ABCL. In the 1920s most doctors still opposed contraception, although increasing numbers were quietly prescribing contraceptives for their private patients. Dr. Robert Latou Dickinson, who in 1923 organized the Committee on Maternal Health, was a leading proponent of family planning. A possible merger of the efforts of Dickinson and Sanger was thwarted, in part, by Sanger's reputation as a radical but mostly by the issue of exclusive physician control of contraceptive clinics. The public outcry in 1929 when police raided the CRB, arresting the staff, seizing records, and taking the names of the patients, showed that contraception was by now generally accepted by the middle class, and police invasion of their medical privacy was not.

Through the 1930s medical resistance faded, as did the force of the Comstock Law. Woman's fertility cycle was clearly mapped in 1924, by the mid-1930s medical schools had introduced instruction in fertility control, and in 1937 the American Medical Association finally gave birth control a qualified endorsement. By 1938 the Supreme Court had exempted doctors from the Comstock Law and had undercut most of the repressive state laws and city ordinances—medical instruction and the sale of contraceptive appliances by prescription were generally permitted. Manufacture and sale of contraceptives were a substantial business.

In 1938 the ABCL and the CRB, estranged since Sanger withdrew from the ABCL in the late 1920s, merged into the Birth Control Federation of America (later, Planned Parenthood Federation of America [PPFA]), returning unity to the movement. With birth control generally accepted, the PPFA now turned to gaining government support for it in public health programs. Some states had already established birth control clinics, and several federal agencies were quietly providing some contraceptive services. In 1942 the U.S. Public Health Service secured the funding necessary to initiate programs.

Through the 1940s and 1950s voluntary agencies such as the PPFA were the major providers of contraceptive services, but strong opposition to clinics run by lay administrators, even though physicians examined and prescribed for patients, severely limited referrals from doctors in private practice and contributed to poor women's having more unwanted children than middle-class women had.

In the 1960s, the use of oral contraceptives brought about a marked drop in fertility rates. Late in the decade increased federal funding for family planning programs seemed to herald success in the PPFA's campaign for government support. However, in May 1991 federal funding of birth control clinics was endangered by the Supreme Court decision that the federal government could refuse funding to clinics that gave advice or information about abortion.

References. Linda Gordon, *Woman's Body, Woman's Right: A Social History of Birth Control in America* (New York, 1976); James Reed, *From Private Vice to Public Virtue: The Birth Control Movement and American Society since 1830* (New York, 1978).

CONTRACEPTIVES are methods, devices, chemicals, or hormones used to prevent conception or implantation of a fertilized ovum as a result of vaginal intercourse. No one method combines 100 percent effectiveness, complete safety, and reversibility. The woman (or the couple) must decide which method is best for her (them) in light of health risks, ethical considerations and sexual needs. Acquired immunodeficiency syndrome (AIDS) has introduced a new factor to be considered in the choice of contraceptive. Unless there is certainty about the health of her partner, the woman must protect herself not just from possible pregnancy but from a fatal disease as well.

Natural methods, which do not involve the use of outside agents, are the least effective. One of the oldest is coitus interruptus, or withdrawal of the penis immediately prior to ejaculation. Withdrawal has a low effectiveness, but some couples use it successfully. When no other method is available, it might be "better than nothing."

Rhythm Methods are based on the natural cycle of the woman's reproductive system.* Theoretically, if the time of ovulation can be pinpointed with any accuracy, then, by factoring in the length of time that the ovum and sperm within the woman's vaginal area remain viable, a monthly schedule of "safe" and "unsafe" periods for intercourse can be determined, and conception can be avoided. All the rhythm methods require careful record keeping and long periods of abstinence. Because each person's body rhythms are different and subject to change, none of the rhythm methods have an effectiveness approaching methods using outside agents. They are especially unreliable during cycle changes, as when women stop breast-feeding and as they approach menopause.*

The calendar rhythm method is based on the assumption that ovulation takes place at the midpoint between menstrual periods. It has been superseded by more sophisticated methods of determining time of ovulation. The thermal, or basal body temperature (BBT), method is based on a rise of temperature of from 0.4 to 0.5 degrees F that occurs at ovulation and persists until menstruation. Daily records of temperature are kept, and a "safe period" is charted. The Billings method is based on observing changes in the cervix and cervical mucus. As ovulation nears, the cervix softens, and mucus increases. The "safe periods" will be periods of dryness before and after menstruation.

The symptothermal method, combining the cervical mucus and the BBT methods, increases effectiveness beyond that obtained by either one used alone. For any success in the use of these natural methods of birth control, careful instruction by a trained counselor is essential.

Methods employing outside agents are intended to control women's reproductive cycles or to prevent conception or implantation of a fertilized ovum during periods of fertility. They include the use of barriers, intra-uterine devices, hormones, and surgical techniques. They do not require the cooperation of the other partner. Condoms and vasectomy are male methods of contraception. The other methods are used by women.

Barrier Methods require the use of material agents to block the passage of sperm or to prevent implantation of fertilized ova. Chemical barriers contain a spermicide in a foam, jelly, cream, or ointment base. Inserted about a half hour before intercourse, they form an occlusive seal, holding the sperm while the spermicide kills them. The woman must remain lying down from the time of insertion until after the coital act.

Barrier devices include the condom, used by men, and the diaphragm, vaginal sponge, and cervical cap, used by women. The condom is a thin sheath of latex or animal membrane that fits over the penis, containing the ejaculate—about a half inch needs to be left at the tip to catch the seminal fluid. It is important to make sure that the condom has no cracks or imperfections. Since use of a latex condom can help prevent the spread of sexually transmitted diseases,* it is strongly recommended as a defense against transmission of the AIDS virus.

The diaphragm is a rounded cup of latex with a flexible rim that is fitted between the pubic bone and the back of the vagina, with the rim going beyond the cervix to rest on the vaginal cul-de-sac. Since it does not completely seal the cervix, a chemical barrier must also be used: spermicidal cream or jelly is placed around the rim and some in the center of the diaphragm. Any sperm getting around the rim will be immobilized and killed by the spermicide. Proper size and rim style to fit the individual, proper placement, and an adequate amount of spermicide are essential to the effectiveness of the diaphragm. It should be left in place for eight hours after intercourse, but a longer period will increase the risk of toxic shock syndrome* and probably vaginitis.*

In 1983 the Food and Drug Administration (FDA) approved over-the-counter sale of the vaginal sponge. It is a disposable disk (about ¾ inch thick) of polyurethane that is moistened, then inserted into the vagina so that the indentation on the top of the cylinder fits over the cervical opening (os). It is held in place by the walls of the vagina and contains a spermicide that releases slowly. A loop of tape on the bottom of the cylinder allows easy removal. Although less effective than the diaphragm, it does not need to be fitted, does not leak, and can be left in place for 24 hours (it must be left in place for 6) and used for repeated intercourse. The results of long-term use are not yet known.

The cervical cap, a latex device that fits over the cervix, was approved for use by the FDA in May 1988. The cervical cap, which has been used in various areas of the world for centuries, was available in the United States earlier in the century but at the time of FDA approval had to be imported. Thimble-shaped, it comes in several sizes and fits over the cervix, forming an almost airtight seal around the OS. It can be left in place for two or three days but cannot be used during menstruation. Most clinics advise the use of small amounts of spermicide; some instructions call for none. Cervical caps must be fitted, and some women may have difficulty finding a proper fit from the sizes available.

Intrauterine Devices (IUD) have been recognized as effective contraceptives for thousands of years, although the way they work is not clear. The prevalent theory is that a foreign object in the uterus stimulates the production of prostaglandins, thereby preventing successful implantation of the fertilized ovum by increasing uterine contractions. IUD use became practicable with the development of plastics and improved insertion techniques in the twentieth century. Plastic devices of various shapes, some with copper or progesterone, were marketed. They appeared so highly effective that in the 1970s they were promoted as an alternative to the—it was thought—more dangerous hormonal method (oral contraceptives).

Pelvic infections, sometimes life-threatening (especially in the case of pregnancy), occur at twice the rate of infections with barrier devices. It is possible to perforate the uterine wall at insertion, and occasionally the device will migrate through the uterine wall after its insertion. Ectopic pregnancies* are abnormally high among IUD users. Pregnancy while the IUD is in place or removal of the IUD once pregnancy is determined runs a high risk of spontaneous abortion. Complaints about serious problems arising from the use of IUDs led the FDA to ban the Dalkon Shield. As lawsuits against its manufacturer mounted, other companies withdrew their products from the U.S. market. Although IUDs are still popular in Europe (e.g., in Sweden about a quarter of contraceptive users use IUDs), in the United

States IUDs were the choice of only 2.3 percent of those using contraceptives in 1990.

The Hormonal Method, oral contraception, or "the Pill" was used by nearly one-half of all those using some form of nonsurgical contraception in the United States in 1990. Approved by the FDA in 1960, it was first hailed as the final answer. These contraceptives contain an estrogen and progestin that together act to prevent conception by suppressing ovulation or, if ovulation does occur, impeding the fertilization and implantation of the ovum. The Pill is taken daily for three weeks, then use is discontinued for seven days.

The use of the Pill can have side effects, some minor, some likely to disappear after several cycles of use, some life-threatening. The latter include increased blood pressure, the possibility of heart attack, stroke, cancer,* and problems with the liver and gallbladder. The possible dangers led to a "Pill scare" and reduction of use in the mid-1970s. Most of the side effects are related to the estrogen. A reduction in the amount of estrogen from a high of 150 micrograms to 50 or, in low-dose pills, to 35–30 micrograms has reduced the risks. In the low-dosage pills, the amount of progestin has also been lowered. The lowered hormone levels have not decreased the effectiveness.

Groups of women at risk have also been identified: women who smoke, older women (risks rise after age 30), those who are diabetic, seriously overweight, or who have a history of heart, liver, or gallbladder problems. Prolonged use combines with other factors to increase the risk. Hence, a healthy nonsmoker under age 35 can use oral contraceptives for 10 to 15 years without accumulating additional risk. Before a woman begins use of the Pill, a careful assessment of benefits and risks in light of the individual's medical history, a thorough physical examination, especially a Pap smear,* and familiarity with the symptoms of the possible serious side effects are essential. So too are a three-month assessment and regular six-month checkups for as long as Pill use continues. For those young, healthy women for whom the Pill poses no serious problems there are additional benefits in its use: reduced risk of ovarian cancer, reduced chance of pelvic inflammatory disease, very regular periods, reduction of menstrual cramping and of blood flow, and, for some, reduction of premenstrual tension.

Minipills, containing only progestin, have been marketed in the United States since 1973 for women who should not, or do not wish to, take estrogen. The low-level progestin pills, which are taken daily, are safer than, but not quite as effective as, low-dose combined pills and cause spotting and irregular bleeding. Few women use the minipill.

A postcoital or morning-after-type contraceptive is the use of combined pills with high progestinal activity (e.g. Ovral). They must be taken as soon as possible after intercourse (no later than 72 hours) and repeated in 12 hours. These pills are marketed by other trade names and available by prescription.

Surgical Methods, or sterilization, prevent reproduction by preventing the delivery of sperm or of ova. Sterilization is an increasingly popular form of fertility control, especially for those over 30 years of age. More women are sterilized than men. The most frequent form of sterilization is tubal ligation or salpingectomy, which can be performed under local anesthesia. Through a small abdominal or vaginal incision, a laparoscopic tube is inserted, the fallopian tubes are cut, then tied or cauterized, thus breaking the passage from the ovaries to the uterus. Although there are very occasional failures in which the cut ends of the tube rejoin, the procedure should be considered irreversible.

Vasectomy, a sterilization procedure for men, is even easier and safer than tubal ligation and is also cheaper. The procedure takes about five minutes under local anesthesia. The vas is tied above the testes, shutting off the sperm portion of the seminal fluid. Theoretically, the operation is reversible but for all practical purposes should be considered irreversible because the tubes are difficult to successfully reconnect, and because the man's body may mount an immune response against his own sperm. Vasectomy and tubal ligation do not interfere with sexual pleasure or menstrual function.

CONVENTION ON THE ELIMINATION OF ALL FORMS OF DISCRIMINATION AGAINST WOMEN was the first treaty to address a broad range of issues related to the position and status of women in society. Originally drafted by the United Nations Commission on the Status of Women, it came into force on September 3, 1981. The goal of the treaty is equality between men and women through nondiscriminatory treatment. Discrimination is defined as any restriction or exclusion made on the basis of sex, and provision is made for affirmative action as a temporary measure aimed at expediting women's equality. The treaty calls for inclusion of the equality principle in national constitutions and the elimination of laws, customs, and regulations that discriminate against women. It covers a full range of subjects, including many that were the basis for earlier, more specific treaties, such as those on slave trade, traffic in women, nationality, education, and employment. It also includes provisions on new subjects, such as shared parental responsibilities, sex-role stereotyping, and the special problems of rural women. The convention provisions are monitored by the Committee on the Elimination of Discrimination against Women, composed of 23 experts, which reviews the reports that states must submit to document their implementation of the treaty. As of January 1996, the treaty had been ratified by 151 states.

NATALIE HEVENER KAUFMAN

CORRECTIONAL OFFICERS AND SUPERINTENDENTS are women who guard inmates in prisons and jails and those who are in charge of prisons and jails. Until the 1960s, women could work only in all-female institutions. Those who served as guards were called matrons, and those who were in charge were called head matrons or superintendents. As a result of the civil rights* and women's rights movements* of the 1960s, laws and court decisions have made discrimination based on sex unconstitutional. Consequently, women now work as correctional officers and superintendents in male as well as female institutions and in top leadership positions in central headquarters.

Careers for women in the correctional system (known as the prison system before the 1960s) began largely through the efforts of women involved in the reform activities of the 1820s to 1870s. These white, well-educated, middle-class women turned to community service, a socially acceptable activity, when they found few other opportunities to utilize their leadership abilities. Many focused their attention on the redemption of fallen women, the prostitutes, vagrants, and alcoholics, whose numbers had increased markedly with the growth of immigration, urbanization, and industrialization that followed the Civil War. Evoking a stereotypical view of woman as highly moral, pious, and virtuous nurturer, they argued that women were better able than men to redeem fallen women and children and that this process should be undertaken in all-female institutions. The first such institution, the Indiana Reformatory for Women and Girls, opened in 1873, creating nontraditional career opportunities for women in what had been an almost exclusively male system. (See PRISON REFORM MOVEMENT, 1870–1930 [U.S.].) The reformers, by arguing that women were innately different from men, had succeeded in creating a matriarchal enclave within the correctional system in which women neither worked with, nor competed with, their male counterparts.

The relatively small all-women's correctional system, which provided the only employment opportunities for women, persisted for almost 100 years. Women received lower salaries than men for similar positions, had fewer opportunities for promotions, and found themselves virtually excluded from major positions of authority in the correctional system. With the 1964 passage of the Civil Rights Act, Title VII,* which outlawed discrimination based on race or sex, women finally had the legal basis upon which to demand equal employment opportunities in all areas of corrections. Even though women had the legal right to equality of opportunity, many of them continued to perpetuate the stereotypical image of women by arguing that women, being more humane, sensitive, and caring, were better able than men to create an atmosphere conducive to the rehabilitation of male as well as female criminals.

In their attempts to achieve equality of opportunity, women met intense opposition from male correctional officers and administrators and male inmates. Male correctional personnel argued that female correctional officers posed security risks in male prisons because of their physical weakness and vulnerability to rape. Male inmates argued that the presence of female correctional officers violated their right to privacy. Both groups of men filed lawsuits to prevent women from working as officers and administrators in male facilities. Both groups failed. In only one case, in 1977, did a court decide that women could be barred from employment in certain male correctional facilities for security reasons. In that case, *Dothard v. Rawlinson*, the U.S. Supreme Court ruled that the bona fide occupational qualification* exception in Title VII could be applied, but that decision failed to establish a precedent. In cases dealing with inmates' right to privacy, courts ruled that male inmates have no constitutional right to privacy when balanced against the objective good of providing equal job opportunities for women.

Most of the employment gains made by women came after 1972 when the authority of the Equal Employment Opportunity Commission* was expanded to cover personnel practices in all branches of government. Departments of corrections were obliged to establish integrated staffs and develop gender-neutral personnel policies and practices. At the same time, a new generation of women in corrections refused to be stereotyped but, rather, viewed themselves as professionals capable of performing all tasks as officers and administrators in male as well as female institutions. By the mid-1990s the federal system and almost all the states had women officers in male institutions, approximately 80 percent of all female correctional officers worked in male institutions, several women had become superintendents of male facilities, and a few had been assigned to central administrative offices in positions of authority and as commissioners.

Black women benefited not just from laws mandating equal opportunity for women but also from the U.S. Supreme Court decision of 1954 in *Brown v. Board of Education*, which declared that segregation based on race is unconstitutional. When racial segregation in prisons and jails ended, black women were hired and promoted on the same basis as were white women. By the mid-1990s, black women constituted more than a third of all female correctional officers.

Despite antidiscrimination policies and practices the correctional system continues to be a male-dominated area of employment. Women constituted approximately 20 percent of all officers in the mid-1990s. Consequently, women who seek equal opportunities in employment and advancement in the system compete with men and often have to deal with hostility and sexual harassment from some of their male colleagues. Nevertheless, women in corrections have successfully dealt with these problems. They have proven that, as professionals, they can handle any job from correctional officer to superintendent in male and female institutions, to administrators and commissioners in central headquarters.

References. Clarice Feinman, *Women in the Criminal Justice System*, 3d ed. (New York, 1994); Joann B. Norton (ed.), *Change, Challenge and Choices: Women's Role in Modern Corrections* (Laurel, Md., 1991).

CLARICE FEINMAN

COURTLY LOVE is a concept invented in 1883, one year after the contraceptive diaphragm, in an attempt to systematize the male–female relationships portrayed in twelfth-century vernacular romances and some other medieval literature. During the late nineteenth and early twentieth centuries, many scholars believed that between 1100 and 1500 there existed a Pan-European code of *amour courtois*, by which a knight declared abject humility and servitude to his chosen lady. Supposedly, he was to tremble and turn pale in her presence, sigh, have trouble eating and sleeping, compose songs offering to die for her, and keep his passion secret from all—particularly from the lady's husband, for courtly love and marriage were mutually exclusive.

In 1883, Gaston Paris (459–534) articulated this concept while reporting on a twelfth-century romance of King Arthur and his Knights of the Round Table, *Lancelot* by Chrétien de Troyes. Paris found supporting evidence for the concept in two places: first, a Latin prose treatise from the same era and region as Chrétien's Old French poem *De amore* (About Love) by Andreas Capellanus; second, some songs in a different vernacular from the south of France a century before Chrétien.

Paris's formulation inspired other scholars to seek courtly love elsewhere in medieval literature. By 1936 C. S. Lewis, in *Allegory of Love*, declared the abrupt emergence in about 1100 of an entirely new human emotion, romantic love. Ever more fascinated, scholars devoted their careers to study of unpublished manuscripts in dusty libraries. Study led to publication of variorum editions, soon followed by abridgments and translations suitable for classroom use. Thus, new generations of medievalists could read far more primary material than had ever been accessible to their teachers and grand-teachers. They could see that courtly love describes only one among the rich variety of male–female relationships portrayed in literature and furthermore that male–female relationships are only one among many social, political, psychological, and artistic concerns of medieval authors.

For example, anyone who now reads a paperback translation of Chrétien's *Lancelot* can see that Gaston Paris was focusing on just one particular relationship. Throughout the poem Lancelot dotes on Queen Guinivere, the lawful wife of his lawful overlord. In private, she sometimes encourages Lancelot and sometimes scorns him; in public, at her commands, he humiliates himself in various ways such as losing jousts.

By treating Lancelot's obsequious attitude as the key to the poem, however, Paris was neglecting much of its action. As it opens, for example, Gawain and Lancelot set out to rescue the queen from abductors. They spend the first night at a castle owned and operated by a fair maiden. At her mocking challenge, Lancelot sleeps successfully in a forbidden bed, despite a flaming lance hurled at him at midnight. Lancelot arrives the second night at the castle of another fair maiden, who extends hospitality only if he will promise to have sex with her. And so on, day by day and night by night: fictional men confront a series of unpredictable, but absolute, rules, prohibitions, and challenges in their behavior toward women.

Since about 1960 literary scholars have increasingly pointed out that although terms meaning "love" and "courtesy" do sometimes occur together in medieval texts, little evidence exists for the codification into *amour courtois* as posited by Paris in 1883. In addition, historians, including Georges Duby, now provide a social context for fictional knightly adventures like Lancelot's. Estates in twelfth-century France were passed entire from eldest son to eldest son. French younger brothers could acquire land only by searching out a bride with no brothers, a girl who would inherit her father's land. These knights without land or wives roamed France in high-spirited, sometimes destructive gangs referred to as *juventi*, (youth).

Old French romances would have appealed to audiences of *juventi*. The verse narratives feature unmarried, landless knights triumphing over arbitrary rules concerning women—though never quite triumphing totally. Lancelot may survive one heiress' spear bed and scorn another's advances, but Guinivere scorns him in turn. His affair with a married woman fails, that is, no matter how hard he tries to please her.

Recent studies likewise provide context for the other evidence of courtly love posited by Gaston Paris: songs in the vernacular of southern France and Andreas' Latin prose treatise. Songs, treatise, and romances all have links to one wealthy family that decided to use expensive parchment to write down secular literature.

Themes and images resembling courtly love occur in tenth-century Arabic literature. They could have passed through Moorish Spain to the south of France with Guillaume IX, duke of Aquitaine (1071–1127), who used writing materials for songs by himself and other composers (i.e., troubadours). A few songs feature a male narrator who declares himself willing to die for love; other songs treat other subjects.

The custom of writing down secular songs may have come north with Guillaume's granddaughter, Eleanor of Aquitaine. She married the king of France; after a divorce, she married the king of England. While queen of England, Eleanor would visit her French daughter, Marie, who had married the count of Champagne. It is to Marie of Champagne that Chrétien de Troyes dedicates *Lancelot*.

Marie appears also in the treatise on love by Andreas, who claims to be her court chaplain. Reworking Ovid's *Art of Love*, written 12 centuries earlier, Andreas replaces Ovid's practical seduction techniques with a series of debates in which men attempt to argue women into sexual intercourse by declaring themselves pale, trembling, sleepless, near death, and so on. Scholars now question whether courtly love was taken seriously even as a theme in fiction in the twelfth century, since Andreas' treatise has lately been proven riddled with obscene Latin puns.

By the fifteenth century social conditions had altered, but the literature on paper remained, paper having replaced expensive parchment so that more and more secular literature could survive. Readers looked back to a golden age of chivalry, as portrayed in books. In one of the clearest cases on record of life imitating art, knights in the real world began imitating those in the stories.

Historical knights' activities mostly involved politics, war, sports such as jousting, and any behavior that might substantiate a property claim by demonstrating that one's ancestors behaved the same way on the same land. It may well be, however, that in the fourteenth and fifteenth centuries some men imitated fictional knights' behavior toward fictional ladies, even including Lancelot's servile idealization of Arthur's wife. Several works by Geoffrey Chaucer, such as the "Knight's Tale" and *Troilus and Criseyde*, show complications that arise when human men and women try to behave like "courtly lovers."

In the twentieth century, it is still quite possible to find songs and other literature in which a male narrator offers to die for his love. It is, indeed, possible to meet real, live men who, supposing that women want to be worshiped, humbly present themselves as inferior and unworthy of love. Apparently some twentieth-century women even respond positively to an attitude of fawning obsequiousness. Perhaps some medieval women did the same.

References. Richard Barber, *The Knight and Chivalry* (1970; rep. New York, 1982); Betsy Bowden, "Introduction to the Second Edition," *The Comedy of Eros; Medieval French Guides to the Art of Love*, trans. Norman R. Shapiro (Urbana, Ill., 1997); Joan M. Ferrante and George D. Economou (eds.), *In Pursuit of Perfection: Courtly Love in Medieval Literature* (Port Washington, N.Y., 1975); David Hult, "Gaston Paris and the Invention of 'Courtly Love,' " in R. Howard Bloch and Stephen G. Nichols (eds.), *Medievalism and the Modernist Temperament* (Baltimore, 1996); Gaston Paris, "Étude sur les romans de la Table Ronde. Lancelot du Lac. II," *Romania* 12 (1883); Mary Francis Wack, *Lovesickness in the Middle Ages: The Viaticum and Its Commentaries* (Philadelphia, 1990).

BETSY BOWDEN

COUVADE, from the French *couver*, "to sit on," "to hatch," is a term that encompasses a wide variety of customs, including activities and restrictions upon activities and diet, by which fathers in a given society ritually take the part of the mother or join with her in childbirth* and the period of recuperation after childbirth.

Such customs have been noted from ancient times. The geographer Strabo in the first century B.C. and travelers in the nineteenth century A.D. wrote of the customs of the Basques in Spain; Marco Polo remarked on the customs of Chinese Turkestan; other medieval and modern travelers amazed and amused readers with reports of men groaning in pain while their wives were in labor. Modern anthropologists have given more staid accounts of practices that stem from what seems a virtually universal concept.

The father's participation in the birth ritual and the duration and severity of the ritual vary widely. The father may perform acts that imitate those of the mother at the various stages of labor, delivery, and recuperation; may be prohibited foods or activities that, if eaten or engaged in by the mother, might harm the child; or may undergo prescribed activities thought to be of benefit to the mother or child. In some cases the father's ritual role may be more important than the mother's. Or both parents may be restricted from work and certain foods for a period, with the mother being more restricted for a longer period.

Couvade emphasizes the importance of the male in the creation and birth of the child but apparently may also assist the wife in having a safe delivery. By refraining from such actions as smoking, scratching, and eating the flesh of animals, the father may be protecting the child from the harm that such actions on the part of the birth-giver might cause. By imitating the actions of the wife in delivery, the father may attract to himself the evil spirits that interfere with delivery, thus keeping them from the wife and child.

COVERTURE is the English law term for the condition of women during marriage.* "[T]he very being or legal existence of the woman is suspended during the marriage, or at least is incorporated and consolidated into that of her husband, under whose wing, protection and cover, she performs everything" (Blackstone's *Commentaries*, 18th century). In England and the common-law states of the United States, this concept of the married couple as a single person at law placed such constraints on the wife as inability to contract, sue, or be sued in her own right and inability to control her own property. It also meant that husband and wife could not contract with, or testify for or against, each other. The disabilities coverture places upon the married woman were fought by early English and American feminists and are still being fought by their late twentieth-century descendants.

CRIMINAL JUSTICE possesses a unique combination of morality and power. Because work within this system involves the coercive enforcement of moral values and behavior, even occupants of entry-level positions in criminal justice exert enormous social power, so it is not surprising that it has been a strongly male enterprise since its inception.

Nevertheless, women have been increasingly employed in the criminal justice professions. Today 9.5 percent of sworn police officers, 21 percent of practicing attorneys, 6–8 percent of state appellate and trial judges, and 9 percent of federal appellate and trial judges are women. In corrections, women comprise 11.3 percent of correctional officers within the Federal

Bureau of Prisons and 17.4 percent of correctional officers in state-level adult facilities.

As with many other professions, women are more likely to work at lower levels, for less pay, and with less authority than men. Only 3 percent of police supervisors are women. The first woman attorney general was appointed only in 1992. Just 8 percent of partners in law firms are women, and their median income is 40 percent lower than that of males. Currently, the two women Supreme Court justices represent a substantial increase, but these appointments have occurred only very recently and still constitute far less than the norm of 50 percent. In corrections, 14 percent of supervisors in adult facilities are women; 13.25 percent of wardens are women; 18.6 percent of juvenile state institutions have female wardens.

Barriers to women's entry include the familiar problems of combining home and marketplace responsibilities in a marketplace shaped to male needs, lack of mentors and role models, and active discrimination, including sexual harassment. Additionally, criminal justice work, especially police work, has been seen as an avenue to establish masculinity, in effect, to "do gender." Thus, not only is the work socially powerful, but it affirms masculine identity. Its male incumbents may be expected to resist strenuously any incursions on territory that not only provides a "male" wage but also affirms masculine identity—so long as it is male only.

As women, nevertheless, began to enter criminal justice system (CJS) work, the first concerns centered around whether women could do the jobs that men do—could they meet male performance standards? Evidence suggests that (1) women can do patrol work as competently and as effectively as men; (2) women handle firearms as effectively or more effectively than men; (3) men are more aggressive prosecutors than women, but women prepare more carefully and win more points with jurors by listening better to witnesses; (4) there are few, if any, gender differences in judicial sentencing; (5) women correctional officers have been rated equally competent with males in most categories of performance, are as effective as males in exercising authority over inmates, and are evaluated similarly by their superiors.

Yet, although full gender integration into the criminal justice professions has been actively sought by women, there are perils involved, for a project of integration contains inherent contradictions. First, insofar as there are a unique woman's perspective and experience of the world, this perspective is abandoned. Existing inequalities are ignored or discounted in an equal treatment approach; as well, genuine difference is ignored.

Second, full integration into the male world is impossible in any case. If men are allowed to continue to set standards for work unilaterally, women will never become more than "junior men" in the enterprise. For example, in policing and corrections, such straightforward standards as those for physical capacity will continue to feature male standards such as upper body strength—requiring women to meet these standards or making special exceptions for women officers. Either move is likely to create or exacerbate women's problems. Unless the special physical qualities of women (e.g., greater endurance, more flexibility) are also considered as standards, women will automatically be disadvantaged.

Third, it is the nature of the system of patriarchy to be built on inter-locking positions of dominance and subordination. Equal rights are not conceivable in a system where the privileges of the "top dogs" are privileges of exploitation. Further, because this hierarchy is built into patriarchy itself, the CJS cannot overcome it alone. No amount of CJS change will alter woman's position as housewife.

Thus, as with most areas of work, to be integrated into an untransformed male world is to work as a male-defined woman under patriarchy. This is difficult enough in most work situations, but within the CJS it is often physically dangerous. There, fully integrated women in a male world are exposed to more danger than are the "good women" who seek protection from male partners or from special rules.

Because of these "perils of integration" women have increasingly sought again to emphasize their differences from men. With two decades of inte-gration, the questions being raised concern whether women have reshaped or can reshape the CJS as an enterprise. Two related questions have emerged: Do women work *as* women, that is, differently from men? and Do they work *for*, or on behalf of, women? These are crucial questions because, to the extent there is sexism in the CJS professions that affects not only workers but also the degree and quality of justice that women citizens served by the CJS receive, only if women are able to transform the system will they be able to effect changes that create justice for women, as well as for men.

Much of the research follows Carol Gilligan's model, which suggests that women and men solve issues of justice in different ways. Male models, based in individual autonomy and hierarchy, are rights- and principle-based, whereas the female approach stresses the primacy of the group over the individual and aims to achieve justice through a more holistic approach featuring harm avoidance and fostering relationships that make a group function.

Gender differences are evident as early as the training stage, where it has been noted that female police academy trainees find that, though they are recognized as having superior interpersonal skills to men, these skills are deliberately de-emphasized, attention being concentrated instead on what they lack in comparison to men. Women law students find the competition and conflict an obstacle since they perform better in cooperative learning environments.

In policing, it was established that citizens responded differently to female officers—they were less likely to resist them and less likely to feel threatened by them, and women complainants in particular responded better to female officers. Women were found to have a less aggressive patrol style, making fewer arrests, issuing fewer traffic citations, and making fewer routine stops for suspicion. Women officers were found to be better at defusing violent situations, at service calls, and at domestic violence calls than were men. Women police were also more likely than men to find community and problem-oriented policing satisfying. Finally, women were less likely to engage in seriously unbecoming conduct than were men.

In corrections it has been found that women workers favor a treatment orientation, while men favor a custody orientation, that women supervise inmates through relationships, while men use formal authority, that women officers ask inmates, while male officers tell inmates, and that women officers explain orders more fully.

In lawyering it has been suggested that women favor a participatory management style and cooperative group work, whereas men prefer a hierarchical style. Women focus more on meeting needs, while men take an adversarial stance to conflict; women are more likely to attempt consensus and are more likely to see themselves in their work as problem solvers rather than rulers. Women appellate judges appear more favorable to criminal rights and to economic liberties than do men; they are also more favorable to issues involving sex discrimination, though they do not favor female over male defendants.

In retrospect we can discern three stages of women's work in the CJS. In the first phase women were employed as specialized task workers (e.g., as police social workers), were paid less, and worked with less authority and upward mobility than did men. In the second phase women sought full integration into a male workplace. In the third phase women seek to create a transformed workplace. We can locate ourselves as currently in this third state, which poses its own special problems.

First, some women fear that different will always mean unequal and/or that the only true differences between men and women are the differences produced by male dominance—hence, to embrace these "slave" characteristics is to admit defeat. Second, transformation is difficult because of the inherent contradictions of affirmative action, which seeks to diversify not just workers but work itself. To the extent that women "act like men," that is, come "up" to a male standard for work, they are more likely to be accepted—to be hired, nurtured, and retained. Yet to transform the workplace requires exactly the sorts of workers who do not conform to current standards.

Perhaps for this reason change that affects women citizens as recipients of criminal justice has, so far, been more likely to come from women working outside the system. Here feminists have succeeded in legislative changes in rape law, in sexual harassment law, in police powers to enforce protection of battered women, and in self-defense law. Feminists have also helped to improve significantly the response of hospitals, police agencies, and the courts to rape and wife battery. The aid that women have established for female crime victims entirely outside the CJS—shelters for victims of wife battery, crisis hot lines and counseling services for victims of rape and other female-victim crimes, aid for women trapped in forced prostitution and for girl runaways—has had an impact on female crime rates, reducing the amount of female homicide; for example, research conducted by women and for women has also had an impact, though it still tends to be marginalized within the academic and policy worlds.

The most pressing need currently is the establishment of links between these outsiders and the new insiders. Such links would have significantly informed and improved the research on effectiveness of presumptive arrest policies for wife batterers, for example. These links are particularly effective and are likely to become increasingly sought in the coming years as more and more women professionals, educated by women professionals, move into decision-making positions in the CJS.

Reference. Carol Gilligan, *In a Different Voice* (Cambridge, 1982).

NANCI KOSER WILSON

CUBA. Without ever reaching total equality, since the 1959 revolution Cuba has been seriously committed to women's emancipation. As actors and beneficiaries of the modernization process, women have performed central roles in the transformation of the socioeconomic and political system. By struggling against a tradition of machismo and gender role casting, women have achieved substantive advances in most areas. But their social gains seemed on the verge of vanishing after the economic crisis that followed the collapse of the Soviet Union and Eastern European regimes in 1989–1991.

Women worried that their social progress could be hindered by the hardships of the 1990s. President Fidel Castro acknowledged their concern at the Sixth Congress of the national (only) women's organization (*Federacion de Mujeres Cubanas*, FMC): "It would be unfair, extremely unfair, if we did not always keep in mind, under the special circumstances we are experiencing, during this special period, the essential weight of the sacrifices being shouldered by the women. [This is in addition to] the burden carried under normal circumstances, which already required special efforts from working women, their work load, and the extreme load of their . . . contributions at home." He also restated the revolution's commitment to women's liberation: "On certain occasions we even said that equality was not even a goal but that we should try to give women more rewards, more rights."

Women's worldwide conditions seemed to Castro comparable to "living under an apartheid system. [This system] still exists in the many discriminatory practices used against women. [But discriminatory practices] could not exist in the Revolution and [then have] disappeared in [Cuba]." Still, Castro admitted that Cuban women were underrepresented in the National Assembly (their delegation was reduced drastically in the 1993 elections), as district delegates, and in other political offices. Notwithstanding its importance, more urgent social and economic problems were affecting and preoccupying the people in general and women in particular.

Although the 1960s saw the eradication of prostitution, the 1990s witnessed the reappearance of prostitutes (or *jineteras*, as they are called), who would sell their sexual favors for U.S. dollars to foreign tourists. Reportedly, in Havana there were approximately 6,000 *jineteras* operating, while their presence also extended to other large cities and foreign-tourist resorts. They had sprung up almost overnight, becoming more obvious once international tourists started to arrive in large numbers.

Prostitution became such a burning issue that it was addressed at the 1996 trade union congress. Vilma Espin, president of the FMC since its foundation in 1960 and a former member of the powerful Communist Party politburo, told the 1,900 delegates present that "sexual tourism is no good, quite the contrary, it attracts the worse kind, the lowest type from other societies instead of good, economically solvent people." The Communist Youth weekly *Juventud Rebelde* acknowledged the issue publicly by interviewing a *jinetera*. It reported that the reappearance of prostitution could be attributed to problems in children's upbringing, nuclear family disintegration, family violence, highly authoritarian or permissive parents, and educational and/or ethical formative deficiencies. Psychologists from Havana University's women's studies program, however, blamed the difficult economic conditions as the main cause of *jineterismo* (prostitution). Many *jineteras*, they argue, have attained a high educational level and hold jobs paid in national currency. But the tourists' dollars allow them to shop in convertible-currency stores, acquiring quality goods not available in national-currency outlets.

The comprehensive social services provided by the regime remained in place. Schools, hospitals, day care, and cultural and sports centers continued functioning but were short of supplies or lacking them altogether. Life became much more difficult but not impossible. The hardships affecting women were more visible at the individual, personal level. Despite the social policies favoring women in the 1975 Family Code, family life dynamics retained some of their traditional patterns, and workingwomen still faced the double shift long after the enactment of the code. As a social aggregate, however, women struggled to safeguard their social gains, but it mostly meant to survive the severity of the special period.

Education. Women in prerevolutionary Cuba had reached a high educational level for Latin American standards. The system was dichotomized on socioeconomic and geographic lines: urban, middle-class, and upper-class women could achieve high school and even college education, while rural, low-income-class women had an illiteracy rate of over 50 percent. The emphasis on education since 1959 benefited the entire population, especially low-income women. In 1981, 53.46 percent of women had completed primary education, 42.3 percent secondary, and 4.3 percent college. Six years later, the figures had improved to 68 percent primary, 63.1 percent secondary, and 4.5 percent college education. Only 1.8 percent of women between the ages of 10 and 49 lacked any schooling. The 1981 illiteracy rate for the entire population was 1.9 percent (it had been 22.3 percent in 1953, but it was drastically reduced to 8 percent by 1961 with the alphabetization campaign).

Distinctions still remained in the late 1980s between urban and rural and between male and female, with the former's ratio higher than the latter's, but by then the differences were minimal. Educational achievement according to the country's racial mix showed that black women had the highest rate at the general secondary (44.4 percent and technical and professional levels (5.2 percent); white women at the primary level (46.5 percent); and Asian women at the higher education level (5.7 percent), while mulatto women trailed shortly behind at all levels. Also, black women had the lowest no-schooling rate among all women (2.2 percent).

Labor Force. Paradoxically, women's share of the labor force decreased from 19.2 percent in 1953 to 18.3 percent in 1970. In reality, a radical labor transformation was taking place. Occupations hitherto closed to women were opened, while their traditional source of employment was radically changed. Women's concentration on domestic work before 1959 ended with domestic workers (and former prostitutes) going to school to learn new trades. This was followed later by a preferential hiring policy that increased women's participation in the labor force to 27.4 percent in 1975, 31.5 percent in 1981, and 38.9 percent in 1990.

The dismal economic conditions of the 1990s reduced women's total labor share and changed their occupations somewhat. They concentrated on the service sector (minus industry) and moved into agricultural work. Over 200,000 women were working in the agricultural contingents of the Food Program (*Programa Alimentario*). Also, they retained technical and professional jobs that have traditionally been occupied by women.

Political Participation. In spite of their high level of political participation and overall involvement in the revolutionary process and the centrality of the FMC as a mass organization, women have not had the electoral success they deserve. Moreover, the election of women as deputies and delegates to the country's political and administrative structure, the Organs of People's Power (OPP), suffered a setback in the last elections. In the different elections held, the Organs of People's Power has followed a curve tracing women's political fortunes (or misfortunes). The electoral trajectory started with a weak showing in 1976 (National Assembly, 21.8 percent; provincial assemblies, 30.8 percent, municipal assemblies, 17.1 percent); and had a drastic fall in 1992–1993 (National Assembly, 22.8 percent, provincial assemblies, 23.9 percent; municipal assemblies, 13.5 percent).

The curve has repeated itself at the national, provincial, and municipal levels, as if a collective will decided whether women should be elected or not—the highest number of elected women to the municipal assemblies in 1992 was in city of Havana province (20.3 percent), and the lowest in Granma province (9.8 percent). The initial 1976–1986 cycle followed an upward trend that was reversed in 1989 at the provincial and municipal elections and continued its downward fall, including the national level in 1992–1993.

The FMC has looked into this matter with concern and conducted an in-depth study in 1994 examining the reasons behind it (Suarez et al.). There are subjective, cultural, and ideological factors involved (i.e., the lingering bias of machismo reinforcing the notion that women are not properly qualified); and objective, socioeconomic factors (i.e., the load of political office interfering with women's burdensome family obligations). Another factor could be the 1992 Electoral Law, which in practice seems to favor men during the candidate selection process, allowing unfavorable attitudes toward women to come into play. The FMC recommended launching a cultural/ideological campaign rectifying outmoded conceptions and stereotypes and selecting more qualified women candidates, with experience in production, service, and administrative jobs, in future elections.

References. F. Castro, "Speech at the Sixth Congress of the Federation of Cuban Women (FMC)," March 4, 1995, *Havana Tele Rebelde and Cuba Vision Networks in Spanish* (FBIS Translated Text); Vilma Espin, *Cuban Women Confront the Future* (New York, 1991); Lois M. Smith and Alfred Padula, *Sex and Revolution—Women in Socialist Cuba* (New York, 1996); K. Lynn Stoner, *From the House to the Streets: The Cuban Woman's Movement for Legal Reform, 1898–1940* (Durham, N.C., 1991); M. Alvarez Suarez et al., *Mujer y Poder: Las Cubanas en el Gobierno Popular*, Federation of Cuban Women (FMC) (Havana, Cuba, 1994); T. Valdes and E. Gomariz (eds.), *CUBA-Mujeres Latinoamericanas en Cifras*, FLACSO (Santiago, Chile, 1992); "Focus on Women's Lives," *CUBA Update* 16, nos. 2–3 (1995): 8–35; J. Weisman, "The Transformations in the Lives of Former Domestic Workers in Cuba," paper delivered at the 19th International Congress of the Latin American Studies Association, Washington, D.C., September 1995.

MAX AZICRI

CULT OF TRUE WOMANHOOD, also known as the Cult of Domesticity, is a term identifying a nineteenth-century ideology that women's nature suited them especially for tasks associated with the home. It identified four characteristics that were supposedly central to women's identity: piety, purity, domesticity, and submissiveness. The cult was first articulated in discussions of women's nature and their proper roles and became prominent in most industrializing societies around 1820; it reached its persuasive height by the 1890s in these areas, while in other European societies it did not begin to gain influence until the turn of the century. Vestiges remain with us today.

The cult dictated that True Women were the moral guardians of the family. They were particularly appropriate for that role because they were spiritually pure—and therefore closer to God. They remained pure because they stayed away from the degrading environment of the outside world, which ruined innocence: moral purity could not withstand the brutality of a world dominated by the unrestrained competition of the free enterprise system. This implied that, since men were constantly participating in the world, they were not as pure as, and therefore were spiritually inferior to, women. It was absolutely necessary for women to cling to the protection of the home. If they left that haven, they lost their innocence, their moral superiority, and ultimately their True Womanhood. Women thus gained their own sphere, which was entirely separate from men's.

A True Woman's role in life was to perform the domestic chores of the household—or oversee their performance by others (usually women) hired for that purpose. She prepared nutritious meals, nurtured her children both physically and spiritually, comforted her husband and soothed away the wounds of his encounters with the outside world, and stood as an invincible sentinel at the portals of the home to keep worldly pollution from entering and despoiling the family.

The idea of True Womanhood was not new, but the self-conscious idea that women should conform to a particular image did not begin to be articulated until the early nineteenth century, when several historical developments prompted its appearance. Enlightenment philosophies made women the conduits through which cultural values (e.g., freedom and social responsibility) passed to future generations. American revolutionary rhetoric formulated that belief more concretely. The idealization of motherhood known as Moral Motherhood or Republican Motherhood emphasized women's natural piety as a basis for the job of instilling republican virtues and attempted to entice women back to the home after their entry into political life during the American Revolution. (See REPUBLICAN MOTHERHOOD.)

The rapid growth of industrialization in the nineteenth century also contributed to the notion that women's special place was in the home. Industrialization moved men outside the home in pursuit of a livelihood. Although in the past women had done a variety of work from farming and husbandry to running inns and publishing newspapers, their traditional work—nurturing and its related duties—took place within, or very close, to the home. Since that job was still essential, and women had "always" done it, they were inevitably the ones who should remain in the home to continue it.

Medical science's definition of women's nature reinforced the idea of their confinement. Doctors believed that women were more fragile than men and that their frailty had to be protected because they were, in effect, the wombs of the nation. Women, therefore, should remain in the home, away from the stress of the world. Social Darwinism's belief that only the fittest could survive reinforced this idea: since women were, by medical definition, not as fit as men, they needed a protected environment. Men, who were by necessity exposed to the outside world and wise in its ways, became women's logical protectors, while women, almost by default, became the keepers of the traditional values embodied by the home. Women's sphere became synonymous with the preindustrial religious and moral values the outside world seemed to have abandoned.

The cult offers a fine illustration of the way in which a phenomenon can interact dialectically with its environment to re-create its environment, reinforce itself, and at the same time redefine itself. True Womanhood encompassed all women. No female was too young or too old to receive instructions from the popular literature that glorified the True Woman. The courts and the churches reinforced women's seclusion in the home through legal decisions and sermons that emphasized women's frailty by dwelling on women's moral purity. But women then claimed this moral superiority as a legitimate platform for reform, which ironically took them outside the home by giving them a public voice in matters of civic virtue and public vice. This stance worked to make the cult both more aggressively oppressive and, simultaneously, less able to confine women in the home. Women's purity argued for strict seclusion from the corruptive elements of the outside world, but that very corruption obligated women to intervene in the male-run world for the good of their men, the community, the nation, and humankind. Thus, the more women accepted the tenets of the cult, the more they were forced to step outside them.

Few women lived up to the dictates of the cult of True Womanhood, even when, at the end of the nineteenth century, it was most binding. Only the newly forming middle class could afford to keep its women at home, but the duties of a True Woman were so many and so idealized that even the most dedicated wife/mother could not fulfill them. Most women had no opportunity to try. Slave women, poor native-born and immigrant women, and working-class women worked outside the home throughout the nineteenth century. Though often their jobs were extensions of domestic tasks, they were performed in factories or in other people's houses, not in the security of their own homes.

The significance of the cult was not that it really described women's lives—recent research indicates that the cult was, in fact, a myth. Its importance is threefold. It limited women's aspirations for themselves; it created a model for life that generated extreme anxiety and stress because it was virtually impossible to live up to; and at the same time, ironically, it contained elements of its own destruction.

Despite the fact that the True Woman was a myth, she was very real in the minds of nineteenth-century people, as is evidenced by the women's magazines and didactic literature of the time. Historians had noted that nineteenth-century women's lives were constricted, but the existence of a cult of True Womanhood was pointed out only in 1966 by Barbara Welter (151–174). Since Welter's trenchant analysis the existence of a cult of True Womanhood has been fully accepted.

Recent works, such as by Norton, and Kerber, have described the origins of the cult during the American Revolution and the early nineteenth century. Other works such as by Cott, *The Bonds of Womanhood* and "Passionlessness" (162–181) and Dublin have attempted to understand how the cult actually affected women.

Other works have explored the cult in its European context. Examples are by Hellerstein, Hume, and Offen; Tilley and Scott; Hall; McMillan; and Smith.

Future work is needed to understand how the cult affected groups that could not achieve the cult's image and, perhaps more important, how the cult maintained its powerful hold on the mind when its image of women's lives was so clearly inaccurate.

References. Nancy F. Cott, *The Bonds of Womanhood* (New Haven, Conn., 1977); Nancy F. Cott, "Passionlessness: An Interpretation of Victorian Sexual Ideology, 1790–1850," in Nancy F. Cott and Elizabeth H. Pleck, *A Heritage of Her Own* (New York, 1979); Thomas Dublin, *Women at Work* (New York, 1979); Catherine Hall, "The Early Formation of Victorian Domestic Ideology," in Sandra Berman (ed.), *Fit Work for Women* (New York, 1979); Erna O. Hellerstein, Leslie P. Hume, and Karen M. Offen (eds.), *Victorian Women* (Stanford, Calif., 1981); Linda Kerber, *Women of the Republic* (Chapel Hill, N.C., 1980); James McMillan, *Housewife or Harlot* (New York, 1981); Mary Beth Norton; *Liberty's Daughters* (Boston, 1980); Bonnie G. Smith, *Ladies of the Leisure Class* (Princeton, 1981); Louise Tilley and Joan W. Scott, *Women, Work and the Family* (New York, 1978); Barbara Welter, "The Cult of True Womanhood, 1820–1860," *American Quarterly* 16 (1996).

KAREN J. TAYLOR

CYSTITIS (inflammation of the bladder) is woman's most common urinary tract infection, which occurs and recurs frequently. Although not usually serious, it is painful and can be embarrassing. The woman may feel the need to urinate frequently. The urine burns painfully during discharge and may also contain blood or pus.

Since a woman's urethra is relatively short (c. 2 in.), it is fairly easy for bacteria to get into the bladder and cause inflammation. Other factors that seem to promote or aggravate cystitis are caffeine, alcohol, decreased fluid intake, not urinating for long periods, and pressure on the urethra from sex or an improperly fitted diaphragm.

Cystitis may disappear without treatment or may respond to self-treatment. However, it should not be allowed to persist beyond 48 hours without medical treatment since it could spread to the kidneys, causing a much more serious infection. If untreated, it could also lead, especially in girls, to muscle damage resulting in inability to "hold urine." In any case, whenever there is blood in the urine, medical attention should be sought within 24 to 48 hours.

Reference. A. Kilmartin, *Cystitis: The Complete Self-Help Guide* (New York, 1980).

CZECH AND SLOVAK REPUBLICS. The Czech lands (Bohemia and Moravia) have long been one of the more industrially developed parts of Europe. The status of Czech women has been conditioned by the region's level of development, as well as by the fact that the area has long had a basically secular culture, high levels of literacy, and political traditions that differed considerably from those found elsewhere in Eastern Europe. Czech women played an important role in the national movement in the nineteenth century and were active in women's as well as partisan and charitable organizations dating from that period. Individual women contributed to Czech cultural and artistic life. Because Czechoslovakia alone of the East European countries retained a democratic form of government for much of the interwar period, Czech and Slovak women, as well as Czech and Slovak men, had greater opportunity to participate in politics than most other East Europeans. However, despite these opportunities and the fact that women were enfranchised in 1919, soon after the founding of the new Czechoslovak state, women were seldom elected to political office during this period.

From 1948, when a communist system was set up in Czechoslovakia, to November 1989, when popular demonstrations ousted it, the status and opportunities of Czech women have been determined less by the country's history than by its political system. Despite the many ways in which Czechoslovakia differed from the Soviet Union, Czechoslovak leaders followed the Soviet example in terms of policy toward women as in other areas. As a result, the status of women in Czechoslovakia currently resembles that of women elsewhere in Central and Eastern Europe and in the Soviet Union. Women's status improved in a number of ways during the communist period, but inequalities remain. There were also numerous obstacles to the development of a feminist movement to challenge the existing situation. Women's gains were most noticeable in terms of educational access and opportunities for participation in paid employment outside the home. However, despite a trend (noticeable among younger age groups in particular) for women's educational levels to approximate those of men, there are significant differences in the educational specializations of men and women at both the secondary and higher levels. Those differences, in turn, are reflected in the labor force, where there is still a significant degree of gender-related occupational segregation. Thus, while women now work in a broader range of occupations, most employed women work in relatively low-priority branches of the economy that have lower-than-average wages. This concentration, in turn, is a major cause of the continued differences in men's and women's wages. Czech women also are far less likely than men to advance to top economic positions.

Czech women's role in the exercise of political power was similarly circumscribed during the communist period. Women voted in numbers equal to those of men in the single-slate elections; they also were well represented in the governmental leadership, particularly as legislators at all levels. However, they were much less frequently found among the group that ruled the country, the Communist Party leadership. Thus, while there were numerous women who were influential party leaders in the interwar period and immediately after 1948, including Marie Švermová, few women achieved such positions, either as Central Committee members or as members of the Presidium of the party, after that time.

Large numbers of women participated in the mass demonstrations that toppled the communist government in November 1989. Young women in particular had also been active in forming independent organizations and organizing unauthorized protests in the two years prior to the Velvet Revolution. Women also played an important part in providing support services for the new political organizations that emerged in November. However, with few exceptions, women have not been chosen for leadership positions in the new parties, movements, or government.

Many of the remaining inequalities that Czech as well as Slovak women face can be traced to a lack of change in women's family roles. As in other socialist countries in Eastern Europe, women's increased educational levels and higher levels of paid employment did not lead to a restructuring of the family or to a redistribution of duties within it. Despite their new roles outside the home, Czech and other Central European as well as Soviet women continue to perform most of the tasks related to caring for children and running the household. The resulting tendency for women to define themselves and be defined by others, first and foremost, by their domestic roles was given added impetus in the last decade and a half by pronatalist policies designed to increase the country's birthrate.

From the mid- to late 1960s, leading Czech women intellectuals began to criticize the leadership's approach to women's issues. This criticism was part of the more general effort to reexamine the foundations of the socialist system in Czechoslovakia that took place during this period. It led to the re-creation of a mass membership for the women's organization, the Czechoslovak Union of Women, which had been reduced to a national committee of prominent women without any organizational links to women at the local level in 1950, and to a reopening of the public discussion of problematic aspects of women's situation in Czechoslovakia. During this period, the women's organization explicitly defined itself as an interest group dedicated to defending women's specific interests. Since Czechoslovakia was invaded by its allies in August 1968, the work of the women's organization has been redirected along the lines more typical of mass organizations in communist states. Czech, as well as Slovak, women thus have had little opportunity to develop autonomous feminist organizations or engage in radical feminist analyses or critiques of women's situation. Issues related to women's situation and policy measures that affect women's interests entered the political arena in Czechoslovakia largely as a result of the activities of specialists and professionals or political leaders who perceived a link between some aspect of women's situation and a higher-priority policy goal.

The restoration of a multiparty democracy in Czechoslovakia has opened up new possibilities for women to articulate their interests and their perspectives on public issues. Women have formed several new independent women's organizations. Most of these, including the Bohemian Mothers, a group of young mothers in Prague, do not define themselves as feminist and appear to have little interest in pressing for women's equality. Instead, their primary interest is in measures that will support women's family roles. This emphasis reflects what appears to be a more widespread reaction against the appropriation of the goal of women's equality by the state and the high levels of employment of women with small children. Many Czechs and Slovaks also regard women's issues as low-priority concerns at present, given the large number of pressing economic and political issues that the democratic government that was legitimated by the June 1990 election now faces. Thus, although political conditions are now much more favorable for efforts by women on their own behalf, it is unlikely that remaining gender inequalities will be significantly reduced in the near future.

References. Karen Johnson Freeze, "Medical Education for Women in Austria: A Study in Politics of the Czech Women's Movement in the 1890s," and Bruce M. Garver, "Women in the First Czechoslovak Republic," in Sharon L. Wolchik and Alfred G. Meyer (eds.), *Women, State, and Party in Eastern Europe* (Durham, N.C., 1985), 51–63, 64–81; Alena Heitlinger, *Women and State Socialism: Sex Inequality in the Soviet Union and Czechoslovakia* (Montreal, 1979); Hilda Scott, *Does Socialism Liberate Women?* (Boston, 1974); Sharon L. Wolchik; "The Status of Women in a Socialist Order: Czechoslovakia, 1948–1978," *Slavic Review* 38, 4 (1979): 583–602; Sharon L. Wolchik, "Women and the State in Eastern Europe and the Soviet Union," in Sue Ellen M. Charlton, Jana Everett, and Kathleen Standt (eds.), *Women, the State, and Development* (Albany, N.Y., 1989), 44–65.

SHARON L. WOLCHIK

D

DANCE. This entry deals with women's contributions as dancers and choreographers to the principal forms of Western theatrical dancing—ballet and modern dance.

Ballet developed from court dances performed by the nobility in Renaissance Italy. By the seventeenth century ballet had evolved into a professional art form, presented in theaters and attended by the general public.

In 1661 the French king, Louis XIV, gave ballet its first official recognition by creating the Académie Royale de Danse, which codified ballet techniques and taught them to both men and women. (Earlier, female roles had been danced by male courtiers; the first professional ballerina was Mlle. de la Fontaine [1655–1738], who made her debut in 1681.)

The eighteenth century marked the rise of the ballet star, including Gaetano Vestris and his female counterparts, Marie-Anne de Cupis de Camargo (1710–1770) and Marie Sallé (1707–1756). Famed for her technical prowess, Camargo shortened her skirt to midcalf to show off her mastery of *entrechats*, jumps in which the feet are crisscrossed quickly in the air, while Sallé developed a reputation for dramatic roles and for replacing the usual, cumbersome wigs and hooped underskirts with simple, loose hairstyles and gowns. Other important eighteenth-century ballerinas were Marie-Madeleine Guimard (1743–1816); Teresa Vestris (1726–1808) (Gaetano's sister); Marie Allard (1742–1802); Barbara Campanini (1721–1799); and Anna Friedrike Heinel (1753–1808).

The nineteenth century is known as the age of the ballerina. As female dancers were called upon to portray mysterious, supernatural characters, their costumes and techniques changed—most notably, through the introduction of *pointe* shoes, enabling them to dance on tiptoe, creating an otherworldly effect. Three of the most famous ballerinas of the day were Italians: Marie Taglioni (1804–1884), whose father, Filippo, choreographed *La Sylphide* (1832) for her; Carlotta Grisi (1819–1899), who created the title role in *Giselle* (1841); and Fanny Cerrito (1817–1909), a particularly dramatic performer. This trio, plus the Danish dancer Lucile Grahn (1819–1907), made a tremendous hit in *Pas de quatre* (1845). During the Romantic period, too, the Viennese ballerina Fanny Elssler (1810–1884) popularized so-called character dances (combining ballet technique with steps taken from Spanish, Hungarian, and other folk forms) and Augusta Maywood (1825–1876) became the first American ballerina to achieve international fame.

Neither Europeans nor Americans but a group of dancers from Russia generated the most excitement during the early twentieth century. In 1910 Anna Pavlova (1881–1931), a *prima ballerina* with the Maryinsky Theatre (a forerunner of Leningrad's Kirov Ballet), formed her own company and toured the world, introducing the classical repertoire to many parts of the world where ballet had never been seen before.

Meanwhile, in 1909 Russian impresario Serge Diaghilev organized the Ballets Russes, which presented Michel Fokine's innovative works—many performed to the radical music of Igor Stravinsky—in Paris. Diaghilev's roster included Tamara Karsavina (1885–1978); Felia Doubrovska (1896–1981); and Alexandra Danilova (b. 1904), plus the celebrated Vaslav Nijinsky. (His sister, Bronislawa Nijinska [1891–1972], was also an important Ballets Russes dancer and choreographer.)

After Diaghilev's death a new generation of Russian dancers toured widely as the Ballet Russe de Monte Carlo, which boasted three young stars called "baby ballerinas": Irina Baronova (b. 1919); Tatiana Riabouchinska (b. 1917); and Tamara Toumanova (b. 1919).

Both major ballet companies in the Soviet Union—the Kirov and Moscow's Bolshoi Ballet—have featured outstanding ballerinas, most notably Galina Ulanova (b. 1910) and Maya Plisetskaya (b. 1925). Several notable Soviet dancers have defected to the West in recent years, including Natalia Makarova (b. 1940) and Galina Panov (b. 1949).

Two former Diaghilev dancers—Dame Marie Rambert (1888–1982) and Dame Ninette de Valois (b. 1889)—can be credited with reviving ballet in England, the former through her Ballet Rambert, which nurtured many prominent dancers and choreographers. De Valois' Vic-Wells Ballet began in 1926 and formed the basis of Britain's Royal Ballet, which featured such luminaries as Dame Alicia Markova (b. 1910) and Dame Margot Fonteyn (b. 1919).

The United States was slow to accept the idea of homegrown ballet. It is not surprising, therefore, that the School of American Ballet was established (in New York in 1934) by a Russian—George Balanchine. His company (later christened the New York City Ballet [NYCB]) has produced an impressive list of ballerinas, including Melissa Hayden (b. 1923); Maria

Tallchief (b. 1925); Allegra Kent (b. 1938); Patricia McBride (b. 1942); Kay Mazzo (b. 1946); Suzanne Farrell (b. 1945); and Gelsey Kirkland (b. 1953). Another venerable company, American Ballet Theatre (ABT), was founded by Lucia Chase (1907–1986) and Oliver Smith in 1940. Whereas NYCB made its reputation with Balanchine's cool, abstract ballets, ABT became known for its productions of probing, psychological compositions by Anthony Tudor and the quintessentially American story ballets of Agnes de Mille (b. 1909). Principal female dancers with ABT have included Janet Reed (b. 1916); Nora Kaye (1920–1987); Lupe Serrano (b. 1930); Toni Lander (b. 1931); Sallie Wilson (b. 1932); Martine van Hamel (b. 1945); Cynthia Gregory (b. 1946); and Marianna Tcherkassky (b. 1955).

Other notable twentieth-century ballerinas are Frenchwoman Violette Verdy (b. 1933), who served as artistic director of both the Paris Opera Ballet and the Boston Ballet; Brazilian Marcia Haydée (b. 1939), since 1961 the star of the Stuttgart Ballet, which she now directs; Alicia Alonso (b. 1921), prima ballerina and director of the National Ballet in her native Cuba; Celia Franca (b. 1921) and Dame Peggy van Praagh (b. 1910), former artistic directors of the National Ballet of Canada and the Australian Ballet, respectively; Vivi Flindt (b. 1943) of the Royal Danish Ballet; and Lydia Abarca (b. 1951), a principal with the Dance Theatre of Harlem.

The early twentieth century was a period of rebellion in all the arts, as painters, writers, and composers searched for innovative forms appropriate to contemporary life. One result of this rebellion was the development of modern dance, a radical new form intended to subvert the bases of classical ballet; instead of melodious music and sumptuous costumes, modern dance typically featured atonal music—or none at all—and accompanying bare-footed dancers in unadorned leotards. Equally important, modern dance tended to tackle difficult, serious themes—not tales of enchanted dolls or swans but violence-filled myths from ancient Greece or hard-hitting socio-political commentary.

Interestingly, most of the giants of modern dance have been women—primarily Americans. The immediate forerunners of modern dance were Isadora Duncan (1877–1927) and Ruth St. Denis (1880–1968), who rejected the rigidity and artifice of ballet, choosing instead to develop their own extremely personal types of movement.

The first true exemplar of modern dance was the German Mary Wigman (1886–1973). Her intense, expressionist choreography was seen all over Europe and the United States during the 1920s and 1930s, until the Nazis closed her school. In 1936 a Wigman pupil, Hanya Holm (b. 1898), formed her own New York company, which produced a number of important dancers (Valerie Bettis [1920–1982], Glen Tetley, Alwin Nikolais). Another influential modern dance pioneer was the American Doris Humphrey (1895–1958), who danced with Denishawn (the company founded by St. Denis and her husband, Ted Shawn), then established her own company with Charles Weidman. One of Humphrey's most famous protégés was José Limón.

The undisputed grande dame of modern dance for over a half century was Martha Graham (1893–1991). In 1929 Graham established a company for which she choreographed well over 150 works and through which have emerged such eminent figures as Erick Hawkins, Merce Cunningham, and Paul Taylor. "Graham technique," taught the world over, is based on the principles of muscular contraction and release; her powerful dance-dramas emphasize striking, angular positions and often feature a female protagonist.

Many members of the next generation of female modern dancers were Graham students, including Anna Sokolow (b. 1912); Jean Erdman (b. 1917); Sophie Maslow (b.?); and Jane Dudley (b. 1912). Younger artists such as Yvonne Rainer (b. 1934) also received their formative training from Graham. Ann Halprin (b. 1920), an important exponent of dance "happenings," was a Humphrey student, and others followed different paths: Bella Lewitzky (b. 1915), a leading West Coast choreographer/dancer, trained with Lester Horton, and Helen Tamiris (1905–1966) was a ballet dancer until the age of 22.

While they did not form their own groups, certain artists have left indelible marks on the companies with which they created key roles: Betty Jones (b. 1926) as Desdemona in José Limón's wrenching *Moor's Pavane*; Carolyn Adams (b. 1943) in Paul Taylor's athletic, exuberant *Esplanade*; and the regal Judith Jamison (b. 1944), for whom Alvin Ailey choreographed the powerful solo *Cry*.

Over the last quarter century modern dance has continued to prosper, largely through the work of small, experimental companies—many headed by women. Two particularly innovative choreographers are Pina Bausch (b. 1940), a leading German expressionist, and Japanese choreographer Kei Takei (b. 1946), whose ambitious dance cycle, *Light*, was begun in 1969. Among younger Americans, Trisha Brown (b. 1936), a founder of the innovative Judson Dance Theatre, has been one of the most successful "postmodern" choreographer/dancers; others include Lucinda Childs (b. 1940); Deborah Hay (b. 1941); Senta Driver (b. 1942); Melissa Fenley (b. 1954); and Johanna Boyce (b. 1954). Since the early 1970s Laura Dean (b. 1945) has been creating intriguing arrangements of obsessively repeated sounds and gestures; Twyla Tharp (b. 1942) has developed a kind of dry, physical humor by combining seemingly casual movements with music by such varied artists as Frank Sinatra and the Beach Boys; and Meredith Monk (b. 1943) has produced remarkably complex theater pieces involving dance, singing, and spoken words.

Reference. Jack Anderson, *Ballet and Modern Dance: A Concise History* (Princeton, 1986).

NANCY G. HELLER

DANISH WRITERS echo the voice of women in premedieval oral tradition. The folktales often feature a female protagonist whose development from childhood through arduous trials, which constitute a rite of passage, brings her to maturity and "happiness ever after" ("King Whitebear"); a passive young woman turns into a person resourceful enough to forge her own destiny. Women, who were often eloquent storytellers, preserved, transmitted, and thereby altered the genre. Those stories inevitably became vehicles for the women's experiences and hopes and perhaps—in the spirit of their Old Nordic ancestresses—even for their prophecies.

The ballad—of which Denmark has one of Europe's largest collections—is a late medieval genre dealing predominantly with the lives of the feudal aristocracy. The first collectors—and possible editors—were women of noble birth, Karen Brahe, Sofia Sandberg, and Ida Gjøe, who recorded the ballads in the late 1500s. Many a ballad features as its central character a woman who is neither pliant nor passive. A few ballads express a female point of view: in "Hr. Ebbe's døtre" (Sir Ebbe's Daughters), the violated young women take revenge in kind.

The Lutheran Reformation brought about the unity of monarchy and state church. Luther's *Cathecismus* (1529) would honor those in authority, and within the family structure that was the male. Latin schools were intended to educate boys of the middle class; girls were limited to little or no education and their mother tongue.

The daughters of the aristocracy were not so limited, and one such was Leonora Christina (1621–1698), a king's daughter who, because of her husband's condemnation for treason, spent 22 years in prison. Her journal, *Jammers Minde* (1674, pub. 1869; A Remembrance of Woe), was written in an honest, direct style that, oral in tone, was eloquent in its description of her imprisonment. There exists only the first of a three-part work, *Hæltinners Pryd* (1684; Heroines' Adornment), on women's contribution to history, demonstrating their natural equality with men with regard to common sense, the ability to learn, the wisdom to govern oneself, and the authority to rule.

Dorothe Engelbretsdatter (1634–1716), born in Norway, which was then a part of Denmark, was the first published poet. Her collections of baroque hymns were enormously popular. (See NORWAY, Norwegian Writers.)

Anna Margrethe Lasson (1659–1738) wrote the first "original" novel in Danish: *Den Beklædte Sandhed* (c. 1715, pub. 1723; The Disguised Truth). In the French baroque tradition, the love story became central. Charlotte Dorothea Biehl (1731–1788) wrote in many genres, but her play *Den listige Optrækkerske* (1765; The Cunning Extortionist), in which there appears a new woman—a deceiver of men—aroused discussion; *Mit ubetydelige Levnetsløb* (1787; My Unimportant Course of Life) described not only her

early battles to read and to make her own choices but also her later years
of isolation.

The nineteenth century, which turned from rationalism to romanticism
and finally to realism/naturalism, was typified by the bourgeois family.
Among the women famous for their intellectual salons was Karen Margrethe Rahbek (1775–1829), whose letters to male friends reflected her
belief in intimate, but platonic, relationships. Thomasine Gyllembourg
(1773–1856), the mother of the famous playwright and critic Johan Ludvig
Heiberg (1791–1860), made her debut at 53. Her slightly romantic stories
discuss problems of love and marriage in the homes of the bourgeoisie.
Ægtestand (1835; Marriage) and "Maria" (1839) support the patriarchal
ideal of woman but maintain a belief in women's right to an education,
the freedom to choose a husband on the basis of love, and the economic
independence of self-support. Gyllembourg's daughter-in-law, Johanne Lu-
ise Heiberg (1812–1890), was one of the age's most admired actresses (with
270 roles). The four-volume work Et liv genoplevet i erindringen (1855–
1890, pub. 1891; A Life Recalled through Memory) was meant to honor
her husband's contribution to literature. In articles she declared that the
male should be the female's disciplinarian and the family should be her
school and that female emancipation would break the sexual biologic order. She interpreted her own longing and melancholy as proceeding from
a religious instinct. Mathilde Fibiger (1830–1872) and Pauline Worm
(1825–1883) viewed marriage as a type of women's welfare and recommended a brotherly-sisterly spiritual and intellectual relationship. Fibiger
in Clara Raphael. 12 breve (1850; Clara Raphael: Twelve Letters) and
Worm in De fornuftige (1857; The Sensible) stressed the function of art in
spiritual liberation, as well as the many shortcomings of female education.
Fibiger's book influenced parliamentary debate, which led to the law to
give unmarried women the rights of adulthood (1857).

Adele Marie (Adda) Ravnkilde (1862–1883) was one of the women encouraged by, and a pupil of, Georg Brandes (1842–1927), the famous critic
who translated John Stuart Mill's The Subjection of Women (1869) and
who introduced into Scandinavia a new literary program that came to be
known as the "Modern Breakthrough," according to which authors were
to place society's problems under debate. Ravnkilde, who wrote three stories—stressing equal rights for women but portraying the sexually masochistic—saw only Judith Fürste (1884) published before she committed
suicide.

A bitter Nordic debate on men's morals opened the eyes of many female
writers to the erotic double standard that existed in "free love," just as in
traditional marriage. The next objective for many was to obtain an identity
for woman as someone with an independent position.

Thit Jensen (1876–1957), however, felt that women had to choose love or work and that love was bound to the motherly, which represented the world's creative energy. Jensen debuted with *To søstre* (1903; Two Sisters) and by 1928 had written 25 books. She was also a zealous promoter of birth control. Agnes Henningsen (1868–1962) made her own life a work of art based on sexuality, the source of creativity, but she thought the Breakthrough's "free love" degrading to women. She wrote a three-volume autobiography, *Kærlighedens åårstider* (1927–1930; Love's Seasons), and an eight-volume memoir, *Let gang på jorden* (1941–1955; Stepping Lightly through Life).

Karin Michaëlis (1872–1950) wrote 70 books, the best known of which were translated into 20 languages. The book arousing greatest notice was *Den farlige alder* (1910; The Dangerous Age), in which a woman tries to escape society's decree that sexual desire is unsuitable for a woman of middle age.

Karen Blixen/Isak Dinesen (1885–1962) first published *Seven Gothic Tales* (1934) in the United States. Though raised in Denmark's upper bourgeoisie, she lived in Africa for many years. *Den afrikanske farm* (1937; Out of Africa) was an autobiographical work about her love and loss of that life. Blixen resumed life in Denmark and wrote with fantasy and an aristocratic understanding of other places and other ages. Believing in destiny, she rejected woman's role in bourgeois life. In her writing, which combines Gestalt and Jungian psychology, her characters seem to be living through the mythic and representing the archetypal.

Tove Ditlevsen (1918–1976), a child of the working class who dreamed of the security and tenderness of a middle-class marriage, was nevertheless a realist. Her lyric writing was reflective of her painful life, from her four marriages (in *Gift* [1971; Poison/Married]), through psychic breakdown (*Ansigterne* [1968; Faces]), to a prophecy of suicide (in *Vilhelms værelse* [1975; William's Room]). She has been called a symbol of the pain of being a woman.

Cecil Bødker (b. 1927), Inger Christensen (b. 1935), and Ulla Ryum (b. 1937) belong to post–World War II modernism. Bødker, who has written several collections of poetry—such as *I vædderens tegn* (1968; In the Sign of the Ram)—short stories, experimental radio plays, and children's books, has received the Critics' Prize for the best prose writer. Her novels include *Tænk på Jolande* (1981; Remember Jolande). Christensen's most famous poetry collection, *Det* (1969; It), has won special praise. *Det* is the story of creation, which begins with "the word," but words begin to obscure the reality they would describe; new words must be found for a new beginning. Ulla Ryum is a novelist, dramatist, and short story writer. Her novels—such as *Natsangersken* (1963; Night Singer) and *Latterfuglen* (1965; The Bird of Laughter)—stress psychoanalytic symbolism and absurdist techniques in tales of sexual cruelty. Elsa Gress (1919–1988), one of the few female members of the Danish Academy (1975), has written novels, essays, memoirs, plays, and film scripts. *Fuglefri og fremmed* (1979; Fancy Free and Foreign) treats the Occupation years.

There was a burst of increased authorial activity in the decade of the 1970s. Among the newer authors are Kirsten Thorup (b. 1942) and Dorrit Willumsen (b. 1940). Thorup's poetry collection *Love from Trieste* (1969) and novel *Baby* (1973) attempt to combine modernism with social realism, both of which tend to "object"-ify the individual. In Willumsen's universe, the women are childish in their dependence, and they seem unable to develop as human beings. Two of her works are the short story collection *Hvis det virkelig var en film* (1978; If It Really Were a Film, 1982) and the novel *Manden som påskud* (1980; The Man as an Excuse).

Artist and socialist Dea Trier Mørch (b. 1941), most famous for *Vinterbørn* (1976; *Winter's Child*, 1986), pictures without mystification, in woodcuts as well as in text, birth and the sisterhood of the hospital. Hanne Marie Svendsen (b. 1933) writes of women who are successful—like Ellen in *Dans under frostmånen* (1979; Dance beneath the Frost Moon)—but who have suppressed certain aspects of their characters to be so. Inge Eriksen (b. 1935) in *Fugletræet* (1980; The Bird Tree) warns against a woman's using her new freedom simply to escape.

If Vita Andersen (b. 1944)—in her poetry *Tryghedsnarkomaner* (1977; Safety Addicts) or short stories *Hold kæft og vær smuk* (1978; Shut Up and Be Beautiful)—reveals women's lives as consisting of superficiality and brutal sexual encounters, Suzanne Brøgger (b. 1944) would transform their limited lives into ideally erotic relationships encompassing mind and body. Brøgger debates modern morals in *Fri os fra kærligheden* (1973; *Deliver Us from Love*, 1976) and describes her effort to live "erotically" in *Crème fraiche* (1978; Sour Cream).

Women writers have tried to describe the "self" as well as to achieve both a communality and a general "fellowship." To that end they have not primarily sought integration into men's histories but have first demanded a recognition of their own history and that of their international sisterhood. There is now a burgeoning generation of critics as well as artists.

Among the new prose writers—Vibeke Grønfeldt, Iris Garnov, Vibeke Vasbo, Suzanne Giese, Jette Drewsen, and so on—and poets—Juliane Preisler, Merete Torp, and Pia Tafdrup—are the following critics: Mette Winge, Pil Dahlerup, Jette Lundbo Levy, Karen Syberg, Lisbet Møller Jensen, Lìsbet Holst, Annagret Heitman, and Anne-Marie Mai.

References. Stig Dalager and Anne-Marie Mai, *Danske kvindelige forfattere*, 2 vols. (Copenhagen, 1982); *I Guds navn: 1000–1800* and *Faderhuset i 1800-tallet*, vols. 1 and 2 of the projected four-volume *Nordisk-kvindelitteraturhistorie*, ed., by Elisabeth Møller Jensen et al. (Copenhagen, 1993), passim; Faith Ingwersen, "Danish and Faroese Women Writers," in Sven H. Rossel (ed.), *A History of Scandinavian Literatures*, vol. 1: *A History of Danish Literature* (Lincoln, Nebr., 1992),

349–371 and passim; Susanna Roxman (ed.), *Kvindelige forfattere. Kvindernes litteraturhistorie fra antikken til vore dage* (Copenhagen, 1985); Bodil Wamberg (ed.), *Out of Denmark: Isak Dinesen/Karen Blixen 1885–1985 and Danish Women Writers Today* (Copenhagen, 1985).

FAITH INGWERSEN

DATE RAPE as a term was coined in 1975 by Susan Brownmiller in reference to a dating situation in which "an aggressor may press his advantage to the point where pleasantness quickly turns to unpleasantness and more than the woman bargained for" (284). More recently, *date rape* has been defined as nonconsensual sex that occurs within a dating context. It is one form of *acquaintance rape* or nonconsensual sex between people who know each other, for example, as friends, neighbors, or coworkers (Parrot and Bechhofer).

Studies concerning the "erotic aggressiveness" experienced by "offended girls" appeared in the scholarly literature as early as the 1950s. For example, Clifford Kirkpatrick and Eugene Kanin discovered that 20 percent of the 291 female college students in their sample experienced "forceful attempts at intercourse" (52–58).

Mary Koss, in conjunction with *Ms.* magazine, conducted one of the largest scientific investigations of date rape (2,972 male and 3,187 female undergraduates on 32 college campuses). College students were selected because they were actively dating and within the age range when rapes most commonly occurred (18–24 years old). The results of the Koss study were published in the first book on date and acquaintance rape that was written for a general audience (Warshaw).

The findings revealed that 8 percent of male respondents either attempted or engaged "in sexual intercourse with a woman when she didn't want to by threatening or using some degree of physical force." One-quarter of female respondents experienced a sexual assault that met the legal definition of rape or attempted rape, that is, unwanted intercourse that was "perpetrated by force, threat of harm, or mental or physical inability to give consent (including intoxication)." More than half (57 percent) of these rapes occurred during dates (Warshaw).

Rape may occur at any point in the dating relationship, from the couple's first date to the more committed stages of the relationship. However, numerous risk factors have been associated with date rape. For example, traditional dating rituals create an imbalance of power between men and women. Thus, it is not surprising that date rape is more common when men initiate the date, pay the expenses, and provide the transportation. For some men, date rape becomes "justifiable" when they are not sexually compensated for the expenses associated with dating. These traditional dating rituals also give men greater power to select activities or isolated locations that are conducive to sexual assault, for instance, "parking" or "making out" in a car (Muehlenhard and Linton, 186–196).

Date rapes are frequently characterized by miscommunication. Men are socialized to view women's behaviors, even friendly gestures, as indicative of sexual interest. These misperceptions are acted out in dating interactions. On dates that culminated in rape, men perceived their dates as "leading them on," for instance, by dressing "suggestively." According to women, this was not intentional. Even when women actively resisted forced sex by fighting back or running away, some men interpreted these behaviors as "token resistance." The belief is that women consent to sex after a brief struggle in order to avoid appearing promiscuous. Heavy alcohol and drug use may further exacerbate this miscommunication. As evidence, date rapes were more frequent when both the victim and assailant are intoxicated (Muehlenhard and Linton).

Rape supportive attitudes further serve to justify forced sex. Among college students date rape was considered "justifiable" under certain circumstances (e.g., if the couple went to a man's apartment, if the man paid for the date) (Muehlenhard, 297–310). Even many high school students endorsed these beliefs. In one study 18 percent of females and 39 percent of males said that forced sex was acceptable if a boy spent a lot of money on a girl or if the girl was drunk (Giarrusso).

These societal attitudes may lead some women to minimize date rape. For example, Mary Koss categorized 76 percent of the date rape victims in her sample as "hidden" victims. While their sexual assault met the legal definition of rape, they responded "no" when asked, "Have you ever been raped?" The reluctance to identify these experiences as rape may explain why none of the hidden victims in this study sought help from the police, hospital, or rape counseling center. In fact, some date rape victims had sex again with the men who assaulted them. However, the majority of victims terminated their relationship with the assailant (Koss, 193–212).

Many victims of date rape eventually recover. However, feelings of shame, fear, and self-blame are common. A sense of betrayal and mistrust may make it difficult to establish future social and romantic relationships. More serious mental health problems, such as depression, anxiety, and sexual dysfunctions, may be experienced as well (Kilpatrick). These problems can be exacerbated if the victim has a history of child sexual abuse (Warshaw).

Societal institutions are beginning to address the prevalence of date rape. In 1994 the Bureau of Justice Statistics redesigned the National Crime Victimization Survey to more accurately assess the number of women who were raped by "intimates," including boyfriends and former boyfriends (Bachman and Saltzman).

In addition, universities are beginning to respond to the problem of campus date rape. For example, in 1992 Antioch College incorporated aspects of the communicative sexuality model in their sexual offense policy. Specifically, students were informed that "verbal consent should be obtained with each new level of physical and/or sexual contact/conduct in any given interaction, regardless of who initiates it." Other date and acquaintance rape prevention programs have included such techniques as "debunking" rape myths and providing sex education. The effectiveness of these policies and interventions awaits further research (Lonsway, 229–265).

Feminists are trying to reduce the prevalence of date rape by addressing miscommunication between women and men. According to Lois Pineau, society should move away from a "forceful-seduction model" of dating where "consent to a caress can be construed as consent to intercourse." Instead, a "communicative sexuality model" should be adopted that encourages partners to "check up as they go along to ensure that different kinds of sexual activity are welcome." This model will reduce miscommunication concerning sexual consent.

More research on date rape should be conducted, particularly with nonstudents, women of color, and lesbians. Despite the research limitations, the existence of date rape has been substantiated. Just like stranger rape, date rape is "real rape" (Estrich).

References. Ola W. Barnett, *Family Violence across the Lifespan* (New York, 1997); Peggy W. Sanday, *A Woman Scorned: Acquaintance Rape on Trial* (New York, 1996); Sally K. Ward, *Acquaintance and Date Rape: An Annotated Bibliography* (Westport, Conn., 1994); Ronet Bachman and Linda Saltzman, *Violence against Women: Estimates from the Redesigned Survey* (Rockville, Md., 1994); Susan Brownmiller, *Against Our Will* (New York, 1975); Susan Estrich, *Real Rape: How the Legal System Victimizes Women Who Say No* (Cambridge, Mass., 1987); R. Giarrusso, *Adolescents' Cues and Signals* (San Diego, 1979); M. Koss, "The Hidden Rape Victim," *Psychology of Women Quarterly* 9 (1985); D. Kilpatrick, "Rape in Marriage and in Dating Relationships: How Bad Is It for Mental Health?" in R. Prentky and V. Quinsey (eds.), *Human Sexual Aggression* (New York, 1988); Clifford Kirkpatrick and Eugene Kanin, "Male Sexual Aggression on a University Campus," *American Sociological Review* 22 (1957); K. Lonsway, "Preventing Acquaintance Rape through Education," *Psychology of Women Quarterly* 20 (1996); C. Muehlenhard, "Is Date Rape Justifiable?" *Psychology of Women Quarterly* 9 (1985); C. Muehlenhard and M. Linton, "Date Rape and Sexual Aggression in Dating Situations," *Journal of Counseling Psychology* (1987); Andrea Parrot and Laurie Bechhofer (eds.) "What Is Acquaintance Rape?" in *Acquaintance Rape: The Hidden Crime* (New York, 1991); Lois Pineau, "Date Rape: A Feminist Analysis," in Leslie Francis (ed.), *Date Rape: Feminism, Philosophy, and the Law* (University Park, Pa., 1996); Robin Warshaw, *I Never Called It Rape* (New York, 1988).

CAROLYN M. WEST

DEATH, WOMEN'S APPROACH TO. Thanatologists frequently note that death is a mirror of life. Death, the common denominator of all human existence, also reflects the differential experiences of men and women.

Women's experiences with death reflect their biological propensity to live longer than men, their capacities of life (birth) and death (miscarriage, abortion), their status within their own particular culture, and their psychosocial sense of connection in their relationships with others. They frequently are treated in death in the same sexist manner in which they were treated in life: infanticide* is more frequently directed toward female babies; women have been expected to entomb or enflame themselves after the deaths of their husbands; widowhood* may represent a time of restricted resources; death rituals may not be as glorious for women as they are for men.

In the United States, research has indicated that gravestones for women are smaller and that there are fewer newspaper obituaries about women. Such obituaries are shorter in length, are rarely accompanied by a photograph, and are likely to appear for women who are related to famous men. It is therefore ironic that women in many cultures are so heavily involved in funerary customs. Mourning rituals are often more severe and/or dramatic for women. They may be expected to wear mourning attire for an extensive period of time, adhere to social restrictions with respect to marriage and negotiations with the outside world, shave off their hair (as found in the Swazi in Africa), inflict themselves with lacerations, or spread dirt and ashes all over their bodies (as found in the Dinka of the Sudan).

In many areas of the world, women are expected to be the death educators—the teachers of ritual and meaning of death. Throughout European history, women have been the caregivers and ministers of comfort and moral support to the dying and yet excluded from legalistic affairs involving the distribution of property and wealth. This tradition of women's tending to the needs of sick and dying family members continues to the present, even for women who may also be employed full-time outside the home. Despite the recent trend of greater male involvement in caregiving for the terminally ill, men are more likely to be funeral directors (in the United States, the percentage is 93 percent, according to recent estimates of the National Funeral Directors Association) and the makers of policy in the social structure of our death system, whereas the proportion of women in hospice, bereavement counseling, and death education far outweighs that of men. Furthermore, this caretaking role has been observed in a number of American ethnic groups (e.g., Mexican Americans, Puerto Ricans, African Americans). Equally important are the many women who rally behind a recently bereaved family to provide meals, housecleaning, baby-sitting services, and the comfort of attentive listening.

Collectively, Western women respond differently to death than do men. Over the past 20 years, the psychological literature has consistently found that women of all ages (beginning at about age 10) report greater death anxiety than do men. What still is unknown, however, is whether such reports actually reflect more anxiety or a willingness to disclose such feelings. Most researchers tend to favor the latter hypothesis. The study of grieving is particularly interesting from the perspective of gender differences. Grief has been alternately explained as a series of stages from loss to recovery or as tasks to be "accomplished" in terms of recognizing the reality of the loss and ultimately developing new social relationships. Many elements to grief are universal and may even be seen in primates and other higher-order animals. With the caveat that one should not look at grief as the greater burden of one sex rather than the other, several dimensions to loss and recovery are more typical for women. For example, losses particular to motherhood (abortion, stillborn death, death due to sudden infant death syndrome) lead to longer periods of grief, yearning, and a profound desire to hold the baby. There is evidence that mothers, when compared to fathers, express more intense grief over the loss of their child.

The *Harvard Bereavement Study*, conducted by Ira Glick, Robert Weiss, and C. Murray Parkes is an examination of how 49 relatively young widows and widowers responded to the death of their spouses. It provides a useful illustration of frequently found sex differences in responses to grief. For example, women typically referred to the death of their husbands in terms of abandonment, whereas men referred to the death of their wives as if it were a dismemberment ("like both my arms were being cut off"). Women also tended to express their grief directly by weeping; the widowers tended to feel "choked up" but actively sought to maintain control over their emotions. Whereas leave-taking ceremonies were typically tolerated (but not necessarily valued) by men, funerals served an important social function for the bereaved women, as such rituals became a public acknowledgment of their new social status as head of the family.

This research also indicated that the long period of grief and mourning that followed were periods of intense pain for both husbands and wives. Yet here, too, there were important gender differences. Women's recovery from grief seemed to follow a more tortured and prolonged path than men's, who appeared to make a faster social recovery. Interestingly, social support systems also seemed to move in gendered pathways; women received more emotional support, and men more help with practical domestic matters. Follow-up research seemed to underscore the distinction between emotional social recovery for men and women. In the long run, women made a more complete emotional recovery than did the men. However, their social recovery took a longer period of time. For many women, social recovery as a widow involves the integration of a new identity within a socioeconomic context that is very different from the one preceding the death of their spouses. But widowed women who assume some of the tasks formerly performed by their deceased husbands, leading to a more "androgynous" lifestyle, apparently experience a greater sense of self-efficacy.

Newer models of grief and mourning refer to differential patterns of grieving as "feminine" and "masculine" grief (see Martin and Doka). Ironically, the feminine pattern, characterized by open emotional expression over the loss, is held as the normative, healthier way to grieve. This notion is questioned by Martin and Doka, who claim that an equally valid pattern (the "masculine" pattern) is found in those people who express their grief through activity and the attenuation of their feelings. The masculine pattern of grieving is typical of males' response to death, but women have also been found to display this form of grieving. In yet another approach to grieving, the stage model, with its idealized ending of recovery and detachment from the deceased, is replaced with the recognition that many bereaved people maintain connections and "continuing bonds" with their dead loved ones (see Klass, Silverman, and Nickman). Whether the continuance of bonds, or the breaking of bonds, also reflect different patterns of grieving for men and women has yet to be determined.

Gender differences extend to the causes of death. Although the leading cause of death for both men and women in the United States is heart disease, factors of lifestyle and/or biology contribute to fewer women than men dying of homicide and motor vehicle accidents. Women are less likely to die of diseases related to smoking (although the gap is narrowing), work-related illnesses and accidents, or suicide. Analysis of suicide statistics shows that more women *attempt* suicide, whereas men tend to kill themselves. The mode of such death also is largely due to the fact that women tend to use methods that leave the door open to discovery and revival. Although there is increased awareness that women's health and disease processes need to be studied in their own right, far too many women are still dying from cancers of the breast, ovaries, and reproductive systems, diseases that are responsible for more female deaths than cardiovascular disease until age 65.

Those who study gender differences are often warned not to maximize the disparities between the sexes in the face of broad similarities. Certainly, this is the case with the experience of death. Death and dying are not gender-specific, and the universal experience of bereavement and grief binds all people. Yet, to some extent, death is a social construction that is interpreted and experienced differently by and for men and women. Cultural and historical traditions that affect women and their relationship to death and dying provide a treasure trove of information that is awaiting exploration by scholars.

References. I. O. Glick, R. S. Weiss, and C. M. Parkes, *The First Year of Bereavement* (New York, 1974); D. Klass, P. R. Silverman, and S. L. Nickman (eds.), *Continuing Bonds: New Understandings of Grief* (Washington, D.C., 1996); T. L. Martin and K. J. Doka, "Revisiting Masculine Grief," in K. J. Doka and J. D. Davidson (eds.), *Living with Grief: Who We Are, How We Grieve* (Philadelphia, 1998), 133–142; K. K. Maybury, "Invisible Lives: Women, Men and Obituaries," *Omega* 32 (1995): 27–37; J. M. Merdinger, "Women, Death, and Dying," in J. K. Parry and A. S. Ryan (eds.), *A Cross-Cultural Look at Death, Dying, and Religion*

(Chicago, 1995); C. M. Parkes and R. S. Weiss, *Recovery from Bereavement* (New York, 1983); J. M. Stillion, *Death and the Sexes* (Washington, D.C.: Hemisphere, 1985).

ILLENE NOPPE

DECLARATION OF SENTIMENTS was written by Elizabeth Cady Stanton and adopted by the Seneca Falls Convention on July 19, 1848. It is based on, and closely copies, the wording and form of the *Declaration of Independence*, even to the point of having the same number (18) of grievances against "all men" that Thomas Jefferson had listed against "King George." The *Declaration* is important as the opening statement of the women's movement and as the basic statement of the goals of the nineteenth-century women's reform movement: the elective franchise; civil existence for married women, including rights to property and guardianship of children; rights to education and employment, including admission to the professions and public participation in the affairs of the church; and elimination of the double moral standard.

DECLARATION OF THE RIGHTS OF WOMAN (LES DROITS DE LA FEMME) was a feminist declaration written in 1791 by Olympe de Gouges, advocating an expansion of French Revolutionary rights to women. Although the *Declaration of the Rights of Woman* should not be considered a manifesto of the women's movement of the late eighteenth century, it is significant because it spelled out a coherent program of feminist concerns that collectively reflected the aims of many French Revolutionary activists.

The document was written by Marie Gouze (1748–1793), the garrulous and quixotic daughter of a butcher and trinket peddler from Montauban, who chose to relocate in Paris after the death of her husband. Changing her name, she embarked upon a short-lived literary career and then began to write political pamphlets.

In more than two dozen pamphlets published between 1790 and 1793, Gouges endorsed social, economic, and political causes, frequently with feminist overtones or in clearly feminist ways. Her social reforms included poor relief, national workshops, the suppression of luxury, and education for women. She initiated a woman's journal and created a second national theater for women. Her political causes, however, were far less progressive and led ultimately to her trial and death. A political conservative with allegiances divided between the monarchy and the National Assembly, she demanded in 1791 that the king's brothers return to France to silence rumors of international conspiracies. In 1792, when Louis XVI was tried for treason, she volunteered to defend him while proclaiming her republicanism. Initially, the popular press mocked her, but her virulent attacks against Maximilien Robespierre brought the wrath of the Jacobins against her. She was arrested, tried for sedition, and executed in November 1793. At the time of her death, the Parisian press no longer mockingly dismissed her as harmless. While journalists and writers argued that her programs and plans for France had been irrational, they also noted that in proposing them she had wanted to be a "statesman." Her crime, the *Feuille du Salut public* reported, was that she had "forgotten the virtues which belonged to her sex." In the misogynistic environment of Jacobian Paris, her feminism and political meddlings were a dangerous combination.

The *Declaration of the Rights of Woman*, which is a mature feminist blending of economic, social, and political aims, was divided into four sections: dedication, challenge to the men of the French Revolution, 27 articles, and postscript. Historically, the least significant section is its dedication to Marie Antoinette, an effort designed to enlist the queen's vanity in order to bring about change.

In the second section of the document, Gouges created the ideological framework for the declaration. First, she challenged men to be just in relinquishing their claims to the oppression of women. Then she rhetorically established that the sexes had never been segregated in nature but rather were found intermingled. Having set forward her claims for equality based on the laws of nature, Gouges then listed the 27 articles of the declaration. Patterned directly after the 1789 *Declaration of the Rights of Man and of the Citizen* and frequently paraphrasing its language, the declaration proclaimed the incontestable rights of woman. Among them were the following: women are born free and shall live equal with men; women are guaranteed the same natural rights as men; women will be treated equally under the law; no distinctions in honors, positions, or public employment will be based on gender; and all citizens, regardless of gender, may play a role in drafting the Constitution. Furthermore, Gouges demanded social reform, including the guarantee that illegitimate children be recognized by their fathers; that women be included in public administration to share in the distribution of goods; that women share in monitoring the determination, base, collection, and duration of taxes; and that property rights be inviolably observed for women, whether married or single. Article X contained Gouges' most famous and most widely quoted demand for political rights: "Woman has the right to mount the scaffold; she must equally have the right to mount the rostrum."

The fourth and final section of the declaration challenged women to demand that the National Assembly take specific action on their needs. In a polemical but practical postscript, Gouges demanded that the government protect morality within the institution of marriage. Her recommendation was a "Social Contract between Man and Woman" that would provide for property rights of women and children, particularly when marriages were dissolved. Gouges included the text of such a social contract in her postscript.

With Gouges' death and the suppression of women's collective and individual rights during the Terror, Directory, and Napoleonic era, the provisions of the *Declaration of the Rights of Woman* were not implemented.

References. Olympe de Gouges, "The Declaration of the Rights of Woman," in Darline Levy, Harriet Applewhite, and Mary Johnson (eds.), *Women in Revolutionary Paris, 1789–1795* (Urbana, Ill., 1979), 87–96; Joan Scott, "French Feminists and the Rights of 'Man': Olympe de Gouges's Declarations," *History Workshop* 28 (Autumn 1989): 1–21.

SUSAN P. CONNER

DECONSTRUCTION. In the latter part of the 1960s, literary theory shifted from structuralism to poststructuralism. Jacques Derrida in "Structure, Sign and Play in the Discourse of the Human Sciences" (1966) and *On Grammatology* (1967) founded the new critical movement called deconstruction, which criticized semiology and structuralism for the continuance of the basic Western philosophical belief in "logocentrism": the concept of structure that depends on stabilizing, fixed, "centers," such as truth, God, consciousness, being, essence, and so on, and the inferior axiological oppositions, such as lie, Satan, unconscious, nonbeing, appearance, and so on. Derrida is primarily concerned with the opposition of speech and writing. He argues that although the spoken word has always been viewed as a "center," with privileged status over its axiological opposite, writing, this is a "violent hierarchy," not only because the two are so similar but also because the hierarchy can be reversed. Reversing such hierarchical opposites is the first stage of deconstruction; the second is to resist asserting a new "violent hierarchy."

Feminists have been attracted to Derridean deconstruction because it demonstrates that thinking in terms of binary opposition has always implied the subordination of the second term to the first. Deconstruction exposed "man" as always occupying the privileged position, as always having set himself up as the central reference point. As deconstruction sought to expose and dismantle the terms and logic through which these claims have been made, many feminist critics have responded to it.

Several French feminist critics have used deconstruction theory in creative ways. For example, Julia Kristeva has looked closely at the opposition between the masculine (and therefore privileged) "closed" rational systems and the feminine, preoedipally formed (hence, a characteristic males also have but in most cases devalue) "open" disruptive irrational systems, the former aligning with her use of the term "symbolic" and the latter with her term "semiotic." The "violent hierarchy" is deconstructed in Kristeva's theories as the poet and revolutionary are shown to rely on what emanates from the drives associated with the body of the mother.

Hélène Cixous mapped out the binary oppositions that privilege man and calls for remapping that places woman as the "center." She advocates only the first stage of deconstruction: the "violent hierarchy" can stay in place, with the female body's plenitude occupying the place of privilege.

Derridean deconstruction has presented two major problems to feminists. First of all, Derrida's resistance to "centers" lies at the base of his theories. Language, he believes, should be—and often is—in constant "play," with no fixed terms or elements that are beyond subversion. Such "play" can disrupt the delimiting effects of "centers." Furthermore, he dismisses linguistic determinacy of form and meaning and stresses that words are constantly deferred as to their meaning. Inasmuch as Derrida believes not only that these things should be operative but also that they have been, he denies what many feminists wish to stress, that is, that men almost totally control the meaning of language.

The second major problem is related to the first in that Derrida gave primary status over all human activities to writing and hence to textuality and the intertextuality of all things. In deconstructionist theory, only writing allows full referrals and shows true differences between and among things because our minds are linguistic. Feminists question how they can imagine a relation between linguistic play and deferral (this engrossing involvement with the signifying processes) and the political and economic action necessary to gain the power for change. Regardless of these drawbacks, feminist critics have found deconstruction a contemporary literary theory that serves them well.

GLORIA STEPHENSON

DENMARK. The status of women in modern Denmark is intertwined with the development of industrial capitalism, organized labor, and the welfare state. The history of women's movements is crosscut by the history of labor movements and the class divisions among women. Current conditions reflect the historic compromises between labor and capital and between women and men that have created this advanced welfare state. When the second wave of Danish feminism began in the 1970s, women already had the luxury of being able to take formal equality and the services of the welfare state for granted.

Current Conditions.

Demography. Denmark's infant mortality rate of 5.4 (per 1,000 people in 1993) and its maternal mortality rate of 3.4 (per 100,000 live births in 1988) are similar to those of other Scandinavian countries. However, stagnation in the Danish life expectancy rates at 72.5 for men and 77.8 for women was the subject of a government report in 1995 that pointed to higher rates of breast and lung cancer among Danish women aged 35–60, resulting in a lower life expectancy than in other Scandinavian countries.

After the fertility rate per woman declined from 2.5 in 1960 to 1.5 in 1985, it increased during the last decade to a rate of 1.8 in 1995. Like the fertility rate, the marriage rate declined from 7.8 in 1960 to 5.2 in 1980 and then slowly started to climb, reaching 6.1 in 1993. The divorce rate stabilized somewhat after increasing from 1.5 in 1960 to 2.5 in 1993. Over half of the adult population lived alone in 1994, with only 14.5 percent of households consisting of a married couple with dependent children.

Economic, Political, and Legal Status. From a 1970 labor force partici-pation rate of 58 percent (of women 15–64), Danish women's rate rose to just under 80 percent in 1995. Women represented 45.5 percent of all those employed in 1994. Denmark has encouraged married women with children to enter the labor force and to expect to place their children in public day care. As a result, in 1990 almost 80 percent of women with preschoolers were employed an average of 34 hours per week. A 1985 survey determined that 60 percent of preschoolers (ages 0–6) were in public day care, 23 percent in private, informal day care, and 17 percent in the care of a parent during the day. In 1987, 81.7 percent of day-care costs were covered by municipalities, with parents contributing 18 percent.

In 1976 Denmark adopted the European Economic Community directive on equal pay for equal work. The Equal Treatment Act was passed in 1978 to prohibit sex discrimination in hiring, promotion, firing, and training. Women's wages in manufacturing jobs were 85 percent of men's in 1992, and in white-collar jobs women earned 71.7 percent of men's salaries in 1989. Differences in wages are largely an artifact of a sex-segregated labor market. Women tend to be overrepresented in lower-paying service jobs. Also, over two-thirds of men work in the private sector, while over two-thirds of women work in the public sector. In the 1980s and 1990s, jobs and wages in the public sector declined relative to those of the private sector, stalling the progress of women as workers in the welfare state.

Denmark and its Nordic neighbors have achieved a level of political rep-resentation of women that makes them more receptive to addressing women's interests. In the 1994 elections, women won 33 percent of the seats in Parliament, up from 17 percent in 1971. In 1990 women's repre-sentation on local councils was 26.4 percent, and on public committees and councils it was 18.5 percent. Since the 1980s women have been more likely to vote left of men and to voice more support for the public sector.

Statutes passed in 1987 and 1989 prohibit discrimination on the basis of sexual orientation in access to public services and give registered same-sex couples all the legal rights of registered opposite-sex couples.

Welfare State Benefits. A partnership has been established between women and the welfare state in which the state supports the dual obliga-tions of mothers to wage work and child care. This partnership is epitom-ized by the extensive system of high-quality, locally organized, and publicly funded day care. In 1989, 47.3 percent of children age 0–2 were in state-sponsored day care, as were 66.1 percent of children 3–6 years of age.

Maternity leave is 14 weeks, plus 4 weeks' pregnancy leave, which must be taken before the birth. Paternity leave is 2 weeks. In addition, there are

10 weeks of parental leave that may be taken by either parent. Pay varies by labor contracts, locality, and private versus public sector employment but is guaranteed up to a maximum maintenance allowance. Since 1994, either parent may also take a paid child care leave of 13 weeks, for each child under age 9, or 26 weeks, if it is taken while the child is under 1 year of age. With the agreement of the employer, child care leave may be extended up to 52 weeks. Families also receive a child allowance for each child up to age 18, regardless of income.

Since 1973 abortion has been legally available upon request during the first 12 weeks of pregnancy and by permission afterward. All expenses of abortion, pregnancy, and birth as well as contraceptive information are free through the national health care system.

History. In 1850, Mathilde Fibiger wrote *Tolv Breve*, a pioneer work of Danish feminist literature. Writing under the name Clara Raphael, she decries the restrictions of her sex and longs for the intellectual freedom that men of her class enjoyed. Physicians and scientists of her time asserted that women's reproductive functions were antithetical to paid labor, intellectual pursuits, or active sexuality. Their ideological reinforcement of middle-class women's confinement to home and children came at the very time when women's lower fertility rate and longer lives would have allowed them more time to pursue education, production, and sexuality and when the development of liberal capitalism with its notions of bourgeois individualism would seem to support women's engagement in work outside the home.

The Danish Women's Society (Dansk Kvindesamfund) was established by Matilde and Frederik Bajer in 1871 to better the position of women in the family and society by improving their access to education and employment. They believed that women should be free to choose employment as long as they remained unmarried or to choose marriage and family, but not both. When nineteenth-century, middle-class women's movements adopted a complementary ideology for married women, as opposed to an equality ideology for unmarried women, it fitted the reality of married women's lives. Reflecting a complementary ideology and reality, the Housewife's Movement became the largest twentieth-century women's movement, larger, by far, than the Danish Women's Society. Both organizations worked to professionalize homemaking.

Poor women had always worked, and their reality was not one of choice about whether to be employed or not. Scientific notions of femininity did not apply to them. For them the struggle was for better working conditions and wages. The General Union of Women Workers (Kvindeligt Arbejderforbund) was established in 1885 to organize unorganized women workers and to improve the working conditions for unskilled women workers. It exists today as an alliance of several women's trade unions with a membership of about 90,000.

Not until the turn of the century did feminism become a movement for political equality. Women achieved full suffrage in 1915. In 1899 the Danish Women's National Council (Danske Kvinders Nationalråd) was formed as an umbrella organization of various women's organizations. It came to be used by the state as the representative of women's interest nationally. It was represented on the 1965–1974 Commission on the Status of Women in Society, which led to the establishment of the Equal Status Council (Ligestillingsråd) in 1978.

Thit Jensen proposed birth control in the 1920s in speeches throughout the country on "voluntary motherhood." She argued that "if women are to achieve anything more than merely formal equality, it is a prerequisite that they themselves should be able to decide how many children they want to have and when to have them."

The Social Democratic Party came to power in 1924 as the political representatives of the labor movement. Social Democrats considered women's inequality to be addressed by the party's class equality policies. They propounded familism as an ideal, including a family wage that would permit working-class women to stay out of the labor force. They created welfare state programs, such as social security, unemployment compensation, and national health care, which improved the position of the working class, including working-class women, while reinforcing the idea that women's interests coincided with those of "family" and children.

Economic growth after World War II increased the demand for married women's labor, and the double shift began to appear in classes other than the poorest of the working class. Denmark's ensuing sex-role debate of the 1960s centered on how to combine women's employment and child rearing. A broad consensus developed that women and men were equally capable of all types of productive work and should have equal opportunity to compete for jobs and to share child-rearing responsibilities. This consensus was deep enough to support an expansion of state-supported day care and transfer payments to families. However, it did not change the everyday forms of gendered labor in the family.

When the new Danish women's movement arose in 1970, the participants fought not for formal equal rights but to discover why practical equality had not followed from the apparent political consensus of the 1960s sex-role debates. The Redstockings, who were the definitive branch of the new women's movement, focused their struggle on the ways oppressive forms of femininity and masculinity were instilled and maintained in the everyday lives of women and men in families and at work. They politicized the personal, created a new gender-conscious political practice, and worked to define the interests of women. Even though they were socialists, their middle-class backgrounds and radical gender analysis made them somewhat suspect from the perspective of working-class women. The lesbian movement arose out of the Redstocking movement in 1974 in solidarity with their goals but signifying that sexual orientation was another important difference among women.

Current Debates. Although neither class nor gender inequalities have been eliminated, the welfare state has mitigated against the worst forms of class and gender oppression. Denmark is now at a turning point. There is growing pressure to reduce the public sector and social expenditures, which some argue would hurt women more than men and the working class more than middle and upper classes. These trends threaten not only the quality of state services but also the welfare state's historic role in promoting greater class and gender equality. On the other hand, Birte Siim sees hopeful signs in the increased number of women politicians, in Denmark's continuing financial commitment to welfare state services, in the mutual dependence of the family and the state, and in an egalitarian political culture that now includes both class equality and gender equality as core national values.

Reference. Birte Siim, "The Gendered Scandinavian Welfare States: The Interplay between Women's Roles as Mothers, Workers and Citizens in Denmark" in Jane Lewis (ed.), *Women and Social Policies in Europe, Work, Family and the State* (Hants, England 1993), 25–48.

LYNN WALTER

DEPENDENCY is a state of needing someone or something for support, comfort, or aid. In Anglo-American culture, dependency is almost a dirty word, a negative condition, associated with female weakness and helplessness, in contrast to the ideal emotional condition of "independence," associated with male strength and autonomy. But in other cultures, such as the Japanese, dependence is regarded as essential in social life; Japanese even has a special word for the need to be attached to, and dependent on, others (*amae*). Research today recognizes the importance of dependency on other people throughout human life, from infancy to old age. For example, theories of adolescent development once emphasized the supposedly key step of "separation" from the parents and becoming "independent" of them. In contrast, new approaches focus on the importance of the adolescent's continued attachment to parents. The young adult learns to be autonomous in certain respects, but this is not the same as being completely "independent."

Popular books have debated whether men or women are the "dependent sex," but the evidence shows that all human beings are dependent on others, though for different things at different times of their lives. In a family,* for example, the spouse who isn't earning an income is financially dependent on the one who is; the spouse who cannot express feelings is emotionally dependent on the one who can; the spouse who has the flu is physically dependent on the one who doesn't.

The stereotype of the emotionally self-reliant, independent male and the clinging, dependent female has a kernel of truth, but it is not the whole cob. Because women have traditionally been financially dependent on men, some observers have concluded that men have not "needed" women as much as women "needed" men. In fact, every relationship is a mosaic of interlocking dependencies that shift and change over time. *Both* sexes, especially in times of trouble, long to be taken care of by others. In exchange for economic security, both men and women have been known to forfeit independence: traditionally women have done so in their marriages, but men have done so in their work. Men are just as dependent on their partners as women, but often they are neither as aware of it nor as willing to admit it. Men have a much more difficult time than women do adjusting to the loss of a spouse through divorce* or death; single men have a higher rate of mental and physical illness than married men. It is as if men are unaware of how dependent they become on their wives for everyday caretaking and emotional support—until they are alone. So striking are the statistics on the frailty of unmarried men that some observers believe that men are the "dependent sex": their apparent autonomy is based on the confidence that they will be cared for. Although women seem dependent and helpless, in this view, they learn from childhood to rely on themselves, to be the caretakers of their children, husbands, friends, and eventually their parents.

In either gender, both extreme dependence and extreme independence carry psychological costs. The excessively dependent person stakes everything on continued support from the partner; if the relationship fails, the individual lacks resources and self-esteem. The excessively independent person risks nothing by trying to remain invulnerable to hurt and rejection; but he or she becomes sealed off from the pleasures and intimacies of close relationships. According to social psychologist Sharon Brehm, both extremes seek the same goal: absolute security. The dependent individual seeks the security of total protection and care; the independent person seeks the security of emotional invulnerability.

But most people do not fall at either extreme. Most men and women continue to depend on their friends, relatives, and lovers throughout their lives for love, moral support, financial aid, and good times.

References. Terri Apter, *Altered Loves: Mothers and Daughters during Adolescence* (New York, 1990); Sharon Brehm, *Intimate Relationships* (New York, 1992); Carol Tavris, *The Mismeasure of Woman* (New York, 1992).

CAROL TAVRIS

DEPRESSION, in mental health usage, is a mood or affective disorder characterized predominantly by pervasive feelings of sadness, hopelessness, and despondency, negative self-image, decrease in ability to experience pleasure, and, in some cases, recurrent thoughts of death or suicide. A depressed person may also report loss of interest in work, decline in productivity, low

energy level, lack of interest in sex, social withdrawal, and sleep and ap-
petite disturbances.

It is important to distinguish depressive illness from normal mood fluctuations. Feelings of sadness, disappointment, and unhappiness are common reactions to the vicissitudes of life experienced by most people at one
time or another. Indeed, it is normal to feel depressed in the face of a major
loss, such as death of a loved one, or to feel "down" or "blue" when things
go wrong in the primary arenas of love and work. The fact that the symptoms of depressive illness are common sometimes makes it difficult to discern when a person has crossed the line into mental illness. The difference
lies in the intensity and severity of the symptoms and in the extent to which
they interfere with the person's functioning.

Theories of Causation. Several theories of the causes of depressive illness
have been proposed, implicating biological, psychological, social, and environmental factors.

Biologically based theories implicate genetic transmission and brain neu-
rochemical activity. Family studies show that depression occurs more often
among the close relatives of depressed patients than in the general population. Twin studies have found that identical twins have a higher concor-
dance rate for depressive illness than nonidentical twins have.

Experimental studies have shown that reduced levels of certain brain
chemicals are associated with depression, while enhanced levels produce
euphoria or even mania. Such chemical interactions are very complex, however, and the causes of fluctuations sufficient to cause mood swings in some
people are not known.

Some theories relate depression to personality needs, such as an overly
punitive superego, resulting in anger and aggression being turned against
the self, taking the form of self-blame and guilt. Such needs could be rooted
in early childhood experiences with dominating and rigid parents who, by
being too judgmental and critical, prevented the child from developing a
positive self-concept and feelings of mastery in meeting life's challenges.

Other theories relate the onset of depression to the stress engendered by
loss of, or separation from, a love object. Researchers such as Rene Spitz
and John Bowlby studied depression in young children who were separated
from their mothers for long periods. Comparative animal studies of monkeys deprived of their mothers indicate that the human capacity for depression as a reaction to loss is part of our evolutionary heritage.

Depression has been related to the thoughts and belief patterns that the
depressed person has. Such persons hold pervasive negative views of themselves, environmental events, and the future. Given the mind-set, they then
misinterpret or distort the meanings of events to fit with, or to confirm,
their worldview, which is basically that life is beset with misfortune and
unhappiness and that nothing good has happened or ever will happen to
them. An example is a young woman who developed herpes after having

sex with a man she met in a bar. On relating what has happened she said, "Every time I try to do something good for myself [e.g., having sex] I get slapped down." For such persons, their depression is a self-fulfilling prophecy* in that every negative event, important or trivial, is interpreted as a confirmation of their basic belief that they are singled out for an unhappy life.

Animal experiments have created a condition of "learned helplessness"* that is quite similar to depression in humans. Dogs subjected to trials of inescapable shock began to accept the shock passively, having learned that no response of theirs would be effective in eliminating the discomfort. The analogy to depression in humans is that a woman who feels unable to control environmental reinforcements may develop a profound pessimism because of her inability to effect positive change in her life. One thinks, for instance, of the battered wife who has learned the futility of any action of hers to protect herself or to remove herself from the situation.

Treatment for depression consists mainly of drugs and some form of psychotherapy, often used together. Certain drugs are effective in alleviating depressions related to brain chemistry. Because depressed persons usually have psychological problems such as negative self-image and feelings of futility and helplessness, psychotherapy is indicated along with drug therapy.

Women and Depression. Many studies have found women to have higher rates of depressive disorders than men have, regardless of the type of disorder. For example, in one study women using outpatient psychiatric facilities had about three times the rate of depressive disorders compared to men in the 25 to 44 age group. Several explanations for this gender-related disparity have been put forth. It has been proposed that the differences in men's and women's lives make women more vulnerable to stress. For example, men may have two major sources of life gratification, their work and their families. Women, by contrast, have traditionally been restricted to only one role, that of the family, thus reducing for them the possibilities for rewards and achievements. Even when women are employed outside the home, most work in low-paying, dead-end jobs that are secondary to their husbands' work role as primary provider. Too, the dependency* of women on men, coupled with their relative lack of resources, could induce in vulnerable women the "learned helplessness" syndrome wherein the woman feels helpless to take action to change an unrewarding situation.

Whereas earlier theories of psychopathology leaned toward locating the source of mental health problems in the afflicted person's psyche, it is now clear that many problems are generated by situational stress, that is, by features of the society and of the person's life over which the individual may have little or no control. Our society, as well as others, has a long history of discrimination* against women and of the relegation of women to second-class status. The incidence of depression is high among oppressed people who feel powerless to alter their situation. While women today have more control over their destinies than did our foremothers, the residuals of the oppressive effects of poverty,* lack of opportunity, and sexual and racial discrimination are still formidable barriers to many. For example, low-income mothers in single-headed households with young children have the highest rate of depression of any demographic group. It is not difficult to appreciate the relationship between environmental stress and depression when we contemplate the difference between the life of such a woman and that of one more affluent with plenty of support and a sense of personal strength and control over her life.

It has been suggested that the preponderance of women over men who are treated for depressive disorders is an artifact reflective of other gender differences. In our society women are freer to express distress than men are and tend to report more symptoms. Women visit doctors more often and get more prescriptions for mood-altering drugs. Also, it may be easier for women to enter the "patient" role because of socialization pressures that foster dependency and reliance on authority for women but not so easy for men, who are encouraged to be strong and stoic.

Another explanation relies on the different coping styles of women and men under stressful conditions. It is possible that, given the same subjective levels of stress, women are more likely to become depressed, while men may handle their distress in other ways, such as substance abuse or acting-out of anger* and frustration. Men do, in fact, have much higher rates of the latter symptoms than women have.

Finally, there is the possibility that some women are more vulnerable to depression because of biological factors. For example, it has been observed that for some women depression tends to be associated with changing hormonal levels of reproductive events, such as menstruation, the postpartum period, and menopause.* Yet most women experience all these events without developing symptoms. Also, mild depressions during the premenstrual or postpartum periods should not be confused with clinical depression, which is usually more severe and longer lasting.

Like most other psychological phenomena, depressive illness in most cases has no single cause. People vary greatly in their resistance to stress, in their vulnerability to the development of mental disorder, and in the circumstances of their lives. Some people develop a clinical depression after exposure to relatively moderate stress; others never do, in spite of extreme emotional and physical pressures.

References. D. D. Burns, *Feeling Good: The New Mood Therapy* (New York, 1980); M. Scarf, *Unfinished Business: Pressure Points in the Lives of Women* (Garden City, N.Y., 1980).

JUANITA H. WILLIAMS

DEPRESSION, THE GREAT, is the economic decline following the stock market crash of 1929, which was marked by increasing numbers of unemployed and decreasing incomes of those working. The economic decline was international in scope and lasted throughout the decade, bringing severe hardship to millions in America and elsewhere throughout the world. Prosperity in the 1920s had been uneven, not shared by tenant farmers, minorities, and the unorganized; and the hard times that followed only widened the gap between the elites and the working class. Among the first to be fired were the unskilled, African Americans, Mexican Americans, and married women in teaching and government service.

Women experienced the depression differently than men did. Whereas males may have suffered the loss of their primary role as breadwinner, women's lives tended to be less disrupted. While there were destitute women—estimates of homeless women run as high as 200,000—they tended to hide and avoid breadlines. The majority of middle-class women experienced the depression as a severe cutback in income. They took up the slack in the family income by increasing their labor for the household, producing more of the family's needs. By mending, canning, conserving, and generally "making do," women carried the family over hard times.

Many wives sought jobs to aid their families. With an increasingly sex-segregated workforce, women's service jobs were not as vulnerable to depression layoffs as were men's manufacturing ones. However, even though they were not in jobs that would be taken by men, there was an effort to blame working wives for the country's unemployment. Campaigns were conducted against the working wife, beginning with the passage of the Federal Economy Act of 1932. Section 213 of this law prohibited federal employment for both spouses, and despite the opposition of women's groups, it was not repealed until 1937. City school systems maintained policies discriminating against married teachers. A National Education Association (NEA) survey found that 77 percent of public school systems would not employ married women as teachers. By the end of the decade, the majority of the nation's banks, insurance companies, and public utilities had restrictions on married women's working. Nonetheless and despite the blatant public hostility toward the working wife, the number of married women in the labor force increased by 50 percent during the decade, continuing a trend begun at the turn of the century. The depression thus sent a double message: by imposing pressure on the family, it pushed married women into wage work at the same time that it fostered a public stance of disapproval.

The depression brought changes to the American family: the divorce rate declined, couples postponed marriage, married couples had fewer children, and often three generations came to live together under one roof. While early research held that the depression changed the patterns of authority within the family, the actual dynamics were more complex. Unemployment for the father of the family did not automatically cause the erosion of his status. Generally, the well-organized family survived the depression best, and this organization was a characteristic of the adjustment of the family members to each other rather than adherence to a particular family pattern. Winifred Wandersee concludes that while women may have gained increased powers and responsibilities in the family, traditional family values were not challenged but rather were strengthened as women abandoned the vision of individual fulfillment advanced in the previous decade.

The record of the Franklin Roosevelt administration and the New Deal on women is mixed. With their advent women gained a spokesperson in Eleanor Roosevelt, who served as a lobbyist for overlooked groups. Through her efforts the new administration called a White House Conference on the Emergency Needs of Women. Women benefited from major programs such as Social Security and the Fair Labor Standards Act. The National Recovery Act codes raised the wages of women in those industries that developed codes but did not award women equal pay. The relief programs also reflected patterns of sex discrimination. Work camps for young women awarded wages of 50¢ a week, while males in Civilian Conservation Corps (CCC) camps earned a dollar a day. Similarly, women employed under the Works Progress Administration (WPA) did not receive equal pay and were forced to relinquish their jobs when the welfare provisions of Social Security were inaugurated.

New Deal programs were also unable to address racial discrimination since most were administered by state and local government. African Americans had not generally shared in the prosperity of the 1920s and faced the hard times of the depression decade with the further handicap of racial discrimination. Almost 40 percent of African American women were in the workforce, the majority of these in domestic service, and were severely affected by the depression. (See AFRICAN AMERICAN WOMEN [SINCE 1865].) Domestics tried unsuccessfully to get a government work code to guarantee a nine-dollar per week pay for a 10-hour, six-day week. During the depression, "slave markets" developed on city street corners, where hungry girls waited to be hired for a day's domestic work for 9 to 15¢ an hour.

The cause of African Americans was advanced through the efforts of Mary McLeod Bethune, educator and founder of the National Council of Negro Women. Given access to the president through Eleanor Roosevelt, Bethune convened an informal group of leaders, the "Black Cabinet," which met weekly at her home to frame policies to urge upon the administration. Greater steps were taken in the later New Deal programs to aid African Americans.

The 1930s was a decade of enormous union growth due to the efforts of the Congress of Industrial Organizations (CIO) to unionize the major mass-production industries. Women workers gained from the unionization of many of these industries, and many women played a role in the unionizing drives of the 1930s. A few women organizers held important positions in the CIO. However, the benefits of unionization did not reach the majority of women workers employed in the sex-segregated economy.

Feminism in the 1930s continued to be dominated by the struggle between the social reform feminists and the National Woman's Party (NWP) over the ratification of the Equal Rights Amendment (ERA). The women active in social reform were crucial to the formulation of much of the New Deal social welfare legislation. Although the NWP made continuous gains in the campaign for the ERA throughout the decade, social feminists feared the loss of protective legislation for workingwomen under the amendment. Mary Anderson of the Women's Bureau attempted to compromise by calling for a Charter for Women's Rights that all women's groups could endorse, but the attempt failed.

As the depression continued, so did the public attack on feminism. The campaign against working wives silenced the earlier proponents of careers for women, who now relied on arguments based on family necessity. Leaders of the Woman's Party feared a U.S. imitation of the "Back to Home" drives of European fascism. Feminism was further eroded by the increasing emphasis on Freudian psychology and the popular reaffirmation of feminine dependence. These values were reflected in the portrayal of women in Hollywood films. Movies featured plots in which strong and competent career women reaffirmed their commitment to the traditional values of marriage and motherhood by the film's end. In the neighborhood theater, as in life, women in the depression played a wider variety of roles yet without challenging tradition.

References. Phyllis Palmer, *Domesticity and Dirt: Housewives and Domestic Servants in the United States, 1920–1945* (Philadelphia, 1989); Lois Scharf, *To Work and to Wed: Female Employment, Feminism and the Great Depression* (Westport, Conn., 1980); Martha Swain, *Ellen Woodward, New Deal Advocate for Women* (Jackson, Miss., 1995); Winifred D. Wandersee, *Women's Work and Family Values, 1920–1940* (Cambridge, 1981); Susan Ware, *Holding Their Own: American Women in the 1930s* (Boston, 1982).

JOAN IVERSEN

DESIGN is an activity that has enormous impact on women's lives, and their relations with it are complex. Women work as designers (of buildings, furniture, textiles, clothes, ceramics, graphics), they consume designed goods, and their identities as women are made visible in the design of fashion and advertising. Design literally shapes how we look and how and where we live, work, and play. It is influenced by social, cultural, political, and economic factors; it makes visible and renders in material form the value systems of the societies within which it is produced and consumed. In Europe and the United States, social structures are still essentially patriarchal, although inevitably patriarchy is mediated by class, race, and ethnicity. In the words of Philippa Goodall "[W]e live in a world designed by men; it is not for nothing that the expression 'man-made' refers to a vast range of objects that have been fashioned from physical material" (50). Design is an activity in which women, particularly those interested in feminism, have sought to contest the definitions, assumptions, and values that, to a large degree, determine who designs, what is designed, and for whom it is designed. This feminist intervention in design has influenced all areas of activity, including architecture, transport, engineering and product design, the decorative arts (textiles, ceramics, furniture, jewelry, metalware), fashion, and graphic design. It is now possible to write of feminist approaches to design, although these vary considerably (see, for e.g., Buckley ["Made in Patriarchy"]; Attfield for a fuller discussion of these theoretical issues). Feminism has also had a significant effect on the ways in which the histories of design are written and the critical context within which design is debated. Since the early 1980s there has been a plethora of research, teaching, conferences, and publishing that has addressed themes relating to women's relationship to design history, theory, and practice, although over the last 10 years the debate has broadened its scope by focusing on gender rather than women. This shift in emphasis reflects the increased interest in gender studies rather than women's studies, and it relates to recent developments within cultural theory (particularly influenced by postmodern and poststructuralist theories). These changes have often reinforced and drawn on the feminist critiques of specific disciplines; however, sometimes they have been at odds with the political goals of feminism. Nevertheless, design has been influenced by these theoretical shifts and reorientations.

Over the last 15 years, women's relationship to design has been the subject of sustained academic work by feminists who have drawn attention to the ways in which patriarchal values have shaped design practice, theory, and history. In a number of specific ways feminists have changed the ways in which writers, critics, teachers, and historians think about design and women's interaction with it. There is now some understanding that women's needs as consumers are not necessarily the same as men's, although there remains a nostalgic commitment to the outmoded notion of the sexual division of labor that locates women in the home and men outside it. This has been mediated by an increased perception that clothes, housing, offices, nurseries, schools, furniture, cars, and the fabricated environment must be designed to meet women's real needs if they are to sell in a competitive marketplace. There is also an acknowledgment that women are not merely passive objects to be manipulated into buying goods, even though it is still possible to see women deployed in advertising in ways that seek to reaffirm traditional notions of feminine identities and female sexuality. But feminist writers and critics have shown that women are discerning and transgressive in their consumption and use of designed objects and that they neither conform nor respond to crude, simplistic stereotypes. Feminists have also shown that women do not design by courtesy of innate, sex-specific skills but rather that these are learned within a patriarchal society, and although women designers remain a minority and are often channeled into specific activities deemed "feminine" (such as fashion and textiles, graphic illustration, pottery decoration, and interior design), qualities such as dexterity, attention to detail, and an interest in surface rather than form are all products of this socializing process, rather than women's biological inheritance. As a consequence, assumptions about women's abilities as designers have to be rethought, and undergraduate and postgraduate training in design has to take account of these in order to enable women to overcome patriarchal bias. Women entering fields of design dominated by men such as architecture, product design, transport, and engineering are working to challenge the assumption that they must acquire the values and outlook of white, middle-class males—the dominant group in these professions—in order to succeed. Finally, feminist historians have helped to show that women have always been involved in design and that they have a rich heritage to discover and appreciate. Research to date has revealed women's widespread participation in design as practitioners, writers, critics, theorists, campaigners, and philanthropists.

Women's place in the history of design has been obscured by the biased methods of design historians who have prioritized certain types, styles, and periods of design and who have emphasized particular design theories such as modernism and the work of a handful of mainly male design "stars." Casualties of these biased historiographical techniques are women designers and the designs that they have produced. For a number of reasons, design activities in which women dominate (fashion, textiles, jewelry, pottery, graphic illustration) have been deemed less significant than those in which men dominate (architecture, furniture, product design, engineering, and transport). Coupled with this, designs have been valued more highly when they are clearly attributed to a named, professional designer, rather than to an amateur who, perhaps, works collaboratively (with other women or with a famous husband), producing work that might be made by hand using traditional methods and/or motifs, typical, for example, of knitting, quilting, embroidery. Designs made within industry for exchange are much more significant within a capitalist economy than those made for home use, and the emphasis within modernist design theory and practice on modernity, progress, and the new technology was essential to stimulate consumption within such an economy. In response to these biased methods, feminists have tried to shift the emphasis in design history. They have aimed, first, to expose old prejudices and value systems, and, second, they have attempted to change the nature of the debate. On one hand, feminist design and cultural historians have outlined women's involvement with design in the broadest sense, showing how women design in particular ways for a host of social, political, economic, and ideological reasons; and, on the other hand, they have tried to write histories of design that reposition the designer as part of a complex web of production and consumption. They have sought to achieve the delicate balance of recovering women's history and mapping out a place for women within it as subjects, while not focusing on the designer to the exclusion of all else—undoubtedly, a complex and enormous task but one worth doing well.

The following references have been selected to give an idea of the range of approaches to the subject, rather than merely a list of the most recent works on the subject.

References. Judith Attfield, "FORM/female FOLLOWS FUNCTION/male: Feminist Critiques of Design," in John Walker (ed.), *Design History and the History of Design* (London, 1989); Judith Attfield and Pat Kirkham, *A View from the Interior. Feminism, Women and Design* (London, 1989); Cheryl Buckley, "Made in Patriarchy: Toward a Feminist Analysis of Women and Design," *Design Issues 3,* 2 (Fall 1986); Cheryl Buckley, *Potters and Paintresses. Women Designers in the Pottery Industry, 1870–1955* (London, 1991); Caroline Evans and Minna Thomton, *Women and Fashion: A New Look* (London, 1989); Elinor Gillian (ed.), *Women and Craft* (London, 1987); Philippa Glanville and Jennifer Faulds Goldsborough, *Women Silversmiths 1685–1845* (London, 1990); Philippa Goodall, "Design and Gender," *Block* 9 (1983); Pat Kirkham, *The Gendered Object* (Manchester, U.K., 1996); Liz McQuiston, *Women in Design, a Contemporary View* (London, 1988).

CHERYL BUCKLEY

DETECTIVE FICTION. Soon after Poe's Dupin tales introduced the detective story proper to English literature in the 1840s, women writers took up the form and have remained in the forefront of the genre ever since. The first two Englishwomen to add to gothic mystery and crime plots the new concept of a central detecting intelligence were Mrs. Henry Wood, née Ellen Price (1814–1887), and Mary Elizabeth Braddon, later Maxwell (1835–1915). Wood, known for the popular *East Lynne* (1861), in *Mrs. Halliburton's Troubles* (1862) used a police sergeant and in *Within the Maze* (1872) used Scotland Yard officials to solve thefts and embezzlements. Braddon's equally popular *Lady Audley's Secret* (1862) borrowed from Wilkie Collins the amateur detective hero who confronts the villain after exhaustive examination of evidence and interviewing of witnesses. Her Robert Audley, an eccentric idler, foreshadows Sherlock Holmes by relying on inference and deduction. *Henry Dunbar* (1864), *Birds of Prey* (1867), and *Charlotte's Inheritance* (1868) are other Braddon novels featuring detectives.

Historians usually credit the American Anna Katharine Green (1846–1935) with writing the first detective novel—Braddon's and Wood's novels having initially appeared in serial form—and her first book, *The Leavenworth Case* (1878), used many elements later to become staples of the form: the suspects all of one household, with the least likely one guilty; an inquest employing ballistics; a diagram of the murder scene. Her police detective Ebenezer Gryce—patient, wise, and looking "not like a detective at all"— set a pattern for fictional professionals. He appears in other novels and in

That Affair Next Door (1897) has a female assistant, Amelia Butterworth, who proves invaluable for her feminine perceptiveness.

Other writers had shown women occasionally detecting, like Collins' clever Marian Halcombe in *The Woman in White*, and even in a professional capacity, as with W. S. Hayward's ladylike police investigator Mrs. Paschal in *The Experiences of a Lady Detective* (1884). Hungarian-born Baroness Emmuska Orczy (1865–1947), whose main contribution to the genre is the armchair detective in *The Old Man in the Corner* (1909), also wrote *Lady Molly of Scotland Yard* (1910) about a beautiful aristocrat who, with her woman assistant, solves crimes while trying to free her imprisoned husband. Like Mrs. Paschal, Lady Molly is intrepid, ingenious, and respected—in her sphere—by male colleagues.

In *The Circular Staircase* (1908) American Mary Roberts Rinehart (1876–1958) has her inquisitive spinster narrator risk her life to unmask a criminal, in what was to become known as the had-I-but-known formula, after the heroine's hindsight realization. The novel was dramatized (as *The Bat*) in several stage and movie versions, and Rinehart used the formula in other novels, such as *Miss Pinkerton* (1932), which featured the nurse-sleuth Hilda Adams. Of a number of women adapting the formula to the gothic mystery, best known is Mignon Eberhart (1899–1996), whose principal sleuth is nurse Sarah Keate in *The Patient in Room 18* (1929) and other novels.

The "golden age" of detective fiction following World War I was dominated by two British women, Dame Agatha Christie (1890–1976) and Dorothy L. Sayers (1893–1957). Between her first novel, *The Mysterious Affair at Styles* (1920), which introduced the Belgian detective Hercule Poirot, and her last published work, *Curtain* (1975), Christie wrote over 80 novels and became the most popular twentieth-century mystery writer. Admired for her skill at constructing puzzles, lively dialogue, and ingenious crimes, as in *Murder on the Orient Express* (1934), she was also criticized for allegedly breaking the rules of fair play in *The Murder of Roger Ackroyd* (1926) by having the narrator turn out to be the murderer. Her other series detective is spinster Jane Marple, seen first in *The Murder at the Vicarage* (1930). In contrast, Sayers wrote only a handful of full-length mysteries, beginning with *Whose Body?* (1923), which introduced her stylishly eccentric Lord Peter Wimsey. In *Gaudy Night* (1935) Wimsey shares the detecting with mystery writer Harriet Vane, whom he marries in *Busman's Honeymoon* (1937). Sayers also wrote many Wimsey short stories, presided over the famous Detection Club, wrote essays on the art of detective fiction, and edited mystery anthologies.

Notable in the next generation of writers are Englishwoman Margery Allingham (1904–1966), whose Albert Campion, "a trifle absent-minded" detective of vaguely aristocratic origins, appears as early as *The Crime at*

Black Dudley (1929) and as late as *The Mind Readers* (1965); the New Zealander Dame Ngaio Marsh (1899–1982), whose Superintendent Roderick Alleyn, also of aristocratic stock, appears in innumerable novels between *A Man Lay Dead* (1934) and *Grave Mistake* (1978), often in theatrical settings where the murders are gruesome; and Scottish-born Elizabeth Mackintosh (1897–1952), who, as Josephine Tey, has rung some original changes on the form in *Miss Pym Disposes* (1946), a moral and psychological study of a student crime, and in *The Daughter of Time* (1951), in which Inspector Alan Grant unravels the fifteenth-century murder of the Princess in the Tower.

Among current British writers Ruth Rendell (b. 1930) has departed somewhat from tradition in making her Chief Inspector Reginald Wexford married, hypertensive, and stationed in Sussex. In novels like *From Doon with Death* (1964) and *Shake Hands Forever* (1975) Rendell mixes strong characterization with social criticism. P. D. James (b. 1920) is noteworthy for her modern settings, such as a home for incurables in *The Black Tower* (1975) and an East Anglian forensic laboratory in *Death of an Expert Witness* (1977). Her series detective is Commander Adam Dalgliesh of Scotland Yard, a published poet, but she also used a young private investigator, Cordelia Gray, in *An Unsuitable Job for a Woman* (1972) and *The Skull beneath the Skin* (1982). Recent American writers include Charlotte Armstrong (1905–1969), whose series character MacDougal Duff probes moral questions in such stories as *Lay On, MacDuff!* (1942); Carolyn Heilbrun (b. 1926), who, writing as Amanda Cross, has the university professor Kate Fansler solving crimes in works like *The James Joyce Murder* (1967); and Patricia Highsmith (1921–1995), who is best known for *Strangers on a Train* (1950) and whose continuing character Tom Ripley is not a detective but a psychopathic killer, as in *Ripley's Game* (1974).

Women's detective fiction over the last century has shown marked differences from men's. Women use less violence and more characterization. Earlier they had, like their male counterparts, seen female detection strengths as intuition and observation; later, more than men, they emphasize women's logic, resourcefulness, and independence. British women favor male detectives, usually professional and upper-class, over female detectives, who tend to be amateurs and middle-class; Americans increasingly choose female private investigators who become personally involved in their cases and are often in physical danger (e.g., Sue Grafton's Kinsey Millhone and Sara Paretsky's V. I. Warshawski). Women's choice of plots involving hidden identities may be connected to personal experiences of pressures to role-play. Braddon, for example, passed for years as the wife of a man already married; Sayers hid the existence of her illegitimate child from even her closest friends. Christie never explained her onetime "amnesiac" disappearance. Women writers often show their protagonist simultaneously solving a crime and resolving a private crisis; by unmasking an impostor, for example, Rinehart's heroine in *The Circular Staircase* comes to a sense of her true self, and Cross' heroine in *The Question of Max* (1976), like Sayers' in *Gaudy Night* almost a half century before, reconciles her feminist principles with love and marriage in the process of unraveling a crime. The inherently conservative nature of detective fiction and the opportunities it allows for inventiveness within formulaic constraints have clearly proven congenial to women writers.

Reference. Kathleen G. Klein, *The Woman Detective: Gender and Genre*, 2d ed. (Champaign, Ill., 1995).

MARY ROSE SULLIVAN

DEVOTIONAL LITERATURE, MEDIEVAL, is probably the most popular of the various types of medieval literature, read or listened to by members of all classes of society; it is defined as literature written for the faithful and intended to develop or heighten feelings of devotion toward God or the saints. Devotional literature is not concerned with teaching theology, but it is didactic in its emphasis on the exemplary Christian life and on the relationship between the individual soul and the divine. Women were some of the best writers of devotional literature; we may also assume that they constituted a large proportion of its audience. Varieties included saints' lives, prayers, hymns or song cycles, guides to prayer, letters of spiritual encouragement, autobiographical narratives of personal spiritual growth, and accounts of women's visions and prophecies.

The prevalence of devotional literature by women attests to the near monopoly on education exercised by the church and to the misogyny in medieval culture that silenced all but the most holy or inspired women. Peter Dronke notes that writing by women "is a response springing from inner needs" resulting in a tone of immediacy; women "look at themselves more concretely and more searchingly than many of the highly accomplished men writers who were their contemporaries" (x). Women who learned to read and write usually did so in convent schools; for them to go on to become writers, they needed the conditions provided by women's communities: scholarly leisure, access to books and materials of book production, economic support, freedom from external responsibilities and from repeated pregnancies and child raising (Wilson, ix). Women without these advantages who felt called to be visionary writers strove to create comparable conditions for themselves so that their ideas and experiences could be written down, even if they had not learned to read and write (Petroff, 27–28).

Women are among the earliest writers of devotional literature. The autobiographical *Passion of Saints Perpetua and Felicity* dates from 203; Egeria's account of her pilgrimage to the holy land (*Itinerarium or Peregrinatio Aetheriae*) dates from the following century. In the eighth century, Frankish nuns write vitae of their famous contemporaries, a practice that continued in French and German convents until the end of the Middle Ages. At about the same time, Anglo-Saxon nuns active in the Christianizing of Germany and in charge of producing the books needed by this mission wrote letters and an epic account of the life of St. Willibald. More famous writers include the dramatist Hrotsvit of Gandersheim and the mystic Hildegard of Bingen.

The type of devotional literature in which women especially excelled is visionary or spiritual autobiography. The earliest example is St. Perpetua's account of her martyrdom, which describes an area of female experience— dreams and prophecies expressing the subjective experience of the divine— that by the twelfth century had become the dominant mode of women's religious writing. Visions, nurtured by the devotional meditations taught to women, provided the structure and content; the visionary was respected in medieval society, and a female visionary could teach others what God or one of the saints had taught her, even when as a woman she ought not to teach in public. Some of these writers are well known to students of mysticism: Mechthild of Magdeburg, Gertrude the Great, Hadewijch, Bea-trijs van Tienen. Others were once influential but now forgotten: Umiltà of Faenza and Marguerite d'Oingt. Several—Marguerite Porete and Na Prous Boneta—were burned at the stake as heretics. Most of the famous mystics of the fourteenth and fifteenth centuries were deeply influenced by this female tradition: Angela of Foligno, Catherine of Siena, Julian of Norwich, Margery Kempe. These autobiographies are also models for the Christian life, prophecies of the future of the church, and guides to devotion. Many of women's devotional writings are among the earliest texts in the vernac-ular languages, a fact that suggests that these writings responded to a felt need among laypeople and religious people of both sexes for guidance to the spiritual life.

Similar autobiographies were often written in the late fifteenth and six-teenth centuries by radical reformers of existing monastic orders. The works of St. Teresa of Ávila are the culmination of this tradition and follow upon the earlier writings of Magdalena Beutler of Freiburg, Catherine of Genoa, and Catherine of Bologna. Scholars are only now identifying and translating women's devotional literature. Many questions remain to be explored: the importance of women writers' bilingualism (their ability to think and/or read and write in both Latin and their own vernacular lan-guage), their combination of oral and written methods of composition, their audience, their awareness of a female visionary tradition.

References. Susan Groag Bell, "Medieval Women Book Owners: Arbiters of Lay Piety and Ambassadors of Culture," *Signs* 7 (1981–1982): 742–769; Peter Dronke; *Women Writers of the Middle Ages* (Cambridge, Mass., 1984); Lina Eckenstein, *Women under Monasticism* (Cambridge, England, 1896; still useful); Elizabeth Pe-troff, *Medieval Women's Visionary Literature* (Oxford, 1986); Kurt Ruh, "Begin-nenmystik: Hadewijch, Mechthild von Magdeburg, Marguerite Porete," *Zeitschrift fur deutsches Altertum und deutsche Literatur* 106 (1977): 265–277; Paul Szarmach (ed.), *An Introduction to the Medieval Mystics of Europe* (Albany, N.Y., 1984); Katharina M. Wilson, *Medieval Women Writers* (Athens, Ga., 1984).

ELIZABETH PETROFF

DIFFERENTIAL SOCIALIZATION is that lifelong process based on social interaction by which individuals develop those attitudes and behaviors considered appropriate to their gender roles.* Every society assigns females and males to differing roles; therefore, every society must include structures and processes to ensure that males and females develop those characteristics assigned to each sex. The predominant agencies of differential socialization include family,* schools, peer groups, the media, and public opinion.

Sex roles and stereotyped expectation begin shaping people's lives even before they are born. When asked whether they had a preference for the sex of their firstborn child, two-thirds of the adults questioned in a survey expressed a preference; 92 percent of those with a preference wanted a boy. The influence of sex-role expectations becomes more apparent after the babies are born; parents tend to have different expectations for sons and daughters from birth. In the study, 30 pairs of parents of newborns were interviewed within 24 hours of their infants' birth. No objective differences between the babies in birth weight, length, or any other physical or neurological characteristics were evident. Fathers were especially influenced by the sex of their child; they described their daughters as more inattentive, delicate, and weak than did the mothers, while the fathers rated their sons as stronger, better coordinated, and more alert than did the mothers. Both mothers and fathers of girls described their infants as little, beautiful, pretty, and cute more often than did parents of boys; parents of boys, on the other hand, were more likely to describe their infants as big. We find, then, that early sex-role expectations set in motion a complex pattern that creates in individuals the characteristics expected. As a classic statement of social psychology—the "self-fulfilling prophecy"*—states, we become what we are called; the labels attached to us create what they describe.

The differential treatment of male and female infants is closely connected to parents' sex-role expectations. For example, mothers of females have been observed to touch their infants more often than mothers of males. They also talked to, and played with, their daughters more often. By 13 months, the girls, in turn, talked to, and touched, their mothers more often than did the boys. This difference in treatment by parents of their sons and daughters can be further seen in children's bedroom furnishings: girls' rooms contain more floral furnishings and more dolls, while boys' rooms contain more animal furnishings, more educational toys, more athletic equipment, more art materials, and more vehicles (see Schaffer).

Most researchers agree that male and female infants show more similarities than differences during infancy and early childhood and that females and males follow similar developmental paths. Despite these developmental similarities, however, young children are being provided the basic information on how girls and boys, women and men, should behave.

During adolescence major differences in sex-role behavior become much stronger, laying the groundwork for adult roles. Socialization pressures become more pronounced, and social reinforcement encourages different behavior from girls and boys. Boys are encouraged to be competitive and assertive and goal seekers, being strongly supported in identifying and pursuing career goals and in developing fully their interpersonal, intellectual, and physical skills and abilities. Girls, on the other hand, often find themselves in a "double-bind"* situation: a conflict between achievement and "femininity"* (Horner). Sex-role prescriptions frequently reward popularity and social ability for girls more than academic and intellectual achievement. Girls are often discouraged from in-depth preparation for a specific career, being urged rather to maintain a flexible identity that will be compatible with their anticipated future roles as wife and mother, while boys are told that they must be successful in a job or career as the way to prepare for shouldering family responsibilities. While parents and family continue to play an important role in differential socialization, during the adolescent years the most important influences are school and peer groups.

While teachers and other school personnel are becoming more sensitive to the detrimental effects of sex-role stereotypes on both boys and girls, the schools continue as powerful agents of differential socialization. Teachers often directly influence sex roles by conveying feelings about appropriate or inappropriate behavior. Throughout their school experience, girls and boys are treated differently. Lisa A. Serbin and K. Daniel O'Leary, for example, report a study of teacher–student classroom interaction where teachers reinforced boys' aggressiveness by responding immediately to boys who misbehaved and by giving them a great deal of attention. All the teachers observed gave the boys more attention and twice as much individual instruction on tasks than they gave girls. Boys were rewarded more for academic achievement, while girls were rewarded for staying close to the teachers and for dependency. Boys were encouraged to take risks, to be creative, to be independent, while teachers were more likely to take over girls' tasks, finishing them for the girls. Numerous studies show that these differential expectations and different patterns of interaction continue through students' sex-role identity as well as affecting academic pursuits. In addition to teachers' expectations and actions, school curricula and textbooks themselves offer powerful, but stereotyped, portraits of appropriate sex-role behavior. Boys and men are far more likely to be characters in school literature, to be used as examples in textbook illustrations and exercises, and to be shown in active, assertive roles, while girls and women are absent, are shown in supportive roles, or act as a passive audience for boys' exploits (see Best; Orenstein).

Especially during adolescence, peer groups are particularly powerful in socializing girls and boys into sex roles. Peer groups typically encourage activities that are greatly influenced by sex-role stereotypes. Acceptance by peer groups entails conforming and subscribing to the values, norms, and goals of the group. Deviance is punished by the threat of withdrawal of support and friendship. The stigmatizing of deviants and the avoidance of them set clear, although unidimensional, standards of what is acceptable. The forces for conformity are probably more intense during adolescence than at any other time during the life cycle (see Taylor, Gilligan, and Sullivan).

The media, particularly television, are potent agencies of differential socialization, especially in their provision of largely stereotyped images of appropriate female and male roles. Television is especially important since nearly everyone in America watches television; for preschool children, viewing television consumes more time than any other activity except sleeping. Studies continue to find marked differences in the portrayal of female and male characters. There are far more male characters on television; further, male characters are shown as aggressive, constructive, helpful, and more likely to be rewarded for their behavior, while female characters are usually portrayed as passive, deferent, and often punished if they were too aggressive or active. This characterization is even more true of television's commercial advertisements (see, e.g., Ang; Courtney and Whipple).

The effects of differential socialization are to produce adults with the knowledge, skills, motivation, and emotional tendencies to perform the sex roles appropriate to their status. Humans are not, of course, automatons, but socialization acts powerfully to produce in us not only the ability but the desire to take on, and enact, our gender roles. Socialization is a lifelong process. Traditional family structures and expectations, schools organized along sexist lines offering stereotyped curricula, peer groups operating as intensifiers and transmitters of traditional culture, and the media and public opinion reinforcing sexist images work to produce humans limited to sex-linked repertoires of acts and feelings. But socialization is also a human process that can be restructured to expand, rather than limit, the human repertoire.

References. I. Ang, *Watching "Dallas": Soap Opera and the Melodramatic Imagination* (London, 1985); R. Best, *We've All Got Scars: What Boys and Girls Learn in Elementary School* (Bloomington, Ind., 1983); A. Courtney and T. Whipple, *Sex Stereotyping in Advertising* (Lexington, Mass., 1983); M. Horner, "Toward an Understanding of Achievement Related Conflict in Women," *Journal of Social Issues* 28 (1972): 157–175; P. Orenstein, *School Girls: Young Women, Self-Esteem, and the Confidence Gap* (New York, 1994), (Rubin, Provenzano, and Luria, "The Eye of the Beholder: Parent's Views on Sex of Newborns," *American Journal of Orthopsychiatry* 44 [1974]: 512–519); K. F. Schaffer, *Sex Roles and Human Behavior* (Cambridge, Mass., 1981); L. A. Serbin and K. D. O'Leary, "How Nursery Schools Teach Girls to Shut Up," *Psychology Today* 9 (1975): 56–58; J. McL. Taylor, C. Gilligan, and A. M. Sullivan, *Between Voice and Silence: Women and Girls, Race and Relationship* (Cambridge, Mass., 1995).

ALLEN SCARBORO

DISCRIMINATION occurs in the context of employment when employers assign similarly qualified men and women to different kinds of jobs, give women lower promotion opportunities than men, or allot women salaries and fringe benefits inferior to those given to similarly qualified men. Discrimination also arises in other economic contexts—women, on account of their sex, are sometimes refused the right to borrow money or buy on credit, to purchase insurance on the same basis as men, to buy or rent a house or apartment, or to try out an automobile that is for sale. Women are sometimes excluded from educational opportunities on account of their gender. They suffer many social snubs, which are damaging in the context of work. Males commonly display a lack of interest in women colleagues' opinions and suggestions. Experiments conducted by psychologists have shown that writing or artwork attributed to a woman is rated as of lower quality than identical work attributed to a man. Sometimes discrimination takes the form of sexual harassment,* in which a woman in a typically male job is hazed by coworkers who annoy her with sexual questions, suggestions, and mock invitations. The "social" forms of discrimination all serve directly or indirectly to impair women's economic opportunities.

Discrimination reduces women's direct access to economic means of self-support, reinforcing the economic disadvantage that women suffer on account of childbirth,* childrearing, and socialization to fit into female roles. Discrimination thus has intensified women's need to form relationships with men in order to gain access to economic goods. For this reason it has been a major cause of women's subordination to men in the family and in society generally.

Full-time women workers in the United States in the 1980s earn 20 to 25 percent less than men of similar education and length of experience. In Japan and Ireland, the gap between men's and women's pay is greater than it is in the United States, but in most of the other developed countries the gap is lower. However, there is no country in which women have parity with men in earnings.

There has been considerable controversy among economists as to how much of the difference in pay between women and men is due to discrimination. Some economists have argued that discrimination against capable women employees in favor of less capable male employees would go counter to the interests of employers. They go on to deduce that discrimination must therefore be rare or nonexistent. These economists attribute women's lower wages not to employer discrimination but to women's own choices. Women's vocational choices are limited, these economists argue, by their willing acceptance of the burden of child care* and housework.* On the other side of the argument is case study material derived from lawsuits, containing testimony to grossly discriminatory practices. Also favoring the hypothesis of pervasive discrimination is the bulk of statistical studies whose authors have looked for evidence that the entire salary gap between the sexes might be explained away innocently but have failed to find it.

Occupational segregation* is the leading symptom of discrimination in employment. Women have been welcomed only in a narrow range of occupations: clerical worker, retail sales worker, nurse, librarian, teacher of young children, and low-level factory and service worker. In the United States in 1985, about half the women workers were employed in those occupations in which the workers were more than three-quarters female. Research that has focused on placement within individual workplaces shows that the isolation of women from men doing the same work is even more extreme than suggested by the occupational statistics. For example, about 20 percent of the workers in the occupation "waiters and waitresses" are men. But the colleagues of the typical waitress are not 20 percent male; on the contrary, restaurants that hire men to wait on tables typically hire no women at all, and those hiring women hire no men.

Discrimination in employment derives from a number of sources. Males have tended to behave in ways that contribute to the maintenance of male superiority. Women are denied the opportunity to have jobs in which they would exercise authority, have high pay, and interact with men as equals. Employers appear to have beliefs about women's incapacity for certain work; as an example, women have been excluded in many instances from jobs in which operating a vehicle, even a passenger car, is part of the duties. Employers have also reasoned that family duties (from which men have been able to keep themselves aloof) make women less desirable employees in certain roles. Employers have not been willing to commit resources to training women on the grounds, now shown to be false, that women are more likely to quit than men.

In the United States, an Equal Pay Act was passed in 1963. It required an individual employer to pay women and men the same wage if they had virtually identical jobs. The following year, the Civil Rights Act was passed, containing far broader provisions barring discrimination in employment on account of sex as well as race, religion, or national origin. The Civil Rights Act makes it unlawful for employers to discriminate in hiring, job assignment, promotion, pay, or fringe benefits. It forbids employers to limit, segregate, or classify employees or applicants by sex in any way that might adversely affect them. The courts have interpreted the Civil Rights Act as forbidding employers to bar women as candidates for any job, even in cases where a considerably smaller proportion of women than men are capable of performing it. Tests given to job candidates that pass a smaller proportion of women than men, unless such tests can be shown to be job-related, also violate the act. The United States has also enacted laws that forbid discrimination in awarding credit and that bar federal support of school programs in which male and female students are treated differently. Through the mid-1980s, complaints to enforcement agencies or court suits brought under these laws have had only a small result in reducing the economic disparities between women and men. More vigorous attacks on job segregation might be mounted through affirmative action plans mandating employers to achieve numerical goals for the hiring of women in all occupations on specific timetables. Such goals and timetables have been a part of the U.S. government program to require firms that sell to it to achieve better representation of workers by race and sex. However, enforcement of the program has been slack.

"Pay equity," or "comparable worth,"* offers a second possibility of accelerating progress against discrimination and its effects. The idea of pay equity is that employers should be required to adjust upward the wages of workers in the traditionally female occupations so as to make them commensurate with the pay of traditionally male occupations requiring similar levels of skill, mental ability, and responsibility. In Australia and England, pay equity adjustments have had considerable success in raising wages of women workers with little discernible adverse effect. In the United States, pay equity campaigns have, for the most part, been targeted against state and local governments in their role as employers.

References. B. R. Bergmann, *The Economic Emergence of Women* (New York, 1986); D. J. Treiman and H. I. Hartmann, *Women, Work and Wages: Equal Pay for Jobs of Equal Value* (Washington, D.C., 1981).

BARBARA R. BERGMANN

DISPLACED HOMEMAKER is a woman whose principal job has been that of unpaid homemaker and who has lost her main source of support because of the dissolution of her marriage or the cessation of income from other sources. (Definitions vary; the preceding is based on the definition in *Displaced Homemakers*). The woman is usually in the 35- to 60-year age span and either has not been in the paid labor force or has earnings below the subsistence level. She either has no marketable skills or has rusty or outdated skills. Usually she is too young (under 60) for Social Security,* and in many cases her youngest child has become too old for public assistance.

Estimates of the number of displaced homemakers in 1983 varied, largely according to definition, from about 2 million to 4 million. The Office of Technical Assessment estimate of displaced homemakers between 35 and 64 years of age was 2.2 million. More than 60 percent were over age 45, and over 60 percent still had children living at home.

Many displaced homemakers just recently have had the wrenching emotional experience of the death of a loved one or a divorce. Many are facing poverty* for the first time in their lives. Feelings of depression* and inadequacy are likely to be heightened as they try to cope with their new life circumstances.

To prepare to support themselves and their families, displaced home-makers need a variety of services, including counseling; training to refresh and/or update skills, learn marketable skills, or acquire basic education; and job placement. Many need financial support for transportation, child care,* or living expenses, and emotional support. Personal counseling is at least as important as vocational counseling, and support groups are im-portant in the transition.

The first displaced homemaker center opened in California in 1975. Since then, with state, very modest federal (until 1985 federal support was not over $10 million at its height), and private funds, the number of centers increased. In 1984, there were at least 425 centers, located in almost every state and the District of Columbia, some independent but most connected with educational institutions, women's centers, organizations such as the Young Men's Christian Association (YMCA). They serve anywhere from a handful to several thousand clients a year and offer services from coun-seling and referral only, to a full range of counseling and support service through training,* to job placement and follow-up (*Displaced Homemak-ers*, 15).

There have always been displaced homemakers, but the rapid increase in divorces coupled with the changes in spousal support that came with no-fault divorce* greatly increased their numbers in the 1970s and 1980s. As more women continue in the workforce after marriage, and the number of full-time homemakers continues to decline, the number of displaced homemakers in need of support services will also decrease. However, bar-ring the very unlikely return to more stringent divorce laws, as long as there are full-time homemakers, the need for support services for women whose long-term marriages have collapsed will continue.

Reference. *Displaced Homemakers: Programs and Policy—An Interim Report* (Washington, D.C., 1985).

DIVORCE IN THE UNITED STATES.

DIVORCE IN THE UNITED STATES. Colonial divorce laws and proce-dures were fundamentally sexist. The laws of the northern colonies, al-though more expansive than those of England, worked in ways that discriminated against women; for example, both men and women could receive divorces on the grounds of adultery,* but men were the chief ben-eficiaries of this law, evidence suggesting the depth of the sexual double standard.* In the South, absolute divorce was proscribed, thereby leaving women at the mercy of their more powerful husbands. This is not to say that the double standard and legal restrictions left colonial women with no recourse. Although only a few hundred colonial women legally dissolved their marriages, several thousand more simply deserted their husbands.

These "self-divorces" reveal a higher level of marital incompatibility than the low divorce rate of the period would suggest: they also prove that thousands of women found the risks of independence more inviting than continued residence with husbands they despised.

During and after the American Revolution, women's situation regarding divorce improved. Wives increasingly included allegations of adultery among their complaints; moreover, most state legislatures expanded the grounds of divorce. Although a variety of new grounds were added to statutory laws, the inclusion of cruelty as a just cause played a key role in fueling the surge of female divorce complaints in the nineteenth century. By 1900, approximately two-thirds of all divorces went to women, and by 1929, 44 percent of all divorces granted to women came on the grounds of cruelty. What is more, judges continually expanded the interpretation of cruelty until some late nineteenth-century jurists began recognizing "mental cruelty" as a sufficient reason for divorce, a development that allowed husbands, but especially wives, to break free of spouses who threatened no violence but who made life miserable nevertheless. The thousands of women who received divorces on the grounds of cruelty and desertion—the two most common late-nineteenth-century complaints—rarely received alimony* or child support but almost always received custody of the children. Thus, divorce for women brought some independence but also the advent of new obligations, dependencies, and financial difficulties.

As the divorce rate continued to rise in the late nineteenth and early twentieth centuries, supporters and opponents of divorce engaged in a protracted debate. On one side stood a handful of feminists and a more numerous group of liberals who supported access to divorce. For feminists like Elizabeth Cady Stanton, women needed divorce to free themselves from fools and tyrants; for liberals, divorce was a remedy in line with their commitments to freedom and happiness. On the other side stood conservatives who viewed divorce as a sign of female selfishness and wider social breakdown: to their mind, tougher laws, an end to divorce havens, and a reinvigoration of traditional morality were needed to stop this fearful erosion of traditional morality and social stability.

Although conservatives had no luck with their hope for a uniform divorce code, they did manage to abolish catchall omnibus clauses, restrict the rights of remarriage, and impose stricter residency requirements on those seeking a divorce, but such reforms could not stand against the small army of petitioners seeking an end to marriage. Fed by rising romantic and sexual expectations within marriage, increased leisure time* and consumption wants, growing female opportunities for economic self-support, and expansive judicial interpretations of statutory laws, the divorce rate continued to rise in the early twentieth century. By 1920 there were 3.41 divorces per 1,000 married population, up from 0.81 in 1870. Almost 150,000 divorces were granted in 1920: the figure a half century earlier was scarcely more than 11,000.

Divorce continued to be a major social issue in the first half of the twentieth century. Progressive reformers shifted the focus away from individual moral failure and toward an emphasis upon the social, economic, political, and demographic changes that produced rising rates of divorce. Progressives believed only fundamental changes could reduce the frequency of divorce; in the meantime, reformers proposed stricter access to marriage, education about marriage* and family life, and even trial marriages to stem the rate of divorce.

Environmental interpretations soon gave way to clinical conceptions of divorce, and from 1910 to 1940, the divorce question was couched in the language of psychopathology and medicine: rejecting earlier moral or environmental explanations, divorce reformers now used psychological and medical terminology to brand divorce seekers as neurotic, infantile, and abnormal. The solution to the divorce problem, reformers now believed, lay in curing the neuroses that produced divorce, but the agent of cure was to be a therapeutic, patriarchal legal system singularly ill equipped for the task. All too easily, legal therapy in the form of family courts, social work investigations, reconciliation sessions, and counseling services simply degenerated into a form of patriarchal state control. Moreover, reformers often found it difficult to implement these reforms in the face of legislative conservatism, splits within the reform camp, and a continued emphasis on divorce as an adversarial rather than a therapeutic procedure.

The post–World War II story is one of sharply rising divorce rates, the emergence of no-fault divorce,* and the growing recognition that no-fault laws have been a disaster for women and children. Beginning with California's no-fault law of 1969, all but two states had some kind of no-fault law in place by the mid-1980s. Promising an end to the fraud, collusion, and acrimony that accompanied the adversarial system of divorce, no-fault was initially hailed as a significant and progressive achievement in the history of divorce litigation. The consequences, however, have left women and their dependents worse off than they were before the change; the reason is that no-fault presupposes an equality between husbands and wives that has no basis in reality. Instead, men's standard of living rises sharply in the first year following divorce, whereas women's and children's declines by over 70 percent, a situation brought on by men's "cashing out" on home sales and by inadequate alimony awards and child support payments. No-fault reflects the erroneous assumption that women—often out of the job market for years and ill equipped by training* or education for today's job market—can readily become self-supporting, independent household heads. Only spousal and child support awards founded on an attempt to achieve parity in standards of living can bring justice to women and their dependents. Until that happens, the divorce revolution of no-fault will be a revolution that made losers of women and children.

References. R. L. Griswold, *Family and Divorce in California, 1850–1890: Victorian Illusions and Everyday Realities* (Albany, 1982); L. Halem, *Divorce Reform: Changing Legal and Social Perspectives* (New York, 1980); E. T. May, *Great Expectations: Marriage and Divorce in Post Victorian America* (Chicago, 1980); W. O'Neill, *Divorce in the Progressive Era* (New Haven, Conn., 1967); L. Weitzman, *The Divorce Revolution: The Unexpected Social and Economic Consequences for Women and Children in America* (New York, 1985).

ROBERT L. GRISWOLD

DOMESTIC NOVEL includes works in the traditional canon, works just on the fringe of it, and scores of second-rate works of popular fiction. This variety reflects the confusion between the use of *domestic novel* as a literary term and its use as a popular one. As a specific term of literary criticism, *domestic novel of manners* is preferable to *domestic novel*. The domestic novel of manners is largely a phenomenon of nineteenth-century British literature and includes a number of texts that have been variously categorized as domestic fiction, domestic romance, social problem novels, governess novels, religious novels, and novels of manners.

The earliest novels that unequivocally idealize domesticity are by Maria Edgeworth, notably *Belinda* (1801) and *Patronage* (1814). The works of Jane Austen share many of the conventions of the domestic novel of manners, although Austen works within the framework of family life without actually idealizing it. The next major works of domestic fiction come in the 1840s and 1850s with the works of Charlotte and Anne Brontë and Elizabeth Gaskell. The novels of all three women show variations on the conventional pattern of the genre yet remain solidly within it. Two novels by George Eliot (*The Mill on the Floss* [1860] and *Middlemarch* [1871–1872]) mark the end of the genre as a major literary category.

The conventional idealization of domesticity is prefigured in *Pamela* (1740), *The Vicar of Wakefield* (1766), and *Evelina* (1778), to cite only three better-known and more substantial examples. These novels, in turn, draw upon an earlier tradition of sentimental romance, the conventional roots of which lie in the Middle Ages and, in the case of some conventions, beyond. Within the sentimental tradition the good female character, the heroine, is a series of negations—purity, ignorance, passive dependence—that must be preserved. This conception of ideal female character is the cornerstone of the primary component of the conventional pattern of the domestic novel of manners: the idealization of domesticity and the sanctification of middle-class, Christian, and family-centered values that dominate characterization, plots, and themes.

The central character, the imaginative heroine, is both an avid reader and a teller of tales, habits that link her closely to her author, reinforcing the textual interpenetration of the genre and its characteristic combination of reading and writing. These texts are not only implicitly parasitic upon earlier texts (and one another) but explicitly so. In early domestic novels of manners self-referentiality is manifest primarily as a preoccupation with literature, especially novels. As the convention evolves during the nineteenth century, it is increasingly preoccupied with language itself, as medium, metaphor, method. Heroines are regularly compared to heroines of fiction and then evaluated in terms of their ability to fulfill conventional requirements. The narrative never fails to call attention to them and consequently to itself, whenever they fall short of, or positively contravene, conventional ideals.

Love is at the heart of all domestic novels of manners in the sense that the plot always revolves around the vicissitudes of the heroine's preparations to love and be loved. The fact that the romantic love she seeks is sanctioned only within the confines of marriage is perhaps the most blatant instance of the idealization of domesticity. Happiness rewards only those characters who love in the right place at the right time, and surprisingly few characters actually achieve this ideal. There are, moreover, very few happily married couples in these texts. The happiest couples are those just on the threshold of married life, as though the conventional "happy ending," the wedding, were actually the end of happiness. As a plot device, the heroine's marriage persists as the traditional closure of the domestic novel of manners long after the authors of these texts have begun to acknowledge its ambivalence explicitly.

The thematic focus of the domestic novel of manners shifts according to subgeneric category. The earliest examples of the genre are often attacks on sentimental or gothic romance. Maria Edgeworth's *Belinda* and Jane Austen's *Northanger Abbey* (1818), for example, parody the conventional characterization of the heroine without seriously questioning traditional standards of female conduct or the pivotal role of marriage in a woman's life. Yet both novels represent a step forward in the concept of female character in that the passivity of absolute purity and ignorance is replaced by the necessity for moral development. Moral development follows the loss of romantic fictional illusions for both Belinda Portman and Catherine Morland. Marriage retains its thematic and narrative importance as both goal and closure.

Between 1830 and 1870 a handful of themes dominated Victorian fiction in general and the domestic novel of manners in particular. The three most pervasive of these themes were the status of women, social reform, and religion. The controversy surrounding the status of women at this time was very often addressed through the character of the governess and the closely related problems of the "fallen woman" and prostitution. Questions of social reform were more various but concentrated on industrial relations, public versus private charity, and the education of the working class. The crucial religious concern of the period might be characterized generally as the struggle between faith and doubt, a struggle that took numerous forms, both publicly and privately.

These three themes became loci for the reformation of many of the conventions of the domestic novel of manners, reformations that contributed to the creation of recognizable subgenres: governess novels, social problem novels, and religious novels. The last category is best represented by the works of Charlotte Yonge, whose domestic novels read rather like Evangelical tracts. In spite of Yonge's achievement, the religious novel, unlike the other significant variants of the domestic novel in this period, contributed little of lasting value to the mainstream tradition.

The governess novel was one of the most common vehicles for literary treatment of the woman question, a unique social problem crossing class lines, regional boundaries, and occupational categories. Although other kinds of workingwomen are occasionally depicted in novels of this period (Elizabeth Gaskell's *Mary Barton* [1848] and Anne Brontë's *The Tenant of Wildfell Hall* [1848], e.g.), the plight of the workingwoman and her salvation through marriage are most often treated in governess novels. Lady Blessington's *The Governess* (1839) is, in many ways, the prototype of this subgenre, but its influence pales beside the sensation made by Charlotte Brontë's *Jane Eyre* (1847).

Elizabeth Gaskell's *North and South* (1854–1855) is the best example of the social problem novel informed by domestic standards and values. It is much superior to Gaskell's earlier novels in this vein, *Mary Barton and Ruth* (1853), and is even more successful than *Jane Eyre* as a novel of manners. In *North and South* Gaskell domesticates the conventions of social relevance in two important ways. First, the explicit analyses of social problems so central to this subgenre are placed in a domestic setting rather than in a mill, in the streets, or in a neutral narrative limbo. Second, household goods and family relationships are used to illustrate the effects of abstract social problems on individual human families.

The ultimate development of the domestic novel of manners comes in the works of George Eliot. *The Mill on the Floss* might be described as a mirror image of a domestic novel of manners, inverting, as it does, the major conventional mode of the genre, the idealization of domesticity. The traditional characteristics of the ideal female character (passivity, ignorance, purity, renunciation) are still in evidence, but the valuation of these traits has been reversed. Acquisition and preservation of these "virtues" reward Maggie Tulliver not with marriage but with death, the epitome of passive self-effacement. Throughout the novel marriage and family life are associated with images of oppression, self-immolation, and death.

In *Middlemarch* Eliot most clearly achieves her desire to render the profound complexities of human character and the lamentably elusive nature of human dreams, including the dream of domestic bliss. The novel's most important themes—marriage, the egoism of perception, and imagination as illusion—shatter the conventional domestic ideals of the genre beyond redemption. Specifically, earlier perceptions of marriage as culmination and conclusion are consistently undermined. Even the marriage of Will and Dorothea fails to provide the conventional perfect fulfillment.

The patterns of characterization, plot, and theme in the domestic novel of manners reveal the close association of that genre with the concept of female bildungsroman (a novel concerned with the formation of the hero's character) in nineteenth-century British literature. The loss of romantic illusions that is so often equated with the heroine's moral development in domestic novels of manners was itself an illusion. Romance was not truly discredited or overthrown; it was institutionalized in the "ideal marriage."

References. Lynne Agress, *The Feminine Irony: Women on Women in Early Nineteenth-Century English Literature* (Cranbury, N.J., 1978); Jenni Calder, *Women and Marriage in Victorian Fiction* (London, 1976); Vineta Colby, *Yesterday's Woman: Domestic Realism in the English Novel* (Princeton, N.J., 1974); Susan Siefert, *The Dilemma of the Talented Heroine: A Study in Nineteenth-Century Fiction* (Montreal, 1977).

ELIZABETH BOYD THOMPSON

DOMESTIC SERVICE is an occupation involving such tasks as cooking, cleaning, washing, ironing, sewing, and child care,* traditionally done by unpaid female family members. In the nineteenth century it emerged as the primary form of gainful employment for women in countries undergoing industrialization. The term "domestic servant" usually referred to someone employed full-time and living on the premises of a private household. By the mid-1800s, in such countries as the United States, France, and England, most domestic servants were women, and in the United States by 1870 over half of all women workers and over two-thirds of all women working in non–farm-related occupations were servants.

The growth of industrial capitalism, urbanization, and a large and increasingly status-conscious urban middle class, with economic changes in rural areas, explains the emergence of domestic service as the primary occupation for women. During the period 1790–1830, these changes began to undermine the household economy throughout England, the United States, and certain regions of Europe, depriving many women of such traditional domestic responsibilities as spinning, while at the same time creating a need for additional family income. These rural and working-class women provided a fairly inexpensive supply of labor just as the growing number of middle-class families began to predicate their status and identities on being able to release their own wives and daughters from all the more onerous aspects of household labor.

Although domestic service was not a new occupation, by the mid-nineteenth century the nature of the job had been transformed. Previously, most domestic servants worked for the nobility of Europe and the wealthiest families of America, where large, complex staffs of servants had been the standard, and male servants usually outnumbered females. This pattern began to change dramatically in the eighteenth century as the commercial and industrial revolutions provided a wide range of jobs outside domestic service for men and as women became available for service at much lower wages. By 1851, less than a third of the servants in France and no more than 10 percent in the United States and England were male. In addition, while it had not been uncommon for less wealthy rural households to hire females to perform domestic chores, prior to the late eighteenth century most of these women were considered "hired help" rather than servants. They were often daughters of neighboring farmers, usually employed for intermittent periods of time and informally incorporated into the family* (sitting down with the family for meals, etc.).

In contrast, the typical domestic servant of the nineteenth century was unlikely to be either a male member of a large domestic staff or a friend of the family acting as temporary "hired help." Instead, she was most likely to be a young, unmarried female who lived and worked alongside, at most, one other servant in a small, middle-class urban household. Although, as was true previously, most domestic servants in England, Europe, and rural America were native-born, in the large northern cities of America, where the bulk of domestic service jobs were found, immigrant women and their daughters predominated, with Irish and Scandinavians more likely than any other group to work as servants.

Although domestic service jobs varied, the majority of servants were "maids-of-all-work" and the only live-in staff. They were responsible for cooking, waiting on tables, washing the dishes, all cleaning and bed making, laundry and ironing, mending, and child care. If a second live-in domestic was hired, it was usually as cook or child's nurse. For all live-in servants the hours were long, on average 11 to 12 a day, seven days a week, and a domestic servant was "on call" 24 hours a day. Domestic servants traditionally got one or two afternoons a week off, but they were expected to have accomplished most of the daily chores, which meant working at least seven hours before leaving. Wages including room and board (which varied considerably in quality) were the same as, or higher than, wages of other unskilled or semiskilled occupations available to women but generally lower than professional or clerical wages.

Wages, however, did not usually determine whether or not a woman chose domestic service employment. Although some women preferred it, particularly newly arrived immigrants who found the assurance of room and board a distinct advantage, most women took the job because lack of education, limited job opportunities in the area, or discrimination* made other jobs inaccessible. Long hours, hard physical labor, cramped living quarters, and bad food made domestic service undesirable; but tense employee–employer relations and the job's low status seem to have represented its major drawbacks. Class, ethnic, and religious differences strained the working relationships of employers and servants. Servants bitterly resented the control their employers exercised over their dress, speech, use of leisure time,* and contact with family and friends.

Just as the early stages of industrialization prompted the emergence of domestic service as the primary form of employment for women, the maturation of industrialization played an important role in its decreasing significance. Between 1890 and 1920, although the demand for domestic servants persisted, the importance of the job for women diminished. Child labor laws and compulsory education that kept the very young out of the workforce, combined with immigration restrictions that cut off the flow of immigrant labor, depleted two of the traditional sources of domestic labor. In addition, as the industrial economies matured, a much wider array of jobs for women became available, and greater proportions of women chose offices, stores, and factories as their place of employment. As a result, in the United States the proportion of women working in domestic service fell from over half in 1870 to less than a fifth in 1920.

The women in, and the nature of, the job changed as well during this period. Women doing household labor were older, less likely to be single, and less likely to be white or foreign-born. The percentage of black domestic servants rose from 24 percent in 1890 to 40 percent in 1920. To a degree, because of these changes, domestic service ceased to be done by women who lived in. A growing proportion of the women in domestic service, like the black women who were denied access to alternative forms of female employment, were married and unwilling to live apart from their own families.

In conclusion, throughout the twentieth century domestic service has become an increasingly marginal job for women in industrialized nations, held by a small percentage of women who generally, for reasons of race, ethnicity, or marital status, cannot obtain other forms of employment. However, for those women still engaged in household employment the disadvantages of long hours, relatively low wages, difficult personal relations with employers, and lack of status have persisted to the modern period.

References. F. E. Dudden, *Serving Women: Household Service in Nineteenth-Century America* (Middletown, Conn., 1983); D. M. Katzman, *Seven Days a Week: Domestic Service in Industrializing America* (New York, 1978); T. McBride, *The Domestic Revolution: The Modernization of Household Service in England and France, 1820–1920* (New York, 1976).

MARY LOU LOCKE

DOMESTIC SPHERE comprises the family* and household and all the duties, activities, and concerns associated with their functioning. In traditional society the domestic sphere has been woman's primary concern. In the sexual segregation of labor, she has usually been responsible for the primary care and rearing of small children, the tasks necessary in cleaning the house, clothing and feeding members of the household, and production for household consumption. On the other hand, the man's primary concern was the public sphere*: production for the market, buying and selling in the market, defense of the home, and relations with the world outside the home.

The duties and concerns of women and men were never exclusive to one sphere, and the spheres themselves overlapped (e.g., what is woman's work in one society might be man's work in another, surpluses from production for household consumption were sold, men purchased items for household use, women influenced public policy, directly or indirectly). However, at the end of the eighteenth and in the early nineteenth centuries, as men's productive activities left the home, and as it became cheaper to buy than to produce more and more items for household consumption, there was a physical separation of production activity from the household. The gap between the public and private spheres appeared so wide that they came to be thought of as "separate spheres." The domestic sphere was "woman's sphere." The ideology of domesticity was developed out of this apparent dichotomy between the home as woman's sphere and the world as man's.

DOMESTIC VIOLENCE is the crime of physical and sexual abuse perpetrated against one family member by another family member, with whom the abuser may or may not reside. The term "domestic violence" is used interchangeably with family violence, spouse abuse, and wife battering. It is a broad term encompassing child abuse, spouse abuse, sibling abuse, abuse of a parent by a child, and abuse of an elderly or handicapped family member. It includes sexual abuse and incest. Domestic violence occurs in all socioeconomic and racial groups. Its victims may be of any age or sex. The family, which ideally is seen as a nurturing and loving environment, is a scene of emotional and physical pain for many people. Domestic violence has been condoned historically because of its occurrence in a domain considered sacred. The home has been protected by the right of privacy, regardless of the fact that the results of abuse impinge on the community at large. Perpetrators of violence may utilize the violent expression of anger in order to control. Their violent behavior may be rooted in learned behaviors or low-stress tolerance. Frequently, they have been abused or have witnessed abuse as children. Cultural factors such as violence in defense, advertising, entertainment, and sports reinforce permissible use of violence to exercise power and control. Loss of such power and control may arouse fear, hurt, anger, jealousy, frustration, and vulnerability. These emotions can be closely linked with violence toward others. The violence continues as long as no one in authority prohibits it.

Child abuse refers to acts of neglect or violence committed against children by adults. Violence has been a fundamental part of the American way of childrearing. It is epitomized by the expression "Spare the rod and spoil the child." Many caregivers of children believe it is permissible and necessary to physically hurt children as a means of discipline. Children are also an available target for the expression of violence-linked feelings. Child abuse may range from deprivation of necessities, to emotional maltreatment, minor physical injuries, sexual abuse, and major injuries, to murder. The Child Abuse Prevention Act of 1974 focused attention on the problem. Its severity has been denied by many, but in 1993 more than 1 million children were deemed victims of maltreatment. The U.S. Advisory Board on Child Abuse and Neglect estimates that about 2,000 infants and young children die from maltreatment each year. Near-fatal abuse and neglect leave another 18,000 children permanently disabled each year.

The most recent estimate of child sexual abuse incidence looks only at the child protective system and finds that, in 1993, there were 330,000 reports of child sexual abuse, of which 150,000 were substantiated. The majority of these children are molested by a family member or someone that they know. Incest and sexual abuse refer to manual, oral, or genital sexual contact that an adult imposes on a child. If the abuse is between two children and an age difference of five years or greater exists, these acts can also be considered abuse. Children may not disclose that abuse is taking place for a variety of reasons, fear being one. There is no uniform impact of sexual abuse. The psychological impact is affected by the intensity, duration, and severity of the abuse, as well as individual and environmental factors. Statutes require that child abuse be reported to the state authority vested with the responsibility of protecting children from abuse.

The term "spouse abuse" refers to acts of violence between intimate partners, who may or may not be married or living together at the time of the abuse. In the 1970s concern voiced by the women's movement gave rise to local, state, and national efforts to end spouse abuse. Those early efforts have resulted in 11 national coalitions, 50 state coalitions, and 1,755 domestic violence intervention programs across the United States. These programs emphasize empowerment, advocacy, and self-determination. Knowledge about domestic violence has increased due to research and information gleaned from the shelter experiences. It is estimated that 4 million women experience severe or life-threatening assault from a male partner (Koss et al., 44). Statistics indicate that men commit 95 percent of reported assaults on spouses (Straus, Gelles, and Steinmetz, 40). In spouse abuse there is an identifiable three-phase cycle of violence that repeats over time. Phase one is a time of tension building. Phase two is violent, focused verbal and/or physical assaults. Phase three is often referred to as the "honeymoon phase," which is a time of contrite and loving behaviors. Battered women grow to believe they deserve and provoke the abuse. Women tend to feel responsibility for the relationship and its maintenance; thus, they may be vulnerable to the third phase of the cycle. At that time men may promise an end to the violence, although they rarely take responsibility for it.

Violence between siblings may be the most common form of domestic violence. One study indicates that sibling violence occurs more frequently than parent–child or husband–wife violence. Since boys of every age tend to be more physically violent than girls, the highest frequency of violence occurs in families that have only boys. While many violent acts are pushing, shoving, and hitting, significant numbers of beatings take place (Straus, Gelles, and Steinmetz, 119–122). Adult children may continue to abuse parents.

The first National Conference on Abuse of Elder Persons was held in 1981. Elder abuse, like other forms of domestic violence, occurs in a repeating pattern. Frail, elderly victims are dependent on others to provide for their living and health needs. The abuser is usually a member of the immediate family responsible for the care of the elderly person and frequently lives in the same house as the victim. Abuse ranges from exploitation of resources, through neglect and threat of physical injury and murder. Victims cluster between ages 75 and 85, with female victims predominating. The victim usually suffers from debilitating physical illness or mental impairment. As with all domestic violence the secrets are kept while the abuse is denied by victims through fear and resignation or through unwillingness to expose a loved one as an abuser.

Mentally retarded, mentally ill, and physically handicapped individuals are also vulnerable as victims of domestic violence. The abusers are again family members or guardians with responsibility for their care. These caregivers may be emotionally, physically, or financially unable or unwilling to care for their elderly or handicapped family members. Medical and social service professionals are taught to recognize the indicators of psychological and physical abuse. They are charged with intervening and offering alternatives. In 48 states some kind of statute now requires mandatory reporting of abuse or suspected abuse of elderly and incapacitated adults and provides protective services for this population.

References. Richard E. Behrman (ed.), *The Future of Children: Sexual Abuse of Children* 4, 2 (Summer/Fall 1994); M. Koss, L. Goodman, A. Browne, L. Fitzgerald, G. Keita, and N. Russo, *No Safe Haven: Male Violence against Women at Home, at Work, and in the Community* (Washington, D.C., 1944); M. D. Pagelow, *Family Violence* (New York, 1984); M. Quinn and S. Tomita, *Elder Abuse and Neglect: Causes, Diagnosis, and Intervention Strategies* (New York, 1986); M. A. Straus, R. J. Gelles, and S. K. Steinmetz, *Behind Closed Doors: Violence in the American Family* (New York, 1980); Lenore Walker, *The Battered Woman* (New York, 1979); National Clearinghouse on Child Abuse and Neglect Information, P.O. Box 1182, Washington, D.C. 20013–1182; (800) FYI-3366.

KATHERINE ST. JOHN and SYLVIA ROBERTSON

DOUBLE BIND. Any situation in which a person is subject to mutually incompatible directives, such that to fulfill one of those directives is ipso facto to have failed to fulfill the other. Thus, no matter what a person does, she or he "cannot win." When first formulated in 1956 by Gregory Bateson et al., the concept was a linchpin of the then newly emerging communications and "family systems" approaches to schizophrenia. Such approaches, which viewed schizophrenia as a strategy of accommodation to intolerably paradoxical expectations within the network of family relationships, in many ways represented a distinct advance over prevailing organic and psychodynamic models.

Double bind theory, however, like most therapeutic models of the post–World War II period, was unable to transcend the gender ideology of the time, which placed the "good" or "bad" mother at the center of family function and dysfunction. Both in theory and practice maternal scapegoating and victim blaming become ubiquitous. The starring role in the family drama nearly always fell to the "schizophrenogenic mother"—typically described as both hostile and emotionally needy, withholding and "engulfing." (The "classic example" of the double bind, cited frequently in textbooks and articles, describes the mother who, visiting her son in his hospital room, stiffens when he embraces her and then, when he withdraws his arm, chides him for not loving her.) Very rarely do paternal "mixed messages" figure in the literature; rather, the father is typically represented as passive bystander to his wife's more actively destructive manipulations. No significance is attached to the social milieu outside the family.

The intensification of feminist consciousness* in the late 1960s and early 1970s generated a good deal of criticism of these early psychiatric uses of the "double bind" concept. At the same time, feminists were able to discern the valuable uses to which Bateson's original insights might be put in describing key conflicts within women's experiences. The "double bind" concept—by now part of our common cultural vocabulary—was pressed into the service of a newly emerging clinical focus on the feminine "role" and the paradoxes and contradictions embedded in it.

At the very center of this theoretical turn was the perception that the prevailing ideology of successful "femininity" was utterly at variance with our high cultural emphasis on self-realization, achievement, and self-reliance. A classic 1970 study of therapeutic attitudes painted the first stroke. In Inge Broverman et al., it was found that most therapists equated mature femininity—much as Freud had—with passivity, vulnerability, helplessness, and submissiveness. At the same time, mature, healthy *adulthood* (sex unspecified) was defined in terms of qualities such as competence, independence, ambitiousness, adventurousness—qualities also strongly associated, by the therapists, with mature masculinity. Thus, not only did there appear to be a gendered double standard* with respect to criteria for mental health but a painful double bind for women clients: to be a healthy, mature woman, in the dominant therapeutic mentality (and certainly in the reigning popular mentality as well), required truncating one's development "as a person"; to be an accomplished, independent adult was ipso facto to have failed to achieve healthy adjustment to the prevailing construction of the feminine role.

Other studies—focusing on sexuality,* the psychology of battered women,* career-related issues, and so on—articulated other binds resulting from the constraints of "femininity." Perhaps the most influential and controversial among them was Martina Horner's study of "achievement anxiety" (popularly known as "fear of success"*). It suggested that such anxiety, which Horner found to be prominent among the college women she interviewed, was the result of historically long-standing notions that to succeed in the public, male world is to become less of a woman, to "lose one's femininity."

Horner's studies, while initially celebrated, drew criticisms in the late 1970s and early 1980s. The ethnocentrism of the study was pointed out; if black women had a "fear of success" (which studies did not show very strongly), *their* "double bind," it was argued, involved anxiety over conflicts between the goals of feminism and the struggle against racism, rather than concern for a white ideal of "femininity." Later criticism, inspired by Carol Gilligan's influential work on gender and moral values, reinterpreted the "fear" of achievement as a rejection of the competitive values associated with achievement in our culture. Attempts in the early 1980s to duplicate Horner's study found little, if any, success anxiety among college women. These, however, cannot be considered to be "refutations" of Horner's findings, since 12 years and a good deal of cultural transformation might well account for the difference in results.

At midpoint in the 1980s, one of the most coercive images spawned from the current gender ideology is that of the "superwoman." The glamour and appeal of superwoman is precisely that she appears to have escaped the demoralizing double binds presented to past generations of women. Rather, she can "have it all"—professional success *and* "femininity," public accomplishment *and* domestic satisfaction. Have the demands of "femininity" and the values of "personhood" in our culture come to be reconciled?

Catherine Steiner Adair's study suggests not. On the basis of a series of interviews, high school women were classified into two groups, one expressing skepticism over the attainability of the superwoman ideal, the other thoroughly aspiring to it. Later administration of diagnostic tests revealed that 94 percent of the "superwoman" group fell into the eating-disordered range of the scale; 100 percent of the other group fell into the non–eating-disordered range. Media images notwithstanding, young women today appear to sense the impossibility of simultaneously meeting the demands of two spheres whose values have been historically defined in utter opposition to each other. Those who do not, it seems, may wind up enacting the tension through the female pathologies of our time. The traditional domestic construction of femininity insists, both literally and metaphorically, that women should learn to feed others, not the self. In her debilitating obsession with diet and self-denial, the eating-disordered woman fulfills this injunction most obediently. Yet with the very same gesture, she rigorously strives to embody those culturally overesteemed values previously reserved for men: control, autonomy, will, and the exercise of power. Far from escaping the double bind of gender, young women in the second half of the twentieth century, it could be argued, have inscribed it on their bodies.

References. Gregory Bateson et al., "Toward a Theory of Schizophrenia," in M. Berger (ed.), *Beyond the Double Bind* (New York, 1978); Inge Broverman et al., "Sex Roles Stereotypes and Clinical Judgments of Mental Health," *Journal of Consulting and Clinical Psychology* 34 (1970): 1–7; S. Brownmiller, *Femininity* (New York, 1984); Carol Gilligan, *In a Different Voice* (Cambridge, Mass., 1982); Martina Horner, "Femininity and Successful Achievement: A Basic Inconsistency," in J. Bardwick et al. (eds.), *Feminine Personality and Conflict* (Belmont, Calif., 1970); E. Howell and M. Bayes (eds.), *Women and Mental Health* (New York, 1981); S. Ohrbach, *Hunger Strike* (New York, 1986); Catherine Steiner Adair, "The Body-Politic: Normal Female Adolescent Development and the Development of Eating Disorders," diss., Harvard University, 1984; R. Unger, *Female and Male Psychological Perspectives* (New York, 1979).

SUSAN BORDO

DOUBLE JEOPARDY is the identification of women of color's subordination within societies as the product of the dual discriminations of sexism* and racism. "Racism" refers to the ideological, structural, and behavioral systems in society that deny and limit opportunities for some groups because of their racial identity in order to create and maintain a racial hierarchy. "Sexism" refers to a system of control that maintains and legitimates a sexual hierarchy in which males are dominant. Both racism and sexism operate in various spheres of society—economic, political, cultural, educational, religious—and both are perpetuated by organizations and individuals in subtle and explicit ways. Individuals who are doubly disadvantaged because of their membership in both the subordinate sexual and racial groups are the victims of double jeopardy. Double jeopardy, then, recognizes the simultaneity of racial and sexual oppressions and the compound consequences of dual discriminations. Frances Beale initially applied the concept to African American women, but it has become generally applicable to all women of color,* including Native Americans, Latinas, and Asian Americans.

As the complexity of various women's circumstances in society has become more fully understood, this notion of multiple discriminations has been further elaborated. In her initial explication of the term, Beale extensively discussed the negative economic ramifications of double jeopardy. Most black women and many women of color are unemployed or underemployed in jobs with low pay, minimal authority, limited opportunities for mobility, and low prestige. Because educational deprivation and economic marginality circumscribe the lives of many women of color, "class," or socioeconomic status, is the most frequent augmentation, expanding the concept to triple jeopardy. In this case, maleness, whiteness, and wealth are independently and collectively advantageous.

The recognition of two major oppressions confounding and intensifying sexism has been a critical development in the comprehension of women's subordination. However, there are certain limitations in its conceptualization. The first and most problematic issue is the continual addition of oppressions. The concept, both theoretically and practically, loses its potency the more broadly and arbitrarily it is applied. Other prejudices and discriminations based on sexual preferences, religion, age, or nationality are substituted or added. Such variations in the components of double or triple jeopardy create confusion and conceptual fussiness. Would quadruple jeopardy refer to "sexism, racism, heterosexism, and ageism" or to "sexism, racism, classism, and heterosexism"?

Second, the approach has led to misguided attempts at ranking the components in terms of their severity and pervasiveness. This has occurred because early discussions of double and triple jeopardy assumed that the relationships among the variables are additive. Increasingly, it appears more useful to conceive of these relationships as dialectical, that is, as multiplicative interactions, with the relative importance of any determined by specific sociohistorical conditions. Thus, linkages among systems of oppression are viewed as dynamically interrelated and varied for those distinct groups of women subject to the double or triple jeopardy of racism, sexism, and class oppression.

References. E. M. Almquist, "Race and Ethnicity in the Lives of Minority Women," in J. Freeman (ed.), *Women: A Feminist Perspective* (Palo Alto, Calif., 1984); Frances Beale, "Double Jeopardy: To Be Black and Female," in T. Cade (ed.), *The Black Woman: An Anthology* (New York, 1970); 90–100; A. Davis, *Women, Race and Class* (New York, 1981); B. T. Dill, "Dialectics of Black Womanhood," *Signs* 4 (1979): 543–555.

DEBORAH K. KING

DOUBLE STANDARD is two different sets of acceptable behavior, one for females and one for males. In patriarchal societies women are allowed less freedom to express their sexuality* than are men and are judged more harshly, not just for sexual activity that, if engaged in by a man, is condoned or even considered normal or desirable but for any conduct or even speech that is considered unsuitable to women's sex role as the caretaker of children.

Women's liability for actions for which men are not punished at all and their harsher punishment for committing some of the same acts that men commit are found in law codes from the second millennium B.C. to the twentieth century A.D. But the chief means of enforcing the double standard has always been through sex-role socialization.*

DOWER is the widow's portion of, or interest in, her deceased husband's real property.

From the ninth century in much of Europe the bridegift* was gradually transformed from property given to a wife at the time of marriage to a promise of the use and profits of a portion, usually a third, of the husband's patrimony. This dower right, the right of a widow to the use of a part of her husband's property, in time became a recognized part of English law.

Under common-law property division, as reformed in the early twentieth century, if a husband dies intestate, the widow receives the dower portion, commonly one-third, sometimes one-half, of her husband's property; or if, by her deceased husband's will, she would receive less than the amount of the dower, she may be able to elect the dower portion. (Of the common-law property states, only Georgia has no statutory provision for dower.) Feminists are working to replace the dower right with the concept of marital property.*

DOWRY is a marriage payment made by the bride's family. It goes with the bride on her marriage* and is administered by her husband for the duration of the marriage. The dowry represents the contribution of the wife's family toward her support, and the profits may be used to that end, but the principal is supposed to be kept intact. After the wife's death it passes to her children or, if there are none, reverts to her family. Upon divorce* the dowry is returned to the wife or her family. In some societies, if there are children, not all the dowry may be returned; or if the wife is guilty of adultery,* she may lose a part or all of it.

The dowry is often considered a form of premarital inheritance. In societies in which the daughters do not inherit except in default of sons, if a man dies before his daughters are married, his sons are expected, although not usually required, to dower their sisters.

Dowry as a system of marriage payment is associated with patrilocal and monogamous marriages and with hypergamy* (the woman's "marrying up") in stratified societies.

DOWRY. Dowry in India changed over time. During the period 1000–500 B.C. bridal gifts among royal families included ornaments, trousseau, livestock, and slave girls. Such wedding presents came from both the families at the time of marriage. However, this was not an equal responsibility. One family had higher obligations than the other. Which family was to become the principal donor depended partly on which regional, cultural, economic, or other factors were predominant at a particular period.

From about the 4th century B.C., it was specified that girls should receive the *stridhana* and *sulka* from the boys or their families. The *stridhana* (literally, a woman's wealth), as it is still known among Hindus, consisted of a fixed sum of maintenance, ornaments, and clothes. The *sulka* remained undefined, with later lawgivers interpreting it as bride-price. Both *stridhana* and *sulka* acted as a security deposit against premarital defects of the partners. If marriage could not take place because of the boy's fault or girl's defect, the aggrieved party retained the *stridhana* and *sulka*. After the wife's death, the *stridhana* went to her children, husband, or his family, and the *sulka* to her natal family.

Whether the marriage was sacred or secular affected a woman's absolute right over her property. In sacred marriage, a husband had limited rights over his wife's property; in secular marriage he had none. The difference in the man's right to control his wife's property reduced the incidence of secular marriages and increased that of sacred marriages, especially among the rich. Consequently, the husband gained, and the wife lost control of her property.

The scope of a woman's property was further restricted when the sacred literature came out strongly against "selling" a daughter through "bride-price" and advocated instead the "gift" of a girl. "Gift" implied not only the permanent transfer of the girl but also that she should not be given empty-handed. Thus, the man was exempted from giving anything to his prospective bride before marriage, and the onus of providing her with the wherewithal for her future life lay entirely with her parents.

This shift from bride-price to dowry occurred sometime between the fourth century B.C. and the second century A.D., when basic socioeconomic changes were taking place. Extension of powerful states over previously independent people, plow cultivation generating an agricultural surplus, and growth of trade, commerce, mining, and other industries increased the social division of labor. Therefore, an elaborate hierarchical social structure was evolved by the brahminical orthodoxy, which returned to power after a short spell of heterodox religious upheaval.

The triumph of orthodoxy was reflected in changes in the status of women. Inheritance of private property by a natural son who alone was entitled to perform ancestor worship became a dominant feature in society. Women were debarred from inheritance and from performing religious rites. Widow marriage was discouraged, and divorce, which had been previously possible under certain circumstances, was totally prohibited. Marriage became an obligatory sacrament for a girl, and the husband became a god. To assure the paternity of the heir, child marriage for girls was preferred. Married young, a woman had no access to education, nor was she equipped for anything other than domestic work. In lieu of the social losses thus suffered, her *stridhana* increased by including whatever she received, in cash or kind from any source, connected with her marriage.

Among the peasantry and the working people, where women worked before and after marriage, bride-price continued for some time. However, women's dependent status eventually percolated downward from upper-class and upper-caste values. Even the Muslims, who settled in India after A.D. 1000 and among whom dowry was unknown, reinterpreted one *surah* of the Koran in favor of dowry. Today, the dowry system is no less prevalent in Pakistan and Bangladesh than in India. (See BANGLADESH and PAKISTAN.) The *Mehr-Namäh* (i.e., pledge money) from the groom's family before the marriage has lost its significance, and now only a token sum is guaranteed to the woman.

Thus, the *stridhana*, once a woman's property given voluntarily by her father, is now a boy's prerogative to demand. It is set in a bargain made between two families before the marriage, and even after the marriage the expectation of more continues. The torture and occasional death of girls on account of inadequate dowry have led to protests against the custom.

The issue became a problem when the Indian Parliament passed legislation in the 1950s outlawing polygamy among the Hindus and giving girls a right to paternal property. In a patriarchal society, inheritance and concentration of private property, continuance of lineage, and ancestor worship are carried through a male heir. Therefore, girls are induced to forego their property claims in favor of their brothers. In this context, dowry is supposed to compensate the girl for giving up her right. Families stretch to their limit to give the daughter jewelry, clothes, cash, and articles for her new home and to give presents to the boy and his family. However, all these "gifts" constituting the dowry belong to the husband and his family, not to the wife. The size of the dowry depends on the boy's qualifications and status. It is erroneously assumed that a substantial dowry will improve the girl's status in her in-laws' family.

The demand for cash before and after marriage is noticeable in the merchant communities, where it is used as capital for business purposes and among other groups as an easy way to acquire expensive consumer goods like videocassette recorders (VCRs), color televisions, and so forth. The Indian Parliament has passed more legislation against dowry, and women's organizations are working to implement the laws. However, the magnitude of the problem is apparent from the fact that in Delhi alone there were 311 cases of burning brides in 1977 and 810 in 1982. Of course, not all cases were related to dowry. Incompatibility, the stigma of divorce, economic and social insecurity, and the absence of support systems for women may be behind some of these deaths. In any case, the number is increasing everywhere.

Reasons for increase in the incidence of dowry are ascribed to greed, consumerism, a quicker way to get rich, and the like. Experience proves that as long as dowry is regarded as a moral or legal problem alone, it will not be eradicated from society. Women activists demand that a woman's property be completely delinked from her husband's. She would thus be the absolute owner, and after her death the property would go to her children or natal family. Women's organizations are also campaigning for giving useful gifts like income-generating assets to a bride instead of such things as ornaments. According to feminists, marriage is neither obligatory nor inviolable and indissoluble. More important, they argue that existing values should change in favor of sex equality.

References. A. S. Altekar, *The Position of Women in Hindu Civilization: From Prehistoric Times to the Present Day* (Delhi, 1962); Elizabeth Bumiller, *May You Be the Mother of a Hundred Sons, a Journey among Women in India* (New York, 1991); Prabhati Mukherjee, *Hindu Women: Normative Models* (New Delhi, 1978); Sakuntala Narasimhan, *Sati: Widow Burning in India* (New York, 1990); Nirjharini Sarkar, *Rachana-samgraha* (in Bengali) (Calcutta, 1991).

PRABHATI MUKHERJEE

DOWRY. In Western Societies. A payment made by the bride's family in cash, goods, or property to the groom. Once married, the wife generally had no access to her dowry, which was controlled by her husband for the duration of the marriage. However, its size and the limited control she could exert might influence her status vis-à-vis her mate. In many instances, the dowry returned to the wife upon the husband's death or (in fewer cases) desertion. Dowries were a means of contributing to the new household. They were also a way of transmitting wealth from parents to children. However, the dowry always signified much more than a transfer of funds: recent investigations of the dowry in various periods and places reveal its centrality to the history of Western women.

The dowry was known by the ancient Hebrews, although bride-price (*môhar*)—the groom's payment to the bride's family—was the legally required settlement. Greek parents gave dowries with their daughters, as did the Romans, but the Germanic invasions in the fifth century caused the Germanic bride-price to take precedence over the dowry in Western Europe for approximately five centuries. However, as early as the sixth century, in Burgundian, Visigothic, and Salic laws, there was a gradual evolution from the bride-price to the bridegift, a marriage payment presented by the groom to the bride rather than to her parents. The bridegift provided for the economic security of women, who were subsequently deprived of their husbands' support. This evolution to bridegift was related to the growth of state power and was one of the most important developments in the history of Merovingian women.

In about the eleventh century, the burgeoning cities of the Mediterranean region abandoned the marriage customs imposed by the Germanic invaders in favor of the dowry. Scholars have underlined the connections between commercial developments, a "crisis of status," and the need for economic and kin alliances (see Hughes). The dowry played a key role in bestowing status and forging alliances. The size of the dowry indicated the bride's family's social and economic standing, and a large endowment could raise the status of the wife and her family.

Evidence suggests that dowries were particularly crucial during a period of economic and social mobility, when those with new money sought status, and those with status sought wealth to either maintain or regain their positions. The commercial revival of the late Middle Ages in Italy is related to the return of the dowry there. This revival first brought increased legal and economic rights to middle- and upper-class women. Later, laws limiting women's rights over their dowries were instituted by men who felt their economic and lineal interests threatened by women's control over property. The dowry often served as a "bridge between women's traditional status in the family and their roles in the new economy" (Reimer). The dowry, which was returned to a woman when her marriage ended, was women's most regular and valuable source of capital for commercial ventures.

Research into dowries in medieval Ragusa (Dubrovnik) (1235–1460) has shown that in the midst of commercial growth, the elite reacted to a period of dowry inflation by using dowries to redistribute property broadly among wealthy families. Thus, the dowry promoted further economic growth and forged cohesive economic and familial alliances. In this process, elite women received an increasingly larger share of their dowries in the form of jewels, ornaments, gold, and silver. This was not only a hedge against financial calamities but, more important, one that women controlled exclusively—an ultimately power-enhancing development for women. Similarly, in early Renaissance Venice (1300–1450) inflated dowries augmented the patrician wife's prestige and power.

These examples, however, should not mislead us into thinking that the assertion of state or elite power necessarily improved women's position. In rural areas outside Italy from the mid-twelfth to the mid-thirteenth centuries, the political order limited women's economic control. Feudal lords, intent on providing economic rights to their vassals, curtailed women's property rights, particularly over their dowries.

Dowries were not only affected by political and economic developments, but, in turn, influenced broader social and demographic patterns. In early modern France and England, for example, the need to save for the dowry resulted in delayed marriages among artisans and peasants. The dowry was a foundation of the family economy, and if peasant or artisan parents could not provide their daughters with dowries, the young women had to wait for their parents' deaths to receive a settlement or had to work until they themselves accumulated enough money or goods. Both alternatives seem to have raised the average age of marriage while also functioning as a kind of birth control. Among the propertyless, however, women generally worked before and during marriage. Among these wage workers, the coming of domestic industry and the concomitant increase in jobs and cash wages as, for instance, in seventeenth-century England, encouraged earlier marriages and more children.

At least until World War I, saving for her dowry was an important aspect of a young workingwoman's life. In parts of Europe, a dowry was even required by law. The Sicilian peasantry, for example, held to the dowry, which provided social status and separated the better-off from the "very poor." To this peasantry, embroidered trousseaux, which were objects of value with significant liquidity, functioned like dowries. They enhanced the social status of the bride and her kin and supported cultural codes of chastity and leisured womanhood by keeping women busy (and, therefore, "virtuous"), but not employed, before marriage.

In France, the dowry was almost a universal institution, even among servants, laborers, and tenant farmers, until the interwar era. Only the poorest urban industrial workers had no dowries, and, as a result, many of them did not marry at all. However, as poorer individuals rose to the ranks of artisans, they, too, accumulated dowries and married. Consequently, marriage was seen by the bourgeoisie as a means of instilling love of property in the poor, a love that was nowhere more open and obvious than in the bourgeois marriages of the late nineteenth century. With the growth of industrial capitalism, the industrialists of the French Nord married off their children to their rivals, thus expanding family business and eliminating competition.

In Imperial Germany (1871–1918), during a period of depression and rapid capital accumulation, dowries took on added meaning for a successful and enterprising bourgeoisie eager to invest, as well as for a caste of nobles and higher civil servants whose fortunes had declined. Parents ensured their family fortunes by arranging marriages, relenting only slowly to the pressures of "romantic love." Women's fate hung on the size of their dowries: the greater the sum, the "better" they married, and the greater their status vis-à-vis their husbands and in-laws.

Ethnic and religious groups often displayed distinct economic profiles and a commitment to endogamy. For the most part, dowries were used to maintain group cohesion and class cohesion within the group, but this did not prevent the wealthiest individuals from using a large dowry to marry out if they wished.

Only after World War I, when women began to reenter the economy as paid workers on a large scale in advanced capitalist societies, did the pursuit of dowries decline. The expectation that a woman would continue to earn a wage during the early years of her marriage relaxed the need for her premarital savings. However, the dowry was not abandoned entirely. The German peasantry continued the tradition of the dowry at least until World War II, with only the poorest families unable to provide some sort of dowry or, at least, a trousseau. Even today, the dowry system is in evidence in less industrialized areas of Europe.

A sketch of the history of the dowry not only reveals the relationship of global forces, such as the economy and the state, to the marriage gift, but the effect this gift had on social relations: the balance of power between wife and husband, between parents and children, and between extended kin. Finally, the marriage endowment reflects the position of women—their status, wealth, and autonomy—as daughters, wives, and mothers. Women's position was shaped by patriarchal society and ideology as well as by the nuclear family. It is within these contexts that the dowry must be examined.

References. Jack Goody, *The Development of the Family and Marriage in Western Europe* (Cambridge, 1983); Diane Owen Hughes, "From Brideprice to Dowry in Mediterranean Europe," in Marion Kaplan (ed.), *The Marriage Bargain* (New York, 1985); Marion A. Kaplan, *The Marriage Bargain: Women and the Dowry in Western Europe* (New York, 1985); Eleanor Reimer, "Women, Dowries, and Capital Investment in Thirteenth-Century Siena," in *The Marriage Bargain* (New York, 1985); Anthony Molho, *Marriage Alliance in Late Medieval Florence* (Cambridge, Mass., 1994).

MARION A. KAPLAN

DRAMA AND THEATRE. British, Nineteenth Century, reflected the changing status of women in society and offered unusual career opportunities at a time when occupations open to women were severely limited.

While melodrama was the dominant genre of the period, the immensely popular pantomime, burlesque, and extravaganza also provided a subliminal means to explore complex, often contradictory attitudes toward power relationships and sexual boundaries. Frequently based on classical myth or fairy tale, these entertainments combined archetypal image with topical reference and emphasized the physical charms of its female performers, who appeared in elaborate costumes often more revealing than contemporary dress. From the 1830s, the breeches role (inherited from the previous century) became a standard feature in these productions as the young male hero was played by an attractive actress (called the "principal boy" from the 1870s). In contrast, the "dame"—an unattractive female character middle-aged or older, often portrayed as a shrew—was frequently played by a male low comedian. Transvestite performance in general was a prominent feature of this period, as women performers played boys and men in both serious and comic, old and new plays.

The public nature of the actress' work made her a conspicuous social figure, as age-old objections to the itinerant nature of the lifestyle, along with the low ebb of theatrical fortunes in the first half of the century, contributed to a general consensus that acting was not a respectable occupation. When a decorous middle-class lifestyle emerged with Victoria's ascension to the throne in 1837, a heavy emphasis on feminine domesticity further highlighted the actress' anomalous position. Exhibition of her talents for gain condemned the average performer to a social category only slightly above that of the prostitute, but if her profession was shameful, it was also alluring. While she suffered ostracism from most polite circles, the actress enjoyed economic independence and a sexual and social freedom denied to more respectable members of her sex. The life was, in many cases, grueling, but those above the profession's lower ranks might enjoy the benefits of a potentially stimulating and lucrative profession that demanded the energetic application of creative talent. In the public imagination, at least, the actress offered a psychic release from the demand that women be self-sacrificing, self-effacing, and confined to the home.

In the first half of the century, most new performers came from the theatrical families that dominated the profession. Actresses frequently married other theatrical personnel and continued to work, often raising large families simultaneously. At midcentury, as financial stability increased, and stage performers were successful in luring a respectable audience back to the theatres, women from middle-class backgrounds began to enter the profession in greater numbers. While the morality of the actress was still under debate late in the century, the most highly suspect were those who performed in light entertainment.

Throughout the period, the great tragediennes were often given the special dispensation of "high art." Undoubtedly, the most revered actress of the period was Sarah Siddons (1755–1831), whose career spanned the late eighteenth and early nineteenth centuries. A member of the Kemble family, she performed in their particular classical style noted for stateliness, dignity, and grace, though she was said to possess greater emotional intensity than the most famous of her siblings, John Philip Kemble. Helen Faucit (1817–1898), who debuted in London in 1836, was particularly concerned with illustrating acceptable feminine qualities in her portrayal of Shakespeare's heroines. Late in the period, the public was willing to overlook the unconventional living arrangements of Ellen Terry (1847–1928), whose liaison with Edward Godwin produced the important twentieth-century theorist Edward Gordon Craig. Terry was named Dame Commander of the British empire, in 1925, following by 30 years the knighthood of her leading man, Henry Irving, the first actor ever to receive such an honor.

The majority of theatrical enterprises in the nineteenth century were controlled by men, but very popular actresses might influence staffing decisions as well as repertoire, while a significant number of women entered the realm of playwriting or management. Dramatic writing was more difficult for women than other, more private forms of authorship, since it required public interaction and collaboration with theatre artists, but women were nonetheless represented as authors, translators, and adapters in the commercial theatre as well as in the "closet" dramatic literature never meant to be performed. Joanna Baillie (1762–1851), perhaps the most widely known female playwright of the period, experimented with the construction of dramas based on one dominant emotion. Her "Plays of the Passions" were greatly admired by readers but achieved only limited success on the stage. The tragedies of Mary Russell Mitford (1787–1855) were performed successfully during the 1820s and 1830s, and *Quid Pro Quo*, by novelist Catherine Grace Frances Gore (1799–1861), was selected as the best comedy submitted to a panel of judges and produced at the Haymarket in 1844.

The hiring, firing, authoritative delegation of work, and financial planning that running a theatre entailed were normally considered masculine responsibilities. In 1831, however, Lucia Elizabeth Bartolozzi Vestris (1797–1856) assumed control of the Olympic Theatre and publicized herself as the first woman manager. This statement was not technically true, since a number of women, both in London and in the provinces, had managed theatres already, but Vestris was by far the most visible and the most important up to that time. A highly successful actress and singer known particularly for transvestite roles, Vestris converted the dirty Olympic into a highly fashionable place of entertainment and reigned there successfully until 1839, building a reputation for innovation in the integration of all production elements and the use of realistic props and detail. With her husband, Charles Mathews, she later managed the Covent Garden (1839–1842) and Lyceum (1847–1856) theatres, mounting several noteworthy Shakespearean revivals and numerous elaborate holiday entertainments.

By the mid-Victorian years, female managers were not uncommon, as women ran theatres alone and with husbands or other family members. Marie Wilton (1839–1921), also a popular breeches role performer, renovated a theatre so filthy that it was known as "the dust hole" and opened it in 1865 as the elegant Prince of Wales'. Two years later she married her leading man, Squire Bancroft, and together they managed the Prince of Wales' until 1879, then the Haymarket from 1880 until their retirement in 1885. Their work with playwright T. W. Robertson marked a new era of realistic production style in Britain, and their managerial methods set the standard for much twentieth-century theatre practice. Noteworthy in a very different context was Sara Lane (1823–1899), who ran the Britannia Theatre in Hoxton with her husband, Sam, until his death in 1871 and then managed it successfully alone until her own death over a quarter of a century later. Revered by the neighborhood working-class people who made up the Britannia audience, Lane wrote eight plays for her own theatre between 1873 and 1881 and played the principal boy in the annual Christmas pantomime until she was in her 70s.

At the end of the century, popular entertainment continued to emphasize female display and sexual fantasy, while women performers, managers, producers, and playwrights participated in the intellectual and theatrical ferment that preceded World War I. In 1889, Janet Achurch (1864–1916), with her husband, Charles Charrington, presented the first significant production of Henrik Ibsen in England when *A Doll's House* was given a private showing. Actresses such as Achurch, Elizabeth Robins (1862–1952), and Florence Farr (1860–1917) found new, challenging roles as complex heroines in Ibsen and the Ibsen-inspired "new drama," often in performances that they themselves produced. Mrs. Patrick Campbell (Beatrice Stella Tanner, 1865–1940) made her reputation as the woman with a past in Arthur Wing Pinero's *The Second Mrs. Tanqueray* and later created Eliza Doolittle for George Bernard Shaw. Of great importance in the renaissance of Irish theatre were Lady Augusta Gregory (1852–1932), playwright and a managing director of the Abbey Theatre, and Annie Elizabeth Fredricka Horniman (1860–1937). After furnishing a permanent home for the Abbey, Horniman formed her own company in Manchester, which became significant in a revival of the repertory system. Theater was enlisted in the campaign for social and political change when the Actresses' Franchise League, founded in 1908, sponsored plays and entertainments designed to further the cause of suffrage. The sweeping changes that came with World War I brought to a close a century of contradictions and evolution in the depiction of women in dramatic literature as well as in the actual contributions of women to the stage.

References. Gwenn Davis and Beverly A. Joyce (eds.), *Women and the Drama to 1900* (London, 1992); Tracy C. Davis, *Actresses as Working Women* (New York, 1991); Linda Fitzsimmons and Viv Gardner (eds.), *New Woman Plays* (London, 1991); Viv Gardner and Susan Rutherford (eds.), *The New Woman and Her Sisters* (Hertfordshire, England, 1992); Adrienne Scullion (ed.), *Female Playwrights of the Nineteenth Century* (London, 1996); Sheila Stowell, *A Stage of Their Own* (Ann Arbor, Mich., 1992).

                                                                KATHY FLETCHER

DRAMA AND THEATRE. British, Twentieth Century. Theatre and drama in Britain have undergone great change and expansion in the twentieth century. The theatre was dominated by a handful of actor-managers at the turn of the century. Prominent among them was Ellen Terry, who, with Henry Irving, operated the Lyceum until 1902. Terry managed the Imperial between 1902 and 1907 and continued to exercise great influence on theater by writing and lecturing until her death in 1928. Major actors of this period include Elizabeth Robins (also a playwright), Madge Kendal (also a manager), and Beatrice Stella (Mrs. Patrick) Campbell.

The repertory movement generated new theatres throughout Great Britain in the early years of the twentieth century. Among them were the Kingsway, started by Lena Ashwell in 1907, and the Little Theatre, begun by Gertrude Kingston in 1910. The most influential of the new theatres included the Old Vic in London, the Gaiety in Manchester, and the Abbey in Dublin. Annie E. Horniman operated a repertory company in Manchester from 1907 to 1921. Occupying the Gaiety Theatre from 1908, Horniman's company produced over 100 new plays, many by local dramatists. Lilian Baylis founded the Old Vic in 1912, developed it into a major center for Shakespearean drama, and managed it until 1936. Baylis, who also presented opera and ballet at Sadlers Wells, is credited with laying the groundwork for today's national theatre, opera, and ballet companies in Britain. Dublin's Abbey Theatre was cofounded by Augusta Gregory (with W. B. Yeats) in 1904. Gregory worked with the Abbey until 1928, both as producer and writer.

After World War II, permanent companies devoted to the classics stabilized, with the help of government subsidy. Major female actors of this period included Peggy Ashcroft, Fabia Drake, Edith Evans, Wendy Hiller, Gertrude Lawrence, Flora Robson, Sybil Thorndike, and Irene Worth. Irene Hentschl was the first woman to direct full-time at the Stratford Memorial (later the Royal Shakespeare). Preeminent among designers were Tanya Moisewitsch, who was known for her innovative architectural settings, Barbara Heseltine, and the all-woman design team Motley.

Theatre in Britain expanded in a new direction when Joan Littlewood moved her Theatre Workshop to London's East End in 1953. Littlewood had founded Theatre Workshop 10 years earlier as a mobile company based in Manchester with the aim of creating plays that would attract and express the concerns of working-class audiences. Littlewood's use of improvisation, adaptation of music hall techniques, and legitimation of working-class perspectives inspired further exploration and experiment. Best known of Littlewood's productions was the collaboratively written *Oh, What a Lovely War!* (1963).

After 1956, the Royal Court Theatre moved to the forefront of new play production in England. During the decade in which it focused on the group of playwrights known as "the angry young men," several women nevertheless launched successful careers there. Jocelyn Herbert is the best-known designer to have emerged at this time, though Margaret Harris and Sophie Devine of Motley also designed some productions, and Deirdre Clancy contributed costume designs. Jane Howell, as associate director from 1965 to 1969, staged major revivals as well as the premiere of Edward Bond's *Narrow Road to the Deep North* (1969). Ann Jellicoe directed a number of plays, while Miriam Brickman, Pam Brighton, and Nancy Meckler directed occasional ones. Female actors who earned acclaim at the Royal Court include Joan Plowright, Jill Bennet, Mary Ure, and Billie Whitelaw.

The political and cultural upheavals of 1968 found expression in the experimental and politically activist companies that performed in small or improvised theatre spaces and became known collectively as the Fringe. Women, active in Fringe companies from the beginning, have, since 1973, organized a number of feminist theatre groups. These include Monstrous Regiment, Mrs. Worthington's Daughters, Bloomers, Spare Tyre, Siren, the Women's Theatre Group, the Birmingham-based Women and Theatre, and the Belfast company Charabanc. The Theatre of Black Women, a company dedicated to theatre by and for black women, was active in the 1980s. Almost Free, Joint Stock, Red Ladder, Gay Sweatshop, Freehold, Paines Plough, Tara Arts, Half Moon, and Wakefield Tricycle are additional Fringe groups that have produced some feminist work. Directors well known for their Fringe productions include Susan Todd, Pam Brighton, Carole Hayman, Pip Broughton, Nancy Meckler, and Paulette Randall. Sue Plummer and Annie Smart are among the Fringe's best-known designers. Female actors who have performed primarily in Fringe venues include Linda Bassett, Amelda Brown, Deborah Findlay, Gillian Hanna, Judith Harte, Carole Hayman, Cecily Hobbs, Tricia Kelly, Patti Love, Miriam Margolyes, Joanne Pearce, Miranda Richardson, Lesley Sharp, Alison Steadman, Jennie Stoller, Meera Syal, and Lou Wakefield.

Government support in the 1960s and 1970s permitted expansion of the Royal Shakespeare Company, stabilization of many regional companies, and establishment of the National Theatre in London. Buzz Goodbody organized and directed in the Royal Shakespeare's Other Place. Di Trevis and Sarah Pia Anderson have directed at the National, while Annie Castledine and Jenny Killick have held artistic director posts in regional theatres. Di Seymour, Alison Chitty, Liz da Costa, Linda Hemming, and Sally Jacobs-Brooks have designed for the National Theatre and the Royal Shakespeare Theatre. Female actors prominent at the two major subsidized theatres, as well as in West End theatre since World War II, include Suzanne Bertish, Claire Bloom, Julie Covington, Sinead Cusack, Frances de la Tour, Judi Dench, Lindsay Duncan, Glenda Jackson, Barbara Jefford, Penelope Keith, Felicity Kendal, Sara Kestelman, Jane Laoptaire, Leslie Manville, Anna Massey, Helen Mirren, Vanessa Redgrave, Beryl Reid, Maggie Smith, Elizabeth Spriggs, Juliet Stevenson, Janet Suzman, Dorothy Tutin, and Zoe Wanamaker.

The development of drama in twentieth-century Britain has paralleled that of theatre, from early realism to contemporary experiment. Augusta Gregory wrote approximately 20 plays, most of which focus on Irish folk and nationalist themes; among the best known are *The Goal Gate* (1906) and *The Rising of the Moon* (1907). Other prewar plays include *Chains* (1909) by Elizabeth Baker, *Rutherford and Son* (1912) by Githa Sowerby, and two religious dramas by Dorothy Sayers. Clemence Dane (pseudonym for Winifred Ashton) wrote successful plays, such as *A Bill of Divorcement* (1921), in the period between the wars. In the decade following the war, both Agatha Christie and Enid Bagnold wrote popular plays; Christie's most famous are *The Mousetrap* (1952) and *Witness for the Prosecution* (1954), while Bagnold's best known is *The Chalk Garden* (1955). Productions in 1958 included Doris Lessing's *Each His Own Wilderness* at the Royal Court and Shelagh Delaney's *A Taste of Honey* at the Theatre Workshop. Ann Jellicoe inaugurated a period of formal experiment with *The Sport of My Mad Mother* (1958) and *The Knack* (1962) at the Royal Court. Margaretta d'Arcy cowrote with John Arden a group of plays dealing with the situation in Northern Ireland. In 1969, conscious feminism made its appearance in two plays: *Rites* by Amureen Duffy, produced by the National, and *Vagina Rex and the Gas Oven*, by Jane Arden, at the Drury Lane Arts Lab.

Since 1970, the number of works by women playwrights produced in Britain has increased. Caryl Churchill, foremost among current Royal Court dramatists, has had 15 plays produced, many of which have won awards in England and the United States. Best known of Churchill's plays are *Cloud Nine* (1979), *Top Girls* (1982), *Fen* (1983), *Serious Money* (1987), and *Mad Forest* (1990). Timberlake Wertenbaker has begun to establish an international reputation with plays such as *Our Country's Good* (1988) and *Three Birds Alighting in a Field* (1991). Sarah Daniels has written feminist plays for a wide range of theatres; most prominent among them are *Ripen Our Darkness* (1981), *Masterpieces* (1983), and *Beside Herself* (1990). Pam Gems has become known for plays about women, including *Piaf* (1978) and *Camille* (1984), both produced by the RSC's Other Place. Scottish playwright Olwen Wymark's *Find Me* (1977) has been widely produced. Winners of the Susan Smith Blackburn Award include Anne Devlin for *Ourselves Alone* (1985) and Lucy Gannon for *Keeping Tom Nice* (1988). Other notable playwrights since 1970 include Kay Adshead, April De Angelis, Nell Dunn, Marcella Evaristi, Catherine Hayes, Charlotte Keatley, Bryony Lavery, Deborah Levy, Liz Lochhead, Clare Luckham, Sharman Macdonald, Rona Munro, Mary O'Malley, Louise Page, Jill Posener, Ayshe Raif, Christina Reid, Jacqueline Rudet, Sue Townsend, Michelene Wandor, and Fay Weldon.

The Women's Playhouse Trust was formed in 1981 to promote equality for women in theatre and drama. It has sponsored productions, training workshops, public debates, and a comprehensive study of women in theatre. The study, published in 1987, showed that women constitute only 15 percent of artistic directors in building-based theatre companies and control only 11 percent of the national arts budget. New playwrights encouraged by the Women's Playhouse Trust include Clare McIntyre, Winsome Pinnock, and Heidi Thomas.

Collections of plays by women include Yvonne Brewster (ed.), *Black Plays* and *Black Plays Two* (London, 1987, 1989); Annie Castledine (ed.), *Plays by Women*, vol. 10 (London, 1991); Jill Davis (ed.), *Lesbian Plays* and *Lesbian Plays Two* (London, 1987, 1989); Linda Fitzsimmons and Vivian Gardner (eds.), *New Woman Plays* (London, 1991); Gillian Hanna (ed.), *Monstrous Regiment: Four Plays and a Celebration* (London, 1991);

Mary Remnant (ed.), *Plays by Women*, vols. 5–9 (London, 1986–1990); Michelene Wandor (ed.), *Plays by Women*, vols. 1–4 (London, 1982–1985).

References. Susan Carlson, *Women and Comedy: Rewriting the British Theatrical Tradition* (Ann Arbor, Mich., 1991); Vivian Gardner and Susan Rutherford, *The New Woman and Her Sisters: Feminism and Theatre, 1850–1914* (Ann Arbor, Mich., 1992); Lisbeth Goodman, *Contemporary Feminist Theatres* (London, 1993); Gillian Hanna, *Feminism and Theatre*, Theatre Papers, 2d series, no. 8 (Dartington, Devon, 1978); Catherine Itzin, *Stages in the Revolution: Political Theatre in Britain since 1968* (London, 1980); Helene Keyssar, *Feminist Theatre* (London, 1984).

AMELIA HOWE KRITZER

DRAMA AND THEATRE. Hispanic Spain and Latin America. Women entered the theatre arena as actresses. Mid-sixteenth-century Spanish women performed in barnstorming troupes, having their position legalized by Phillip II's 1587 proclamation allowing women onstage, provided they were married and wore no male costume. Over three centuries later some actresses were heading their own companies. The Catalonian Margarita Xirgú (Spain/Uruguay, 1888–1969), who acted in Catalonian and Spanish, formed her own company, traveled to Argentina, and excelled at female roles created by Frederico García Lorca, some specifically for her. Xirgú became a director and founded a theatre school in Uruguay. María Guerrero (Spain, 1868–1928) formed a touring company that premiered about 150 plays throughout Europe, the United States, and Spanish America, contributing to the splendor of Spanish theatre. The Cervantes Theatre in Buenos Aires was built through her initiative and financial support. Virginia Fábregas (b. María Barragán, 1880–1950) and María Teresa Montoya (b. 1902) were two Mexican actresses heading their own companies. They toured Europe, the United States, and Spanish America. In Argentina several actresses affirmed their independence by forming their own companies: Angelina Pagano (1888–1962); Blanca Podestá (b. 1889); Camila Quiroga (1896–1942), who toured the United States with her company; Elsa O'Connor (b. Elsa Asunción Celestino de Hartich, 1906–1947); Lola Membrives (1883–1968), for whom Jacinto Benavente wrote several of his female roles; and Paulina Singerman (1910–1984) and her sister Berta Singerman (b. 1897), who specialized in solo poetry recitals and who founded and directed a chamber theatre group.

Many actresses created memorable female characters: María Luisa Robledo (Spain/Argentina); Nuria Espert (Spain); Argentine Eva Franco, president of Casa del Teatro; Mexican Carmen Montejo; and Chilean Delfina Guzmán, actress and codirector of the theatre group Ictus. Of the present generation, Argentine actresses Norma Aleandro and Soledad Silveyra have shown an interest in scripts that examine women's issues. Noted in their special fields are the bilingual (Yiddish and Spanish) actress Jordana Fain of Argentina; the actress and mentor Hedy Crilla (Germany/Argentina, b. Hedwig Schlichter de Crilla, 1899–1984); puppet creator and director Mané Bernardo (Argentina); the Chilean folklorist, performer, and writer of protest songs Violeta Parra; Argentine performer and songwriter María Elena Walsh; Venezuelan puppeteer Carmen Delia Bencomo; Brazilian Maria Clara Machado and Peruvian Sara Joffré, both devoted to children's theatre; and the Argentine dancer/choreographers Iris Scaccheri and Ana María Stekelman, the latter director of the Buenos Aires Municipal Ballet.

As directing opened to women, actresses became directors, showing an interest in sociopolitical concerns of which women's status is a part. Examples are the Argentines Inda Ledesma, Marcela Solá, Norma Aleandro, Laura Yusem, Beatriz Matar, and Alejandra Boero; the Cuban director and playwright Karla Barro; the Costa Rican Bélgica Castro; the Venezuelan Germana Quintana; and the Mexican Martha Luna. Film director and producer María Luisa Bemberg (Argentina), a dedicated feminist, earned international recognition for her films *Camila, Miss Mary*, and *Sor Juana*. Graciela Galán (Argentina), scene and costume designer for theatre and opera, collaborated in these films. Other scene designers who entered this mostly male-dominated arena are the Mexican Félida Medina and Argentines María Julia Bertotto, Mayenco Hlousek, and Renatha Schussheim, painter and designer.

The richest and most lasting contribution comes from playwrights. Sor Juana Inés de la Cruz (Mexico, b. Juana Inés de Asbaje, 1648–1695), often called the "first feminist of Hispanic America," entered a convent as the only means to assert her right to an education. Though her plays *Los empeños de una casa* (The Labors of Home), *El divino Narciso* (The Divine Narcissus), and *San Hermenegildo* conform to the "comedia" and miracle play format of her time, her feminism is implicit in her participation in a field restricted to men in the seventeenth century and explicit in her approach to writing. Alfonsina Storni (1892–1938), Argentine writer, teacher, and committed feminist, wrote children's plays and some controversial adult plays: *The Master of the World, Cimbelline in 1900*, and *Polixena and the Little Cook*. Two strong female voices are Clorinda Matto de Turner (Peru, pseud. Carlota Dimont, 1852–1909), who wrote *Hima Sumac* (1892), and Gertrudis Gómez de Avellaneda (Cuba, 1814–1873) author of *La hija de las flores* (The Flowers' Daughter), *Saúl*, and *Tres amores* (Three Loves). The Mexican Rosario Castellanos (1925–1974) is an important feminist voice. In *El eterno femenino* (1975; The Eternal Feminine) she uses verbal and theatrical clichés to expose and satirize ingrained stereotypes of the Mexican culture.

A psychological, rather than a social female, perspective is typical of Elena Garro (Mexico) in *La señora en su balcón* (1960; The Lady at Her Balcony) and *La mudanza* (1959; The Move) and of Luisa Josefina Hernández (Mexico), author of *Los frutos caídos* (1976; The Fallen Fruit). The

Argentine Griselda Gambaro's recurrent theme is the relationship between victim and victimizer, which she sometimes illustrates with a male/female dyad, as in *El campo* (1967) (*The Camp*, 1970), *La malasangre* (1982; Evil Blood), and *Del sol naciente* (1984; Of the Rising Sun). Gambaro has perceived the need to make her female characters less peripheral and more dynamic from a female perspective. Myrna Casas (Puerto Rico) deals with the problem of female roles in *Absurdos en soledad* (1964; Absurd in Solitude) and *Eugenia Victoria Herrera* (1964).

The following contemporary playwrights concern themselves with the larger sociopolitical issues of their times and environment, reflecting them in various styles: in Spain, Laura Olmo and Ana Diosdado; in Mexico, Maruxa Vilalta (Spain/Mexico), Carlota O'Neill, and Sabina Berman; in Argentina, Malena Sándor (1913–1968), Roma Mahieu (Poland/Argentina), Beatriz Mosquera, Marta Lehmann, Aida Bortnik, Nelly Fernández Tiscornia, and Rosa Diana Raznovich; in Chile, Isidora Aquirre and María Asunción Requena; in Venezuela, Elizabeth Schön and Mariela Romero; in Cuba, María Alvarez Ríos, Gloria Parrado, and Ingrid González; in Brazil, Maria Wanderley Menezes; in Haiti, Mona Guérin; in Paraguay, Josefina Pla; in Peru, Sarina Helfgott; and in Costa Rica/Salvador, Carmen Naranjo. Though these dramatists examine women's status only tangentially, their voices merit careful attention.

References. Luiza Barreto Leite, *A mulher no teatro brasileiro* (Rio de Janeiro, 1965); Doris Meyer and Margarita Fernández Olmos (eds.), *Contemporary Women Authors of Latin America*, 2 vols. (Brooklyn, 1983); Yvette E. Miller and Charles M. Tatum (eds.), *Latin American Women Writers: Yesterday and Today* (Pittsburgh, 1977); Lily Sosa de Newton, *Diccionario biográfico de mujeres Argentinas* (Buenos Aires, 1986).

                                                                    EDITH E. PROSS

DRAMA AND THEATRE. United States. This field for women has inspired not only a popular list of actresses in a steady stream since 1752 but, beginning with the American Revolution, has provided a sporadic collection of important playwrights and managers and, more recently, creative directors and designers. Acting has long been for women a road to financial and creative independence. The other theatrical occupations have always been much more difficult to enter, and success within them has been an infrequent accomplishment. In two waves, however, c. 1890–1929 and c. 1960–present, women have made great strides in breaking the sexist barriers in the professional American theatre. Furthermore, it might be said in overview that from 1752 to c. 1890 women were primarily working to establish themselves in the marketplace of the theatre.

With the arrival from England of Mrs. Lewis Hallam (d. 1773) in 1752, colonists enjoyed the first prominent woman on the professional American stage. As the leading actress of the Hallam troupe, she was important in helping to establish the British classical and contemporary repertory, tastes, and performance styles that remained the prominent dramatic model in American theatres throughout much of the nineteenth century. Many more talented and popular British-born actresses, such as tragediennes Anne Brunton Merry (1769–1808) and Mary Ann Duff (1794–1857), followed in subsequent decades and dominated the stage until the rise of native stars in the 1840s. Merry even broke a masculine barrier briefly when her second husband died, and she took his place in co-managing for two years the Chestnut Theatre, the most important American playhouse until after 1810.

Although the eighteenth century produced few female playwrights, the fervor of the impending revolution inspired Mercy Otis Warren (1728–1814) to join the propagandistic war of belles lettres with her satirical *The Adulateur* (1773) and *The Group* (1775). After the Revolution plays by women were periodically produced in Philadelphia and Boston and subsequently published, most notably, the topical response to Barbary pirates *Slaves in Algiers* (1794) by actress/novelist Susanna Haswell Rowson (1762–1824).

Throughout much of the nineteenth century actresses found themselves in a disadvantageous social position. Recognized by many in church and society as immodest purveyors of deception and lasciviousness, working actresses might be ostracized from church services and the parlors of the best society, but economically they often worked on an equal footing with men. Although avenues to management and playwriting were more difficult, actresses grew in both numbers and prominence as the century progressed.

Despite the social and religious taboos, many women flocked to acting as a means of making a decent living, supporting a family, or attaining economic freedom. One of the most dynamic among those seeking independence was America's first native-born acting star, who not incidentally often portrayed male roles. Charlotte Cushman (1816–1876), who became a star by 1843, performed primarily from the standard repertory and was particularly admired as Lady Macbeth. Although many actresses in England and America habitually played breeches roles in the nineteenth century, Cushman's harsh physiognomy, deep voice, and authoritative manner led her to prominence in roles such as Cardinal Wolsey, Hamlet, and, especially, Romeo. Cushman made great strides in convincing the public that the stage could serve as a center for great artistic achievement.

Throughout the nineteenth century fewer American women writers ventured into drama than those who opted for other literary forms. Although plays written by women were infrequently produced professionally before 1915, the work of two women was quite successful. Young Louisa Medina (c. 1813–1838) created the first long runs at the Bowery Theatre in New York with her spectacular melodramas, such as *The Last Days of Pompeii* (1835) and *Nick of the Woods* (1838), adapted from recent novels. An unusually brave and talented woman, Anna Cora Mowatt (1819–1870), wrote *Fashion* (1845), a frequently revived comedy of manners effectually satirizing the nouveau riche and one of the finest plays of the century. Mowatt "betrayed" her social class by entering the acting profession in order to retrieve financial security after her husband lost his fortune. At the time she was accused of setting a bad, even depraved, example for women of gentle breeding. The second half of the nineteenth century witnessed the advent of important actress-managers who forged successful careers at the head of large companies and controlled their own theatres. Laura Keene (c. 1820–1873) and Louisa Lane Drew (1820–1897), both British-born, encountered difficulties from men who found the idea of women managers unseemly. Inspired by the example of Madame Vestris in London, Keene, also a successful actress, ran the Laura Keene Theatre in New York (1855–1863), apparently the first long-term solo management by a woman in America. Drew not only performed and ran an excellent stock company and the Arch Street Theatre in Philadelphia with resounding success for 32 years beginning in 1860 but also was the matriarch of the Barrymore theatrical dynasty.

As the nineteenth century approached its end, two actresses made important strides toward improving women's rights, Mary Shaw (1860–1929) as an activist and Minnie Maddern Fiske (1865–1932) as an independent actress/manager. Both were dedicated to important social issues in drama and nearly stood alone in championing the social dramas of Henrik Ibsen and Bernard Shaw in America. Under her own direction Fiske performed many of Ibsen's heroines, most notably, Nora and Hedda, often giving the plays the only unbowdlerized versions available in this country. With her husband she managed a superior acting company in the Manhattan Theatre (beginning 1901), thus making inroads against the stranglehold that the conservative Theatrical Syndicate had on professional theatre from 1896 to 1915.

As a suffragist and feminist, Mary Shaw became an important public speaker and crusader while touring the country in Ibsen's *Ghosts* beginning in 1899. In addition, she was arrested for playing the title role in the first American version of *Mrs. Warren's Profession* (1905), adjudged grossly immoral by the New York police. After starring in a suffragist play, *Votes for Women* (1909) by Elizabeth Robins, she attempted to found the Woman's National Theatre, which, if successful, would have had an all-woman management and artistic staff.

Before the 1920s most women who wrote with any success for the stage created light comedies celebrating conventional values. As suffrage approached, however, and with the arrival of the little theatre movement, which encouraged women to write for the stage, talented playwrights such as Rachel Crothers (1878–1958; *A Man's World* [1909]) and Susan Glaspell (1882–1948; *The Verge* [1921]) began to explore seriously women's problems such as the double standard, professionalism versus a career, and madness grown from social patterning. Glaspell was also instrumental in founding the Provincetown Players in 1915, the same year that Irene (c. 1894–1944) and Alice Lewisohn (c. 1883–1972) established the Neighborhood Playhouse, both influential little theatres that gave impetus to the first serious advance of artistic theatre off-Broadway.

In the 1920s one of America's finest actress-directors emerged in Eva Le Gallienne (1899–1991). Her privately subsidized Civic Repertory Theatre (1926–1932) and American Repertory Theatre (1946–1948), led by Le Gallienne with producer Cheryl Crawford (1902–1986) and director Margaret Webster (1905–1972), were dedicated to producing important revivals of modern classics like Ibsen and Chekhov, establishing permanent acting companies, and making the theatre affordable to all economic classes.

Le Gallienne's values and experiments anticipated the spirit of the regional theatre movement. Three of the most important nonprofit regional theatres dependent on subsidy were initiated by intrepid women: Margo Jones (1913–1955), Nina Vance (c. 1912–1980), and Zelda Fichandler (b. 1924), who popularized theatre-in-the-round, developed new playwrights, and demonstrated dedication to the classics with Theatre '47 in Dallas; the still-thriving Alley Theatre in Houston, begun in 1947; and the very active Arena Stage, founded in Washington, D.C., in 1950.

The only instance of federally subsidized theatre in the history of America was led by a woman. Hallie Flanagan Davis (1890–1969) directed the Federal Theatre Project (1935–1939) under the Works Progress Administration. During the Great Depression this project, which established theatres all over the country, employed thousands of actors, directors, playwrights, designers, and stagehands, who presented hundreds of productions. Davis insisted on including children's, black, classic, contemporary, and experimental theatre companies.

Undoubtedly America's most celebrated woman playwright, Lillian Hellman (1905–1984) stands as a symbol of the independent, professional woman both in her plays and in her life. *The Children's Hour* (1934) presents particular suffering in the lives of two unmarried professional women at the hands of a malicious child. Despite attention drawn to Hellman's work, few women playwrights emerged before the women's movement of the 1960s. After growing beyond the retrenchment following the success of suffrage, the shock of the depression, and the effort of World War II, women again became significant in all aspects of theatre with the performance groups and experiments in dramatic form characteristic of the 1960s. Megan Terry (b. 1932), for example, appeared with the Open Theatre and produced not only strong feminist statements in her plays like *Calm Down Mother* (1965) but also explored transformational character. Following the example of Terry's experiments with form and style, feminist writers began to break away from the traditional forms followed by Hellman and her predecessors. As women have discovered that many of their problems with identity, personal and professional needs, and emotional stability differ significantly from men's, so have the playwrights departed from the structure and methods created by men. Not only the subject matter has changed in women's plays, but the methodology as well.

Much off- and off-off-Broadway activity in the 1960s was inspired by women such as actress/director Judith Malina (b. 1926), who codirected the political Living Theatre (the primary inspiration for a host of performance groups), and Ellen Steward (n.d.), who in 1961 opened La Mama Experimental Theatre, the home for a myriad of young playwrights. Among the most important playwrights following such off-Broadway development are Maria Irene Fornes (b. 1930; *Fefu and Her Friends* [1977], an experiment in theatrical space demonstrating the effect of home environment on the female personality); Tina Howe (b. 1937; *Painting Churches* [1983], a generational conflict exploring art and the family); Marsha Norman (b. 1947; *'Night, Mother* [1982], an examination of suicide and mother–daughter relations); and Wendy Wasserstein (b. 1950; *The Heidi Chronicles* [1989], an art historian's search for self that also traces the women's movement across several decades). A host of important African American women have also commanded attention as playwrights, beginning with traditional Lorraine Hansberry (1936–1965) and continuing with the rituals and choreopoems of Adrienne Kennedy (b. 1931) and Ntozake Shange (b. 1948). (See AFRICAN AMERICAN PROSE WRITERS.)

Contemporary, postmodern directing in America has had no more dynamic exponent than JoAnne Akalaitis (b. 1937), whose work has featured both groundbreaking deconstructions and disturbing visual reinterpretations of modern classics like *Endgame* (1983). Controversies over performance art have persisted since the late 1980s with the self-explorations of Karen Finley (b. 1956) in such critiques of oppressive society as *We Keep Our Victims Ready* (1989). The union of theatre with dance found near perfect expression in the imagistic productions of Martha Clarke (b. 1944), whose *Vienna Lusthaus* (1986) disturbingly, but beautifully, explored the forbidden and the pleasurable.

During the 1970s many feminist theatres, notably the Omaha Magic Theatre, At the Foot of the Mountain (Minneapolis), and the Women's Project of the American Place Theatre (New York), sometimes working completely outside the commercial and professional world, emerged. The goals have included creating new plays by and about women while escaping the competitive nature of mainstream theatre by involving audiences in deconstructions of the familiar, bizarre, postmodern staging, frequent cross-dressing and gender blurring, ritual reconstructions of shared women's experiences, and improvisational or testimonial performances. Much of the work is also highly politicized and transcends gender differences to explore the once-forbidden territory of lesbian sexuality, as seen in the work of

Split Britches in New York beginning in 1981. One dynamic result of feminist theatre activity has been the burgeoning of poststructuralist, feminist theory and criticism since the mid-1980s, most markedly in the work of Jill Dolan (b. 1957) and Sue-Ellen Case (b. 1942). Such work has clearly transformed the larger field of theatrical criticism while affecting contemporary professional theatre practice. (See also PLAYWRIGHTS, U.S. [TWENTIETH-CENTURY].)

References. Albert Auster, *Actresses and Suffragists: Women in the American Theatre, 1890–1920* (New York, 1984); Sue-Ellen Case, *Feminism and Theatre* (New York, 1988); Helen Krich Chinoy and Linda Walsh Jenkins, *Women in American Theatre* (New York, 1981); Jill Dolan, *Presence and Desire* (Ann Arbor, 1993); Claudia D. Johnson, *American Actress: Perspective on the Nineteenth Century* (Chicago, 1984); Amelia Howe Kritzer, *Plays by Early American Women, 1775–1850* (Ann Arbor, 1995).

RONALD H. WAINSCOTT

DUAL-CAREER COUPLES are partners in a relationship in which both members pursue jobs that require commitment and training and have advancement potential. Such couples can be married or cohabiting, heterosexual or homosexual.

Two-thirds of all married women work outside the home. In 9 out of 10 such marriages, the husband has the major career interest, and the wife views her employment as secondary to her family responsibilities. However, the percentage of couples in dual-career marriages (a term coined by Rapoport and Rapoport) is rising. Couples most likely to be in dual-career relationships are college-educated, with strong needs for achievement and self-esteem and a belief in egalitarian gender roles.* Women are more likely to desire such relationships than are men.

Dual-career relationships are difficult, especially if children are involved, since child care responsibilities traditionally have fallen on the mother, and most careers are patterned for individuals without such concerns (traditionally, men). Societal attitudes also cause stress since most people believe a woman should put her husband and children ahead of her career. However, dual-career relationships seem to have clear economic, intellectual, and psychological benefits, particularly for women. Wives in dual-career marriages tend to have higher self-esteem, a greater sense of competence, and greater relationship satisfaction than wives in the labor force solely out of economic necessity or wives not in the labor force.

Reference. Rhona Rapoport and Robert Rapoport, *Dual-Career Families* (Harmondsworth, England, 1971).

SUSAN A. BASOW

DUAL ROLE is the double job of the woman who is employed full-time and also has the complete or major responsibility for the care of home and children. A growing number of women who head single-parent households

must not only provide all, or the major share of, income for the family*
but, after finishing a full day's work, assume all the duties and responsibilities of a homemaker.

In marriages in which both husband and wife work an equal length of
time producing income, the husband rarely spends an equal, or anywhere
nearly equal, time in doing housework.* Since the wife usually earns less
than the husband, her job tends to be considered less important and so
does not entitle her to more than minimum assistance in the home—helping
to clear the table and emptying the dishwasher, perhaps. Even when the
wife and husband earn comparable salaries, or the wife earns more than
the husband, she may still have the major responsibility for homemaking,
although in such marriages the husband is more likely to share more of the
housework than in marriages in which he is the primary breadwinner.

DUTCH WRITERS are women from Holland or the Flemish part of Belgium who write in Dutch or "Netherlandic." Until recently, there was no
female tradition in Dutch literature or any genuine awareness of women's
literary achievement. In 1920, however, Maurits Basse drew attention to
numerous, hitherto ignored women writers from the Middle Ages to the
nineteenth century. In 1934 Annie Romein-Verschoor published her dis-
sertation about female novelists after 1880. Lately, Hannemieke Stamper-
ius, Hanneke van Buuren, Truus Pinkster, Anja Meulenbelt, and others
have been studying women writers from a feminist perspective.

Among the oldest Dutch texts preserved are the biography and some
religious poems of Sister Beatrijs van Nazareth (c. 1200–1268) and numerous letters, poems, and "visions" of the mystic Hadewijch, who wrote
in the vernacular.

The Catholic sixteenth-century poet Anna Bijns (1493–1575), an Antwerp schoolmistress, produced three collections of poetry and a number
of plays. *Mariken van Nieumeghen* has been attributed to her. She participated fully in the literary life of her day, knew the leading figures of the
Chambers of Rhetoric, and wrote, in addition to very candid love poems,
virulent polemical verse attacking the Reformation and, especially, Luther.
Because it is inspired by deep personal feeling, Anna Bijns' poetry is better
than that of most *Rederijkers* (members of the Chambers of Rhetoric). The
poetry of her contemporary Katharina Boudewijn, who was out of touch
with literary fashions, represents a weak, late blooming of medieval religious verse.

The seventeenth century produced the pious Anna-Maria van Schuurman
(1607–1678), a scholar and artist known throughout Europe as a prodigy.
She was a staunch Calvinist and was extraordinarily learned, attended the
University of Utrecht, and wrote a Latin treatise discussing the usefulness
of intellectual training for girls. It was immediately translated into French
and English. She later rejected the ideas of this *Amica dissertatio* (1638),

however, and concentrated exclusively on theology and biblical exegesis. In Dutch she published an explanation of the first three chapters of Genesis, *Uitbreidingsrer de drie eerste capittels van Genesis* (1632); a contemplative essay about death, *Paelsteen van den tijt onzes levens* (1639); and her autobiography, *Eucleria of Uitkiezing van het beste deel* (1684; Eucleria or The Best Part).

After Anna-Maria van Schuurman there was a hiatus of about a century in which no female voices were heard. Then the eighteenth century peaks with *De Historie van Mejuffrouw Sara Burgerhart* (1782; The History of Miss Sara Burgerhart) about a middle-class girl in trouble who needs help and moral instruction. This book is the first modern Dutch novel and the first book written for and by women. The writers Betje Wolff (1738–1804) and Aagje Deken (1741–1804) promoted reason and virtue and described Dutch life with revolutionary realism and naturalness. They were influenced by Samuel Richardson and, like him, used the epistolary form. Before teaming up with Deken, Wolff produced poetry and numerous prose pieces, of which only *De Menuet en de dominees pruik* (1772; The Minuet and the Minister's Wig) is still read. Together with Deken she also wrote *Historie van den Heer Willem Leevend* (1784–1785; The History of Mr. Willem Leevend), *De brieven van Abraham Blankaart* (1887; The Letters of A. B.), and *Historie van Mejuffrouw Cornelia Widschut of de gevolgen van de opvoeding* (1793–1796; Story of C. W. or The Consequences of Education), all inferior to *Sara Burgerhart*, which provides an unsurpassed portrait of Dutch life in the eighteenth century.

Wolff and Deken were realists, not feminists, but they were thoroughly in touch with their time. Geertruida Bosboom-Toussaint, on the other hand, used history and aristocratic settings in other countries to escape her own milieu. Well known are her historical novels *Het huis Lauernesse* (1840; The House of Lauernesse) and the *Leycester* trilogy (1845–1855). The didactic novel *Majoor Frans* (1874; Major Frans), about the "masculine" and independent young woman Frans, seems modern but is hardly a denunciation of nineteenth-century morality. That Bosboom-Toussaint had no direct followers may be significant, for in the next 50 years novel writing by women increased dramatically. As the labor movement spread, the women's question also surfaced increasingly and was dealt with in novels by many women writers.

Mina Kruseman's *Een huwelijk in Indie* (1873; A Marriage in Indonesia), though of doubtful quality, is truly feminist and modern. It was the first of a large number of "emancipation novels" that form the first wave of Dutch feminism and include Anna de Savornin-Lohman's *Het eenige nodige* (1897; The Only Thing One Needs), Cécile Goedkoop's *Hilda van Suylenburg* (1898), and Cornélie Huygens' *Barthold Meryan* (1897). This trend is continued by the feminist Jo van Ammers-Küller (1887–1966) but stops as a general phenomenon around World War II.

In the first half of the twentieth century the vast majority of writing women concerned themselves with the so-called small genres, especially children's books and religious and didactic work. Many contributors of the Catholic journal *Van Onzen Tijd* (Our Time) and the Protestant weekly *Ons Tijdschrift* (Our Journal) were women. Serious literature was still almost entirely a male preserve. Notable early exceptions are the novelist Virginie Loveling (1836–1923), a foremost representative of Flemish realism; the poet Hélène Swarth (1859–1944); the realist novelist Carry van Bruggen (1881–1932); and the poet Henriette Roland Holst-van der Schalk (1869–1952), editor of the socialist journal *De Nieuwe Tijd* (A New Time) and author of a vast oeuvre, including the poetry collection *Tussen tijd en eeuwigheid* (1934; Between Time and Eternity).

World War II has been recorded in the diaries of two of its victims, Anne Frank (1929–1945) and Etty Hilesum (1914–1943), and is a major theme in postwar fiction, especially the novels of Marga Minco (b. 1920), Hanny Michaelis (b. 1922), and Mischa de Vreede (b. 1936). Also important is a preoccupation with the colonial past and life in the colonies of Surinam (described by Miep Diekman, Sonia Germers, Bea Vianen, Thea Doelwijt, and Diane Lebacs) and Indonesia (Augusta de Wit, Maria Dermoût, Beb Vuyk, Margaretha Ferguson, and Marion Bloem). The novelist Anna Blaman (1905–1960), the author of *Vrouw en vriend* (1941; Woman and Friend), *Eenzaam avontuur* (1948; Lonely Adventure), and *Op leven en dood* (1954; A Matter of Life and Death), was influenced by the French existentialists and described unsatisfactory relationships of people afraid of loneliness and death. Her analyses of the psychology of sex and eroticism met with great resistance.

Serious modern poets of quality are Ida Gerhardt (b. 1908), Clara Eggink (b. 1906), Vasalis (b. 1909; was awarded the P. C. Hooft Prijs and the Constantijn Huygens Prijs), Ellen Warmond (b. 1930), Maria de Groot (b. 1937), and the feminist poet Elly de Waard (b. 1940).

The second wave of feminism has occasioned an outburst of female writing on topics ranging from divorce (L. Stassaert, A. Meulenbelt, Dolores Thijs), celibate motherhood (Aleida Leeuwenberg, Gertje Gort) and giving up a child (Christine Kraft), to lesbianism (Blaman, Burnier, Meulenbelt) and sex-change operations (Dirkje Kuik). There are two main tendencies: (1) social, where the focus is on the immediate, honest expression of lived or observed experience, as in Anja Meulenbelt's *No More Shame* (1976) and (2) literary, where the author's feminism is interwoven with her search for new forms and techniques, as in the novels of Andreas Burnier (b. 1931) and Monika van Paemel (b. 1945) and in the poetic feminism exemplified by Lucienne Stassaert (b. 1936). Less academic but no less literary are Hannes Meinkema (b. 1943), Mensje van Keulen (b. 1946), Doeschka Meysing (b. 1947), and Hester Albach (b. 1954). The sales figures indicate that these young writers strike a responsive chord in the population.

MAYA BIJVOET WILLIAMSON

DYSTOPIAS are literary works depicting an imaginary society in which conditions are worse than in the author's experience, as opposed to a *utopia*, in which conditions are better. (*Dystopia* means "bad place" or "evil place," *utopia* means "good place.") While some dystopias by women deal with many of the same issues as dystopias by men, feminist dystopias focus upon how extreme forms of patriarchy affect women's lives.

Like the utopia, the dystopia uses certain traditional narrative strategies. One of the most basic is the fantastic journey to an alternative world, an unknown land, another planet, or, most frequently, to the future. Another is the philosophical dialogue. Also, the dystopia frequently uses satire and irony to contrast present with future conditions that, the dystopia implies, will occur if current evils go unchecked.

Two of the most important dystopian novels by women written before World War II are *Swastika Night* by Katharine Burdekin (pen name Murray Constantine; 1937, repr. 1985) and *Kallocain*, by the Swedish poet Karin Boye (1940; Eng. trans., 1966). *Swastika Night*, published 12 years before Orwell's *1984* (which it resembles), portrays a grim future three centuries hence in which Nazism has conquered the world. Burdekin draws a clear parallel between woman hating and other forms of oppression. In *Kallocain*, a male chemist creates a "truth" drug that empowers the state to read minds and thus to destroy the last vestiges of individual privacy.

The 1960s, 1970s, and 1980s have seen a flowering of speculative fiction by women, including many utopias and dystopias. Although women's dystopias show many of the usual concerns of men's, they also focus upon women's lives under patriarchy. They deal with the rise of the religious Right, the loss of women's control over their bodies, the persecution of minorities, and the loss of women's recent political gains.

Women's oppression is justified by religious fundamentalism in *The Handmaid's Tale* by Canadian Margaret Atwood (1986) and *Native Tongue* by Suzette Hadin Elgin (1984). In English author Zoe Fairbairn's *Benefits* (1979), the state seizes control of women's reproductive ability. The legally sanctioned oppressing of minorities appears in *The Handmaid's Tale* and in *The Godmothers* by Canadian Sandi Hall (1982). Atwood and Elgin, in particular, show in nightmarish detail how the oppressive world they describe is already germinating in the 1980s.

Many utopian works also have dystopian elements, for example, Ursula K. LeGuin's *The Dispossessed* (1974), Joanna Russ' *The Female Man* (1975), Marge Piercy's *Woman on the Edge of Time* (1976), and Sally Miller Gearhart's *The Wanderground* (1979). Russ and Gearhart both show destruction of the environment, loss of individual freedom, and extreme polarizing of male and female gender roles, all occurring as male aggression goes unchecked.

Many women's dystopias, unlike men's, assume that women's oppression under patriarchy is related to other forms of oppression and that patriarchy oppresses men as well. Male authors often assume that the desire for power is part of human nature and that oppression is thus inevitable. As a result, they conclude that the desire for utopia itself leads to worse conditions than those it seeks to correct (e.g., Huxley in *Brave New World* and Evgeny Zamyatin in *We* [*Nous autres*]). But because many women authors see the urge for power as stemming from patriarchal ideology and not as existing as an immutable part of human nature, they are frequently more optimistic about the possibility of change.

References. Carol Farley Kessler (ed.), *Daring to Dream: Utopian Stories by United States Women, 1836–1919* (crit. bib. and annot. bib. 1836–1983; London, 1984); Ruby Rohrlich and Elaine Hoffman Baruch (eds.), *Women in Search of Utopia: Mavericks and Mythmakers* (New York, 1984).

CHARLENE BALL

E

EAST CENTRAL EUROPEAN WRITERS (EARLY). In Eastern Europe political history has determined the place of women writers more obviously than in Western European nation-states, where unified languages simplified the growth of national literatures. The multinational Austro-Hungarian empire included peoples with old cultures and languages but without political status. In addition, the Turkish Ottoman empire occupied over half of the area for two to five centuries. When the discovery of sea routes to Asia ended the early prosperity of Eastern Europe based on the "silk roads," economic stagnation and political conservatism created general problems crying out for commentary by women writers as well as by men. Thus, social themes tended to predominate, though intermixed with religious and personal moral concerns.

No medieval Latin works are known from women authors, though certain wealthy convents apparently had schools and extensive libraries. Vernacular medieval literature by women is also unknown, even in the Czech language, which showed the most intensive development during Hussite emphasis upon vernacular religious texts under the influence of Wycliffe's followers at Oxford. The wider development of vernacular literatures in the Renaissance and Reformation stimulated women writers among the literate nobility. Research is still incomplete, but a few secular lyrics are found in private letters, and more numerous religious hymns are attributed tentatively to women who were important patrons, if not authors. Both epistolary practice and literary patronage appear as steps toward personal affirmation in literature. More is known of the baroque period (seventeenth and eighteenth centuries), particularly about religious hymnists or memoir writers. An interesting memoirist was the Magyar Kata Bethlen (1700–1759), who felt forced into a Catholic marriage in violation of her Calvinist conscience. The prayer book of Katarina Frankopan Zrinski (1625–1673),

Putni Tovarus, expressing her hope and despair at the anti-Hapsburg rebellion she took part in, was the first Croatian writing by a woman. Related by family connections to Zrinski and part of the same continuing rebellion was Kata-Szidonia Petroczy, whose Magyar hymns (written to Slovak and German melodies as well as Magyar) included political themes against the Austrian throne (1690–1708). Another type of hymn gave moralistic advice against seduction by the Slovak Rebeka Leskova in 1798 in the first literary work by a woman in the newly restored Czech language. Such a complex of political and cultural relations was characteristic of Eastern Europe. Numerous women collected songbooks of anonymous authorship to which they may have contributed. Another group of women known to be literate and literary were the printers' wives working with their husbands or as widows, but it is difficult to know whether they composed or only edited the many anonymous hymns and poems they printed.

A quite different treasury exists in the thousands of extant folk lyrics, alternately merry, teasing, exhortative, and hauntingly sad, which were once sung while women and girls worked, birthed, married, mourned, and died. Though anonymous, they were indubitably created by the women who sang them.

NORMA L. RUDINSKY

EAST CENTRAL EUROPEAN WRITERS (FROM THE NINETEENTH CENTURY). Two trends emerged in women's literature of the early nineteenth century and have persisted to the present. In the struggle to form national states from the multinational empires that characterized this region, both men and women writers felt called upon to serve as prophets and guides. Thus, political and social themes usually predominated. Periodically, however, this engagé tradition was abandoned for intensely personal lyric expression of erotic, feminist, or domestic subjects indistinguishable from women's concerns elsewhere.

One of the earliest prose writers was the Czech Bozena Nemcova (1820–1862), who can be compared to George Sand. Her one novel, stories, and sketches are early examples of realism and Romantic feminism. After the failed revolutions of 1848 and with the increasing women's movement, writers explicitly sought to reveal women's function in the national movement. Katarina Svetla's first novel in 1861 pictured an inspirational mother of two Czech revolutionaries, and Elena Marothy-Soltesova created a Slovak woman inspiring her renegade husband to return to his nation. In much fiction the nationalist heroines were schoolteachers bravely maintaining their students' language and identity. The Czech poet Eliska Krasnohorska and the Slovak Terezia Vansova were also important as editors of the earliest women's magazines in their languages. Czech dramatist Gabriela Preissova depicted sharply realistic village women, and the prose of Marie Majerova (1882–1967) showed her strong social concerns. Rebellious women forced by financial need into unhappy marriages characterized the powerfully perceptive satires of Slovak Bozena Slancikova Timrava. Historical novels and nationalist poetry were chosen by Maria Kubasec and Mina Witkojc, respectively, the first women writers of the restored Lusatian Sorbian language in its tiny enclave in eastern Germany.

Izadora Sekulic (1877–1958) wrote psychological novels and essays that helped develop modern Serbian prose, while Ivana Brlic-Mazuranic (b. 1874) chose mythic themes. Queen Elisabeth of Romania (1843–1916), though not of Romanian descent, translated Romanian folk literature into French and German under the pseudonym Carmen Sylvia. A popular saga by Hortensia Papadat-Bengescu followed a single family, and she is considered the founder of the Romanian urban novel. The first major Magyar novelist, Margit Kaffka (1880–1919), showed apparently autobiographical portraits of female characters unable to find a place in the slowly modernizing world. Strong females in a changing world also characterize the novels of Magda Szabo (b. 1917). Historical novels were written by Cecile Tormay and Eren Gulacsy, as well as the expressionistic Slovak Margita Figuli (1909–1996) during World War II. The Bulgarian Blaga Dimitrova (b. 1921) wrote powerful fiction and poetry as well as essays, and emigrée Julia Kristeva has become famous for her place in French psychoanalytic and semiotic literary theory.

The personal lyric tradition was influenced by French modernism. The Magyar Minka Czobel cultivated symbolist poetry at the turn of the century, and Renee Erdos expressed erotic details in both poetry and fiction. Ludmila Podjavorinska returned to the Slovak ballad as a sensitive vehicle of personal emotions, and the ostensibly simple lyrics of Masa Halamova (1908–1995) beautifully condensed elemental experiences of love and death. The Serbian lyric poet Desanko Maksimovic (b. 1898) published several volumes on highly individualized themes, then changed to patriotic poetry in World War II. The Bulgarian poet Elisaveta Bagryana (1893–1991) wrote moving, intimate, and feminist poetry until the war turned her also to political concerns.

Socialist feminism, following Karl Marx and August Bebel, traditionally considered sex discrimination as a capitalist contradiction that socialist society cures. Thus, the post–World War II communist governments of Eastern Europe, led by the former Soviet Union, provided unprecedented educational and employment opportunities but allowed no women's studies as such. Unofficial women's movements existed, however, and revealed perceived problems, as did dissident writers, though their reflection in socialist realist literature seldom exceeded typical workingwomen's concerns with child care and domestic burdens. The collapse of all those governments in 1989 offered new opportunities for expression, but it also radically disrupted the established parameters of literary creation, both internal and external. The sudden freedom from censorship, from taboo subjects, proscribed authors, prescribed styles, and so on also paradoxically destroyed the value of subtle Aesopian language, which had been carefully and courageously constructed to both hide and reveal political resistance through encoded symbolism, fables, historical parallels, or simply an ironic authorial persona. Everything could now be said openly and directly. Besides this loss of what had been practically a predominant genre, writers were replaced in their unique mission as public spokespersons by politicoeconomic celebrities in the new governments and the suddenly independent journalistic media. External changes further diminished literary production, as state-supported publishers dissolved or commercialized their output with quick translations of Western pulp fiction. The economic transition also became personally disruptive through unemployment, inflation, and decreased social benefits, which seem to have hit women hardest.

Some writers are meeting the new challenges by publishing full versions of older works or by accepting direct political roles. In Romania the highly respected opposition poet Ana Blandiana (b. 1942) has also actively participated in civil protests against post-Ceauşescu injustices. The poet Daniela Crasnaru (b. 1950), elected to Parliament in 1990, is publishing works that were previously secreted. In Bulgaria Blaga Dimitrova (b. 1922) published in 1991 the full version of her 1981 novel *Litze* (Face/Person), which, even though shortened, had been withdrawn from circulation. Very active in politics, she was elected vice president of Bulgaria in 1992 but resigned in 1994. Other writers remain observers, not participants. Recent prose of the versatile Dubravka Ugresic (b. 1949) includes her ironic reflections on the tragic war in Croatia as seen from the United States, where she was working. Certain former dissidents have continued, for example, the Czech Eva Kanturkova, whose memoir details her prison stay with criminal women as "friends from a funeral parlor." Zdena Frybova's novel series satirizing post-1989 economic changes, new forms of corruption, Mafia activities, and public disappointment with "freedom" in Prague became popular for its veracity. Among Slovak authors Milka Zimková's sequel to her prizewinning film *Pasla kone na beton* (She Pastured the Horses on Concrete) shows the same comic family in eastern Slovakia after 1989, and Maria Batorova emphasizes intellectuals' engagement of national questions in the new democracy. The very young Albanian Mimoza Ahmeti (b. 1963) has written lyrical psychological work.

A dynamic new element for these women writers exists in their many organizations and networks as women alone, in contrast to the former communist writers, which were unions tightly organized by men. For a typical example, in Slovakia at least two groups are publishing theoretical works, reviews, and general women's studies as well as prose and poetry in original and translation. They organize workshops and conferences, travel to international gender centers such as *Europa vor ort* in Berlin, and prepare materials for school and university use. All such groups very actively network with each other and with informed women's groups in Western Europe and the United States. The Internet is essential, especially for such tiny groups as the Albanian women in the Kosovo region of Serbia and generally for the war-torn former Yugoslavia, where gender center activities extend to rape victim support, peace leagues, and refugee assistance, as well as literary activities.

Though relatively little post-1989 literature has yet appeared, the current rapid increase in such texts with a wider register of formerly taboo themes and, in general, the wealth and variety of women's activities suggest that the initial culture shock has been overcome. One can eventually expect a rich literary synthesis of the former dissidents' openness, the nuance and sophistication of writer and reader underlying and fostering Aesopian language, and the interaction of Eastern and Western formal and thematic experiments that (on both sides) were inaccessible or unappreciated in the past. The decade after 1989 will ultimately be recognized as a time of creative chaos and fruitful incubation.

NORMA L. RUDINSKY and ETELA FARKÁŠOVÁ

ECTOPIC PREGNANCY is a pregnancy outside the uterus, most usually in the fallopian tube but also possible in other locations, such as the ovary, abdominal cavity, or cervix. Untreated ectopic pregnancies are the major cause of maternal deaths in early pregnancy.

In an ectopic pregnancy the fertilized egg does not complete its normal passage down the fallopian tube to the uterus but attaches itself to tissue outside the uterus. In most cases, the journey is stopped by an obstruction in the tube, such as scar tissue or a malformation. Unable to proceed, it implants itself on the tube wall. Failure of the egg to reach the uterus can also be caused by impairment of the muscle activity of the tube, inhibiting the contractions necessary to move the egg, or the fertilized egg may have implanted on endometrial tissue (the tissue lining the uterine cavity) in the tube wall (endometriosis*). In some cases a fertilized egg may have passed into the pelvic cavity instead of entering the tube, or a tubal pregnancy may have aborted and traveled back up the tube into the pelvic cavity, to replant on the abdominal wall. In all cases the site and tissue are not suited for the development of a fetus.

All ectopic pregnancies are life-threatening and need to be discovered and treated surgically as early as possible. In tubal pregnancies, if not aborted early or removed surgically, the fetus will rupture the tube, usually within 8 to 12 weeks. Modern technologies have greatly increased early diagnosis and treatment. Before the mid-1970s over three-quarters of tubal pregnancies ruptured before being discovered; by the mid-1980s, around three-quarters were being treated before rupture. If the pregnancy is discovered before it ruptures the tube, the tube can be saved. An incision is made in the tube, and the conceptus is removed, or possibly it can be "milked out" without incision. A ruptured tube must be removed. There have been instances of pregnancies in other locations going near to term, but the delivery of a normal infant is rare.

The number of ectopic pregnancies has been rising. The use of contraceptive intrauterine devices and the increasing occurrence of pelvic inflammatory disease with resulting scarring of the fallopian tubes are thought to be responsible for much of the increase. Older estimates put the incidence at about 1 in 300 pregnancies. Some estimates in the early 1980s have run as high as 1 in 40. After an ectopic pregnancy, about 60 percent of women retain the ability to reproduce, but they are at risk for a recurrence of ectopic pregnancy or for miscarriage.

Reference. L. Madaras and J. Patterson with P. Shick, *WomanCare: A Gynecological Guide to Your Body*, 2d ed. (New York, 1984), 683–692.

EDUCATION. In Western civilization, education constitutes, first of all, the traditional molding of character by which societies inculcate their mores into their young. With respect to women, the aim has been to produce obedient daughters, chaste maidens, willing workers, faithful wives, and nurturing mothers. Training has most often been given in the home and/or under religious auspices.

Athenian women of the golden age did not participate in the great intellectual advances of their time; daughters of citizens received no education at all. But among the Romans upper-class young women were often tutored along with their brothers in order to enhance their role as mothers of soldiers and statesmen. In the early Christian era, St. Jerome agreed that women should be educated, by which he meant schooled in their religion. During the medieval period convent life was the only source of learning for women. Some nuns were highly educated and were able to manage abbeys, corresponding with educated men. Some upper-class women during the Renaissance were also learned; their male relatives displayed them along with their palaces, their art, and their libraries.

Women's education, like that of men, varied according to the roles individual women were expected to play in the society—servant, court lady, bourgeois helpmate, worker. The common denominator, however, for almost all women's education in the past was the intention of inculcating the religious virtues considered proper to their sex: chastity and obedience. Any additional learning was mainly for the purpose of enhancing the role of the males in their families.

Even when not tied to religion, in periods of enlightenment and change the ideal aims of women's education remained the same. In the mid-eighteenth century, Jean-Jacques Rousseau wrote in *Émile* (1762) that women should be trained in relation to men "to please them, be useful to them, be loved and honored by them, raise them when young, care for them when grown, counsel them, console them, render life sweet and agreeable to them." This purpose might be interpreted more or less broadly in different periods but remained at the heart of the education afforded to women.

Instruction, formerly a secondary goal of education, assumed greater importance as the division of labor created more complex societies. But, for the most part, women were instructed only in domestic skills, including the handwork required for the family clothing or, later, for the trade practiced by the family. However, in early modern times upper-class young women of all countries were taught "accomplishments" (dancing, fine needlework, music, drawing, and foreign languages) in order to enhance their value on the marriage market. During the seventeenth and eighteenth centuries some women, after marriage, were able to further their education by opening salons that attracted learned men able to converse with them.

Reading was a luxury of leisured women until the Reformation prescribed elementary education for all in Protestant countries for the purpose of reading the Bible. From that time on, the primary education of women has been closely tied to that of the lowest classes in general. With individual exceptions, societies that did not educate the poorest males did not provide formal instruction for women.

The needs of an expanding economy arising from the commercial revolution and Industrial Revolution in modern times led to the extension of secondary education for men, but not for women. As a result, the relative position of women declined in the centuries of modernization. Their lack of education made women lower-class, whatever their family, and unskilled workers, whatever their trade.

At the end of the Enlightenment Mary Wollstonecraft had challenged Rousseau's position that women should be trained only for their marital and maternal roles. In her *Vindication of the Rights of Women* (1792) she noted the frivolity and silliness of upper-class women and attributed them to the woeful inadequacy of their intellectual training. Others, from Christine de Pisan in the fourteenth century to Catherine Macauley Graham in the eighteenth, had made the same point. But Wollstonecraft was the first to call for a system of universal coeducation in which the intelligence of women would be trained equally with that of men. She maintained that women could not even be good wives and mothers without instruction. She suggested that women who did not have family duties might become doctors, managers, even legislators if their faculties were fully developed.

During the French Revolution the Marquis de Condorcet submitted to the Convention a plan for primary school coeducation on a national level. He maintained that without it there could be no equality within the family and therefore none in the society. But he also insisted that women be given equal access to education as a matter of simple justice. However, Rousseau's views on women continued to dominate, in some form, the nineteenth-century developments in women's education. Even those who admitted the theory of equality between the sexes insisted on differences in their training. "Separate but equal," the most liberal position on women's education for all but a few, ensured inferior education for women well into the twentieth century, even when the "women's sphere" was broadened to include practical subjects like home economics and business courses.

Western elites justified the inferior education given women, as they did that given the lower classes, on the basis of their supposed biological inferiority. Aristotle was only one of many to identify the male with form, the female with matter; the male as active, the female as passive. The brains of females were said to be either smaller or more fragile—in general, incapable of grasping abstract ideas. In early modern times the clergy was convinced that reading and writing would lead women only to moral harm; they would read evil literature and write love letters. In the nineteenth century women were admonished that exposure to higher education would render them unfit to bear children. Despite these strictures, women sought education, and the necessities of the modern world gradually increased the amount and quality of the education they received.

Progress differed among nations. In general, there was more awareness of the necessity to educate as many people as possible in those nations that were economically more advanced. But in the nineteenth century this awareness did not always extend to women. Nor did the other argument for universal education after the extension of suffrage—"educating our rulers," as Gladstone put it—apply to women. Therefore the adoption of female education in different countries or parts of countries was often tied to some particular situation.

The German states were far ahead in primary education because of their Protestant background; Russia, in need of doctors, gladly opened its medical schools to women. In France, women's secondary education was part of a republican effort to decrease the influence of the Catholic Church because of the church's opposition to liberal political development; women's secondary education was not, however, intended to lead to higher education or careers. In Spain and Italy, church influence maintained the traditional forms of female education, in home and convent.

This unwillingness to alter tradition was manifest in England and the United States, where education was not controlled by the national governments. Left to themselves, most communities did not choose to educate women beyond the three Rs. In England, where secondary education was primarily for elite males, women's education lagged far behind, despite the founding of a few colleges in London, Oxford, and Cambridge. Major American cities established high schools during the nineteenth century, serving both men and women, and women's colleges (really secondary schools) were founded under private auspices. Only in the land-grant colleges of some of the states did American women receive the same higher education as men. The relative deprivation of women in this area is often obscured by the large numbers of women who were attending school in the United States.

In general, the modern experience is that women, like minority groups, are ensured an equal education only when the national government is committed to an education that guarantees it to them. The Protestant German states had achieved almost complete literacy of their population, male and female, by the end of the eighteenth century. However, Germany was the last of the industrialized nations to allow women into universities. France initiated universal education in the late nineteenth century, including female secondary education. But women had great difficulty enrolling in French universities until after World War I. Russia, in great need of doctors and administrators, had allowed women to attend universities in the late nineteenth century but installed universal education only under the communist regime.

By 1950, communist countries had equal numbers of men and women (per hundred thousand population) in universities, followed closely by France. Germany maintained its more restrictive policies on women in higher education until later in the century. In 1990 the former East Germany, like most communist countries, had almost equal numbers of men and women in universities, while in the former West Germany the proportion of women to men was less than two-thirds. The USSR had fallen behind, with a percentage of women to men of only 87 percent. In the same year France had more women than men in higher education. In England and the United States, where democratic local control of schooling has prevailed, persistence of traditional views was long responsible for the undereducation of females on all levels of the educational ladder. In 1990 the United Kingdom had roughly the same percentage of women to men in higher education as the USSR, 87 percent.

The other important factor in equal educational opportunity for women is also related to government. Where schooling is provided without cost, the proportion of males and females at all levels moves toward equality, particularly if education to a certain level is obligatory. Where parents must contribute, fewer girls than boys are enrolled in primary schools. Child labor laws must also be enforced to ensure attendance. The same principle of cost applies to women's access to higher education. The proportion of women in universities in the United States long lagged behind that in nations where university education was provided by the state without cost. Since midcentury this situation has been rectified somewhat by government loan and scholarship policies. In 1990 there were more women than men (per hundred thousand) in higher education.

Even when the optimum conditions are met, traditional views of what courses of study are appropriate for women may result in educational inequality. Until recently, science and mathematics courses were considered less appropriate for women than for men because the high-level careers to which they led were viewed as masculine. This is also clear on the level of university teaching, long a masculine preserve. In no developed country were women more than 40 percent of the teachers in universities in 1990. Those where they were more than 30 percent were all ex-communist. In the United Kingdom the percentage was 19; in the United States, 27.

Education of women for particular professions tends also, because of the assumption of female intellectual inferiority, to result in the devaluation of those professions and the curricula that lead to them (i.e., teaching in the United States, medicine in the USSR). However, the presence of large numbers of educated women in a society tends to break down the traditional views of gender and leads to better opportunities for the next generation of women. The United Nations has recognized that one of the most important elements in the development of Third World nations is the education of their women. Illiteracy rates for women age 15 to 24 in undeveloped countries range from 28 percent in Tunisia, to 49 percent in Haiti, to 88 percent in Yemen. In all regions of the world there are more illiterate women than men. The enrollment of females in primary and secondary schools is now climbing faster in most areas of the world than that of males. Even so, the World Bank announced in 1995 that it intended to devote a proportion of its budget specifically for the primary education of women.

References. Phyllis Stock, *Better than Rubies, a History of Women's Education* (New York, 1978); United Nations, *The World's Women 1995, Trends and Statistics* (New York, 1995).

PHYLLIS H. STOCK-MORTON

EDUCATION. Higher Education. Women have a young history in higher education compared to the general history of higher education in America, which began in 1636 with the founding of Harvard, a liberal arts college for men. The express purpose of college was to train the religious leaders and statesmen of the new nation. Women, not included in the ruling elite, were not considered potential students of higher education.

In the eighteenth and nineteenth centuries the purpose of men's colleges broadened to include preprofessional and, eventually, graduate training in medicine, law, and teaching. When, in the 1830s, coeducational experiments were introduced into American higher education, and the first women's colleges were chartered, it was not the aim or purpose of higher education for women to produce civic leaders as such or to prepare women for the professions. By law and by custom no professional careers were open to women until well into the twentieth century. When "exceptional" women did earn law or medical degrees, their femininity was subject to considerable speculation. Regardless of sanctions against women in the professions, some women did practice law and medicine before the turn of the century.

The impetus for higher education for women derived from complex interactions among economic, social, and political factors in the nineteenth century, among them the following: industrialization with its consequent shifts in the role and status of the family and the growth of class differentiation; the diffusion of democratic ideals and institutions that nurtured the growth of public schools and fostered ideas of the dignity of labor; and the spirit of humanistic reform, spawned by the European Enlightenment and modified to deal with the economic and social institutions peculiar to nineteenth-century American culture.

Two schools of thought on advanced education for women emerged. First, advocates of education for women per se called for the education of women to fill their "true sphere" as wives, mothers, and guardians of the nation's morality. Actually, with rapidly changing economic structures, growing urbanization, and revolutionizing discoveries in natural science, the American family and women's role in it were in the process of major change. However, the assumption remained throughout the nineteenth century that every daughter of the middle class should be prepared thoroughly for her future as wife and mother. The impact of this domestic goal on vocational training in postsecondary institutions of learning, including colleges, was to introduce greatly expanded domestic curricula into departments of home sciences (home economics).

Second, opponents of higher education for women also fastened onto the issue of women's proper sphere; the best interests of society, the opponents said, are threatened by a college education that leads women away from their domestic duties. The elite women's colleges, offering curricula modeled on those of Harvard and Yale, were urged to raise domesticity to curricular emphasis, and to the extent that Vassar (1860), Smith and Wellesley (1875), Bryn Mawr (1880), and Mount Holyoke (1888) ignored that urging, they were attacked for unsexing their students, for endangering the frail health of young women, and for subversively intending to undermine the family and, thus, the nation.

Concurrently, the nation's expanding systems of public elementary and secondary schools needed teachers. For the first time in the nation's history, women as a class, a separate group distinguished solely on the basis of gender, were assigned a "legitimate" public role and function as teachers.

The Civil War marked the critical point in women's participation in higher education. During the war and in the years following, colleges faced financial crisis. As male enrollment declined, revenues from student fees, the major source of income, shrank dramatically. Suddenly, women emerged as the viable source of financial rescue for struggling men's colleges. Coeducational experiments at previously all-male bastions were inaugurated, and land-grant colleges that proliferated after the Civil War initiated coeducation as they opened. By 1890, 70 percent of female college students were enrolled in coeducational institutions.

Many women could pay for their own college education with earnings from teaching, dressmaking, and domestic work. Middle-class parents were "able and willing to finance daughters' advanced schooling in an era of smaller families, rising age of marriage, lessened domestic duties, and demographic imbalances that left many women permanently unmarried" (Clifford).

Progress was tempered, however, by those who questioned the *value* of higher education for women, thus continuing the earlier debate into the first 60 years of the twentieth century. The debate evolved from the prescriptive ideal of womanhood, rooted in Victorian principles of separate domains for women and men, clouding the economic realities of women's lives, on one hand and, on the other, highlighting those economic realities by offering separate kinds of education for class-distinguished women. The elite women's colleges expected to serve exclusively the daughters of the upper and upwardly mobile middle classes. The home economics and normal departments of state-supported institutions and second-echelon private colleges, normal schools, and trade institutes enrolled working girls and the daughters of less affluent families, as well as young women of middle-class affluence. Embedded within the argument about women's education was the corollary issue of the nature of learning itself vis-à-vis assumed biological sex differences.

By the early 1900s native white women were routinely accepted as college students by the public. Still the way was difficult for nonnative whites and for blacks. Black women constituted only 0.3 percent of the female student population in institutions of higher education in 1910. Liberal arts colleges rarely were integrated, and black colleges had few women in the liberal arts course. Those black women who did gain access to postsecondary education usually received teacher or industrial training (Solomon).

The prescriptive ideal of womanhood prevailed in all echelons of higher education among black women as well as white as late as the 1950s. In reality, graduates of women's colleges were educated to become enlightened mothers and socially exemplary wives, models to inspire women of the working classes. Working-class women sought training to better their lot through access to the only occupations offering upward mobility to women: commerce, some trades, and, above all, teaching. The interests of the state were best served by providing access to that training; thus, the status quo was protected. Women were granted access to higher education, but the most highly educated women by male-dominated standards of classical liberal education and its by-product of professional training in no way threatened male hegemony in the public sphere of law, politics, medicine, business, religion, and college teaching. While it is true that women pioneers emerged in all the professions, not until the 1970s did college-educated women make significant gains in professional fields outside teaching. The early 1980s ushered in a new era as female undergraduate students became, for the first time in history, the majority of college students nationwide. (See also WOMEN'S COLLEGES.)

References. C. J. Clifford, "Shaking Dangerous Questions from the Crease: Gender and American Higher Education," *Feminist Issues* 3 (1983): 30; M. Newcomer, *A Century of Higher Education for American Women* (New York, 1959); B. M. Solomon, *In the Company of Educated Women* (New Haven, Conn., 1985), 76–77.

CAROL O. PERKINS

EDUCATION, ECONOMICS OF WOMEN'S. Education is an important determinant of the nature of, and rewards to, women's work* both in the market and in the home. Women's probability of being in the labor force, continuity of participation over the life cycle, earnings, occupational attainment, fertility, and allocation of time across household tasks all vary with educational attainment. Highly educated women have been offered employment opportunities in the growing white-collar occupations and have been able to take advantage of the breakdown in occupational segregation* in the professions since 1970.

If one simply looks at school attendance, educational experience will be seen to have varied much more by race and class than it has by gender, at least since the early nineteenth century. Earlier there had been substantial gender differences among whites. While both girls and boys were taught to read the Bible, only about half as many girls as boys were taught to write. Colleges and universities barred all women no matter what their scholastic abilities, thirst for knowledge, wealth, or social standing.

The spread of academies and the growth of the common schools in the early nineteenth century, however, greatly expanded educational opportunities for white women and tended to equalize the educational attainment of women and men. By 1850 the attendance rate of white girls in primary schools nearly equaled that of boys. By the turn of the century girls outnumbered boys in the high schools. Higher education became available to women in the 1830s, and by the turn of the century white women accounted for 20 percent of all college students. The proportion of female high school graduates attending college grew steadily through the twentieth century so that by 1983 women accounted for over half (51.7 percent) of degree credit enrollment.

Black women shared the educational discrimination facing black men. Under slavery, education was prohibited. After emancipation, poverty and discriminatory school boards kept black women's and men's educational attainment far below that of whites. Within these limitations, black girls were far more likely than boys to attend school. In 1900, 216 black women graduated from high school for every 100 black men who did so. Among whites the gender imbalance was not so great: 139 white women graduated for every 100 white men (Carter and Prus). Relative improvement in educational opportunities for black women did not occur until segregated schools were outlawed, and antidiscrimination legislation brought about by the civil rights movement was implemented. In 1960 median educational attainment of blacks was only 73 percent of that of whites. By 1982 it had risen to 97 percent.

Class continues to have an important influence on the attendance patterns of both women and men. A study of the high school class of 1972 revealed that among high school graduates whose fathers had received at least some college education, 60.4 percent of white males and 57.6 percent of white females enrolled in college. Among those whose fathers did not complete high school the enrollment rates were 24.6 percent and 20.1 percent, respectively. Similar differentials exist for blacks. These differences appear to be due to the influence of family status on the quality of elementary and high school educational attainment and the importance of family income in financing college attendance (Thomas, Alexander, and Eckland).

The relative equality between women and men in enrollment rates, however, conceals tremendous differences within and across institutions, in motivation for, and constraints inhibiting, attendance. While scholastically able women from well-to-do families are about as likely to attend college as similarly situated men, able women from poorer families are much less likely than their brothers to do so. In one sample the college enrollment rate for academically able men from upper-income families was 98 percent as compared with 89 percent for those from lower-income families. Among women, however, the enrollment rates are 95 percent and 65 percent, respectively. The greater effect of family income on daughters' attendance rates may be due to women's low wages in the labor market, which make it more difficult for women to repay college loans and put themselves through school and/or to less willingness of families to finance daughters' education (Blakemore and Low).

Among those who attend, women are more likely to enroll in two-year colleges. In 1983 women accounted for 55 percent of those enrolled in two-year colleges as compared with 52 percent of all degree credit enrollment. Women's share of enrollments falls progressively as one moves to four-year colleges, research universities, and graduate programs. It took federal legislation to enable women to gain access to education for particularly prestigious and lucrative fields like medicine and law (Radour, Strasburg, and Lipman-Blumen.)

Within institutions women are concentrated in traditionally female fields. As late as 1970 over half of the female undergraduates received their degrees in the fields of education, English, languages, and fine arts. However, in the 1970s large numbers of women began moving into formerly male fields so that by 1980 the four traditionally female fields listed earlier accounted for only 30 percent of women's bachelor's degrees. Even in the same classroom, however, women and men often have very different educational experiences. Attitudes of teachers and classmates may discourage women from class participation, result in less feedback on their work, and cause them to lower their career aspirations and lose self-confidence in the process. The curriculum may make it difficult for women to learn to think for themselves and develop a consciousness of themselves as independent intellects.

There are a number of theoretical perspectives on these issues. Neo-classical economic theorists have focused on the differences in attendance patterns between women and men. The decision to go to school, or the demand for education, is modeled as an investment undertaken on the expectation of monetary and nonmonetary returns. The payoff to education is greater the greater the earnings differential between educated and uneducated labor, the longer the expected time in the labor force, the greater the benefits of education in nonmarket activities, and the lower the educational costs.

According to this approach, women would be expected to take less education than men to the extent that expected lifetime labor force participation* was less. As women's expected labor force participation has risen, so has their optimal level of education. In this view changing patterns in the educational attainment of women result from women's choices in the context of changing conditions.

Feminists tend to view changes in women's school attendance rates as the outcome of political and social struggles. Women would generally be expected to have preferred far more education than they, in fact, were able to obtain. Rising educational attainment, the institution of women's studies, and the mainstreaming of feminist scholarship are evidence of success in wresting control over access to educational institutions and programs from patriarchal forces. Such victories, however, are not permanent, as evidenced by the backlash against coeducation around the turn of the century, the fall in women's share of graduate students in the 1930s, and the efforts to restrict the impact of Title IX* in the *Grove City College v. Bell* decision.

Reproduction of labor power theorists tend to focus on the curriculum and to view schools as institutions for maintaining gender inequalities over time. By portraying the gender-based division of labor as natural, training women for their traditional roles, and failing to develop women's capacity to view these patterns critically, the schools have reinforced women's subordinate position in the larger society. In this view, schools will help liberate women only if critical feminist scholarship is developed and taught.

References. A. E. Blakemore and S. A. Low, "Scholarship Policy and Race-Sex Differences in the Demand for Higher Education," *Economic Inquiry* 21 (1983): 504–519; S. B. Carter and M. Prus, "The Labor Market and the American High

School Girl 1890–1928," *Journal of Economic History* 47 (1982): 163–171; G. J. Clifford, " 'Shaking Dangerous Questions from the Crease': Gender and American Higher Education," *Feminist Issues* 3 (1983): 3–62; C. B. Lloyd and B. T. Neimi, *The Economics of Sex Differentials* (New York, 1979); B. M. Solomon, *In the Company of Educated Women: A History of Women and Higher Education in America* (New Haven, Conn., 1985); P. J. Perum (ed.), *The Undergraduate Woman: Issues in Educational Equity* (Lexington, Mass., 1982); M. L. Radour, G. L. Strasburg, and J. Lipman-Blumen, "Women in Higher Education: Trends in Enrollments and Degrees Earned," *Harvard Educational Review* 52 (1982): 189–202; G. E. Thomas, K. L. Alexander, and B. K. Eckland, "Access to Higher Education: The Importance of Race, Sex, Social Class, and Academic Credentials," *School Review* (February 1979): 133–156.

SUSAN B. CARTER

EDUCATION AMENDMENTS OF 1972. See TITLE IX

EGYPT (ANCIENT). Women in ancient Egypt are a section of society that is well documented in both representational and textual material, most of which relates to women belonging to the elite families of male officials. The evidence from art and literature shows that women, within their appointed roles, held a respected position. This was partly because of the importance attached in that culture to fertility; also, there is no trace of the misogyny that bedeviled the lives of their Greek and Christian sisters.

The wives and mothers of officials featured prominently in the decoration of the monuments of their sons and husbands. It was far less common for them to possess their own monuments, and they were usually buried in their husbands' tombs. As with all important figures in Egyptian art, the image of these women is idealized, so that both wife and mother are shown as youthfully mature and attractive with little distinction between them. The relative importance of figures is encoded by scale. Women, especially in the Old Kingdom (c. 2600–c. 2180 B.C.), were often drawn much smaller than men, but couples might also be depicted with the man and woman the same height or with the woman shorter than the man by a realistic amount. Individual figures, for the most part, reflected natural proportions, so that women were shown as more slender than men with shorter backs and more spreading buttocks.

Advancement in society leading to an administrative post depended on an ability to read and write. Probably only 1 percent of the population was literate, and there is little evidence to suggest that reading and writing were taught to women; thus, women were, in the main, debarred from the administration, and very few are recorded with any sort of administrative title. In the Old and Middle Kingdoms (c. 2600–c. 1780 B.C.), one of the few titles common among upper-class women was "priestess of the goddess

Hathor," and women could also be funerary priests. There were no female overseers of priests or female lector priests, since this office involved literacy. The priestesses probably provided music in the temples and may have taken part in some rituals. By the New Kingdom (c. 1570–c. 1070 B.C.), the priesthood had become a professional body in which a man could make his career; women with the title of "priestess" are no longer found. Instead, upper-class women frequently bore the title "chantress" of a particular deity. Apart from possible duties in the temples, the domain of the upper-class woman seems to have been in the home. While men were depicted with a reddish-brown skin tanned by exposure to the sun, women were shown with a yellow skin that had been protected from the sun, presumably because they mostly remained indoors.

Thus, the roles of men and women were perceived as very different in what was basically a male-dominated society. It is interesting, therefore, to discover from legal and business documents that men and women, within their class, had equal legal rights. Like men, women could own private property, being free to administer and dispose of it as they liked. They could inherit; make a will; adopt heirs; own, hire out, and free slaves; and go to court and testify at law, all in their own right, whether married or unmarried.

Little evidence survives on the contraction of marriage or choice of marriage partner. Monogamy was normal and polygyny rare (except for the king), but because of low life expectancy and divorce, both men and women might have more than one marriage partner in a lifetime. There is no evidence for legal or religious ceremonies to sanction marriage, which seems to have consisted basically of a couple setting up house together. Divorce occurred when one partner left the home. Economic settlements were drawn up to provide for the wife's subsistence during marriage and for the disposal of property after the marriage had ended, whether by divorce or death. These arrangements limited the husband's rights in administering and disposing of the property; equally, the wife could not do as she liked with property that was held in common. In general, at the death of the husband, one-third of his property went unconditionally to his wife, while the other two-thirds was divided among his children. In the case of divorce, a repudiated woman retained the property she had brought into the marriage and received maintenance. However, if she were found guilty of adultery, which was regarded very seriously, her financial rights would lapse.

The human sexual act was not depicted overtly in formal art, although sketches of copulating couples are preserved on *ostraka* (pottery shards and flakes of limestone) and in graffiti, and one papyrus explicitly depicts the adventures of a man with a prostitute. When about to give birth, women removed to a specially constructed shelter where they remained until they were purified after the birth had taken place. A number of *ostraka* feature women in these buildings nursing a child, and such scenes may have also formed part of house decoration.

Owing to the bias inherent in the material, we know most about women belonging to official families, but the monuments also show scenes of musicians, dancers, and acrobats, including women, entertaining the official classes at banquets or forming a part of temple processions or festivals. Other scenes depict female servants spinning, weaving, baking, brewing, and waiting on guests at table. Peasant women are sometimes shown in agricultural scenes, gleaning after the reapers, harvesting flax, and bringing food to the workers. Since the vast majority of the population, both men and women, were unable to leave records concerning themselves, we cannot examine their lives in any depth.

The most important female members of the royal family were the king's mother, his principal wife, and, to a lesser extent, some of his daughters. The king was polygynous, but little is known of his secondary wives, whose status is uncertain, although their sons could inherit the throne. A number of kings married their (half) sisters. From this it was for a long time supposed that the right to the throne passed through a line of royal women, although power was exercised by the man whom the current "heiress" married. According to this theory, for the throne to pass from father to son, brother–sister marriage had to be practiced. However, no "heiress" is mentioned in the mythology of kingship; instead, the living king is identified with the god Horus, son of the god Osiris, who is identified with the dead king; in myth, Horus succeeds to the throne as the son and heir of Osiris. Further, a number of principal wives and king's mothers were of nonroyal birth, so that there was, in fact, no line of "heiresses." The importance of brother–sister marriage was that such marriages were not practiced by ordinary people but were found only among the gods. By marrying his (half) sister, the king distanced himself from his subjects and drew closer to the divine sphere.

Some royal women from the 18th dynasty onward bore the title "god's wife of Amun." The title was a priestly one settled on the women of the royal family at the beginning of the 18th dynasty (c. 1570 B.C.). It could be held by a king's principal wife, daughter, or mother and gave the holder an important position in the cult of the god Amun at Thebes. From about 870 B.C., the god's wife, now often called "divine adoratrice," was always the daughter of a king, who never married but adopted her successor. She held vast estates at Thebes, and it is possible that such a powerful woman learned to read and write.

The role of the king as validated by mythology was a male one, yet a few women took the title of king. The most important of these was Hatshepsut (fifteenth century B.C.), who ruled Egypt for almost 22 years, first as regent for the boy Thutmose III and then as king. After her death, her name was removed from the monuments and was never included in later king lists. The reason for this hostility against her is uncertain, but the aim may have been to expunge from the records all memory of a woman who dared occupy the male office of kingship.

References. Henry G. Fischer, *Egyptian Women of the Old Kingdom and the Heracleopolitan Period* (New York, 1989); P. W. Pestman, *Marriage and Matrimonial Property in Ancient Egypt* (Leiden, Netherlands, 1961); Gay Robins, "Some Images of Women in New Kingdom Art and Literature," in B. Lesko (ed.), *Women's Earliest Records from Ancient Egypt and Western Asia* (Atlanta, 1989), 105–116; "While the Woman Looks On: Gender Inequalities in New Kingdom Egypt," *KTM: A Modern Journal of Ancient Egypt* 1 (1990): 18–21, 64–65; Gay Robins, *Women in Ancient Egypt* (Cambridge, Mass. 1993).

GAY ROBINS

EGYPT (ANCIENT). Pharaonic Royal Women frequently exercised considerable power and influence and, on rare occasions, reigned. Generalizations about them are difficult and often incorrect.

The "heiress theory," the commonly held belief that the right to the throne in Egypt passed through the female line, and the king had to legitimize his position by marrying the royal "heiress," the daughter of the previous king and his principal wife (and ordinarily his own full or half sister), dates to the nineteenth century and is founded on incorrect assumptions about Egyptian society. Several earlier scholars had questioned aspects of this theory, but Robins has mounted a persuasive case against the evidence for the theory; its correctness should no longer be assumed. There was, however, a stress on female kinship in ancient Egypt.

While the "heiress theory" is, at best, questionable, it is demonstrable that at least as early as the Middle Kingdom (2050–1786 [all dates are B.C. and approximate]; no evidence survives for the Old Kingdom, 2700–2200) many Egyptian kings married their full or half sisters. Although royal sibling marriage was not practiced without exception (mortality rates alone would make this impossible), sibling marriage did distinguish royalty from nonroyalty who did not commonly practice it. Such royal sibling marriages apparently imitated those of the gods, thus reconfirming the king's divinity.

Pharaonic queens (kings' principal wives and kings' mothers) used an assortment of titles and had their names enclosed in cartouches, as did the kings, but any other kind of public recognition or role for royal women should not be assumed, though such a role frequently existed, particularly in the New Kingdom (1575–1087).

Some would deny that queens regularly had a role in religious ritual, although it is likely that the king's principal wife did play a part in several ceremonies, particularly the harvest festival for Min, a god who personified the generative force of nature. Queens were buried with royal splendor, and late in the Old Kingdom the pyramid texts, once a monopoly of the king, began to appear in their burials. Some cults of queens are known from the early Old Kingdom on, but it is difficult to say whether all principal wives of kings received worship after their deaths. Only a few royal women are known to have had cults in their lifetimes, a regular practice with kings. The title "god's wife of Amun" had a brief period of popularity with queens at the beginning of the eighteenth dynasty. Earlier and late usage of the term differs, but in the eighteenth dynasty it seems to have been a priestly office bringing with it considerable property and prominence.

Queens, even those not of royal birth, often played a part in power politics. Instances from both the Old and New Kingdoms are recorded in which royal women participated in attempted palace revolutions meant to replace the reigning king. More typical are queens who played important public roles in both their husbands' and sons' reigns. Ahmose (1575–1545), founder of the eighteenth dynasty, said that his mother helped him in driving the Hyksos out of Egypt (that the help was military aid is not ruled out). Ahmose's principal wife, Nofretary, like her mother-in-law, was involved in her husband's building program, particularly buildings of a religious nature. Nofretary's involvement continued into the reign of her son, who honored her with a separate mortuary temple for her funerary cult. Even under her son's successor, a man probably not related to her by blood, she received public recognition. Teye, principal wife of Amenhotep III (1398–1361) and mother of Akhnaton (1369–1353), although herself not of royal birth, played an unusually prominent role in both men's reigns. A colossal statue shows her equal in size to her husband (this was unusual in royal art). The king of the Mitanni suggested that Akhnaton should consult his mother on matters of foreign policy because she was the most knowledgeable person on that subject.

Much rarer were female rulers, whether regents or female kings. While the names of several other women appear on various king lists (e.g., Nitocris, said to have been regent late in the Old Kingdom), Hatshepsut (1490–1468) is the only well-documented case. The daughter of Thutmose I (1525–1495) and his chief wife, Hatshepsut, married Thutmose II (1495–1490), a son of her father by another wife. When her half brother/husband died, his son by another wife, Thutmose III (1490–1436), was made king, although he was still a child. At first Hatshepsut seems to have acted as regent for her stepson, but after several years she began to use the full titular of a king and to appear with the male costume of a king. She claimed that her father had chosen her as his successor. For some 20 years Hatshepsut reigned, and her coruler, although not deposed, remained obscure. Much is controversial about Hatshepsut's reign, but it is not true that she rejected the military expansionism of her immediate predecessors. She engaged in considerable temple building, and her mortuary temple at Dier el-

Bahri is particularly well known. After her death (cause unknown) her stepson reigned alone and restored the earlier policy of imperialism.

In general, the role of royal women in public life increased from the Old to the New Kingdom (although this perception may be affected by the paucity of evidence in the earlier period). They were particularly prominent in the eighteenth dynasty. This prominence probably stems from the high legal, economic, and social position (compared to other ancient cultures) enjoyed by all Egyptian women and from the tremendous power and prestige of what is arguably the most absolute monarchy in history, a prestige that tended to elevate the importance of all members of the royal family.

References. V. C. Callender, "A Critical Examination of the Reign of Hatshetsup," *Ancient History* 18 (1988): 86–102; Gay Robins, *Women in Ancient Egypt* (Cambridge, Mass., 1993); Gay Robins, "A Critical Examination of the Theory That the Right to the Throne of Ancient Egypt Passed through the Female Line in the 18th Dynasty," *Gottinger Miszellen* 62 (1983): 67–77; L. Troy, *Patterns of Queenship in Ancient Egyptian Myth and History* (Stockholm/Uppsala, 1986, Uppsala Studies in Ancient Mediterranean and Near Eastern Civilization 14).

ELIZABETH CARNEY

ELVIRA, COUNCIL OF, was the earliest known synod of the Catholic Church in Spain. It produced the oldest extant disciplinary canons, almost half of which are concerned directly with the control of sexuality. The misogyny of the late Roman and medieval Church is evidenced in its directives toward women.

Held at Elvira, near modern Grenada, either between A.D. 300 and 303 or in A.D. 309, the council was attended by 45 clergymen (19 bishops and 26 priests), all but 5 of whom were from southern Spain. It apparently was called primarily to deal with the problems of apostasy and of Christians holding public office in a pagan state; but the canons reveal that, consciously or unconsciously, the clergy were most concerned with defining the character of Christian life and their own role and status within a Christian community whose membership had been rapidly increasing in size and social importance. That 14 of its 81 canons were among those approved at councils at Arles, Nicaea, and Sardica within the next half century attests both to the importance of the Council of Elvira and to the communality of belief in control over the lives of members of the Christian community by the Christian clergy.

The decisions of the council show that the clergy was establishing itself as an elite marked off from the laity by a much stricter sexual asceticism: marital sex was forbidden in the oldest known legislation on clerical continence, and the clergy and consecrated virgins were more rigorously punished for sexual transgressions than were the laity. However, in canon after canon, the Church fathers also tried to regulate the sexual lives of the entire community, dealing with adultery, fornication, divorce, abortion, prostitution, homosexuality, pimping, premarital lovemaking, betrothal, and the arranging of marriages. In the majority of cases, commission of the cited offense brought, in addition to an occasional mention that penance was undergone, the denial of communion for a term of years, until the point of death, or even permanently, with the offender not being readmitted to communion even at the point of death (*nec in finem*). Of the 20 *nec in finem* punishments in the canons, 15 were for sexual offenses.

Twenty-two of the canons are directed specifically at women. This large number and the severity of the punishments show marked hostility toward, and a need to punish, women. Of the canons directed toward women, only one is positive: immediate acceptance of the reformed prostitute. This contrasts with the permanent excommunication of the lapsed consecrated virgin. Another very revealing contrast can be seen in comparing the seven-year excommunication of the woman who purposely beats her female slave to death with the *nec in finem* excommunication of a woman who leaves her husband for another man. Of the 15 *nec in finem* punishments, 6 are directed at women; 1 is directed at parents who give a daughter in marriage to a pagan priest; and 2 are directed at men who do not throw their wives out of their homes when they know that those women have committed adultery.

Reference. Samuel Laeuchli, *Power and Sexuality: The Emergence of Canon Law at the Synod of Elvira* (Philadelphia, 1972).

EMBRYO, in human development, is the term for the developing human organism during its early stage of differentiation and growth, the stage during which the organ system and the basic body structure are established. By about the end of the eighth week after conception, at which time the body structure becomes recognizably human, the embryonic stage is completed, and gestation has entered the fetal stage.

EMPTY NEST SYNDROME is the name given to feelings of depression caused by the loss of the mother role when a woman's children leave home. Its prevalence among women has been greatly exaggerated. A woman whose identity is dependent on her role as mother and who has lived her life through her children often feels that her life is purposeless when she loses her role. However, most women whose children have left home find that they are happier than they have been in years.

Reference. E. Hall, "Motherhood," in C. Tavris (ed.), *EveryWoman's Emotional Well-Being* (Garden City, N.Y., 1986).

ENDOGAMY/EXOGAMY. Endogamy is a term for marriage* within a defined group. Marriage within the group may be preferred or may be required by custom or law. The group may be defined by kinship or fictive kinship ties; for instance, a clan or tribe might be based on some other social division, such as village, socioeconomic class, ethnic, racial, or religious group.

Exogamy is the opposite of endogamy: marriage outside the defined group. Marriage outside the defined group may be discouraged, or it may be prohibited by law or custom.

ENDOMETRIAL CYCLE is the monthly renewal of the lining of the uterus (endometrium) in order to support a developing fetus* and the subsequent breakdown and shedding of the lining when no conception takes place.

The regenerative phase of the cycle begins about the fifth day of menstruation and lasts until after ovulation. Under the stimulus of estrogen new glandular cell tissue covers the base layer of the endometrium (which remains unchanged throughout the cycle). The progestational or secretory phase begins after ovulation when progesterone stimulates glandular secretion of nutrients. The lining doubles in thickness, becoming rich and soft. If no fertilization takes place, after about 12 days estrogen and progesterone decline. Without hormonal stimulus, the lining begins to break down. As blood circulation slows, blood vessels constrict; without blood, tissue dies. As the weakened blood vessels dilate again, some blood escapes. Blood, glandular secretions, and dead tissue flow from the uterus into the vagina, and menstruation begins.

ENDOMETRIOSIS is a condition in which endometrial tissue (the tissue that lines the uterus) grows in locations outside the uterus, usually on surfaces within the pelvic cavity, especially on the ovaries but also on other areas, such as the fallopian tubes, intestines, and so on, occasionally, even outside the pelvic cavity, as on lung, thigh, or upper arm. When the endometrial tissue bleeds during menstruation, blood trapped in the pelvic cavity can cause internal bleeding, cysts, inflammation, and, subsequently, scar tissue, obstructions, adhesions, and, often, intense, chronic pain.

Endometriosis can affect women from menarche* to menopause,* but the most severely affected are aged 25 to 45. The bits of "misplaced endometrium" vary in size and extent; they may be confined to one area or be found in different areas. Some women have no symptoms; others have a great deal of pain, before or during menstruation and during sexual intercourse—and the severity (or absence) of pain is not related to the extent of the endometriosis. It may be related to the size of cysts, the frequency of cyst breakage, and the amount of scar tissue.

Endometriosis is one of the major causes of infertility* in women. Why is not always clear. Nor are the causes of endometriosis known. Various theories have been proposed to explain how it could be spread from the uterus. It has also been suggested that some cells in the tissue of other organs in the pelvic cavity may, under hormonal stimulus, undergo modification, resulting in bits of endometrium among other tissue. There is also support for a genetic explanation (it may run in families).

The type of treatment or whether there should be treatment depends on whether the woman wishes to have children, the severity of the symptoms, and the woman's age. When there is no or little pain, a woman nearing menopause has little to gain by treatment. Oral contraceptives will relieve symptoms but are not a satisfactory solution for a woman who wishes to have children or for someone at risk from oral contraceptives. A synthetic steroid, Danazol, is effective in arresting and reducing the condition and has had some success in allowing fertility, but the condition is likely to recur after its use is discontinued. Danazol is also quite expensive and has side effects, possibly including cardiovascular risk. Surgery is sometimes used, usually cutting the tissue out, scraping, or cauterizing it. Hysterectomy, with or without removal of ovaries and fallopian tubes, is usually resorted to only when the condition is widespread and the pain acute and debilitating. (Ovaries should be removed only when recommended by two independent physicians. Also, removal without hormone replacement increases cardiovascular risk.)

The Endometrius Association (PO Box 92181, Milwaukee 53202) was formed in 1980 as a self-help group and clearinghouse for information, and support.

Reference. Julia Older, *Endometriosis* (New York, 1985).

ENLIGHTENMENT was an eighteenth-century cultural phenomenon, the result of two centuries of intellectual ferment. In its purist form, it was primarily the preserve of a small group of philosophers and writers; but its aim was to free the human mind and spirit everywhere from ignorance, superstition, and traditionally accepted wisdom. It was seen by its proponents as heralding for everyone a new way of life based on rationalism and enlightened thought. Women were touched by the Enlightenment in two ways. They were the focus of discussion by certain philosophers exploring the rational universe; and when those philosophers failed to provide a place for women in their rational world, women formed their own private corners of the Enlightenment.

The philosophers appeared generally unconcerned with the status of women. Their preoccupation with the concepts of liberty and equality did not usually extend to women. In some cases, philosophers searching for general enlightenment in humanity actually argued for the traditionally inferior status of women. Those who argued for equality often did so persuasively, but the philosophers' position was to observe and criticize, not to create a social revolution. Their observations on equality therefore went unheeded.

The strongest Enlightenment voice in favor of women's equality was the Marquis de Condorcet. He insisted that women of property should have the right to vote and hold office. One of the few thinkers who blamed women's inferior status on education and society, Condorcet suggested that faulty socialization might explain women's seeming physical and mental inadequacies.

Other voices were weaker. The Baron de Montesquieu, in *The Spirit of the Laws*, urged states to allow men and women equality in opening divorce proceedings. While Montesquieu displayed a sympathy to the plight of women in traditional society, their equality was not a priority for him. In the midcentury *Encyclopédie*, writers did not even agree about the position of women. One article on women and natural law argued for female liberation from male authority in marriage, noting the natural equality of all human beings, the gender-free nature of wisdom, and strength and the equality between Adam and Eve before the Fall; an article on women and morality, however, compared women unfavorably with men in wisdom, strength, virtue, and personal character. In his essay "On Women," Denis Diderot stated that a woman was dominated by her uterus, an organ that left her physically weak and mentally helpless. Jean-Jacques Rousseau not only believed that women were decidedly inferior to men in every way but urged the separation of the sexes. The Baron d'Holbach agreed with Rousseau in his praise of girls educated at home and his criticism of libertinism and the theater as damaging to middle-class values and female sensibility.

The cursory concern with women by the philosophers forced women to create their own Enlightenment. Many writers and thinkers rose from the female ranks. It was not uncommon for an educated woman of the era to write extensively in her journal and even earn her own living by writing. Women produced the majority of all novels published in England in the second half of the eighteenth century, and French writers like Mme. de Genlis were universally recognized as witty and clever in print. In England, Mary Astell and Mary Wollstonecraft were feminist intellectuals, both using the power of reason in their arguments. In *A Serious Proposal to the Ladies*, Mary Astell tried to persuade unmarried women to contribute their dowry money to educate themselves. In a second work on the subject, she urged them to discipline their minds and use reason as their method of thought. Mary Wollstonecraft also tackled the problem of women's training in *A Vindication of the Rights of Women* in 1792 (See *VINDICATION OF THE RIGHTS OF WOMAN, A.*) Many upper-class women in France established salons where the highest Enlightenment ideas were discussed and popularized. (See *Salonière*.) Theatre groups became very popular, with women playing various parts and often organizing and running the entire organization: the Duchesse du Maine's *Mouche à Miel* was a combination theater group, salon, and secret society.

Beyond the obvious ranks of writer, philosopher, and salonière, the Enlightenment reached less dramatically. Women read the words of the philosophers; in London some women in the publishing trades circulated political tracts; and mixed-gender charitable organizations were formed by women. In French Freemasonry mixed-gender lodges were formed in which women masons took part in rituals emphasizing certain Enlightenment ideals. In these ways women, who were denied full participation in the intellectual ferment, produced their own windows to the Enlightenment.

Reference. Margaret Hunt, Margaret Jacob, Phyllis Mack, and Ruth Perry, "Women and the Enlightenment," *Women and History*, special issue (Spring 1984).

JANET M. BURKE

EPICS, MEDIEVAL. Heroic Epics in Middle High German are about 20 epics based on material from the native oral tradition, popular in what later became southern Germany and Austria from the early thirteenth to the late sixteenth centuries. Women are depicted variously in the epics according to the purpose of the (usually anonymous) author and the expectations of the audience. The *Nibelungenlied* (Song of the Nibelungs), earliest and most influential, was meant to warn a noble audience steeped in Arthurian romance of real dangers of moral and political corruption. In contrast to Arthurian romance, in which a male hero perfects himself and then improves society, the hero of the *Nibelungenlied* is Kriemhild, a Burgundian princess, who, victimized by the corruption of her society, brings about its destruction as well as her own. Her marriage to Siegfried is allowed only because it is politically expedient. When this expediency is no longer the case, he is murdered, and his fortune is stolen from her. Only remarriage to King Etzel of the Huns gives her the means of avenging the murder and robbery. Brünhild, the *Nibelungenlied*'s other important woman, is also the pawn of political interests. At first a powerful queen, she is duped by Siegfried into marriage to Kriemhild's weak brother, Gunther, whereupon she loses all strength. When she learns of the deceit, she instigates Siegfried's murder in order to protect Gunther's image.

Virtually all other epics respond explicitly or implicitly to the *Nibelungenlied*; the roles of women in them reflect a reaction to Kriemhild and Brünhild. The *Nibelungenklage* (Lament of the Nibelungs), composed in the first third of the thirteenth century, attempts to excuse Kriemhild because her revenge was motivated by love for Siegfried. *Der grosse Rosengarten zu Worms* (The Large Rose Garden at Worms), composed at the turn of the fourteenth century, parodies the *Nibelungenlied* and the Arthurian romance alike by depicting Kriemhild as a woman who issues unreasonable challenges, for which in one version (A) she is punished by having her face scratched by a hero's beard as she rewards him with kisses. By the sixteenth century the material had become completely trivialized: in *Das Lied von hürnen Seyfrid* (The Song of Seyfrid with the Horny Skin), circulated for popular entertainment, Kriemhild has become a stereotypical abducted princess, rescued by, then married to, Siegfried.

Kudrun, composed c. 1230–1240, uses the abduction plot to present a courtly alternative to the *Nibelungenlied*. Womanly virtue is depicted as passivity coupled with efforts to reconcile opposing forces. Hilde, Kudrun's mother, allows her fiancé to stage elopement as abduction but later makes peace between her husband and father. Betrothed to Herwig but abducted by Hartmut, Kudrun spends years at hard labor because she refuses to marry Hartmut. When Herwig rescues her, she makes peace between them. This is possible because her suffering has not been caused by Hartmut but by his mother Gerlind, whose assertive behavior is severely punished.

Twelve narratives, including *Rosengarten*, are called Dietrich epics because Dietrich von Bern, a supporting character in the *Nibelungenlied*, plays an important role in them. Three were composed for the nobility of the late thirteenth century to protest the tyranny of princes over lesser nobles. The others, more literary than political in focus, either uphold or criticize courtly values. Many literary epics became staples of popular entertainment by the fifteenth century. Two non-Dietrich epics, *Ortnit* and *Wolfdietrich*, parallel this group in focus and transmission. Women's roles are small in all these narratives.

Epics of the political group, like the *Nibelungenlied*, depict the suffering of women as pawns of political interests. In *Das Buch von Bern* (The Book of Bern) Dietrich reluctantly agrees to marry Herrat in order to get military aid from Etzel. In *Alpharts Tod* (Alphart's Death) Amelgart, brought from Sweden to marry Alphart, cannot dissuade him from going to his death in battle. In *Die Rabenschlacht* (The Battle of Ravenna) Helche, Etzel's first wife, who, in implicit contrast to Kriemhild and Brunhild, maintains harmony at court at any cost, forgives Dietrich, even though he is indirectly responsible for the deaths of her sons. In Dietrich epics of the literary group such as *Laurin, Virginal*, and Albrecht von Kemenaten's fragmentary *Goldemar*, which uphold courtly values, women do not transcend the abducted princess stereotype. The same is true of the non-Dietrich epics *Ortnit, Wolfdietrich*, and the fragmentary *Walther und Hildegund*. The maiden pursued by a monster in *Der Wunderer* (The Monster) is a partial exception. She recruits Dietrich to defend her, saying later that she is Lady Luck, thus implying she can reward him for his action. Like *Rosengarten A, Eckenlied d* (Song of Ecke) criticizes courtly values. Queen Seburg sends Ecke to duel with Dietrich, who has done no harm to either. Dietrich, unwilling to fight without just cause, nonetheless punishes both Ecke's foolishness and Seburg's unreasonable challenge.

References. Ruth Angress, "German Studies: The Woman's Perspective," in Walter F. W. Lohnes and Valters Nollendorfs (eds.), *German Studies in the United States: Assessment and Outlook (Monatshefte* Occasional vol. 1; Madison, Wis., 1976), 247–251; Joseph R. Strayer (ed.), *Dictionary of the Middle Ages*, 9 vols. to date (New York, 1982–), for individual epics.

RUTH FIRESTONE

EQUAL EMPLOYMENT OPPORTUNITY LAWS. Regulation and Enforcement. Since 1978, the responsibilities for developing regulations for, and enforcing, equal employment opportunity laws and orders have been consolidated with the Equal Employment Opportunity Commission (EEOC), which is appointed by the president, the Office of Federal Contract Compliance Programs (OFCCP) of the U.S. Department of Labor, the Justice Department, and the Department of Education. EEOC's authority covers all public and private employers and unions, as well as the federal government as an employer. In addition, EEOC enforces the Equal Pay Act, the Age Discrimination Act, and the Americans with Disabilities Act (1990). The Family and Medical Leave Act (1993) is enforced by the Department of Labor Employment Standards Administration (ESA). OFCCP enforces Executive Order 11246* as amended and deals with all federal contractors. The Justice Department is responsible for litigation against state and local governments under Title VII* of the Civil Rights Act of 1964 and represents the federal government when suits are brought against federal contractors. Title IX* of the Education Amendments of 1972 is enforced by the Department of Education. In 1978, EEOC, the Labor Department, and the Justice Department jointly issued the *Uniform Guidelines on Employee Selection Procedures*.

References. E. Kirby, *Yes You Can: The Working Woman's Guide to Her Legal Rights, Fair Employment and Equal Pay* (Englewood Cliffs, N.J., 1984); J. Ralph Lindgren, *The Law of Sex Discrimination* (St. Paul, 1993); U.S. Department of Labor Women's Bureau, *A Working Woman's Guide to Her Job Rights* (Leaflet 55) (Washington, D.C., 1992).

DAYLE MANDELSON

EQUAL RIGHTS AMENDMENT (ERA), first proposed in Congress in 1923, was passed by both Houses of Congress in 1971 (House) and 1972 (Senate) and defeated at the expiration of the state ratification deadline on June 30, 1982. Written by suffragist Alice Paul, founder and head of the National Woman's Party, the ERA was not considered on the floor of both houses until 1970–1972. Three attempts at substitution of the ERA by language supporting women's "traditional" roles were made in 1947, 1950, and 1971 but were defeated. The wording of the ERA that passed the House in 1971 and the Senate in June 1972 was "equality of rights under the law shall not be denied or abridged by the United States or by any State on account of sex." The ERA was originally given a seven-year state ratification deadline. In 1978, a coalition of proponent groups, led by the National Organization for Women (NOW) persuaded Congress to extend the state ratification deadline. While they hoped the new deadline would include the 1982 election, to enable the public to vote on legislators' behavior, the deadline was set for June 1982. Unfortunately, no additional states ratified during the extension period; thus the last state to ratify was Indiana in 1977. The ERA was officially 3 states short of the 38 states required and was defeated in the southern states, Utah and Nevada, and

Illinois. In 1983, then–Speaker of the U.S. House, Thomas P. "Tip" O'Neill tried to achieve passage of the ERA to hold legislators accountable in the 1984 election. The measure failed by six votes (Harrison).

Historical Alliances on the ERA. The national party positions on the ERA underlined and reflected the congressional parties' tension over the relationship between the ERA, seemingly promising "absolute equality," and gender-specific state protective labor laws. These laws were upheld by the Supreme Court in 1908 (*Muller v. Oreaon*, 208 U.S. 412). The Republican Party, which was the first to include the ERA in its platform in 1940, tended to support the ERA as a way to minimize corporate costs associated with protective legislation. Until women-only protective labor laws were outlawed by judicial interpretation in 1970 of Title VII of the 1964 Civil Rights Act, the Democratic Party was divided over the ERA. As noted by Harrison, liberal, pro-labor Democrats tended not to favor the ERA, while conservatives did. The Democrats adopted the ERA in their national platform in 1944. With the new judicial interpretations of protective labor laws in the early 1970s, conservatives and liberals generally reevaluated their position on the ERA. Conservatives began to overwhelmingly oppose it, while enough liberal support could be found in Congress to pass the ERA for the first time.

Arguments For and Against the ERA. Deborah Rhode has characterized the arguments on both sides of the ERA as "instrumental" and "symbolic." Instrumental themes were found in arguments about whether the ERA was the best means to improve women's legal status in areas such as employment, education, family law, and the military, or if a more piecemeal approach through legal reform would be better. Symbolic arguments on both sides moved beyond the issue of discrimination faced by women and claimed that women's social roles could change under the ERA.

ERA opponents such as Republican activist Phyllis Schlafly, leader of the Eagle Forum and STOP ERA, tried to "have it both ways," raising arguments that were framed as instrumental but rested largely upon symbolic fears. On one hand, Schlafly and others stated that women still enjoyed unique "protections" under the law in the 1970s. However, judicial action striking down gender-specific labor protections, alimony, custody, and child-support laws suggested otherwise. On the other side, Schlafly argued that the ERA would entail an "absolutist" standard, denying courts any discretion in construing what "sex" meant under the law. The examples of social ills that would purportedly ensue included a broadening of homosexual rights, the requirement that women fight in the military, and the mandating of unisex bathrooms in public places. These arguments ignored the courts' ability to retain discretion in two key areas. As discussed in Brown et al., these areas of discretion included "physical characteristics unique to one sex" and those relating to "privacy between the two sexes."

In her arguments, Schlafly incorrectly assumed that, if ERA passed, the concept of gender would be treated by the courts in exactly the same fashion as they treat the concept of race. Since the 1930s, statutory and administrative distinctions based on race were elevated to the highest level of judicial scrutiny under the equal protection clause of the Fourteenth Amendment outlawing state-level discrimination. In ruling racial discrimination "suspect," the Supreme Court has stated that the purpose of a racial classification in law or practice must be "compelling" and that the classification must have a "necessary" relationship to the compelling state purpose (*U.S. v. Carolene Products*, 304 U.S. 144 [1938]; *Korematsu v. U.S.*, 323 U.S. 214 [1944]).

Gender classifications have received less stringent scrutiny under equal protection review. Not until 1971 was a state law differentiating between the sexes found to violate the equal protection clause, at the lowest standard of judicial review, that of "minimal" scrutiny or the "rational-basis" test *(Reed vs. Reed*, 404 U.S. 71 [1971]). In 1976, the Supreme Court articulated the equal protection test for gender, that of "intermediate" scrutiny, where a law or practice classifying by gender must bear a "substantial" relationship to an "important" state purpose (*Craig v. Boren*, 429 U.S. 190 [1976]). Without the ERA, gender rights are included at this ambiguous level of equal protection review, located in between the lowest and highest levels of judicial scrutiny. Mezey shows that since 1976, gender-based classifications brought to the Supreme Court for review have been upheld and overturned an equal number of times. Most of the cases upholding sex-based classifications have concerned the parental rights of unmarried partners.

It is not clear that the ERA debate should have been based on the question of whether a constitutional amendment, rather than legal reform, was necessary. An examination of constitutional gender interpretation since 1976 shows the equal protection clause to be an inadequate substitute for the ERA and that constitutional and legal reforms are both necessary. Also, a comparison of the evolution of gender and racial rights shows that Schlafly was incorrect to hypothetically compare sex-based rights under the ERA, which would have allowed for some physiological exemptions, to race-based rights under the equal protection clause, which do not allow for such exceptions.

The Women's Movement and Electoral Politics. The pattern of party voting in Congress on the ERA was often replicated in the state legislatures during the 1972–1982 state ratification campaign. Proponents felt that ERA votes were determined less by feminist considerations than by the question of being on the "right side" of corporate power. In part, evidence cited for this was the fact that neither party put all of its weight behind the ERA. Within the U.S. party system, lacking the framework of "responsible" government, members of Congress and state legislators were often free to vote as they pleased, independent of both the national party platform and of their constituents' wishes. During the last election to be held during the state ratification campaign, the Republican Party shifted its national platform away from its historic support of the ERA to a position "opposing federal interference or pressure" on unratified states. In a study of four targeted state legislatures (Illinois, Florida, North Carolina, and Oklahoma), NOW found that 17 percent of Republican legislators in those states voted for the ERA, against their party's national platform. Conversely, two-thirds of Democrats in those legislatures voted for the ERA, with the other third voting against their national party platform supporting the amendment. The majority of legislatures defeating the ERA were Democrat-controlled.

Proponents, led by NOW from the mid-1970s onward, responded by targeting legislators in particular states for defeat, attempting to persuade states that had enacted "supermajority" requirements to change them and, after 1980, trying to find a way to hold the Republican Party generally and some anti-ERA Democrats accountable for the ERA's defeat.

The electoral strategy begun by NOW in 1980 has had long-term ramifications. Based, in large part, on the Republican Party shift and presidential nominee Ronald Reagan's avowed opposition to the ERA, women's movement analysts noted a significant 8 percent gap in male and female support for candidate Reagan. The "gender gap" in male–female support for both Republican and Democratic presidential candidates has continued through the 1990s, as has women's higher voting turnout rate since 1980. Based on gender gap mobilization, in the 1982 elections NOW helped elect more pro-ERA state legislators in Illinois and Florida, two states that narrowly defeated the ERA. In that same election year the NOW PAC endorsed 109 pro-ERA congressional candidates, 66 of whom were elected (Langer).

References. Janet Boles, *The Politics of the Equal Rights Amendment* (New York, 1979); Barbara A. Brown, Thomas I. Emerson, Gail Falk, and Ann E. Freedman, "The Equal Rights Amendment: A Constitutional Basis for Equal Rights for Women," *Yale Law Journal* 80 (April 1971): 871–986; Cynthia Harrison, *On Account of Sex: The Politics of Women's Issues, 1945–1968* (Berkeley, Calif., 1989); Cynthia Harrison, "Politics and Law," in Sarah Pritchard (ed.), *The Women's Annual 4* (1984): 155; Howard Langer, "The Women's Movement: What N.O.W.?" *Social Education* (February 1983): 114; Jane J. Mansbridge, *Why We Lost the ERA* (Chicago, 1986); Susan G. Mezey, *In Pursuit of Equality* (New York, 1992); Deborah L. Rhode, *Justice and Gender* (Cambridge, 1989).

MELISSA HAUSSMAN

EUROPEAN UNION (EU) LAW is an independent legal system that establishes rights and obligations affecting women workers in countries belonging to the EU. To the basic law, the Treaty of Rome, the founding instrument of the EU signed March 25, 1957, have been added regulations, decisions, and directives of the Council of Ministers and other community institutions.

Women are affected primarily by Article 119 of the treaty, which establishes "the principle that men and women should receive equal pay for equal work" in member states. The article was not adopted in the interests of fair treatment of women but to prevent unfair competition through the use of cheap female labor. However, when social concerns became an issue in the 1970s (out of concern for political stability), this article was used as the basis for directives aimed at improving working conditions for women.

Five directives on women were adopted from 1975 through 1986: in 1975 on equal pay, in 1976 on equal treatment, in 1978 on equality in government Social Security programs, in July 1986 in occupational Social Security programs, and in December 1986 on equal treatment in self-employed occupations and protection of self-employed women during pregnancy and motherhood.

The EU Commission also set up two action programs to spur progress toward the objectives of equality between men and women in access to employment, training, advancement, working conditions, and pay. An action program from 1982 to 1985 was designed to promote equal opportunity, and a Committee for Equal Opportunity was set up to advise the community on policy.

In 1986 a second action program was approved for 1986 through 1990. Since some states have delayed implementation of directives or have differed considerably in their interpretation, a major goal of the program was to improve the application of already existing directives. Adequate provision for child care and the increased use of parental leave were also goals. Since in most member states it is necessary for a woman to go to court to prove discrimination, very few cases have been instituted. In 1988 the commission recommended that the burden of proof should be placed on the employer.

A number of bureaus and commissions have been set up to aid and to monitor the implementation of the directives and action programs. Besides the Committee for Equal Opportunity, a women's information bureau and a women's employment bureau have been established, and the equal pay unit has been expanded to include representatives of employers, unions, and a few mainline women's organizations.

Although EU policy cannot go beyond what the member governments of the community will agree to, it can be an important source for change, and it has provided real benefits for some women workers. Since EU law takes precedence over national law, it can bring a measure of reform where governments are disinclined to pass equal rights legislation.

EVALUATION BIAS is discrimination* based on gender when judging an individual's competence.

Women are less likely than men to attain high levels of achievement in our society despite the fact that there appear to be few, if any, substantive differences between the sexes in intelligence or competence in a wide variety of situations. One explanation for the difference in achievement is that females often are evaluated as less competent than males with identical or equal accomplishments and qualifications.

In Goldberg's landmark study female college students evaluated journal articles from either traditionally masculine, feminine, or neutral fields. For half the subjects, a given article was said to have a female author; for the other half, a male author. Male-authored articles received more favorable ratings than female-authored ones, especially in masculine fields.

Since 1968, many studies have shown that both female and male evaluators, children as well as adults, show similar antifemale bias when judging the quality of articles, essays, paintings, and applicants for managerial, scientific, academic, and semiskilled positions. In addition to bias regarding performance or qualifications, studies reveal that devaluation may extend to personal and social traits as well. Competent women have been judged to be less likable and less preferred as coworkers than equally competent men. Competent women also have been judged less "feminine" and more "masculine" than less competent women.

Not all studies find evaluation bias, however, and in some cases the bias is pro-female. Factors other than gender influence evaluation bias in complex ways. These include the gender association of the field or task, characteristics of those being rated, and characteristics of the raters. Devaluation of women is more likely to occur in fields traditionally dominated by men, whereas women are often evaluated more favorably than men in tasks or jobs typically associated with females.

The level of competence of the person being rated may influence the nature of evaluation bias as well. When there is external evidence that an individual possesses outstanding credentials or achievements, antifemale bias diminishes or disappears. Moreover, some studies have found that women who are portrayed as being highly successful in traditionally male occupations are judged more competent than males in the same occupation. This has been called the "talking platypus phenomenon"; that is, it makes little difference what the platypus says; the amazing thing is that it can talk at all. But even when the competence of a successful woman is recognized, the explanations offered for her success may differ markedly from those offered to explain a man's success. His successful performance generally is attributed to the stable, internal attribute of skill, while the same performance by a woman is attributed to such unstable or external factors as luck, effort, or ease of task.

At the other end of the competency continuum, males of low competence often are evaluated more poorly than females of low competence. In the middle range of average competence, which includes most people, antifemale bias is the rule, however,

In general, the more relevant the information that raters are provided about those being judged, the less likely they are to devalue women. For example, women are likely to be rated as competent as men when performance is judged on the basis of clear, explicit criteria. Moreover, antifemale bias is least likely when raters are evaluating someone they know well or with whom they have worked and interacted.

Other characteristics that affect evaluation bias include sex, sex-role attitudes, and the nature of the sample (e.g., college students versus employers). Males are more likely than females to show antifemale bias. Males with traditional attitudes toward women, in particular, are apt to devalue women.

Studies that ask college students to evaluate hypothetical persons are less likely to find consistent evidence of evaluation bias against women than are studies in which actual employers, managers, or recruiters are asked to judge prospective employees in hypothetical or actual decision-making situations. It has been suggested that employers, unlike students, are making their judgments in a more realistic context in which they have a potential stake in the outcome.

To sum up, evaluation bias is a complex phenomenon that depends not only on the gender of the person being judged but also on other characteristics of the individual, the social context, and characteristics of the evaluator.

References. J. Archer, "Sex Bias in Evaluations at College and Work, *The Psychologist: Bulletin of the British Psychological Society* 5 (1992): 200–204; Susan A. Basow, *Gender Stereotypes: Traditions and Alternatives,* 2d ed. (Belmont, Calif., 1986), ch. 11; Philip Goldberg, "Are Some Women Prejudiced against Women?" *Transaction* 5, no. 5 (April 5, 1968): 28–30; B. Lott, "The Devaluation of Women's Competence," *Journal of Social Issues* 41 (1985): 43–60; T. J. Top, "Sex Bias in the Evaluation of Performance in the Scientific, Artistic, and Literary Professions: A Review," *Sex Roles* 24: 73–106; B. S. Wallston and V. E. O'Leary, "Sex Makes a Difference: Differential Perceptions of Women and Men," in L. Wheeler (ed.), *Review of Personality and Social Psychology* (Beverly Hills, Calif., 1981), 2, 9–41.

CLAIRE ETAUGH

EVE AND MARY are the authors of damnation and redemption for the human race. A symbolic contrast between Eve, the first woman, and Mary, "the second Eve," was drawn in the second century and freely elaborated in the Middle Ages. As early as 155, the apologist Justin Martyr contrasted Eve's "conception" by the serpent with Mary's conception by the Holy Spirit. St. Irenaeus (c. 177) observed that "whereas the former had disobeyed God, the latter was persuaded to obey God, that the Virgin Mary might become an advocate for the virgin Eve" (*Against Heresies* 5:19.1). Such parallels extended Paul's understanding of Christ as the second Adam: Mary, as the second Eve, became Christ's helpmate in the work of salvation. After the third century, almost all Greek and Latin church fathers adopted the parallel. Through Eve came sickness, through Mary healing; through Eve sorrow, through Mary joy; death through Eve, life through Mary. Eve sold the human race to the serpent or Satan, but Mary crushed his head (Gen. 3:15) when she gave birth to Christ.

In the fourth century, St. Ambrose signaled a change of tone. Previous writers had emphasized a symmetry between the two women, but Ambrose remarked, "Through a *woman* came folly, through a *virgin* wisdom" (*On Luke* 4:7). The term "woman" (*mulier*) had the connotation of sexual experience. Although Genesis gives no indication that Eve tempted Adam sexually, she could now be associated with the "foolish woman" or harlot portrayed in the book of Proverbs. The Virgin Mary, on the other hand, was assimilated to the goddesslike figure of Wisdom. Henceforth, contrasts between the two women very often focused on Eve's sensuality and Mary's purity. The pains of childbirth (including menstruation) and the subordination of wives were taken as legitimate penalties for Eve's sin (Gen. 3: 16). Male advocates of virginity proposed them as due punishments for female sexual activity, holding up the horrors of childbearing and male dominance as arguments for chastity. Eve's very name (Latin *Eva*) was declared to be an anagram of *vae* (woe), or an imitation of the newborn infant's wail.

However, when Gabriel saluted Mary with the greeting *Ave* (hail), he reversed the name and plight of Eve. The Virgin was said to be physically intact not only before but also during and after the birth of Christ. Freed from concupiscence, the curse of Eve, she bore her son without pain or defilement. Because of this miraculous childbearing, Mary could not serve as a model for ordinary mothers who followed Eve's path. Her perfect virginity, however, set a standard for the consecrated nun. Virgins were advised to bear Christ in their hearts as Mary bore him in her womb. Their spiritual fertility would be more pleasing to God than the physical fertility of their sisters.

This conviction may account for the difficulties experienced by several married women who wished to lead holy lives, transferring themselves from Eve's role to Mary's. The Italian mystic Angela of Foligno (d. 1309) enjoyed an ecstatic vision in which the Virgin handed the infant Jesus into her arms. However, her natural motherhood was so abhorrent to her that she prayed for the deaths of her husband and all her children and rejoiced when God granted her prayer. The autobiography of Margery Kempe (c. 1436) illustrates a similar devotion to the baby Jesus, together with a total indifference to her own 14 children. The dominant interpretation of Eve and Mary undoubtedly contributed to the denigration of motherhood and exaltation of virginity throughout the medieval period.

Other writers used the parallel in a more liberating way to stress the transformation of Eve into Mary, the negative female into the positive. Peter Abelard, who believed that women were inferior to men by nature, used Mary's example to argue that they were more privileged in grace because God honors the weaker vessel. Eve's fall could be considered fortunate not only because it led to the birth of Christ but specifically because it would be reversed by Mary, thereby raising the status of all women. Hildegard of Bingen, in the mid-twelfth century, wrote that in Mary the "form of woman" had "graced the heavens more than she once disgraced the earth" (*Symphonia*, 11). A fifteenth-century English song runs, "Ne hadde the apple taken been,/ The apple taken been,/ Ne hadde never our Lady/ A been hevene-queen." From this perspective Eve was deserving of forgiveness, almost of gratitude. Medieval legends held that she and Adam did penance after their fall and were delivered by Christ at the harrowing of hell. In Canto 32 of the *Paradiso* Dante Alighieri portrays Eve sitting at Mary's feet among the blessed.

Both the reproach of Eve and the celebration of Mary became literary conventions. With respect to the net image of woman, their extremities of praise and blame probably canceled each other out. However, the powerful dichotomizing tendency at work in this parallel is evidence of a general taste for binary images of woman. Allegorical Vices and Virtues were universally portrayed as female. Literary types like the shrewish wife, the adulteress, and the demon in female guise bear a family resemblance to Eve. Mary is imaged by the virgin martyr and the nun, and to some degree by the courtly lady. Scholars have often noted a similarity between hymns in praise of Mary and troubadour lyrics in honor of a lady; but these resemblances seldom extend beyond stock praise of feminine beauty and worth.

Eve and Mary are represented in innumerable paintings, sculptures, and stained glass windows. The subject seems to have been especially popular in the fifteenth and sixteenth centuries. One iconographic type features an angel driving Adam and Eve out of Paradise in the background while, in the foreground, an angel delivers his message to the Virgin. Fra Angelico's *Annunciation* is a fine example. Alternatively, a painting or relief of Adam and Eve may decorate a wall in the room where the Annunciation takes place, lending a more naturalistic flavor. The motif of Mary crushing the serpent occurs in a number of Renaissance sculptures that portray the Virgin as the "woman clothed with the sun, with the moon under her feet" (*Rev.* 12:1). Beneath the moon is a woman's head or a figure of Eve with the serpent, forming the pedestal on which Mary is glorified.

The Eve–Mary theme could also be combined with the motif of the Cross as Tree of Life, balancing the Tree of Knowledge of which Eve partook. A fifteenth-century miniature from the missal of Bernhard von Rohr sums up all the theological aspects of the image. It depicts a single tree bearing both apples and eucharistic hosts; in one side of the foliage is a crucifix, and in the other is a skull. On the skull side stands a nude, lascivious Eve, taking apples from the serpent coiled around the tree and feeding them to a crowd of kneeling sinners. Beneath the crucifix stands Mary, fully clothed and crowned, plucking hosts and offering Communion. A naked Adam sits dazed at the foot of the tree, symbolizing man who must eternally choose between death through Eve or life through the Virgin.

After the Renaissance, the Eve–Mary theme lost some of its popularity in the face of newer forms of devotion. However, it is still the heart of symbolic Mariology in the Catholic and Orthodox Communions.

References. Hilda Graef, *Mary: A History of Doctrine and Devotion* (New York, 1963); John Phillips, *Eve: The History of an Idea* (San Francisco, 1984); Rosemary Ruether, *Mary—The Feminine Face of the Church* (Philadelphia, 1977); Marina Warner, *Alone of All Her Sex: The Myth and the Cult of the Virgin Mary* (New York, 1976).

BARBARA NEWMAN

EXCESSIVE FEMALE MORTALITY (EFM) results when the care and treatment of infants and children differ by sex to the extent that girls have a higher death rate than boys. Whereas in developed countries girls have a higher survival rate at birth and longer life expectancy than boys, in areas where girls are devalued in comparison with boys, the death rate of girls is considerably higher than that of boys. Where infanticide is not permitted, unwanted girls may be kept, but they might be treated differently than are boys, given less food, less medical attention, less attention to their physical and emotional needs. The girls will, therefore, be more susceptible to parasitic and infectious diseases than the better-cared-for male children. Underinvestment of resources in children is often referred to as delayed or deferred infanticide. (Young girls who suffer from such underinvestment of resources but survive to marriageable age are very likely to suffer from anemia, an important factor in the very high maternal mortality rates in developing countries.)

Much of the evidence for underinvestment in females is indirect, being inferred from demographic evidence of excessive female mortality (EFM). Johansson relates evidence of EFM in childhood and adolescence with the beginnings of commercial agriculture in colonial America and areas of nineteenth-century Europe. Since women and girls were concerned with agriculture for domestic consumption, and men and boys with cash crop agriculture, girls were devalued during this period. Once industrialization opened jobs for young girls and women, EFM during childhood and adolescence disappeared.

Demographic evidence shows EFM during childhood and premarital adolescence in many developing countries, and field research has demonstrated its socioeconomic causes—poorer nourishment, medical care, and emotional investment for girls. In the Mideast EFM has been found among girls aged 1 to 5 in Jordan, Lebanon, and Syria, and among the Palestinian Arabs and in the Sahara. There is less evidence of EFM in Africa and Latin America, but it has been demonstrated in much of South Asia, including

Burma, Pakistan, Sarawak, Sri Lanka, and Thailand. In many areas of India and in Bangladesh EFM is especially marked among girls under 4.

Reference. Sheila Johansson, "Deferred Infanticide: Excess Female Mortality during Childhood," in G. Hausfater and S. B. Hrdy (eds.), *Infanticide: Comparative and Evolutionary Perspectives* (New York, 1984).

EXECUTIVE ORDER 11246 was issued by President Johnson in 1965. It prohibits discrimination* on the basis of race, color, sex, religion, or national origin in all terms and conditions of employment and requires affirmative action* for women and minorities by agencies and institutions with federal contracts. In 1971, Revised Order Number 4, applying to firms with contracts over $50,000 and with 50 or more employees, mandated the development and implementation of written affirmative action plans, including goals and timetables and requiring "good faith" effort in order to "remedy the effects of past discrimination" and to eliminate present discrimination. In 1985 and 1986, President Reagan considered the repeal or substantial revision of Executive Order 11246, including the elimination of goals and timetables, but, although the administration did little to enforce the order, it was not substantially changed. Authority for the enforcement of Executive Order 11246, as amended by Executive Orders 12086 and 11375, is held by the Office of Federal Contract Compliance Programs of the U.S. Department of Labor.

DAYLE MANDELSON

F

FABLIAUX are medieval comic tales in verse, usually indecent or at least irreverent in language and spirit. In the strict sense the term "fabliaux" refers only to some 150 Old French poems composed between about 1200 and 1340, but these poems have obvious affinities with bawdy narratives told in other centuries and other languages, notably, the tales of the Miller, Reeve, Summoner, Merchant, and Shipman in Chaucer's *Canterbury Tales*.

Fabliaux make extensive use of certain, easily recognizable types of characters, including lecherous priests, poor, but clever, students (clerks), newly rich peasants, ignorant virgins, jealous husbands, and resourceful wives. The typical plot pits two of these types against each other in a contest for sexual gratification, power, money, or revenge—or sometimes all four. Victory tends to be won by some ingenious stratagem. The female characters are worthy adversaries in these contests; in sharp contrast with courtly literature, in fact, fabliaux generally portray women as formidably aggressive, clever, and determined to get what they want.

What are we to make of the aggressive women in fabliaux? Critics have sometimes interpreted them all as hostile stereotypes, expressions of deep-seated fears of female sexuality and power. There are fabliaux that clearly exhibit this kind of antifeminism. In "Porcelet" (Piglet) and "La Dame qui aveine demandoit pour Morel" (The Lady Who Demanded Oats for the Black Horse), for example, crude, scatological punishments are devised for wives whose sexual demands are excessive. "Sire Hain et Dame Anieuse" (Sir Hate and Lady Scold) emphatically recommends that a husband tame a disobedient wife by beating her. "La Dame escoillee" (The Castrated Lady) relates a more imaginative and extreme use of violence to reform domineering wives and concludes with a general curse on women who defy men's authority.

Reassertions of traditional male prerogatives are less typical of this genre, however, than stories that encourage identification with the rebellious woman. Thus, a number of fabliaux use the motif of an intolerable husband whose wife eventually turns the tables on him. One nice example is the suspicious peasant in "Le Vilain mire" (The Peasant Doctor) who decides to beat his wellborn wife every day because she might be unfaithful if she weren't weeping. After a few days of this treatment, the wife retaliates by persuading the king's messengers, who are seeking a great physician, that her husband can cure almost any malady if he's given a good beating first. The boastful coward in "Berengier au lonc cul" (Berengier of the Long Ass) demands a more humiliating comeuppance: he lords it over his aristocratic wife, pretending that he is a great warrior, until she disguises herself as a knight and forces him to choose between meeting her in battle and kissing her ass.

To applaud such heroines obviously requires one to dispense, at least temporarily, with conventional notions of proper female conduct. Indeed, fabliaux seem to have their own ethos, one that has little in common with either courtly ideals of polite behavior or Christian ideals of virtue. This point becomes particularly important when one considers the largest and most controversial group of women in fabliaux: wives who get away with infidelity by tricking their husbands. In another context such behavior would be the stuff of bitter satire, if not tragedy, and even the tellers of fabliaux often include some conventional moralizing against female deceit. But recent critics have argued persuasively that the real thrust of these stories is aesthetic rather than moral: the delight in a great piece of invention for its own sake, hence, the recurrent note of competitiveness. Can the woman manage simultaneously to have her husband cuckolded, beaten, and pleased with her (as in "La Borgoise d'Orliens" [The Townswoman of Orleans])? Can she tell him the whole truth, in language that he won't understand ("La Saineresse" [The Female Doctor])? Can she rise to the occasion when he finds her lover's clothes ("Les Braies au Cordelier" [The Friar's Breeches])? Which of three women deserves the prize for most cleverly deceiving her husband ("Les Trois Dames qui troverent l'anel" [The Three Ladies Who Found the Ring])? The ingenuity celebrated in such stories is not confined to women, of course. There are similar fabliaux about the exploits of peasants and especially clerks—other disadvantaged members of medieval society who become heroes, in these comic tales, by completely outsmarting their betters.

Reference. Charles Muscatine, *The Old French Fabliaux* (New Haven, Conn., 1986).

SHERRY L. REAMES

FAMILY is "a married couple or other group of adult kinfolk who cooperate economically and in the upbringing of children, and all or most of whom share a common dwelling" (Gough). Gough's definition is one of many attempts to identify essential, universal components and functions of the family, a social form and cultural construction that varies considerably through time and space. Much controversy exists over whether the family is universal, what functions it must or should perform, what structural components are essential, whether it should be understood as culturally constructed (i.e., from an emic perspective) or cross-culturally, and how and why it varies and changes.

Anthropological definitions of the family are devised to develop specific argumentation about these controversies. For example, the debate over whether the family is universal is bound up with the question of how to define it. Spiro argued that the family does not exist within the Israeli kibbutz because parents and children do not share a common residence, and husband and wife do not form a basic economic unit, two essential characteristics of the family as defined by Murdock's now classic definition: "a social group characterized by common residence, economic cooperation, and reproduction. It includes adults of both sexes, at least two of whom maintain a socially approved sexual relationship, and one or more children, own or adopted, of the sexually cohabiting adults." However, Spiro later reformulated his argument to suggest that Murdock's definition be revised to reflect the existence of the family within the kibbutz, where it performs essential psychological functions.

The commonly accepted view among anthropologists today is that the family is universal and that definitions of "the" family should reflect its universality. This concurrence is based, in part, upon arguments by early twentieth-century anthropologists, principally Bronislaw Malinowski, against those nineteenth-century social evolutionary theorists who questioned the existence of marriage* and the family in primitive societies (e.g., Engels). By distinguishing between sexual and conjugal relationships and conceptualizing "social fatherhood" (where the husband of the mother is considered to be the father of the child), anthropologists rejected the idea that group marriage and promiscuity characterize primitive, non-Western societies.

Within this consensus about the universality of the family, general agreement exists that its functions are economic cooperation as well as reproduction and socialization of children and that its structural components include the incest taboo, kinship, marriage, the nuclear family, common residence, and a gender-based division of labor.

Largely from the last characteristic—a gender-based division of labor—feminist anthropologists have derived a renewed critique of the universality of the family. In mid–twentieth-century America it was popularly assumed that the family was a natural institution and that women's place within it was naturally fixed—that the nurturing and expressive functions of the family were best performed by women who, by their nature, were suited for it. Placing women's primary functions and identity within the family meant a lesser role for women in public life and, concomitantly, a universally subordinate position relative to men.

The feminist critique is that "family" is best understood as a culturally constructed concept as opposed to a cross-cultural imperative and concrete institution. For example, Collier, Rosaldo, and Yanagisako examine American ideas of the family from this perspective and conclude, "The Family is not a concrete 'thing' that fulfills concrete 'needs' but an ideological construct with moral implications" (37). They propose that analyzing the family as a cultural construct rather than as a functional imperative will lead to better understanding and explanation of the moral and symbolic weight placed upon the concept of family in America today and its symbolic significance in other cultures.

Historians of the family have also challenged the usefulness of universal definitions of the family for analyzing changes in family forms, relationships, and attitudes.

To account for such critiques and obvious cultural variations while proposing cross-cultural generalizations, anthropologists have developed an extensive vocabulary of terms related to family, marriage, and kinship. With the proviso that the definitions of these terms are also debatable, some of the more important ones are the following:

Nuclear Family. A married couple and their dependent children.

Extended Family: Three or more generations of kin (a *stem family*) or two or more adult siblings, their spouses, and dependent children (a *joint family*), all of whom share a common dwelling and cooperate economically.

Compound Family (or *Polygamous Family*): A person and his or her spouses (two or more) and their dependent children.

Family of Orientation (or *Natal Family*): The family in which one is born and raised, including one's parents and siblings.

Family of Procreation (or *Conjugal Family*): The family one forms at marriage, including one's spouse and children.

Household (or *Domestic Group*): A group of people who share a common residence and cooperate economically.

References. Jane Collier, Michelle Rosaldo, and Sylvia Yanagisako, "Is There a Family? New Anthropological Views," in B. Thorne (ed.), *Rethinking the Family, Some Feminist Questions* (New York, 1982), 25–39; K. Gough, "The Origin of the Family," *Journal of Marriage and the Family* 33 (1971): 760–771; Friedrich Engels, *The Origin of the Family, Private Property, and the State* (New York, 1970); George Murdock, *Social Structure* (New York, 1949), 1; Melford Spiro, "Is the Family Universal?" *American Anthropologist* 56 (1954): 839–846.

LYNN WALTER

FAMILY (AS A SOCIOECONOMIC UNIT). The social institution that exerts profound influence on the construction of gender, the socialization of children into gender roles,* and the organization of sexuality. Although the family shapes relationships of power and dominance, as well as cooperation and affection, in all societies, there are great differences across societies in the ways in which the family is connected to social and economic life. For example, some societies make a sharp distinction between economic life and domestic life; in other societies, the family is the location where productive labor takes place. In some cultures large families and complex households are encouraged; in other cultures, the norm is small families and simple households. Women are expected to manage the work of running the household in most societies, yet some societies encourage all members of the family to share household tasks. To understand the position of women in a society at any historical period, it is important to analyze the structure of the household and family and the way the family relates to the social, economic, political, and legal systems of that society. These factors reveal a great deal about how gender roles and sexual stratification function in a particular society.

Feminist scholarship has profoundly reshaped the analysis of the family as a socioeconomic unit. This reshaping has occurred in several ways. First, feminist research has raised the possibility of understanding the family as an *ideology*, rather than as a social unit. In most societies, norms of who should live together, share resources, form affectional ties, and engage in sexual relationships are used to define the family unit. Such normative definitions then serve to justify restrictions on the social access and privileges of women, children, and the aged and to restrict alternative forms of family and household arrangements. The ideology of family in modern life in the Western industrial world emphasizes a division between public and private life in which women's place is defined as the private sphere of home and family, and men's place is defined as the public sphere* of economic and political life. Such an ideology of family is consistent with a sex/gender system in which gender is constructed so that the aspirations, personalities, opportunities, and emotional makeup of women are seen as being greatly different from those of men. As an ideology, the family also has been a potent political issue. Historically, calls to "save the family" have been used both to justify the restriction of rights and protections for women and children and to motivate labor, community, and personal struggles against oppressive conditions.

Second, feminists have challenged the assumption that the family is a monolithic social unit and that there is a harmony of interests within the family. Feminists have argued that different members of the family experience life within the family in different ways. Although members of the family may share common interests or work toward common goals, such commonality cannot be assumed. Often, perceived harmony disguises intense differences of power and resources within the family and the monopolization of control and decision-making by the most powerful member(s).

This is most apparent in the exercise of power and violence within the family. Women, children, and the elderly have been the most common victims of family violence, reflecting their relative lack of power and resources in the home and in the larger society. The divergent interests of family members, often separating along lines of sex and age, are reflected in many other areas of family life as well. Decisions about employment of family members, childbearing, residential location, and ties to extended family members are examples of areas in which family members may have different interests and goals.

Third, feminist scholarship suggests that the family is intimately connected to a variety of other structures of society. Although the family sometimes is portrayed as a "haven" from the heartless, impersonal world of work and commercialized relationships, feminists argue that family life, too, is permeated by judgments of worth and value from the larger society and economy. In societies divided by social class distinctions, the family acts to perpetuate these distinctions over time by socializing children and by preparing its members to assume a class-prescribed place in the economic, social, and legal systems. Moreover, the family contributes directly to the economic system through the invisible, unpaid work of women within the family and home. New research on the labor of housework* indicates the enormous economic contribution of household labor to the functioning of the economic system. Moreover, feminist research has affirmed the inseparability of production (work) and reproduction (family/ home) in modern life. Understanding the lives of women—or the lives of men—requires attention to both the paid labor of public economic life and the unpaid labor of life within the household. In modern societies, the family is the social unit that bridges production and reproduction since within the family consumption of goods and services is organized. Thus, the family affects, and is affected by, many aspects of the economy and society.

Fourth, feminist scholarship has affirmed the importance of understanding the structure of the family and household in a historical perspective. A central interest in this area has been the nature of nurturance, especially female mothering in Western, industrial societies. Research on the "reproduction of mothering" indicates that the predominance of female nurturance of young children in modern Western society has long-term consequences for adult personality development and sex/gender relationships. In societies in which the primary social bond of infants and children is developed mainly through adult female mothering, gender begins to be shaped at a very early age. Girls, with whom mothers identify closely, tend to develop facility with emotional life and relationships but may have difficulty establishing a sense of autonomy and personal boundaries in adulthood. Boys, for whom separateness from mothers is easier, tend to possess a sense of independence and autonomy but often have difficulty with emotional relationships. This divergence of gender is reinforced through socialization processes in the family that encourage boys to specialize in skills for a future work life and girls to specialize in skills for a future family life. The success of sex-defined mothering and sex-role socialization* pressures is evident in the strength of gender roles within and outside the family. Despite a great deal of publicity about changes in the male sex role, the participation of adult men in housework and child care* has changed very little over time in Western societies. In modern industrial societies, women continue to be the primary caretakers of children, and men continue to predominate in the world of work.

Fifth, feminist historians have pointed to the impact of changes in household and family composition upon the lives and opportunities of women and men in the family. In modern Western societies, households typically have been nuclear in composition (i.e., consisting of an adult couple and their children), although it is not uncommon for households to stretch to accommodate additional members during times of economic or personal crisis. Yet the size of the household and family has changed significantly over time. For the most part, family size (especially the number of children born) has declined in Western industrial societies. This has freed women for activities other than childrearing for a greater period of their lives. Moreover, the functions of the family have changed. Productive activities that used to be centered in the household are now usually found outside the home, creating a dichotomy between the public world of work and the private world of home and family, but ultimately freeing women for labor in the public sphere. Other functions that the family performed in earlier times, such as training and educating children, increasingly have become the province of the state, with mixed results for the lives and power of women within the family.

Finally, feminist analysis points to the wide variety of forms, functions, and processes of family life over time, across cultures, and within any society. Although general patterns in family structure and family relations can be discerned within specific historical societies, differences across racial, ethnic, religious, cultural, and geographic boundaries are complex and numerous. Indeed, a major contribution of feminist scholarship is to make clear that the family is not a monolithic entity. The forms that the family takes (nuclear, extended, childless, or other) and the relationships that underlie family life (monogamous or polygamous; heterosexual or homosexual; privatized or communal) are neither "natural" nor inevitable. Families, like other relationships of intimacy, are the product of constant negotiation and change in every society.

References. Lillian Rubin, *Families on the Fault Line* (New York, 1994); Arlene Skolnick, *Embattled Paradise: The American Family in an Age of Uncertainty* (New York, 1991); Carol Stack, *All Our Kin: Strategies for Survival in a Black Community* (New York, 1974).

KATHLEEN M. BLEE

THE FAMILY AND MEDICAL LEAVE ACT OF 1993 entitles eligible employees to take up to 12 weeks of *unpaid* leave each year for the birth, adoption, or placement for foster care of a child; the care of a spouse, son, or daughter with a serious health condition; or an employee's own serious health condition. The law covers all public sector employers and private employers with 50 or more employees within a 75-mile radius of the firm and employees who have worked for a covered employer for at least one year and 1,250 hours over the previous 12 months. Employers are required to maintain health insurance coverage for employees on leave on the same terms it was provided before the leave. Also, under most circumstances, employees are entitled to return to their original or equivalent positions after the leave with no loss of benefits. Exceptions are made for *key* employees who are among an employer's highest paid 10 percent. The law is enforced by the Employment Standards Administration, Wage and Hour Division of the U.S. Department of Labor.

The Family and Medical Leave Act was designed to respond to the needs of a changing labor force, especially with respect to the increasing labor force participation of women, and its passage was very controversial in terms of its potential effects on employers. In 1996, the Bipartisan Commission on Family and Medical Leave evaluated the impact of the law's first one and a half years. The commission's report showed that between 1.5 and 3 million people took family or medical leave between January 1994 and July 1995, that is, less than 4 percent of eligible employees. Of those taking leave, 59 percent took leaves for their own medical conditions; 25 percent for the birth, adoption, or serious illness of a child; and 10 percent for spouses' or parents' medical conditions. Employees with family incomes of $20,000 to $30,000 were more likely to take leaves than those with higher incomes. Notably, between 89 percent and 98 percent of the covered employers surveyed reported little or no extra cost associated with their compliance with the law.

References. U.S. Department of Labor Women's Bureau, *Family and Medical Leave: Know Your Rights* (Washington, D.C., 1994). Internet: http://gatekeeper. dol.gov/dol/esa/public/regs/statutes/whd/fmla.htm or Internet: http://gatekeeper.dol. gov/dol/esa/public/regs/cfr/29cfr/toc__Part500–899/0825__toc.htm

DAYLE MANDELSON

FEAR OF RAPE. Women fear rape more than any other offense (including murder, assault, and robbery). Early studies repeatedly documented women's greater fear of crime, especially rape. Women report levels of fear of rape three times higher than those of men. Women's fear of rape results in their use of more precautionary actions than men use, especially isolation behaviors such as not leaving the house. Women's fears are most likely to result in avoidance of discretionary activities, those activities they enjoy most, such as visiting friends or going out for evening entertainment. Riger and Gordon (1989) report that women engage in many self-imposed restrictive behaviors intended primarily to avoid rape. Such findings have lead both theorists and researchers to conclude that the fear of rape is a means of social control, a way to keep women in their place, at home, or under male protection.

How does fear of rape develop among girls and women? Studies that attempt to explain women's fear of rape have come to several conclusions. Women fear rape because (1) women are the primary victims of rape and other forms of male sexual violence, (2) women perceive a high likelihood of becoming victimized, (3) women are socialized to be vulnerable to rape and to fear it, and (4) the social and institutional systems reinforce fear of rape by placing blame on the victim.

Fear of rape seems to develop early in life. Rozee ("Freedom from Fear") reports that as girls between the ages of 2 and 12, the women in her study remembered receiving parental warnings about avoiding strangers. Women continue to receive warnings through a number of sources throughout their lives from parents, boyfriends, friends, and, of course, the media. These warnings communicate a sense of danger for women.

Women's assessment of the risk of rape is based on a background of other experiences of victimization. Alina Holgate found that all the women in her sample had experienced sexual intrusions or harassment and that such intrusions were significantly related to reported fear of rape. Every woman had been honked at, whistled at, leered at, propositioned, and commented upon sexually. Nearly all the women (two-thirds or more) reported that they had been followed, physically restrained, pressured for sex, hassled by men in hotels, subjected to obscene phone calls, rubbed against, grabbed or fondled, witness to a flasher or masturbator, or in a possible rape situation. From these and other experiences women assess their level of sexual vulnerability; from this assessment comes their level of fear.

Situational or environmental factors can also elicit fear of rape. The physical environment is one of the strongest factors in exacerbating fear of rape and enacting protective strategies among women. Situational factors in the workplace, such as poor lighting, lack of security in parking areas, and sexual harassment, contribute to women's fear of rape.

Rozee (1996) suggests that women who perceive themselves as having a high likelihood of being raped report more fear of rape. Media depictions of women as the victims of all manner of brutal sex crimes heighten women's perception of the likelihood of rape. Media reports give the impression that rape happens so often that women have little or no chance of escaping a would-be rapist. This couldn't be further from the truth. In fact, most women do escape. Riger and Gordon illustrate this media bias in a comparison of the ratio of attempted rapes to completed rapes. A random sample survey of households conducted by the National Crime

Victimization Survey (NCVS) for the Census Bureau found that there were four attempted rapes for every completed rape (4:1). Examination of newspaper stories shows that the press covers 1 attempted rape for every 13 completed rapes it covers (1:13). Thus, the media report that there are far more completed rapes than attempted rapes (1:13), while the reverse is actually true according to the NCVS (4:1). Why is this important? Because an attempted rape is a rape where the victim fought back, escaped, and was not raped. Women are four times more likely to fight back and escape their would-be rapists than they are to be raped (4:1). Such sensationalist reporting does a disservice to women because it exaggerates the actual rape rate and instills a lack of confidence in the ability to fight back.

The media portrayal of rapists as disproportionately black men as well as the greater frequency of arrests of black men due to inequities in the criminal justice system lead white women to especially fear black men. In truth, most violent crimes are intraracial, occurring primarily between people of the same race and socioeconomic class, according to several reports, most notably, O'Brien's.

Many authors have pointed to the tendency to socialize girls as weak and passive and boys as strong and aggressive. Many women are still raised to defer to men, to support men in their goals, and to expect men to take care of them and protect them. Girls are expected to be ladylike, timid, dependent and quiet and never to embarrass anyone by making a scene. Many of these socialized traits are in direct opposition to being able to successfully defend oneself. They may also leave women with negative perceptions of their physical competence and a perceived lack of physical strength and endurance. Women's negative perceptions of their own physical competence play a part in their levels of fear.

Another contributor to women's fear of rape is the pervasive atmosphere of victim blaming in our society. Every woman knows that, unlike nearly any other violent crime, if she is raped, the blame will be directed at her. Not only does this add to the trauma of a rape victim, but it also instills a sense of fear in all women.

Social and institutional forces that tend to engender fear of rape include the "revictimization" of rape victims by police, hospitals, and the courts. These are male-controlled systems that regulate violence against women in the guise of protecting women (Rozee, "Forbidden or Forgiven"). All women are taught to be dependent for protection on the very system that enables violence against women to go essentially unpunished.

Successful reductions of women's fear of rape require that we address all of the mechanisms through which women learn their fear and all the institutions (and people) that maintain it.

References. Aline Holgate, "Sexual Harassment as a Determinate of Women's Fear of Rape," *Australian Journal of Sex, Marriage and Family* 10 (2) (1989); 21–28; R. M. O'Brien, "The Interracial Nature of Violent Crimes: A Reexamination,"

American Journal of Sociology 92 (1987): 817–835; S. Riger and M. Gordon, *The Female Fear* (New York, 1989); P. D. Rozee, "Freedom from Fear: The Missing Link in Women's Freedom," in J. Chrisler, C. Golden, and P. D. Rozee (eds.), *Lectures on the Psychology of Women* (New York, 1996); P. D. Rozee, "Forbidden or Forgiven: Rape in Cross-Cultural Perspective," *Psychology of Women Quarterly* 17 (1993): 499–514; E. Stanko, "Ordinary Fear: Women, Violence, and Personal Safety," in P. Bart and E. Moran (eds.), *Violence against Women: The Bloody Footprints* (Newbury Park, Calif., 1993), 155–165.

PATRICIA D. ROZEE

FEAR OF SUCCESS (FOS) is a concept invoked to explain the vicissitudes of women's achievement. Originally proposed by Horner, it is defined as the fear that the attainment of success can have negative consequences. An avoidance motive, learned in early childhood in conjunction with sex-role identity, it is most salient for bright, competent women who are highly motivated to achieve. As Margaret Mead noted many years before Horner, "Men are unsexed by failure, while women are unsexed by success."

Horner was working within a dominant paradigm in psychology, the Atkinson–McClelland theory of achievement motivation, which had defined and studied achievement as a masculine characteristic. In the measure that Horner devised, college women wrote stories about Anne, a woman who was first in her class in medical school. Anne was described by college women in very negative terms as currently or ultimately suffering negative consequences (e.g., loss of friend) or as having attained her success unfairly (e.g., by cheating or in cutthroat competition).

The introduction of FOS helped trigger a new look in the study of women's achievement motivation and behavior. It was a stimulus, very much in tune with the zeitgeist of the late 1960s and early 1970s, for a surge of research on social-psychological underpinnings of women's achievement behavior. Since its introduction, the concept has received great attention from researchers, clinicians, and general observers of the social scene. The scientific context and definition have been frequently overlooked, particularly in lay discussions about the question of whether women, in general, have or do not have fear of success. The term took on a life of its own and was for some time a media event, a much-touted explanation for why women don't achieve.

Hundreds of studies have examined the reliability and validity of the concept and its measures. Arguments center on the questions of how to assess the construct (e.g., thematic imagery versus questionnaire) and on whether there are sex differences. Researchers have asked whether FOS reflects an accurate observation by all people of a cultural attitude (i.e., a stereotype), a motive, an *intrapsychic* disposition to certain kinds of behavior, or a logical response to specific situations (e.g., stress of competition, or intellectual evaluation).

While early studies upheld the validity of the idea and the measure, later ones did not. Questionnaire and imagery methods have both met with mixed success and inconsistent results. These may be due, in part, to changes in social perceptions that affected the meaning of the measures. For example, Anne, the successful medical student, is certainly no longer a deviant. The inconsistencies may also reflect researchers' expectation that FOS involves *all* women rather than only the high-ability achievement strivers whom Horner talked about, as well as real changes in the cohorts being studied.

Studies have included men as well as women and have varied class, age, ethnicity, and race. One review summarized 20 studies of African American women done between 1970 and 1982. Also examined have been personality characteristics such as identity stage, self-esteem, Type A, locus of control,* and psychological femininity.* FOS has been looked at in relation to competition, causal attribution, task sex typing, level of aspiration, peer or public acceptance or rejection, and a host of achievement-related behavioral variables. While interest during the 1980s abated, it did not cease; a search of the 1980s literature uncovered about 40 new references.

In conclusion, FOS has a heuristic value; it sparked an area of research and forced within psychology a new look at women's achievement strivings. As a scientific concept, its status is now shaky. This is due, in part, to inadequate attention to the complexity of the causes of women's achievement behavior.

Reference. Martina Horner, "Femininity and Successful Achievement: A Basic Inconsistency," in J. Bardwick et al., *Feminine Personality and Conflict* (Belmont, Calif., 1970).

MARTHA T. MEDNICK

FEMALE COMPLAINTS. A nineteenth-century catchall term used to describe women's ailments ranging from painful menstruation to prolapsed uterus. Writing in 1868, the French historian Jules Michelet characterized the nineteenth century as the "Age of the Womb," an observation borne out in the century's pervasive concern with women's health. Popular medical literature in America caricatured women as the victims of a host of female complaints. Like all caricatures, the image distorted reality by exaggeration. Women could and did suffer from a variety of diseases of the reproductive organs that nineteenth-century medicine only dimly understood. However, the emphasis on women's weakness had as much to do with social as with medical reality. Throughout the century, men facing the pressures and conflicts engendered by urban industrialization tended to project their fears and anxieties onto women by warning that material progress, far from bettering women's lot, only enfeebled them and led to female complaints.

The early nineteenth century witnessed the constriction of women's activities into a prescribed "woman's sphere." At the same time, doctors focused, with obsessive concern, on women's reproductive systems. Indeed, their "scientific" dicta helped to explain and justify the need for restricting women's sphere to the household. The distinguished British physician Henry Maudsley argued that females were no more than "mutilated males" who by virtue of their maimed organs could never expect to be as vital and active as men.

The relationship between medical theory and social theory has rarely been more obvious than in the way doctors used disease as a sanction to restrict women's lives. The female reproductive system came to be seen as a sacred trust, so delicate and temperamental that a woman must constantly work to preserve it in the interest of the race. Physicians hinted darkly that women who attempted to step out of traditional roles as wives and mothers could expect their organs to rise up against them.

Among the most common female complaints were those surrounding menstruation. The medical explanation of the periodicity of menstruation was taken by doctors to prove conclusively that women's bodies were out of control. While men struggled to master their animal lust, women, judged passionless, were nevertheless viewed as victims of a power so strong it could not be held in check by any degree of moral or mental exertion. Like it or not, they were once each month caught up in the throes of their reproductive systems. Thus, not simply the accidents or diseases of their sex but its normal exercise and functions came to be seen as pathological. Dr. Robert Battey gained notoriety by advocating the removal of healthy ovaries to spare women the ravages of menstruation.

In a society intent upon seeing women as inherently weak and infirm, it was not surprising that female complaints became so common. The medical specialty of gynecology developed in the late nineteenth century and promised by surgery and local treatment to cure various uterine complaints. Because of its accessibility, doctors frequently overtreated and maltreated the uterus. Although there was no effective treatment for prolapsed uterus, doctors nevertheless experimented with procedures ranging from intravaginal pessaries to surgical excision of the womb.

Critics labeled gynecological surgery "mutilation" and charged that physicians performed unnecessary operations. Patent medicine makers, seizing on the therapeutic confusion, cashed in with medicines like Lydia Pinkham's Vegetable Compound, which promised to cure prolapsed uterus and a host of other female complaints "without the knife." However exaggerated and self-serving, patent medicine advertising provided a sensational, but frequently sound, critique of nineteenth-century gynecology.

References. John S. Haller and Robin Haller, *The Physician and Sexuality in Victorian America* (New York, 1974); Sarah Stage, *Female Complaints: Lydia Pinkham and the Business of Women's Medicine* (New York, 1979).

SARAH STAGE

FEMALE DEVELOPMENT. A Life Span Approach. Contemporary theories and research on female development consider how the personality, cognitive construction of gender identity, and gender roles evolve over the entire life span. Additionally, acknowledgment of cultural diversity as a significant factor in developmental processes has begun to influence work on the development of women from infancy through old age. Throughout the course of life there are both change and continuity in women's development, as well as an expanding array of alternative lifestyles and pathways to be forged by individual women. With these qualifications in mind, the following description focuses on major themes that characterize the experience of being a Western female from birth through old age.

Infancy and Childhood. During the early years, a major developmental task involves the child's construction of a gender identity and gender schema. Even prior to a cognitive awareness of gender, however, is the socialization into a gender role that begins before birth with parental attitudes and expectations. For example, a majority of U.S. parents still prefer that their firstborn child be male (a worldwide attitude frequently based on religious traditions and economic circumstances). Parental perceptions of their newborn infants involve the view that their female offspring are more delicate, sensitive, and fearful than male babies. Although many aspects of the caregiving relationship are not differentiated on the basis of the baby's gender, communication patterns, independence training, activities, and toys set in motion key divergent paths for male and female infants. Mothers tend to be more responsive to the emotional expressions of their daughters and to ignore bids for comfort from their sons. Fathers, on the other hand, spend more time interacting with their sons than with their daughters. The outcome of these patterns may be female toddlers who handle stress and read social cues more effectively than their male counterparts, whose independence has been encouraged to a greater degree. Layered over the socialization process is a sophisticated cognitive developmental system that enables children to classify faces by sex by the latter part of the first year of life and to classify activities by gender by age 3. By the time a girl is 3 years old, she may manifest different preferences for activities and toys than do her male peers. She has learned to label herself as a girl and is very much aware of the normative expectations that her culture has of her gender.

Girls as well as boys develop their concepts of gender from a variety of sources. According to cognitive developmental theory, the acquisition of a gender identity reflects an active intellectual process whereby the child learns to label herself as a "girl" and then to seek out confirmatory experiences that help to define the gender label. For example, she may pay particular attention to gender-typed behaviors of significant females (her mother and teachers) and female peers. Her mimicry of their gender-typed behavior will be more likely to occur if there is a reward in doing so. Because classification by sex is so salient in our culture, children learn very early on to categorize information about their social world into "male" and "female." Such categorization evolves into a general knowledge structure, or *gender schema*, that becomes the repository for information about the two genders, their different activities and preferences, and expectations for behavior. A gender schema is an important construction for the child because it guides her observations and learning into what she may consider appropriate for her. Ultimately, she learns to recognize that her gender is immutable through time and to superficial changes in appearance. Thus, behavioral patterns, preferences, and schema that are different for boys and girls occur very early in the life span and reflect emotional and cognitive processes as well as behavioral learning via imitation and reward. Gender identity and gender schemata become a significant dimension of the child's overall concept of self.

Girls learn their gender roles not only from their parents, but also from a number of powerful extrafamilial sources of information and reward with respect to gender. Eleanor Maccoby, a scholar of gender-role development who has made a significant contribution to our understanding of the process, has become increasingly convinced that contemporary children learn more about their respective genders from their peers than from their elders. American children find themselves in age- and sex-segregated peer groups to a much greater extent than in the past. Maccoby claims that this context of play patterns, systems of influence, and social structures of boy and girl groups truly teaches the lessons of gender. In addition to the peer group, gender development is greatly influenced by television and classroom interactions. Television has consistently depicted women in stereotyped roles. Women typically are portrayed in romantic, married, or family roles— rarely are they seen as achievers or leaders. Unfortunately, there is a strong relationship between heavy televiewing among children and their degree of gender-role stereotyping. The evidence also suggests that girls and boys are treated differently in school. Girls generally have a positive elementary school experience because they are rewarded for behaviors that are consistent with gendered behaviors such as neatness, compliance, and affectionate closeness to the teacher. Achievement prior to adolescence is not viewed as a negative attribute for girls. However, research also shows that teachers prefer the intellectual challenge and stimulation provided by boys and reward them more for their competence. Girls are praised for their cooperation; their teachers generally do not focus on the intellectual quality of their work.

Adolescence. A central task of the adolescent years involves the crystallization of identity. Identity issues are intertwined with the dramatic changes of puberty, involving the growth spurt, onset of menstruation,* development of secondary sex characteristics,* and heightened sexual arousal. Thus, self-conception partially is defined in terms of becoming a mature woman or man. For adolescent males, identity is often focused upon future career goals; however, the female identity typically is confounded by both personal goals and present and future intimacy needs. Frequently, social acceptance is based on physical appearance and sexual appeal. Bolstered by the images of glamorous and unrealistic bodies in the media (especially the sexual content of music videos so closely watched by adolescents) and the pressures of the peer group, adolescent girls fight the emerging rounded contours of their bodies with diets and strict adherence to the whims of fashion. A perceived incompatibility between academic achievement and femininity heralds a downward spiral in academic achievement for many adolescent girls, particularly in the sciences and computer technology. It is no wonder that the small sex differences observed for certain cognitive abilities are manifested during the adolescent years. Such findings apparently are more typical of the white female adolescent; recent research has found that African American female adolescents receive much more encouragement from parents and schools to excel academically. The interpersonal focus of adolescent girls' identity formation is manifested in many dimensions of her life. From her interviews with girls aged 6 to 18, Carol Gilligan learned that girls are highly attuned to their relationships, define themselves within the context of these relationships, and judge themselves in terms of their ability to care. Their "different voice," emphasizing connection with others, is seen in contrast to the male goals of achievement and independence, which are nurtured by solitude. Fearing that their "voices" are not as respected as those of boys, many adolescent girls become "silent" as they hide their talents and abilities.

Early and Middle Adulthood. For adult women, the roles of wife and mother are central to their identities. Although gender stereotypes still adhere to the perception of these roles as the primary activities for women (the so-called motherhood-mandate), the reality of the 1990s is that fully 75 percent of U.S. women between the ages of 25 and 54 hold paying jobs. This sets the stage for a number of possibilities in the life patterns of adult women.

An older (but not necessarily invalid) theory of gendered behavior by David Guttman suggests that men's and women's behavior becomes more stereotyped because of the *parental imperative,* which dictates that women become "passive-accommodative" and nurturant (in contrast to the instrumental actions of men) because such division of behavior optimizes the development of children. Although not everyone agrees that such gendered division of household tasks is an evolutionary mandate, many women do still perform the majority of household tasks and experience role conflict and overload in their attempt to balance the demands of work and family. Adult women's commitments to relationships extend beyond their mothering role. Within the family, often the woman maintains intergenerational relationships and the management of social activities.

While the centrality of motherhood is indisputable in many cultures, contemporary Western women are offered a number of variations on the family and work themes. There is an increase in the numbers of women who are single, who are married and child-free, or divorced with and without children. The quest for personal fulfillment and economic necessity has led to an increase in the numbers of women who are returning to college, a reversal of the adolescent aversion to educational and intellectual achievement. The downside of such changes is reflected in the "feminization of poverty," a significant decrease in the standard of living for many divorced women who do not receive alimony payments and cannot maintain the same standard of living experienced when they were married.

For many women, the centrality of the themes of intimacy and work continues through the midlife years. In contrast to older notions that midlife represented a crisis heralded by the "empty nest syndrome"* and the onset of the climacteric,* the 60th decade of life may be the "prime years" for many women. Once children achieve some measure of independence, many women delight in the rediscovery of talents and abilities that have been neglected during the years of demanding child rearing. This seems to be true even for women who have maintained a traditional lifestyle while raising their children. As Guttman noted, the parental imperative wanes, allowing women to reclaim a more androgynous personality. Also supporting this finding are the positive attitudes that many postmenopausal women express toward the cessation of menstruation. Unlike popular cultural and medical stereotypes, many women do not view menopause as the signpost of a major life transition or a biological crisis. In many non-Western cultures, postmenopausal women experience a gain in social stature.

Later Life. While a number of issues are particularly salient for elderly women, it is important to note that the effects of aging on women are mediated by cohort effects. Divorce, continuing education, the pursuit of a career, and planned parenthood were not options for elderly women who were born in the early part of this century. Currently, 66 percent of women over age 75 are widowed. When their husbands die, many women lose not only their friends and companions but their economic security (further contributing to the feminization of poverty) and their sources of identity. Many widows, however, derive psychological comfort and support from well-established networks of intimate friendships, typically with other women. Women also retain continuity in their roles within the context of home and family. For many older women, grandparenthood is a meaningful and joyful experience. For a variety of reasons, there is an increase in the numbers of older women who are assuming primary responsibility for the rearing of their young grandchildren, certainly a mixed blessing. Research findings suggest that this is a more common experience among older African American women than for white women.

Susan Sontag has suggested that women experience a "double standard of aging." Women continue to be appreciated for their sexual, reproductive, and nurturing functions, all of which are valued within the context of youth. An aging man becomes more handsome and dignified, but an aging woman is a has-been as a mother and sexual partner. Drastic measures such as cosmetic surgery and hormone replacement therapies have reflected such attitudes. Hopefully, as the "baby boomer" generation ages, new standards of women's beauty will replace current negative stereotypes of older women.

Finally, the impact of retirement* upon the aging woman is a psychosocial event that will warrant increasing attention as women continue to enter the workforce. Will the issues they face be the same as those for retired men, or will the unique mosaic of work and family lead to a different set of concerns and role transitions as women change their work status? For example, women who began working once their children were of school age may be at the height of their careers just when they are expected to retire. Current models of retirement still tend to view the process from the male perspective, and relatively little is known about how women experience their retirement.

In summary, it is evident that female development involves the tensions between personal identity, family relations, cultural expectations, adaptability to social constraints, and the flexibility of alternative lifestyles. Such issues underscore the theme that the life stages of women reflect an ongoing process of change and development.

References. American Association of University Women (AAUW), *The AAUW Report: How Schools Shortchange Girls* (Washington, D.C., 1992); C. R. Beal, *Boys and Girls: The Development of Gender Roles* (New York, 1994); Carol Gilligan, *In a Different Voice: Psychological Theory and Women's Development* (Cambridge, MA, 1982); David Guttman, "Parenthood: A Key to the Comparative Study of the Life Cycle?" in N. Datan and L. Ginsberg (eds.), *Life-span Developmental Psychology: Normative Life Crises* (New York, 1975); E. E. Maccoby, "Gender and Relationships," *American Psychologist* 45 (1990): 513–520; S. Sontag, "The Double Standard of Aging," in J. Williams (ed.), *Psychology of Women: Selected Readings* (New York, 1979), 462–478; M. R. Stevenson, *Gender Roles through the Life Span* (Muncie, Ind., 1994); R. Unger and M. Crawford, *Women and Gender: A Feminist Psychology* (New York, 1992).

ILLENE NOPPE

FEMICIDE. The term "femicide" was first coined in England in 1801 to signify "the killing of a woman." In 1848, femicide appeared in Wharton's *Law Lexicon*, suggesting that it had become a prosecutable offense (*The Oxford English Dictionary*, 825). I was totally unaware of this history when I defined femicide to mean the "killing of a female because of her gender" (Radford and Russell). Such a word is needed to remove the obscuring veil of nongendered terms such as homicide and murder and to facilitate recognition of the worldwide problem of womanslaughter.

Femicide is not synonymous with *gynocide*, a concept first introduced by Mary Daly in 1973 and later defined by Dworkin to refer to "the systematic crippling, raping, and/or killing of women by men . . . the relentless violence perpetrated by the gender class men on the gender class women" (16).

Gynocide is a much broader concept than femicide, including, but not limited to, the misogynist killing of women and girls. Also, unlike femicide, the term "gynocide" never applies to a single case of womanslaughter.

Misogynist murders are the most obvious examples of femicide. These include mutilation murder, rape murder, woman battery that escalates into wife killing, the immolation of witches in Western Europe and of brides and widows in India, and "honor crimes" in some Latin and Middle Eastern countries, where women believed to have lost their virginity are murdered by their male relatives.

In the United States, women living with their husbands and children are most at risk of being murdered. Given that the family is the fundamental unit of this society (and perhaps of all societies) and that it is often regarded as a haven from the dangers and stresses of the nondomestic world, the frequency of femicide in marriage assumes a sinister irony.

Some cases of wife murder do not qualify as femicide, as when husbands murder their wives for economic reasons. However, many men murder their wives in a jealous rage or in outrage that women whom they regard as their possessions plan to leave them. The nuclear family is a prison for millions of girls and women. Some husbands and fathers act as full-time guards who threaten to kill if defied—a threat all too often carried out. For example, as a case of *familicide* motivated by femicide is the following:

"Dedicated Bible reader" John List was convicted for mass murder in New Jersey in 1990 after escaping detection for 18 years. In a letter to his pastor, List complained that his wife refused to attend church, an action which he "knew would harm the children." Moreover, his daughter wanted to pursue an acting career, making him "fearful as to what that might do to her continuing to be a Christian." In a rage over his loss of control of his family, this supposedly godly man slaughtered his wife, daughter, mother, and two sons. (Caputi and Russell, 36–37)

Our sex-and-violence culture is a breeding ground for the amateur torturers and executioners who have emerged as the shock troops of male dominance.

Although there is no way yet to ascertain what percentage of murders of women by men are cases of femicide, I believe that most of them are, not only because mens' misogynist attitudes are so widespread but also because the culture promotes femicide. For example, when women report to the police that their husbands are threatening to kill them, law enforcement personnel typically fail to protect them no matter how well documented the man's threats and his violent history. The police and the public are much more willing to assist women who are attacked by strangers than women who are attacked by their husbands. The still-widespread assumption that women are the property of their husbands contributes to the high rate of wife femicides.

While the murder of wives is the most common form of femicide, the percentage of prostitutes who are casualties of femicide is much higher than the percentage of wives or any other grouping of women or girls. Prostitutes are among the safest femicidal targets because of their devaluation by police and public alike.

Femicides committed by serial killers have become more frequent since the late 1970s. Although precise figures are not available reports that by the mid-1980s, police officials' estimate of the total number of serial killings had risen to 4,000 a year. While some serial murderers kill males, most experts agree that the vast majority of victims are female (203).

Femicide is on the extreme end of a continuum of antifemale terror that includes such verbal and physical abuse as rape, torture, mutilation, female sexual slavery (particularly forced marriage and prostitution), incestuous and extrafamilial child sexual abuse, physical and emotional battery, and genital mutilation. Whenever these forms of terrorism result in death, they become femicides.

One theory is that growing numbers of men are committing femicide because rape and other lesser forms of violent abuse have failed to keep women subservient. A slightly different formulation of this theory is that the escalating violence against females is part of male backlash against women's becoming more liberated as a result of feminism and various socioeconomic forces. This doesn't mean it is the *fault* of feminism. Patriarchal culture terrorizes women whether or not they fight back. Nevertheless, when male supremacy is seriously challenged, the terror is intensified. Many law enforcement officials have commented on the growing viciousness in slayings. As Justice Department official Robert Heck said: "We've got people [sic] out there now killing 20 and 30 people [sic] and more, and some of them don't just kill. They torture their victims in terrible ways and mutilate them before they kill them." (Caputi, 2), for example:

Teenager Shirley Ledford screamed for mercy while Roy Norris and Lawrence Bittaker of Los Angeles raped and mutilated her with a pair of locking pliers, hit her with a sledgehammer, and jabbed her in her ear with an ice pick. The men audiotaped the torture-femicide from beginning to end. One victim of a sexual femicide was found with stab wounds in her vagina and groin and with her throat slashed.

Her nipples had been removed and her face severely beaten; and her cut-off hair was found hanging from a nearby branch. (Caputi and Russell, 36)

Femicide goes beyond the legal category of murder. It includes woman killing—or women being permitted to die—because of misogynistic attitudes, practices, and/or social institutions. For example, wherever the right of women to choose to be mothers is not recognized, thousands of women die from botched abortions. Writing about the United States in 1970, during a period in which the death penalty had been ruled unconstitutional by the U.S. Supreme Court, Millett pointed out: "Indirectly, one form of 'death penalty' still obtains even in America today. Patriarchal legal systems in depriving women of control over their own bodies drive them to illegal abortions; it is estimated that between two and five thousand women die each year from this cause [in the United States]" (43–44). Other examples of culturally sanctioned femicide include economic discrimination against women in poor communities and countries, resulting in the deaths of disproportional numbers of women and girls; deaths from unnecessary surgeries such as hysterectomies, genital excision, and infibulation; and a preference for boys, leading to countless deaths of girls from neglect, illness, starvation, and infanticide in nations such as China and India.

Just as many people have denied the reality of the Nazi Holocaust, most Americans refuse to recognize the gynocidal period in which we are living—and dying—today. While many women who stepped out of line in early modern Europe were grotesquely tortured and killed as witches (with estimates ranging from 30,000 to 9 million killed (Daly, footnote, 183), today such women are regarded as cunts or bitches, deserving whatever happens to them (Caputi and Russell). "Why is it wrong to get rid of some fuckin' cunts?" Kenneth Bianchi, convicted "Hillside Strangler," demanded to know (Caputi, 33).

When murderers select their victims because they are members of an oppressed group, the murders must be recognized as political hate crimes. Just as the concept of racist murder facilitates our recognition of the racist element in some murders, the word "femicide" serves the same purpose in the case of misogynist woman killing, and just as the federal government treats racist murders as more heinous than murders free of racism by defining them as civil rights violations as well as homicides, femicides deserve similar recognition and treatment.

Acknowledgment. I am greatly indebted to Jane Caputi for her contribution to this article. We coauthored some of the material contained in it for an article in *Ms.* (1990).

References. Claudia Brenner and Hannah Ashley, *Eight Bullets* (Ithaca, N.Y, 1995); Deborah Cameron and Elizabeth Frazer, *The Lust to Kill* (New York, 1987); Jane Caputi, *The Age of Sex Crime* (Bowling Green, Ohio, 1987); Jane Caputi and Diana E. H. Russell, " 'Femicide': Speaking the Unspeakable," *Ms.* (September/October 1990); Mary Daly, *Gyn/ecology* (Boston, 1978); Andrea Dworkin, *Our Blood* (New York, 1976); Willard Gaylin, *The Killing of Bonnie Garland* (New York, 1982); Elliot Leyton, *Hunting Humans: Inside the Minds of Mass Murderers* (New York, 1986); Louise Malette and Marie Chalouh (eds.), *The Montreal Massacre* (Charlottetown, Prince Edward Island, 1981); Kate Millett, *Sexual Politics* (New York, 1970); Jill Radford and Diana E. H. Russell, *Femicide: The Politics of Woman Killing* (New York, 1991); Robert Ressler, Ann Burgess, and John Douglas, *Sexual Homicide* (Lexington, Mass., 1988).

DIANA E. H. RUSSELL

FEMININITY means the characteristics claimed to constitute femaleness. Femaleness and maleness, those traits that differentiate males and females, have received increasing attention in Western culture over the last 300 years. During the nineteenth century these traits were examined primarily through three genres: characterization in fiction (women's sensibilities), prescriptions for appropriate social and moral arrangements (the idea of separate spheres), and research on the biological bases of such characteristics (sex differences* in cranial size, special functions of the reproductive organs).

These genres of knowing contributed to refined conceptions of male and female and particularly to a discursive sense of the attributes of masculinity and femininity. By the end of the century interest in these special sexual attributes shifted toward the psychological realm, and eventually the primary locus of examining sexual difference became an *intrapsychic* one. The terms "femininity" and "masculinity" came to signify the mental characteristics, often unconscious traits, that differentiated females and males. Sex differences came to be equated, more often than not, with psychological properties. Although not available to ready observation and measurement in the same way that cranial and physical strength are, such mental differences nevertheless were taken as *real*. In other words, they were fundamental, enduring, and essential properties.

These essential psychological properties of masculinity and femininity came under scrutiny through psychoanalysis and scientific psychology. With psychoanalysis, Sigmund Freud set the tone for a universal, although sometimes ambiguous, conception of the feminine psyche. While Freud maintained that the libido is the same in males and females, he believed it to be basically masculine. Feminine sexuality is a specific variant of masculine libido: it results from the girl's realization that she has no penis and her consequential repression of masculine (active) desires for feminine (passive) ones of penis substitution. Other analysts have amended Freud's interpretation of the origins of the feminine psyche. Some argue that libido itself is sex-specific. That is, males and females have fundamentally different psychological experiences due to physical differences—males' experiences being phallic or outward-oriented and females' being concentric or inward-oriented. Taking this perspective, Erik Erikson developed notions of the feminine sense of "inner space" (and masculine sense of "outer space"). Taking another approach, analysts of an object relations perspective attribute essential sex-specific characteristics to the earliest relations between mother and infant. For instance, Chodorow has suggested that the girl's interior world reflects her earliest environmental experiences: psychosexual traits arise when the mother continues to promote a sense of unity or connectedness with female infants while promoting separation or independence with male infants. By internalizing a world of connectedness with others, girls acquire psychological traits of attachment, dependence, and passivity.

Scientific psychology has rejected psychoanalytic models but, nevertheless, has developed conceptualizations of femininity and masculinity that are strikingly congruent with psychoanalytic theory. During the early twentieth century psychologists began experimental investigations into the nature of sex differences. The initial findings were equivocal: differences in various psychological abilities were variable and often not found at all. The search continued with construction of psychometric tests that purportedly measured more essential mental functions, those of femininity and masculinity. The first such masculinity–femininity test was published in 1936 by Lewis Terman and Catherine Cox Miles. By the 1960s dozens of scales had been created to assess these supposedly deeply embedded, frequently concealed traits. The tests also were used to identify abnormal deviations that were thought to be predictors of psychopathology, notably, latent homosexuality* or poor adult adjustment. Like the psychoanalytic models, these conceptualizations associated femininity with passivity, emotionality, dependence, and involvement in personal relationships, while masculinity was associated with activity, independence, rationality, and interest in objects.

These ideal types hardly differed from their nineteenth-century counterparts. They are held to be universal, fixed, essential, and intrapsychic features of men and women. They are features that are ascribed according to biological sex rather than achieved by performance or activities. In most theories, the types also are prescribed as characteristics of healthy functioning in adults, and they have fitted well with the structure of existing social relations. On one level, this duality of personality types matches the occupational roles accorded to the sexes in society. The feminine personality complements the role demands intimated in the nineteenth-century conception of "expressive" roles (as opposed to "instrumental" or task-oriented ones): mothering, caregiving, attending to social and environmental "housekeeping," and so on.

Feminist theorists have identified another level at which the duality of masculinity and femininity relates to societal forms. Masculinity is the ideal that is represented in cultural forms generally: the masculine personality corresponds to the enshrined rationality, disinterestedness, the objectivity (distance) of scientific epistemology; the autonomy and individualism of liberal political doctrines; and the object orientation and aggressiveness of the modern technological workplace. Femininity represents the "other," that category that is not achievement, that is not representative of cultural progress. Yet femininity remains absolutely essential to maintaining social and emotional relations. From this perspective many feminist theorists see femininity as a cultural construction that is constitutive in maintaining social relations in societies where differential status and options are accorded to men and women.

The concepts of femininity and the feminine personality type, therefore, are themselves cultural contradictions. While femininity represents the "other," or the absence of traits valued in postindustrial conceptions of personhood, it also contains qualities (passion, caring, intuition) that are sometimes recognized as virtues. Those feminists who advocate women-centered models as correctives to patriarchal conditions face this contradiction. Other feminist theorists have attempted to resolve the cultural contradiction by advocating "androgyny,"* for the androgynous personality encompasses desirable traits of both femininity and masculinity. The androgynous being can be independent, assertive, and rationally motivated in one situation and caring, receptive, and emotional in another. The androgynous person has a psychological repertoire that allows him or her to respond to a wide range of situational demands. However, the androgynous being is too often presented as a protean *man*, a disarmingly transient personality that manifests primarily masculine virtues or at least is accorded stature and power for displaying masculine attributes.

Recent feminist scholarship has moved toward revealing the feminine personality as a social construction: femininity can be seen as a manufactured status or state that serves maintenance of particular social systems. However, this move only challenges existing social discourse and practice. Further transformations are needed to establish the future possibilities regarding femininity, for until such time, femininity will be attributed to fixed, intrapsychic characteristics, and the recognition of feminine behavior will be restricted in its social value and power.

References. N. Chodorow, *The Reproduction of Mothering* (Berkeley, 1978); J. G. Morawski, "The Troubled Quest for Masculinity, Femininity and Androgyny," in P. Shaver (ed.), *Review of Personality and Social Psychology* 7 (Beverly Hills, Calif., 1987); C. Smith-Rosenberg, *Disorderly Conduct: Visions of Gender in Victorian America* (New York, 1985); R. Steele, "Paradigm Lost: Psychoanalysis after Freud," in C. Buxton (ed.), *Points of View in the History of Modern Psychology* (Orlando, 1985).

JILL G. MORAWSKI

"FEMININITY" was the title of an influential essay by Sigmund Freud that was first published in his *New Introductory Lectures on Psychoanalysis* (1933). It draws on ideas from two of his earlier essays—"Some Psychological Consequences of the Anatomical Distinction between the Sexes" (1925) and "Female Sexuality" (1931)—in an attempt to provide a coherent psychoanalytic theory of women. Freud predicts in the essay that feminists will likely object to his solution to what he calls "the riddle of femininity," and, indeed, many prominent feminist thinkers—among them Simone de Beauvoir, Betty Friedan, Germaine Greer, and Kate Millett—have taken pains to denounce Freud's theory as a classic illustration of sexism. Doubtless, Freud's views do bespeak sexism, but that sexism belongs as much to Freud's Victorian and Jewish cultural heritage as to Freud himself, and it seems possible, especially in light of Mitchell's reassessment, to regard his theory less as a pseudoscientific distortion of the true lives of women than as an accurate description of the process by which society has traditionally molded women to accept subordinate status.

Certainly "Femininity" needs to be read in the context of the overall evolution of Freud's thought, particularly the elaboration of the so-called second topography in *The Ego and the Id* (1925). This treatise marks an important transition in Freud's thought away from the analysis of the libidinal instincts and the id and toward the analysis of the cultural forces that repress these instincts, represented internally by the ego and the superego. With the development of the theory of narcissism in the mid-1910s Freud was able to explain more precisely how the male child resolves the Oedipus crisis. Previously Freud had maintained that the boy's oedipal love for his mother and rivalry with his father ended with the awakening of castration fear, which prompted the boy to identify himself with his father and repress his maternal attachment. In the new model of the mind, the boy's identification with the father establishes a permanent precipitate in the ego—Freud calls it the superego—that internalizes the commanding presence of the father and provides the son with the psychological strength to renounce his incestuous wishes. Thereafter, the superego shapes the character of the young man, imbuing him with the father's stern moral prohibitions, cultural standards, and thrusting, propagating ways.

The essays on female sexuality that follow *The Ego and the Id* derive from Freud's belated recognition that the Oedipus complex in girls could not be said to follow a course parallel to that in boys. In the female complex the girl loves her father and hates her mother, but since Freud wished to assert that infants of both sexes originally love their mother, the girl must, at some point, unlike the boy, switch the object of her libidinal interest, a two-stage developmental scheme that Freud found congenial with his longstanding belief that the clitoris precedes the vagina as the sexual organ of the girl's phallic phase. In Freud's new theory, the shift in love interest and sexual organs occurs when the girl discovers the inferiority of her clitoris to the phallus and experiences the female version of castration anxiety, penis envy. Under its influence the girl turns in rage against her mother, who is similarly inferior; renounces clitoral masturbation; and bestows her love on her father. Her femininity is established when, through the unconscious equation between a penis and a baby, she substitutes her wish to have her father's penis for a wish to have a baby by him.

The chief significance for Freud in this theory lies in another important difference it indicates between the psychosexual history of men and women: Whereas castration fear terminates the male Oedipus complex, penis envy initiates the female complex. Women, in other words, never undergo the dramatic repression of their oedipal loves in the way men do; they remain within the complex for a longer period of time and demolish it less completely. "In these circumstances, the formation of the superego must suffer," Freud observes in "Femininity." As a consequence women remain closer to the world of nature than culture; they are more instinctive and narcissistic, less attuned to the demands of reality and conscience, less capable of sublimation. A young man of 30, Freud notes, strikes an analyst as largely unformed and alert to possibilities of psychological development; a woman of the same age, however, "frightens us by her psychical rigidity and unchangeability. Her libido has taken up fixed positions and seems incapable of substituting them for others."

Condescending as Freud's tone may be, his theory does, nevertheless, register the phallic orientation of Victorian cultural values. By indicating the lack of superego development as the chief psychological characteristic of women, he acknowledges their alienation from the deepest springs of that culture. Furthermore, the decisive role of castration fear in both masculine and feminine development may be regarded as a telling comment on the way patriarchal societies define men and women. Both achieve their psychological identity through the fear of phallic inferiority, the fear of being feminine.

References. T. Brennan (ed.), *Between Feminism and Psychoanalysis* (New York, 1989); R. Feldstein and J. Roof (eds.), *Feminism and Psychoanalysis* (Ithaca, N.Y., 1989); J. Gallop, *The Daughter's Seduction* (Ithaca, N.Y., 1982); L. Irigaray, *Speculum of the Other Woman* (Ithaca, N.Y., 1985); Juliet Mitchell, *Women, the Longest Revolution: Essays on Feminism, Literature and Psychoanalysis* (London, 1984); J. Strouse (ed.), *Women and Analysis: Dialogues on Psychoanalytic Views of Femininity* (New York, 1974).

JON HARNED

FEMINISM affirms the value of women and women's contributions to social life and anticipates a future where barriers to women's full participation in public life will be removed. Within feminism are many different political agendas, philosophical positions, values, ideologies, and viewpoints. However, feminists share five general commitments: (1) valuing women and their specific contributions to society; (2) critically analyzing the past to understand how patriarchal practices have devalued women; (3) analyzing sex-gender constructions that emphasize male–female differences and examining differences among women, especially in terms of race, ethnicity, sexuality, class, age, body shape, and religion, as well as other categories of identity that are used to denigrate, dismiss, or delegitimate persons without consideration of the merit of their actions, thoughts, or character; (4) formulating new understandings that can transform social, political, and personal practices on the basis of women's contributions, values, and experiences; and (5) working toward social and personal transformations through political activities designed to enable women to participate as full citizens in public life. This understanding of feminism develops out of Western thought, takes shape in the context of English-speaking feminist conversations in the later part of the twentieth century, and is informed by worldwide conversations about women's status.

Working on behalf of these five commitments involves feminists in two central activities. First, while feminists often argue for woman's autonomy and endeavor to secure for women the same political rights granted to Western men, they seek full citizenship by going beyond equal rights to an equal share of public power. Second, because feminists are suspicious of abstractions like "humanity" that may actually articulate only male experiences, especially the experiences of white, middle-class, heterosexual males, who are assumed to represent all of humanity, feminists affirm the specificity of women's lives and experiences. Within this specificity, feminists frequently assert the importance of daily life and personal experiences, and they emphasize the links between public and private spheres of social existence.

While feminists share these five commitments, there are important differences in the ways in which feminist activists, whose primary activity is political work, and feminist academics, whose primary activity is analysis, realize these commitments. While vital connections exist between feminist activists and feminist academics, feminism takes different forms in the context of these two activities.

Feminist activism is political work that focuses on advocating for women by eliminating discrimination against persons because they are female. In English the word "feminism" first appears in the late nineteenth century. Shortly after its introduction, it was used to refer to one branch of the nineteenth-century U.S. women's movement that sought general social change. This distinguished it from the other branch, which sought woman suffrage and legal rights. In the later twentieth-century women's movement, the term "feminist" has been used to designate all persons who work as political advocates on behalf of women and women's values. Women's values are most frequently characterized as including democratic processes, egalitarian supportive relationships, self-definitions, caring relationships, contextualized knowledge practices, and collaborative organizational work. Thus, feminist activists critique authoritarian practices, hierarchical power relationships, and competitively structured relationships.

Feminist activists often find that issues of gender, race, ethnicity, class, and sexuality are woven together. Accordingly, feminist political work struggles against systems of oppression generated by racism, sexism, heterosexuality, and class, and often examines how women and other identity groups, based on race, sexual orientation, age, and class, have been marginalized by social practices. The concept "woman as other," developed by Simone de Beauvoir, has been used to explain such marginalizations, which respond to identifying characteristics rather than to actions taken by such persons. Feminist activists work to undo institutional structures, habits, and social practices that create second-class citizens. While marginalization produces political disenfranchisement, the marginalized are often able to develop richer and more accurate social understandings than are forthcoming from those in the center. Thus, listening to the analyses developed by those marginalized citizens facilitates feminist work. Feminists often find themselves working against international systems of injustice in the effort to create equality for all the world's women. Furthermore, experiences associated with colonization and its undoing can serve as models for feminist emancipation. Bell hooks, for example, argues that feminist work includes decolonizing thought.

Academic feminism comprises a body of thought that builds upon the five commitments previously mentioned. It is sometimes referred to as feminist theory, feminist scholarship, or gender analysis. In the later twentieth century, the institutionalization of women's studies and the introduction of gender analyses into universities have produced the term "academic feminism," which distinguishes this body of thought from the activities involved in direct feminist political work. Feminist scholars develop a value-oriented analysis that they understand as a contribution to political thought. In this sense, their goal is to make the world more just. They may or may not be directly involved in other types of political work.

A part of the politics of feminist scholarship involves showing how adding women to existing theoretical frameworks forces alterations in fundamental concepts, relationships, and epistemological concerns, because such theories have been formulated on the basis of assumptions that come from men's experiences. Feminist scholarship, feminism, and/or feminist theory house a multiplicity of philosophical positions and epistemological strategies. Feminist philosophical positions have aspirations and commitments that go beyond immediate social goals and interest group politics. A variety of feminist approaches to scholarship have emerged with differing assumptions about human nature, social values, political goals, epistemological strategies, and analyses of gender power relationships. Alison Jaggar develops a typology that analyzes four philosophical positions—liberal feminism, Marxist feminism, radical feminism, and socialist feminism. These philosophical positions go far in explaining and informing the political agendas of the women's movement. Feminist scholars have expanded this typology to include psychoanalytical feminism, postmodern feminism, cultural feminism, existential feminism, ecofeminism, theological feminism, and conservative feminism, among others. However, some scholars argue that such hyphenated feminisms are inadequate, because feminism requires a more focused commitment to women than can be developed and maintained by using schools of thought originating in patriarchal contexts.

Another way of understanding feminist thought is to consider two of its key aspects which have transformed Western political thought. The first is the assumption that women's contributions are as significant as men's. Working from such an assumption alters basic Western concepts. For example, understandings of work need to include activities such as homemaking and housework. Understandings of class need to move beyond constructing women in terms of their husband's employment and education. Understandings of art expand to include quilt making and weaving. Thus, valuing women alters many basic Western concepts that have been built upon men's activities.

A second key aspect of feminist thought is suspicion of abstractions that may hide patriarchal assumptions. Feminist scholars emphasize the particularity of women's experiences. Even postmodern feminist scholars like Donna Haraway, who critique experience as a category of analysis, embrace the specificity of women's lives. An epistemological implication of this specificity is that empiricism is to be respected, even though positivism and the notion of a value-free analytical viewpoint are rejected. Scholars like Nancy Hartsock, Patricia Hill Collins, and Sandra Harding argue for feminist standpoints that recognize the social-political situation of analyses. They argue that all analyses are shaped by theoretical assumptions, social conditions, and values.

Similar fundamental changes occur in the cases where "feminist" has been used as an adjective to indicate the way in which particular disciplines or disciplinary approaches have been changed by infusions of feminist analyses. This produces such concepts as feminist pedagogy, feminist epistemology, feminist aesthetics, feminist history, feminist science, feminist literary theory, feminist legal theory, feminist philosophy, feminist spirituality, feminist leadership, feminist art, and other combinations. Academic feminists use feminist values to reform academic practices so that they can be transformed to include women and women's values.

In reforming social life, feminist scholars use four major approaches. First, some feminist scholars understand their work as including women in analyses to produce gender-inclusive work. New feminist empirical theory is one example. A second approach is used by those who consider themselves radical feminists. They begin with women's experiences to reform social thought from the bottom up. Radical feminists begin with women's lives to theorize about society without depending on the grand theories based on men's lives. They emphasize the ways in which women-identified-women can work with each other to develop new ways of thinking, new ways of symbolizing social life, and new ways of living. One form taken by this approach is represented in the notion that "feminism is the theory; lesbianism is the practice," a phrase coined by Ti-Grace Atkinson. However, lesbian theory, like feminist theory, has developed a rich and diverse tradition and may include reformulations of "lesbianism" that emphasize commitments to women rather than to a type of sexual activity. Lesbian theory and queer theory play central roles in shaping feminist theory. A third approach to feminist scholarship hopes to reform society by building on women's values. Developed as the care model, this approach emphasizes the way in which women's values, especially the value women place on relationships and connections, can be used to restructure society. Building on the work of Nancy Chodorow and Carol Gilligan, these feminists focus on the ways in which the values found in child rearing, family relationships, and/or intimate friendships can be used as models for a new social/political order that offers a moral world in which citizens care for one another. A fourth approach to feminist scholarship, represented by postmodern feminists, seeks political transformation through the analysis and interrogation of discourse, the creation of new metaphors, and the deconstruction of reified theories of representation. This approach avoids fundamental claims to universal knowledge and instead favors contextualized knowledge claims. While these four approaches are not exhaustive, they suggest the major ways in which contemporary feminist scholars see themselves as being involved in transforming societies.

Thus, academic feminists represent diverse approaches to understanding women's situation. Nevertheless, they share an understanding that a sex-gender system permeates human existence. Feminists point to the cultural emphasis on categorizing babies as male or female to illustrate the centrality of the sex-gender system. Exposing the social construction of sex/gender systems, these academics critique the way in which biology has been used to determine women's status. In the 1990s postmodern feminists have emerged as academic feminists who deconstruct the category "woman" in order to show how gender is a performance rather than an essential characteristic of an individual body. They emphasize the way in which language and speech practices construct notions of gender and sex as well as understandings of a sex-gender system. These feminists problematize the male/female distinction, offer critiques of the ways in which women have been essentialized, and celebrate the diversity within feminism. They include such feminists as Judith Butler, Gayatri Chakravorty Spivak, Drucilla Cornell, Joan W. Scott, and Donna Haraway. Rather than seeking a cohesive, united front, designed to undo patriarchy, these postmodern feminists argue that coalitions help feminists to build action on the basis of differences. Rather than seeking a unified understanding of the self and "woman," they argue for analyses that privilege fragmentations of the self and the multiplicity of social life. While academic feminists represent diverse methodologies, epistemological strategies, disciplinary commitments, and values, they share a commitment to analyses of women's status. They argue that scholarship is value-laden and see themselves as engaged in social change in the interests of enhanced gender equity. They employ a praxis model that emphasizes a dialogical connection between theory and action. Both academic feminists and activist feminists seek connections between theory and action, and thus both groups value dialogues that bring such connections into focus. Both those engaged in feminist political work and those engaged by feminist analyses often accept all who identify themselves as feminists, because both activities value democratic processes and self-definition.

Because of the important symbolic role the term "feminism" plays in the women's movement and in academic work, it is the subject of debate and controversy. Many women may accept the values and political goals of feminism while rejecting the label. Some activists and scholars reject calling themselves "feminists" and instead describe themselves as advocates for feminism. The term "womanist" is sometimes preferred, especially by some African American writers such as Alice Walker. Some feminists claim that only women-identified-women, who understand themselves in terms of their relationships to women rather than to men and who commit themselves primarily to improving women's lives, can be called feminists. Some feminists insist that only women can be feminists because women must speak for themselves. Others argue that men can be feminists because anyone who works politically toward improving women's status merits the name. The politicization of this term has contributed to debates about its definition and led to efforts to police its use.

Feminism is used to refer both to political work and to analysis. While political work emphasizes change and action, analysis emphasizes truth and reflection. Because feminist activists demand new analyses as a basis for their work and because feminist academics require that their work contribute to the improvement of women's status, the two activities are intimately connected. In many cases, academic feminists engage in feminist activism, and activists contribute to feminist scholarship. Productive connections between feminist scholarship and feminist social/political action are at the center of contemporary feminism. Feminists share a vision of the world in which women live as full citizens and a commitment to realize that world.

ELOISE A. BUKER

FEMINIST CONSCIOUSNESS is an awareness that the individual woman is part of a larger social group and that her personal problems, as a woman, are problems that affect all women and, hence, are political problems—that the personal is political.

Feminist consciousness is an awareness that women's experiences must be examined and interpreted, and the nature of women's oppression must be understood as a necessary precondition for social change.

FEMINIST MOVEMENT (1960 THROUGH EARLY 1970) is the re-emergence of an active feminist movement, often referred to as the "second wave" of the women's movement. The first wave of feminism became virtually dormant after the passage of the suffrage amendment in 1920.

Composition of the Second Wave. Early activists, mostly white, middle-class, and well educated, entered the movement as two distinct groups. Scholars distinguish them as the women's rights and women's liberation groups, the older and younger branches, or the bureaucratic and collectivist strands. In this entry the terms "bureaucratic" and "collectivist" will be used.

The bureaucratic part of the movement consisted of national organizations such as the National Organization for Women (NOW), National Women's Political Caucus (NWPC), Women's Equity Action League (WEAL), and Federally Employed Women (FEW), organizations that concentrated on ending legal and economic discrimination against women by using traditional forms of political action.

The bureaucratic group was older than the collectivist in terms of its starting date and the average age of its initiators. The initiators were established professionals of the depression generation, in which higher education for women was a rarity. (See DEPRESSION, THE GREAT.) Though an elite few, they suffered from employment discrimination and social devaluation of any women's roles other than wife and mother.

The feminist organizations created by these professional women reflected the conventional organizations and occupations they worked in. They were bureaucratic, hierarchical, impersonal, and achievement-oriented and drew strength from their members' skills and resources.

The collectivist branch consisted of groups of younger women from the baby boom generation, primarily students and housewives living in the 1960s-style counterculture in university communities. Higher education for women was common by their generation, and, with the increase in labor force participation by married women, many grew up in households with employed mothers. Thus, they had high expectations for success in the job market, but their expectations were tempered by the same discrimination faced by women of the bureaucratic branch.

With the counterculture many collectivist women experienced the sexual revolution of the 1960s and found that sexual liberation without gender equality left them more vulnerable than ever. Consequently, they fought gender inequality within personal relationships as well as within the broader political, economic, and social arena.

The collectivist part of the second wave was mass based without national organization; its politics were formed by the experiences of its leaders in the New Left and civil rights movements. Collectivist women established nonhierarchical, personalized, and informal groups with few rules, minimal divisions of labor, and experimental structures. New, egalitarian forms of functioning were considered important accomplishments, not simply means to achieving substantive goals.

The collectivists lacked the professional skills and resources of the bureaucratic women, but they more freely exercised boldness, creativity, and even flamboyance in their work.

The two parts of the movement were never entirely separate and became more intertwined over the years. From the first, they complemented each other. The collectivist branch stimulated the bureaucratic with bold experiments and attentiveness to humanism and nonhierarchical organizational forms. The bureaucratic part worked effectively to change the existing legal and political system. Over time, both became more action-oriented, and the bureaucratic part incorporated features of the collectivist portion, such as consciousness-raising groups and attention to gay and lesbian rights.

Beginnings of the Second Wave. Early activity was initiated by the bureaucratic part and focused on legal and economic issues. A research-oriented President's Commission on the Status of Women was appointed in 1961. Its report, published in 1963, documented widespread discrimination against women but had little effect. However, commission by-products, state commissions on the status of women, played an important role in the feminist movement.

Two important pieces of federal legislation were passed in the early 1960s, the 1963 Equal Pay Act and the Civil Rights Act of 1964 (neither as a result of concerted efforts by organized feminists). The Equal Pay Act mandated equal pay for equal work. It was effectively implemented but had limited impact because it covered only those few instances in which men and women work at the same jobs. Title VII of the Civil Rights Act prohibited employment discrimination based on sex or race. The bill had been introduced in Congress as a response to the civil rights movement and at first covered only racial discrimination. Sex discrimination was added to the bill due to the efforts of two legislators: a woman who sought to promote women's rights and a southern man who incorrectly thought the addition would prevent passage of the bill.

The EEOC (Equal Employment Opportunity Commission) was created to implement all of Title VII, but it enforced the law only as it applied to race discrimination. Delegates to the Third National Conference of the [State] Commissions on the Status of Women tried to pass a resolution urging the EEOC to treat sex discrimination as seriously as race discrimination, but conference officials refused to allow the resolution to come to the floor. As a result, on June 30, 1966, dissatisfied delegates under the leadership of Betty Friedan founded the National Organization for Women

(NOW). As an organization of women and men working for woman's rights, NOW was intended to be for women what the National Association for the Advancement of Colored People (NAACP) was for blacks.

Over the next few years, numerous woman's rights organizations were established. In 1968, conservatives in NOW resigned over the abortion issue and founded the Women's Equity Action League. WEAL concentrated on legal and economic issues, especially in employment and education. That same year Human Rights for Women, a legal defense fund, also was founded. The National Women's Political Caucus was founded in 1971 by Bella Abzug, Shirley Chisholm, Gloria Steinem, and Betty Friedan. Many special-purpose and single-interest groups such as Federally Employed Women and the National Coalition of American Nuns were formed during the late 1960s and early 1970s. At the same time, other organizations such as the National Federation of Business and Professional Women's Clubs and the American Association of University Professors' Committee on the Status of Women were reactivated. Participation in these organizations grew quickly. In 1967, for example, NOW had 14 chapters, 700 members, and a budget of $6,888. By 1974, it had 1,000 chapters, 40,000 members, and a budget of $605,650.

The collectivist part of the feminist movement also developed during the 1960s. Women working in the New Left and civil rights movements became dissatisfied because movements that sought to further the rights of blacks, workers, welfare recipients, and others had failed to recognize women's rights as a legitimate political goal. Furthermore, sex discrimination was rampant within these very movements. Women were rarely in leadership positions and were often relegated to traditional female roles such as secretary or cook. (This problem was more acute in the New Left than in the civil rights movement.) Women also felt exploited by the sexual relationships within these movements. By the late 1960s these women had developed the determination and the ability to fight sexism. They found inspiration in the lives of black women in the civil rights movement who broke with sexual stereotypes and became the first to express criticism of sexist practices. Through their political work, they developed organizational skills and a loose national network.

At first, collectivist women responded to sexism with written analyses of the problem to try to stimulate discussions within their organizations. They were unsuccessful. When Stokely Carmichael cut off debate about sexism at a 1964 SNCC (Student Nonviolent Coordinating Committee) convention by saying that "the only position for women in SNCC is prone," he expressed the attitude of many men in the civil rights movement and the New Left. Consequently, women called for the formation of an autonomous women's movement.

The development of an autonomous women's movement was further stimulated by developments that limited the roles white women could play in the civil rights movement or the New Left. By 1965, black militancy had become the motivating factor of the civil rights movement, and whites were no longer welcome. By 1966, the New Left had adopted draft resistance as its primary work. Since women were not drafted, all they could do was offer draft counseling from the sidelines. White, middle-class women, marginalized in both movements, had little impetus to fight sexism within them. Thus, by 1967 or 1968, women's liberation groups were being formed throughout the country. Women from organizations such as SDS (Students for a Democratic Society), the Socialist Workers Party, SNCC, and even NOW formed women's liberation groups, as did previously apolitical women.

Two important concepts came from the small groups in this sector of the movement: consciousness-raising* and "the personal is political." Implicit in their egalitarian goals and experimental devices, such as rotating jobs or limiting the time any single woman could speak at meetings, was an antileadership bias that eventually affected the entire women's movement.

From the collectivist sector came the name "women's liberation movement," popularized by the first national newsletter, *Voice of the Women's Liberation Movement*, which was published for 16 months in 1968 and 1969.

By 1969, the media had been forced to recognize the women's movement. Media accounts often referred to feminists as "bra burners," a term coined at a Miss America Contest protest sponsored by WITCH (Women's International Terrorist Conspiracy from Hell). The protest featured a "freedom trash can" into which bras, girdles, false eyelashes, and other instruments of female oppression were dropped; no bras were burned.

In 1970 NOW organized a march to commemorate the 50th anniversary of the passage of the Nineteenth (suffrage) Amendment. It was supported by almost every other women's organization, received good media coverage, and had a huge turnout. NOW membership increased, particularly among clerical workers and women who were disaffected with "the feminine mystique." The movement had fully come into its own.

Activities of the Early Years. Achievements in the legal and legislative arenas during the 1960s and early 1970s were limited but set the stage for more significant victories in subsequent years. NOW's first action, in 1967, was to get President Lyndon B. Johnson to amend Executive Order 11246 to prohibit sex discrimination by federal contractors. That year, also as a result of NOW's efforts, the EEOC prohibited airlines from automatically retiring female flight attendants at age 32 and prohibited employers from using protective legislation as a rationale for denying equal opportunity to women. In 1970, WEAL filed a class action complaint against all colleges and universities with federal contracts. The Equal Rights Amendment was approved in the House in 1970 and in the Senate in 1972 (but was eventually defeated in 1982 because it was not ratified by enough states for passage).

During these years, the collectivist sector of the movement worked to develop many feminist services and alternative institutions for women, such as women's centers, rape crisis centers, and feminist gynecological clinics, production companies, restaurants, and theater groups.

Women's publications increased rapidly. By 1971, there were over 100 women's liberation journals and newspapers. Important books included Betty Friedan's *Feminine Mystique* (1963), Kate Millett's *Sexual Politics* (1970), Germaine Greer's *Female Eunuch* (1970), Robin Morgan's *Sisterhood Is Powerful* (1970), Shulamith Firestone's *Dialectic of Sex* (1970), Edith Hoshino Altbach's *From Feminism to Liberation* (1971), and Vivian Gornick and Barbara K. Moran's *Women in Sexist Society* (1971).

Once the movement was established, women of color and working-class women who were reluctant to join predominantly white, middle-class, feminist groups formed separate organizations. Chicana women had established a center for workingwomen in California by 1971. In 1972 the National Conference of Puerto Rican Women was organized; in 1973 the National Black Feminist Organization and Black Women United for Action were founded. The Coalition of Labor Union Women was started in 1974, as was the National Mexican American Women's Association. In 1977 the National Alliance of Black Feminists and the National Association of Black Professional Women began, and the first American Indian Women's Conference was held.

Continuing Issues. From the outset, the second wave has been divided by controversial issues. Should lesbian rights be treated as a feminist issue? Should feminists support women's right to abortion? Should pornography be outlawed? Should feminists work with men? What criteria should be used to determine whether to endorse candidates for public office? How should feminists deal with racism and anti-Semitism? (See ANTI-SEMITISM.) These issues and others continue to be unresolved within the feminist movement.

Social gains for women have been extensive, though not complete, and economic gains have been limited. Consequently, the movement's work continues.

References. Sara Evans, *Personal Politics* (New York, 1979); Myra Marx Ferree and Beth B. Hess, *Controversy and Coalition: The New Feminist Movement* (Boston, 1985); Jo Freeman, *The Politics of Women's Liberation* (New York, 1975).

PAM E. GOLDMAN

FEMINIST PEDAGOGY. See PEDAGOGY, FEMINIST

FEMINIST THEOLOGY. See THEOLOGY, FEMINIST

FEMINIST THEORY is the philosophical analysis of the concept of gender and the meaning of sexual difference. Feminist theory critically evaluates the claim that gender is determined directly by biology. Generally, feminist analysis depends on the premise that gender is a socially constructed, historically changing reality.

The central project of feminist theory is fourfold: (1) to evaluate critically the claim that gender is determined directly by biology; (2) to explore the ways that sexist assumptions have distorted the meaning of gender so that women's experiences either have been rendered invisible or have been undervalued; (3) to challenge the claims to truth of science and the humanities on the grounds that their metatheoretical foundations are sexist; and (4) to propose an alternative, more inclusive epistemological framework.

Feminist theory claims that to acknowledge the gender bias of traditional theory is to transform radically the structure of our knowledge of reality. Since thinking is a human activity engaged in by sex-gendered beings, whose specific historical identity influences their perceptual capacity, then knowledge—the product of that activity—is always bounded by this fact. Feminist theorists differ both in the extent to which they accept the idea of a unique, gender-determined knowledge and in their recommendations for the reconstruction of scientific and nonscientific discourses. To some, the assertion of "female" ways of knowing is the reproduction of sexist thinking, while to others "female" discourse is the epitome of undistorted communication. Earlier feminist theory tended to subscribe to the former point of view. More recent theorists, especially those influenced by French feminist writings and contemporary philosophies of deconstruction* and hermeneutics, tend to endorse the latter position.

Contemporary feminist theory has developed through several stages of inquiry. It began with the project of exploring the *origins* of women's oppression. Early work during this stage concentrated on considering the ways that women's reproductive biology and women's roles in the family* were used throughout history to segregate women as a group (class) and to isolate them from the full range of human activity. The concept of patriarchy* was introduced to this debate about the root causes of the exploitation of women and became a central category of analysis. For example, early work in anthropology demonstrated how the development of surplus production contributed to the institutionalization of patriarchal property systems. Since kinship and property systems were structured through male lines, women's position in these exchange systems became defined by their position in relation to the male-dominated family/property nexus. Although women's activity was important to the daily life of the community, both economically and socially, women appeared to wield little official power, being absent from most positions of recognized leadership. Theorists in anthropology and other fields continue to debate the question of women's relative powerlessness. Some contend that anthropological fieldwork focuses on male experience and interprets social reality from a masculinist perspective, thus obscuring or distorting the significance of women's roles.

During this earlier stage of theory building, major disputes developed among liberal, socialist, radical, and lesbian feminists, with each school claiming to have identified the basic cause of patriarchy. For liberals, it was the lack of equal rights and opportunities to participate in mainstream activities that led to the exploitation of women. Socialists saw relations of property under capitalism as the motor of patriarchal ideas and practices in the modern era. Radical feminists argued that women's biology was the root cause of patriarchy. Lesbian feminists challenged compulsory heterosexuality* as the mainstay of patriarchal relations.

Later, feminist theorists attempted to treat the concept of patriarchy with greater historical rigor, claiming that patriarchy was not a universal, unchanging phenomenon but had a history and a material foundation that empirical analysis could uncover. This stage of theory shifted debate away from the question of origins to the question of how patriarchy was maintained. Feminist historians researched women's multifarious activities in different epochs. They challenged the extent to which history had provided an accurate picture of either the pattern of development of civilization or the relative value of women's contributions to that development. Contending that most historical models had been based on unfounded assumptions about the ways that women's biology had impaired their participation in state or economy building, feminist historians reviewed existing records and discovered new archival materials to substantiate their argument that women had made important political and economic contributions. Since women had been "hidden from history" by distorted models of social change that privileged male-dominated activities, these theorists contended that reinserting women into the historical record altered substantially both the way that history would be written and the image of women as a silent and inactive oppressed group.

Most recently, feminist theorists have been reassessing the concept of patriarchy and debating the relevance of the "oppressed group" model for describing women's experiences. Once again, the nature of sexual differences and the role they play in defining gender have become central to the debate. But the emphasis on difference is different. Some theorists argue that gender differences need to be emphasized, so that the uniqueness of female experiences and values can be recognized and appreciated. For example, scholars like Adrienne Rich and Sara Ruddick redefine mothering as a culturally progressive and potentially subversive institution whose values and practices could challenge the male system of power and hierarchy if it were structured along gynocentric lines. Artists and literary critics claim that women's visions and voices are unique because of the historical segregation of male and female activities. Rather than attempt to imitate male styles, women's creativity should flourish in different ways. Other theorists react strongly against this reasoning because they contend that it defines women as ontologically distinguishable from men. To these theorists any renewed emphasis on differences, especially by feminists, is politically dangerous because it contributes to the reestablishment of sociopolitical hierarchies that disadvantage or oppress women. Eradication of differences is the goal for this group.

The issue behind all of these debates is the epistemological challenge that feminist theory represents by its endeavor to create a theory of knowledge that is more inclusive of the full range of human experience. Regardless of their divergent political ideologies, feminist theorists share this project. By critically evaluating and redefining the basic methods of science and interpretation and by developing new categories of analysis, feminist theory has made seminal contributions to the philosophy of science and the humanities.

KATHLEEN B. JONES

FEMINIST THERAPY emerged in the mid-1970s as a reflection of feminist criticism of psychiatry, of efforts to rid psychiatry of sexist biases, such as its double standard and the hierarchical relation between practitioner and client, which too often replicates the source of the client's problem, and of new research and new insights into women's psychology. Feminist therapists have no one technique but share common underlying principles and common goals. These are incorporated in the ethical code of the Feminist Therapist Institute, Inc., adopted in 1987 as guidelines for feminist therapists and to indicate to the public the accountability of institute members.

FEMINIZATION OF POVERTY. Since the 1960s in the United States the poor have been more likely to be single females, members of female-headed households, and elderly females than to be single men, members of male-headed households, and elderly men. There has been a great increase in female-headed families, and over 40 percent of those living in female-headed families are poor. Less than 10 percent of persons living in male-headed households live in poverty.*

Higher female poverty has long been a fact of life of colonial capitalism, especially in Africa. As men were coerced to work in mines or on settler farms, women, children, and the elderly were left to eke out a living on infertile reservation lands. Male migrant workers were paid a subsistence wage for only one person.

FEMINOLOGY. Literally, the science of women, feminology is an alternative term used to signify women's studies in some countries, notably Scandinavia. Used at the Royal Library in Copenhagen since 1971, this word was invented by librarian Nynne Koch for the ease with which it would be adapted to numerous languages and used in both substantive and adjectival forms as well as for its neutral, scientific connotations and its ability to project "a new image of the scientific landscape." The term is not, however, altogether new, for it was used decades earlier to designate a prototypical women's studies course offered at the *Collège libre des sciences sociales* (Free College of Social Sciences) in Paris between 1900 and 1905. Taught by a Frenchwoman of letters, Mme. Marguerite Souley-Darqué, this "course on feminology" resembled contemporary women's studies courses in its content, institutional innovativeness, and diversity of student audience. Cross-disciplinary, it combined philosophical, sociological, and historical approaches to understanding the "nature," experience, and perceptions of women. Similar to the early women's studies courses offered in community-based "free schools," it was housed in an institution established in 1895 to foster innovative research and teaching, especially for the new "social scientists" who sought to apply scientific methods to the solution of social problems. Also like many of the first women's studies courses, instructors taught, and students attended voluntarily, without recompense other than the intrinsic value of educational experimentation. Feminology then as now attracted students of both sexes and diverse ages and conditions. It was likewise placed under a rubric of "feminist education." Influenced by Darwinism, Mme. Souley-Darqué was concerned primarily with demonstrating that women's social inferiority was explicable as a response to past environmental conditions that industrial capitalism made obsolete. Her course, which disappeared with the decline of the *Collège libre* (and the increasing acceptance of social sciences in established universities), demonstrates the continuity of feminist effort to revise definitions of femininity grounded in bias or ignorance.

References. S. G. Bell and M. S. Rosenhan, "A Problem in Naming: Women Studies—Women's Studies?" *Signs* 6 (1981): 540–542; M. J. Boxer, "For and about Women: The Theory and Practice of Women's Studies in the United States," *Signs* 7 (1982): 660–695, esp. 664–665, n. 11; M. J. Boxer, "Women's Studies in France circa 1902: A Course on Feminology," *International Supplement to the Women's Studies Quarterly* 1 (1982): 25–27.

MARILYN J. BOXER

FERTILIZATION of an ovum (egg) takes place during a period of about 12 to 24 hours after ovulation. After about a day, an unfertilized ovum will begin to deteriorate and die.

After ovulation the egg is taken up by the funnel-shaped end of the fallopian tube and is then moved toward the uterus by muscular contraction of the tube (oviduct) wall. Sperm passing through the cervical opening (os) move through the uterus into the tube. When sperm meet egg in the outer third of the tube, and a sperm unites with the egg, the combined chromosomes from egg and sperm form a zygote, the beginning of a new individual. The union itself is called conception. After conception, the fertilized ovum continues down the tube into the uterus, a trip of several days. There, after a period of floating within the uterus, the conceptus is implanted in the lining, and the embryonic development begins. From ovulation to implantation takes about a week.

FETUS, the term for an unborn vertebrate, is sometimes used to refer to the human organism during the entire period of its development from conception to birth. It is also used more specifically of the second, or fetal, stage of development, beginning around the ninth week, after the body structure has become recognizably human. The preceding stage of development is the embryonic.

FIBER ARTS. Women have always been involved in the making and embellishment of items for practical use. In the Middle Ages, much elaborate embroidery with silver-gilt thread and semiprecious stones was created for church use. The Church was also the repository of works such as the 230-foot Bayeux Tapestry, an elaborately embroidered frieze, almost certainly created by teams of women working from plans of a single, unknown designer.

The division "fine" and "applied" arts or "crafts" developed in the Renaissance, reflecting hierarchical patterns found in the society at large, with "women's work" being afforded a different status from that of men's accomplishments. Architecture, sculpture, and painting were arts restricted largely to men. The "home arts" of decoration of clothing and household furnishings became more nearly the limits of women's creative outlets and were assigned less value than the "fine arts." This division has modified within the twentieth century.

Fiber arts are founded on traditions. Late twentieth-century women make many objects, using similar material and processes, that were made by early American women, but while there have been many carryovers, there have also been notable developments. Changes have occurred in the status of these objects and their makers relative to the fine arts, in the materials and processes, in their value, and in the goals of their makers.

In early America women worked in traditional areas of weaving, quilting, embroidery, and needlepoint. In colonial times professional weavers, a few of whom were women, made coverlets and other things for the home and dyed the fibers. The efforts needed for survival left little time for leisure or for self-expression in decorative work. Products were intended for practical use to add to the comfort and decoration of the home.

The scarcity of textiles made every scrap of material precious. Homemakers joined scraps of fabric to make bedcovers. The odd-shaped bits were joined into random, varicolored patterns by stitching them together to form a top layer for the crazy quilt. The top, an insulating layer, and a backing were joined by knots of string tied here and there across the top or by rows of small stitches—the quilting.

The pieced quilt was composed of tiny pieces arranged in geometric patterns within squares that were then joined to make the top. The quilting stitches enhanced the pattern either by following it or by creating a kind of counterpoint in their own design. In school or at home, girls were taught at an early age to make the small, even stitches prized in quilting. The piecing of the squares was usually done alone, but once a top was finished, the quilting often became a collaborative effort. Quilting was an excuse to socialize with neighbors who might live hours away. Pioneer women centered a large part of their social life on the quilting bee, a purely American custom.

As life became more settled and prosperous, women had more time, and decorative detail became more prevalent. Country fairs encouraged competitiveness in design, color, and craft. One tradition for brides was a chest with 13 quilts. A girl would begin when quite young on her first quilt in a simple pattern and progress till the last ones, of greater intricacy, would show off the skills of the young woman. The 13th quilt was the wedding quilt.

While the geometric quilt remained a favorite, appliqué was also popular. In appliqué technique, a plain background cloth has pictorial pieces sewn onto the surface. They are sometimes elaborately quilted and may be embroidered as well. In the style called "whitework" (regardless of color), two fabrics are quilted together, and the design comes entirely from the stitching. Trapunto is a version of whitework in which the two pieces are quilted together. Shapes of the design are made to stand out by pushing an opening in the backing cloth and forcing small amounts of stuffing into the shapes, producing a sculptured effect.

In the 1870s home-crafted items and quilting were largely replaced with manufactured goods. However, an 1876 exhibit of eighteenth-century quilts brought a revival of interest. In the late nineteenth and early twentieth centuries, articles and books on needlework brought about an increase in popularity of quilting and other handwork. *Godey's Lady's Book* published quilting patterns frequently. The first author to devote an entire book to quilts was Mary Webster (*Quilts: Their Story and How to Make Them*, 1915). Journalist and feminist Ruth Finley collected quilts and told their stories in *Old Patchwork Quilts and the Women Who Made Them* (Newton Centre, Mass., 1929).

After World War I, women played major roles in reestablishing the relevance of their crafts both to the art world and to design, especially in industry. Much of what we now take for granted in design was developed at the Bauhaus Design School, founded in Germany in 1919. When the Bauhaus closed with World War II, many of its masters emigrated to America, settling at Black Mountain College in North Carolina. These European émigrés played important roles in art and fine arts education in succeeding years. Leaders in weaving, Anni Albers and Trudi Guermonprez influenced a reevaluation of the loom as a tool for expression in functional and non-functional works of art. Loja Saarinen, as director of the weaving school at the Cranbrook Academy in Michigan, carried on her commitment to the connection among art, crafts, and architecture. Educational programs, crafts organizations, and crafts guilds appeared all across the country: in 1922, the Boston Weavers Guild; in 1924, the Shuttle Craft Guild, founded by Mary M. Atwater; in 1930, the Southern Highland Handicraft Guild; and in 1943, the American Crafts Council, started by Arleen O. Webb. Some who kept the fiber arts alive were Berta Frey, Trudi Guermonprez, Gunta Stoltzl, Mary M. Atwater, and Harriett Tidball.

After World War II, industrial designers became trendsetters for the textile market. In the 1950s there was an explosion of interest. The textile industry turned to artists for ideas, engaging designers responsible for many exciting textiles produced for mass production, such as Anni Albers, Dorothy Lieves, Pola Stout, and Hella Skowronksi. A variety of materials was explored for home and architectural use: newly developed synthetics, plastics, metals, leather, beads, and so on. In New York, the Museum of Modern Art held an exhibit of weavings by Anni Albers, breaking the old tradition of exclusive concentration on the traditional fine arts.

At the same time, there was a new awareness of Third World art objects. These objects, intended for practical use, were revalued as art and influenced the making of more art. Master of fine arts programs in weaving and textile design began to appear throughout the country. Ruth Asawa, a West Coast artist, was showing looped, three-dimensional, and wire-interlaced forms, the first indication of contemporary woven sculpture. The trend toward three-dimensional reliefs and sculpture in fibers included work by artists Kay Sekimachi, Sheila Hicks, and Lenore Tawney. In 1957, the Staten Island Museum in New York held a major one-person show by Lenore Tawney.

The boom in crafts activities is often credited to the 1960s counterculture, with its emphasis on handwork and crafts for everyone. But it also shares its genesis with the liberation of the homemaker, who, with more leisure time, education, and exposure to contemporary art forms, began to seek avenues of personal expression. Fibers were a natural choice of media because of familiarity with them in homemaking roles. Classes in fiber arts areas sprang up across the country. Crafts were everywhere. The 1960s and 1970s saw a slow growth of the acceptance of crafts media within the fine arts. By the middle 1960s fiber arts were often shown with other arts media. By the beginning of the 1980s, a number of New York art galleries, previously inhospitable to this work, began to hold exhibits by artists working in crafts media.

The 1980s crafts artwork reflects broader art trends in the use of a variety of materials and the crossing of old barriers, combining needlework with papermaking, painting, and quilting and using of plastics, wire, found objects, and other items. Many artists worked in ways that combine the old understanding of "craft" with the values of fine arts. The division of "arts" and "crafts" has been largely erased.

Weaving, for example, has become a generalized term encompassing all ways of constructing textiles, including the knotted structures of Diane Itter and the sculptural forms of Claire Zeisler. Materials have also changed. Arline Fisch and Mary Lee Hu apply textile technique to metal instead of to the traditional yarns and threads. Cynthia Schira uses an ikat warp with brocading elements of predyed cotton tapes. Embroidery from past centuries is certainly the root of the technique but has little in common with the finished forms of Mary Bero's small, brilliantly hued, intricately embroidered and painted faces.

Papermaking, another craft from the distant past, has had a recent revival in work by artists such as Nance O'Banion. Her powerful basket forms that combine paper with sticks and other materials have been influential for other artists. Lissa Hunter makes constructions of handmade paper, using basketry structure and lamination; surfaces are embellished with drawing materials and pigments. The purity of the sculptural forms of Ferne Jacobs makes her work seem almost totemlike. Felting is another ancient craft revived in service of contemporary artists' work. Joan Livingstone makes three-dimensional forms by combining painted wood and felt.

Tapestry has a long European tradition but little early history in the United States. Helena Hernmarck works from, and uses, imagery of photographs in huge photorealism tapestries.

The work of many of the artists could be called "mixed-media," as would Jane Lackey's wall relief images, made in combinations like wire and wood. Neda Al Hilali, as if creating her own canvases, plaits with processed paper, then paints and dyes the resulting surfaces. Another trend is called "installations." Magdalena Abakanowicz makes molded body forms in multiples and arranges them to fill large gallery spaces, as well as making many woven forms, huge and powerful environmental pieces. Collaboration, as in the cooperative group efforts of the early quilters, is also seen in Judy Chicago's "The Dinner Party," with dozens of people working together to produce the multiple parts, including ceramic plates and embroidered runners, which together celebrate women in history. Shiela Hicks has been influential in getting fiber arts into the architectural setting. Thus, we can see the change in women's fiber art from mostly utilitarian objects done primarily in isolation, such as a quilt top, to works that hang in art galleries.

Quilting still survives, now as an art form, with artists using the intense colors of fabrics to create pieced and quilted works. The collaborative team of Gayl Fraas and Duncan W. Slade uses architectural elements and landscape vistas in quilts. Nancy Crow's intense colors and intricate geometric designs make looking at her quilts like looking at a kaleidoscope.

By the 1980s fiber arts expanded in many ways. Artists have begun to deal with subjects beyond the decorative and to treat subject matter heretofore dealt with in the fine arts but not in those media often called "crafts." Fiber artists are using their media to express and interpret ideas, emerging as artists free to deal with all possible concepts and sources of creative energy, including humor. The issue of fine arts versus crafts should no longer be a problem. When one realizes that it is not technique or materials that make an object fine art, then any medium can be elevated to an art form if its concerns are with concepts, questions, and inner visions. Artists working in fibers deal with the same issues as artists working in other media—art is a matter of quality.

References. Mildred Constantine and Jack Lenor Larson, *Beyond Craft: The Art Fabric* (New York, 1986); Wendy Slatkin, *Women Artists in History* (Englewood Cliffs, N.J., 1985); J. Paul Smith and Edward Lacy Smith, *American Craft Today: The Poetry of the Physical* (American Craft Museum, 1986); Naomi Whiting Towner, *Filaments of the Imagination* (essay, catalog for exhibition, University of Hawaii Art Gallery, 1981).

KAYE WINDER

FIBROCYSTIC DISEASE is a catchall term for several different kinds of benign tumors of the breast (cystic mastitis, mammary dysplasia, fibroadenoma, and so on) (Sloane, 187–190). Whether or not they are "diseases" is questionable.

The causes of fibrocystic disease are not known but appear to be related to cyclic hormonal stimulation of breast tissue to prepare it for milk production. In cystic conditions sacs of fluid or semifluid material develop, with more or less associated tenderness and pain, peaking the week before menstruation, then receding once menstruation begins. The size and location of the cysts help to determine the discomfort. In one type of cystic condition, one or more large lumps appear, often in just one breast. Although there is some cyclic change in size, it is not as noticeable as in other types. These larger cysts tend to be very tender and painful, and the pain often persists through much of the cycle. Fibroadenomas (adenofibromas) are solid tumors that most frequently develop in women in their late teens or early 20s and that do not undergo cyclic growth and retardation. They usually are small, grow slowly, and are not tender and painful. Occasionally, a large or faster growing one must be removed because it distorts the shape of the breast or interferes with blood vessels.

The belief that women with fibrocystic disease have an increased risk of cancer has been called into question. But fibrocystic disease does need to be distinguished from cancer. Certain types of cancer and fibroadenomas are very similar in appearance, and hard cystic tumors and malignant tumors can be distinguished only by biopsy. A more serious problem is that a malignant growth may be hidden among other lumps.

Fibrocystic disease can be a nuisance or it can make the breast very tender and painful for a large portion of each month. Formerly, treatment consisted only of needle biopsy to aspirate cysts or surgical removal of cysts or solid tumors. Today there are options. Hormonal contraceptives reduce the chances of developing fibrocystic conditions, and various hormonal treatments have been tried with varying results. Danazol, a synthetic steroid, has had promising results, but its high cost and side effects make it preferable to try other things first. Dietary changes, elimination of caffeine, and vitamin supplements have all shown promising results in clinical tests (Sloane, 189–190). Many doctors still recommend periodic removal of cysts and solid tumors to manage cancer risk and needle biopsy of cysts to investigate precancer cell changes, despite the fact that the link between benign breast disease and cancer is highly questionable.

Reference. Ethel Sloane, *Biology of Women*, 3d ed. (Albany, N.Y., 1993).

FIBROIDS, UTERINE, are benign tumors that grow from the muscular wall of the uterus outward (subserous), inward (submucus), or within the wall (intramural or interstitial). The most common are the intramural.

Their cause is unknown, except that it is estrogen-related and possibly genetic. Fibroids are more common among black than among other women; they are most common in women over 30 and shrink after menopause. Until then they continue to grow, but most grow slowly. They should be checked for signs of growth during routine pelvic examinations.

There are records of fibroids of immense size, but today they are usually removed before getting very large. As long as they are small, painless, and do not interfere with pregnancy, there is no reason for treatment. Large ones can cause abdominal or back pain and menstrual irregularity. They might also encroach on other pelvic organs and can interfere with pregnancy by obstructing the opening of the fallopian tube, preventing the proper implantation of the conceptus, or blocking the birth canal.

If they do cause excessive bleeding, urinary difficulties, or problems with pregnancy, they are removed surgically. A D&C (dilating the cervical opening and scraping the uterus with a curette) can occasionally be used. A myomectomy, removing the fibroid while leaving the uterus intact, will allow the woman to retain childbearing capabilities; however, fibroids may recur. If keeping childbearing capability is not a factor, many doctors recommend hysterectomy. Since fibroids are the leading cause of unnecessary hysterectomies, a second opinion should always be sought and may be required by the insurance company or the hospital.

FILM AND FEMINISM. Writing in the mid-1980s for *Signs*, Judith Mayne noted "two possible directions for feminist film criticism: encouraging filmmakers to formulate another kind of cinema with a feminist perspective, or encouraging film viewers to understand cinema as symptomatic of women's contradictory investments in patriarchal society" (88). From the 1910s, feminist women involved in social activism have perceived film's power and have attempted to use it for their purposes, from Jane Addams to the National Woman Suffrage Association. For a discussion of women's relation to mainstream film production, see "Filmmakers and Mainstream Production"; this entry focuses on alternatives to mainstream film production, on one hand, and on the feminist reception of films, on the other.

From the point at which mainstream cinema was established, and alternatives to it could be identified, women have played an important role in the development of such alternatives. In Germany, Lotte Reiniger used scissors to cut out silhouette figures, hundreds and thousands per film, eventually creating *The Adventures of Prince Achmed* (1923–1926), the first feature-length animation film. In France, Germaine Dulac produced surrealist works that were controversial among the men of the movement for her feminist inflections of their material, for example, *The Seashell and the Clergyman* (1928). In the United States, Maya Deren's short experimental films, especially *Meshes of the Afternoon* (1943), are usually cited as founding works of U.S. avant-garde cinema.

In the 1960s, two trends became apparent, one more inward-looking or personal in nature and the other deliberately outward-looking and political in intent. Initially, given their different starting points, the two groups of filmmakers involved worked in different genres, with different styles, and for different purposes. A small number of women who had worked originally in other art forms, some of whom gained their film training through academic programs affiliated with art schools, began to produce films as personal expressions of their subjective visions. Members of this group include Gunvor Nelson (*Schmeerguntz*; 1965–1966) and Storm de Hirsch, whose *Goodbye in the Mirror* (1964) "is perhaps the first full-length American independent film of directly feminist interest" (Kay and Peary, 231). A few other women, most notably, Shirley Clarke, worked within an existing and developing tradition of alternative cinema, influenced by the technology that had made cinema verité possible. However, Clarke pulled her *Portrait of Jason* (1967) out of a major New York festival of films by women because she "didn't want to be known as a women's filmmaker" (Rosenberg, 55). She was probably motivated by a justifiable concern that such an identification would ghettoize and further restrict her opportunities to work.

Meanwhile, the rise of feminism led women, many of whom had no prior film experience, to appropriate the medium for purposes of social activism. Most of these self-identified feminist filmmakers espoused realism as a preferred style and documentary as either a preferred or a necessary genre. Landmarks of the era include *The Life and Times of Rosie the Riveter*

(Connie Field, 1980), *Janie's Jane* (New York Newsreel, 1971), *With Babies and Banners* (Lorraine Gray, 1978), and *Union Maids* (Julia Reichert and James Klein, 1976), all films that gave voices to working-class women and their stories. The strategy was to put stories on screen that male filmmakers had neglected and to counter the negative images of women prevalent in mainstream media.

"Real" images of women were the order of the day, and documentary—traditionally, a realist form—was both easier to fund and technically more accessible to novice independent filmmakers. However, early in the 1970s, feminist film scholars began to argue that simply replacing bad images with good would not be sufficient, since agreement over what constitutes a good image is not always possible, given the diversity even among self-identified feminists. Attention began to turn away from images of women to study the process of imaging, that is, to the specificity of cinema as a representational medium.

With the appearance of Laura Mulvey's "Visual Pleasure and Narrative Cinema" (originally published in 1975 and anthologized widely, including Penley's *Feminism and Film Theory* psychoanalytic theory), especially in combination with the earlier lessons of semiotic-and Marxist-informed film theory, became a primary tool for feminist film theory. Unique among academic disciplines, film studies became driven for 10–15 years in the 1970s and 1980s largely by feminist issues, and female film scholars achieved an importance unmatched elsewhere in the university. Mulvey's essay itself is probably the most frequently cited work of film theory, and its influence has spread to other disciplines, throughout the humanities, and into the social sciences.

Mulvey rejects the normative ego psychology of the 1950s (that had given psychoanalysis a bad name among feminists, especially in the United States in favor of Lacanian psychoanalysis, a rereading of Freud in light of twentieth-century linguistic research. From this standpoint, Mulvey analyzed mainstream Hollywood-style cinema in terms of the Oedipus complex and castration anxiety: woman's function is to be looked at either as part of a punitive investigation or a defensive fetishization. Using Marlene Dietrich for one of her examples, Mulvey noted that narrative action tends to pause while the female star appears on screen, picking up again when the male protagonist appears.

As important as Mulvey's essay is, it has not gone unchallenged. Among the first objections was Mulvey's presupposition of a male spectator, and discussion of this point—and what positions might be open to female spectators—contributed to the development of spectator studies as a dominant subject in film studies for something like a decade. For example, if mainstream feature films are narratively and rhetorically structured with male spectators in mind, then must female spectators adopt a masochistic or a transvestite position in order to enjoy these films? Counterobservations that chipped away at Mulvey's argument include the fact that traditions do exist of presenting male performers to be looked at (Bergstrom) and that the genre known as the woman's film intentionally attempts to appeal to predominantly female audiences. Later arguments based in a Deleuzian understanding of psychoanalytic concepts have accused Mulvey of emphasizing sadistic responses over masochistic impulses. From the beginning, detractors have argued against the ahistorical, universalistic aspects of psychoanalysis that would seem to preclude any possibility for change in the everyday lives of women.

As feminism itself has become more fragmented by demands for multiple and multicultural voices to be represented, and film studies has merged increasingly with media or cultural studies, the era of work epitomized by Mulvey's essay has passed, although her analysis, in its popularized form, continues to inform writing by critics such as Suzanne Moore in Great Britain or cultural studies scholars such as Suzanna Walters in the United States.

Filmmakers can also be said to have learned the lessons of 1970s and 1980s feminist film theory. "Visual Pleasure and Narrative Cinema" ends with a call to reject mainstream cinema in favor of an avant-garde cinema more open to women's concerns, and Mulvey herself, working with Peter Wollen, has made a number of films, including *Riddles of the Sphinx* (1977). Even before film theory became important for feminist filmmakers, the films themselves suggest a coming together of the concerns of social activists and artists in the early 1970s in what Rosenberg has called "portrait films" (61–74), for example, Joyce Chopra's documentary *Joyce at 34* (1972, made in collaboration with Claudia Weill), about her own pregnancy.

Chopra has noted how extraordinary it was for the filmmaker to turn the camera on herself, but the mix of personal and political, not surprisingly, has characterized much feminist filmmaking since then. Michelle Citron's *Daughter Rite* (1978) uses home movie footage to explore relations between mothers and daughters and between sisters, while Su Friedrich's *Sink or Swim* (1990) uses similar home movie footage to explore the relation between her father and herself. Both filmmakers engage in various formal concerns. Citron's later film, *What You Take for Granted* (1983), while apparently a documentary, gradually reveals itself to be a performance of a documentary by actors. The sort of irony underlying Citron's film contributes to later developments in feminist filmmaking, for example, Mitch McCabe's *Playing the Part* (1994), a short film about a white, upper-middle-class lesbian's difficulties coming out to her Grosse Pointe, Michigan, family.

Made in a less ironic era, Alile Sharon Larkin's *A Different Image* (1979) presents an African American woman's attempt to assert her own identity rather than have it imposed on her by the culture around her. Julie Dash's

Illusions (1983) features an African American woman's efforts to pass for white while working as a production figure in a World War II–era Hollywood studio. Dash's extraordinary feature-length *Daughters of the Dust* (1991) continues the exploration of African American identity by women.

Outside the United States, a number of women filmmakers have produced a large body of films that belong to the avant-garde, countercinema, or independent and alternative strand of filmmaking. Sally Potter's *Thriller* (1979) is an important direct response to the concerns of feminist film theory; it can, in fact, be called a "theory film." In it, Potter analyzes traditional narrative constraints—here represented by *La Bohème* and Hitchcock's *Psycho*—that typically require the female protagonist's death in order to sustain the male hero's romanticized concept of self. In Australia, Laleen Jayamanne's *A Song of Ceylon* (1985) deals, among other things, with the fetishism of female bodies and colonialization.

What often characterizes these intensely theoretical films, including work in the United States by Yvonne Rainer (e.g., *Film about a Woman Who . . .* [1974], *Kristina Talking Pictures* [1976], *Journeys from Berlin/1971* [1980], *The Man Who Envied Women* [1985], and *Privilege* [1990]) and Vietnamese-born, French-educated, and U.S.-based Trinh T. Minh-ha (*Reassemblage* [1982]) is a consideration of the relation between sound and image. More specifically, many of these filmmakers attempt to redirect the spectator's understanding of that relation away from its mainstream patriarchal tendencies to represent women in negative ways and toward an empowering representation of women.

While festivals of women's films in the early 1970s encouraged feminists to make films, distribution of work by women has always been problematic. In the late 1960s and early 1970s, many women producing films intended to further social activism; these women often had to distribute their films themselves, often accompanying them and participating held in the consciousness-raising sessions associated with their screening held in church basements, women's crisis centers, and other alternative venues. Alternative distribution networks have been set up in the United States and elsewhere, including companies attempting to specialize in women's work. The most successful and long-lived of these is now Women Make Movies, headquartered in New York City, but increasingly including international work as part of its catalog.

References. Janet Bergstrom, "Sexuality at a Loss: The Films of F. W. Murnau," *Poetics Today* 6, 1–2 (1985); Diane Carson, Linda Dittmar, and Janice R. Welsch (eds.), *Multiple Voices in Feminist Film Criticism* (Minneapolis, 1994); Miriam Hansen, *Babel and Babylon: Spectatorship in American Silent Film* (Cambridge, Harvard University Press, 1991); Karyn Kay and Gerald Peary (eds.), *Women and the Cinema: A Critical Anthology* (New York, 1977); Judith Mayne, "Feminist Film Theory and Criticism," *Signs* 11 (1985): 88; Suzanne Moore, *Looking for Trouble: On Shopping, Gender and the Cinema* (London: Serpent's Tail, 1991); Constance

Penley, *Feminism and Film Theory* (New York, 1988); Jan Rosenberg, *Women's Reflections: The Feminist Film Movement* (Ann Arbor, 1983); Suzanne Walters, *Material Girls: Making Sense of Feminist Cultural Theory* (Berkeley, Calif., 1995).
                                                           HARRIET MARGOLIS

FILMMAKERS AND MAINSTREAM PRODUCTION. Women have been involved in film production, both behind and in front of the camera, since the medium's inception. Research by women such as Allie Acker and Gwendolyn Foster Dixon has reclaimed some of the lost history of directors such as Alice Guy Blaché, Lois Weber, Mrs. Wallace Reid, and Ida Lupino. We have learned that women such as Adela Rogers St. Johns and Frances Marion significantly altered and developed Hollywood's scriptwriting process (McCreadie) and that Mary Pickford rearranged the relation between actors and producers, leaving behind United Artists as the living legacy of her financial acumen (Balio, 153–172).

Since the origins of feminist film studies in the 1970s, scholars have analyzed repeatedly the body of films that Dorothy Arzner edited and directed (Mayne). Of the many women working during the silent era, Arzner was the only woman director who survived the transition from silent to sound cinema within the Hollywood studio system. She thus has a unique position in women's film history. Similarly, Ida Lupino stands out as a Hollywood actress who directed a small number of independently produced films dealing with controversial subjects such as rape and bigamy during the 1950s, a time when women were not directing feature films. She also worked as a pioneer director of television drama, producing a substantial body of work in her lengthy association with the newer medium.

From the 1970s, women around the world have increased their roles behind the camera as producers, directors, and technicians. Janis Cole and Holly Dale's *Calling the Shots* (documentary film, Canada, 1988) presents excerpts of interviews with women directors and producers (primarily North Americans) that provide an excellent survey of the women and issues involved. Alexis Krasilovsky's collection of interviews with U.S.-based female cinematographers, both celebrates women's increasing involvement in an aspect of filmmaking heretofore closed to women and notes the obstacles yet remaining. Organizations such as Women behind the Lens and Women in Film and Television have had an international influence on women's involvement in film production, providing professional information, job training, and general networking opportunities.

Such behind-the-camera roles for women in the industry matter, it has been argued, because women's voices need to be heard, telling women's stories and expressing a female point of view, both of which would otherwise go ignored. Yet such assertions face objections for their essentialist tendency to associate gender with a monolithic and specific point of view or with specific sorts of stories, with the attendant characters, settings, themes, budgets, and presumed audiences associated with such stories. That is, saying that it takes women to relate certain sorts of stories would seem to relegate women to a limited form of filmmaking. Kathryn Bigelow, for example, has defied Hollywood's usual practice of restricting women to domestic melodramas that tell stories about other women in domestic settings, typically featuring female characters. Instead, Bigelow has worked in various genres, telling stories about men as well as women, and her settings and budgets have reflected such differences. As director Penelope Spheeris has noted, not all women working in film are interested in telling what have traditionally been considered women's stories.

Yet the traditional sort of woman's film has an obvious appeal for women actors. As Molly Haskell noted, the woman's film features a woman at the center of the universe. In a world of film production that offers few roles for women (most of which have more to do with an actor's looks than her talent and skill) any film that allows a woman to practice her art, especially as she grows older, can seem desirable. Barbra Streisand, for example, has produced and directed a number of films that hark back to the sort of drama that used to be Hollywood's staple. *The Mirror Has Two Faces* (1996) not only features Streisand herself but gives Lauren Bacall, Mimi Rogers, and Brenda Vaccaro large parts in a film that indulges in female fantasy but also addresses such feminist issues as the tyranny of contemporary standards of beauty and romantic relations.

Goldie Hawn is another actress who has produced a number of films, many of which deal with burning social issues of their day. While Hawn often continues to play the dumb blond character with which she established her career in *Laugh In*, the 1960s television success that helped Lily Tomlin and others to achieve international fame, films such as *Protocol* (1984) and *Housesitter* (1992) deliberately echo socially conscious films of the 1930s by Frank Capra and others. The populist appeal of Hawn's films makes her treatment of issues such as self-esteem, the pursuit of a career, single mothers, and the homeless especially important, since she is able to bring this material before viewers who might not otherwise bother with more blatantly feminist filmmaking efforts.

Certainly, the women who have succeeded as Hollywood producers have not generally "green-lighted" strikingly different projects from those of their male counterparts. Dawn Steele, head of production briefly at Columbia, is probably better known to the general public for her autobiographical account of how she used her marketing skills to become a producer only to have the rug pulled out from under her by her male colleagues while she was giving birth. Gale Ann Hurd has produced a number of big-budget special effects films, including *Terminator* (1984; also cowriter), *Terminator 2* (1991), and *The Abyss* (1989). Perhaps the most controversial as well as the most successful of the mainstream women producers is Sherry Lansing. Although her *The Accused* (1988) deals sensitively with the issue of gang rape and responsibility, her *Fatal Attraction* (1987) has famously incited male audiences to yell "kill the bitch," leaving female audience members feeling threatened and vulnerable.

In contrast, less-well-known producers have made significant if less controversial contributions to the body of work by women. At MGM, Paula Weinstein was responsible for producing *9 to 5* (1980) and *Yentl* (1983), while at Orion Barbara Boyle approved production of director Susan Seidelman's *Desperately Seeking Susan* (1985). *Susan*'s producers also included director Sarah Pillsbury and Midge Sanford, a team whose joint works include many of John Sayles' films as well as *River's Edge* (1986) and *How to Make an American Quilt* (1995). Their successful financial track record, rather than whatever politics they espouse, is surely what has kept them all employed in the industry.

A number of U.S. women directors have moved from making documentaries into mainstream feature filmmaking. Many women who began their film careers in the late 1960s and early 1970s were part of a women's liberation movement–inspired attempt to appropriate the cinema as a medium for feminist social action. Martha Coolidge, for example, who has since directed such films as *Valley Girl* (1983), *Joy of Sex* (1984), and *Real Genius* (1985), earlier made *Not a Pretty Picture* (1975), her transition film that mixed a fictional re-creation of her own date rape* with conversations between herself and the actress who plays her (the actress herself having had a similar experience).

Others who made the transition from documentary filmmaking to features include Donna Deitch, Penelope Spheeris, and Amy Jones. Spheeris made documentaries on the heavy metal rock scene; her first, low-budget features deal with violence (*The Boys Next Door*, aka *Big Shots*, 1986) and homelessness for teenagers (*Suburbia*, aka *The Wild Side*, 1983). The commercial success of *Wayne's World* (1992; again about young men) opened the door to her for directing and producing within the Hollywood community. As Amy Jones has observed, it's virtually impossible for anyone outside a few television network staff members to earn a living making documentaries. Jones acknowledges early help making the transition into feature film directing from Roger Corman, the king of independent, low-budget film producers, who has always been notably open to hiring women in production roles. However, unlike Spheeris, Jones has not produced a film sufficiently successful in financial terms to keep her in the director's role. She continues to work in the industry as a writer, but her career points to a truism about the difference between male and female directors: if in Hollywood you're only as good as the box office on your last film, then this goes double for women, whose films can earn large profits relative to their production costs and yet be perceived as less successful than male-directed films that earn a larger gross but a smaller net profit because their original costs were higher.

Meanwhile, outside the United States, various women directors have achieved international successes. Polish-born Agnieszka Holland received critical acclaim for tense adult dramas dealing with Europe's twentieth-century history, many of which she wrote as well; she has also made *The Secret Garden* (1993), an English-language film based on an English children's classic that pleases young and old alike. German director Margarete von Trotta has also established the sort of reputation that gets her films widespread distribution. After making such hard-hitting feminist films as *A Question of Silence* (1983) and *Broken Mirrors* (1984), Dutch director Marleen Gorris has made *Antonia's Line* (1995), an amusing, lighter, and less controversial story, as well as adapting Virginia Woolf's *Mrs. Dalloway* (1997). Sally Potter has also moved from making challenging avant-garde feminist films couched within English feminist film theory to the more accessible *Orlando* (1993), again from Woolf's original.

Within the United States, nonmainstream voices are also getting heard. Julie Dash's *Daughters of the Dust* (1991), Leslie Harris' *Just Another Girl on the I.R.T.* (1993), Darnell Martin's *I Like It Like That* (1994), and Allison Anders' *Mi Vida Loca* (1993) are films by members of ethnic and class groups not often represented in Hollywood. Maria Maggenti's *The Incredibly True Adventures of Two Girls in Love* (1996) and Rose Troche's *Go Fish* (1994) manage to present lesbian relations in a positive light in popular feature films. From Canada, Mina Shum's *Double Happiness* (1994) has used the same sort of ironic, media-sophisticated style to deal with immigration, multiculturalism, and family loyalties.

The Australian-based women filmmakers, though, have perhaps had the most visible success, critically, financially, and in terms of retaining their national and political integrity. Historically, women played important roles in the development of Australia's silent film industry, only to lose their positions of influence with the coming of sound, as in the United States. When the Australian government actively promoted the renascence of its national film industry in the 1970s, a few women were positioned to benefit. The first Australian woman to direct a feature film in the 45 years since Paulette McDonough's *The Cheaters* (1929), Gillian Armstrong burst on the international circuit with her third feature, *My Brilliant Career* (1979), but her first attempt at Hollywood filmmaking, *Mrs. Soffel* (1984), was a failure, financially and critically. Returning to Australia, she continued to produce successful films there and was again called to Hollywood. She now alternates between working in Australia and Hollywood, and her most recent U.S. film, *Little Women* (1994), garnered at least three Academy Award nominations.

Perhaps the most interesting Antipodean film to hit the international scene, though, is *The Piano*, which shared top honors at Cannes in 1993. Written and directed by New Zealand–born but Australian-trained and based Jane Campion, *The Piano* struck a nerve for most of its viewers.

Featuring a heroine whom we never see speak but whose choices override those of the men who seek to control her, *The Piano* breaks with the traditional woman's film and the more contemporary feminist film in its representation of a female protagonist's subjectivity as well as her relations to other characters.

As the body of films by women directors and producers grows, it will increasingly be possible to assess the influence of women on the industry. However, the day of equal power within the medium remains a milestone for the future.

References. Allie Acker, *Reel Women* (New York, 1991); Tino Balio, "Stars in Business: The Founding of United Artists," in Tino Balio (ed.), *The American Film Industry*, rev. ed. (Madison, Wis., 1985); Gwendolyn Foster Dixon, *Women Who Made the Movies* (documentary film, U.S., 1991); Molly Haskell, *From Reverence to Rape*, 2d ed. (Chicago, 1987); Alexis Krasilovsky, *The New Cinematographers: Women behind the Camera* (Westport, Conn., 1997); Judith Mayne, *Directed by Dorothy Arzner* (Bloomington, Ind., 1994); Marsha McCreadie, *The Women Who Write the Movies: From Frances Marion to Nora Ephron* (New York, 1994).

HARRIET MARGOLIS

FINLAND. Women fare extremely well if suffrage, political representation, or participation in paid labor are any measures of emancipation. Finland was in 1906 the first European country and the third in the world to grant women a right to vote in parliamentary elections. Finnish women have a long tradition of gainful employment. Already in 1910, 28 percent of factory workers were women and, in 1950, 45 percent of married women worked outside the home. In the late 1980s, 61 percent of women and 69 percent of men were employed, 88 percent of the women full-time, in contrast to their Nordic sisters, many of whom work part-time. However, researchers have questioned whether these figures accurately measure the degree of women's emancipation.

The campaign for universal suffrage, for instance, was more a class than a gender issue. It did not result from a fierce feminist struggle as in Great Britain. Finland, in 1906 an autonomous Grand Duchy of Russia, had managed to retain its Swedish legal, administrative, and educational system after its separation from Sweden in 1809. As these systems signaled the country's separate identity, to maintain them, intact if possible, became a matter of pride and survival. However, by the turn of the century the old forms no longer corresponded to social realities, and three-fourths of the population were entirely without political representation. Under these circumstances women as well as men mobilized to demand a radical democratic reform. While women's active participation in the struggle has been attributed to Finland's strong agricultural heritage and rather harmonious gender relations, the relatively smooth passing of this, "Europe's most radical parliamentary reform," can at least partly be explained by the stiff

Russification measures imposed upon Finland and by Russia's internal turmoil. It was essential for the Finns to present a united front and for the Russians to avoid any further social upheaval.

The agricultural tradition accounts also for the early employment of Finnish women. Up to the repeal of the so-called Vagrancy Law in 1883, all unmarried women in the countryside were forced to work for others in order to acquire legal protection. Even after that date, most women were driven by economic need into paid labor. Rather than a right, then, employment for these women was a necessity and an enslaving necessity at that, as one researcher put it. In fact, the concept of a housewife, a woman as a family being with the private sphere as her domain, did not prevail in Finland until World War II. Although not measures of women's emancipation nor results of it, the early suffrage and women's high participation in work life have surely contributed to the development of gender equality in Finland.

Although Finland proportionately has more women artists than any other European country, women entering the artistic field continue to face greater obstacles than men. Their own educational background at least equals that of men, and very few of them hail from the working class. In the words of one researcher, women need more social and cultural capital than men. Whereas women have always been strongly represented among painters, their ranks among writers have steadily grown since the 1880s, when they first entered the literary scene, simultaneously with the first wave of the women's movement. These early writers, like the dramatist Minna Canth (1844–1897), dwelt on the many social ills such as economic exploitation of the lower classes, married women's property rights, and the lack of solidarity between women of different social classes. A number of the legal reforms in the 1880s and 1890s came as a direct result of their polemical writings. The next generation of women writers, who made their debut in the 1910s, shifted their focus to women's inner lives and their problems with sexuality and female identity. During the modernistic decade of the 1950s and the socially active 1960s women faded again to the background, only to make a forceful comeback in the 1970s. Today women writers dominate within all genres, from lyric poetry to the epic novel.

The educational level of Finnish women is high. Since the end of the 1940s a higher percentage of women than men have finished high school and well over half of all university students are women. In fact, the new equality concern is the weak academic performance of boys in senior high school. Critics claim that the whole educational system is designed to favor women. Nonetheless, only 7 percent of full professors are women, while they constitute 40 percent of university lecturers. Moreover, gender distribution between different disciplines, in academe as well as in work life, is uneven. About half of all Finns work in largely unisex work environments. In technical fields only 18 percent of students are women, whereas their percentage in health-related fields, excluding physicians, is 98. Nevertheless, many professions that in the United States are heavily male-dominated have in Finland attracted women for a long time, for example, 59 percent of medical and 72 percent of dental students are women. Their most recent territorial gain is veterinary medicine, where 80 percent of the students are female compared to only 36 percent in 1970.

Largely because of the gender-segregated job market, women continue to earn less than men, receiving on the average only 78 percent of men's earnings. Furthermore, the wage gap is greater in the private than in the public sector. Thus, while formal equality has been achieved, old attitudes persist. One of the last formal hindrances to equality was removed in 1988, when women gained the right to serve as pastors in the state Lutheran Church. Only the military remains closed to them, but even there the current minister of defense is a woman.

According to the official ideology, men and women possess equal rights and responsibilities in terms of work, family, and civic duties. For this goal to be realized, numerous social benefits have been legislated in recent years: public day care for children, the possibility of a shortened workday for parents of young children, family allowances, fatherhood leaves, and, as a matter of course, pregnancy leaves for mothers. Perhaps because of the high degree of formal gender equality and women's early political and economic gains, the remaining deep-seated inequalities have been slow to surface and even slower to be remedied. The most recent wave of feminism reached Finland rather late; the very word "feminist" carries a bigger stigma there than in the United States, and feminist research at the universities was relatively slow to establish itself. In the 1990s, work on comparative worth holds perhaps the greatest promises of genuine choice of employment for men and women and equal compensation for their work.

References. Finland. Tilastokeskus, *Position of Women*, Statistical Surveys 72 (Helsinki, 1984); Elina Haavio-Mannila et al., *Unfinished Democracy: Women in Nordic Politics* (Oxford, 1985); Merja Manninen and Päivi Setälä (eds.), *The Lady with the Bow* (Helsinki, 1990).

VIRPI ZUCK

FOLKLORE and "women" are terms that have been linked in scholarship only recently. Expressive, artistic behavior, whether verbal or plastic, used to be considered an activity exclusive to men. Women's expressive behavior was assigned categories such as "decorative" or "utilitarian," thus denying the conscious manipulation of form and content for effect or aesthetics.

In 1888 the American Folklore Society was founded; from the beginning women scholars were represented in its publications as well as in other popular and scholarly publications of the time. However, the perceptions of women's contributions, whether as scholars or consultant/informers, were limited by prevailing ideas about women and their abilities. Today, women are actively challenging the preconceptions about themselves and their scholarship, sometimes with a strident rhetoric, sometimes with a comical or ironic attitude, but always with a plethora of knowledge and references. Indeed, the adage of women's having to be "better than" to be considered "equal to" is demonstrated repeatedly in women's reports of their difficulties in being taken seriously and being published in premier outlets. While we like to think that our times are considerably different from those of 100 years ago, in practice we now find many similarities to the situation obtaining when folklore first became a scholarly presence on the American scene.

Early collectors, whether men or women, preferred to gather stories from men, unless, of course, the stories concerned hearth and home, charms or lullabies, children's games or cooking, which were the province of women, it was believed. Despite the fact that the Grimm brothers reported collecting their fairy tales primarily from serving-women, men were believed to be the bearers of the important and lengthy traditions, while women were believed to be more capable of, and interested in, things that surrounded what was considered to be their primary role: household and child care. Even when women's knowledge was demonstrated to be superior to that of men in a particular genre, the words of men were preferred.

Gradually, during the 1950s and 1960s, information about women in journals or books was expanded to include their roles in cultures other than those founded on Western European models. At times some of this information related to folklore. But usually it was folklore *about* women rather then the kinds of expressive behavior in which women engaged, whether in groups of women, women with children, or mixed gender groups. Occasionally, there was a single publication focusing on the repertoire of this female storyteller or that woman singer; such publications were exceptions to an otherwise firm rule that significant folklore study was predicated on working with men's knowledge.

By the late 1960s and the early 1970s the situation was changing rapidly. It is not a coincidence that this change occurred coterminously with the so-called women's movement and court cases affirming the rights of minorities and women. Many graduate school programs, previously de facto closed to women, began to reserve slots for women in order to ensure the continuance of federal funding for other sectors of the university. Older women, those with children, and those who lived on the margins longing for the opportunities of their brothers and husbands were represented in disproportionate numbers in these early graduate classes. These women, predominantly in our country at the University of Texas in Austin, at Stanford University, at the University of Pennsylvania, and at Indiana University–Bloomington, had life experiences and artistic/folkloristic repertoires that were neither described in literature nor accorded legitimacy. These women began to be heard in the mid-1970s, when there was a sudden explosion of literature about women, their folklore, their roles, their self-perceptions, and even their bawdy jokes, stories, and tales—more often than not with men as the butt. With the increasing availability of funding for women and their concerns, stories began to circulate of the women's folklore from this country or that and its similarities and differences compared with American folklore. Much of this cross-cultural work, however, was not published until the late 1970s and early 1980s.

Also during the late 1960s and early 1970s women's groups were formed; originally these were consciousness-raising* or rap groups, but now they are termed support groups and have generalized to the society as a whole. Women delighted in finding their commonalities, especially in sharing their ways of relating experiences about such commonalities in these groups. Some of the earlier published and scholarly work in women's folklore grew from such associations of women.

The numbers of books, articles, and chapters on women and their folk-lore being produced in the mid- and later 1980s reached such proportions as to make it impossible for any one person to keep adequate track of the literature without devoting full time to it. Primarily the work has focused on women's roles and women's expressions of and about them in cultures throughout the world as well as in our own country. There has also been a coming together of feminism and scholarship. Women have been freed, one hopes permanently, from the bonds of being passive to the recognition that women are active agents, often agencies as well, for the enactment of their lives. Even in repressed situations, such as can be seen in some back-to-the-past Middle Eastern cultures, women scholars are demonstrating the expressive ways in which women manipulate and comment upon their condition through folkloristic resources.

Theoretical work in women's folklore currently follows the same trends and paradigms as does any other subject in an academic discipline. There are those studies that focus on ethnography, on a Marxist perspective, on a structural presentation, on a semiotic interpretation, or on a performance enactment, as well as those that take a tone of literary criticism; additionally, many works reinterpret past canon on the basis of contemporary insight. Previously taboo topics, such as lesbianism, receive their fair share of scholarly attention and are now publishable, whereas a few years ago they were not—save in the so-called underground press. What were once accepted social "facts," as, for instance, the concept of universal male dominance, have recently been shown to be as much a product of our own mythology concerning proper roles of men and women as they were social reality. The genres and paradigms that have been utilized to discuss women and their folklore or to trivialize them both are more reflective of the scholars and the zeitgeist than they are of the actual situation obtaining in any one time or place.

In the late 1980s attention is being given to the effects of colonialism, of cultural recidivism, of feminism, of text versus performance, of performance of text, and of alphabetic literacy on the production, recording, and interpretation of folklore and women. The topic of folklore and women now encompasses folklore of women, folklore about women, women's folklore, and metafolklore—the folklore about the folklore.

In 1888 understanding of folklore and women was a foregone conclusion: everyone knew the kinds of folklore women had and the areas in which they could be expected to demonstrate competency, and everyone knew that real folklore was a possession of men. It took almost 100 years, until 1972, before the first scholarly session on women's folklore was presented at the American Folklore Society; two years later, in 1974, the interest was so intense that there was a double session (four hours of papers). In 1986 the society's annual meeting featured an entire day of scholarly papers on women's folklore, with multiple sessions running concurrently. Unfortunately, few men attended the sessions. This précis of the American Folklore Society's record concerning folklore and women replicates the situation in other disciplines and scholarship in general.

Four works have had a significant impact upon the thinking of those who write about folklore and women. Barbara Babcock's contains two of her essays, the Introduction, and "Liberty's a Whole," which are seminal. Claire R. Farrer's has articles repeatedly cited. Marta Weigle's presents images of women from many cultures throughout history. Finally, Michelle Zimbalist Rosaldo and Louise Lamphere, although in an anthropological collection, provided the stimulus for much of the research now seeing the light of publication.

References. Barbara Babcock (ed.), *The Reversible World* (Ithaca, N.Y., 1978); Claire R. Farrer (ed.), *Women and Folklore: Images and Genres* (Prospect Heights, Ill., 1986); Marta Weigle, *Spiders and Spinsters* (Albuquerque, 1982); Michelle Zimbalist Rosaldo and Louise Lamphere (eds.), *Women, Culture and Society* (Stanford, Calif., 1974).

CLAIRE R. FARRER

FOOD AND EATING DISORDERS. Responsibility for food preparation continues to be a central part of women's lives. A North American study has shown that even though one-fifth of household work is now "shared" by family members, the woman carries out 88 percent of meal preparation tasks and 86 percent of the chores related to cleaning up after food preparation. Even in "progressive" families, men and children "help," while the woman manages what is seen to be her responsibility.

Food preparation is distinctly different from other domestic responsibilities. Unlike child care,* which is a building process, with each day's work adding to a growing product, food preparation is a process that constantly starts from the beginning. Responsibilities for child care gradually diminish as society assumes some role through nurseries and schools and as the child

can take care of itself. In contrast, work required for feeding the family*
increases as children grow and make individual demands. Housework* is
different from food preparation in that it can be delayed or organized into
times that fit into a busy schedule. Meal times impose constant deadlines.
No one will die if windows are not cleaned regularly, but feeding the family
is literally a life-or-death responsibility.

Industrialization has changed the work women do as food producers.
Unlike our sisters in the Third World, the North American woman's role
has changed from producing food on the land to buying food. A shift has
occurred from time spent cooking food to time spent shopping for food. A
woman's identity has become increasingly connected to her role as consumer.

Technology in the home may *increase* women's workload. Rather than
reducing work, appliances seem to raise the standards of domestic labor.
Studies have shown a direct correlation between the number of appliances
owned and the time spent on housework. In the urban United States, time
spent per week on housework increased from 51 hours in 1929 to 77 hours
in 1971. Appliances are also used as a substitute for a more equal division
of household chores; that is, men and children are more likely to do the
dishes if a home does *not* have a dishwasher.

Women have ambivalent feelings about their roles as food producers.
Many women get great satisfaction from cooking and find it more reward-
ing than other household tasks. For many women, food production is their
principal source of identity, a prime way to express creativity, an ideal way
to show love and caring for others, and their major source of power and
control in the world. Food then takes on an enormous significance. Food
becomes symbolic of a woman's love for her family. She is unable to let
down high standards of meal preparation, perpetuated by advertising and
the media, without feeling she is reneging on her expected caring role.
Rejecting or accepting mother's food is seen as rejecting or accepting
mother. Food becomes the channel through which power struggles in the
family are fought.

In violent homes, power and control issues often get expressed in relation
to food preparation duties and body image issues. Abusers punish women
when the buying, cooking, or serving of food is not carried out according
to their demands, and criticisms about body weight or management of food
preparation are extremely common forms of the verbal/emotional continuum. The kitchen is the most dangerous room in violent homes because of
the many objects that can be used as weapons, so safety planning with
battered women* often includes a discussion of getting out of the kitchen
if the abuser is getting violent.

Fear of Fat. Women's responsibility for food preparation is an important
part of the domestic division of labor that restricts women from making
their maximum contribution to society and to changing that society. But,

on a day-to-day basis, most women are far more aware of the conflict between their role as producer/consumer and the pressure on women to be thin.

An abundance of food, particularly low-fiber, high-fat, high-sugar foods, means that many people are plump. Plumpness is common, so slimness is valued, and there is extreme prejudice against fat people. Obesity is the most stigmatized, by all age groups, physical feature except skin color. The prejudice against fat people is exaggerated because obesity is thought to be a voluntary choice, even though metabolic factors and physical exercise have more to do with body weight than eating habits.

The fear of getting fat or staying fat is much more a concern for women than for men. Women's roles as food producers mean that they can never get away from thinking about, and dealing with, food. Women need relatively fewer calories (an average of 1,600 to 2,400 calories needed per day compared to 2,300 to 3,100 for men), and hormonal changes make them more susceptible to weight gain. Women are judged by their appearance far more than men and live with constant reminders of the narrow range of body images acceptable for the "ideal woman." There is less pressure on men to diet, but when men decide to lose weight, they do so more easily, partly because of the support they get from women.

Eating Disorders. Anorexia nervosa,* bulimia,* compulsive eating, and dieting are all women's issues symbolic of contradictions in women's relationship to food as preparers and consumers.

The eating disorders literature (both research and reports of mental health professionals) has often focused on young, white, middle-class women, particularly those who have been labeled as "overachievers." It is now recognized that this emphasis is more a reflection of who calls upon mental health services than an accurate picture of the occurrence of eating disorders. Groundbreaking work in the 1990s has put a new emphasis on making sure eating disorders are addressed for a much more diverse population of women (see Thompson; Fallon, Katzman, and Wooley). This work has paved the way for looking more closely at eating issues as responses (sometimes "survival strategies") related to violence and various forms of oppression in women's lives.

Anorexia is defined as self-starvation, a loss of weight of 20 to 25 percent of initial body weight. Ninety-five percent of anorexics are women. Anorexia is common only in societies where there is an abundance of food and where thinness is valued. Health professionals are most aware of anorexia in white, middle-class young women, labeled as "overachievers," though this may be more a reflection of who calls upon the mental health services than an accurate picture of the occurrence of anorexia. Although anorexia is predominantly a mental health issue, there are serious physical consequences of the extreme weight loss. There is an absence of menstruation, the risk of sterility, extreme susceptibility to infection, and a wasting away of vital muscle (including heart) tissue. It is estimated that 15 to 20 percent of anorexics die because of their eating disorders.

Bulimia is defined as a cycle of binging and purging. Bulimics get rid of food by vomiting, fasting, or using diuretics, laxatives, or amphetamines. Eighty-five percent of bulimics are women, and studies indicate that 15 to 20 percent of college women are bulimic. Many bulimics do not seek professional help and are of "normal" weight without weight fluctuations, so the incidence may be even more common. Physical health problems include rotting teeth (from stomach acids), dehydration causing long-term mineral imbalances, and increased infections.

Compulsive eating is usually defined as having an addiction to food, feeling out of control about one's eating habits, or eating without regard for the physical body signals of hunger and satiety.

What Is Ordered Eating? The preceding conditions are usually labeled as eating disorders. Instead of viewing them as extreme conditions, it is probably more useful to view them as extensions of a continuum of problematic relationships women have with eating habits, weight control, and their role in this society. Sophisticated psychological tests (used for diagnosis and treatment of anorexia) find little difference between ordinary weight-preoccupied women and anorexics. Indeed, the goal of treatment for anorexia is that the person is "no more neurotic about food than anyone else."

References. Patricia Fallon, Malanie A. Katzman, and Susan C. Wooley, *Feminist Perspectives on Eating Disorders* (New York, 1994); Becky M. Thompson, *A Hunger So Wide and So Deep* (Minneapolis, 1994).

NANCY WORCESTER

FOOT-BINDING is the traditional Chinese practice of tightly wrapping the feet of young girls in order to prevent natural growth and ensure "attractive" small feet. This crippling practice originated around the tenth or eleventh century A.D. It appears to have been inspired by palace dancers whose small shoes with upward pointing toes were seen as especially attractive. The custom spread particularly among the upper classes, where women's bound feet were seen as beautiful and erotic symbols of status and wealth. The rising popularity of foot-binding coincided with a general decline in women's status in Chinese society and was inspired in part by the concern of patriarchal Confucians to exert tighter control over women's lives.

Foot-binding was the most painful of many manifestations of the subordination of women to men in late traditional China (roughly from A.D. 1100 to 1900). A young girl (from 4 to 8 years old) would have four toes (all except the big toe) bent under the foot and pulled back toward the heel by bindings of cotton or silk wrapped very tightly. As the foot's natural growth was thus stunted, the toes would putrefy and sometimes even drop off. With circulation hampered by the tight bindings, there was always a danger of blood poisoning and other infections. The arch of the foot would be broken, and the foot would be permanently crippled. The pain this caused was excruciating for at least a year as the foot was transformed into a withered stump. Once permanently maimed, the foot could not be unbound without intensifying the pain. Walking was difficult without assistance.

The tiny, curved, bound foot became a symbol of women's dependence on men, of the wealth and status of their families, and of "feminine beauty and elegance." Large feet were seen as ugly, clumsy, and even suggestive of loose morals; small feet were associated with virtue, refinement, and (somewhat contradictorily) eroticism. Bound feet were said to enhance the female gait (not unlike high heels); male aesthetes found it sexually exciting to unwrap and fondle the small crippled foot; even the smell of the bound foot was proclaimed by some as a strong sexual stimulant. Beyond the status benefits and the sexual connotations of foot-binding, the custom had the very practical consequences of ensuring a family's control over its women. They could easily be confined to the boudoir, their economic dependence on the family was total, and their "market value" in marriage was relatively high.

Foot-binding was never universally practiced in China, though it became especially popular from the sixteenth through the nineteenth centuries. The very poor could not afford such drastic disabilities, and there was widespread regional variation. Generally speaking, the custom was less widespread in the southern half of the country, where labor-intensive rice cultivation and sericulture made women's labor more essential to family income. Even so, foot-binding was practiced by many poor families in hopes of achieving marriage alliances with higher-status families. There were always a few vocal critics of the cruelty of foot-binding, but they were an ineffective minority until the twentieth century, when the custom was finally abolished as part of numerous social reform efforts following the fall of the Manchu dynasty in 1911.

Reference. Howard S. Levy, *Chinese Footbinding: The History of a Curious Erotic Custom* (New York, 1966; dated, but the only extensive published study available).

PAUL S. ROPP

FRANCE. Code Napoléon was the far-reaching civil code promulgated in 1804 by Napoléon Bonaparte that affected all aspects of civil law and French society. Ratified on March 21, 1804, the code was a collaborative effort between Napoléon, a four-member select committee of attorneys, and the Conseil d'Etat (council of state). Attempting to create a body of laws that would provide unity of legislation and retain the separation of civil law from religious law, the framers designed a comprehensive code containing a total of 2,281 articles.

While attempting to bring order to the haphazard French legal system, the framers also imposed their personal views of society on the code. In particular, Napoléon was insistent that the prerevolutionary strength of the family unit be restored and the authority of the father within the family be assured. Napoléon and many of his closest advisers were convinced that the French Revolution had destroyed societal order and the family by liberalizing divorce, granting rights to illegitimate children, and restricting the powers of the father over inheritance and control of the family. The code in its final form, therefore, systematically destroyed gains that women had made in the previous decade and, by eliminating class distinctions, also suppressed property and legal rights that women of the religious and lay nobility had held under the ancien régime. As of 1804, women actually enjoyed fewer rights than they had had during the eighteenth century.

The code is generally praised for its brevity, clarity, and unity; and it has been described as the fulfillment of the "aspirations of 1789." A number of significant reforms, in fact, were legislated, including the suppression of the hereditary nobility, recognition of civil equality (without regard to social class), and provisions for equality of inheritance. For men, the code was a progressive document that firmly ended the abuses of the ancien régime and retained many of the contributions of the revolutionary period. For women, for the most part, the code was reactionary. Only in sections dealing with inheritance and a woman's right to guardianship of her children in the event of the husband/father's death did the French law benefit women. In those cases, Frenchwomen gained rights their contemporaries across the Channel did not have.

In every section of the code, women were affected by sweeping measures intended to create a "domestic monarchy." Among the most important provisions were those that dealt with the authority of the father within the family and women's rights to make contracts, hold property, and dissolve their marriages.

In the code, the power of the husband/father was considered absolute. For example, fathers were allowed to imprison their children without cause, with the length of detention not to exceed one month for children under 16 or six months for children between the ages of 16 and 21. The mother was granted no rights to discipline her offspring; in fact, she was treated as a minor, like her children. Article 213 specified: "The husband owes protection to his wife, and the wife owes obedience to her husband."

Although the Code Napoléon is generally cited as a model for community property laws, it carried a mixed message for women. In the section dealing with marriage contracts, the code precisely spelled out the meaning of community property and how it would be administered. First, community property was defined to mean properties (intangibles and real estate) that were acquired by either spouse during the marriage. In effect, the husband and wife became coowners of their joint wealth. Real estate held by either partner prior to the marriage could be kept separate from the community property. Second, Article 1388 of the code expressly defined the husband as head of the household. In that capacity he had sole right to administer all household belongings—community property, his personal property, and his wife's personal property. Although community property was coowned by the spouses (providing a married woman with a right not previously held), she had no rights to control the property she legally coowned. Under the code, no wife could give, sell, or mortgage any of the property, nor could she acquire property without her husband's written consent. Article 1124 specifically declared that married women, children, and persons of unsound mind were incapable of making contracts. Only under extraordinary circumstances could a woman with her own business or trade engage in contracts without her husband's consent.

The right to divorce, which was the subject of heated debate, emerged as a compromise in the final draft of the code (Articles 231–233). Under revolutionary law, divorce had been liberally granted in three manners: divorce by mutual consent, divorce for incompatibility (on demand of either spouse), and divorce for "grave causes." The Code Napoléon, however, took a far more limited position. Only adultery, cruelty, and conviction of one spouse for a felony were considered "grave causes." In those cases, testimony from the family council and evidence would have to be presented in court for the divorce decree to be granted. Alimony was allowed only in cases of "grave cause" if the duration of the marriage was at least 20 years, and the wife had not attained the age of 45. When adultery was cited, a double standard prevailed: a husband had the right to divorce his wife for one isolated act, but a wife could divorce her husband only if he introduced a permanent mistress into the household.

The right to divorce on grounds of incompatibility was suppressed completely by the Code Napoléon, and divorce by mutual consent was severely restricted. Only if a marriage had endured less than 10 years could mutual consent be considered, and a person could have no more than one divorce. A three-year waiting period applied to remarriage for divorced persons.

When Napoléon dictated his memoirs from St. Helena after the first French empire had fallen, the former emperor cited the code as one of his greatest accomplishments, greater even than 40 of his battlefield victories. It had been part of his plan to bring order from chaos and to create a lasting, consistent, and unified legal system. Napoléon's armies had swept across Europe and taken the code with them when their leader created satellite kingdoms; later codes written in Egypt, Canada, portions of Central and South America, and Japan bore its influence.

Napoléon's defeat and the restoration of Louis XVIII to the French throne did little to change French law. The application of the law to French society, including the basic provisions concerning women, remained substantially intact until after World War II, nearly a century and a half later. The French revolutionary rhetoric of social equality, which Napoléon claimed he had preserved and guaranteed for generations to come, was only a myth to women.

References. *The Code Napoléon; or, The French Civil Code*, trans. George Spence (New York, 1841); H.A.L. Fisher, "The Codes," *Cambridge Modern History* 9 (1969): 148–159; Claire Goldberg Moses, *French Feminism in the Nineteenth Century* (Albany, N.Y., 1984).

SUSAN P. CONNER

FRANCE. Feminism and the Women's Liberation Movement. The contemporary women's liberation movement emerged in France after the student and worker revolt of May 1968. Women activists in "revolutionary" organizations rebelled against the reproduction of sexism within these groups, which were to have engendered their generation's vision and commitment to change. In May 1970, "Combat pour la liberation des femmes" was published in the new left journal *L'Idiot International*. Subsequently, all-women's meetings were held, disrupted at first when men tried to participate. On August 26, 1970, at the Arc de Triomphe, several women attempted to place flowers on the Tomb of the Unknown Soldier in memory of his wife, who is even less known than he. This first public protest and successful media event is generally considered to mark the birth of the *Mouvement de Liberation des Femmes* (MLF).

The term "movement" reflects the MLF's theoretical and political diversity, the proliferation of groups in France's major cities, the multiplication of the themes of action and reflection, and the variety of publications. The MLF can nevertheless be characterized by several basic principles: male exclusion, rejection of hierarchy and leadership, autonomy of its groups, and independence from political parties.

In the early years, although there was a strong sense of unity in the MLF, it contained several different strands, formalized to varying degrees into groups or "currents."

Psychanalyse et Politique, a group constituted at the very beginning of the movement, set itself the goal of "eradicating the masculine" within women to create a veritable "female identity." This group has officially proclaimed its opposition to feminism. Feminism, equated with the demand for equality, was rejected as a phallocentric, reformist strategy. After years of conflicts, the vast majority of movement groups united to condemn *Psychanalyse et Politique* when it claimed possession of the term "women's liberation movement" by founding an association by that name and registering *Mouvement de Liberation des Femmes* and MLF as a trademark. *Psychanalyse et Politique* is the founder of "des femmes" publishing house, several journals and bookstores, and, in 1989, the *Alliance des Femmes pour la Démocratisation*.

The *Lutte de Classes* (class struggle) current was created by activists from far left, often Trotskyist, organizations. Each of its components, such as *Le Cercle Dimitriev*, *Les Petroleuses*, and *Les Femmes Travailleuses En Lutte*, was set up by women from a given organization. The *Lutte de Classes* current, as its name indicates, saw women's struggle as subordinate to class struggle, although, over the following years, many *Lutte de Classes* activists left their organizations, as had the early founders of the MLF. It spawned numerous neighborhood women's groups as outreach to working-class women, a series of national coordinating congresses, and several journals.

The *Féministes Révolutionnaires*, less structured than the other groups, exemplified the radical feminist current. They analyzed men's domination of women as that of one sex-class over another and insisted that the struggle against patriarchy could not be secondary to the fight against capitalism. This perspective has given birth to numerous groups throughout the history of the MLF.

In 1970, the *Torchon Brûle*, the first MLF journal, appeared as a joint project of the *Féministes Révolutionnaires, Psychanalyse et Politique*, and a number of unaligned women (seven issues, 1970 to 1973). A multitude of other publications followed—special issues of journals, collective works, publications of specific task forces or currents, mimeographed newsletters, monthly reviews sold at newsstands, theoretical journals, and so forth.

Abortion was illegal in France in the early years of the MLF, and feminists rapidly mobilized around this issue. The *Manifeste des 343*, in which 343 women (some famous, and others unknown) declared that they had undergone abortions, was published in April 1971 in the left-wing, mass-distribution weekly *Le Nouvel Observateur*. In 1972, feminists organized support for a minor who was arrested for having had an illegal abortion and for her mother, who was charged with collusion. Protests were staged, celebrities spoke out at the trial in Bobigny, and the girl was acquitted. The struggle for free abortion on demand continued, including in cosexual groups, such as those that, despite the legal risks involved, performed abortions. It culminated in 1974 with the adoption of a five-year law legalizing abortion. This law was made permanent in 1979 following an impressive feminist demonstration in Paris; after 1982, abortion fees were covered by the national health plan.

The demand for bodily self-determination went much further than rejecting compulsory motherhood. The fight against rape, the extreme form of physical coercion to which women are subjected, was another landmark for the MLF. As early as 1970, feminists denounced all forms of violence against women, but only after 1976 did the issue go public through a host of actions such as conferences, speak-outs, take-back-the-night protests, and public support of rape victims in court. The debate on rape brought out theoretical rifts. A part of the *Lutte de Classes* current opposed involvement in the "bourgeois" criminal justice system and refused to sanction a "policy of repression" that put rapists in jail; for the *Féministes Révolutionnaires*, rape was an integral part of the system of social control of women and should be seen and punished as a crime. Several years later, the *Lesbiennes Radicales* directly challenged heterosexuality, as their slogan, "All men are rapists, all men are men," shows.

The first lesbian group in the MLF, the *Gouines Rouges* (Red Dykes), started in 1971 (and led to the forming of the *Front Homosexuel d'Action Révolutionnaire*, which rapidly became a male organization). Rarely involved in the gay movement, which they denounced as misogynist, lesbians were never, on the other hand, fully accepted in the feminist movement, which they criticized for heterocentrism. From 1975 on, several lesbian groups were created in different cities, and a journal, *Quand les femmes s'aiment* (1978–1980), was produced by the *Groupe Lesbiennes* in Lyon. The *Lesbiennes Radicales'* critique of heterosexuality, considered to be women's collaboration with men as a class, led to the creation of a movement outside the MLF and a split in the radical-feminist journal *Questions féministes*.

The impact of the MLF was also felt in labor unions, where feminists organized women's caucuses. In left-wing political parties, feminists created their own groups, which were critical of their party's positions (in 1978, the *Courant G* in the Socialist Party and *Elles Voient Rouge* in the Communist Party).

After the socialists came to power in 1981, a Woman's Rights Ministry with a small, but significant, budget replaced the previous government's advisory commission on the status of women. While most officials were Socialist Party politicians, adding to feminists' ambivalence, cooperation was established on a number of projects. The ministry was responsible for various legal changes and educational campaigns.

Today, while the MLF no longer exists in its early form, numerous feminist and lesbian groups remain engaged in the movement for women's liberation, even if the connections among them have weakened. Some run alternative institutions such as battered women's shelters, women's centers, feminist archives and information centers, women's cafés, and film programs. Some work against specific facets of women's oppression such as legal discrimination, sexual mutilation, sexual harassment, and rape. Some publish journals, such as the *Cahiers du féminisme, Cahiers du GRIF, Nouvelles questions féministes*, and *Lesbia*. Feminist studies have gained legitimacy in several universities, and, despite the lack of enthusiasm from governmental and academic institutions, courses are taught, conferences are held, and the number of research programs continues to grow. Since 1989, a national women's studies association, *Association Nationale de Etudes*

Féminists (ANEF) has brought together students and scholars and links the regional associations that were started after the first national women's studies conference in Toulouse in 1982. With the advent of the European Community, French feminists are participating in the European women's studies networks currently being created. In all these initiatives, theoretical research as well as feminist practice continue to be marked by the tensions between the different feminist currents of thought—Marxist feminism, feminitude (stressing women's natural differences with men, *la différence*), and radical feminism.

References. For French feminist documents translated into English, see Claire Duchen, *French Connections: Voices from the Women's Movement in France* (London, 1987), companion volume to Claire Duchen, *Feminism in France: From May '68 to Mitterrand* (London, 1986), and *Feminist Issues* (Berkeley, Calif., a radical feminist journal). Féministes (Catherine Guinchard, Annick Houel, Brigitte Lhomond, Patricia Mercader, Helga Sobota, and Michèle Bridoux), *Chronique d'une passion, le Mouvement de Libération des Femmes à Lyon* (Paris, 1989); Annie de Pisan and Anne Tristan, *Histoires du M.L.F.* (Paris, 1977); Monique Remy, *Histoire des mouvements de femmes* (Paris, 1990); Marthe Rosenfeld, "Splits in French Feminism/Lesbianism," in Sarah Lucia Hoagland and Julia Penelope (eds.), *For Lesbians Only, a Separatist Anthology* (London, 1988).

BRIGITTE LHOMOND, with aid and translating by JUDITH EZEKIEL

FRANCE. French Revolution is a decade (1789–1799) in which the fabric of French society was altered but in which women were not the beneficiaries of that change.

The French Revolution, in fact, represents a leading example of feminist theory on revolution. It provides evidence that periods of progressive change for men restrict women rather than broadening their opportunities; and it challenges historians to use gender, like class, as a category for the historical analysis of society during revolutionary periods.

Although the outcome of the revolutionary period was the repression of women, the early years were characterized by significant contributions of women to the concept of popular sovereignty. Long before the revolution, women had participated in collective action and popular demonstrations when provisions were scarce. Bread riots and examples of *taxation populaire* punctuated the century; it was not uncommon for women to appropriate goods, set up their own markets, and sell those goods on a scale that they themselves set. Prerevolutionary demonstrations, however, lacked the explicit political motivation that characterized later demonstrations.

Contemporary with these prerevolutionary demonstrations, a conspicuously feminist literature promoted citizenship and expanded opportunities for women. Among the women writers, Mme. de Puisieulx, Mme. de Galien, and Mme. Gacon-Dufour struck at the myths and misconceptions that perpetuated the inequality of the sexes. Mme. Gacon-Dufour noted that the difference between the sexes could be found only in the biological act of propagating the species. Another writer, Mme. de Coicy, pointed out that economic difficulties were a result of the antiwoman bias of French law and society.

In this environment, women of the popular classes began to assert themselves. The *cashiers de doléance* (lists of grievances) were the first clear indication that concerns about bread and constitutional questions were merging. In these lists, which were directed to the Estates-Général in 1789, a new consciousness emerged. Demands included legal equality; education; reform in the laws dealing with marriage, divorce, and inheritance; relief from economic distress; guaranteed employment; and the suppression of prostitution.

Once these ideas had been articulated, it was only one step further to action. In October 1789 women of the markets (*dames des Halles*) marched to Versailles to demand subsistence and the king's consent to constitutional reform. Many of the marchers were seasoned veterans of women's activities. Some had already participated in petitioning, strikes, and market demonstrations; others had exercised their right to attend the debates of the Constituent Assembly or had formed deputations to address the king. Contemporaries viewed the women's march to Versailles in conflicting ways. Some members of the assembly, while heralding the return of the king to Paris, denounced the participants as rabble, the vile, lowest class. Others singled out heroines who were portrayed as larger than life; they were exceptional women, not models for others to emulate. Regardless of the interpretation, women were reminded that they should avoid public activities, should not drink in excess or appear to be entertainers or actresses, and should avoid public marches and displays because such behavior was not consistent with the woman's role. Already a bourgeois morality governing the private and public sphere was beginning to emerge.

As debates concerning the Constitution of 1791 took place, questions about active and passive citizenship and the right to petition were discussed. In the streets, pamphlets like Olympe de Gouges' "Declaration of the Rights of Woman" circulated, advocating that women throw off their bonds and obtain political equality and a social contract with men. (See DECLARATION OF THE RIGHTS OF WOMAN.) The Marquis de Condorcet's "Sur l'admission des femmes aux droits de la cité" (1792) dismantled sexist arguments that women who had political opportunities would neglect their domestic duties. Although women were excluded from active citizenship, the right to petition was affirmed so long as the petitions were individually signed. Other legislation broadened the right to divorce, liberalized inheritance, and granted rights to illegitimate offspring.

During 1792 and 1793, women continued their collective action in the streets, in the galleries of the assemblies, and in the political clubs. In May 1793, a group of women went before the municipal authorities of Paris to charter the first society exclusively for women. It was known as the

Société des Républicaines révolutionnaires. (See SOCIÉTÉ DES RÉPUBLI-
CAINES RÉVOLUTIONNAIRES.) Its leadership advocated radical social
reform. Initially, the *Républicaines révolutionnaires* were welcomed into
the political arena by Jacobin colleagues. It is likely that the Jacobins consciously used the *Républicaines révolutionnaires* in their efforts to consolidate their hold on political power. The cooperative efforts of the Jacobins
and *Républicaines révolutionnaires* were useful in expelling moderate Gi-
rondins from political power in May and June 1793. During the summer
of 1793, however, it became clear to the Jacobins that the women's society
was demanding far more change than the Jacobins were willing to author-
ize. Too radical in their program, the *Républicaines révolutionnaires* were
hounded from the corridors of government and legislated into oblivion a
few months later. On October 30, 1793, after scarcely six months in existence, the revolutionary women and all women were refused the right to
organize. The National Convention (1792–1795) asserted that the suppression of women's organizations did not violate the intent of the revolution; individual rights remained intact.

Among the most vocal of the conventioners was André Amar, who condemned the *Républicaines révolutionnaires* as unnatural women. He
charged them with counterrevolutionary activities and with creating dysfunction in society and lawlessness in the streets. Their demands that all
women wear the revolutionary cockade and their occasional appearance in
revolutionary costumes and pantaloons were cited as further evidence of
their danger to society. In his clearly misogynistic remarks he noted that
women were incapable of governing because they had neither the physical
nor the mental constitution for it. When Pierre Prudhomme reported the
convention's decree banning all women's organizations in his *Révolutions
de Paris*, he challenged women to be "honest and diligent girls, tender and
modest wives" and to avoid activities that tended to "disorganize society
by changing sexes."

While some women engaged in political activity to bring about economic
and social change and to guarantee subsistence, other women took a more
personal position. They spoke about their patriotic duty to support their
country while they looked for employment less affected by shifts in the
economy; the military provided that option. When foreign armies threatened the frontiers in the summer of 1792, women began to enlist in the
French army. There was no law to exclude them from the military, the
assembly noted in July 1792, and laws that suspended height and age requirements made enlistment more readily available to women.

Although members of the *Société des Républicaines révolutionnaires* had
petitioned to form battalions, no women's corps had been created. Instead,
individual women were mustered into the military in various capacities.
Women cited a number of reasons for enlistment: stable employment, the
security of rations, the means to provide for a family, failures of men to

heed the call, the desire to follow a loved one, or the need to support the nation. According to extant military records, most of the women soldiers were from the provinces rather than from Paris. There was no pattern to their marital status or to the roles they played in the military. They served in the national guard, in the cavalry, as aides-de-camp, and in the heavy artillery.

For the most part, the government was ambivalent about the enlistment of women. However, as the economy worsened, it was reported that thousands had flocked to army encampments where requisitions were plentiful and where they could ply their trades as laundresses, traders, and prostitutes. In all likelihood the migration was a product of economic dislocation and war, but representatives of the government speculated that a new morality, or perhaps lack of morality, was the cause. In the confused, often virulent, speeches condemning the "scourge which was destroying the armies," the government made no distinction between women soldiers and women who were camp followers. In the same environment that suppressed the politically active clubwomen, women soldiers were condemned and discharged from the military. The final decree was issued on December 12, 1793.

According to the Jacobins, the decrees issued in 1793 had censured only "unnatural women." As the Jacobins professed their Republic of Virtue in 1794, market women and working-class women, who were not identified with the radical women, believed that they would now serve as models of virtue and order for the new society and believed that social equality included them. When the laws against hoarders were not enforced as stringently as women of the popular classes desired, they sent deputations to the government and protested against inadequate policing of the streets. By the end of 1794, their continued activities to "govern" the streets placed them in jeopardy; Jacobin centralization left little room for their vision of popular sovereignty and justice.

Only once more during the revolutionary decade did women organize. When hoarding and speculation ran rampant, and inflation reached new levels after the fall of the Jacobins, women sansculottes returned to the streets to demand change. Disturbances in breadlines were common; *taxation populaire* recurred, and women demanded constitutional reform. They used every method of popular collective action they had learned previously, but the new government took harsh measures. No woman could visit the assembly, action was taken for the slightest, indiscreet comment against the government, and the mobility of women was hampered by increased police action.

Gradually, a bourgeois morality, promoted by the government, redefined women. In 1804 those sentiments received legislative sanction in the Code Napoléon, which finalized the fate of women. Civic housekeeping, which had earlier been applauded, was no longer within the woman's sphere. Even for the wage-earning woman, her "natural domain" was domestic house-keeping. Her model was to be the *femme au foyer* of writer Louis de Bonald—the woman who cared for her home as a man cared for the affairs of state.

References. Carol Berkin and Clara Lovett (eds.), *Women, War and Revolution* (New York, 1980); Marie-France Brive (ed.), *Les Femmes et la Révolution française* 3 vols. (Toulouse, 1989–1991); Olwen Hufton, *Women and the Limits of Citizenship in the French Revolution* (Toronto, 1992); Joan Landes, *Women and the Public Sphere in the Age of the French Revolution* (Ithaca, N.Y., 1988); Darlene Levy, Harriet Applewhite, and Mary Johnson (eds.), *Women in Revolutionary Paris* (Urbana, Ill., 1979); Candice Proctor, *Women, Equality and the French Revolution* (Westport, Conn., 1990).

                                                                     SUSAN P. CONNER

FRANCE. New French Feminisms. In 1979, Elaine Marks and Isabelle de Courtivron published an anthology of translations in English of French theoretical writings, emphasizing especially those literary and philosophical texts that drew from current tendencies in French philosophy, notably the poststructuralists like Jacques Lacan, Jacques Derrida, and Jean François Lyotard. Among English-language academics, the title of this widely read book, *New French Feminisms*, or, more often and more simply, the term "French feminist theory," became a kind of shorthand for the poststructuralist theorists, even though there are actually in France, as in other countries, many feminist perspectives and many, especially those that are derived from the thought of Simone de Beauvoir, that would seem much more familiar to U.S. feminists. The best known of the new French feminists are Hélène Cixous, Luce Irigaray, Monique Wittig, Claudine Herrman, and Catherine Clement. Whereas Beauvoirians call for equal rights for women in the existing patriarchal order with, of course, the purpose of transforming it, the advocates of *la différence* (those who believe that the biological differences between men and women are fundamental) call for more radical measures: having reached the conclusion that "woman is absent," that "only man has been represented," and that "the projection of male libidinal economy in all patriarchal systems—language, capitalism, socialism, monotheism—has been total," they advocate the dismantling of "phallocentric order" or the way society places man at the center of everything and in a position of authority (Marks and de Courtivron).

Like most contemporary theorists in France, new French feminists dwell on a variety of theories dealing mostly with *le discours* (language). These are more or less linked with Lacanian psychoanalysis, with Derridean "deconstruction," or with Lyotard's theory of "libidinal economy." They derive from structuralist and semiological trends (Ferdinand de Saussure, Michel Claude Levi-Strauss, Foucault, Roland Barthes), which contributed to the systematic questioning of the fundamental "structures" that make up our culture and, in particular, the questioning of what anthropologists call "the symbolic order," of which language is a part. They expose the fact that the "symbolic order" represents exclusively the "Law of the Father," or patriarchal power. Hélène Cixous, Luce Irigaray, and others who have learned the strategies of "deconstruction" from Lacan or Derrida have taken the opportunity to use precisely such theoretical discourse in order to discredit the Law of the Father and the symbolic order it generates. "Let the priests tremble, we are going to show them our sexts [a blending of "sex" and "texts"]!" threatens Hélène Cixous. By the same token, they strive to define a specifically feminine order. They stress the importance of rediscovering, rehabilitating, or inventing a language particular to *féminité* (being a woman) and free of all phallocentric patterns. They also are the most theoretical writers among the feminists. Each, in her own style, attacks phallocentrism at its very roots; the conceptual, the philosophical, and the psychoanalytical. From Sigmund Freud and Lacan to Plato, they deconstruct the scholarly reasoning of humanism, sever psychoanalysis from its Freudian roots, and demystify masculine models of moral and aesthetic heritage (Marks and de Courtivron).

Whereas de Beauvoir used current language as an unequivocal system referring to reality, the new generation of feminists, who are used to a structuralist approach, question the validity of language as a guaranteed referential tool. Instead, they play with words, handle puns, and look for the unconscious in wordplay, well aware of the primordial role of the subconscious in the shaping of language.

The psychoanalytic perspective is somewhat lacking in de Beauvoir's writings. Nevertheless, thanks to her, feminism has evolved the way it has in France. The new French feminisms are much indebted to her ideas, whether or not they diverge from them. *The Second Sex* (1949) still represents the only exhaustive fundamental analysis of the subject. We owe to it the idea, central to all feminist protests, that women's value is universally based on their desirability according to the law of exchange on which our society has set its foundations. De Beauvoir—who was the first to philosophically demonstrate the very mechanisms of woman's oppression—showed that it stems from woman's being *objectified* by man and that in the unavoidable interactions of subject/object and dominating/dominated that regulate social interplay, woman represents the *object*, the dominated, *l'autre* (the other). Objectification of woman leads to society's appropriation of her work and of her body and its reproductive functions. It leads to the appropriation of her psyche as well.

As a consequence, de Beauvoir has denounced the relationship existing between the capitalistic order and the organization of human relationships around the patriarchal law that establishes man as sovereign, as the possessor, and woman as a commodity bought, exchanged, and disposed of. We are ever reminded of such an order by the wedding rites, when the daughter is "given away" by her father to a husband; when she is expected to "give" children (preferably male) to her new protector and provider; and when she is supposed to "give birth" (and not take or keep that birth for herself) in a system where she cannot possess because she is being possessed. Luce Irigaray similarly unraveled the varied consequences of phallocentric order as it affects women's lives, but she did so from a psychoanalytical perspective, beyond the Marxist viewpoint: "Woman is traditionally use-value for man, exchange-value among men. [As m]erchandise, then . . . [w]omen are marked phallically by their fathers, husbands, procurers" (*Ce sexe qui n'en est pas un* [This Sex Which Is Not One] [Paris, 1977]; translated in *NFF*, 105).

Appropriation of woman means also occultation of woman. De Beauvoir had, before the new feminists, pointed out that woman's sexuality has been exclusively explained from the male's point of view. She had also shown how in woman's sexual pleasure the clitoris has been obscured in favor of the vagina, which is associated with the reproductive function of the womb. In the language of the new feminists, the womb is said to be appropriated and glorified, while the clitoris, as the "signifier of an autonomous subject" free of any reproductive function and of dependence on man, is kept secret, unmentioned: a systematic, but subtle, symbolic clitoridectomy.

Having researched beyond philosophy into psychoanalysis for the causes of woman's oppression, Irigaray, Cixous, and others found that woman "is outside the symbolic"—that is, she "does not exist," because she does not enjoy "what orders masculinity," the castration complex, and therefore lacks phallus, the transcendental signifier. In Cixous' words, woman supposedly "lacks lack" and such "lack of lack" would be translated as lack of desire (*jouissance*), or, at least, the inability to express it (Lacan), hence, the obliteration of woman's libidinal economy in patriarchal order. "Outside the symbolic" also means "outside language," which is the place of the Law of the Father: woman is absent as the maker of meaning.

De Beauvoir dismissed theoretical discourse as being impractical, since it divorced facts from expression and since it was, in her Marxist views, purely an elitist occupation from which the masses were excluded. That is why later in her life she found *The Second Sex* too theoretical and felt closer to North American feminists for being more pragmatic than the French. That is also why her writing took an activist turn. The review *Nouvelles Questions féministes* (New Feminist Issues), which she directed until her death, dealt mostly with militant issues on woman's rights such as protests against rape, economic or judicial inequities, and discriminating practices and action for free abortion.

De Beauvoir, who insisted that *féminité* is the result of conditioning and not of essence, has, to some extent, tended to minimize the particularity of female biology and its role in woman's life. Moreover, although she later conceded that biology is by no means a negligible factor in the feminine condition, she still did not see it as being determinant. In this, she opposed the advocates of *la différence* and thus failed to take into account the fact that woman's specific "libidinal economy" of biological nature makes her desire, imagine, and create differently than man does. Above all, de Beauvoir was concerned that the concept of *différence* constituted a trap, a double-edged representation geared to justify man as the parameter and woman as the nonessential counterpart and, therefore, geared to justify woman's state of oppression.

To sum up, de Beauvoir thought within the existing symbolic order, whereas the new French feminists, steeped in the climate of deconstruction, have no difficulty in envisioning a radical reconstruction that would start with the symbolic, particularly with language.

Indeed, "the question of language" has become central to feminist debates, since the French language reflects and glorifies the oppressive phallocentric order, based as it is on a conventionally binary division of the world into masculine and feminine, active and passive, and so forth. Words stab femininity in the back through a continuous process of inferiorization, objectification, or exclusion. The French language could not represent a better example of such a process, with its "mute e," which is intended to designate the feminine, and its gender structure, which calls for the masculine to supersede the feminine. Since everything in the end is filtered through language, and since language is phallocentric, women, in the eyes of the new feminists, should reject language as the instrument of their colonization. Indeed, if woman wants to exist as a sovereign, autonomous subject and not as an object, she must invent a discourse of her own, signs of her own that accurately render her own experience, her own perceptions, her imaginary world, her subconscious, and her "true" sexuality. In short, she must create her own symbolic order.

It has always been true that, within the male symbolic order, women demonstrate a lack of logic and assertiveness, for their language reflects their insecurity and their dependence. "Woman never speaks the same," said Luce Irigaray, "What she emits is fluent, fluctuating, swindling [*flouant*] and no one listens to her, 'lest one lose the proper meaning of things and sense of what is proper' ('sinon à y perdre le sens [du] propre')" ("La mécanique des fluides" in *Le sexe qui n'en est pas un*). The language that theorists look for is the one women would use within a symbolic domain of their own, where they would perceive themselves as subjects. Such a language would defiantly define itself through nonlinearity and nonbinarity.

"Women have been turned away from their bodies . . . so let them win their bodies back" and "discover the natural rhythms of their pulsations"; let them open the gate to "the untold," wrote Cixous ("Le rire de la Méduse," 245), a text now considered as the manifesto of *nouveau féminisme: NFF*, 245).

Although in France the production of women's writings has considerably increased in the last 15 years, only a few women writers have answered Cixous' call *à la lettre*, or, like Wittig, have experimented with *l'écriture du corps* in defiance of order. The "un-doing," "unleashing" (*dé-lire, dé-rive*, Cixous) of words and language does not appeal to Beauvoirians, who dismiss this kind of writing as a "narcissistic" exercise and a dangerous one, since it would, in their opinion, reintegrate woman in the ghetto of the body in which she has been imprisoned for so long, whereas Cixous and Irigaray believe that the body, as speaking subject and not object, being the prime signifier of libidinal economy, the body, as speaking subject and not object, is the place to start.

References. Hélène Cixous, *La jeune née* [For a New Woman] (Paris, 1975); E. Marks and I. de Courtivron, *New French Feminisms* (New York, 1981); Hélène Cixous, "Le rire de la Méduse," [Laugh of the Medusa], in E. Marks and I. de Courtivron, *New French Feminisms* (New York, 1981); Simone de Beauvoir, *The Second Sex* (Paris, 1994).

FRANCE. Since 1945. In 1945 Frenchwomen finally enjoyed one of the basic rights of citizenship in a democracy: the right to vote. In 1944 Algiers-based politicians and leaders of Resistance to the Nazi occupation and collaborationist Vichy regime ended the political deadlock that blocked woman suffrage in interwar France. The first elected women deputies numbered 5–6 percent of the two postwar constitutional assemblies and the first legislature of the Fourth Republic (1946–1958), the majority of them Communist Party members. Not until the March 1986 elections would as many women again serve in the National Assembly—33 out of 555—and in 1986, 21 were socialists. Léon Blum's Popular Front government (1936–1937) set the important precedent of appointing three woman undersecretaries, even before women had the vote, and in 1947–1948 the first woman minister joined a French government: Mme. Germaine Poinso-Chapuis, a Christian Democrat, served as minister of public health. There would not be another woman minister until 1974, when Auschwitz survivor Simone Veil received the health portfolio, although four women were undersecretaries between 1946 and 1974.

Not surprisingly, during the half century after 1945, social, economic, and cultural changes had greater impact on Frenchwomen's lives than did their limited participation in elected assemblies, even though women's representation on many locally elected councils was greater than at the national level. During the traumatic years of German occupation, women's role in the labor force increased, but after the war, as in the United States, many women left the workplace, voluntarily or involuntarily. A French "baby boom," long the well-publicized goal of Third Republic (1870–1940) natalists alarmed by France's low birthrate in comparison to that of Germany, also materialized. After wartime travails, couples turned with relief to the joys of private life and took advantage of an expanded system of social insurance, which built on prewar programs and the 1939 Family Code but provided larger benefits to families with children. The birthrate rose from a 1938 low of 14.6 per 1,000 population to a postwar peak of 21.3 in 1947 and remained about 18 per 1,000 during the 1950s. In turn, women's place in the labor force between 1946 and 1962 dropped from 38 to 33 percent, and married women's participation rate declined from 41 to 32.5 percent. A 1958 survey of attitudes in the Paris region toward women's roles revealed that respondents were closely divided on the question, "Should women work?" 41.6 percent said yes, and 41.3 percent no, but women approved of women's employment far more often than men—57 percent, as compared to 27 percent of men.

In the context of the "30 *glorieuses*," today's familiar designation for the three decades of impressive postwar economic growth now halted, many families encouraged daughters to take advantage of the much-expanded secondary school system and to enroll in universities. In 1959, the new Fifth Republic (1958–) raised the legal school-leaving age from 14 to 16, and by 1968, the number of young women receiving the "baccalauréate," the secondary school diploma required for university entry, exceeded that for males. During the 1970s women university students became as numerous as men, although they less often selected scientific and engineering specialties.

The social and cultural changes of the 1960s proved more significant for women than the constitutional change of 1958, prompted by France's controversial war in Algeria (1954–1962) and the return to power of Charles de Gaulle, the provisional postwar president (1944–1946) and Fifth Republic president until 1969. Even before new women's liberation groups appeared in the wake of the famous student protests and labor upheavals of May 1968, more women displayed impatience when traditional notions of femininity were utilized to limit their participation in the workplace or larger society. A French counterpart to the 1960s American Commission on the Status of Women was a committee appointed in 1965 to study the situation of women workers. Some socialist women also organized the Women's Democratic Movement (MDF). The 1968 census recorded the first increase in women's workforce participation since 1946, and close analysis revealed that the postwar decline in women's employment had stemmed largely from the diminished importance of agriculture and that their employment in the service sector, including government services, actually rose steadily since the war. Also indicative of changing mores were a declining birthrate—dropping to 16.7 per 1,000 by 1968—and the 1967 Neuwirth law, which ended the long-ignored 1920 ban on contraceptive devices for women.

During the later 1960s and the 1970s many women discovered or rediscovered Simone de Beauvoir's 1949 feminist classic *The Second Sex* (*Le deuxième sexe*), and as of 1966 they could read a French translation of Betty Friedan's *Feminine Mystique* (1963). Sociologists like Evelyne Sullerot and civil servants like Pierrette Sartin also published new studies on women's roles in society and the workplace and were initially surprised by both the size of the market for such books and the publicity they generated.

Against this backdrop, President Valéry Giscard d'Estaing (1974–1981) created a new secretariat for the "Feminine Condition," headed initially by journalist Françoise Giroud. Also precedent-setting in the cabinet of Giscard's first premier, Gaullist Jacques Chirac, was the number of women: Veil as health minister and four women secretaries of state. Veil sponsored the January 17, 1975, legalizing of abortion, soon known as the "Veil law." Other mid-1970s landmarks included the opening to women of two of the last all-male bastions of administrative power: the inspectorate of finance and the corps of prefects and deputy prefects, the national government's chief representatives at the departmental level. In 1972 women were finally admitted to the Ecole Polytechnique, the most prestigious training ground for engineers. The Education Ministry also called for eliminating sexist language and imagery from schoolbooks. By the end of the 1970s, Nicole Pasquier, a secretary of state at the Labor Ministry, recognized that solving "the fundamental problem of women depends upon the evolution of attitudes," but she identified employment as their major practical problem, particularly "the reconciliation of work and motherhood." Women workers long had benefitted from paid maternity leaves (since 1913) and from publicly funded nursery schools, but obtaining care for infants and young children remained a dilemma. Facilities at crèches were limited, and nursery schools typically admitted children at age 3 or 4 rather than at the legal minimum age of 2, due to space limitations as well as to families' own preferences.

Since their enfranchisement in 1944, women had voted more often for parties of the Right than had men, but in 1981 a majority of women preferred socialist candidates, thus participating in socialist François Mitterrand's victory over Giscard for the presidency and the return of a large socialist legislative majority. Mitterrand promptly upgraded the woman's rights office to the status of a ministry, appointing MDF veteran Yvette Roudy, who had a budget 10 times larger than that of her predecessor and a staff of 400. The Woman's Rights Ministry soon published a report on *Women in France in a Society of Inequalities* (1982) and achieved its major legislative success with the passage of the 1983 "Roudy law" on equality in the workplace. Defeated, however, was Roudy's much-discussed effort to eliminate sexist language, particularly from advertising; and after the conservatives' legislative victory in 1986, the woman's rights office lost ministerial status, which it did not regain when the Left again controlled the legislature and government (1988–1993). Although Mitterrand's second presidential term (1988–1995) produced the landmark appointment of France's first woman prime minister (premier), Edith Cresson, she held office for only 11 months in 1991–1992, and her personal "style" was much criticized.

Ministerial appointments and legislative landmarks notwithstanding, two experts on women's position in contemporary France—Jane Jenson and Mariette Sineau—judged in 1995 that women's encounter with the Mitterrand presidency was a "missed opportunity." The critical verdict stemmed not only from the loss of ministerial status for the woman's rights advocate but also from the proliferation of part-time jobs more often held by women than by men, inadequate provision of child care facilities, and society's general denigration of the term "feminism," which the government seemed disinterested in countering. Another study similarly faulted the official failure to develop effective methods to enforce French equal employment policies since the 1970s. Nonetheless, women's place in the workforce has increased steadily since 1968 and by the late 1980s totaled 45 percent. In the civil service, historically more receptive to providing women with new opportunities than the private sector, women were 51 percent of all employees by 1986. Critiques of the French state's shortcomings with regard to women thus reflected a long tradition of expectations for the state to be the model employer of women; for example, women teachers were the first women workers to enjoy paid maternity leaves before World War I. Viewed from the United States, France's provision of health insurance, maternity leaves, child allowances, and nursery schools is enviable because it eases the challenge of combining work and family responsibilities, even if the official rhetoric surrounding such measures sometimes seems to envision women as only mothers. More illustrative of cultural resistance to feminist perspectives are the attitudinal and administrative obstacles sometimes hindering efforts to implant women's studies offerings in French educational institutions. However, the launching of the women's history journal *Clio* in 1995 is a hopeful sign of change.

References. Linda L. Clark, *Schooling the Daughters of Marianne: Textbooks and the Socialization of Girls in Modern French Primary Schools* (Albany, N.Y., 1984); Claire Duchen, *Feminism in France from May '68 to Mitterrand* (London, 1986) and *Women's Rights and Women's Lives in France 1944–1968* (London, 1994); Jane Jenson and Mariette Sineau, "François Mitterrand and French Women: *Un rendez-vous manqué*," *French Politics and Society* 12 (Fall 1994); Amy G. Mazur, *Gender Bias and the State: Symbolic Reform at Work in Fifth Republic France* (Pittsburgh, 1996); Karen Offen, "Women, Citizenship, and Suffrage with a French Twist, 1789–1993," in Caroline Daley and Melanie Nolan (eds.), *Suffrage and Beyond: International Feminist Perspectives* (Auckland, 1994); Dorothy McBride Stetson, *Women's Rights in France* (Westport, Conn., 1987).

LINDA L. CLARK

FRANCE. The Third Republic (1870–1940), one of the most enduring regimes in French history, was marked by the ongoing struggle of Frenchwomen for equality before the law. Spanning the period between 1870 and 1940, the Third Republic witnessed a vigorous debate on women's political and civil rights. Discussion of the "woman question" was intimately tied to widely held assumptions about the family and women's role within it. These assumptions—that the family constituted the basic socioeconomic and political unit and that the needs of the family, including a strict sexual division of labor, took precedence over the interests of individuals—shaped the attitudes of policymakers and public figures from across the political spectrum.

In the early years of the Third Republic, these assumptions about women were common among otherwise contentious groups. During the troubled years before World War I, the two most important antagonistic groups that kept the new democratic republic politically divided were supporters of the Catholic Church, the main organized religious group in France, and secular leaders from the scientific community and the republican legal, educational, and political establishments. Within these groups centuries-old attitudes about women's nature were reformulated and eventually passed along to leaders of political parties on both the Left and Right in the twentieth century.

Prior to the Great War, Catholics not only rejected the new political forms and limited social aims of the republic but also condemned many aspects of modern life. Catholic opinion regarding the place of women in society was clearly established in the papal addresses and letters issued by Leo XIII, Benedict XV, Pius XI, and Pius XII, as well as the Canon Law of 1918. These papal encyclicals reflected a belief that women should devote themselves to their families, taking Mary as their feminine role model, and that married women should not seek wage employment. While official Catholic opinion upheld as the ideal the chaste and devout mother modeled on the Virgin Mary, there remained a general fear and distrust of women's sexuality. The irresponsible sexuality of Eve in the Garden of Eden led many to conclude that women, despite their redemption by the Virgin Mary, still required constant surveillance and control by a superior male authority. Insistence by Catholic educators that girls must be separately educated from boys and carefully monitored reflected this belief in women's dual nature.

The belief in the dual nature of women was common among anticlerical republicans as well. The founders of the Third Republic adhered to a traditional patriarchal model of the separation of spheres and functions for the sexes. Women's role in society would still largely be determined by the rigidities of the Napoleonic Code of 1804, which reflected attitudes that were as strictly functionalist as those held by the Catholic Church.

At the heart of the secular debate about women in the early Third Republic was the problem of redefining woman's social function in the new state and preparing her to fulfill it. In formulating the new sociopolitical order, the leaders of the Third Republic were highly influenced by prevailing notions about the physical, mental, and emotional differences between the sexes. Research by doctors, physical anthropologists, psychologists, and sociologists was used to justify old arguments for women's subordination, substituting scientific truths for religious ones. Women were seen primarily as reproductive creatures controlled by their wombs and in need of social control, particularly by the male head of household. For the secular leaders of the Third Republic, like their Catholic counterparts, the sexes were to occupy exclusive, separate spheres: women were to remain within the private sphere of the home, concerning themselves with reproduction and the moral upbringing of their children, while men—both citizens and heads of household—were to occupy the public sphere of politics, business, and law. This sexual division of labor influenced much of the social legislation of the Third Republic at the turn of the century.

Despite the functionalist rhetoric about women's place in French society, women made up between 25 and 45 percent of the French labor force between 1870 and 1940. During the early twentieth century, the extensive employment of women was of great concern to secular republicans, Catholics, workingmen, and their political parties on the Left. Although political parties of the Left, such as the socialists (SFIO) and the communists (PCF), endorsed political and civil equality for women, they tended to support a patriarchal notion of the working-class family that would enhance women's reproductive and domestic role. At the same time that formal vocational training for women was expanded, measures were taken to promote domesticity. In 1913, amid a nationalistic climate and fears about depopulation, measures for maternity benefits as well as a shortened workweek for female wage laborers were enacted.

Within this persistent set of assumptions and attitudes about women, the struggle for women's political and civil rights in France is best understood. Women's role in French society between 1870 and 1940 continued to be largely determined by the patriarchal family model established by the French Civil Code. Napoleon and his ministers had created a system whereby women could not vote, hold public office, act as witnesses in civil acts, serve on juries, or take a job without their husbands' consent. Women were stripped of all formal control of their property, their persons, and their children. Even though among the wealthy and educated classes male authority was tempered by women's moral authority within the home, such informal power was of little use within the existing legal system.

Protests against women's inferior status had begun with the promulgation of the Civil Code in 1804. By the early Third Republic, the debate on the woman question became more marked as proponents of woman's rights challenged the leadership of the new republic to reexamine the implications for women of the republic's founding principles of *liberté, égalité, fraternité*. Advocates of women's equality, such as Maria Deraismes, Léon

Richer, and Jeanne Schmahl, challenged the provisions of the Civil Code that governed the status of women. These efforts yielded piecemeal reforms, including the reestablishment of civil divorce in 1884, the authorization in 1897 of women to act as witnesses to civil acts, and admission to the legal profession in 1900.

By the turn of the century, women's rights advocates were demanding more drastic reform of the Civil Code. Without formal political rights, however, many feared that comprehensive reform would be thwarted by men fearful of the loss of power over their wives and family. French feminists such as Julie-Victoire Daubié and Hubertine Auclert renewed the call for woman suffrage,* which dated back to the 1790s. By 1900 Marguerite Durand had convened an international congress on woman's rights in Paris, and woman suffrage became a major political issue. During the first decade of the twentieth century two major woman suffrage bills were introduced in the Chamber of Deputies, and organizations like the Union française pour le suffrage des femmes (UFSF) gave the movement added momentum. Yet votes for women did not obtain support in the French legislature. Polarization of partisan political life and prevailing attitudes about the role of women in society left the issue of woman suffrage stalemated in the French legislature on the eve of World War I.

In the interwar period, little progress was made in changing women's civil and political status in the Third Republic. Steady population decline exacerbated by the massive losses of young Frenchmen during World War I resulted in national policy objectives that sought to reinforce women's domestic and reproductive functions, placing a renewed emphasis on separate sexual spheres. In the interwar years, the combination of depopulation, a new nationalism that emphasized traditional patriarchal values, and a renewal of the church–state conflict hindered progress in reforming laws regarding women's civil and political status. By 1920 fears of depopulation and a more general social conservatism led to the prohibition of contraceptive sales and tough new laws against abortion providers by 1920. Pronatalist advocates agitated for the end of employment of married women, and the percentage of Frenchwomen in the labor force declined between 1919 and 1936.

Léon Blum brought three women into his Popular Front cabinet in 1936. Yet women still could not vote. Despite a new wave of suffrage agitation led by Louise Weiss in the 1930s, the issue of voting rights for women remained stalled in the French legislature. Following the lead of earlier republican opponents of voting rights for women, the Left argued that enfranchised women would vote for pro-church parties that would undermine the secular republic. Bills to give women the right to vote were repeatedly blocked (1919, 1929, 1932, and 1935) in the French Senate. Moreover, reform of the legal code that would ultimately give civil rights to women made little progress before the fall of the Third Republic. As the Third Republic entered its final crisis years, women's political and civil status remained stalemated. Only after war and liberation would the French nation make the significant changes necessary to include women in the long-overdue promise of *liberté* and *égalité*.

References. Susan Groag Bell and Karen Offen, *Women, the Family, and Freedom* (Stanford, Calif., 1983); Steven Hause and Anne R. Kenney, *Women's Suffrage and Social Politics in the French Third Republic* (Princeton, 1984); Theresa McBride, *The Domestic Revolution* (New York, 1976).

KOLLEEN M. GUY

FRENCH ACADEMIC ARTISTS painted in accordance with the standards of the French Royal Academy (Académie Royale de Peinture et de Sculpture), founded in 1848 as France began its cultural ascendancy in the reign of Louis XIV. For over 200 years it was the dominant force in French art; its École des Beaux-Arts trained artists in the approved styles, and its annual salons exhibited only art that met its standards. Very few women were members, and those who were members were not in full standing—they could not attend the École or compete for the Prix de Rome until the end of the nineteenth century, could not hold office, and from 1791 held only honorary rank—but to achieve success, women artists, members or not, adhered to its standards. There were no radicals until the impressionist movement in the late nineteenth century.

The number of women professional artists was inconsiderable in the seventeenth century but grew thereafter. By the end of the eighteenth century not only were some women artists earning a good—sometimes an excellent—living from painting, but the idea that well-bred young ladies should have "accomplishments" (i.e., know something of music and drawing as well as needlework) meant others could support themselves by lessons in private homes or convent schools.

Most women artists were painters who confined themselves to portraiture, still life, and genre scenes, which earned less prestige and less money than the large historical, religious, and allegorical works commissioned by public institutions. Their training was restricted: they could not attend art schools until after the mid-nineteenth century or study from live nude models until the 1870s; until the Louvre was opened to the public after the Revolution, most could not study the old masters. Few attempted large-scale, multifigure works that required knowledge of male anatomy, and when landscape became popular, women could not travel freely through the countryside. But within their limited confines, women were successful. As long as they "kept their place" within the genres classified as minor and did not threaten male artists economically and especially if they were of pleasing appearance and manners, they were accepted. If, however, they successfully vied for commissions for large-scale works or made too much money, they might find themselves accused of having had men retouch or actually paint their canvases.

In the seventeenth century almost all women artists came from families of artists and were trained by fathers or other family members, but in the eighteenth century exceptions were more numerous. From the latter part of the century the atelier system of studio instruction evolved, and women sought instruction in the studios of both male and female artists. A few women artists remained single, often the sole support of their families. Most married, usually to other artists. For some, marriage ended their careers; others continued, but production often declined sharply as childbirth and increasing domestic duties interfered.

Although Royal Academy salons were open only to members, public exhibitions were possible through the less restrictive provincial academies and, in Paris, through the Academy of St. Luke (Académie de Saint-Luc), until its closure in 1777. St. Luke's lacked the prestige of the Royal Academy, but women could earn a reputation and with it some financial success through its exhibitions.

The first woman elected to the Royal Academy was Catherine Duchemin in 1663. Over the next 20 years, six other women were admitted, then no others for almost 40 years. The best-known woman painter of the seventeenth century was not a member; Louise Moillon (1610–1696) had probably ceased painting before the academy was founded (her first child was born in 1642). She was one of the earliest French still-life artists, painting fruit (and sometimes vegetable) still life with an almost classic simplicity of arrangement. Other Frenchwomen artists of the seventeenth century include Madeleine Boullogne, still-life artist, and her sister Génevieve, about whom nothing is known, academy members in 1679; Catherine Perrot, admitted 1682; Sophie Chéron, who is best known for her allegorical portraits and who supported her family by her art; still-life artists Charlotte Vignon and Marie Blancour; Suzanne de Court, enameler; and Claudin and Antoinette Bouzonnet Stelle, engravers.

From 1720, when Italian pastelist Rosalba Carriera was admitted, to 1769, four women were elected to the academy, only one of whom was French, miniaturist Marie Thérèse Reoul. When, in 1770, admittance of two women—Anne Vallayer Coster and Marie Suzanne Girout-Roslin— meant there were four women academicians, fears were raised, and it was decided never to exceed that number. Not until 1783 were women again admitted: the very successful painters Adélaïde Labille-Guirard and Elisabeth Vigée-Lebrun.

Marie-Suzanne Giroust-Roslin (1734–1772), one of the two finest French pastelists of the eighteenth century, in her short career painted mostly family and friends. She died of breast cancer at 38. Anne Vallayer-Coster (1744–1818), on the other hand, one of the best eighteenth-century still-life painters, had a long career: 26 when elected to the academy, she entered her last salon the year before her death. One of her finest works is *The White Soup Bowl* (1771), a steaming white bowl of soup with dark bread and wine.

Adélaïde Labille-Guirard (1749–1803) and Elisabeth Vigée-Lebrun (1755–1842) were admitted to the academy at the same time and were apparently competitors. Both, because of their success and their lifestyles, were accused of immorality and of having men paint or retouch their work. Labille-Guirard over her long career showed continued growth, moving on to another genre after succeeding in a previous one (from miniatures to pastels to oils), and at the time of the Revolution she was moving into large canvases. Her best work was her portraits in oils, but her lack of flattery meant that Vigée-Lebrun was more in demand than she. First winning success in the Academy of St. Luke, in 1785 she created a sensation at the Royal Academy with her *Portrait of the Artist with Two Pupils*. She moved easily from painter of royalty in the 1780s to painter of revolutionary leaders in the 1790s.

Elisabeth-Louise Vigée-Lebrun was enormously popular. Beginning at age 15, her talents were exploited first by her stepfather, then by her husband, until she divorced him in 1794. Her highly flattering portraits, combining rococo and neo-classical style, made her the most sought after painter in Paris and, during 12 years of exile, 1789–1801, in whatever city she visited. As official painter of the queen she did many portraits of Marie Antoinette, the last *Marie Antoinette and Her Children* in 1778 having been an official attempt to counter the virulent attacks being made on the queen's morals. After her return from exile her career did not resume its former prominence.

Marie-Ann Collot (1748–1821) was one of the few eighteenth-century women sculptors. She did many portrait busts during a long stay in Russia, where she went with her teacher Etienne Falconet. Later, when Falconet had a stroke, she left her husband, Falconet's son, and her career to take care of him.

All prerevolutionary academies were abolished in 1793. When they were later reestablished under the Institut de France, the Académie de Peinture et Sculpture admitted women only to an honorary rank, as had been decided in 1791. Since they could exhibit in salons, and since they had been little more than honorary members before, numbers of women artists gained a practical advantage at the expense of prestige for a very few. Throughout the nineteenth century there was a continued increase in the number of women who exhibited in academy salons. In the second half of the century, as opposition to the academy and its conservative standards grew, women found it easier to exhibit and, as academy prizes became more meaningless, to gain more of them.

From the late eighteenth century the sentimental genre became highly popular with male and female artists. More women were also trying historical paintings now, especially pupils and followers of Jacques Louis David, although the first classes with nude models were not open to them until late in the nineteenth century. (See ART EDUCATION, Europe in the Nineteenth Century.)

Marguerite Gérard (1761–1847), sister-in-law and student of rococo painter Jean Honoré Fragonard, painted mostly genre scenes but without the excessive sentimentality of so many paintings of the period. Prints helped popularize her work and spread her reputation, as they did also for Antoinette Haudebourt-Lescot (1784–1845), whose early paintings, genre scenes set in Italy, were so much in demand her work suffered from haste. Later she turned to portraits and in her 40s abandoned genre painting. Pauline Angou (1775–1835), who entered her first salon at 18, combined sentimental genre with history in paintings of Marie Louise, commissioned by Napoleon as part of his efforts to promote the empire.

Of painters reputed to have been pupils of Jacques Louis David, one of the most gifted was Constance Marie Charpentier (1767–1849). Her work includes portraits of women and children, genre scenes, and allegory. Marie Guilhelmine Benoist (1768–1826), student of Vigée-Lebrun and David, is the painter of the outstanding *Portrait of a Negress* (1800). When her husband was given a high government post after the Restoration, he ordered her to retire from professional painting. She was then at the height of her success. Also associated with David was Nanine Vallain, painter of classical and allegorical canvases, whose republican sympathies are clearly marked in her *Liberty* (1793–1794).

Félicie de Fauveau (1802–1886), best woman sculptor of nineteenth-century France, was an active political supporter of the monarchy, imprisoned for her activity during the July Revolution (1830). Interested in the medieval, she is an early figure in the gothic revival.

The animal paintings of Rosa Bonheur (1822–1899), the most successful painter of the nineteenth century, were more popular in England and the United States than in France. Her realistic portrayal of animals, the result of thorough studies from life, found a wide audience. Her most famous paintings, *Plowing in Nivernais* (1849), *Horse Fair* (1853), and *Haymaking in Auvergne* (1855) gained her national and international fame. Through prints her paintings appeared in homes and schoolrooms all over Europe and America. When she was denied the Cross of the Legion of Honor because of her sex, Empress Eugenie, acting as regent for Napoleon III in 1864, got it for her and delivered it personally. She was the first woman to receive this honor and the first to be made Officer of the Legion of Honor. Her success and her unconventional behavior—she smoked, cut her hair short, and wore trousers—caused resentment and ridicule.

Among other painters of the eighteenth and nineteenth centuries are Gabrielle Capet, pupil of Labille-Guirard, best known for miniatures; Marie

Victoire Lemoine, a student of Vigée-Lebrun; Marie Geneviève Bouliar, portraitist; Elisabeth Chaudet, painter of children with animals and other sentimental themes; Jeanne Philiberte Ledoux, painter of children and young girls; Marie Eléonore Godefroid, portraitist; Adrienne Marie Grandpierre-Deverzy, painter of interiors and literary subjects.

References. Elsa Honig Fine, *Women and Art: A History of Women Painters and Sculptors from the Renaissance to the 20th Century* (Montclair, N.J., 1978); Anne Sutherland Harris and Linda Nochlin, *Women Artists: 1550–1950* (New York, 1976); Charlotte Yeldham, *Women Artists in Nineteenth-Century France and England*, 2 vols. (New York, 1984).

FRENCH IMPRESSIONIST PAINTERS. In 1874 a group of dissident artists declared their independence from the French academic art world and held their own exhibition. The original group of impressionists included Claude Monet, Pierre Auguste Renoir, Camille Pisarro, Alfred Sisley, Edgar Degas, Paul Cézanne, Jean Guillaumin, and Berthe Morisot (1841–1895). Others similarly dissatisfied later joined them, including Mary Cassatt (1844–1926) in 1879. Some, although associated with the group and sharing a similar aesthetic, did not exhibit with them, as was the case with Edouard Manet and Eva Gonzales (1849–1883). Suzanne Valadon (1865–1938) is a postimpressionist with strong ties to the impressionists.

The artists loosely grouped under the label impressionist shared a basic need to escape from the narrow confines of academic orthodoxy and an overriding interest in light and color. They shared a common interest in the contemporary, in painting figures caught in a moment of ordinary activity.

Berthe Morisot and Mary Cassatt were fully accepted by their male colleagues. The limitations placed upon them as women were the limitations they themselves subscribed to. They were professional artists, and they were revolutionaries within their profession, but they were also thoroughly upper-middle-class nineteenth-century women.

Berthe Morisot's *plein air* landscapes had been accepted for salon exhibition before, in 1868, she met Manet and, through him, the young rebels who gathered at the Café Guerbois. After this time her interests turned to figures in landscapes and domestic settings. The often-reproduced *Mother and Sister of the Artist* comes from this early period (1869). Her painting achieved full maturity in the 1870s. *The Cradle* (1872) is characteristic of her treatment of interior light, here filtered through drapery onto the netting over the cradle, and of her mother–child paintings, with the mother in a protective posture.

In 1874 Morisot helped organize the first impressionist exhibition and also entered into a successful marriage with Eugéne Manet, younger brother of the artist. Their beloved daughter Julia was a model for many of her paintings.

In the 1880s Morisot's brush stroke becomes more marked, detail fades away, and definition becomes minimal, as light threatens to dissolve all forms. In *The Dining Room* (1886) woman and room seem to meld into one. Then in 1890 she began to change her technique. She makes many preliminary sketches, colors become more brilliant, figures more defined (e.g., *The Cherry Pickers*). While she was not a commercial success in her own day, her reputation grew in the twentieth century, while that of more successful nineteenth-century artists, such as Rosa Bonheur, declined.

Mary Cassatt, from a well-to-do Pennsylvania family, studied with the fashionable academic Charles Chaplin and in Holland, Spain, and Italy. Although she exhibited in successive salons from 1872 to 1876, two rejections soured her on the selection method. When Degas in 1878 invited her to exhibit with the impressionists, she was ready to do so. Her entry in the 1879 exhibition is one of her best impressionist paintings, *In the Loge*, with its play of gaslight on the figure and dress of her sister Lydia relaxing during intermission at the opera.

Cassatt's paintings show a cool, detached realism, the complete lack of sentimentality that marked her life as it did her work. Among paintings exhibited from 1879 to 1886 were *The Cup of Tea* (1880), the portrait of her mother reading *Le Figaro* (1883), and mother–child paintings, on which she concentrated in the 1880s and 1890s. Mother–child paintings were popular with artists, male and female, during the period. Her many paintings of children may reflect the fact that a proper Victorian maiden lady was limited in the subject matter available to her. The completely unsentimental renderings of children do not bespeak the deep maternal longings male critics tried to read into them. Among her best impressionist works is *A Mother About to Wash Her Sleepy Child* (1880).

Like Morisot, she too grew dissatisfied with impressionism. In the late 1880s and early 1890s her painting shows renewed concern for clear definition, disappearance of the obvious brush stroke, brighter color, and more structure. The effect of spontaneity is eliminated in favor of the timeless pose. Two outstanding mother-and-child paintings from this period are *The Bath* (1891) and *The Boating Party* (1893–1894).

Influenced by Japanese woodcuts, in 1891 she produced a set of color aquatints, using her own technique. These superb prints (e.g., *La toilette*) help establish Cassatt's place in the history of art. In 1904 the French government awarded her the Legion of Honor.

Eva Gonzales, also upper-middle-class and, like Cassatt, a student of Chaplin, in 1869 met Manet and became his model, student, and protégée. Like Manet she exhibited through the official salon, refusing to join the impressionists, but, like the impressionists, she was interested in scenes from everyday life and the effect of light on figures in the open air. However, in the definition of figures and the use of color she does not follow their lead. One of her finest works is *Reading in the Forest* (1879). She died at age 34, after giving birth to a son.

Suzanne Valadon was of a very different background from that of Morisot, Cassatt, and Gonzales and lived the very different life of a Montmarte bohemian. Growing up on the streets and on her own from at least age 10, in the early 1880s she became a very successful model. From her association with artists, many connected with the impressionist movement, she picked up technique, and, when she began drawing c. 1883, Toulouse-Lautrec and then Degas took an interest in her work.

Her earliest paintings date from 1892–1893, but until 1909 she did mostly drawings and prints. Her first prints, etchings of various phases of the toilette, were done in Degas' atelier under his direction. Not until she was 44 did she turn exclusively to painting. Her nudes (she was one of the first women to paint male nudes), portraits, and still lifes were drawn and painted in an original style—she claimed not to have been influenced by any other artist—and her bold color, strong line, and earthy realism contribute a vitality and forcefulness that stamp all her work.

References. Elsa Honig Fine, *Women and Art* (Montclair, N.J., 1978); Ann Sutherland Harris, *Women Artists, 1550–1950* (New York, 1977).

FRENCH RESISTANCE. Women played a significant role in the struggle against the Germans who occupied France from 1940 to 1944 and against the indigenous Vichy, or collaboration government, which abolished the republic in favor of an authoritarian French "state." From its uncertain beginnings in 1940 until the Liberation in 1944 (when Frenchwomen were finally granted the vote), the Resistance was characterized by unique forms of political action, protest, and combat. French resisters were joined by Jews and political refugees from other European countries. Although the struggle was waged jointly by men and women who worked together within the different Resistance formations (groups, parties, networks, and movements), some forms of action were gender-integrated, while others were gender-specific. Women did participate at all levels and in all sectors of the movement, including armed combat, the traditional preserve of men. A few notable women, like Marie-Madeleine Fourcade of *Alliance* and Lucie Aubrac of *Libération Sud*, even had leadership roles. Despite varying practices among different groups, however, the division of tasks on the basis of gender seems to have prevailed within the Resistance as a whole.

Full-time underground activists assumed new identities and were forced to leave homes, families, and friends to protect themselves from discovery and arrest. Part-timers, many of whom were women, served as crucial links in the movement (transmitting intelligence, providing social services, recruiting other members) while carrying on with the rest of their aboveground lives as normally as possible. Ironically, such rear-guard support has rendered the mass of female resisters invisible because part-time and support functions have rarely received recognition, despite the commitment and risk they demanded. Resistance involvement, however, was widely interpreted by the German and Vichy authorities to include support services often provided by women.

Women served as couriers, "letter boxes," and safehouse keepers. They collected information; provided invaluable support to other resisters in the form of food, shelter, and supplies; produced and distributed underground newspapers and broadsheets; formed escape lines across the border for Allied soldiers and others; participated in sabotage and fighting. The female resister is typified by the ubiquitous "liaison agent," who ran missions, transmitted messages, and transported precious arms to those in hiding. Liaison agents were commonly women because they were less likely than men to draw suspicion from the enemy.

The so-called women's work of the Resistance mobilized underground and aboveground activists on both full- and part-time bases. The task of caring for, and protecting, other resisters devolved upon women, whose traditional roles in the family and in the workplace became politicized in service to the cause. Many of these women performed functions that were crucial to the survival of the movement, though unfortunately they were not always considered full-fledged members of the group themselves.

All-women groups were also formed, primarily under the aegis of the then-banned French Communist Party, which organized housewives and others in women's committees (comités populaires féminins) for public demonstrations and other protest actions to demand higher food rations, to press for the return of prisoners, and to lobby (often by illegal means) for the expulsion of the Germans and the end of the Vichy regime. A clandestine women's press appeared throughout France, especially in cities in both the northern (occupied) and southern (unoccupied until November 1942) zones.

The price of participation was enormous. Resisters suffered arrest, imprisonment, interrogation and sometimes torture, and deportation to concentration camps as political prisoners. La Roquette women's prison in Paris figured on many a woman's itinerary; another larger women's facility in Rennes grouped women resisters from the entire northern zone. From prisons in France, many were shipped to camps farther east, where they perished from disease, starvation, exhaustion, beatings, or more systematic forms of extermination. Many Frenchwomen were sent to Ravensbrück, the concentration camp for women east of Berlin. Jewish resisters and those deemed particularly dangerous were also sent to Auschwitz in eastern Poland; this is the case of the famous convoy known as the "31,000" (the series tatooed on their arm upon arrival), which included many prominent communists such as Marie-Claude Vaillant-Couturier and Maïe Politzer. Unlike their male counterparts, women as a rule were not executed in

France for political crimes; a few (Berty Albrecht of *Combat*, France Bloch of the *Front National*), however, are known to have been executed in Germany.

Women now hold an important place in the collective memory of the French Resistance. Heroic martyrs Danielle Casanova and Berty Albrecht have come to personify the Resistance legacy *au féminin* for communists and Gaullists, respectively. Scholarly memory, on the other hand, has not been partial to women; although the presence of women at all levels and in groups on both Left and Right is woven throughout monographs, memoirs, and oral testimony, historians have paid only passing attention to their role in the movement, less still to the specificity of their involvement.

References. Marie-Louise Coudert, *Elles, la Résistance* (Paris, 1988); Vera Laska (ed.), *Women in the Resistance and in the Holocaust: The Voices of Eyewitnesses* (Westport, Conn., 1983); Paula Schwartz, " 'Partisanes' and Gender Politics in Vichy France," *French Historical Studies* 16, 1 (Spring 1989): 126–151; Union des Femmes Francaises (ed.), *Les Femmes dans la Résistance* (Paris, 1975).

PAULA SCHWARTZ

FRENCH WRITERS. Marie de France's *Lais* (c. 1155) remain the earliest known works in *langue d'oil*, the northern dialect that evolved into modern French. Inspired by Gallic bards, Marie probably lived at the Anglo-Norman court and introduced the Arthurian cycle into France. Her twelfth-century contemporaries, the *trobairitz* (women troubadours) wrote in the southern *langue d'oc*. Tibors, the countess of Dia, Maria de Ventadorn, Lombarda, and Castelloza sang about love, expressing personal emotions like desire, uncertainty, and anger at being jilted. (See TROUBADOR LITERATURE.) A century later, Christine de Pisan (c. 1363–1431) became the first Frenchwoman to live by her pen. Her numerous courtly, didactic, and autobiographical works include *The Book of the City of Ladies* (1404).

The sixteenth-century French Renaissance fostered women's talent and intellect; its patrons included Francis I and his sister, Marguerite de Navarre (1492–1549). Sheltering humanists in her court at Nérac, Marguerite also wrote poetry, letters, and a religious treatise condemned by the Sorbonne; and Boccaccio's *Decameron* inspired her *Heptaméron* (1558). Renaissance ideals also inspired a group of Lyon poets, including Louise Labé (1526–1566) and Pernette du Guillet (1520–1545), who helped revive lyric poetry. Another humanist circle flourished in the Poitiers salon of Madeleine des Roches (c. 1520–1587) and her daughter, Catherine (1542–1587).

The best-known women writers of the Old Regime held salons, which played key roles in French literary development. (See SALONIÈRE.) Madame de Rambouillet (1588–1665) dominated seventeenth-century Paris and planted the seeds of preciosity. The *Précieuses** marked an important step in feminism, as they emphasized women's value through rules of polite speech. Prolific novelist Madeleine de Scudéry (1608–1701) typifies the precious writer. Important sociohistorical documents of post-Fronde aristocratic society, her multivolume romans à clef, rampant with euphemism and metaphor, include *Clélie* (1654). Its "Map of Tendre" illustrates "civilized" behavior: in this fictional land, women dictate the rules, and men must comply if they wish success, social or amorous.

Many society hostesses engaged in correspondences or kept journals; these genres reflected women's "proper" realm, the private sphere. Marie-Louise Rabutin de Sévigné (1626–1696) elevated the letter to an art form. Publication was stigmatized as an improper display of the female self, so many women published anonymously, used male pseudonyms, or, like Sévigné, waited for posthumous publication. Yet, many memoirs reveal individual experiences that subvert traditional gender roles; Anne-Marie d'Orléans de Montpensier (1627–1693), the "Grande Mademoiselle," cousin of Louis XIV, led Fronde rebellions against Mazarin, and Catherine de La Guette (1613–1676) dressed like a man to fight in the Wars of Religion.

Excluded from the highest literary forms (theater, history, and poetry), women developed the realm of fiction, dominating the novel until the nineteenth century. Critics generally consider Marie-Madeleine de Lafayette's (1634–1693) *Princesse de Clèves* (1677) the first modern novel in French. Both Lafayette and contemporary Marie-Catherine de Villedieu (1640–1683) examine the relationship between love and politics at court, exposing the fiction of an ideological split between male/public and female/private worlds.

Women writers cultivated the newly popular fairy tale during the late Old Regime. Suffering from financial problems, unhappy marriages, or both, aristocrats like Marie-Catherine d'Aulnoy (1650–1705), Jeanne-Marie Leprince de Beaumont (1711–1780), and Gabrielle-Suzanne de Villeneuve (1685–1755) supplemented their incomes, creating familiar classics like *Beauty and the Beast*. Catherine Durand (c. 1650–1712), Catherine Bernard (1662–1712), Sophie Cottin (1770–1807), and others published highly popular novels. Françoise de Graffigny's (1695–1758) *Lettres d'une Péruvienne* (1747) has recently been rediscovered as a potential classic, and her *Cénie* (1750) represents a rare success for a woman playwright.

Greater freedom after the death of Louis XIV encouraged Enlightenment philosophy's development in aristocratic and bourgeois salons of Madame de Tencin (1681–1749), Madame Geoffrin (1699–1777), Madame d'Épinay (d. 1783), and many others. Until their execution in 1793, Revolutionary writers Madame Roland (1754–1793) and Olympe de Gouges (1748–1793) campaigned for political reform from their salons.

Didactic literature for children also came under the purview of women writers. Society protested when the duke of Orleans named former mistress Stéphanie de Genlis (1746–1830), governor of his sons, but her moralistic novels like *Adèle et Théodore* (1782) reveal pedagogical theories inspired by Madame de Maintenon (1635–1719). The comtesse de Ségur (1799–1874), a Russian émigré, carried on their tradition; her autobiographical *Sophie's Misfortunes* (1860) sought to socialize children through amusing negative examples.

Germaine Necker de Staël (1766–1817) grew up in her mother's Enlightenment salon. Influenced by her precocious childhood, Staël created a liberated heroine who influenced an entire generation with *Corinne* (1807). Her critical works like *On Germany* (1810) contributed to Romanticism's development in France. Others influenced by Romanticism include Claire de Duras (1777–1823), whose novels like *Ourika* (1823) feature social misfits. Poets Amable Tastu (b. 1798), Louise Colet (1810–1876), and Delphine Gay de Girardin (c. 1815–1855) remain obscure. Marceline Desbordes-Valmore (1786–1859) drew from the hardships of her life to create lyrics lamenting lost love and lost children.

Ideologically, women fared poorly throughout the nineteenth century, relegated to roles of virgin, mother, muse, or whore; the *femme auteur* became an anomalous object of ridicule. George Sand (Aurore Dupin, 1804–1876) protested these roles by dressing and choosing lovers with the freedom of a man. *Indiana* (1832) shocked audiences with its critical look at marriage, and her pastoral and socialist novels portrayed peasants and workers idealistically. Contemporary Daniel Stern (Marie d'Agoult, 1805–1876) recounted her affair with Liszt in *Nalida* (1846) but gained respect for stepping into a "male" genre with *Histoire de la Révolution de 1848* (1850–1853). Activist and organizer Flora Tristan (1803–1844) wrote to improve the lot of women and workers in *The Workers' Union* (1843). Although women had broken into journalism in the eighteenth century, feminist periodicals first appeared in the 1830s, and later Marguerite Durand edited *La Fronde* (1897–1903), whose contributors included Séverine (Caroline Rémy, 1855–1929).

The years 1880 to 1914 marked a transition; progressive legislation, new economic forces, and an accompanying moral crisis opened new avenues of expression to women. Gyp (Sibylle-Gabrielle de Mirabeau, 1849–1932) identified with men to obtain greater freedom. Her saucy adolescent, *Little Bob* (1882), lampooned bourgeois mores, but her reactionary politics and anti-Semitism were attacked. Rachilde (Marguerite Eyméry, 1860–1953) scandalized the public with novels like *Monsieur Vénus* (1884), which reverses sex roles and highlights sexual perversion. The Sapphic Group formed in Paris, including lesbian artists and writers like Renée Vivien (Pauline Mary Tarn, 1877–1909), an Anglophone who adopted the French language. With Anna de Noailles (1876–1933), Vivien remains among the very few women poets who attract critical attention today.

The *Femme Nouvelle*, the new woman, came into her own through increasing educational and career opportunities. While seventeenth- and eighteenth-century novels explored concerns about arranged marriage versus marriage for love, women's novels at the turn of the century looked at problems of career versus marriage. Lucie Delarue-Mardrus (1880–1945), Gabrielle Réval, Marcelle Tinayre (1877–1948), and Colette Yver (1874–1953) wrote about young professional women, unwed mothers, equality in marriage, proposing reform but occasionally defending traditional roles. Sidonie-Gabrielle Colette (1873–1954) began her career at the turn of the century with the autobiographical Claudine series (1900–1903). Married young to a celebrated journalist, then separated, Colette soon lost her illusions in the fast life of the Paris music halls. Her journalism, theater criticism, and best-selling novels intimately portray human psychology.

By 1950 women's writing takes on a completely modern character. The German Occupation and French Resistance affected intellectuals Simone Weil (1909–1943) and Elsa Triolet (1896–1970), who wrote to support social reform. Simone de Beauvoir (1908–1986) also began her influential career at this time, publishing *Le Deuxième Sexe* in 1949. (See *SECOND SEX, THE.*) Nathalie Sarraute (b. 1902) expressed the uncertainties of modernity through the new novel, *le nouveau roman.* Breaking down the traditions of realist fiction, Sarraute plays with narrative viewpoint and uses types rather than developing individual characters in *Portrait d'un inconnu* (1949). Marguerite Duras (1914–1996) reworks similar situations and characters in novels like *L'Amante anglaise* (1967) and *The Ravishing of Lol V. Stein* (1964), subverting the notion of the completed literary work. Christiane Rochefort (b. 1917) and Francoise Sagan (b. 1935) realistically portray lives of young women from both working-class and privileged milieus. But Marguerite Yourcenar's (b. 1903) less controversial historical fictions garnered her the first woman's chair in the Académie Française.

Fed up with the constrained conformity of the de Gaulle era, French students revolted in May 1968. A complete reexamination of cultural values ensued, spurring a feminist renaissance in the early 1970s; Monique Wittig's (b. 1935) lesbian utopia *Les Guérillères* appeared in 1969, and key works by Hélène Cixous (b. 1937), Luce Irigaray (b. 1930), and Julia Kristeva (b. 1941), in 1975. Feminist theory and notions of feminine writing influenced many contemporary novelists and playwrights. Chantal Chawaf (b. 1943) and Jeanne Hyvrard (b. 1945) reveal mother–daughter relationships in an exploratory style, highlighting language's role in the development of the individual. Annie Ernaux's *The Frozen Woman* (1981) provides an autobiographical account of the struggle to live up to traditional notions of the feminine while competing in the career world.

While the 1980s and 1990s have been viewed as periods of backlash or postfeminism, writers like Sylvie Germain (b. 1954) continue to describe experiences and realities pertinent to women. Her *Medusa Child* (1991) tells of an abused little girl's fantasy of revenge and final redemption. Enriching the tapestry, unique voices rise from the vestiges of the French colonial empire, as Caribbean novelists Maryse Condé (b. 1937) and Simone

Schwarz-Bart (b. 1938) and playwright Ina Césaire (b. 1941) gain recognition. Another rising group, the *Beurettes* (Parisian slang for North African women), reveals the unique problems of women immigrants who juggle several identities in the face of discrimination. This theme recurs in the novels and plays of Assia Djebbar (b. 1936), Fatima Gallaire-Bouroga, and Soraya Nini.

Over the centuries writing has provided French-speaking women the means toward fulfilling two main ends: an outlet for self-expression and a weapon in the fight to better the quality of their lives.

References. Roland Bonnel and Catherine Rubinger (eds.), *Femmes Savantes et Femmes d'Esprit: Women Intellectuals of the French Eighteenth Century* (New York, 1994); Joan de Jean, *Tender Geographies: Women and the Origins of the Novel in France* (New York, 1991); Alice Jardine and Anne Menke (eds.), *Shifting Scenes: Interviews on Women, Writing, and Politics in Post-68 France* (New York, 1991); Jennifer Waelti-Walters, *Feminist Novelists of the Belle Epoque* (Bloomington, Ind., 1990); Katharina M. Wilson (ed.), *Women Writers of the Renaissance and Reformation* (Athens, Ga., 1987).

AMY J. RANSOM

ISBN 0-313-31071-8